Beyond the San Francisco System

Young-Ho Kim • Tae-Jin Yi
Wada Haruki • Dekun Hu • Alexis Dudden
Editors

Beyond the San Francisco System

Springer

Editors
Young-Ho Kim
Department of Economics
Kyungpook National University
Daegu, Korea (Republic of)

Tae-Jin Yi
Department of History
Seoul National University
Seoul, Korea (Republic of)

Wada Haruki
Institute of Social Science
University of Tokyo
Tokyo, Japan

Dekun Hu
Institute of Boundary and Ocean Studies
Wuhan University
Wuhan, China

Alexis Dudden
Department of History
University of Connecticut
Mansfield, USA

ISBN 978-981-95-3327-5 ISBN 978-981-95-3328-2 (eBook)
https://doi.org/10.1007/978-981-95-3328-2

This Springer imprint is published by the registered company Springer Nature Singapore Pte Ltd.
The registered company address is: 152 Beach Road, #21-01/04 Gateway East, Singapore 189721, Singapore

Preface

It is said that "The path to paradise begins in hell." This phrase is widely known to represent the theme of *Inferno*, a part of the epic poem *The Divine Comedy* by the Italian poet Dante Alighieri.

The modern history of East Asia after the Second World War began with the San Francisco Peace Treaty. The San Francisco System, an Asia-Pacific Cold War regime formed and expanded by that treaty, has remained firmly in place for over 72 years. It is often said that with the Treaty of Versailles, the Allied powers imposed excessively harsh punishments on the defeated Germany, and the resulting backlash later gave rise to Nazism. Conversely, the San Francisco Peace Treaty was so lenient that it effectively became an economic revival treaty, making it impossible to reckon with the past—that is, to address the crimes of war criminals and colonialism. As a result, the rulers of the old regime became the protagonists of Japan's postwar economic reconstruction, leading them not to reflect on the past but rather to rationalize or even glorify it from the position of a war victim. The economist J.M. Keynes argued at the time of the Treaty of Versailles that helping the defeated nations rebuild their economies would be more advantageous for the victorious nations, but his views did not prevail. In the San Francisco Peace Treaty, however, his ideas were revived as part of a Cold War strategy, becoming an Asian version of the Marshall Plan that brought about the postwar economic revival of East Asia. The price, however, was an economic boom devoid of reflection on war crimes and colonial atrocities.

Consequently, conservative forces in Japan, in alliance with the US military-industrial-financial complex, are reinforcing the San Francisco System as an Asia-Pacific Cold War regime. Meanwhile, in places like South Korea and Taiwan, economic growth has been accompanied by democratic progress, bringing to the fore major human rights issues such as those of the "comfort women" and conscripted laborers, leading to a direct clash with the San Francisco System.

In stark contrast, the UN World Conference against Racism, Racial Discrimination, Xenophobia and Related Intolerance was held in Durban, South Africa, in 2001, to address the legacies of slavery and colonialism. At the Durban conference, the Durban Declaration was issued, defining the slave trade and colonialism as a "crime against humanity." This declaration was a conference of justice that upheld the spirit of the Universal Declaration of Human Rights, but unlike the San Francisco System, it was not linked to economic revival.

The problem now is that as we move beyond the San Francisco System, a new peace regime is not being formed. Instead, the rivalry between the United States and the Soviet Union has been replaced by one between the United States and China, giving rise to an Indo-Pacific system as part of a strategy to contain China. Furthermore, as plans for a "NATO-ization" of the Indo-Pacific system advance, the San Francisco System is showing signs of being reinforced. While the hypothesis from neo-dependency theory that "the periphery of the periphery is still the periphery" was once popular, a situation where "San Francisco 2.0" succeeds "San Francisco 1.0" is now becoming a reality. Recently, China and Japan have been experiencing frictions, and China appears to be attempting to connect these to the end of the San Francisco system. We are paying close attention to this point. It may have been unavoidable that the path to paradise began in hell, but for that path to culminate in war is something that East Asian civil society and its intellectual community cannot accept.

With the dream of transitioning to a new peace system, where the San Francisco System is overcome and civil society matures alongside economic growth in Asia, we have repeatedly held international conferences to explore a kind of "Durban System 2.0."

From 2016 to 2023, we held a series of five international conferences over a total of eight years—with a three-year hiatus due to the COVID-19 pandemic—with experts from Japan, China, the United States, South Korea, Canada, Australia, Russia, and other countries, all under the consistent theme of "Overcoming the San Francisco System." The content was overwhelmingly critical, effectively becoming a collective international indictment of the San Francisco System. We would like to express our sincere gratitude to the institutions that have co-hosted these academic conferences: The Center for Korean Research (Director, Charles Armstrong) at Columbia University for the first conference; the James Joo-Jin Kim Program in Korean Studies (Director, Eugene Y. Park) at the University of Pennsylvania for the second; the Institute of Boundary and Ocean Studies (Director, Dekun Hu) at Wuhan University in China for the third; the Northeast Asia Peace Center (Director, Young-Ho Kim) for the fourth conference in Seoul; and the Asiatic Research Institute (Director, Lee Jin-han) at Korea University for the fifth. The Northeast Asia Peace Center was the permanent host on the Korean side for all five conferences, and we received financial support from the Northeast Asian History Foundation (Chairman, Kim Dohyung) from the first to the fifth conference, for which we express our profound gratitude. We also thank the Dodam Cultural Foundation and the ERA Foundation for their support with simultaneous interpretation expenses. Professor Dekun Hu of Wuhan University declined all support from the very beginning and covered all his expenses himself. Despite these challenges, distinguished senior scholars such as Gavan McCormack and Wada Haruki graciously endured flying in economy class. There was a palpable sense of mission.

We sought to publish the outcomes of these five conferences in a single volume, going beyond the proceedings prepared for each event. The Korean edition, compiling the results of the first four conferences, was published by Medici Media in 2022. This Korean edition was selected as a 2023 "Year Book" in the social sciences category by The Hankyoreh, a leading liberal newspaper in Korea. This English book is an updated version that incorporates the results of the fifth conference. We are delighted that it is being published by the renowned publisher Springer. Dr. Hitoshi Hirakawa from Nagoya University introduced us to Springer for the publication of our manuscripts and provided a review of the content. We would like to express our heartfelt gratitude. We are especially grateful for the kind editorial guidance and thoughtful consideration of Mr. Yutaka Hirachi and Ms. Manonmani Pradeepkumar at Springer.

Although the title is similar to the Korean edition, the content is substantially different, having been more carefully curated and significantly updated. All manuscripts were first presented at our academic conferences, and the publication rights belong to us. However, as considerable time has passed, some parts may have been published in other journals or may overlap with other works by the authors. We wish to state this in advance and ask for your understanding. The authors take individual responsibility for their own articles. In the process of publishing this book, Dr. Hee Jung Chung provided tremendous assistance with the editorial work. We express our deep gratitude through these pages.

January 2026
The Editorial Committee
Young-Ho Kim, Tae-Jin Yi, Wada Haruki, Dekun Hu, Alexis Dudden.

Contents

About the Editors

Young-Ho Kim (金泳鎬) was born in 1940 in Hap-chun, Korea. After graduating from Kyungpook National University, he received his Ph.D. at Osaka City University. He has served as a professor in the Department of Economics at Kyungpook National University, Dean of the College of Business Administration at Kyungpook National University, and professor at the University of Tokyo in Japan. Additionally, he has served as Minister of Industry and Resources of the South Korean Government and as President of Yuhan University.

Among his major publications are *East Asian Industrialization and World Capitalism*(東アジア工業化と世界資本主義)(Tokyo: Toyo Keizai Inc. 東京: 東洋経済新報社, 1988) and *Dasan Studies in the World History*(세계사 속의 다산학)(Seoul: Knowledge Industry Co., Ltd. 서울: 지식산업사, 2021).

He has received multiple awards, including the Award of Dasan Economics.

Tae-Jin Yi (李泰鎭, b.1943) is Professor Emeritus of Seoul National University where he had taught since 1973 who was retired in 2009.

He is the author of over three hundred articles and over twenty books including Han'guk sahoesa yongu, *Studies on the Social History of Korea* (1986), Chosun yugyo sahoe saron, *The Social History of Confucianism in Chosun* (1989), and Kojong sid'ae ui chaejomyong, *Reexamination of the History of the King Kojong Era 1864~1907* (2000). In 2022 he published two books on the Japanese Empire historians' founding of the 'Toyoshi' (東洋史) and 'Tohogaku' (東方學) in the purpose of the establishment of the East Asian world ruled by the emperor of Japan.

He was in charge of Chairman of National Institute of Korean History 2010~2013. In 2007 he was nominated as a member of the National Academy of Sciences Republic of Korea. He was honorably elected as the Bureau member of the Union Académique Internationale(UAI) in 2015. He has also received multiple awards, including the prestigious 3·1 Cultural Award.

Wada Haruki (和田春樹) was born in 1938 in Osaka, Japan. After graduating from the University of Tokyo and receiving his Ph.D. there, he served as a professor at the University of Tokyo and was the director of its Institute of Social Sciences. He has published over ten books including *A Complete History of the Korean War* (朝鮮戦争全史)(Tokyo: Iwanami Shoten Publishers東京: 株式会社岩波書店, 2002) and *Origins and Outbreak of the Russo-Japanese War* (日露戦争 起源と開戦(上・下))(Tokyo: Iwanami Shoten Publishers東京: 株式会社岩波書店, 2009-2010). He is also a recipient of awards such as the Kim Dae-jung Academic Award.

Dekun Hu (胡德坤), born in 1946 in Suizhou, Hubei Province, graduated from the Department of History at Wuhan University in 1969 and remained at the university to teach. He was a visiting scholar at Kyoto University, Japan, in 1980, and at Soka University, Japan, in 1991. He was promoted to professor in 1988 and was appointed Senior Professor of Humanities and Social Sciences at Wuhan University in 2010. He previously served as Vice President of Wuhan University, Dean of the School of History, and Director of the Institute of China's Borders and Oceans, among other academic positions. He also served as President of the Chinese Society for the Study of the History of World War II.

He has published 15 books and 160 academic papers, including *Research on China and the World during the Anti-Fascist War Period*(反法西斯战争时期的中国与世界研究(九卷本, 主编))(Wuhan: Wuhan University Press 武汉: 武汉大学出版社, 2010) and *The Historical Status of China's War of Resistance in the World Anti-Fascist War*(中国抗战在世界反法西斯战争中的历史地位)(Beijing: Economic Science Press 北京: 经济科学出版社, 2013).

Alexis Dudden is a professor in the Department of History at the University of Connecticut. She is currently on leave and is also serving as a visiting professor in the Department of Japanese Studies at the National University of Singapore from 2024 to 2026.

She graduated from Columbia University (B.A.) and the University of Chicago (M.A.), and then completed her Ph.D. at the University of Chicago. Her research focuses on modern Japan, Korea, and East Asian history, with an emphasis on empire, nationalism, and reconciliation.

Among her major publications are *The Opening and Closing of Japan, 1850-2020* (under contract with Oxford University Press) and *Troubled Apologies Among Japan, Korea, and the United States* (Columbia University Press, 2008). She has received multiple awards, including the Manhae International Peace Prize.

Explanation: The Formation, Process and Results of the San Francisco System

Young-Ho Kim

1 From the Japan-Korea Basic Treaty to the San Francisco Peace Treaty

In 2010, marking the 100th anniversary of Korea's annexation, we issued a joint statement by Korean and Japanese intellectuals declaring the 1910 Treaty of Annexation of Korea as illegally null and void, which also became a core issue in the 1965 Japan-Korea Basic Treaty. A key issue in the normalization of diplomatic relations between Korea and Japan was how to interpret the series of treaties leading up to Korea's annexation, especially the meaning and starting point of "already null and void" in Article 2. The Korean position was that the treaties were null and void from the time they were signed, and that Japan's colonial rule was therefore illegal and void, while the Japanese position was that the treaties were legal and valid at the time they were signed, but became null and void upon the Liberation or the signing of the Treaty of San Francisco.

These two positions were irreconcilable at the time, and the result was the "already" in Article 2, and the compromise behind it was that South Korea would interpret it in a South Korean way and Japan would interpret it in a Japanese way. This was a "cowardly" compromise that glossed over the problem, but on the other hand, normalization of diplomatic relations could not have been achieved otherwise, so it was considered by some to be a "wise" compromise. Such measures may be temporary or superficially acceptable, but in the long run and inherently unsustainable. The Joint Statement of Korean and Japanese Intellectuals was to provide a

Supplementary Information The online version contains supplementary material available at https://doi.org/10.1007/978-981-95-3328-2_1.

Y.-H. Kim (✉)
Department of Economics, Kyungpook National University,
Daegu, Korea (Republic of)

Y.-H. Kim et al. (eds.), *Beyond the San Francisco System*,
https://doi.org/10.1007/978-981-95-3328-2_1

certain direction of resolution to this problem. Fortunately, 1000 Korean and Japanese intellectuals proposed that the Korean-Japanese Merger Treaty was illegal and null and void from the outset, and that the arbitrary interpretation of Article 2 of the Korean-Japanese Basic Treaty should be unified with the Korean interpretation. At that time, the number of signatures of Korean and Japanese intellectuals exceeded 1000, and the two countries stopped it at 1200. Among the intellectuals, historians overwhelmingly participated, which meant that the consensus was reached by the most expert among the intellectuals. At the same time, the "Naoto Kan Discourse" by Naoto Kan, the prime minister of Japan at the time, was published after a cabinet meeting. Although it did not reach the level of the Joint Statement of Korean and Japanese Intellectuals, it certainly surpassed the level of the previous prime minister's discourse and was influenced by the Joint Statement of Korean and Japanese Intellectuals.

We pursued the realization of the 2010 Joint Statement by travelling back and forth between Seoul and Tokyo under the slogan "Promises of 2010, Expectations of 2015", but again, with the return of former Prime Minister Abe in late 2012 and the radicalization of Japanese society and politics, we were frustrated by the wall of the 1965 Japan-Korea Basic Treaty. We secured support for the legitimacy of our claims in 2015 with the Joint Statement of Korean, Japanese and World Intellectuals, which included intellectuals such as Professor Noam Chomsky of the Massachusetts Institute of Technology.

We recognize the historical limitation that such a framework for the Japan-Korea Basic Treaty was in fact unavoidable within the framework of the San Francisco Peace Treaty. Given the nature of the San Francisco Enhancement Treaty, the Japan-Korea Framework Treaty could only be achieved in this way. Therefore, we shared the view that the problem should not be the nature of the Japan-Korea Framework Treaty, but the San Francisco Enhancement Treaty, which is the basis of the Japan-Korea Framework Treaty. Thus, our tagline "2010 Promises 2015 Expectations" became "Beyond the San Francisco System". We were fortunate to have very active participation from China, which, along with South Korea, is arguably the biggest victim of the San Francisco System.

The first conference, "Beyond the San Francisco System", was held at Columbia University in 2016 with the participation of experts from China, United States, Japan and Korea; the second conference was held at the University of Pennsylvania in 2017 with the participation of scholars from China, the United States, Japan and Korea; the third conference was held at Wuhan University in China with the participation of scholars from Korea, China, the United States, Japan, Russia and Canada; and the fourth conference was held in Seoul in November 2019 with the participation of scholars from Korea, China, the United States, Australia and Canada. The fifth meeting was planned to be held at the University of Waterloo in Canada, but has been postponed twice due to the COVID-19 pandemic. In the winter of 2024. while preparing for the meeting at the University of Waterloo, the organizer Professor Kimie Hara was hospitalized for health problem, so the date and venue were changed and the meeting was held in December at Korea University in Korea, co-hosted with the Asiatic Research Institute of Korea University.

On the occasion of the 70th anniversary of the San Francisco Treaty in 2021, the Korean edition titled "Beyond the San Francisco System" (Medici Media, 2023) was published as a collection of papers presented at four conferences. The Korean edition was selected as "the book of the year"in the social science category in 2023 by the Hankyoreh newspaper. The English version of this book is expected to be published in 2025, which reflected the results of the fifth conference and updated the contents again.

2 The Formation and Changing Nature of the San Francisco System

In its preamble, the San Francisco Covenant states that it is "committed to adhere to the principles of the Charter of the United Nations and to implement the goals of the Universal Declaration of Human Rights in all circumstances". It consists of seven chapters and 27 articles, signed at the end by representatives of 48 invited countries. South Korea and China, two of the biggest victims of Japanese fascism, were not invited and did not become signatories. It has been said that South Korea was not invited because of Japan's obstruction, but it has been confirmed that the United States persuaded Japan to send a letter of invitation to South Korea, citing the need to strengthen South Korea's position during the Korean War while maintaining its stance of recognizing South Korea as a member of the Allied forces that fought against Japan. In the midst of the Korean War, President Syngman Rhee's reply to the U.S. representative showed that he did not understand the change in the U.S. position and took an ultra-hardline stance against Japan, which embarrassed the United States. In the end, Britain, which represented Japan's position, convinced the United States that if Korea was invited, the Soviet Union would demand an invitation to North Korea, which would be difficult to refuse. The British representative at the San Francisco Conference took the exact opposite position from W. Churchill's at the Cairo Conference. The result was that Korea was placed at a disadvantageous position under the San Francisco Treaty than Poland under the Versailles Pact or Libya under the Italian Pact.

However, at this conference, it was reaffirmed that the United States officially recognized the Korean Independence Army as part of the Allied forces fighting alongside Chiang Kai-shek's Nationalist government against Japan, and that the United States ultimately withdrew its invitation to Korea due to persistent British opposition at Japan's request. Both of those were discoveries of significant historical facts.[1]

[1]Yi, T.-J. (2025). A Case for the Modifiability of the San Francisco Peace Treaty: Examining the Varying Positions of the U.S. and Britain over South Korean Participation. In *Beyond the San*

In fact, as its preamble makes clear, the San Francisco Treaty was concluded between the Allies and Japan to "settle the questions which still remain unsettled as a result of the existence of a state of war" between the Allies and Japan, i.e., to deal with the aftermath of the Second World War. Japan's aggression in Asia and its colonial and semi-colonial responsibilities, including its invasion of Korea and its colonial crimes, were not even envisaged as issues to be resolved. This was not the intention from the outset.

In fact, the San Francisco Treaty changed its character in three phases. The first phase was in 1945–1947, when the United States pushed for the early conclusion of a full reinforcement. The goal of the Allies was to dismantle the war criminal Japanese fascism and turn Japan into an agricultural nation in Asia. However, as the U.S.-Soviet confrontation intensified and the Cold War intensified, the Soviet Union opposed the early strengthening of Japan and opposed the early strengthening, so the United States changed its policy to prioritize confrontation with the Soviet Union, and its policy towards Japan changed radically. In the second phase of 1948–1950, the United States sought to strengthen Japan alone, to the exclusion of the Soviet Union.

In Young-Ho Kim's paper "The Collision between Historical Legacy and Regional Integration in the San Francisco System",[2] it is analysed that the San Francisco system was a Keynesian policy world. After the war, the demands for reparations from the victorious countries towards the defeated countries were traditionally harsh. After the Punic Wars between Rome and Carthage in the second century BC, the victorious Rome imposed reparations on the defeated Carthage that were at a level of destruction that rendered recovery impossible, and most defeated nations faced a Carthaginian-type destruction. Even after the establishment of modern capitalism, after the war between Prussia and France, France paid a Carthaginian debt, and the Treaty of Versailles among the victorious nations of World War I, including the United States, Britain and France, and the defeated Germany, also included harsh reparations conditions. John Maynard Keynes, a young representative from Britain participating in this conference, emphasized that minimizing Germany's reparations and instead supporting the reconstruction of Germany's economy would benefit the economic prosperity of the Allies. This argument was published in his book *The Economic Consequences of the Peace* (1919). The United States aimed for the revival of the Japanese economy in the third stage of the San Francisco Peace Treaty. The United States had already implemented Keynesian economic policies with the New Deal in 1929 and was conducting the Keynesian Marshall Plan in Europe. Coincidentally, due to the security necessity of preventing the communization of East Asia, an Asian version of the Marshall Plan followed. The Korean War was the pinnacle of the Asian Marshall Plan. The San Francisco Peace Treaty was the world's first treaty for the economic revival of a defeated

Francisco System. Springer.

[2] Kim, Y.-H. (2016). The collision of the historical legacy and the economic integration in the San Francisco system. Paper presented at the *first Conference of Beyond the San Francisco*, Columbia University.

nation. The rapid economic growth of Korea, Taiwan, Singapore and China following Japan after the war is difficult to explain without considering the direct and indirect connections to the San Francisco Peace Treaty.

At the National Security Council (NSC13/2), which deals with the basics of U.S. foreign policy, the "Report on the Policy of the United States Towards Japan" was effectively decided and signed by the President in October 1948. This was the core of a policy of intensification aimed at the de facto reconstruction of Japan. The overarching goal of U.S. policy towards Japan was "economic revival beyond reform". The third phase, which began with the Korean War, settled the U.S. possession of Okinawa and the stationing of U.S. troops in Japan, and led to the signing of a security treaty along with a peace treaty. NSC13/2 was the Japanese version of the Marshall Plan for Western Europe. To revive Japan's economy, the reparations to be paid by Japan were drastically reduced from 2.42 billion yen to one-fourth, and 90% of the money was allocated to military production facilities, thus halting the reduction of Japanese production facilities (Dulles' Seven Principles for Strengthening Japan, September 1950, decided by John Foster Dulles when he became the President's special envoy for the peace treaty) and resulting in a generous strengthening treaty that recognized Japan as a partner in the Cold War rather than a defeated nation. The United States drastically reduced the number of chaebol to be broken up to democratize Japan's economy from 257 to 17. The U.S.-Japan defence treaty also ensured that the Japanese economy would bear little of the burden of military expenditure and, most notably, that Japan would have a near monopoly on the extraordinary benefits of the Korean War. The Korean War was a Marshall Plan for Japan. He also pushed for the strict implementation of the Nine Principles of Economic Stability, brought inflation under control in the short term with the Dodge Line, and dismantled radical unions to lay the political foundations for the postwar conservative system in Japan.

This Japanese version of the Marshall Plan led to the so-called miracle of Japanese economic growth after the Korean War, which provided both the opportunity for postwar East Asian economic growth and the opportunity for Japanese economic subordination. Through the San Francisco Reinforcement Treaty, the United States froze Japan's assets in its former empire in East Asia so that they could be used as the basis for post-war economic reconstruction in East Asian countries, and implemented land reforms to eliminate the semi-feudal legacy in Korea and redirect economic activity to the non-agricultural sector. In addition, through the process of national reconciliation with Japan, reparations or quasi-reparations were paid, which became a source of new investment funds for economic development. And by opening up the U.S. consumer market, cheap goods from developing countries were freely imported, which prevented domestic inflation and established export-led industrialization in East Asia. At the same time, the New International Economic Order was formed under the auspices of the United Nations (UN) in the 1960s, which gave preferential tariffs to the export of manufactured goods from the East Asian empires to promote export-led industrialization. As a result, the so-called East Asian NICs (Newly Industrialized Countries) such as South Korea, Taiwan, Hong Kong and Singapore emerged.

The transition from Japan's economic miracle to East Asia's high growth to China's high growth cannot be seen as a linear continuation of the economic achievements of the San Francisco system. However, it is also true that it is difficult to discuss the economic development of East Asia without ignoring the economic consequences of the San Francisco system.

It should be emphasized initially that the San Francisco Peace Treaty was an international agreement to resolve issues arising from the conclusion of World War II. Importantly, it was not intended to address Japan's aggression in East Asia or its colonial and semi-colonial crimes. The treaty imposed only limited responsibility for war on Japan, while not holding Japan directly accountable for its acts of aggression and colonial rule. Nevertheless, Japan's history of aggression in East Asia is not merely a historical event but an ongoing unresolved issue with profound implications for both the present and the future.

We have repeatedly seen in international conferences that the San Francisco Reinforcement Treaty does little to reflect the Cairo and Potsdam Declarations made at the end of the Second World War. On 1 December 1943, President Roosevelt of the United States, Prime Minister Churchill of the United Kingdom, and Premier Chiang Kai-shek of China met in Cairo and jointly issued the Cairo Declaration. The core values of the Cairo Declaration were to "crush and punish the Japanese aggressor", "restore the sovereignty of colonized and illegally occupied territories", and "improve human rights".

Here, the issue of restoring territorial sovereignty was twofold: the restoration of China's territorial sovereignty and the restoration of DPRK's territorial sovereignty. Professor Dekun HU and Professor Shu Yong, on the Chinese side, argued that the current San Francisco Treaty of Enhanced Cooperation is illegal and null and void with no historical basis, and that China does not recognize the treaty and expects the return of several South China Sea islands (including the Diaoyu Diaoyu Islands) and Okinawa to China as promised by the United States.

Below is the original Korean text excerpt.

> Japan shall also be expelled from all territories which she has taken by violence and greed. The above three Powers are mindful of the enslaved condition of the Korean people and resolve to make them free and independent by due process of law.

The core values of the Cairo Declaration were reaffirmed in paragraph 8 of the Potsdam Declaration of July 1945, and moved from political declaration to international law with Japan's unconditional acceptance of the Potsdam Declaration in its surrender document of 10 August 1945 and the signing of the surrender document on 2 September that year. The relevant parts of the Japanese surrender document are as follows:

> We (Japan) accept the provisions set forth in the Declaration issued at Potsdam on 26 July 1945 by the Heads of Government of the United States, China and Great Britain and subsequently endorsed by the Soviet Union. We pledge that the Government of Japan and its successors hereafter will faithfully carry out the provisions of the Potsdam Declaration.

This had the effect of retroactively and explicitly confirming the Dokdo clause, which had been implied but not specifically stated in the Cairo and Potsdam Declarations. Again in 1946, Supreme Allied Powers Supreme Command (SCAPIN) 677 specified that Dokdo should be excluded from Japanese territory and returned to Korea, and notified the Provisional Government of Japan. This was a directive from MacArthur's command that retroactively confirmed that Dokdo was included in the list of islands to be returned to Japan in the Cairo and Potsdam Declarations.[3]

However, the core values of the Cairo Declaration and Potsdam Declaration were lost during the second phase of the San Francisco Treaty. The omission of Dokdo from the list of islands to be returned to Korea by Japan in Articles 2(1) and 9(d) of the San Francisco Treaty provided the basis for Japan's subsequent claim to the islands. Professor Alexis Durden highlights the role of Mr. Seibold, a pro-Japanese adviser to McArthur, in this process. The United States has always sided with Japan in historical disputes between Korea and Japan, not just over Dokdo, making the United States the de facto leader and arbiter of the disputes between Korea and Japan. This is what calls the "dirty secret of American diplomacy".[4]

At a Columbia University conference, Professor Jung meticulously traced the process of attribution of the disputed islands and publicly exposed photographs of U.S. military officers and their wives wearing Japanese kimonos and enjoying private parties with Japanese political figures.[5]

In fact, it was revealed that the US delegates to the San Francisco Treaty of Enrichment used tactics to foster and capitalize on Japanese superiority over Asians. This is the "dirty secret" of the San Francisco Treaty, as Professor Durden puts it. In addition, the value of the Cairo Declaration's recognition of the enslavement of the Korean people and the value of human rights improvements to the Korean people have been lost in the focus on war responsibility for the Second World War and the neglect of colonial responsibility.[6]

It can be said that the road to resolving the comfort women issue and the issue of forced labourers is blocked today because of the wall of the San Francisco Peace Treaty. When normalizing diplomatic relations with former imperialist countries

---

[3] Lee, J.-H. (2025). The Core Values of Cairo Declaration and an Exit Strategy to Overcome the Limitations of the San Francisco Peace Treaty, In *Beyond the San Francisco System*. Springer.

Hu, D. (2025). Transcending the San Francisco System requires the elimination of colonial remnants—with a focus on post-war territorial disputes in Northeast Asia, In *Beyond the San Francisco System*. Springer.

Xu, Y. (2025). A Study on Modern Japanese Colonialism and Ryukyu Restoration, In *Beyond the San Francisco System*. Springer.

[4] Dudden, A. (2022). Trouble among East Asian allies? America's dirty secret. Paper presented at the Seoul conference, 2019. In *Beyond the San Francisco System* (샌프란시스코 체제를 너머서) *(Korean edition)*. Medici Media.

[5] Jung, B. J. (2025). The San Francisco Peace Treaty and Territorial Issues: Information Pamphlets on Territorial Issues from the Japanese Ministry of Foreign Affairs and Their Impact, In *Beyond the San Francisco System*. Springer.

[6] Lee, J.-H. (2025). The Core Values of Cairo Declaration and an Exit Strategy to Overcome the Limitations of the San Francisco Peace Treaty, In *Beyond the San Francisco System*. Springer.

after the war, it is a common practice to express apologies for their past aggression and fascist domination, but the Japan-Korea Basic Treaty is a very rare case where there is no such expression at all.

Japan did not insert a tariff clause in the Treaty of Ganghwa Island (1876), the first modern treaty in the opening period, making it a tariff-free treaty unprecedented in modern world trade treaties: the so-called Eunsa Protection Treaty in Korean did not even have the substance of a treaty: and the so-called Korean Annexation Treaty was an incomplete treaty without the approval of the Korean head of state, the King. However, the Treaty of Normalisation of Diplomatic Relations after liberation did not express apology for colonial crimes.

Japan's colonization of Korea is a special case in world history. Japan did not plunge into imperialist aggression until after the international movement for peace had already begun with some reflection on the harms of imperialism, leading to the Hague Universal Peace Conference (1908). Western imperialism generally invaded and colonized distant Asia and Africa in the nineteenth century, where people of different races and cultures from the West were common. Japan colonized a neighbouring country with which it had shared a state religion for over a thousand years. Japan insists that other powers would have invaded Korea even if Japan hadn't, but after the Sino-Japanese and Russo-Japanese wars, there was no other power on earth that could stand up to the United States and British-backed Japan. The defeat of the Russo-Japanese War revealed that the Russia of the eve of the Revolution had neither the ambition nor the ability to enter Korea.

Professor John W. Dower, a leading authority on the modern history of East Asia in the United States, summarizes the legacy of the San Francisco system in eight ways.[7] Okinawa and two Japan: territorial disputes with Korea, China and Russia: U.S. military bases in Japan: the Japanese treasury and the U.S. nuclear umbrella: historical issues: the Chinese blockade and Japan's disengagement from Asia: and Japan's subordinate independence.

All eight of these issues are relevant to Korea, but the territorial and historical issues of Dokdo are particularly important. In the process of reopening diplomatic relations in post-war world history, treaties were signed without apology for the history of colonial aggression. The Korean-Japanese Basic Treaty and the Convention on Claims were concluded as subsystems within the framework of the San Francisco Peace Treaty and its guidelines and enforcement. And in response to South Korea's recent attempts to rectify this unequal treaty, the Japanese government has denounced it as a violation of the Convention on the Rights of Claims and a reneging on the promises made between the countries, and has not hesitated to retaliate with trade.

In the San Francisco Treaty, the crimes of colonization committed by Japan in Korea between 1910 and 1945 were never envisaged as an issue to be addressed. The word colony itself does not appear anywhere in the treaty. Article 21 stipulates that Korea is not a signatory to the treaty but enjoys the benefits of Articles 2, 4 and

[7] Dower, J. W. (2014). The San Francisco system: Past, present, future in U.S.–Japan–China relations. *Asia-Pacific Journal: Japan Focus, 12*(8), e2.

12. Professor Kang says that legally "to enjoy a benefit, it must literally be a benefit, and it cannot impose an obligation. Denying the right to compensation based on a treaty that was not attended is not a benefit, but an obligation", he said.[8]

Article 2 (a) provides that "Japan recognizes the independence of the Korean Peninsula and renounces its rights and claims to the Korean Peninsula, including Geomun Island and Ulleung Island in Jeju Province", which is a formal link to the Cairo Declaration. The purpose and structure of the treaty suggests that recognition of Korean independence does not mean that Japan is entitled to pursue accountability for its colonial crimes, but only that the financial and civil claims arising from the partition of the territory have been resolved.

Here we see that the United States facilitated Japan's annexation of Korea through the secret Teft-Katsura agreement: that after World War 1, Korea, inspired by President Wilson's national self-determination, raised the March 1 movement and asked for support, only to have it callously crushed in favour of Japan: and that the San Francisco Reinforcement Treaty thoroughly blocked Korea's avenues for pursuing Japanese fascism's colonial crimes. It has been suggested that the original sin behind this was the U.S. invasion and colonization of Hawaii. In fact, at the beginning of the U.S.-Soviet Cold War, Jewish organizations and the UN War Crimes Commission presented 36,000 allegations of Nazi crimes, but the U.S. government, under the influence of McCarthyism at the time, swept them under the rug as a logical response to the Cold War. The timing is almost coincidental. Since then, diplomatic tensions have risen between the Park, Geun-hye and Abe governments over the comfort women issue, and when President Obama of the United States was busy mediating, we argued that the United States should apologize to the grandmothers of the comfort women before Japan, citing the case of the U.S. Senate and House of Representatives, which passed a resolution to apologize for the forced occupation of Hawaii in 1992, the 100th anniversary of the occupation.

The San Francisco Peace Treaty completely ignored colonial crimes and only superficially addressed the war crimes of World War II. The Claims Convention was limited to civil and financial claims arising from the geographical division and partition of national territory; thus, it did not establish colonial crimes as a historical or legal basis for claims. If the Japan-Korea Agreement was a treaty modelled on the San Francisco Treaty, then the Japan-Korea Basic Treaty and the Claims Convention, which are the basis of the so-called 1965 system between Japan and Korea, are treaties that have nothing to do with colonial crimes. In other words, the crimes of colonization have not yet been addressed by the two countries and remain a historical issue between Japan and South Korea. While the South Korean government is dealing with the comfort women issue and the issue of forced labourers in the context of settling colonial crimes, the Japanese government is dealing with the issue in the context of settling claims that were incidental to the geographical separation of Japan and South Korea following the end of World War II. Is the issue of settlement of colonial crimes and the issue of claims completely separate?

[8] Kang, B.-K. (2018). The impact of the 1951 San Francisco Peace Treaty on the Korean Peninsula: Focusing on territorial issues and war reparations. Paper presented at the third Conference of Wuhan University, China.

3 Continuity and Discontinuity of the San Francisco System: A Series of Workout Patterns That Will Take You Beyond the San Francisco System

The historical consequences of the San Francisco system contrast sharply with those of the Versailles system. The Treaty of Versailles, signed by the British, French and Russian belligerents with defeated Germany at the end of World War I, was extremely harsh. They imposed excessive reparations, separated resources such as Alsace-Lorraine (population 6.74 million) from Germany, returned German-controlled overseas colonies to the belligerents, disbanded the General Staff, which had a large army, and banned the possession of heavy weapons. The Treaty of Versailles was deeply resented by the German people, and it was this resentment that would later give birth to Hitler's Nazism.[9]

The San Francisco Treaty, in contrast to the Versailles Treaty, was a strategic response to the communication of mainland China and the Korean War, and as a result, the United States punished the war criminal Japan too lightly. As a result, war criminals were given a free pass, and the United States was rewarded for rebuilding Japan's economy through extraordinary economic assistance and special aid for the Korean War, which ultimately spurred Japan to "reverse course" and return to its pre-war status quo. As support and authority for the post-war peace regime strengthened and became more generalized, the degree of glorification and affirmation of the pre-war regime weakened and became a minority, but as time passed in the post-war period. Japanese society's support and evaluation of the post-war regime weakened and the degree of glorification and affirmation of the pre-war regime increased. The post-war peace constitution was not established by the will of the Japanese people, but by the unilateral coercion of the occupying forces, and Japan has marked the day of the signing of the San Francisco Treaty as the day of the restoration of Japanese sovereignty, and has seen a resurgence of conservative politics in Japan, with Prime Minister Shinzo Abe formally declaring constitutional revision as a goal of his administration. Emphasizing that prewar Japan was a model to be admired rather than something to be reflected upon. While the Abe administration has not succeeded in amending Article 9, the core of the Peace Constitution, the Right to Collective Self-Defence Law, which effectively renders Article 9 ineffective, is now in place. This has been criticized by lawyer Masatoshi Uchida as a coup against the constitution.[10]

---

[9] Kim, S. W. (2025). Hasty Peace, Nasty Greed: Analyzing the Defects of the 1951 Treaty of San Francisco in Comparison with the 1919 Treaty of Versailles, In *Beyond the San Francisco System*. Springer.

Kim, Y.-H. (2025). From the Joint Statement by Korean and Japanese Intellectuals to the End of the San Francisco System Evaluation Conferences—Toward a Durban Conference of East-Asian Intellectuals, In *Beyond the San Francisco System*. Springer.

[10] Uchida, M. (2022). Abe "encouraged" the Armitage Report: The "revision" of Article 9 of the Constitution to allow the exercise of the right of collective self-defence(아베 '개헌'을 '독려'한 아

In terms of the resurgence of Japanese conservative politics and the revival of the pre-war system, it is actually operating beyond the San Francisco system, and although it has not succeeded in amending Article 9 of the Constitution, it has succeeded in neutralizing it. Here, we can say that if the result of the Versailles Reinforcement Treaty, which was very harsh on Germany, the defeated country of World War I, led to Hitler's Nazism, the result of the San Francisco Reinforcement Treaty, which was very lenient on Japan, the defeated country of World War II. led to a new revival of Japanese wartime fascism. Humanity had to spend most of the second half of the twentieth century overcoming Nazism. Now, humanity may have to spend the placenta of the twenty-first century overcoming Japan's re-emergence of fascism.

We are experiencing the transition from San Francisco System 1.0 to San Francisco System 2.0 as we witness the resurgence of pre-war fascism in a post-war democracy with Japan's general rightward shift.

In the United States, the Japanese version of the Marshall Plan, based on the National Security Council's (NSC) "Report on U.S. Policy Towards Japan" (NSC13/2), which was the economic substance of the San Francisco Enhancement Treaty, was initiated, and the Japanese economy began to grow at a high rate due to the intensive benefits of the Korean War. The San Francisco system was to make Japan a strategic base for the United States in response to the communization of mainland China and the outbreak of war in Korea, while at the same time making it a showcase for capitalism and reorganizing the East Asian empire into a peripheral part of the Japanese economy. U.S. policy therefore developed according to the framework of the San Francisco system. Post-war U.S. aid and frozen Japanese assets in the East Asian empire provided the basis for post-war East Asian economic reconstruction, while land reform allowed for the release of rural excess labour, which, combined with the entry of Japanese capital, enabled dependent industrialization to take place.

At the same time, the United States opened up its domestic market to curb post-war inflation and stimulated import demand from the East Asian empires. The unlimited supply of capital from the United States, Japan and other countries, combined with the unlimited supply of domestic labour from the East Asian empires, led to the export-led industrialization of East Asia, and the emergence of the Newly Industrialised Countries (NICs) such as South Korea. Taiwan, Singapore and Hong Kong. In 1972, the municipal authority of Okinawa was returned to Japan, heralding a change in the San Francisco system. The "Nixon Shock" of 1972 normalized U.S.-China relations, and around this time, Sino-Japanese diplomatic relations were restored, and the 1988 Seoul Olympics led to diplomatic relations with 45 communist countries, including the normalization of diplomatic relations with South Korea and China, as part of the Roh Tae-woo government's so-called Northern Diplomacy. North Korea-Japan relations also improved in 2002 with

---

미티지 리포트: 집단적 자위권 행사 용인은 헌법 9조의 '개변'), In *Beyond the San Francisco System* (샌프란시스코 체제를 너머서) (Korean version). Medichi Media.

Prime Minister Koizumi's visit to Pyongyang and the Pyongyang Declaration. As China became the world's largest market, with intra-regional trade exceeding 50%, intra-regional investment followed suit and with intra-regional trade exceeding 55 per cent in 2020, there was a parallel regionalization of finance. The East Asian region, which had been divided and confrontational under the San Francisco system, has slowly begun to integrate. The ASEAN+3 (China, Japan, Korea) community was formed and Australia and New Zealand joined the grouping, which evolved into a regular summit system. The "Chiang Mai Initiative" radicalized regional monetary and financial integration, and the Regional Comprehensive Economic Partnership (RCEP) was promoted and finally ratified in the context of trade and investment finance integration. The trilateral summits were also regularized and a trilateral cooperation secretariat was established. Has East Asian economic integration passed the point of no return? Does the establishment of the East Asian Community mark the end of the San Francisco system? The maturation of the East Asian Community is another pattern of graduation from the San Francisco system.

However, the situation was complex. Karl Deutsch, a prominent sociologist, had proposed the so-called "Karl Deutsch Hypothesis" that the more frequent contact and communication between countries, the greater the degree of integration. In East Asia, the prevailing view was that economic exchanges and contacts had exploded, leading to greater integration and a full-fledged community, but the situation was reversed. The "unsolved problems" of the San Francisco Treaty of Enhanced Cooperation, centred on historical disputes and territorial issues such as the disputed islands, have continued to be raised and have set back political and economic cooperation. This reverse phenomenon is known as the "Paradox of East Asia". In Western Europe, the establishment of the European Union (EU) was possible because "historical reconciliation made European integration possible" as European intellectual Jacques Attali testified. So, while the San Francisco Treaty has led to a steady path of economic growth in East Asia, has it also opened the way for continued intra-East Asian conflict? Professor Kimie Hara of the University of Waterloo, Canada, presented a surprising conclusion at the Seoul Conference in 2019, suggesting that the United States may have strategically planted the seeds of historical and territorial disputes in the San Francisco Treaty in order to induce imperial conflict in East Asia.[11]

> The ambiguities of the Enhanced Treaty were not the result of inadvertence or mistake. Rather, they were deliberately left unresolved.

[11] Hara, K. (2005). サンフランシスコ平和条約の盲点: アジア太平洋地域の冷戦と『戦後未解決の諸問題』 [The blind spot of the San Francisco Peace Treaty: The Cold War in the Asia-Pacific Region and 'Unresolved postwar issues']. 渓水社.

Hara, K. (2022). Keys for correct resolution and reconciliation: Beyond the San Francisco system(올바른 해결과 화해를 위한 열쇠들: 샌프란시스코 체제를 넘어서), In *Beyond the San Francisco System*(샌프란시스코 체제를 넘어서) (Korean edition). Medici Media.

Hara, K. (2025). Beyond the San Francisco System: An Inspiration from Canada, In *Beyond the San Francisco System*. Springer.

Professor Kimie Hara views the recent territorial dispute settlement process between Canada and Denmark as a notable example of historicization and decolonization with the involvement of the native of Canada, providing valuable insights into territorial dispute resolution under the San Francisco system.

Moreover, the United States has strategically supported former Japanese Prime Minister Abe's campaign to revise the Peace Constitution. The Peace Constitution is an important achievement and pillar of the San Francisco system, so why support its revision? The answer, of course, is to actively draw Japan into the anti-China camp in the U.S.-China hegemonic confrontation. The United States and Japan have established the so-called QUAD alliance, a security cooperation between the United States, Japan, India and Australia in the Indo-Pacific system, aiming to create an Asia-Pacific version of NATO (North Atlantic Treaty Organization). In the theory of emergent genus, there is a proposition that the next in line of the periphery is also the periphery. Professor Lee Jong-won (Waseda University) calls the San Francisco system 2.0, which is not a graduation of the San Francisco system but a new San Francisco system called the Indo-Pacific system.[12] Professor Lee Jong-won (Waseda University) notes that Prime Minister Abe's speech to the U.S. Congress in 2015 argued that Japan was a war criminal and a loser in World War II, but a winner in the Cold War, and that it had a joint responsibility to build a vast sea of freedom from the Pacific Ocean to the Indian Ocean with the United States, The fact that it is based on the Armitage Report, the U.S. government's strategy of containment of the People's Republic of China, and its close ties to historical revisionism in Japan make it what Professor Lee calls the San Francisco System 2.0.0.

The Abe discourse of the last 50 years has effectively "overwritten" the Murayama discourse, if not outright repudiated it. As Professor Gavan MaCormack, who attended the 2019 Seoul conference, points out.[13]

"The San Francisco Treaty/Cold War system is approaching the end of its useful life, some 70 years after it was established. Abe is now focused on maintaining that framework, grovelling to Washington for much of his efforts, while constantly ramping up war preparations in confrontation with China, Russia and North Korea".

In his paper, Professor Gavan MaCormack sharply analyses the growing Cold War ties between Japan and Australia, warning that "citizens, especially on the Korean peninsula and around Okinawa, are experiencing first-hand how precious peace can be", and pointing out that only by focusing on peace-building, rather than war-making, can we move away from the nuclear threat and begin to address the historic challenges of climate change.

Abe has signalled a break from the past by completely ignoring the discourse of Naoto Kan. Although South Korea has become politically and economically advanced, its security system remains relegated to the periphery of the San Francisco system, caught between the U.S.-China confrontation. South Korea, once

[12] Lee, J.-W. (2025). Beyond the San Francisco system, to where? Contending visions for the region-building in East Asia, In *Beyond the San Francisco System,* Springer.

[13] MacCormack, G. (2025). Clientelism forever? Contemplating the San Francisco Treaty settlement 72 years on, In *Beyond the San Francisco System,* Springer.

victimized as a periphery of the San Francisco system when that confrontation started immediately post-World War II, is now again repositioned as a victim in the emerging San Francisco system 2.0 amid full-scale U.S.-China rivalry, making it increasingly important to turn this crisis into an opportunity.

When human rights and democracy blossom in East Asia, they tend to clash with the San Francisco system, which has a tendency to turn a blind eye to democracy and make it difficult to get along. We will take the case of South Korea as an example. The post-liberation land reforms created a low-cost labour supply from the rural overpopulation, and under the developmental dictatorship of the military government, the combination of chaebol capital and an unlimited supply of foreign capital, including loans and claims funding from Japan, led to a decade of export-led economic growth that turned the country into a middle-income country, which in turn became a newly industrialized country (NIC) in the decade of the new millennium, which in turn created a middle-income-oriented civil society in the decade of the new millennium. Dissident forces that had already been formed in resistance to developmental dictatorships grew and partnered with the citizenry to win democracy through the Gwangju Uprising and the June Uprising. Here, the solidarity between the dissident movement and the middle class (the tie force) fostered by the developmental dictatorship is important. In post-war history, we have seen the evolution of economic growth, new industrial countries, civil society and democracy, but in Japan, human rights were emphasized in the civil society stage of the democratic system, and the current emphasis on human rights has heightened criticism of human rights violations in history. Therefore, the more democratic Korea becomes, the more sensitive the issue of colonial past history becomes, and the more conservative Japan becomes, the more it goes against historical reflection, making historical conflicts between Korea and Japan almost inevitable. As South Korea's democracy has grown, the level of aggression has increased, including the comfort women issue, the issue of forced labourers, the history of human rights abuses in the colonial past, and the issue of revising the Unequal Treaty. With the establishment of democracy in South Korea, the testimony of Kim Hak-soon, a former comfort women victim, on 14 August 1991. and the demand rallies that brought the issue of comfort women to the world's attention began in January 1992. The issue of post-war liquidation was raised in earnest as a social issue, and the issue of annulling or revising the unequal treaty with former Japanese colonial power Japan was raised. Finally, in 2010, on the 100th anniversary of the annexation of Korea, the "Joint Statement of Korean and Japanese Intellectuals" was released. in which more than 1000 Korean and Japanese intellectuals participated. Under its influence, the "Discourse of Prime Minister Naoto Kan" was published, which evolved further.

The Joint Statement of Korean and Japanese Intellectuals was widely reported in the media, especially in South Korea, and its impact was felt in the immediate aftermath of the Constitutional Court's 2011 ruling on the unconstitutionality of the state's actions in the comfort women's trials, and the Supreme Court's 2012 ruling that Japan's colonial rule was illegal and that the right to compensation for damages caused by state intervention was not covered by the Convention on the Rights of Claims. This had a direct and decisive impact on the November 2018 ruling on compensation for victims of forced labour. The Supreme Court‘s November 2018 ruling stated that “the right to compensation for crimes against humanity by Japanese companies directly related to the Japanese government‘s illegal colonization and waging of wars of aggression is not covered by the Japan-Korea Claims Settlement Agreement, and therefore, the right to compensation for victims of forced mobilisation against Japanese companies exists”. At its core, the ruling stipulates that Japan’s colonial policies were illegal, which is in line with the Joint Statement of Korean and Japanese Intellectuals and in direct opposition to the San Francisco Peace Treaty. This ruling was groundbreaking. According to Do Shi Hwan’s research, South Korean high courts have traditionally accepted the judgements of the Supreme Court of Japan under the doctrine of stare decisis. Even in the recent appeals of the Japanese forced labour cases in February and July 2009, the Korean High Court upheld the 2007 ruling of the Supreme Court of Japan, which had ruled in favour of the plaintiffs in the case. After the joint statement by Korean and Japanese intellectuals, a completely new ruling by the Constitutional Court on comfort women and a ruling by the Supreme Court on recruiters were issued.[14]

While the judiciary’s own judgement was significant, the Joint Statement of Korean and Japanese intellectuals had already altered the course of history. “The Japanese courts did their best to preserve the seal with the flawed logic of eliminating the right to sue”, says Professor Kim Chang-rok...... The US courts also joined in. citing “sovereign immunity” or “political issues” to keep the seal in place. This is why the rulings of the South Korean Constitutional Court and Supreme Court are particularly noteworthy. Their rulings meant breaking the “seal” of the San Francisco Treaty, which was established 60 years ago.

And then there were reports of criticism coming out of the State Department that it was a violation of international law. Not to mention the violation of international law, it is a violation of the San Francisco Peace Treaty. The San Francisco system is destined to end with the maturation of democracy in East Asia, but on the contrary, it can be said that East Asian democracy is under the constraints of the San Francisco system.

After the Supreme Court‘s decision on the issue of internment, the issue of individual claims by internees emerged as a focus of attention. The San Francisco Peace Treaty prohibits individual claims, whether by comfort women or forced labour recruits, while the rising prominence of international human rights law, led by the United Nations, pushed increasingly in favour of recognizing individual claims. The international legal basis for the U.S. military administration’s decision to allow the unrecognized Korean Provisional Government to return home in an individual capacity immediately after liberation was the U.S. government’s policy that would later culminate in the San Francisco Peace Treaty. The Korean comfort women and forced labour recruits have never had their individual claims recognized by the

---

[14] Do, S.-H. (2020). The 2010 joint statement of Korean and Japanese intellectuals and the task of defining history. *The News of the East North Korea History Foundation, 165.*

Japanese judiciary. However, shortly after the 1965 claims settlement, the head of the Treaty Division of the Japanese Ministry of Foreign Affairs stated in a reply to the Japanese Diet that only the state's diplomatic protection of the victims' human rights had been terminated, and that individual claims remained alive. This principle was reaffirmed by Japan's Foreign Minister in November 2018, shortly after the Supreme Court's comfort women trial, and in a statement by Japanese lawyers in support of the South Korean Supreme Court trial. In addition, not only has Japan recognized the individual claims of the survivors of the atomic bombings of Hiroshima and Nagasaki in the past, but China has also recognized the individual claims of Chinese forced labourers in the case of Nishimatsu Construction and Mitsubishi Mining after a diplomatic settlement with Japan to resume diplomatic relations. This confirms the basic principle that diplomatic consultations between states only affect the right to diplomatic protection of individual human rights, and that individual claims themselves are not subject to state intervention. This confirms the basic principle that citizens and peoples in East Asia are relatively independent of the state. While there are many practical constraints that make it difficult for this principle to work, it is important to affirm and realistically expand this principle. This principle can be a starting point for East Asia's billion-plus middle class and smart people to realize that they are not passive guests in East Asia, but sovereign hosts, and to move towards a Civil Asia.

As a starting point, the argument for the establishment of the International Court of Human Rights in East Asia is drawing attention. The establishment of an International Court of Human Rights is urgent given that the results of Military Sexual Slavery's trial are the opposite in Korea and Japan.

When we put aside the Joint Statement of the Korean and Japanese Intellectuals and dealt with the issue of the San Francisco system, we naturally saw a major new development on the issue of the old Korean-Japanese Agreement. Having already shared the research results that the Korean Annexation Treaty of 1910 was a fictitious treaty without the approval of Emperor Sunjong, a series of international academic conferences produced a touching scene in which surprising fact that the so-called Protection Treaty of 1905 was a fictitious treaty that did not exist was raised by Professor Yi Tae-Jin and confirmed by Professor Totsuka/Lawyer(Japan) through independent research and agreed by all participants.[15]

This is a major event that undermines the prerequisites and historical basis for the existence of the 1910 Korean Annexation Treaty.

There is no original copy of the Protection Treaty of 1905 on the planet today.

This is a historical event. In addition, one of the pioneers of international law, Fransis Lay of France, in his book The International Situation of Korea (1905), cited the 1905 Japanese-Korean Protection Treaty as one of the three representative

[15]At the third conference held at Wuhan University in China on October 27–28, 2018, Professor Tae-Jin Yi's presentation, entitled **"Expectations for the New International Order of East Asia in the twenty-first Century,"** was followed by Professor Etsuro Totsuka's moving examination of the absence of a treaty on the protection of historical property, entitled **"A Way Towards Japan's Defreezing of Its Decolonisation Process."**

examples of the invalidity of treaties made under duress, and Professor Manley Ottmer Hudson of Harvard University cited the 1905 Korean-Japanese Protection Treaty as one of the five representative examples of international treaties made under duress.[16] Both of these treaties were not motivated by nationalistic motives, but rather by the spirit of pure international law, and were published as the Harvard Law School Report in the name of the League of Nations' Committee of Experts. This, in turn, was resolved by the UN International Law Commission and formally passed by the UN General Assembly in 1963.[17] This further strengthens the legitimacy of the Joint Statement of Korean and Japanese Intellectuals. Furthermore, it is not only the fact that the San Francisco Reinforcement Treaty fundamentally denies the legitimacy of Japan's colonial history in Korea, but also the context of the UN General Assembly's denial of the very core of the legitimacy of the San Francisco system.

4 Closing Remarks

In its preamble, the San Francisco Peace Treaty states that it is "committed to upholding the UN Charter and implementing the goals of the Universal Declaration of Human Rights in all circumstances". The preamble is about adhering to the UN Charter and implementing the goals of the Universal Declaration of Human Rights. The post-war strengthening treaties have a lifespan of 70 years.

In particular, it is difficult to overlook the contribution of the San Francisco Treaty, both directly and indirectly, to the economic growth of East Asia. While it imposed some punishment on the war criminals who had fought against the United States in the pre-war period, it imposed almost no punishment at all on the fascist violence of invasion and colonization of East Asian empires. Not only did the United States tolerate Japanese fascism, but it not only partnered with Japan in the communication of China and in its response to the Six-Day War, but it also made Japan the new ruler of its postwar East Asian empire. The United States kept Japanese fascism alive through the San Francisco system. This is what Professor Alexis Dudden has exposed as the "dirty secret" of U.S. diplomacy.[18]

---

[16] Yi, T.-J. (2025). A Case for the Modifiability of the San Francisco Peace Treaty: Examining the Varying Positions of the U.S. and Britain over South Korean Participation. In *Beyond the San Francisco System*. Springer.

[17] United Nations. (1963). Article 35: Personal coercion of representatives of states. In *Yearbook of the International Law Commission* (Vol. 26).

Totsuka, E. (2025). Unlawfulness of Japan's Colonization of Korean Peninsula—Korea' Declaration of January 21, 1904 and Japan's Violation of International Law. In *Beyond the San Francisco System*. Springer.

[18] Dudden, A. (2022). Trouble among East Asian allies? America's dirty secret. Paper presented at the Seoul conference, 2019. In *Beyond the San Francisco System (샌프란시스코 체제를 너머서) (Korean edition)*. Medici Media.

This is contrary to the treaty's preamble, which states that it is committed to the UN Charter and to the goals of the Universal Declaration of Human Rights. In August–September 2001, the UN held a World Conference against Humanitarian Racial Exclusionism and Related Intolerance in Durban, Africa, which identified slavery, slave trade and colonialism as "crimes against humanity".

In addition, the International Criminal Court (ICC) Statute formally established the crime of aggression in 2010, and the UN General Assembly unanimously adopted "victim-centeredness" in 2005, making clear the basic principle of victims' rights. However, in the San Francisco system, the issue of comfort women and forced labourers is not covered by these "crimes against humanity", "crimes of aggression" and "victim-centeredness" principles at all.

A foundational principle of modern international law is that victims of crimes against humanity and war crimes are entitled to truth, compensation, reparation and guarantees of non-recurrence, while perpetrators are obligated to provide adequate redress. The argument that the Korea-Japan Claims Agreement prevents comfort women and forced labour victims from seeking redress from Japanese corporations ignores fundamental principles of international law.

According to the core principle of the Vienna Convention, if the Korea-Japan Claims Agreement were to justify provisions contrary to fundamental international norms, such provisions or even the agreement itself would lack validity. Therefore, there is no basis for interpreting the Claims Agreement otherwise.[19] Professor Baik Tae-Ung said that he was very puzzled by the almost diametrically opposed rulings of the Civil Division 34 of the Seoul Central District Court (Presiding Judge Kim Jung-gon) on 8 January 2021 on a claim for damages filed by 12 former comfort women and the Civil Division 15 of the Seoul Central District Court (Presiding Judge Min Sung-cheol) on 21 April 2021 on a claim for damages filed by two former comfort women and their survivors. The former is highly praised as "a noteworthy ruling that stands in the same vein as new human rights jurisprudence in countries such as Belgium. Spain and Italy, which have recognised universal jurisdiction over crimes against humanity and war crimes and have actively responded to remedies for human rights violations, and reflects the trend of expanding human rights protection and remedies that began after the Second World War", and the latter is sternly rebuked as "a misguided nationalistic approach that is unacceptable in light of international law and recent trends in international human rights law".[20]

The San Francisco system underwent a major transformation following U.S. President Nixon's visit to China in February 1972, with the establishment of Sino-Japanese diplomatic relations in September and the return of Okinawa municipal authority to Japan in the same year. The reconstruction of the San Francisco system through the Obama administration's "Pivot to Asia" policy and the invention of a new adversary. China by Trump-Abe is culminating in today's Quad alliance of

[19] Baik, T.-U. (2025). Remedies for the Victims of Crimes against Humanity: The Case of Comfort Woman and Forced Labor. In *Beyond the San Francisco System*. Springer.

[20] Baik, T.-U. (2025). Remedies for the Victims of Crimes against Humanity: The Case of Comfort Woman and Forced Labor. In *Beyond the San Francisco System*. Springer.

the United States, India, Australia and Japan in the Indo-Pacific region. There are signs that the San Francisco System 2.0 may be taking shape in the form of an expanded and strengthened quad alliance. Had the inter-Korean rapprochement that followed the Pyeongchang Winter Olympics in South Korea, and the subsequent Singapore and Hanoi talks, been successful, would the tensions between the San Francisco system and North Korea have been overcome? Professors Gavan McCormack and Wada Haruki conclude from the Seoul meeting that genuine denuclearization of North Korea cannot be separated from the denuclearization of the entire San Francisco. System (including the U.S. military bases in Okinawa).[21] Professor Wada Haruki states that the new image beyond the San Francisco system is one in which "all three countries, North Korea, South Korea and Japan, are denuclearized and neutralized" and "the three nuclear powers, the United States, China and the United States, establish a Northeast Asian security community under a pledge not to attack the Korean Peninsula and the Japanese islands".[22] Professor Shi Yuan Hwa of China emphasizes the importance of restoring the September 19 Joint Statement of the Six-Party Talks in 2005, and calls for starting over with the construction of the Northeast Asian Economic Corridor, with China, Japan and North Korea at the centre, and with the participation of Northern China.[23]

Professor Young-Ho Kim stresses that the transition from the San Fransico systems to the Durban System of East Asia is important.[24]

We would like to note, among other things, that as a result of East Asian industrialization, more than a billion middle class and even more smart people have been created, and that the citizens or people of the three countries have been given a tenuous recognition of their individual claims, which they have interpreted to mean the restoration of their relative autonomy from the state. Now, they are not guests of East Asia or puppets of their respective populisms, but rather, just as the citizens of Germany during the reunification process broke out shouting "Wir sind das Volk" (We are the sovereign people), so we are the masters of East Asia, and a new sky will open for East Asia when we break out of the San Francisco prison that holds the masters of East Asia. If we do the "Woke Citizen" thing right, populism will have no footing. "A master makes friends rather than enemies" and if the Woke Citizen's master event is held in solidarity with the goals of the UN Charter and the Declaration of Sofit Human Rights, we can replace the San Francisco system with the Civil Asia "Durban" system.

---

[21] MaCormac, G. (2025). Clientelism For Ever?- Contemplating the San Francisco Peace Treaty Settlement 72 Years On. In *Beyond the San Francisco System*. Springer.

[22] Wada, H. (2025). Beyond the San Francisco System: A Japanese View. In *Beyond the San Francisco System*. Springer.

[23] Shi, Y. H. (2019). San Francisco system and the strategic interaction between China and US on the Korean Peninsula. Paper presented at the fourth Seoul Conference.

[24] Kim, Y.-H. (2025). From the Joint Statement by Korean and Japanese Intellectuals to the End of the San Francisco System Evaluation Conferences—Toward a Durban Conference of East-Asian Intellectuals, In *Beyond the San Francisco System*. Springer.

The San Francisco System in the Postwar World Order

Clientelism Forever? Contemplating the San Francisco Treaty Settlement 72 Years Ago

Gavan McCormack

Abstract This paper examines the enduring legacy and contemporary relevance of the San Francisco Treaty system, established over seventy years ago in the aftermath of World War II. It argues that despite profound global changes, the framework of US hegemony and clientelism persists in East Asia, particularly in Japan and South Korea. The analysis situates this system within the context of escalating existential threats—nuclear war and climate crisis—compounded by intensifying geopolitical tensions. The paper traces the shifting economic balance, highlighting China's dramatic rise and the relative decline of US and Japanese economic dominance. It explores the concept of the "client state," focusing on Japan's structured subordination to US interests, ongoing militarization, and the erosion of sovereignty and democracy. The study also considers the broader implications for regional stability, noting similar patterns of dependency in other US allies. Ultimately, the paper questions the sustainability of the San Francisco system in a multipolar world and calls for a fundamental rethinking of East Asia's security and political order.

Keywords San Francisco Treaty · US Hegemony · Client state · East Asia · Geopolitical tensions · Nuclear threat · Climate crisis · China's rise · Regional stability · Sovereignty erosion

1 72 Years

Ours is a troubled time. Humanity in our generation contemplates something it has not previously known: the threat of extinction, on two fronts—nuclear and climate. The hands of the nuclear Doomsday Clock were set in 2023 at ninety-seconds to midnight, and the gap to midnight is likely only to narrow further in 2024. Meanwhile, the ecological crisis deepens: carbon dioxide levels in the atmosphere

G. McCormack (✉)
Australian National University, Acton, ACT, Australia
e-mail: Gavan.McCormack@anu.edu.au

Y.-H. Kim et al. (eds.), *Beyond the San Francisco System*,
https://doi.org/10.1007/978-981-95-3328-2_2

rise to their highest level in three million years (421 ppm in 2022); the oceans rise, acidify, and groan from the spread of plastics and other types of pollution; the glacial and polar ice shrink; forests burn; deserts spread; storms rage; and multiple species are lost. The nuclear and climate crises are exacerbated by geopolitical tensions as Palestine and Ukraine are laid waste and military build-up and war preparation continue on many other fronts, including the East and South China Seas.

Facing these multiple crises, the frame of inter-state relationships in early twenty-first-century East Asia remains as it was set more than 70 years ago by the San Francisco Treaty in the wake of World War 2. The United States then was the undisputed master of the world, accounting for about half its GDP. China was divided, enfeebled and excluded, Korea was divided and at war, and Russia (the Soviet Union) was excluded. In Japan, the apparatus of occupation, bases, and US hegemony was unquestioned and seen as crucial to maintaining regional and global security, a linchpin of the system. This overarching inter-state framework became known as the "San Francisco Treaty system."[1]

While the system, after more than seven decades, remains intact, its economic underpinnings are rudely shaken. The United States' share of global GDP, about half at the time of San Francisco, is about 16% today, and is expected to decline further, to around 12% by 2050. China, insignificant as it reached the nadir of its civil conflict at the time of San Francisco, grew then, by a remarkable fifteen times in the two decades from 1995. From a still relative low at that point of about 4%, it soared to 18.3% in 2021 before falling slightly in 2023 (to 16.9%). Some believed this presaged a long-term negative trend, pointing to seemingly intractable problems such as the shrinking and ageing of the population (expected to halve to about 779 million in the remaining years of the twenty-first century), sharpening social inequality (as measured by GINI Co-Efficient level),[2] and burgeoning public and private debt. The OECD, however, sticks to its 2018 predictions that global GDP would continue to grow, quadrupling between 2011 and 2060, "largely driven," by China which it expects will account for about 27% of the world during the 2030s before slowly declining to around 20% in 2060."[3]

As for Japan, under the San Francisco formula it too was divided, comprising a war state under US absolute control (Okinawa) and a nominal "peace state," mainland Japan, which was also semi-occupied at the time of San Francisco. Constituting then mere 3% of global GDP, it rose by 1994 to 18% but then began a slow but

[1] Kimie Hara, ed., *The San Francisco System and Its Legacies: Continuation, Transformation, and Historical Reconciliation in the Asia-Pacific,* New York and London, Routledge, 2014. See also John W. Dower, "The San Francisco System: Past, Present, Future in U.S-.Japan-China Relations," Asia-Pacific Journal: Japan Focus, 23 February 2014. https://apjjf.org/2014/12/8/John-W.-Dower/4079/article.html/.

[2] Japan's Nikkei estimated even in 2010 that China's GINI Coefficient was already at "world's worst," and "critical" level, in excess of 0.60. (See "Chugoku no shotoku kakusa, kiken iki bodo hinpatsu no haikei ni," *Nihon Keizai Shimbun,* 11 December 2012.)

[3] OECD, "The Long View: Scenarios for the World Economy to 2060," 2018, http://www.oecd.org/economy/growth/scenarios-for-the-world-economy-to-2060.html/.

steady decline. By the early 2020s it was back, remarkably, to its 1950 level, about 3% once again.[4]

China, excluded altogether in 1951, by 2022 had become the world's biggest economy. In 2023 the CIA calculated that it accounted for $24.2 trillion of the global economy as against the US's $20.8 trillion.[5] Chinese GDP, one-quarter that of Japan in 1991, surpassed it in 2001 and quadrupled it by 2018, with the gap continuing to widen.[6] Provided broad continuance of current trends, China by 2035 might be as much as *eight* (sic) times greater than Japan.[7]

When "sovereignty" was restored to Japan at San Francisco, it came at a price. As John Foster Dulles put it when arriving in Tokyo to negotiate the deal:

> Do we get the right to station as many troops in Japan as we want, where we want and for as long as we want? That is the principal question.[8]

Provision of a chain of military bases throughout the Japanese archipelago may have seemed a modest price to pay for Japan's privileged position within the US-dominated world system but the price gets heavier as time passes. The chain of bases on which Dulles insisted then played a key role in wars from Korea in the 1950s and Vietnam in the 1960s to the Middle East and North Africa since then, and now prepare for the ultimate conflict, against China.

The San Francisco system was predicated on a unipolar, US-dominated global system, such as has long ceased to exist. The incongruity is plain. Yet if there is an underlying keynote to US policy, it would be that China's rise must be stopped, or even reversed.

The US has to be the primary power. Its "grand strategy," since its founding, has been to acquire and maintain preeminent power over any rivals, anywhere in the world. Its "National Security Doctrine" from 2017 insists on global "full-spectrum [land, sea, air, space] dominance." But its global footprint has steadily shrunk, and the sometime scion of the free and democratic world morphed gradually into a lawless or outlaw state. As a renowned British literary figure, Harold Pinter, put it in accepting the 2005 Nobel Prize,

> The United States supported, and in many cases engendered, every right-wing military dictatorship in the world after the end of the Second World War. I refer to Indonesia, Greece, Uruguay, Brazil, Paraguay, Haiti, Turkey, the Philippines, Guatemala, El Salvador, and of

---

[4] Terashima Jitsuro, "Noryoku no ressun," No 258, "Nijuichi seiki, miraiken no Nihon saisei e no koso," *Sekai*, December 2023, pp. 125–130; ibid., No 262, "Nijjuichi seiki, shisutemu o Nihon wa do ikiru ka," *Sekai*, April, 2024, pp. 164–167.

[5] CIA, *World Factbook*, 2023.

[6] Terashima Jitsuro, "Noryoku no ressun," No 192, "Chugoku no kyodaika kyokenka o seishi suru Nihon no kakugo," *Sekai*, April 2018, pp. 42–47 at p. 42.

[7] Australian government estimates, see Hugh White, "Sleepwalk to war: Australia's unthinking alliance with America, *Quarterly Essay, No.* 86, 2022, *p. 62.*

[8] Minutes, Dulles Mission Staff Meeting, 26 January 1951, Department of State, *Foreign Relations of the United States*, 1951, vol. 6, p. 812.

> course Chile. The crimes of the United States have been systematic, constant, vicious, remorseless....[9]

To update that harsh assessment, it would only be necessary to add the crimes of torture and murder, and to the geographic scope, at least Iraq, Afghanistan, Yemen, and Syria. The US alone ignores or defies international law and the United Nations, scrapping major multilateral or treaty commitments such as the Paris Accord on Climate Change, the Trans-Pacific Partnership (TPP) trade agreement, the Treaty of Rome (1999) and the International Criminal Court, the Joint Comprehensive Plan of Action (JCPOA) Iran nuclear deal and the INF intermediate range missile agreement, defying or vetoing international agreements while stepping up nuclear weapon development.

In March 2019, upon completing his term as head of the CIA, Mike Pompeo addressed Texas A&M University, saying,

> What is the motto at West Point? You will not lie, cheat, or steal, or tolerate those who do. I was the CIA director. We lied, we cheated, we stole. We had entire training courses.

After a brief pause, he went on,

> It reminds you of the glory of the American spirit.[10]

In other words, all and any acts, however otherwise illegal or criminal, are permitted to agents of the American state.

In like vein, retiring in 2023 from 20 years as president of the prestigious Council on Foreign Relations, Richard Haass saw "the most serious danger to the security of the world" as none other than the United States. "It's us," he said.[11] He was speaking before the US became complicit in what looks increasingly like the "crime of crimes," genocide, by Israel against the people of Palestine.[12]

Meanwhile, China is seen as the challenge, or threat, that must be put down. As the walls of containment designed to accomplish that goal grow higher, so the tighter does it insist on enveloping its San Francisco camp dependent states into containment (potentially rollback) roles. The insistence on US global hegemony and determination to put China down is of course counter to the principles of the United Nations[13]; strictly speaking, illegal. Still, Japan today (and other dependent states) swallow pride and principle and prepare for a potentially catastrophic military clash with China, in effect entrusting their national destiny to the Pentagon.

---

[9] Harold Pinter—Nobel Lecture. 7 December 2005. https://www.nobelprize.org/prizes/literature/2005/pinter/lecture/.

[10] Tyler Durden "I was the CIA director—we lied, we cheated we stole," *Zerohedge*, 15 April 2019. https://www.zerohedge.com/news/2019-04-21/i-was-cia-director-we-lied-we-cheated-we-stole/.

[11] Peter Baker, "To foreign policy veteran, the real danger is at home," *New York Times*, 1 July 2023. https://www.nytimes.com/2023/07/01/us/politics/richard-haass-biden-trump-foreign-policy.html/.

[12] Complicity in genocide is proscribed under Article 3 of the 1949 (1951) Genocide Convention.

[13] Jeffrey Sachs, for one, points this out. ("The need for a new US foreign policy," The New World Economy, 13 April 2023. https://www.jeffsachs.org/newspaper-articles/the-need-for-a-new-us-foreign-policy/).

While the United States consolidated its military chain of bases strung out along the Japanese archipelago, especially Okinawa, over time Japan's own armed forces grew to supplement them, surpassing those of the UK, Germany, or France, while it also subsidized the Pentagon and its war machine to the tune of multi-billions of dollars each year.[14] Despite its constitutional commitment to pacifism, Japan came to be a major military power, possessing latest generation fighter aircraft, battleships and submarines, even an aircraft carrier, and cooperating not only in "conventional" US military programs but also in those designed to establish hegemonic control over space and cyber-space.

This process of militarizing Japan gathers pace. Kishida Fumio's government in 2022 legislated to *double* defence expenditure to the (nominal) NATO level of 2% of GDP. It is to spend 43 trillion yen ($330 billion) on its military over the 5 years to 2027. It would thereby become world No 3 military power (after only the US and China).

The shift in relative weight vis-à-vis the United States and China disturbs and challenges Japan. Following San Francisco, successive governments accepted the status of subordinate/protectorate and/or national division. Okinawa at the time of San Francisco was a spoil of war, occupied and controlled by the US military and not returned to Japan for the next two decades and then within the frame of an American military colony. Ever since that *faux* reversion, Okinawans have struggled against the militarized and colonial status assigned to their islands.

So, 72 years after San Francisco, it is astonishing that a design to preserve US hegemony as it was in the 1950s should still be in place. The incongruity is plain. The system is ripe for comprehensive rejigging.[15] But is it happening?

2 Client States

From 2006, I have been employing the "client state" (Japanese: *zokkoku*) concept to understand Japan.[16] By "client state" I mean one that adopts a posture of structured submissiveness [to the United States], one that *chooses* servitude.[17] For Japan, alliance with the United States has de facto priority over the constitution and the US military presence in Japan (especially Okinawa) is absolutely privileged.

---

[14] For details, Gavan McCormack, *The State of the Japanese State: Contested Identity, Direction and Role*, Folkstone, Kent, Renaissance Press, 2018.

[15] Gavan McCormack, "Japan, Australia, and the rejigging of Asia-Pacific alliances," The Asia-Pacific Journal—Japan Focus, 15 November 2021. https://apjjf.org/2020/22/McCormack.html/.

[16] *Client State: Japan in the American Embrace*, London and New York, Verso, 2006 (Japanese Korean, and Chinese editions in 2007/2008); *The State of the Japanese State: Contested Identity, Direction and Role*, Folkestone, Kent: Renaissance Books, 2018.

[17] Nishitani Osamu, "Jihatsuteki reiju o koeyo—jiritsuteki seiji no ippo," *Sekai, F*ebruary 2010, pp. 126.

The US enjoyment of being surrounded by a web of client states is crucial to its status as hegemon. Breakouts from alliance bonds are not tolerated. It also means that US "client states" (Japan and Australia prominent among them) are at least morally responsible for acts committed by the master-state, including multiple wars, 11 since 2000 (one every 2 years and commonly without UN authorization),[18] and crimes (including torture and assassination) for which the US itself refuses to be held responsible. US client states stand with, and support, the arch-criminal United States.

Consent on the part of its "clients" to US regional and global policy and strategic direction within the San Francisco framework was sine qua non to US action, including its successive wars. "Client States" were and are complicit states.

The Client State phenomenon is not confined to Japan. Australia likewise fits the bill,[19] probably the UK likewise.[20] Both Russia and China have their own dependent ring of satellite states that function in similar way, mirroring the San Francisco states, and French president Emmanuel Macron's recent call for Europe to assert its strategic autonomy and avoid becoming a "vassal" in the confrontation between United States and China showed that he thought of clientelism in like terms (but as something to be avoided at all cost).[21]

Post-1945 leaders from Hirohito (emperor 1926–1989) to the three successive twenty-first-century Prime Ministers, Abe Shinzo (2006–2007 and 2012–2020), Suga Yoshihide (2020–2021) and Kishida Fumio (2021-) fudged national sovereignty by adopting submission to the United States as core national policy. Submission to the global super-power sat uneasily with Japanese pride but made some sense on the assumption that the United States would retain its global dominance of 1951, and its benevolent disposition towards Japan.

Within such a frame, being only semi-sovereign, the number one priority of national policy is to follow the United States, at whatever the cost. The Japanese state is a dependent rather than sovereign entity, resting on unstable foundations and heading in an un- or anti-democratic direction. This structural deformity, commonly neglected in the Western literature or media reporting on Japan, is at odds with the image presented by Japan's leaders to multiple audiences, including the United Nations and the US Congress, of a democratic, law-governed, constitutional state.

---

[18] Joseph Camilleri, "Australia adrift and a foreign minister all at sea," Pearls and Irritations, 20 April 2023. https://johnmenadue.com/australia-adrift-and-a-foreign-minister-all-at-sea/.

[19] One former Prime Minister (1975–1983) who in retirement became deeply concerned at Australian dependence on the US was Malcolm Fraser, *Dangerous Allies*, Melbourne University Press, 2014. Malaysia leader Mahathir Mohammed was blunt: "Malaysian labels Australia a US puppet," ABC (Australia) News, 16 October 2003. https://www.abc.net.au/news/2003-10-17/malaysian-labels-australia-a-us-puppet/1494508/.

[20] David Leigh and Richard Norton-Taylor, "We are now a 'client state'," *The Guardian*, 17 July 2003, https://www.theguardian.com/politics/2003/jul/17/usa.world/ and Seumas Milne, "70 years of foreign troops? We should close the bases," *The Guardian*, 23 January 2014. https://www.theguardian.com/commentisfree/2014/jan/23/seventy-years-time-close-us-bases/.

[21] "Macron sparks anger by saying Europe should not be 'vassal' in US-China clash," *The Guardian*, 10 April 2023.

Not coincidentally, Japan's militarization exacts a growing price on the rest of the economy. National debt, at a staggering 265% of GDP, is far and away world No 1. Henceforth, taxes must be raised, and health, education and welfare budgets cut to cover the costs of militarization.

It is no longer shocking to think or write in Client State terms. Despite the generally warm and positive image of Japan internationally, there is within Japan itself a burgeoning dystopian literature. Prominent public intellectuals adopt the Client State *(zokkoku)* category (whether or not using the actual word) to refer to Japan. Subsequent to my 2006 book (which I revisited in 2018),[22] others have employed a similar framework, with works by Nishitani Osamu (2010),[23] Magosaki Ukeru (2012),[24] Shirai Satoshi and Uchida Tatsuru (2016),[25] Shirai Satoshi (2018),[26] Nakano Koichi (2018),[27] Koseki Shoichi (2020),[28] and Matsuda Takeshi (2022).[29] Prominent public intellectuals refer to contemporary Japan as an "extreme rightist" country,[30] subject to a "fascism of indifference" in which the Japanese voters are like frogs in slowly heating fascist water,[31] others see it as no longer law-governed or democratic but moving towards becoming "a dark society and a fascist state,"[32] where a "fundamental corruption of politics" spreads through every nook and cranny of Japanese society,[33] as it begins the "steep decline towards civilizational collapse."[34] One scholar argues that there is a close correlation between the emperor-centred *Kokutai* or national polity of pre-war (fascist) Japan and today's US-dominated Japan, both polities absolutist and in time becoming exhausted, plunging Japan into existential crisis.[35] Former diplomat Amaki Naoto, who resigned

[22] McCormack, *The State of the Japanese State*, op. cit.

[23] Nishitani, op. cit.

[24] Magosaki Ukeru, *Sengoshi no shotai, 1945–2012*, Sogensha, 2012.

[25] Uchida Tatsuru and Shirai Satoshi, *Zokkoku minshushugi*, (Client State Democracy), Tokyo, Toyo keizai, 2016.

[26] Shirai Satoshi, *Kokutai-ron—Kiku to seijoki*, Tokyo, Shueisha shinsho, 2018. And for a short statement of his thesis, "Okinawa to kokutai," *Days Japan*, vol. 15, No. 10, October 2018, pp. 4–11.

[27] Nakano refers to Japan's as an "appropriated" (or "privatised" *shibutsuka*) state, *Shibutsuka sareru kokka: Shihai to fukuju no Nihon seiji*, Kadokawa, 2018.

[28] Koseki Shoichi, *Taibei juzoku no kozo*, Misuzu, 2020.

[29] Matsuda Takeshi, *Jihatsuteki reiju no Nichibei kankeishi*, Iwanami, 2022.

[30] Takahashi Tetsuya [Tokyo University philosopher], "Kyokuu ka suru seiji," *Sekai*, January 2015, pp. 150–161.

[31] Soda Kazuhiro [film-maker and journalist], *Nekkyo-naki fuashizumu—Nippon no mukanshin o kansatsu suru*, Kawade shobo shinsha, 2014. Also, "Nekkyo-naki fuashizumu e no shohosen," *Sekai*, February 2015, pp. 81–95, at p. 89.

[32] Kimura Akira [Kagoshima University], "Hatoyama seiken hokai to Higashi Ajia kyodotai koso—atarashii Ajia gaiko to ampo, kichi seisaku o chushin ni," in Kimura Akira and Shindo Eiichi, *Okinawa jiritsu to Higashi Ajia kyodotai*, Kadensha, 2016, pp. 202–230, at p. 230.

[33] Yamaguchi Izumi [author], "Matsurowanu kuni kara no tegami," *Ryukyu shimpo*, 21 October 2016.

[34] Yamaguchi Jiro [Hosei University], "Bunmei no owari?" *Tokyo shimbun*, 22 May 2016.

[35] Shirai Satoshi [Kyoto Seika University], *Kokutairon—Kiku to Seijoki*, Tokyo: Shueisha shinsho (2018).

from the Foreign Ministry in 2003 in protest against Japan's support for the Iraq War) sees the country as being in the grasp of a cabal of US neocons.[36] Critic Aoki Osamu, even more savagely, refers to Japan's leaders as sticking to their US masters like a trail of faeces behind a goldfish.[37]

As for Korea, like Japan its basic institutions were set in place to serve US interest at a time when both were occupied by US forces. While the defeated enemy, Japan, was treated to a soft peace and granted a privileged position as US subordinate within the San Francisco Treaty system, Korea, the former Japanese colony, was no sooner "liberated" than divided and subjected to harsh suppression of its incipient democratic movement.

While Japan followed the San Francisco settlement by thereafter gradually deepening its character as a client state, South Korea as divided state went through successive mass uprisings, in 1960, 1980, 1987, and 2016–7, rejecting military dictatorships imposed and maintained by the United States (and aided by Japan) for four and a half decades, culminating with the democratic mass movement known as the "candlelight revolution" of 2016–17).[38] That movement may have faltered with the victory of Yoon Seok-Yeol in the 2022 presidential election, but whether or not one uses the term "client state" of his government at least it may be said that his major policy settings have been clientelist.

The question of South Korea's dependence is intimately tied to the fact of division of the peninsula into Northern and Southern states, now in its eighth decade. So long as division and hostile militarism prevails, the US occupation of bases and insistence on South Korean submission cannot but continue. Below I attach a separate discussion of "the North Korea question."

3 Beyond Clientelism?

Since the end of the Cold War, an awareness has spread in Japan on the part of both "conservatives" and "progressives," and much of civil society, that it is inappropriate for Japan, as a democracy and great economic power to remain locked in servility to its erstwhile conqueror and occupier, that it is time to move from subservience to autonomy.[39] At least twice in the post-Cold War era, governments have taken office oriented towards renegotiating the US relationship.

Quite apart from the overt struggles against clientelism during the governments of Hosokawa Morihiro [1993–4] and Hatoyama Yukio [2009–2010]), clientelism in

[36] Amaki Naoto, "Amaki Naoto no meru magajin," 13 November 2023.

[37] Aoki Osamu, TBS "Sande moningu," 19 November 2023.

[38] Paik Nak-chung, "South Korea's candlelight revolution and the future of the Korean peninsula," *The Asia-Pacific Journal—Japan Focus,* 1 December 2018. See aso Kim Ho-gi, "Kankoku ni rosoku kakumei o rekishi ni ijizukeru," *Sekai*, February 2019, pp. 150–156.

[39] See my "Zokkoku-ron maku 2," in Kimura Akira, ed., *Okinawa kara tou higashi Ajia kyodotai—gunji no kaname kara heiwa no kaname e*, Kadensha, 2019, pp. 144–163.

Japan has been resisted or contested even by some of those commonly seen as the system's nominally most committed proponents. Thus, former Prime Minister Abe Shinzo (2006–2007, 2012–2020), first seated in the Diet in 1993, just after the "end" of the Cold War, began to call for an end to the "post-war regime" and for fundamental revision of the US-imposed post-war system. What he and other proponents of what they called the "beautiful" or "new" Japan found most offensive about the post-war Japanese state was its democratic, citizen-based, anti-militarist qualities and its admission of responsibility for war and crimes of war by pre-war and wartime Japan.

Shinto values above all the pure and the pristine. Neo-Shinto-ists such as Abe could not tolerate the stain on Japanese history of crimes such as the mass abduction and rape of women throughout Asia, the so-called "comfort women" system, in the 1930s and 1940s. Critical of the post-war state's liberal democracy, Abe preferred instead a blend of neo-nationalism, historical revisionism, and Shinto, rooted in the *kokutai* or national polity of pre-war and wartime Japan (though preferring to call it *kunigara*). He imagined Japan, beneath the emperor, as a unique, superior, "beautiful country." In his first term of office (2006–2007), he spoke of "taking Japan back" (*Nihon o torimodosu*). When he denied or equivocated about war responsibility, Comfort Women and Nanjing, and insisted on rewriting Japanese history to make people proud, he appears to have believed it possible to "cast off" post-war strictures and become a "normal" state (with a fresh constitution and unshackled armed forces) while yet somehow continuing Japan's "client state" relationship to the United States.

Such an Abe agenda was at odds with that of Washington's "Japan handlers" (as they came to be known). A 1995 Centre for Strategic and International Studies (CSIS) report spelt out the principles appropriate to a Japanese client state. Any diminution of US military hegemony was unthinkable since East Asian security depended on the "oxygen" of US military presence and therefore on preservation of the bases, retaining 100,000 US soldiers in Japan and Korea. It meant denial of full sovereignty to both East Asian countries. The essence of the San Francisco system as redefined by the CSIS's Joseph Nye and Richard Armitage was that the United States retained the right to dictate policy.

CSIS followed that 1995 report by others in 2000, 2007, 2012, and 2018,[40] spelling out the legal and institutional reforms required to reinforce the Alliance and consolidate Japan's servility. Separately, the US government between 1994 and 2017 issued its Japanese counterpart an annual statement of the "reforms" it wanted to have Tokyo implement, expanding its domestic market and energizing the country by deregulation, privatization, and structural reform.[41] Whether in the form of the CSIS "recommendations" or the "Desiderata" statements I know of no parallel

---

[40] Richard L. Armitage and Joseph S. Nye, eds, "More Important than Ever: Renewing the US-Japan Alliance for the twenty-first Century," Washington, CSIS, October 2018, https://www.csis.org/analysis/more-important-ever/.

[41] See my *The State of the Japanese State*, p. 53.

in inter-state relations of such a charter of submission, renewed under one name or another until the advent of Donald Trump in 2017.

In 2012 just months before Abe's return to office, CSIS cautioned Japan to think carefully as to whether or not it wanted to remain a "tier-one" nation. By that it meant was Japan ready to do what was required of it by the United States, to "stand shoulder-to-shoulder," send naval groups to the Persian Gulf and the South China Sea, relax its restrictions on arms exports, increase its defence budget and military personnel numbers, maintain/increase its annual subsidy to the Pentagon, press ahead with construction of new base facilities in Okinawa, Guam, and the Mariana Islands, and revise either its constitution or the way it was interpreted so as to facilitate "collective self-defence." If Japan baulked at any of this, Washington intimated, it would simply slide into "tier-two" status, and that, clearly, would be beneath contempt.

Abe did not baulk. Following his December 2012 electoral triumph he hastened to Washington to assure the CSIS "Japan handlers" that he and his government would do as they were told. Thereafter, Japan's defence expenditure rose steadily, the ban on arms exports was relaxed and major security and secrecy legislation adopted making it possible to despatch the Self-Defense Forces to aid the United States or other friendly nations in case of an armed attack against them, even if not itself directly under attack. The country's constitutional scholars overwhelmingly declared the 2015 security bills unconstitutional.[42]

Furthermore, as Abe admitted in a 2016 interview with veteran journalist Tahara Soichiro, once the 2015 package of security bills authorizing Japan to act on the principle of "collective security" was adopted (September 2015) there was "absolutely no need to revise the constitution."[43] In other words, Abe's signature cause of constitutional revision, often viewed as a mark of his nationalism, was actually the opposite: a policy of servility demanded by Japan's American masters.

It did not make sense to think, like Abe, of liquidating the post-war, American-granted regime and comprehensively revising the constitution to reflect the Shintoist, "beautiful," "new" and emperor-centred Japan while simultaneously declaring unqualified support ("100% *shiji*") for the Trump (or Biden) "America First" agenda. So, in the years that remained of his government, he abandoned his radical constitutional agenda and neo-nationalist principles to perform a purer form of submission, while concentrating on widening state prerogatives, circumscribing citizen rights, and reinforcing national security.

The sometime nationalist fire-brand intent on remaking the state in accord with a grand post-Cold War, post-servile programme morphed during his later years in office into a faithful servant of the US cause. He may have *wished* for a pristine,

---

[42] *Asahi shimbun* on 11 July reported that 104 of 122 constitutional scholars saw the Abe security legislation package as unconstitutional, while just two defended it. ("Ampo hoan 'iken' 104 nin, 'goken' futari kempo gakusha tachi ra," *Asahi shmbun*, 11 July 2015. https://www.asahi.com/articles/ASH797JMJH79ULZU01W.html/).

[43] Tahara Soichiro, "Waga sokatsu—(13) Abe ikkyo taisei to seiji no henshitsu," *Sekai*, January 2020, pp. 243–25, at p.244.

independent Japan, but he came to realize in his first term as Prime Minister (2006–2007) that the United States would not permit it. There was no alternative to clientelism.

During his second term in office (from 2012), Abe abandoned his radical constitutional agenda and neo-nationalist principles. No more did he talk of "taking Japan back" or of "going beyond the post-war system." Instead, he deepened Japan's submission, adopting a revised form of clientelism (Clientelism Mark 2). His popularity in the US rose steadily.

On 28 May 2019, as the culmination of President Donald Trump's four-day visit to Japan, Trump and Abe stood on the deck of the Japanese helicopter carrier, Kaga, to declare the alliance "more robust than ever." It was in essence an act of ritual submission by Japan's government and armed forces to their American Commander-in-Chief, calling to mind the "other" Japanese surrender, 74 years earlier, on the US Battleship Missouri. Any "beyond clientelism" agenda for Japan would have to wait for a future Prime Minister prepared to take the risk of dissenting from the United States and articulating a "Japanese" (rather than American) national interest.

4 League of Clients: Quad and AUKUS

From around the turn of century, Japan and Australia became the US's pre-eminent client states. Australia cooperated with Japan in UN Peacekeeping operations in Cambodia and East Timor in the 1990s and in the 2000s the Australian Navy and the Japanese Maritime Self Defense Forces (MSDF) joined in US-led South China Sea and Persian Gulf patrols, while the Australian Air Force cooperated with the USAF out of Kadena base in Okinawa on so-called "UN-patrols" to enforce UN-imposed sanctions on North Korea.[44]

In March of 2007Australian Prime Minister John Howard signed with his Japanese counterpart (Abe Shinzo) a "Joint Declaration on Security Cooperation."[45] India too was included in proposals for an Asia-Pacific Democratic League or "Strategic Dialogue" and Abe was acclaimed for declaring that vision before the Indian parliament in August 2007.[46] It was to take another decade to come to fruition. Meanwhile, Australia's Tony Abbott (Prime Minister 2013–2015) and Japan's Abe Shinzo (Prime Minister 2006–2007, 2012–2020) in 2014 elevated the bilateral relationship to the unique category of "special strategic partnership" (a hair's

[44] "Monitoring and surveillance activities by Australia against illicit maritime activities including ship-to-ship transfers," Department of Foreign Affairs, 17 September 2020. https://www.mofa.go.jp/press/release/press4e_002905.html/.

[45] "Australia-Japan Joint Declaration on Security Cooperation," Australian Government, Department of Foreign Affairs and Trade, 13 March 2007, http://www.dfat.gov.au/geo/japan/aus_jap_securitydec.html/.

[46] Shinzo Abe, "Confluence of the Two Seas," speech to the parliament of the Republic of India, 22 August 2007. https://www.mofa.go.jp/region/asia-paci/pmv0708/speech-2.html/.

breadth short of full alliance). In 2022, the Japan-Australia Reciprocal Access Agreement (RAA) brought the two sides closer to merger.

Turning a blind eye to the US's violent, lawless, and war-addicted character, Australia and Japan, as US "allies" (read: client states) would join it in an "Arc of Freedom and Prosperity," dealing with challenges to US hegemony in the Asia-Pacific region and encircling and constraining China.

The loose 2007 grouping inclusive of India took time to take shape, not till 2019 becoming a "quadrilateral [US-Japan-Australia-India] security dialogue," commonly "the Quad." US Secretary of State Mike Pompeo confirmed the US intent to consolidate the Quad into "a true security framework," spearheading the struggle against the Chinese Communist Party's "exploitation, corruption, and coercion … in the south, in the East China Sea, the Mekong, the Himalayas, the Taiwan straits."[47] It would, said Pompeo, be a struggle "for the soul of the world," no less.[48] A "Quad-plus" grouping soon came to include a second tier of countries such as (from March 2000) South Korea, New Zealand, and Vietnam, and even, from May 2021, Brazil and Israel.[49]

A (potentially) momentous alliance was thus negotiated at a high state level with zero participation on the part of the people who stood to be affected by it. The exclusive bilateral US security relationships in the Asia-Pacific that had existed since the San Francisco Treaty settlement of 1951 (and the US-Australia ANZUS of the same year) and through the Cold War were thus renegotiated in the third decade of the twenty-first century and transformed into a multinational alliance system. Australia and Japan (along with South Korea and New Zealand) both well-established NATO "partners" (implicitly accepting its nuclear character) participated from 2022 in annual NATO Conferences.[50]

Former Australian Prime Minister, Paul Keating (1991–1996) spoke sarcastically of the Quad as "a reliable bunch of Deputy Sheriffs, Japan, Korea, Australia and India" that would "contain" China and keep it in its place."[51] He lamented Australia's "timidity." To come of age, he said a little later, "Australia has to have a new and altogether different view of itself."[52]

---

[47] Kyodo, "'Quad' nations vow to step up coordination for free and open Indo-Pacific," https://www.japantimes.co.jp/news/2020/10/06/national/politics-diplomacy/quad-free-open-indo-pacific-china/.

[48] Ibid.

[49] Wikipedia, "Quadrilateral Security Dialogue," https://en.wikipedia.org/wiki/Quadilateral_security-dialogue/.

[50] Gavan McCormack, "Global agendas 2022—NATO and RIMPAC, The Asia-Pacific Journal—Japan Focus, 1 July 2022. https://apjjf.org/2022/20/13/Gavan-McCormack/5720.html/.

[51] "AUKUS Statement by PJ Keating," National Press Club, 15 March 2023. https://www.whitehouse.gov/briefing-room/statements-releases/2023/03/13/fact-sheet-trilateral-Ausralia-Uk-US-partnership-on-nuclear-powered-submarines/.

[52] "It is time for Australia to break out of its timidity: Keating," *Australian Financial Review*, 21 February 2024.

Military planning and coordination and regular war "games" became increasingly common. From 2016 the US Marine Corps rotated its Pacific forces through northern Australia on a regular basis, effectively adding Darwin to its global empire of bases, a mini-Okinawa (minus a pesky anti-base movement), and from 2023, Tindal, near Darwin was designated host to a squadron of nuclear-capable B-52 bombers, ready, if required, to take off for China. In 2019, Australian Air Force crews cooperated in combat drill exercises with Japan's Self-Defence Forces in northern Hokkaido.[53] In 2023, Japan's F-35s were deployed to Australia and Australia's F-35s to Japan.[54]

Japan, Australia, and India were thus assigned (and claimed) a key role in a NATO-esque military alliance designed to shore up US hegemony in the Asia-Pacific.[55] Australia appeared to welcome unreservedly Japan's transition from constitutional peace state to fully "normalized" military great power. Japan, while proclaiming democracy, human rights, and rule of law as values supposedly shared with the United States, Australia, and India, was simultaneously committed to revision of the basic instruments (including the "peace" constitution) that underpinned those same principles. Together, while declaring their commitment to the "rules-based international order," Canberra, Tokyo and Delhi would serve the US alliance and constitute the bulwark of multinational, China-containing coalitions.

Paralleling the Quad, late in 2021 AUKUS (the Australia-UK-US Trilateral Security Partnership) emerged.[56] It was a strictly "white" grouping that spanned the world's oceans and promised merger of Australia's military with the global force projection capacities of the UK and United States. Central to the design would be the provision of nuclear-powered submarines by United States and UK to Australia. Australia would pay a humungous sum (at least $A368 billion) for eight such submarines. Most would be second-hand US "Virginia" models but at least one was to be newly built to a design that has yet to be drawn. Delivery, currently anticipated between the late 2030s and early 2040s, was almost certain to be even further delayed by technical and political difficulties.

In 2023, a House of Commons Foreign Affairs Committee recommended that Japan and (South) Korea should both be invited to join an AUKUS "Second Pillar"

---

[53] "Japan's first air combat drills with Australia contribute to peace, says Defense Minister Taro Kono," *Japan Times*, 25 September 2019, https://www.japantimes.co.jp/news/2019/09/25/national/japan-says-first-air-combat-drill-australia-contributes-peace/#.XZFcd4VOKUI/, https://www.stripes.com/news/surveillance-planes-from-australia-and-new-zealand-to-help-enforce-n-korea-sanctions-1.546371/).

[54] Government of Australia, Ministry of Defence, "Australia and Japan deepen defence ties," 14 August 2023. https://www.minister.defence.gov.au/media-releases/2023-08-14/australia-and-japan-deepen-defence-ties/.

[55] Emma Chanlett-Avery, Caitlin Campbell, and Joshua A. Williams, "The US-Japan Alliance," Congressional Research Service (CRS), June 13, 2019, CRS RL33740, p. 17.

[56] For an official three-sided Statement as of 13 March 2023, "FACT SHEET: Trilateral Australia-UK-US Partnership on Nuclear-Powered Submarines," https://www.whitehouse.gov/briefing-room/statements-releases/2023/03/13/fact-sheet-trilateral-australia-uk-us-partnership-on-nuclear-powered-submarines/.

agreement on technological defence cooperation,[57] and Japan's Deputy Prime Minister Aso Taro floated a proposal for the inclusion of Japan in the agreement proper, transforming AUKUS to JAWKUS.[58] For rightists such as Aso, there could be no higher goal for Japan than incorporation in the US/Anglo-Saxon bloc.

For Australia, and conceivably in future for Japan, incorporation in AUKUS—even as "support and even respect for the West at large" collapses globally and a US-sponsored and armed regime in Israel continues its "pitiless assault" on Palestine—promises incorporation for at least the next generation on "the wrong side of history."[59]

5 Okinawa and the East China Sea

The loosely knit San Francisco frame was thus gradually tightened and shaped by US direction. Far from there being any transcendence of the San Francisco frame, its basic principle of US hegemony was refined and concentrated. As the US-led agenda of China containment gathered momentum, over and under the East China Sea battleships and aircraft carriers, missile and counter-missile systems, fighter jets and submarines—not only Japanese and American but also British, French, Australian, Canadian, and German—proliferate and rehearse a possible future war between a US-led coalition of the willing and China.

The Quad (from 2020) and AUKUS (from 2021) were markers of this new phase, and the Camp David Declaration (2023) by leaders of the United States, Japan,and South Korea was a statement of common purpose.[60]

China must be brought down, its wings clipped, the United States believe. There is no secret as to the East China Sea design: to "bottle up" Chinese forces and deny them access or egress to or from the Pacific Ocean in the event of some "Taiwan event." In preparation, Japan has over the past decade concentrated on militarizing its Southwest frontier islands, converting them into a giant maritime great wall that stretches from Kagoshima City (Kyushu) via Mage, Amami, Okinawa, Miyako,

[57] UK Parliament, "Foreign Affairs Committee reviews government's tilt to the Indo-Pacific," 30 August 2923. https://committees.parliament.uk/committee/78/foreign-affairs-committee/news/197226/foreign-affairs-committee-reviews-governments-tilt-to-the-indopacific/. Corey Lee Bell, "Australia should support Japan and South Korea's accession into AUKUS," *The Diplomat*, 19 October 2023. Australia Should Support Japan and South Korea's Accession into AUKUS – The Diplomat/.

[58] Ryosuke Hanada, "No, Japan is not ready for AUKUS," *The Strategist*, 7 December 2023, https://www.aspistrategist.org.au/no-japan-is-not-ready-for-aukus/.

[59] Henry Reynolds, "Australia's brutal 'Rules-Based International Order' is on display in Gaza," Pearls and Irritations, 17 January 2024.

[60] The White House, The Spirit of Camp David: Joint Statement of Japan, the Republic of Korea, and the United States," 18 August 2023, https://www.whitehouse.gov/briefing-room/statements-releases/2023/08/18/the-spirit-of-camp-david-joint-statement-of-japan-the-republic-of-korea-and-the-united-states/.

Ishigaki, and Yonaguni Islands, to Taiwan. For Washington and Tokyo, the key *raison d'être* for these Southwestern islands has to be as a joint US-Japan bastion projecting force where required for the regional and global hegemonic project, ultimately for "containing" China and addressing any "Taiwan Contingency" or war over Taiwan. Over the past decade, therefore, Japan has reinforced its military (Self Defence Force) presence on these islands, deploying missile and counter-missile units and intelligence-gathering units in a series of new or under construction bases,[61] rushing missile and anti-missile units to the Southwest islands, placing an order late in 2022 for 400 "off the shelf" Tomahawk Land Attack Missiles (capable of attack on targets within 1500-kilometre radius (including major centres in Russia, China, and North Korea).

Should circumstances require it, Japan's missiles (fighters, submarines, etc.) would be called on to cooperate with US Airforce and Marine units from Okinawa main island in blocking Chinese naval entry or egress to the Pacific via the international waters of Miyako Strait (between Okinawa Island and Miyako Island). That of course would be an act of war.

Far from offering reassurance to people living on these islands, the centrality of Okinawa to war designs guarantees its inclusion on potential target lists such as are undoubtedly being drawn up on the other side of the East China Sea.

Mage Island, till recently an unnoticed, unpopulated island offshore from Kyushu, may be seen as key to the overall project. Construction, expected to take 4 years, commenced in January 2023 on a joint facility to accommodate all three wings of Japan's military (Ground, Sea and Air Self Defence Forces) together with unspecified numbers of their US counterparts.[62] The sharing arrangement would ensure ultimate Pentagon coordination, control, and command of Japanese military operations throughout the adjacent seas.

As this war preparedness proceeds, it pays to recall the early years of US occupation when, with Okinawa under complete US military control, up to 1300 nuclear weapons were stored there and in other US bases and Pentagon planners contemplated scenarios for the defence of the "free world" involving the destruction of *all* major cities in the then Soviet Union and China, killing around 600 million people (sic) and very possibly bringing human civilization itself to an end.[63] Nuclear weapon-based "security" today threatens a no less global catastrophe.

While Prime Minister Abe insisted that Japan was a country governed by law, the militarization of these islands that his government (followed by the Suga and Kishida governments) was enforcing was a trampling on law and constitution.

---

[61] Gavan McCormack, "Japan on the path to becoming a military great(er) power," Pearls and Irritations (John Menadue's Public Policy Journal), 24 April 2023, https://johnmenadue.com/japan-on-the-path-to-becoming-a-military-greater-power/.

[62] For background and early stages of this project, Gavan McCormack, *The State of the Japanese State*, pp. 155–157.

[63] Daniel Ellsberg, *The Doomsday Machine: Confessions of a Nuclear War Planner*, London, Bloomsbury Publications, 2017, and Ellsberg in conversation with Peter Hannam, "Setting the world alight," *Sydney Morning Herald*, 9 March 2018.

Okinawan Governor Onaga Takeshi (in office 2014–2018) was acclaimed by Okinawans when he berated the national government as "condescending," "outrageous," "childish," "depraved," [*rifujin, otonagenai, daraku shita*] and "ignoring the people's will."[64]

The long-sustained Okinawan anti-base struggle is at the forefront of the global movement for a non-war future. If a peaceful East Asian community of nations is to be constructed, it is certain that Okinawa will be its centre, and if it cannot be constructed, Okinawa, together with much of the world, is doomed.

Okinawa has to find a path from its Cold War role as "keystone" in US military strategy to "bridge stone" linking Japan and its neighbours. In place of the role assigned to Okinawa under successive national defence plans since 2010, calling for steady military build-up and confrontation with China, Okinawans therefore talk of an Okinawa-centred demilitarized "livelihood zone," of "a space for co-existence, co-living by Japan, China, and Taiwan, and a symbol of goodwill." They would turn Okinawa itself into a "peace hub for Asia,"[65] extending the Okinawan principle of grassroots democracy so as to negotiate a new kind of future for the East China Sea communities.

6 Korea North

North Korea, not represented at San Francisco, has for 70 years been the "other" to the United States and its San Francisco allies.[66] For 70 years peace on the peninsula has rested on the fragile ceasefire of 1953. The UN has never repeated its Korean experience of waging war, but neither has it ever acknowledged responsibility for war crimes committed both during and after this conflict.

For any resolution of the "Korean problem" (division), the UN will have to play a role. As an organization it bears a peculiar responsibility for creating the problem in the first place, by dividing the country and establishing an anti-communist bastion in the south in 1947–1948,[67] and then by going to war against North Korea in

[64] For sources, Gavan McCormack and Satoko Norimatsu, *Resistant Islands: Okinawa Confronts Japan and the United States*, 2012, pp. 278–9 (Japanese, Korean, and Chinese translations of this book in 2013, 2014, and 2015 respectively).

[65] "Urgent Appeal: To Transform Senkaku islands into a Shared Livelihood Zone for Japan, China, and Taiwan," by the Okinawa-based "Committee of One Hundred," 10 January 2013, see http://peacephilosophy.blogspot.ca/2013/02/an-urgent-appealfrom-Okinawa-to-turn.html/.

[66] For my general perspective, see T*arget North Korea: Pushing North Korea to the Brink of Nuclear Catastrophe*, New York and Sydney, 2004, Japanese translation from Heibonsha 2004, Korean translation from Icarus Media 2006. For two more recent essays: "Human rights and humanitarian Intervention: The North Korean Case," *Journal of Political Criticism* (Seoul: the Korean Association for Political Criticism), Vol. 16, May 2015, pp. 151–171, and "Storm Clouds over Korea," *Journal of Political Criticism*, Vol. 18, June 2016, pp. 193–200.

[67] The UN could only do this because two countries on the UN Temporary Commission for Korea (UNTCOK), Australia and Canada, reversed their position and bowed to US pressure to endorse

1950 (entrusting military and political control to the United States), allowing the slaughter of 100,000 people by "our" (i.e., United States, South Korean, and other) forces under the UN flag just in the first year of war, and many other victims of incidents likely constituting war crimes.[68] Some of the most horrendous incidents, which were then simply blamed on the "communists," were revealed much later to have been committed by forces on the UN side.[69] Carpet bombing and the destruction of the infrastructure of daily life, including dams, dykes and power stations, were all evident war crimes.

Then, after the war and in breach of the Armistice agreement, the United States refused to engage in peace talks and (in 1958) introduced nuclear weapons to South Korea in an attempt to intimidate and compel North Korea to submit. Thereafter, the United States refused to take seriously its obligations under the Non-Proliferation Treaty of 1968 to "negotiate in good faith to achieve a precise result – nuclear disarmament in all its aspects," and included North Korea on its nuclear target list, also in breach of the Treaty. It persisted in unremitting nuclear intimidation of North Korea thereafter.

North Korea has been a kind of pariah state for almost the entirety (since 1948) of its existence. It may be the most reviled country in modern history, the ultimate "other" to which the word "evil" has commonly and unquestioningly been applied. Yet for virtually the entire period from San Francisco 1951 to today North Korea has been a nuclear *victim* state (subject to nuclear intimidation). If anything might be calculated to drive a people "mad," feeding an obsession with security, it would surely be prolonged exposure to existential nuclear threat such as North Korea has faced. But so long as the threat was directed *at* North Korea, not *from* it, the world showed no interest. Only when North Korea succeeded in developing its own deterrent, signalled by a flurry of tests in 2017 (continuing to this day), would the world pay attention.

There is a second reason for including brief reference to Korea. It is because the extraordinary events of 2018 showed a way beyond San Francisco, an alternative future, remedying the egregious flaws of the San Francisco system, not least its inattention to Korea. President Trump, responding to North Korean overtures, began to treat it with respect, endorsing the need for a treaty to end the Korean War. The Koreas of North and South, together with US President Trump, agreed on a shared strategic objective—peace, denuclearization, and comprehensive cooperation for the Koreas. The outcome, ever so briefly, was the spectacle of two Korean leaders chatting in the spring sunshine at Panmunjom, ushering each other back and forth

---

separate elections in South Korea. See my *Cold War Hot War—An Australian Perspective on the Korean War*, Sydney, Hale and Iremonger, 1983.

[68] Truth and Reconciliation Commission, Republic of Korea, Comprehensive Report, Vol 1, 2010.

[69] Kim Dong-choon, The Truth and Reconciliation Commission of Korea: Uncovering the hidden history of the Korean War," *The Asia-Pacific Journal—Japan Focus,* March 1, 2010. http://apjjf.org/-kim-dong-choon/3314/article.html/. For a full study of these grim events, see Su-Kyoung Hwang, *Korea's Grievous War*, University of Pennsylvania Press, 2016.

across the line dividing their two zones.[70] Shortly after meeting with Kim Jong-un in Singapore, Trump declared, "We will be stopping the war games, which will save us a tremendous amount of money … Plus, I think it's very provocative."[71] He went on in terms of unusual eloquence:

> The past does not have to define the future. Yesterday's conflict does not have to be tomorrow's war. And as history has proven over and over again, adversaries can indeed become friends. We can honor the sacrifice of our forefathers by replacing the horrors of battle with the blessings of peace. And that's what we're doing and that's what we have done.[72]

Sadly, the blessings of peace were no sooner glimpsed than they disappeared again. The series of high-level international conferences in 2018 addressing Korean issues nevertheless demonstrated just how suddenly war preparation could give way to peace cooperation and long-frozen diplomatic logjams break-up. If a peace treaty to end the Korean War can be put onto the bargaining table (as for a time under Trump it was), so can the closure and return of the American bases in Okinawa, and the liquidation of the dominance of Japan and Korea by the United States.[73] Clientelism need not be forever.

While the condition of human rights in North Korea may be deplorable, and the threat of its nuclear and missile systems to the region and the world is real and serious, these are essentially the symptoms of the underlying problem: Korean division. World citizens and scholars, and indeed the United Nations, must pay attention to the essential justice of the demand that North Korea makes of the world: for a peace treaty to end the Korean War, the "normalization" of relations with Japan and the United States, and a lifting of the multiple punitive sanctions under which it labours. These are necessary, even urgent, demands, yet in the three-sided Camp David Declaration of 2023 there was no sign of readiness to meet them.

Despite the almost universal belief that North Korea is to blame for the isolation it suffers from, the South Korean president who did much (in 2018) to try to overcome is clear that "at every pivotal 'hinge point' when the North Korean nuclear issue could have been resolved or at least kept in check with diplomacy [actors] have missed opportunities and made the situation worse through excessively ideological political decisions rather than rational choices."[74] It has been the "the abandonment of agreements and suspension of dialogue" on the part of the United States

[70] President Moon handed Chairman Kim a USB containing multiple plans and suggestions for a united future, something unthinkable at any time in the past seven decades. Equally unthinkable, Kim Jong-un accepted it and it presumably informed subsequent South-North discussions.

[71] Press Conference by President Trump, Singapore, June 12, 2018, https://www.whitehouse.gov/briefings-statements/press-conference-president-trump/.

[72] For the you-tube coverage of this speech, 30 September 2018, see https://www.bing.com/videos/search?q=trump%2c+kim+jong-un%2c+%22love%22&view=detail&mid=2C5079B1CC64334C9DB02C5079B1CC64334C9DB0&FORM=VIRE.

[73] On 1947 and 1995, McCormack and Norimatsu, *Resistant Islands*, pp. 6, 64–5.

[74] "Scrapping pacts, cutting off dialogue has hastened N. Korea's nuclear development," says Moon. *Hankyoreh*, 11 December 2023. https://english.hani.co.kr/arti/english_edition/e_northkorea/1119931.html/.

and other hostile states that has hastened North Korea's nuclear development. Hostility on the part of the United States and its allies has been only barely concealed by the periodic calls by Japan's Kishida and Korea's Yoon for a summit meeting with North Korean Chair Kim Jong-un.[75]

7 Conclusion

Though nominally aimed to preserve peace and the "rules-based" international order, the structure of confronting alliances—US-Japan-South Korea versus China-Russia-North Korea—threatens to spiral into conflict, like the early twentieth-century alliances that were supposed to guarantee peace but instead brought Europe to disaster in 1914.

Neither the Quad, nor AUKUS, nor the Camp David Declaration formula for reorganizing the San Francisco world order, had room for climate change, civilizational sustainability, or nuclear disarmament. The likelihood of global warming by at least two, perhaps even three, degrees Celsius by the end of the century grows. As the collapse of the ice-sheets gathers momentum, rising sea-levels will come to threaten the world's (including Japan's) ocean-front cities. The real costs of prolonged abdication and clientelism, dividing the world into allies and enemies and pressing for military confrontation and weapons purchase, will then be apparent, missiles, fighter aircraft and submarines a useless irrelevance.

As the twenty-first century evolves, the logic that in the twentieth century guided Japan's rulers to embrace clientelist status because it seemed to offer best promise of protection in an uncertain world no longer holds sway. The military-industrial [and intelligence] complex against which then President Eisenhower warned (in 1961) becomes manifest both domestically and internationally. Dependence for national security in the twenty-first century on the erratic and war-prone United States makes little sense for countries such as Japan, Australia, and South Korea.

Kishida Fumio, Japan's fourth Prime Minister of this twenty-first century, now in his third year of office, faces catastrophically slumping poll figures, multiple scandals, and a generally unhappy country. His government's major commitment is to continue doing whatever is demanded of him by his US superiors, building new bases for the Marine Corps, militarizing Japan itself and subjecting its armed forces to US direction. At huge cost he will turn the country into the world's number three military force. He shows no sign of understanding that the deep problem Japan faces is the one held over from San Francisco 72 years ago: to recover sovereignty and the peace constitution or to remain on the path of dependence and military greatness.

In Australia, the country's seventh Prime Minister of this century, Anthony Albanese, like Kishida, is clear that his government's number one priority is to serve

[75] Wada Haruki, "Normalization of relations between Japan and North Korea: why is it necessary and how could it be accomplished," edited and translated by Gavan McCormack, The Asia-Pacific Journal—Japan Focus, 27 December 2023. https://apjjf.org/2023/12/Wada-McCormack.html/.

the United States, be faithful to the Quad and AUKUS, and cooperate closely with NATO. He appears to relish the role of [US] "Deputy Sheriff." Under Albanese, the major state project for his and succeeding governments will be the purchase or construction of nuclear-powered submarines, signifying Australian commitment to hostility for the emerging superpower of China through at least mid-twenty-first century.

For the Cold War knots tied by the San Francisco settlement around East Asia—especially tightly around the Korean peninsula and the Okinawan archipelago—to be untied, foreign troop occupations will one day have to be ended and war drums silenced. Only by doing so can the door be opened to a comprehensive, post-San Francisco Treaty regional order. It will have to be a post-US hegemony order. On the Korean peninsula and in Okinawa in particular citizens know from experience how precious is peace. The desire for peace has to be passed on across the generations. Only by turning from war preparation to peace construction is it likely that the nuclear and climate change challenges with which this paper began can be met.

The Core Values of the Cairo Declaration and an Exit Strategy to Overcome the Limitations of the San Francisco Peace Treaty

L. E. E. Jang-Hie

Abstract The core values of the Declaration were not sufficiently reflected in reality, and were distorted in the drafting of the San Francisco Peace Treaty for legal termination of the Pacific War. In addition, countries that were colonies & victims of the war such as the Republic of Korea (ROK) and Taiwan were not included as treaty signatory nations. One reason for their exclusion can be traced back to the fundamental changes in US foreign policy towards East Asia in the Cold War order since The Truman Doctrine (March 12, 1947). Additionally, Japan's persistent lobbying (e.g., by William Sebald) of the US Government, along with security considerations such as the building of weather and radar stations on Dokdo Island, also contributed to the exclusion.

As a result, the San Francisco Peace Treaty did not become a punishment treaty, but rather an indulgence treaty that failed to punish Japanese war criminals and address the issue of compensation for victims. The war criminals were mostly released from the Tokyo War Criminal Trial (1946–1948). Such failures demonstrate that the San Francisco Peace Treaty was a relic of the Cold War order of the 1950s, and failed to implement the core values of the Cairo Declaration.

Today, East Asia is drifting in uncertainty due to conflicts over regional territorial and history. Institutionalization of an East Asia peace community is a long way off. The effects of surviving colonialism have made regional collaboration among countries very difficult. The long division of the ROK and the Democratic People's Republic of Korea (North Korea) created a new Cold War structure in East Asia,

This article has been written with update and changes, based on the author's English article, "The Core Values of the Cairo Declaration and Exit Strategy to overcome the limitations of the San Francisco Peace Treaty"(Article), Korean Yearbook of International Law, Vol.8, The Korean Branch of International Law Association, 2020.9. pp. 19–38.

L. E. E. Jang-Hie (✉)
Hankuk University of Foreign Studies, Law School, Seoul, Republic of Korea

Y.-H. Kim et al. (eds.), *Beyond the San Francisco System*,
https://doi.org/10.1007/978-981-95-3328-2_3

further hindering regional collaboration. Finally, the remnants of colonialism and the long division of the Korean Peninsula can be traced to the limitations of the San Francisco Peace Treaty, which was based on the Cold War order. Likewise, the Korean Armistice (1953) and the Korea-Japan Agreement (1965) are also by-products of the Cold War order. These historical disputes in East Asia come from the limitations of the San Francisco Peace Treaty. This paper suggests exit strategies to overcome such limitations. Action plans include "adopting the Civil Society Charter" towards peace and human rights in East Asia to overcome the San Francisco Peace Treaty system on the basis of universal norms and values for a peaceful East Asian community.

Keywords Cairo Declaration · Harry Lloyd Hopkins · Franklin Delano Roosevelt · Winston Churchill · Chiang Kai-shek · Potsdam Declaration · San Francisco Peace Treaty · Korean independence · Civil Society Charter · Peaceful East Asian Community · Asian NGO peace–network

1 Core Values of the Cairo Declaration and Its Implementation Failure in the San Francisco Peace Treaty

The current year of 2024 marks the 81st anniversary of the Cairo Declaration, which was made on December 1, 1943.[1] To tackle the current issues of East Asia such as unresolved territorial and colonial disputes, we need to develop a deep understanding of the historical background and the core values of the Cairo Declaration.

1.1 Background of the Cairo Declaration

The Cairo Declaration was made by three leaders: President Franklin Delano Roosevelt of the United States, Prime Minister Winston Churchill of the United Kingdom, and General Chiang Kai-shek of China (signed the Cairo Declaration later in the Tehran talks, followed by Stalin of the Soviet Union) in the Cairo Mena district of Egypt (1943.22–27) and then, on December 1, 1943, after the four-day Tehran talks (1943.27–30) with the participation of Stalin instead of Chiang Kai-Shek, the three Allies announced the Cairo Declaration with the Tehran Communiqué.[2] The most pressing issue was how to quickly and efficiently destroy Japan and Germany through military operations. A second priority was to develop

[1] The Cairo Declaration from the conferences at Cairo and Tehran, 1943, available at http://digital.library.wise.edu./1711.dl/FRRUS/FRUS1943 (Accessed October 20, 2019). See TEXT: Appendix 1: The Cairo Declaration (1943.12.1.).

[2] June Harry Hopkins, Sudden Hero, Brash Reformer,Pargave,(Macmillian,1999), pp. 27–28.

friendship among the heads of the Allied forces and their staff while discussing strategy and tactics to employ against Japanese imperialism and the German Nazis. The original purpose of the Cairo talks was to discuss strategic military tactics that would quickly punish Hitler and Japanese fascism. Stalin's initial absence from the Cairo talks, replaced by the attendance of Chiang Kai-shek, resulted in many changes during the drafting of the Cairo Declaration.[3]

The Cairo talks had to be moved to the Tehran talks, so there was no clear conclusion on the big principles and plans in Cairo, but the issues were understood by all parties. The Cairo Declaration was initially drafted by Harry Lloyd Hopkins (1890–1946), Roosevelt's longtime companion and special adviser. The first draft included the fact that the Allies must pressure Japan into surrendering unconditionally through a fierce military attack, the need to restore China's old territory, consideration of the slave status of Koreans, the need for the freedom and independence of Korea in due course ("at the earliest possible moment"), and the list of attending military commanders and staff members from the three countries that attended. The first draft was not the [Joint Declaration], but the [Joint Communiqué]; Hopkins' first draft was passed to Roosevelt; Roosevelt did not touch the Hopkins draft itself, but amended five points. First, the statement "it will be a vigorous attack" on Japan was adjusted to a "continuous and increasingly vigorous attack." Second, the sentences related to "the meeting place" were deleted. Third, the Korean independence question was marked to change the line and start a new one, and at the same time, the "(at the earliest possible moment)" was changed to "at the proper moment." The Korean clause remained. Fifth, the name of Song Mi-ryeong was erased from the list of participants in developing the draft.[4]

The declaration, which the Hopkins draft had been corrected and reorganized by Roosevelt, was formally confirmed as the United States' draft regarding the Cairo Declaration, and this confirmed American draft was then passed on to Chiang Kai-Shek and Churchill.[5]

The British made five revisions:

First, time limitations were added by appending "since the beginning of the first World War in 1914" to the term "confiscation of the Pacific occupied islands of Japan."[6]

Secondly, the word "treacherously" was taken from among the "treacherously stolen" in the passage of returning the All Chinese territory that had been treacherously stolen by Japan.[7]

Third, the sentence "All conquered territories taken by violence and greed by the Japanese will be freed from their clutches" has been replaced with a more refined

[3] Ibid., pp. 29–30.

[4] Jung Il Hwa, The Cairo Declaration, (Covenant Press, 2009.12), pp. 46–47.

[5] Ibid., pp. 47–48.

[6] Winston Churchill, The Second World War: Their Finest Hour, (The Riverside Press,Cambridge, 1949), p. 543.

[7] Ibid.,p.544.

expression "Japan will also be expelled from all other territories which she has taken by violence and greed.".[8]

Fourth, the Hopkins original draft "... determined that at the earliest possible moment Korea shall be become free and independent" was modified by Roosevelt as "at the proper moment" back to "in due course" by Churchill. The term " in due course" is a commonly used term by Churchill.[9]

Fifth, instead of the word "we", the subject that started the article of Korean independence was changed to the more responsible word "the aforesaid three Great Powers".[10]

1.2 *The Core Values of the Cairo Declaration*

The Cairo Declaration is the first international "gentlemen's agreement" in which the Three Allies compromised in determining the core values. The main core values of the Cairo Declaration include "punishing the Japanese aggressor," "recovery of territorial sovereignty of China, all islands in the Pacific & Korea," and "Independence and Freedom of Korean People" and "mindful of enslavement of the people of Korea" in due course to address the military aggression and colonialism of imperial Japan.

The core values of the Cairo Declaration were accepted in the Potsdam Declaration (July 26, 1945).[11] Japan accepted it unconditionally (August 10, 1945) and signed the surrender instrument unconditionally (September 2, 1945). Since then, the Cairo Declaration has had a legally binding force on Japan. The mandate that "the terms of the Cairo Declaration shall be carried out and Japanese sovereignty shall be limited to the Islands of Honshu, Hokkaido, Kyushu, Shikoku, and such minor as we determine"[12] was again actually carried out by SCAPIN[13] 677 on January 29, 1946, and on June 22, in SCAPIN 1033.[14]

However, the core values of the Declaration were not sufficiently reflected and ultimately were distorted in the drafting of the San Francisco Peace Treaty for the legal termination of the Pacific War. In addition, countries that were invaded and victimized by colonialism such as Korea and Taiwan were not treaty signatories. One reason for this can be traced to fundamental changes in US foreign policy in

[8] Ibid., p.545.

[9] Ibid.,p.546.

[10] Ibid.,p.547.

[11] Potsdam Declaration, Proclamation Defining Terms for Japanese Surrender Issues, at Potsdam, July 26, available at: https://www.digital.ndl.go.jp/constitution/e/etc/c06.html (Accessed October 20, 2019): See Text: Appendix 2: Potsdam Declaration 1945.12.1.).

[12] Article 8, The Potsdam Declaration (1945).

[13] SCAPIN (Supreme Commander for the Allies Powers Instruction).

[14] In SCAPIN 677 & SCAPIN 1033 of 1946, after World War II, The Allied Powers occupying both Japan and Korea issued instructions that separated Dokdo from Japanese territory.

East Asia regarding the Cold War since the Truman Doctrine of 1947.[15] Another factor is persistent Japanese lobbying of the US Government with security considerations, such as the building of weather and radar stations on Dokdo Island.

As a result, the San Francisco treaty became a treaty not of punishment, but almost of indulgence of Japanese war criminals with regard to the issues of "punishing the Japanese aggressor" and "compensation for victims." War criminals were mostly released from the Tokyo War Crimes Trials (1946–1948).[16]

The issue of "recovery of territorial sovereignty" was very ambiguous as stipulated in the Treaty. This ambiguity lies in the roots of current territorial disputes in Korea, China, and the Pacific.[17] The last goal for the "independence and freedom of Korean people" is the peaceful unification of the Korean Peninsula, which has experienced the terrible pain of division for the past 78 years.

The term "mindful of enslavement of the people of Korea" provides a legal basis for the protection of human rights with regard to military sexual slavery (the so-called "comfort women" program) by Japan. However, the Japanese government has not yet legally apologized to Korean victims, and no legal compensation has been provided.

As such, the San Francisco Peace Treaty was trapped in the Cold War Order of the 1950s. The above core values of the Cairo Declaration were distorted and all but ignored in Article 2(a) of the San Francisco Peace Treaty (1951)[18] concerning the territory of Dokdo Island. The 1951 peace treaty between Japan and the Allied Powers made no specific mention of Dokdo. Perhaps this is due to the Korean War and the dynamics of Cold War politics. Article 2(a) of the San Francisco Peace Treaty has been invoked by Japan to claim sovereignty over Dokdo, based on an argument that the paragraph does not specify Dokdo. But Korea did not sign this treaty.[19]

As a result, the San Francisco Peace Treaty ultimately tolerated and justified Japanese colonialism and imperialism without deeply considering their victims.

---

[15] The Truman Doctrine(March 12,1947) was an American foreign policy with the primary goal of containing Soviet geopolitical expansion during the Cold War. It was announced to Congress by President Harry S. Trumann on March 12,1947, and further developed on July 4,1948 when he pledged to contain the communist uprisings in Greece and Turkey. The Truman Doctrine became the foundation of the American foreign policy, and led, in 1949,to the formation of NATO, military alliance that still exists. Historians often use Truman's speech to date the start of the Cold War. Michael Beschloss, Our Documents:100, Milestone Documents From The National Archives,(Oxford University Press,2006),pp.194–99.

[16] Jang-Hie Lee, "A Comparative Study on the Nurenberg War Crimes Trial & the Tokyo War Crimes Trial from the International Law Pint of View", Dongbuga Yeoksa Nonchong,(Journal of Northeast Asian History),Vol.25(2009.9.), pp.222–223.

[17] Dekun Hu, "Analysis on Why the San Francisco Peace Treaty Changed the Allies' Disposal of East Asian Territories", Beyond The San Francisco System, the second international conference(December1,2017,Perry World House, University of Pennsylvania, USA), Proceedings of Papers, pp.70–71.

[18] TREATY OF PEACE WITH JAPAN /Sept. 8, 1951 CHAPTER II TERRITORY: Article 2: (a) Japan recognizing the independence of Korea, renounces all right, title and claim to Korea, including the islands of Quelpart, Port Hamilton and Dagelet.

[19] http://dokdo.mofa.go.kr/eng/include/print.jsp.

2 Present Situation in East Asia

It has been over 30 years, almost an entire generation, since the international community entered the post-Cold War and post-colonial era in the 1990s. Now, East Asia is drifting in uncertainty due to regional territorial and historical conflicts. Institutionalization of an East Asia peace community is still a long way off. The long-term effects of having survived colonialism have made regional collaboration between countries very difficult. The long division of the ROK and North Korea created a new Cold War structure in East Asia, further hindering regional collaboration. Ultimately, the remnants of colonialism and the long division of the Korean Peninsula can be traced back to the limitations of the San Francisco Peace Treaty on the basis of the Cold War order. Likewise, the Korean Armistice (1953) and the Korea-Japan Agreement (1965) are by-products of the Cold War order.

Let us look at this in greater detail. The root causes of many of the distortions and territorial disputes among Japan, Korea, China, and other Asian countries can be traced back to the times of Japanese colonialism and imperialism. In addition, there are still unresolved issues regarding compensation due to the victims of colonialism and the Pacific War. In particular, at the end of the Pacific War the United States, seeking an early end of the Pacific War, overestimated the Japanese Kwandong army in Manchuria, and strongly demanded the Soviet Union participate in the Pacific War as an alternative. The Soviet Union's entry into the war led to the eventual division of the Korean peninsula. The division of the Korean peninsula has been a major obstacle to establishing historical justice, a peace regime, and the development of democracy on the Korean Peninsula.

In particular, East Asian countries, including Korea and China, are currently quite concerned about the extreme right-wing government of Japanese Prime Minister Abe Shinzo. His foreign policy is mainly focused on a resurgence of colonial militarism. Today, the Japanese government is still trying to justify its history of colonial occupation, and the Chinese government also tries to distort ancient history. These historical disputes in East Asia come from the limitations of the San Francisco Peace Treaty.

As a concrete argument, the San Francisco Peace Treaty did not clearly state the illegality and criminality of Japanese colonial invasion of territory and crimes against humanity in order to implement the core values of the Cairo Declaration. Following that, the 1965 Korea-Japan agreement system was created, premised on the legalization of Japanese colonial rule. Japan complains that Korea has violated international law on the basis of the 1965 Korea-Japan Agreement, which can exempt the Japanese government from legal and state responsibility.

What actions should be taken to resolve this situation? What should the exit strategy be to overcome the limitations of the San Francisco Peace Treaty?

3 Initiative Actor to Build a Peaceful East Asian Community

First of all, who should lead the way to end colonialism and the division of the Korean Peninsula? The early resolution of issues related to colonialism is a critical matter for East Asian countries; once they pass this step, they can recover and establish rightful cultural and historical identities so that a peaceful East Asian community can be built in the twenty-first century. However, we should not leave this matter in the hands of East Asian sovereign states seeking national interests. Non-governmental organizations (NGO) that pursue peace and justice in ways that transcend selfish national interests must take the initiative in this matter. Therefore, the role of NGOs such as the "Asian NGO Peace Network" (hereafter ANPN) as a "Non-State Actor" with initiative and drive is necessary to bring about historical reconciliation and regional peace.

Second, in what way should this problem be handled? It should be pointed out that East Asian countries have numerous cultural and historical heritages. Therefore, the first step in building a peaceful East Asia is establishing "universal norms and values" based on the culture and history of East Asia. Instead of taking various nationalistic views, we should take an East Asian point of view based on a shared culture and history. By establishing shared norms and values, East Asia should play a central role in making a peaceful East Asian community. Non-state actors should initiate the measures and encourage member countries to accept them through persuasion and pressure.

Third, what are the difficulties? Who will take on the leadership role? Who takes the initiative is a critical matter in establishing the shared rules and values of an East Asian community. As is well known, East Asia has a heterogeneous nature in terms of culture, economic status, and geography. Korea, China, and Japan, however, are close to each other geographically, culturally and economically; the three countries should start with regional collaborations and gradually expand these to the ten ASEAN countries. Of the three countries, Korea is the only one that has never been a threat to the other two. For this reason, Korea is the most suitable candidate to be a mediator. East Asia has not been able to recover its unique historical and cultural identities, both spiritually and culturally. We should now take a leap forward in establishing historical and cultural identities, and establish the shared rules and values of East Asia rather than simply seeking economic prosperity.

Fourth, we must learn how to overcome historical and ethnic conflicts by studying the experiences of multiple European countries.[20] There was a very strong movement among European countries to institutionalize hope for the peace and prosperity of Europe through historical reconciliations among themselves. The first attempt was made in May 1949 when the Council of Europe was formed with ten

---

[20] Dennis Sammut, "European expression in attaining human rights, civic values, and universal norms", 2011 International NGOs Conference on History and Peace, Specialists Round Table 1 (August 18–22, 2011, Younsei University, Seoul), Materials Book, pp. 161–162.

member states.[21] Now, the number of member states has grown to 47. European countries founded the Council of Europe (May 5, 1949) and established the European Court of Human and Rights as a separate entity from the Council based on the European Convention on Human Rights (November 1950)[22] and the Commissioner for Human Rights that makes suggestions on the human rights report. The Council of Europe's most famous achievement is the European Convention on Human Rights, which was adopted in 1950 following a report by the Council of Europe's Parliamentary Assembly, and followed on from the United Nations "Universal Declaration of Human Rights" (UDHR). The Convention created the European Court of Human Rights in Strasbourg.

Also, European countries intentionally adopted the European Social Charters in 1961 at the Council of Europe in order to protect economic, social and cultural rights that were not included in the European Convention on Human Rights. The European Committee of Social Rights was also established to monitor the implementation of the European Social Charter.

Also, the Helsinki Final Act of the Conference on Security and Cooperation in Europe (CSCE),[23] established in 1975, has contributed to regional collaboration and regional integration, both directly and indirectly. A total of 35 participating states, including all of the then-existing European countries as well as the United States and Canada, signed the Final Act in an attempt to improve the détente between the Soviet bloc and the West.[24] CSCE in particular played a critical role in the German unification process.[25] It is noteworthy that non-state actors such as civic groups and church organizations worked actively to build public support for regional collaboration, and took on a role in founding the Council of Europe[26] and CSCE.[27] East Asia should pursue the multilateral approach adopted by the Council of Europe and CSCE rather than the bilateralism as an approach to regional cooperation.

---

[21] The Treaty of London or the Statute of the Council of Europe was signed in London on that day by ten states: Belgium, Denmark, France, Ireland, Italy, Luxembourg, the Netherlands, Norway, Sweden and the United Kingdom. Many other states followed, especially after the democratic transitions in central and eastern Europe during the early 1990s, and the Council of Europe now includes all European states except Belarus, Vatican City and European territories with limited recognition such as Artsakh, Abkhazia, South Ossetia, Northern Cyprus, Transnistria, and Kosovo.

[22] The Court supervises compliance with the European Convention on Human Rights and thus functions as the highest European court. It is to this court that Europeans can bring cases if they believe that a member country has violated their fundamental rights and freedoms.

[23] CSCE has been changed to OSCE (Organization for Security and Cooperation in Europe) since 1994. Please refer to OSCE Handbook, third edition, June 2000.

[24] Encyclopedia Britannica, Helsinki Accords: available at: http://www.britanica.com/EBchecked/topics/260615/Helsinki-Accords.

[25] Theodor Schweisfurth, "Einfuehring", KSZE, Dokumente der KSZE, Beck-Texte im dtv, pp. XI–LXIV.

[26] The first attempt was made in May 1949 by creating the Council of Europe for the peace and prosperity of Europe through historical reconsilkation through among themselves. Jang-Hie Lee, "Tasks for Adopting 'the Civil Society Charter' towards Peace and Human Rights in East Asia",KYIL,Vol.5, 2017,pp.161–162.

[27] Ibid.

4 Tasks for Adopting "The Civil Society Charter" Towards Peace and Human Rights in East Asia to Overcome the Shortcomings of the San Francisco Peace Treaty

What are the details of the shared norms and values[28] related to adopting the Asian Social Charter at the NGOs level as the foundations of the East Asian peace community, and the specific action plans?

The values pursued by East Asia—Peace, Prosperity, and Human Rights—should go beyond the nationalistic perspective and acquire a new identity from an East Asian perspective. The Asian Social Charter at the level of NGOs should be based on the shared norms and values of East Asia.

- Shared norms: Common peace, prosperity, and human rights in East Asia based on international law
- Shared values: Cultural identity of East Asia, civil values of East Asia
- Principles of action: Complete elimination of colonialism, resolution of historical conflicts, international social responsibilities of the private sector (observance of ISO 26,000).[29]
- Adoption of "the Civil Society Charter" in "East Asia NGOs Conference on Peace and Human Rights".
- Specific tasks:

  (a) Publication of a common East Asian history textbook
  (b) Publication of a survey of historical conflicts in East Asia
  (c) Exchange and cooperation project to enhance cultural understanding
  (d) Establishment of the East Asia Peace Education Center
  (e) Establishment of East Asia University
  (f) Development of East Asian history reconciliation index and peace index

- Initiative Organization: "Asian NGO Peace Network" (ANPN) as Non-State Actors.

  (a) Members of ANPN: NGOs from "ASEAN+ 3".
  (b) Utilization of the human resource network of those who participate in the "International NGOs Conference on History and Peace".[30]
  (c) Cooperation with UNESCO Asia Pacific members

[28] Ki-Joon Hong, "Two Track approaches to Common Norm Building in North east Asia", 2013 International NGOs Conference on History and Peace, Specialists & NGOs Workshop (July 22–25, 2011, Kyung Hee Univ. Seoul), Materials Book, pp. 294–298.

[29] Martin Neureiter, "ISO 26000-the future global Standard on Social Responsibility", International Conference, Convergence of Corporate Governance & Social Responsibility (January 28, 2011), hosted by Institute for Legal Studies, Sogang University Law School, Material Book, pp. 12–22.

[30] Example: The 2016 International NGO Conference on History Education for Peace in East Asia and Europe (6–10 July 2016, The Hague, Leiden, Utrecht, Amsterdam, The Netherlands) co-organized by History NGO Forum for Peace in East Asia and European Association of History Education.

- Road map: Four steps toward a "Council of Asia".
- first step: ANPN: Steering Committee for NGOs: Universal Norms & Values.
- second step: East Asia NGOs Conference on Peace, Prosperity, and Human Right (Adopting the Civil Society Charter).
- third step: Strong Campaign through Programs Education by ANPN.
- - fourth step: Establishment of "Council of Asia"[31] at the Government Organization level.

  (Ex.: Council of Europe)

- Final Objective:
- Institutionalization of shared rules and values of East Asia and principles of action by adopting the Asian Social Charter in "East Asia NGOs Conference on Peace, Prosperity, and Human Rights."
- Declaration of East Asian version of [Durban Declaration, 2001][32]: [Action Plans]; establishment of a permanent acting organization: Campaign to establish Council of Asia at the Government Organization level.

5 Exit Strategy to Overcome the Limitations of the San Francisco System

East Asia, once devastated by colonialism and imperialism, has become economically prosperous. The rich East Asian countries must develop the correct historical and philosophical perspective based on East Asian values in order to make ongoing contributions to peace, prosperity, and human rights, both in Asia and in the broader international community. If East Asian countries show an uncritical obeisance to neo-liberalism, chasing after competitiveness and material prosperity, that choice will act as a big hindrance to the development of East Asia. To build a long-standing, peaceful East Asia, we must start by establishing shared norms and values based on Asian cultural identity.

This task will never be achieved if we rely solely on the selfish pursuit of our own national interests. In this era of the global community, where the cultural heritage of a nation is protected and preserved as the world's cultural heritage, people need to change their self-centred view of history. We must learn lessons from the European experience. The European Union is now dreaming of a European Federation.

---

[31] Council of Asia member states maintain their full sovereignty but commit themselves through the Asian Social Charter and cooperate on the basis of common values and common political decisions.

[32] The 2001 World Conference against Racism (WCAR) also known as Durban I, was held at the Durban International Convention Center in Durban, South Africa, under UN auspices, from31 August to 8 September 2001. The conference covered several issues, including redress for transatlantic slavery and the Second class citizenry issues in Palestine-Israel. https://www.hrw.org/legacy/campairns/race/

In this regard, the "Asian NGO Peace-Network (ANPN),"[33] as a non-state actor aspiring towards peace, prosperity and human rights beyond national boundaries, should come forward with an action program and a road map. The Asian NGO Peace Network must put pressure on their own governments and organize regional collaboration campaigns in order to establish and institutionalize our hope for the peace, prosperity and human rights of East Asians. As a result, the Council of Asia, the Asian Court of Human Rights at the Government Organization level, and the Asian Social Charter on the NGOs level should gradually be institutionalized. We must make an Asian version of the Durban Declaration (2001) among the ASEAN+3 countries, and the Asian NGO Peace Network must take the initiative in this process. Another option is to organize the Regional Steering Committee by networking with all of the professional participants in the many gatherings of the International NGOs Conference on History and Peace. ANPN should devise a multilateral peace mechanism (Ex.: OSCE) within the Conference on Peace and Human Rights in East Asia, which could coincide with the individual peace interests of the participating states. ANPN would enable fundamental peace, historical reconciliation, and regional cooperation in East Asia, not to mention promote the relationship between Japan and Korea. For the sake of future generations' interests, let us look at the world from the perspective of practical interests, peace and human rights rather than being stuck in ideologies. NGOs must lead the path towards peace and human rights and historical reconciliation in East Asia.

In conclusion, this matter should not be left in the hands of East Asian sovereign states that are pursuing their own national interests. Non-governmental organizations (NGOs) that support universal peace, human rights and justice in a way that goes beyond selfish national interests must take the initiative in this matter. Therefore, the role of NGOs such as "Asian NGO Peace–Network" (ANPN), as non-State actors with initiative and drive, is necessary to bring about historical reconciliation and regional peace in East Asia.

Appendix 1: The Cairo Declaration (1943.12.1.)

Declaration of the Three Powers-Great Britain, the United States and China Regarding Japan Signed at Cairo, November 27, 1943

President F D Roosevelt, Generalissimo Chiang Kai-Shek (Jiang Jieshi) and Prime Minister Mr. Winston Churchill, together with their respective military and diplomatic advisers, have completed a conference in North Africa.

[33] Jang-Hie Lee, "Tasks for Adopting the Civil Society Charter" towards Peace and Human Rights in East Asia: Overcoming The San Francisco Treaty System," Korean Yearbook of International Law, Vol. 5 (2017), pp. 154–156.

The following general statement was issued:

The several military missions have agreed upon future military operations against Japan. The Three Great Allies expressed their resolve to bring unrelenting pressure against their brutal enemies by sea, land, and air. This pressure is already rising.

The Three Great Allies are fighting this war to restrain and punish the aggression of Japan.

They covet no gain for themselves and have no thought of territorial expansion.

It is their purpose that Japan shall be stripped of all the islands in the Pacific which she has seized or occupied since the beginning of the First World War in 1914, and that all the territories Japan has stolen from the Chinese, such as Manchuria, Formosa and the Pescadores, shall be restored to the Republic of China.

Japan will also be expelled from all other territories which she has taken by violence and greed.

The aforesaid three great powers, mindful of the enslavement of the people of Korea, are determined that in due course Korea shall become free and independent.

With these objectives in view the three Allies, in harmony with those of the United Nations at war with Japan, will continue to persevere in the serious and prolonged operations necessary to procure the unconditional surrender of Japan.

Appendix 2: Potsdam Declaration 1945.12.1

Proclamation Defining Terms for Japanese Surrender

Issued, at Potsdam, July 26, 1945

We-the President of the United States, the President of the National Government of the Republic of China, and the Prime Minister of Great Britain, representing the hundreds of millions of our countrymen, have conferred and agree that Japan shall be given an opportunity to end this war.

The prodigious land, sea and air forces of the United States, the British Empire and of China, many times reinforced by their armies and air fleets from the west, are poised to strike the final blows upon Japan. This military power is sustained and inspired by the determination of all the Allied Nations to prosecute the war against Japan until she ceases to resist.

The result of the futile and senseless German resistance to the might of the aroused free peoples of the world stands forth in awful clarity as an example to the people of Japan. The might that now converges on Japan is immeasurably greater than that which, when applied to the resisting Nazis, necessarily laid waste to the lands, the industry and the method of life of the whole German people. The full application of our military power, backed by our resolve, will mean the inevitable and complete destruction of the Japanese armed forces and just as inevitably the utter devastation of the Japanese homeland.

The time has come for Japan to decide whether she will continue to be controlled by those self-willed militaristic advisers whose unintelligent calculations have brought the Empire of Japan to the threshold of annihilation, or whether she will follow the path of reason.

The following are our terms. We will not deviate from them. There are no alternatives. We shall brook no delay.

There must be eliminated for all time the authority and influence of those who have deceived and misled the people of Japan into embarking on world conquest, for we insist that a new order of peace, security and justice will be impossible until irresponsible militarism is driven from the world.

Until such a new order is established and until there is convincing proof that Japan's war-making power is destroyed, points in Japanese territory to be designated by the Allies shall be occupied to secure the achievement of the basic objectives we are here setting forth.

The terms of the Cairo Declaration shall be carried out and Japanese sovereignty shall be limited to the islands of Honshu, Hokkaido, Kyushu, Shikoku and such minor islands as we determine.

The Japanese military forces, after being completely disarmed, shall be permitted to return to their homes with the opportunity to lead peaceful and productive lives.

We do not intend that the Japanese shall be enslaved as a race or destroyed as a nation, but stern justice shall be meted out to all war criminals, including those who have visited cruelties upon our prisoners. The Japanese Government shall remove all obstacles to the revival and strengthening of democratic tendencies among the Japanese people. Freedom of speech, of religion, and of thought, as well as respect for the fundamental human rights shall be established.

Japan shall be permitted to maintain such industries as will sustain her economy and permit the exaction of just reparations in kind, but not those which would enable her to re-arm for war. To this end, access to, as distinguished from control of, raw materials shall be permitted. Eventual Japanese participation in world trade relations shall be permitted.

The occupying forces of the Allies shall be withdrawn from Japan as soon as these objectives have been accomplished and there has been established in accordance with the freely expressed will of the Japanese people a peacefully inclined and responsible government.

We call upon the government of Japan to proclaim now the unconditional surrender of all Japanese armed forces, and to provide proper and adequate assurances of their good faith in such action. The alternative for Japan is prompt and utter destruction.

(The Ministry of Foreign Affairs "Nihon Gaiko Nenpyo Narabini Shuyo Bunsho: 1840-1945" vol. 2, 1966)

A Case for the Modifiability of the San Francisco Peace Treaty: Examining the Varying Positions of the United States and Britain Over South Korean Participation

Tae-Jin Yi

Abstract This paper explores the modifiability of the San Francisco Peace Treaty, focusing on the issue of South Korea's participation and analyzing the differing positions of the United States and the UK. It reveals that while the United States initially favored South Korea's involvement during the treaty-making process that began in 1949, the UK consistently opposed it on the grounds that Korea had been a Japanese territory before 1945 and that South Korea was not a fully sovereign state even after liberation. Following the outbreak of the Korean War, the U.S. position evolved, and discussions regarding South Korea's signing of the treaty advanced. However, due to complex reasons including comparisons with Poland's Treaty of Versailles case and the lack of international recognition of the Korean Provisional Government, the United States ultimately accepted the British opposition, leading to South Korea's exclusion as a signatory. This study traces these developments through official documents and meeting records, offering implications for the legal and political nature of the treaty, diplomatic coordination among the Allied powers, and the possibilities for amendment and interpretation of the San Francisco Peace Treaty.

Keywords Allied powers · Diplomacy · Korean War · Modifiability · Recognition · Republic of Korea · San Francisco Peace Treaty · Signatory · Sovereignty · United States

---

T.-J. Yi (✉)
Department of History, Seoul National University, Seoul, Korea (Republic of)
e-mail: tjyi@snu.ac.kr

Y.-H. Kim et al. (eds.), *Beyond the San Francisco System*,
https://doi.org/10.1007/978-981-95-3328-2_4

1 Introduction

After the coerced annexation on August 29, 1910, Koreans carried out various anti-Japanese campaigns in and outside the Korean peninsula, and U.S. President Wilson's proclamation of the doctrine of national self-determination prompted a nationwide demonstration for independence on March 1, 1919, which marked a turning point in the movement for the restoration of national sovereignty. Even as the cry for independence continued within the peninsula, anti-Japanese activists gathered on April 11 in the Shanghai French Concession, set up the National Assembly, and established the Provisional Government of the Republic of Korea (Daehan Minguk), which was named after the Great Korean Empire (Daehan Jeguk) to signify its intent to succeed the Empire.

While conducting research on the Korean Provisional Government (KPG)'s efforts to engage the leaders of the great powers with a view to restoring Korea's national sovereignty, I came to recognize the historic import and relevance of The League of Nations. What caught the interest of me in particular was the codification of international law that was suggested and executed by Professor Manley Otto Hudson of the Harvard Law School from 1927 to 1935, which elevated the status of international law, previously regarded as mere academic theories postulated by individual jurists, to the sphere of public law. This was intended to lay the foundation for a break with the ills of territorial expansionism that the great powers pursued through secret agreements even up until the early twentieth century. The Report on the Law of Treaties, reported by Professor James Garner of the University of Illinois who was acting under the aegis of Professor Hudson, lists among those treaties that were without any legal effect: (1) the 1773 Treaty of Partition that Russia coerced on the members of the Diet of Poland; (2) the 1905 "Protectorate Treaty" that Japan coerced on the Korean emperor and high officials; and (3) the 1915 Treaty that the U.S. coerced on the Haitian national assembly by surrounding it with the U.S. Marines. The 1905 "Protectorate Treaty" was the treaty that, by depriving the Great Korean Empire of its foreign relations power, paved the way for its annexation.

This achievement, made under the initiative of Professor Hudson, was handed over to the International Law Commission of the United Nations newly launched in 1946. Having inherited the 1935 Report on the Law of Treaties from the League of Nations, this Commission conducted supplementary work and submitted a new report to the UN General Assembly in 1963, which adopted it in Resolution 1902 (XVIII) of November 1963. In this report, the Commission added the Munich Agreement (Munich Betrayal) of September 1938, which was pursued by Nazi Germany in order to partition Czechoslovakia, to the above list of the three coercive treaties that were without any legal effect. "The Grotian spirit of international law in the 20th century" was upheld and retained also in the United Nations.

I sincerely feel the need to examine whether the Japanese Peace Treaty signed in San Francisco on September 6, 1951 was in keeping with the spirit of international law as embodied by the League of Nations and the United Nations. However, it is difficult to find the spirit of the League of Nations and the United Nations in the

Peace Treaty with Japan. Neither the preamble to the treaty nor the text of the treaty has little, if any, reference or allusion to the spirit behind the establishment of the United Nations. If the "Report on the Law of Treaty" in 1935 and its successor, i.e., the International Law Commission Report (item 69 of its 15th session) adopted in 1963 by the United Nations General Assembly Resolution 1902 of its 18th session, found Japan's protectorate treaty with Korea *void* ab initio and the consequent Japanese rule of Korea *ipso facto* illegal, it follows that Korea should have been allowed to participate as a signatory and ratifying state to the Japanese peace treaty in order to remedy such an illegality. Eventually, however, Korea was excluded on the grounds that it was a part of Japanese territory during 1910–45 and that it was not a belligerent state in the war against Japan.

Recognizing these problems, I have a critical opinion that the substance of the treaty was dictated by the exigencies under the Cold War system and that as such, it does not contain sufficient merit to be worthy of permanent compliance. At the conclusion of this presentation, I'd like to note that in the early negotiation process, the United States insisted that South Korea must participate in signing and ratifying the treaty, and briefly examine why and how the British and Japanese opposition to South Korean participation eventually led to the exclusion of South Korea from the treaty.

2 The Korean War in 1950 and the Chinese Red Army's Entry into War: Impetus for the San Francisco Peace Treaty

The Pacific War ended on August 15, 1945, when Emperor Hirohito of the Japanese Empire declared Japan's "unconditional surrender." On August 21, the U.S. government proposed the establishment of The Far Eastern Advisory Commission to the Soviet, British, and Chinese governments as an organization for the control of the defeated Japan. With this proposal, the council of representatives from the four countries renamed the Commission the Far Eastern Commission (FEC), giving the U.S. government the function of policy recommendation to implement the various provisions of the Japanese Instrument of Surrender. From July 10, 1947 to December 23, 1948, the FEC did in fact determine the 13 policies on disarmament, democratization, and economic recovery.

Efforts toward devising a peace treaty to restore Japan to the community of peaceful nations made very little headway among the countries concerned until 1949.[1] In September of the same year, U.S. Secretary of State Dean Acheson and

---

[1] From November 1945 to May 1947, 'The Board of Governors for the Research of the Peace Treaty Issues' 平和條約問題研究幹事會 was established within the Japanese government, and preparations for drafting the treaty were made by 'the Working Group on Japan Treaty' in the U.S. State Department from 1947 to 1948. See Jeong Byung-jun 鄭秉峻, *Dokdo 1947* 독도 1947 [Liancourt Rocks 1947] (Seoul: Dolbege, 2010), chapters 3 and 4.

British Foreign Minister Ernest Bevin met in Washington to agree in principle on a peace conference, excluding the Soviet Union. At this point the peace conference was under preparation, but no real progress was forthcoming. On January 12, 1950, the Acheson Line of defense was declared, and on January 15, a group of Japanese intellectuals known as the Discussion Group on the Matters of Peace 平和問題 討論會 issued the Statement on Peace Issues. But actual progress remained elusive. In February, the opposition Republican Party in the U.S. Congress condemned the failure of the Truman administration on its China policy. Then McCarthyism erupted, and President Truman pursued bipartisan diplomacy. In April, the president named Republican George Foster Dulles as a consultant to the Secretary of State and in May, the president officially appointed him special representative of the President to negotiate the Japanese peace treaty.[2] After visiting Tokyo, Dulles traveled to Seoul for 3 days from June 18 to carry out his mission, and on June 25, the North Korean People's Army crossed the 38th parallel into South Korea and initiated a war. Thus, the beginning of negotiations for the Japanese Peace Treaty coincided with the breakout of the Korean War. Thereafter, it took months for Dulles to devise and present his own strategy. After the Chinese intervention in the Korean War in late October, he insisted on the urgency of signing the peace treaty with Japan.

John Moore Allison, a senior officer for Far Eastern Affairs in the U.S. State Department, sent a memorandum of December 2, 1950 titled "Japanese Peace Treaty" to the Consultant to the Secretary of State, John Foster Dulles.[3]

The memorandum states as follows:

1. I have been thinking over our conversation yesterday with particular reference to that portion in which you [Dulles] suggest we should make an immediate study of Far Eastern Commission decisions and the surrender instrument with Japan with a view to ascertaining how far we can go without a Treaty toward giving Japan freedom of action in local and international affairs, I believe the time has come and the situation is so serious that more drastic measures are necessary.
2. In my opinion, attempts by the United States to give Japan a larger degree of freedom than she now possesses within the limits of existing FEC policy decisions would not only be extremely difficult, but would expose us to a charge of insincerity by our allies and would not, in fact, get the results desired.
3. Exhaustive studies have been made as to what can be done within the framework of present FEC directives and they have shown it is comparatively little. Also, General MacArthur has vigorously opposed this conception. I do not believe the Japanese would be satisfied with what we could do in this limited way.

[2] See Fukunaga Fumio 福永文夫, "Sanfuranshisuko kōwa - senryō no shūketsu" サンフランシスコ講和 - 占領の終結 [San Francisco Peace Conference-The End of Occupation], in *Nihon senryōshi, 1945–1952: Tōkyō, Washington, Okinawa* 日本占領史-1945-1952, 東京·ワシントン·沖縄 [A History of the Occupation of Japan, 1945–1952: Tokyo, Washington, Okinawa] (Tōkyō: Chūkō Shinsho, 2014).

[3] J. M. Allison to John Forster Dulles, December 2, 1950, microfilm, USE Micro-copy No. Coo 4 3 (UPA) Roll No. (s) 1, Declassified NND 867209 RG 59 Entry Japanese peace treaty 1947–52 Box 1, (copies to Mr. Rusk, Colonel Babcok, NA-Mr. Johnson), pp. 55 ~ 66.

4. Therefore, serious consideration should now be given to going to our friends on the FEC and pointing out frankly and forcefully that the present situation is so serious and present conditions so utterly different from those contemplated at the time the Far Eastern Commission was set up, that we are no longer in a position to abide by the terms of reference of the Far Eastern Commission or its previous decisions. This would be an honest straightforward position to take, and I believe would be understood by our friends. We would naturally want to assure them that we have no intention of allowing Japan to become a threat in any way to this interest, and that we would take steps to see that such a situation did not develop.

Having noted that after the end of the Pacific War, the United States followed the FEC decisions concerning Japan, Allison went on to argue that a new strategy should be adopted to take into consideration the drastic changes that occurred—presumably upon the outbreak of the Korean War. The memorandum then continues with the following recommendation:

5. I believe we would then be in a position to recommend to them that they acquiesce in our desire to bring Japan into our family of nations as a free and independent member, with which we could make agreements for military assistance on a basis of equality in an attempt to get Japan on our side voluntarily and not by force. In my opinion, we should endeavor to get the Japanese to agree, with respect to their own defense and the defense of the Japan area, to furnish ground forces (the U.S. furnishing ground forces only until Japanese forces could take over) while the United States and such other of our allies as agreed with us and would come in on our terms, would furnish air and naval forces. The fact that Japan would not have air and naval forces would go far, it seems to me, toward reassuring our allies that Japan would not be in a position to threaten their interests, and that the arrangement would be one primarily for defense of Japan and the Japanese area. This agreement should be couched in U.N. Charter terms in so far as possible and considerations might well be given to having Japan become a co-signatory of any possible mutual defense arrangements which might be entered into with New Zealand, Australia, and the Philippines.

Attached to this memorandum was a draft of an agreement between the United States and Japan. To be precise, it was titled the "Agreement between the United States and Japan for Collective Self-defense made pursuant to the Treaty of Peace between Japan and the Allied Powers and the provisions of Article 51 of the Charter of the United Nations." The draft agreement consists of a preamble with 5 points and a text comprising 4 clauses. Also included was the "Jurisdictional Status of United States Forces Abroad." It is logical to assume that this was a preliminary draft of "The Security Treaty Between the United States and Japan" signed between the United States and Japan on the same day as the San Francisco Peace Treaty, which in turn formed the basis for the security treaty.

The North Korean People's Army, which had crossed the 38th parallel southward on June 25, 1950, began to retreat to the north on September 15, following the success of the UN forces' amphibious landing behind North Korean lines at Inchon, executed under the command of General MacArthur. On September 28, the UN forces restored Seoul, crossed the 38th parallel northward, and captured Pyongyang on October 19, and a band of the Korean army arrived at the Yalu River. On October 19, however, the Chinese troops intervened and penetrated into Korean soil through a mountain route between Ganggye and Hamheung in Hamgyeong Province. Allison's memorandum was issued on December 2, 1950, when the UN forces were being driven back south by the Chinese Red Army. As the memorandum states, the situation of the Far East at the time could no longer be bound by the FEC's policies and decisions, which were based on a sanction regime against the defeated Japan. Under the circumstances where the four main members of the Committee (the United States, Britain, the Soviet Union, and China) split in half and waged war against each other, the FEC policies could not be maintained any further. U.S. State Department Far Eastern Affairs officer Allison's proposal focused on military preparedness to protect Japan's mainland. The Chinese intervention in the Korean War made the possibility of a Soviet invasion of Japanese territory through Sakhalin appear more realistic, giving urgency to timely preparation against such a possibility. This was why the San Francisco Peace Treaty was accompanied by the U.S.-Japan Security Treaty. The U.S. government was deeply concerned that China and the Soviet Union might attack both Japan and South Korea in an all-out war against the free world.

On January 4, 1951, the ROK forces failed to repel the southward thrust of the Chinese Red Army and decided to withdraw from Seoul. The same day (January 4), consultant John Foster Dulles sent a letter to Secretary of State Dean Gooderham Acheson about the situation of the Far East.[4] Having said that he had a discussion the day before with Rusk, Allison, and the Joint Chiefs of Staff regarding how to proceed to a Japanese peace settlement, Dulles presented his opinions in detail as follows:

First, although the joint memorandum of the Secretary of State and the Secretary of Defense, dated September 7, 1950, which was approved by the President and issued as the Presidential directive of September seventh, stipulated that there should be no definitive Japanese peace settlement "until after favorable resolution of the present United States military situation in Korea," the Chinese Communist intervention in Korea has made it seem unlikely that there would be any such "favorable resolution." And, in consequence, active negotiations have necessarily been in suspense for about 6 weeks pending modification of the Presidential directive of September 7th. This delay has worked against the long-range interests of the United States in relation to Japan in the sense that:

1. The Japanese people and their leaders are coming increasingly to feel the danger of throwing in their lot with us in view of the fact that Communist power seemed

[4] John Foster Dulles to Dean Gooderham Acheson, January 4, 1951, microfilm, USE Microcopy No. Coo 43 (UPA) Roll No. (s) 1, Declassified NND 867209 RG 59 Entry Japanese peace treaty 1947–52 Box 1 (copies to Mr. Rusk, Colonel Babcok, NA-Mr. Johnson), pp. 13–16. The "top secret" mark on the top of this document has been crossed out.

to be closing in upon them, and also upon their normal sources of food supply from French Indochina, Siam, and Burma. It would be difficult to assuage such increasing doubt on the part of the Japanese leaders as to the wisdom of any definitive commitment to our cause at the present time unless perhaps under conditions as to military and economic security which it would not be easy for us to fulfill.

2. The United Kingdom is seeking to gain the initiative and is itself drafting a Japanese peace treaty. This apparently is being now considered in London by the Commonwealth Prime Ministers, who are also reported to be considering a Pacific Pact. The British policy in relation to the Far East is different in many essential respects from ours, and the British Commonwealth proposals probably will not adequately take account of our vital interests in this area.[5] In sum, the delay in our delaying the Japanese peace settlement has not worked to our advantage.

Dulles then related two principal reasons why the Joint Chiefs of Staff desired further delay as follows:

1. To preserve our existing authority in Japan until after the Korean affair is liquidated.
2. To reinforce Japan with additional United States land forces lest the Soviet might move its own armed forces into Japan either as an "occupying" power under the Surrender Terms or on the theory that the Sino-Soviet Treaty of February 1950 requires this because of the remilitarization of Japan.

To this, Dulles stated that neither of these reasons was valid in his opinion: "In my opinion, further delay will substantially increase the risk that it will be impossible to obtain an unreserved Japanese commital, in fact as well as form, to our cause on conditions which we would regard as acceptable." This letter was sent also to the secretarial office of Defense Secretary George C. Marshall.

According to the letter of Dulles, the U.S. officials were very concerned about the Soviets' possible entry into Japanese territory following Chinese intervention in the Korean War. Clearly, heightened concern about a possible Soviet invasion of Japan was a decisive factor in hastening the signing of the San Francisco Peace Treaty and the U.S.-Japan Security Treaty in September 1951.

[5] The United Kingdom held Commonwealth Conferences, such as the Canberra Conference in 1947 and the Colombo Conference in January 1950. In the meantime, the British government was in contact with the US State Department, discussing stabilization in Southeast Asia and the rearmament of Japan. The Colombo Conference was marked with differing opinions among Commonwealth members, and a separate Commonwealth Working Committee was formed to delegate consultations. But especially with regard to the issue of rearmament of Japan in a proposed 'Pacific pact,' a series of difficulties in proceedings arose amid strong opposition from India, Australia, and New Zealand. See Kibata Yōichi 木畑洋一, "Tainichi kōwa to ikirisu no ashia sēsaku" 對日講和とイキリスのアシア政策 [Japanese Peace Treaty and Britain's Asia Policy], in *Sanfuranshisuko kōwa* サンフランシスコ講和 [San Francisco Peace Treaty], ed. Watanabe Akio and Miyazato Sēgen (Tōkyō: Tōkyō Daigaku Shuppan-kai, 1986).

3 The Differing Positions of the United States and the UK on Korean Participation

3.1 A Review of Their Changing Positions.

After the memorandum of Dulles dated January 4, 1951, the U.S. government consulted with the British government for the early conclusion of a Japanese peace treaty and an accompanying U.S.-Japan security treaty. The two countries disagreed over the issue of South Korea's participation in signing and ratifying the peace treaty. Table 1 summarizes the changing opinions of the U.S. and British governments—since the Japanese Empire's declaration of unconditional surrender on August 15, 1945—on whether a South Korean representative should be invited to participate in the signing of a peace treaty between the Allied Powers and Japan. The table also includes the South Korean government's expressions of its will to participate.[6]

The United States, as the representative of the Allied Powers, launched in October 1945 a task force in the State Department to conclude a peace treaty, but the treaty development process moved at a glacial pace for more than 2 years. This was also the case with the FEC, which was launched in July 1947 as the body responsible for the decisions of the Allied States on their rule over Japan. On August 29, 1947, the interim Legislative Assembly of South Korea conveyed to the U.S. State Department its desire to participate in the anticipated peace conference with Japan.[7] But in the words of U.S. Secretary of State Dean Acheson, "The United States and British Governments, as well as others, attempted in 1947 to bring about a peace conference and failed."[8] For the better part of the year 1948, much attention was concentrated in the International Military Tribunal for the Far East (May 3, 1946–November 12, 1948).

The draft peace treaty with Japan that the United States disclosed in December 1949 included South Korea as a signatory. To this, the UK expressed its opposition for the first time in the same month.[9] As described below, the UK did not agree with

[6] Except for the asterisked sections, Table 1 is based on Kang Seong Mo, "Great Britain's Postwar Insecurity and the Question of South Korean Participation in the Japanese Peace Treaty," *Seoul Journal of Korean Studies* vol. 28–2, (2015): 153–179.

[7] "The Political Adviser in Korea (Jacobs) to the Secretary of State, Seoul, 29 August 1947," Foreign Relations of the United States (FRUS), 1947, Vol. VI (Washington DC: Government Printing Office, 1972), 511.

[8] "The Secretary of State to Certain Diplomatic Offices, Washington, 27 December 1949," Foreign Relations of the United States (FRUS), 1949, The Far East and Australasia, Vol. VII, Part 2, 931.

[9] In response to the U.S. move to allow Korean participation in the treaty, the British side prepared in January 1950 a series of documents on the issue, one of which stated, "There is no doubt that Korea was a territory of Japan, and there is room for doubt as to whether or not it is a complete and single nation even today." This was reportedly the opinion of Gerald C. Fitzmaurice, second Legal Counsel. See Kim Minsoo 金民樹, "Tainichi kōwa jōyaku to Kankoku sanka mondai" 対日講和条約と韓国参加問題 [The Debate over Korean Participation in the Japanese Peace Treaty],

Table 1 Shifting stances of the United States and the United Kingdom over South Korean participation in the Japanese Peace Treaty

Dates	United States	United Kingdom	Notes
Oct. 1945			A working group for the treaty was established in the U.S. State Department
August 29, 1947			The interim legislative assembly of South Korea conveyed to the U.S. State Department its desire to participate in the anticipated peace conference with Japan
Dec. 1949	Permitted south Korean participation		A U.S. draft treaty included South Korea as a signatory state.
Jan. 1950		opposed south Korean participation	The grounds for the British opposition: (1) Korea was a territory of Japan before 1945; (2) it remained doubtful whether South Korea was a complete, single sovereign state even after liberation
Jun. 18–20	Well-disposed to south Korean participation		This was expressed during John Foster Dulles' visit to South Korea
Jun. 25	North Korean army crossed the 38th parallel. The Korean war broke out		
Jul.	Favorable appraisal for south Korean participation		The U.S. State Department noted added stature to be gained by the south Korean government from signing the treaty
Oct. 29, 1950	The Chinese red Army entered the Korean war		
Jan. 1951 Jan.-May 1951	The Chinese red Army crossed the 38th parallel and occupied Seoul		
Jan. 26	Permitted south Korean participation		Dulles confirmed to south Korean ambassador to the U.S. Chang Myon the U.S. intention for a continued support for south Korean participation in the peace treaty and for efforts to dissuade Britain and Japan from opposing south Korean participation
Mar. 11		Opposed south Korean participation	Britain drafted a note stating its concern for the Soviet Union to manipulate the situation of two Koreas
Mar. 14	Seoul was recaptured by the allied forces		
Mar. 21	Permitted south Korean participation	Opposed south Korean participation	U.S. delegate John M. Allison expressed his wish to distribute the draft peace treaty to South Korea. British delegate Robert H. Scott conveyed British opposition on the grounds of Korea's different legal status

Table 1 (continued)

Dates	United States	United Kingdom	Notes
Mar. 23	Permitted south Korean participation		The U.S. government delivered the draft treaty to South Korea
Apr. 16		Entertained reserved acceptance of south Korean participation	British foreign minister Herbert Morrison's memo: "If the US government attach importance to south Korean participation, we need not insist on our view."
Apr. 23	Permitted south Korean participation		In a meeting between Yoshida Shigeru and Dulles, Dulles indicated that the United States wished to build up the prestige of the south Korean government but that Japan's concerns over the Koreans in Japan (with many communists among them) and the issue of compensation rights for them should be addressed
May 01–04	Permitted south Korean participation	Opposed south Korean participation	U.S. delegate Allison: Given an aggression against South Korea (i.e., the Korean war), there would be political advantages to allowing South Korea to sign British delegate F.S. Tomlinson: Korea had not been a belligerent, and most of the terms of the Japanese peace treaty did not apply to Korea
			South Korea advised the United States that Korea should be a signatory, following the case of Poland signing the treaty of Versailles in 1919
May 09	Opposed south Korean participation		The U.S. State Department found South Korea's argument unconvincing on the grounds that the KPG lacked the recognition the polish provisional government had received from the principal western powers, thus rendering Koreans' fight against Japan in China of "no bearing."
May 16	Opposed south Korean participation		The U.S. government noted that it was "inclined to accept the UK" position
Jun. 01	Opposed south Korean participation		In the draft dated June 1, the United States officially agreed with the British position on the grounds that the KPG was not recognized by the Western allied Powers including the United States during world war II. Korea was excluded from the list of signatory states, but article 10 states, "the Republic of Korea shall be deemed an 'allied Power' for the purposes of articles 5, 10 (to be 11) and 13 (to be 14) of the present treaty, effective at the time that the treaty first comes into force."*

(continued)

Table 1 (continued)

Dates	United States	United Kingdom	Notes
Jun. 14	Opposed south Korean participation	Opposed south Korean participation	In the joint Anglo-American draft dated June 14, Korean exclusion from the list of signatory states was maintained, and article 10 of the U.S. draft dated June 1, "the Republic of Korea shall be deemed an 'allied power,' was excised therefrom*
Jul. 09	Opposed south Korean participation	Opposed south Korean participation	The decision to exclude South Korea was conveyed to the South Korean government. Dulles stated that only the signatory states of the United Nations Declaration of January 1942 would sign the treaty

Source: Kang Seong Mo, "Great Britain's Postwar Insecurity and the Question of South Korean Participation in the Japanese Peace Treaty," *Seoul Journal of Korean Studies* 28–2, (2015): 153–179

the United States on Korean participation due to its intention to establish diplomatic ties with the new communist People's Republic of China declared after the Chinese mainland fell to the communists in 1949. The rationale for the British opposition was that Korea was part of Japan's territory before 1945 and that it is difficult to view it as a complete, single state, presumably referring to the situation of the two divided Koreas. Nevertheless, the U.S. intention to allow South Korean participation was maintained during Dulles's visit to Korea on June 18–20, 1950.

On June 25, 1950, the North Korean People's Army crossed the 38th parallel into the South and started a war. It was 5 days after Dulles visited Seoul. Despite, or perhaps because of, the extremely unfavorable war situation at the time, the U.S. State Department expressed its willingness to review South Korea's participation favorably again in July. As mentioned earlier, on January 4, 1951, the day the Chinese troops recaptured Seoul, Dulles sent a letter to State Secretary Acheson, advising that a peace treaty with Japan be swiftly concluded to orient Japan to the path of a peace-loving nation and that a security arrangement be urgently made in in Japan at the same time, with a view to guaranteeing Japan a measure of confidence in its relationship with the United States against a possible Soviet-communist aggression.[10] In the face of Chinese intervention in the Korean War, the U.S. government took seriously the possibility of Soviet troops entering Japan through Hokkaido and hastened to set up a policy aimed at the dual goals of making Japan a liberal democracy and assuring Japan of sufficient security arrangements with the cooperation of the U.S. military. It is well known that this U.S. policy was embodied in the San Francisco Peace Treaty and the U.S.-Japan Security Treaty that were signed in

Kokusai seiji 國際政治 131 (2002): 139. The appearance of these British documents coincided with the U.K.'s official recognition of the People's Republic of China on 6 January 1950, which, according Wolf (1983), was driven principally by the U.K.'s desire to "secure conditions favorable to British trade." See Wolf, David C. "'To Secure a Convenience': Britain Recognizes China—1950,' Journal of Contemporary History 18, no. 2 (1983): 299–326.

[10] See Footnote 5.

San Francisco in September of the same year. But it is worth noting that the impetus came from the Korean War, and especially from the Chinese intervention in that war.

Since January 1951, Dulles repeatedly expressed his intention to allow South Korean participation, citing two reasons. The first was that the Provisional Government of the Republic of Korea participated in the anti-Japanese war with China's Kuomintang government. The second was the need to raise the political stature of Korea, which was then fighting the communist forces.[11] This argument in favor of South Korean participation was expressed five times after the Chinese intervention in January 1951, as shown in Table 1, until May 4. On the other hand, Britain opposed South Korean participation four times during the same period.[12] On one occasion in April 16, British Foreign Minister Herbert Morrison stated in a Cabinet memorandum that "… if the U.S. Government attach importance to this, we need not insist upon our view."[13] But this opinion was quickly overruled, and Britain continued in its opposition.[14] The United States, which was consistently in favor of South Korean participation, leaned toward accepting the British opinion after May 9, and Korea was eventually unable to attend the San Francisco Peace Conference held in September.

3.2 Reasons for the British Opposition: Maintaining Ties with the Chinese

Britain opposed South Korean participation ostensibly because it would provoke the People's Republic of China (China) and the Soviet Union. In actuality, the priorities seem to have lain in protecting the British commercial and political stakes in China and Southeast Asia that had been maintained since the era of imperialism. In particular, the economic importance of China and Hong Kong took priority.[15] In protecting these interests, the UK was faced with two major challenges: to establish

[11] The United Nations recognized the Republic of Korea in 1948. The United States played a central role in this by successfully overcoming the opposition of the Soviet Union. At the time, it was none other than Dulles who was the representative of the United States. The United States was aware of the Cairo Declaration (November 27, 1943), which noted the "slave status" of Koreans under Japanese rule, and the fact that the Korean Provisional Government had declared war against Japan on December 10, 1941. See Kim Minsoo (2002), 138.

[12] A study suggests that after the U.S. draft was released in March 1951, the United Kingdom objected once more on April 11 to Article 18 regarding South Korea's participation as a signatory state. See Tsukamoto Takashi 塚本孝, "Kankoku no tainichi hēwa jōyaku shomē mondai - Nitchō kōshō, sengo hoshō mondai ni kanren shite" 韓國の對日平和條約署名問題 - 日朝交涉, 戰後補償問題に關聯して [The Issue of Korea's signing of the Peace Treaty with Japan: Japan-North Korea Negotiations, On Post-war Compensation], *References* レファレェンス 3 (1992).

[13] Kang (2015), p. 160.

[14] Kang (2015), p. 160.

[15] For the economic concerns of the UK in Southeast and East Asia, see Kibata Yōichi (1986).

amicable relations with China's new communist regime and to drive a wedge between China and the Soviet Union in order to prevent communist solidarity.[16]

At the end of World War II, the UK was facing a total economic ruin. Unlike that of the United States, the British economy was based on the economic structure of a colonial network. Economic relations with China, Hong Kong, and Malaya had significant implications for the world, especially the United Kingdom. China was a country with immense raw materials and trade potential. In 1949, British merchants and companies had substantial business interests in China for commercial trading. Hong Kong was one of the world's most important, thriving ports and markets. Shipbuilding and ship repairing there were of great import.[17] It was politically and psychologically significant also as a base for anti-communism. Malaya was also of great importance to the Western economy as an area with such important resources as rubber, tin, and foods. The UK attempted to overcome its economic crisis by regaining the influence it had established in these areas before the war. At the same time, the UK tried to prevent the Chinese from aligning too closely with the Soviet Union. The combined forces of the Soviet Union's formidable military strength and China's massive land forces would pose a major threat to the West. Communist rule of China was indeed "repugnant," but maintaining ties with China was unavoidable as a geopolitical exigency.

Dulles, who was negotiating the peace treaty with multilateral parties including the UK, decided to forgo the U.S. insistence on South Korean participation—presumably on the premise that British ties with China would help negate the Soviet predominance in the Far East. A Soviet invasion of Japan through Hokkaido was one of the most worrisome possibilities the United States contemplated, and apparently it was concluded that concurring with British policy would help prevent this. The United States thereupon officially changed its position from that espousing South Korean participation in the treaty as a signatory on the grounds of political advantages to that concurring with the British opposition to South Korean participation. In order to counter the British opposition, the South Korean government argued that South Korea should be a signatory just as Poland was in the 1919 Treaty of

[16] The following description on the reasons for British opposition to Korean participation is based on Kang (2015).

[17] At the end of January 1951, there was a discussion between Dulles and the British Embassy in Tokyo about the size of shipbuilding facilities in Japan. In other words, the United States inquired about the size of the shipbuilding facilities identified thus far in order to hand over to Japan the shipbuilding facilities managed by the UK until then. According to a telegram (cryptograph) sent to the British Foreign Service Officer in Tokyo (C.P. Scott) to Sir A. Gascoigne of the British Foreign Office in London, the person responsible for the shipbuilding said that his shipbuilding adviser reported 700,000 tons of annual shipbuilding capacity. But it was reported that he believed it should be lowered to 400,000 tons. This was a preliminary arrangement by the UK to prevent Japan's shipbuilding industry from outperforming Hong Kong's after Japan's restoration to the status of a free, sovereign state by limiting Japan's capacity to not more than 400,000 tons per annum. Public Record Office, F.O. 371 closed until 1982, 92,530. 1951, Far Eastern Department, Japan J 1022/36, From Tokyo to Foreign Office 38, Sir A. Gascoigne No. 111, 30th January 1951. The United Kingdom was also wary of the resurgence of Japan's textile industry.

Versailles. On July 9, however, "Ambassador Dulles pointed out to the Korean Ambassador that the ROK Government would not be a signatory to the treaty, since only those nations in a state of war with Japan and which were signatories of the United Nations Declaration of January 1942 the United Nations Declaration of January 1942 would sign the treaty."[18]

This reasoning was explained in more detail in the "Japanese Peace Treaty: Working Draft and Commentary Prepared in the Department of State" dated June 1, 1951, which states, "Article 10 The Republic of Korea shall be deemed an 'Allied Power' for the purposes of Articles 5, 10 (to be 11) and 13 (to be 14) of the present Treaty, effective at the time that the Treaty first comes into force. The reason for this proposal is that the United States now considers, in agreement with the British position, that Korea is not entitled to be a signatory to the treaty. The U.S. and other major powers deliberately refrained from recognizing the "Provisional Government of Korea" as having any status whatsoever during World War II. The facts that that government declared war on Japan, and that Korean elements, mostly longtime resident in China, fought with the Chinese forces, do not, therefore, have any bearing on the question. The Korean Government has cited the fact that Poland was permitted to sign the Versailles Treaty. On examination, however, Korea's case for participation in the Japanese treaty does not gain much support from this example. The Polish National Committee set up in Paris in 1917 under Paderewski was "recognized" and dealt with by all the principal western Allies."[19]

4 Problems of Justification for Opposing Korean Participation: Inverse of the Spirit of International Law Under the UN

When the United States notified the South Korean government of its final decision to exclude South Korea from the Japanese peace treaty, fierce battles were being raged along the 38th parallel. On March 14, 1951, when the UN forces pushed out the Chinese and restored Seoul, Commander MacArthur ordered the crossing of the 38th parallel to the north, and on June 25, the Soviet delegation to the UN proposed an armistice talk. But South Korean President Syngman Rhee refused and argued for "a unification of Korea." On April 10, U.S. President Truman dismissed Commander MacArthur, who had preferred a more aggressive strategy against the Chinese intervention, and on June 29, ordered Commander Matthew Bunker Ridgway, who had succeeded MacArthur, to commence ceasefire negotiations. Amid the intense fighting between the UN forces and the communist forces that continued throughout the ceasefire negotiations, South Korea's hope to participate

[18] "Memorandum of Conversation, by the Officer in Charge of Korean Affairs in the Office of Northeast Affairs (Emmons), 9 July 1951," FRUS, 1951, Asia and the Pacific, Vol. VI, Part 1, 1183.

[19] "Japanese Peace Treaty: Working Draft and Commentary Prepared in the Department of State, 1 June 1951," FRUS, 1951, Asia and the Pacific, Vol. VI, Part 1, 1068–1069.

in the peace treaty with Japan was forsaken largely due to the British opposition, which in turn was driven by its policy not to antagonize Communist China.

Is Korea's exclusion justified? Is there a convincing argument for such a decision? To examine this, we need to compare the differing positions of the United States and the UK.

On November 23, 1949, the U.S. Acting Secretary of State sent a telegram to the U.S. Embassy in Korea inquiring the U.S. Ambassador's "views as to whether and to what extent provision [should] be made for Korean participation in [Japanese] treaty."[20] On December 3, 1949, U.S. Ambassador in Korea John J. Muccio suggested to the US State Secretary, "We are strongly of view ROK should be included in some capacity among nations participating in Japanese peace treaty. ... Accordingly, we do not anticipate Korean participation in negotiation of peace settlement would be serious source of embarrassment to other negotiating powers. Before extending any invitation to ROK to participate we could, if desired, privately inform ROK invitation contingent upon not presenting further reparations claim. In this connection we feel Korean eagerness to be signatory is such that ROK would agree to foregoing terms."[21] This appears to have been the first instance of a U.S. official speaking in favor of Korean participation. The U.S. government maintained this view when Dulles negotiated with Britain between January 1951 and the first half of April.[22] More specifically, it was mentioned that the Korean Provisional Government participated in the anti-Japanese war with China's Chiang Kai-shek Nationalist government.[23] This is a view that officially acknowledges the anti-Japanese struggle of the KPG, which was established in Shanghai in April 1919.

On the other hand, when the U.S. State Department prepared a U.S. draft treaty reflecting the recommendation from the U.S. Ambassador Muccio in Korea and presented it to the British government in December 1949, the British government opposed Korean participation in January 1950 on the following two grounds: (1) before 1945, Korea was a part of Japanese territory and (2) it was difficult to view it

[20] "The Acting Secretary of State to the Embassy in Korea, 23 November 1949," FRUS, 1949, The Far East and Australasia, Vol. VII, Part 2, 904.

[21] "The Ambassador in Korea (Muccio) to the Secretary of State, 3 December 1949," FRUS, 1949, The Far East and Australasia, Vol. VII, Part 2.

[22] "Ambassador Dulles said that it has always been the U.S. position that Korea should participate, and that he has held as full discussion with the Korean Government regarding the treaty as with most FEC countries. He explained that with the initial discussions with our Allies completed, he had come to Japan to obtain the views of the Japanese Government on the United States seven-point statement of principles, following which he planned to talk again with representatives of the FEC nations, Indonesia, Korea and Ceylon. He said that the procedure of bilateral discussions had been adopted largely in order to deprive certain nations of opportunity to maintain that the North Korean and Chinese Communist regimes, rather than the Republic of Korea and the Chinese National Government, should represent Korea and China in the negotiations, and that the United States would continue to support the right of the ROK to participate in the Japanese peace settlement." "Memorandum of Conversation, by Mr. Robert A. Fearey of the Office of Northeast Asian Affairs, 26 January 1951," FRUS, 1951, Asia and the Pacific, Vol. VI, Part 1 (Washington DC: Government Printing Office, 1977), 817.

[23] Kim Minsoo (2002).

as a complete, single state even after liberation. On April 23, 1951, Japanese Prime Minister Yoshida Shigeru offered a similar opinion in the "Korea and Peace Treaty "presented to Dulles who visited Tokyo at the time. Yoshida Shigeru added that if South Korea were to become a signatory, property rights and reparations for nearly one million Koreans residing in Japan would be a problem. He also mentioned that most of those Koreans were communists.[24]

The U.S. view emphasized the fact that Korea's Chongqing Provisional Government established the Korean Liberation Army and participated in the anti-Japanese front with the support and cooperation of the Chiang Kai-shek' KMT government forces. It was remembered that the Liberation Army established operations with U.S. or British troops in western China. The British would also have remembered this but turned away for other reasons. As noted above, finding it critical to maintain post-war economic relations with China, the British disregarded the facts. They were concerned that Korean participation would provoke China and the Soviet Union, which might cause friction with these two countries.

It is true that the Korean Provisional Government did not receive official recognition from the League of Nations before August 1945. However, the situation in East Asia caused by Japan's Mukden (Manchurian) Incident in 1931 deprived the League of Nations of any opportunity to do so. At the time of the Incident, the League of Nations had just secured a legal basis for dealing with international disputes and sent the Lytton Commission to the area in dispute to investigate the incident. In 1932, the Commission found Japan's action as aggression violating international law and "recommended" a restoration to the state prior to the Incident. But the Japanese Empire rejected the Commission's findings and withdrew from the League of Nations. Japan thereupon moved itself into the path of militarism and soon launched the Second Sino-Japanese War and then the Pacific War. Under these circumstances, it was hardly feasible for the Korean Provisional Government to be formally recognized by the League of Nations, which barely started reviewing wrongful deeds of aggressor states such as the Japanese Empire. In fact, however, a remarkable achievement was made when the 1935 Report on the Law of Treaties identified the 1905 "Protection Treaty" as a treaty without any legal effect due to its patently coercive nature. It would be fair to say that if such a major work of the League of Nations concluded that the treaty by which the Japanese Empire, for all practical purposes, turned Korea into its "colony" was indeed without any legal effect from its inception (void ab initio), then it follows that the League of Nations found the consequent Japanese occupation of Korea ipso facto illegal. Such a conclusion was tantamount to a tacit acknowledgement of the Korean Provisional Government that was fighting against Japan's "illegal" occupation of Korea. Around that time, Germany and Italy, which followed the path of fascism after Japan, withdrew from the League of Nations one after another, and the world reentered the phase of an impending world war. In this historical context, the significance of the

[24] Kang (2015), p. 160.

1935 Report on the Law of Treaties cannot be ignored.[25] This is especially the case if the report was inherited, as it was, by the newly formed United Nations that assumed the mantle of the League of Nations after World War II.

The League of Nations was credited with promoting international law to the status of public law, but its weakness was that it had no sanctions regime against aggressor states. To remedy this defect, the formation process of the United Nations began in 1942, and the new organization officially commenced in December 1946. The following year the League of Nations voluntarily dissolved. The League's codification of international law had been led by Manly Hudson, and Hudson once again became the driving force behind the formation of the International Law Committee under the UN, which accepted the results of the League's codification project in toto, as mentioned above. In 1963, the UN International Law Committee supplemented the Report on Treaty Law of the League of Nations and submitted this supplemented report to the UN General Assembly, which adopted it in Resolution 1902. In this new report, Nazi Germany's coercive treaty for the partition of Czechoslovakia was added to the list of the above-mentioned three treaties that the 1935 Report viewed as without legal effect ab initio on the grounds that they were extracted under duress.

The United States is the nation that led the creation of the League of Nations and the United Nations. Professor Manly Hudson, who spearheaded the codification of international law as carried out under the auspices of the League of Nations, described this work as "the realization of the Grotian spirit in the 20th century." Premised on the requirement of full disclosure of all treaties to be signed, this codification effort was pursued in order to bring an end to the unlawful and illicit practice of using secret agreements between great powers, which was spurred on by fierce colonial competition prevalent at the turn of the century. International law that had existed until then as

[25] The Report on the Law of Treaties, a result of the League of Nations' codification of international law, based its findings about the 1905 Protectorate Treaty on Francis Rey's study on the Treaty titled "La situation internationale de la Corée", *Revue Générale de Droit International Public*, Tome XIII (Paris: 1906). Francis Rey was a member of the delegation of France at the 1919 Paris Peace Conference and later served as the Secretary General of the International Committee of the Donau River. Yi Tae-jin 李泰鎭, Kkeutnaji anheun yeoksa - sikminjibae cheongsan-eul wihan yeoksainsik 끝나지 않은 歷史-植民支配 淸算을 爲한 歷史認識 [Unfinished History: Historical Perspective on Settling Issues with Colonial Rule], (Seoul: Taehaksa, 2017), 257–58. James Garner, a reporter of the Report on the Law of Treaties, was a professor at the University of Illinois in the United States, but he was fluent in French and spent much of his time conducting academic activities in France. Thus, it is highly likely that James Garner was in contact with Francis Rey. When a delegation from the Korean Provisional Government submitted its appeal to the 1919 Paris Peace Conference, the Secretary-General sent a reply at the end of the Conference stating that this was a matter that should be addressed by the League of Nations soon to be established. If so, the determination of the 1905 Protectorate Treaty as void ab initio in the Report on the Law of Treaties can be construed as the League's public reply to the KPG's appeal. Yi (2017). Yi Tae-Jin, "San Francisco Peace Treaty with Japan and the Problems with the 'Colony' Korea: Criticizing the Unjust Condoning of the Japanese Colonization of Korea Despite the Judgements of Illegality of the 1905 'Protectorate Treaty' by the League of Nations and the United Nations," Proceedings of the international conference, "Beyond the San Francisco System: Seeking a Peace Regime in East Asia," October 28, 2016.

mere academic theories became recognized as belonging to the sphere of public law. "Grotian spirit" thus represented was concerned with the pursuit of international justice, rather than the maximization of the interests of great powers. From this perspective, it was perfectly reasonable for the U.S. government to argue that Korea should participate as a signatory state in the San Francisco Peace Treaty. And it was a grave error to change its position and eventually accept Britain's argument against Korean participation, due to concerns arising from a possible Soviet aggression against Japan following the Chinese intervention in the Korean War. One cannot but wonder if the influence Britain and Japan exerted to bring about this change was not a throwback to the imperialistic era, where imperial self-interest was placed above all else. Regarding the British involvement in the U.S.-led peace settlement with Japan, there is a noteworthy comment as follows: "The British government, still regarding itself as a great imperial power in East Asia and the Pacific, endeavored to intervene in the U.S.-led peace treaty from the position equal to that of the U.S. as much as possible."[26]

5 Conclusion: Modifiability of the San Francisco Peace Treaty

The Japanese Empire initiated four major wars during the span of 60 years from the end of the nineteenth century to the first half of the twentieth century: the First Sino-Japanese War in 1894, the Russo-Japanese War in 1904, the Second Sino-Japanese War in 1937, and the Pacific War in 1941. Japan has attempted to explain away all these wars as unavoidably caused by unexpected upheavals in international affairs. However, initial plans were laid well before the actual launching of these wars of aggression, which were in fact executed methodically by the Chōshū clique, after they overthrew the shogunate and established the Meiji government in accordance with the teachings of their deceased master Yoshida Shōin, who was executed in 1859 for his failed attempt to overthrow the shogunate. A master plan of foreign expansion propagated by Yoshida Shōin, as delineated in his 1854 book titled *Record From Prison* (Yūshūroku幽囚録), eerily matches the actual progression of wars the Chōshū clique treaded ever since the Meiji Reform. Suddenly faced with encroaching steamships, Yoshida Shōin writes, Japan, an island country, is made vulnerable and must act quickly before it falls victim to Western conquest. His solution: Absorb advanced technologies of Western powers fast and then conquer neighboring countries first before the Western powers do. He even mapped out the sequence of such military conquests: Hokkaido, Kamchatka, Ryukyu islands, Taiwan, Korea, Manchuria, Mongolia, and China. His next goal was continued expansion into Australia and California to make the Pacific the sea of Japan.[27] In

[26] Kibata Yōichi (1986), p. 185.

[27] See Yi (2017), 145, and Yi Tae-Jin 李泰鎭, "Yoshida shōin to Tokutomi Sohō - kindainihon ni yoru Kankoku shinryaku no shisō-teki kitei" 吉田松陰と德富蘇峰-近代日本による韓國侵略

hindsight, it would be more apt to describe these wars, all of which were faithfully carried out one after another as per Yoshida's master plan, as "premeditated warfare."

If the San Francisco Peace Treaty could be called a treaty for a true peace, Japan should have been held accountable for all these wars. While the Japan Peace Treaty of 1951 is said to have been concerned only with the Second Sino-Japanese War and the Pacific War, even that is not quite right because one party to the former, China, was absent. Korea arguably suffered the greatest damage from these four wars, but it was not even invited to the peace conference because it was "annexed" to Japan in 1910 and became a part of its territory. The Russo-Japanese War of 1904 was a war that Japan launched to make Korea a protectorate. On the basis of the Japan's victory over Russia, a "protection treaty" was coerced upon Korea, and based on this treaty, the coercive annexation of Korea was carried out in 1910. Koreans' active pursuit of the recovery of their national sovereignty attracted great attention at the Second Hague Peace Conference in 1907 and the Paris Peace Conference in 1919. There also exists the historic 1935 Report on the Law of Treaties, in which the 1905 Protectorate Treaty was designated as one of the three treaties that were void from their inception. Nevertheless, those responsible for the San Francisco Peace Conference ignored all this and resorted to the coerced annexation and the consequent occupation of Korea, i.e., the argument "that Korea was a part of Japanese territory," as the grounds for the exclusion of Korea from the peace treaty. A peace conference that should have penalized acts of aggression ended up justifying acts of aggression. The drafters of the San Francisco Peace Treaty, unaware of the reasons why the Second Sino-Japanese War and the Pacific War occurred, ended up giving preferential treatment to the aggressor.

The San Francisco Peace Treaty was a treaty devised to save Japan from Soviet-communist threat within the context of the Cold War system, rather than a treaty intended to bring its war crimes to justice. At the opening of the conference, President Truman of the United States, who hosted the Peace Conference, stressed, "The treaty recognizes the principle that Japan should make reparations to the countries which suffered from its aggression. But it does not saddle the Japanese people with a hopeless burden of reparations which would crush their economy in the years to come." The San Francisco Peace Treaty aimed to make Japan a sovereign state capable of entering into treaties needed for defense against the threat of communist aggression then looming large in Northeast Asia. In other words, it was a prerequisite step toward the conclusion of the U.S.-Japan Security Treaty that immediately followed it. Even if this strategic judgment of the United States and the UK was unavoidable in the face of the formidable communist menace in Northeast Asia, "the principle that Japan should make reparations to the countries which suffered from its aggression" should have been honored properly. Was Korea not the country that suffered the most by the aggression of the Japanese Empire? Was South Korea

---

の思想的基底 [Yoshida Shoin and Tokutomi Soho—Modern Japan's Ideological Base in the Colonization of Korea], Tsuru Bunka Daigaku Kenkyū Kiyō 都留文科大學研究紀要 80 (2007): 175–202.

not the country battling against the Communists at the forefront? If all these problems remain unrectified, this treaty will live in infamy in the history of treaties.

The San Francisco Peace Treaty, as a multilateral treaty, also had many problems in form. Unlike Korea, which was not invited on the grounds that it was part of its territory as a Japanese colony, Pakistan, India, Ceylon, Indonesia, Vietnam, Laos, Cambodia, and others became treaty signatories on the grounds that those countries were former colonies of the Allied Powers (UK, the Netherlands, and France). It was "a far cry from fair or rational decision making."[28] It was an unfair dealing brought about through the influence of the UK, which once possessed the largest number of colonies in history. It is also important to remember that the Italy voiced dissatisfaction with the preferential treatment Japan received in the San Francisco Peace Treaty, terms of which was far more lenient than those of the Treaty of Peace with Italy signed on February 10, 1947. This led to a public outcry in Italy for demanding a revision of the Treaty of Peace with Italy.[29]

The extent of Britain's involvement in the San Francisco Peace Treaty was excessive considering Britain's actual contribution to the Pacific War. This has already been criticized as a result of "having failed to break with its self-identification as a great imperial power in the East Asia-Pacific region", but the error caused by the exercise of the undue influence should be corrected. Above all, if the British argument provided an opportunity for Prime Minister Shigeru Yoshida to activate his imperialistic mentality, that must be considered significant.

In conclusion, the San Francisco Peace Treaty produced a result in which the Cold War logic and the imperial mindset intermingle, and this unreasonableness still acts as one of the major causes of geopolitical instability in Northeast Asia. For the true peace of East Asia, new efforts will have to be made in the name of the United Nations and in the "Grotian spirit of international law in the 21st century" (22 September 2019).

[28] Jeong Byeongjun 鄭秉峻, *Saenpeulansiseuko pyeonghwa joyag-ui hanbando gwanlyeon johang-gwa hangug jeongbu-ui daeeung* 샌프란시스코 平和條約의 韓半島 關聯 條項과 韓國政府의 對應 [Articles on the Korean Peninsula in the San Francisco Peace Treaty and Responses from the Korean Government thereto] (Seoul: Center for Diplomatic History Studies of the Korea National Diplomatic Academy, 2018), 122.

[29] Kim (2002), 137. A study suggests that the handling of territorial issues in the Peace Treaty with Japan was not as sufficiently detailed as that in the Peace Treaty with Italy. See Kang Pyung-Keun 강병근, "Pyeonghwa joyag nae yeongto johang-e gwanhan yeongu—daeil pyeonghwa joyag-gwa dae itaeli pyeonghwa joyag-eul jungsim-euro" 平和條約 內 領土條項에 關한 研究 - 對日平和條約과 對이태리 平和條約을 中心으로- [A Comparative Study on the Provisions on Territories in the Peace Treaty with Italy in 1947 and the Peace Treaty with Japan in 1951], Gukje Beophakhoe Nonchong 國際法學會論叢 63(4) (2018): 217–245.

References

Dudden, A. (2008). *Troubled apologies among Japan, Korea, and the United States*. Columbia University Press.

Fukunaga, F. 福永文夫. (2014). 日本占領史 *1945–1952;* 東京·ワシントン·沖縄 *[A history of the occupation of Japan, 1945–1952: Tokyo, Washington, Okinawa]*. 中央公論新社.

Hara, K. 原貴美惠. (2012). サンフランシスコ平和条約の盲点 (新幀版). 溪水社.

ジョン·ダウ. (1991). 吉田茂とその時代 (上)(下) (大窪愿二 譯). 中公文庫.

渡辺昭夫, 宮里政玄 (編). (1986). サンフランシスコ講和. 東京大學出版會.

三浦陽一. (1996). 吉田茂とサンフランシスコ講和. 大月書店.

福永文夫. (2014). 日本占領史 *1945–1952* 東京·ワシントン·沖縄. 中公新書.

徐相文. (2004). 毛澤東과 *6·25*戰爭*:* 派兵決定過程과 介入動機. 國防部 軍事編纂研究所.

鄭秉峻. (2010). 독도 獨島 *1947*. 돌베개.

鄭秉峻. (2019, August). 샌프란시스코 평화조약의 한반도 관련 조항과 한국정부의 대응. 국립외교원 외교사 연구센터.

남기정. (2016). 기지 국가의 탄생—일본이 치른 한국전쟁. 서울대학교 출판문화원.

李泰鎭. (2017). 끝나지 않은 역사—식민지배 청산을 위한 역사인식. 태학사.

Challenges to the Post-War Asia-Pacific International Order

Charles Armstrong

Abstract More than seventy years after the end of World War II, the boundaries between and relationships among the states of the Asia-Pacific remain largely within the order established under US hegemony in the late 1940s and early 1950s. This paper examines the formation of that post-war order and discusses the ways in which it is being challenged by contemporary global and regional developments. In particular, it asks whether the Chinese-led Belt and Road Initiative is an alternative or complement to the idea of the Asia-Pacific, and how both concepts reflect changing geo-economic, technological, and territorial forces.

Keywords Asia-Pacific · Belt and road initiative · China · Eurasia · Geopolitics · International order · Post-war · San Francisco system · United States · US Hegemony

1 Introduction

In recent years many commentators in the United States in particular, and Western countries in general, have expressed deep concern about the decline of the so-called "post-war liberal international order."[1] While there are differing views regarding the content, as well as the value, of this liberal order, it is often thought to include a generally free international trading system, a set of agreed-upon rules regulating trade and international disputes, respect for international institutions, and stable military alliances. This order is embodied in a set of institutions established under

[1] See for example the expert survey in *Foreign Affairs*, the representative journal of the US foreign policy establishment, on the question, "Is the Liberal Order in Peril?" https://www.foreignaffairs.com/ask-the-experts/liberal-order-peril.

C. Armstrong (✉)
Independent Scholar, New York, NY, USA
e-mail: cra10@columbia.edu

Y.-H. Kim et al. (eds.), *Beyond the San Francisco System*,
https://doi.org/10.1007/978-981-95-3328-2_5

US leadership at the end of World War II, in particular the United Nations, the World Bank, and the International Monetary Fund, as well as later the World Trade Organization (WTO). Although this "liberal international order" (liberal in both the political but perhaps especially in the economic sense) has certain roots in British global dominance in the late nineteenth and early twentieth centuries, the contemporary liberal order is closely associated with, and to some extent even defined by, US leadership. Thus, concern about the decline of the post-war international order is closely related to anxiety over the decline of American leadership and global power. American power and leadership are seen to be declining relative to other regional and potentially global "non-liberal" powers, especially China.

There is considerable evidence that American power and influence is in relative decline, except in terms of sheer military strength, and that elements of the post-war order are facing a number of serious challenges. In this paper I will focus not on the economic and political aspects of the post-war order and its challengers, but rather their spatial configurations and orientations, with a focus on the Asia-Pacific. At the center of this analysis is the question of why the post-1945, US-led Asia-Pacific international order, established to resolve the settlement of World War II, still remains largely in place today and whether it can last in the face of rapid change in Asia-Pacific and Eurasian relations. This paper takes a historical perspective reflecting on the evolution of concepts of global and regional spatial order, arguing that there is a deep structure of thought underlying contemporary American approaches to international order, including arrangements in the Asia-Pacific. This underlying deep structure can be identified with the nineteenth and twentieth-century strategic tradition known as Geopolitics, which has undergone a considerable revival in the US today. I begin with a brief introduction to the history of geopolitical thinking in Europe and the United States, and the rise of the United States as a Pacific and world power that coincided with this history. I then examine the establishment of the United States as an East Asian power in the aftermath of World War II, the establishment of the US alliance system and demarcation of boundaries in the 1950s, and the emergence of the Asia-Pacific as a geo-economic macro-region from about the 1970s onward. Finally, the paper discusses the Chinese-led Belt and Road Initiative (BRI) and discusses how this relates to the Asia-Pacific order: whether the growing integration of Eurasia associated with the BRI is a challenge, an alternative, or a complement to the Asia-Pacific. My preliminary conclusion is that the BRI and Asia-Pacific order are not exactly comparable, as they are based on very different sets of principles and institutions, and that viewing the BRI through the traditional Anglo-American lens of geopolitics may lend itself to misunderstanding or even conflict. The paper concludes with some thoughts on the viability of the post-war, US-led Asia-Pacific order in the context of rapidly changing relations in East Asia and Eurasia.

2 Geopolitics: Territory, Technology, and Power

As mentioned, there has been a marked revival in popularity of geopolitics in the US and other English-speaking countries in the twenty-first century, as measured by the appearance of the term in books, academic papers, university courses, and the popular media.[2] Space, once thought to be conquered by technology (including the Internet), global communications, and economic convergence after the Cold War, has returned as a key problem in global politics. This revival results from many real-world events, including the rise of ethnic conflict in the post-Cold War period, territorial clashes in many parts of the world including East Asia and Eastern Europe, the threat of global terrorism, and other factors. Geopolitics can be defined as the strategic application of military force, technology, and other forms of power across space and territory in regional and global competition.[3] The term was invented by the Swedish politician Rudolf Kjellen in 1899, was popularized in Germany, and soon took hold in Britain. Its most famous British proponent was the scholar and politician Halford Mackinder, whose 1904 essay "The Geographical Pivot of History," presented at the Royal Geographic Society, would a profound effect on Anglo-America worldviews and foreign policy, not least during the Cold War. Not by accident did the concept of geopolitics become popularized at the peak of British power in the late nineteenth century, offering as it did a way of seeing the world as one of power competition and influence over territory that could serve British imperial interests. At the same time, the United States was extending its own power overseas, especially in the Caribbean and the Pacific. For Americans, it was the naval strategist Alfred Thayer Mahan rather than Mackinder who would exert a stronger influence, prioritizing as Mahan did oceanic rather than terrestrial power projection. Mahan's most important book *The Influence of Sea Power on History* (1890) was required reading for US navy officers and has apparently become widely read in China in recent years as well.[4]

---

[2]The work of Robert D. Kaplan has been particularly influential, in works such as *The Revenge of Geography: What the Maps Tell Us About Coming Conflicts and the Battle Against Fate* (New York: Random House, 2013).

[3]There are a number of different definitions of geopolitics but most convergence around the key forces of territory, technology and power. See among others John Agnew, *Geopolitics: Re-Visioning World Politics*, second edition (Routledge 2003), Saul Bernard Cohen *Geopolitics: The Geography of International Relations* (Rowman & Littlefield, 2009), and Klaus Dodds, *Geopolitics: A Very Short Introduction* (Oxford 2014).

[4]"China's Indo-Pacific Strategy: The Problems of Success," *Journal of Territorial and Maritime Studies* vol. 6 no. 2 (Summer/Fall 2019), p. 103.

3 The US as a Pacific Power, 1890s—World War II

As Mahan and Mackinder laid the foundation of what would become the intellectual tradition of geopolitics, the United States was developing into a Pacific power. The United States had a long history of trans-Pacific trade, going back to the "China clippers" that sailed from New England to the China coast in the eighteenth century. With the coming of the steamship in the nineteenth century, US military and economic expansion across the Pacific took off, among the most important moments being the opening of Japan to trade and diplomatic relations with the United States in 1854. But it was the Spanish-American War of 1898 that made the United States a Pacific power and gave it a permanent presence in Asia by taking over the former Spanish colony of the Philippines. Along with the possession of Guam, also taken from defeated Spain, and the annexation of the formerly independent kingdom of Hawaii in 1898, the United States was for the first time an Asia-Pacific power by the beginning of the twentieth century. To this day the United States possesses a collection of islands across the Pacific, territories that are American but whose residents do not have the voting rights of normal US citizens, a fact that many Americans do not even know.

As the twentieth century progressed, the United States eclipsed the European nations that had established their presence in the Pacific—Britain, France, Russia, for a brief time Germany—and by the 1920s the only serious rival for influence in the Pacific was Japan. Most infamously—at least for Koreans—the United States entered a secret agreement with Japan in 1906, after Japan defeated Russia in the Russo-Japanese War, to allow Japan to dominate Korea in exchange for Japan not interfering with the United States in the Philippines. After World War I, Japan as a member of the victorious Allies received the former German possessions in the South Pacific. The clash of empires finally came, of course, at Pearl Harbor in Hawaii in 1941. When the Pacific War ended with Japan's defeat four years later, the United States had unchallenged pre-eminence in the Pacific, overseeing the transition from colonial rule not only in Japan's Pacific island territories but its continental possessions as well—Korea (with the shared responsibility of the Soviet Union), Taiwan, and Southern Sakhalin. In contrast to Europe, where four allies oversaw the post-war order, in the Asia-Pacific the United States would (with the partial exception of Korea) unilaterally set the terms of the peace, including the territorial boundaries among the postwar nations.

4 The Post-War Pacific Order: The "San Francisco System"

Even before World War II came to an end, the outlines of the US geopolitical imaginary of the subsequent Cold War were emerging. The person whose ideas most prefigured this new American geopolitics was the Dutch-born political scientist Nicolas Spykman. In 1942, Spykman's *America's Strategy in World Politics* updated and revised Mackinder's image of the "world-island." Like Mackinder, Spykman's geopolitics focused on the Eurasian space, but he reversed the relative importance of the interior or "heartland" and the exterior or "rimland," what Mackinder had called the "outer crescent." Hearkening back to Mahan, and emphasizing America's position as an offshore power removed from Eurasia, Spykman declared that control of the seas was the key to global power.[5] Control of the rimland was the key, and America was in a unique position to exert that control because of its geographical position, its awesome military and economic might, and its removal from the power struggles of the Eurasian land mass. Spykman's view was to be prophetic, as America came to dominate the Western and Eastern peripheries of Eurasia, the Atlantic and the Pacific edges, after Europe and Asia had both exhausted themselves in war. This rimland/heartland dichotomy was reflected, in part by deliberate design, in the policy of "containment"—of the Soviet Union and then China—that would be central to Cold War policy from 1947 onward. We can also see an echo of this geographical idea in the idea of the "Great Crescent" articulated by Secretary of State Dean Acheson: it did not matter that the United States lacked influence over the vast interior spaces of Eurasia dominated by the Soviet Union. Far more important was that the United States had control of the industrialized and resource-rich peripheries, a great crescent—or rather two intersecting crescents—stretching from Britain and Western Europe through Turkey and the Middle East on one side, and from Japan through Southeast Asia on the other.[6]

The situation in Europe and the developing transatlantic alliance were America's key concerns in the post-war period, but East Asia in the aftermath of Japan's defeat was an important secondary concern. The US position as the dominant military power in the Pacific was consolidated in the decade after the end of World War II, from 1945 until the mid-1950s. This was the birth of the post-war, US-led Asia-Pacific international order. The transition from war to post-war/Cold War in the Pacific was signified above all by the end of the US occupation of Japan, a process accelerated by the outbreak of the Korean War in June 1950. The San Francisco Treaty of 1951 formalized the end of the US occupation and the beginning of the Asia-Pacific alliance system. There is no space here to go into the details of the San Francisco system, but in brief, the Treaty of San Francisco established the formal independence, with continued US military presence, of the Japanese main islands (Okinawa would remain under US military control until 1972); declared that Japan "renounced" control of its erstwhile colonial possessions; and established the territorial boundaries between Japan and its neighboring states, among others. Significantly, no Korean or Chinese government was represented at the San Francisco conference—North Korea, South Korea, the People's Republic of China, or the Republic of China on Taiwan. Thus, the territorial boundaries and other issues directly impacting these states were decided without Korean or Chinese interests

[5] Nicolas Spykman, *America's Strategy in World Politics: The United States and the Balance of Power* (Harcourt, Brace & World, 1942).

[6] Michael Schaller, "Securing the Great Crescent: Occupied Japan and the Origins of Containment in Southeast Asia," *The Journal of American History*, vol. 69, no. 2 (September 1982), pp. 382–414.

represented, and the effects of this remain salient to East Asia to this day, not least in the territorial disputes over Tokto/Takeshima between South Korea and Japan, and the Diaoyu/Senkaku islands between China and Japan.

Following from the San Francisco Treaty were the set of mutual defense treaties signed between the United States and its East Asian allies: Japan, the Republic of Korea, and the Philippines, treaties which are still in effect, as well as Taiwan and South Vietnam, which are now moot. Along with Australia, New Zealand, and Thailand, the East Asian alliances formed the "hub and spoke" system of bilateral alliances that characterize the Asia-Pacific alliance system. Unlike the multilateral trans-Atlantic alliance system, embodied in NATO, the trans-Pacific system was never codified in a multilateral alliance, despite some failed attempts. Originally intended to contain an allegedly expansive Soviet Union and China, this trans-Pacific alliance system has proven remarkably long-lived, although recently it has begun to be re-conceptualized as an "Indo-Pacific" strategic alliance, to be discussed below.

Throughout the Cold War period, the post-World War II, American-led order in the Asia-Pacific remained in place more or less unchanged despite the events that reshaped the region during the Cold War years. The stand-off in Korea; the American defeat in Vietnam; the economic rise of nations on the East Asian rim, beginning with Japan and followed by Taiwan; and even normalization of relations between the United States and China, the economic integration of China into the US-dominated parts of the region and the extraordinary economic growth of China since reform and opening—none of this has fundamentally reshaped the Asia-Pacific international order until now. In part, this is because there has been no viable alternative to which all parties could agree. Until now, despite frictions and occasional dissatisfactions, a set of boundaries and relationships designed to resolve the post-war disposition of the Japanese empire and serving America's interest in the Cold War remains in place.

The dominant US approach to the Asia-Pacific in the years following the end of the Cold War was that China would be a "stakeholder" in the post-war liberal order still under American leadership, and indeed China became increasingly integrated into the capitalist world economy, including membership in the World Trade Organization in 2001. With the advance of the Asian economies in the 1980s and 1990s, the Asia-Pacific became characterized as an economic entity as much as a military alliance system. This was institutionalized in the formation of the Asia-Pacific Economic Cooperation forum (APEC) in 1989, coinciding with the end of the Cold War. APEC, born out of Japan-US cooperation as much as anything, is a preeminently liberal organization founded on the principle of free trade among its members. While the relative strength of its Asian members has changed, the Asia-Pacific could still be said to be a US-led international order at the beginning of the twenty-first century. This however is beginning to change.

5 Alternatives to the Asia-Pacific: Belt and Road, Eurasia, and the Indo-Pacific

The second decade of the twenty-first century has seen perhaps the most serious challenges to date for the postwar Asia-Pacific international order. While some signs of alternatives to the US-led international order were apparent well before, it was the global financial crisis of 2007–8 that marked the transition to new relationships and networks among East Asian and Eurasian nations. New terms were coined or repurposed to articulate new strategies, initiatives, or institutions led by the United States, China, and Russia respectively: the Indo-Pacific, beginning in 2011; One Belt One Road or the Belt and Road Initiative (BRI) in 2013; and the Eurasian Economic Union (EEU), signed among Russia, Belarus, Kazakhstan Kyrgyztan, and Armenia in 2014. While all three emerged at roughly the same time and reflect changing spatial orientations across the greater Pacific-Eurasian space, they are not really compatible and are in fact very different from each other. The BRI is a loose set of investment and infrastructure projects, the EEU is a treaty-based economic union, and the Indo-Pacific is a strategic zone that essentially projects the post-war US alliance system farther West to include a strategically aligned (but not allied) India. The Indo-Pacific is, in short, a geographical extension of the US-led Asia-Pacific alliance system designed to counter a rising China.

At first glance, the contrast between the Asia-Pacific and the Eurasia/Belt and Road geographies suggests the re-mergence of the classic conflict of traditional geopolitics, from Mahan and Mackinder to Spykman: maritime power vs. terrestrial power, "Rimland" vs. "Heartland." In fact however there is no necessary reason they should compete, although they could. It does not seem to be the case that the Belt and Road Initiative is imagined as a *geopolitical* strategy, in that the economic and the military appear quite separate. The Belt and Road extends westward across the Eurasian terrestrial space, whereas China's military concerns remain defensive and focused on its coastal territories on the East and South, and it is not at all obvious that China is attempting to challenge US preeminence in East Asia as a whole, much less at a global level. On the one hand, the BRI is associated with new institutions that are reminiscent of the post-war institutions set up under US leadership, such as the Chinese-led Asian Infrastructure Investment Bank, a kind of localized equivalent of the World Bank. But China has indicated no intention, much less has it taken concrete steps, in establishing military dominance or sets of alliances along the postwar US model.

The Belt and Road Initiative led by China, part of the growing integration of Eurasia as whole, does not necessarily undermine the US-led Asia-Pacific order; the two theoretically can co-exist in a complementary fashion. But while continentalist integration under the Belt and Road does not compete directly with the Asia-Pacific order, it may decenter it. Under the BRI there has been a reorientation of transportation and economic flows across Eurasia, facilitating the unprecedented integration of the Eurasian “supercontinent”.[7] For decades now America’s Asian allies have become more oriented toward China economically while remaining strongly tied to the US military. This will only accelerate as Eurasia becomes increasingly interconnected. The relative strength of the Asia-Pacific and Eurasian economic macro-regions is perhaps the most important development in the long term. Europe and Asia combined represent 61.93% of global GDP nominally, or 69.41% by purchasing power parity.[8] As Eurasia becomes more integrated internally, the trans-Atlantic and trans-Pacific relationships that underpinned American post-war prominence will inevitably decline in relative terms.

6 Conclusion

The post-war international order in the Asia-Pacific has been in some respects remarkably resilient over the past seventy years. The territorial boundaries established under the San Francisco Treaty remain in place, and the system of US bilateral alliances continues to be the only significant military alliance system in the Asia-Pacific. However, this international order faces increasing strains and challenges. Territorial disputes over unresolved issues remaining from post-war boundary-making, including disputes between South Korea and Japan and in the East and South China, are acute and growing ever more so. South Korea and Japan, America’s most important allies in East Asia, are now facing their most serious confrontation since the two normalized relations with each other more than a half-century ago. The value of America’s military alliance in Asia, as well as in Europe, is being openly questioned by the current US President. It is an open question how long the post-war order can withstand these strains without fundamental change.

Above all, changes in relations on the Eurasian continent challenge the older US-led Asia-Pacific regional order. If in the worst-case scenario China and the United States “decouple” their relationship as a result of ongoing trade disputes, the US presence in East Asia is sure to rapidly decline. The United States seems unwilling in the foreseeable future to invest the kind of economic resources necessary to maintain a balance against China. Short of this extreme scenario, the balance between the Pacific orientation and continental orientation is clearly tilting toward the latter. For now the Asia-Pacific order is changing but toward what we cannot yet know. BRI is not an alternative, much less a geopolitical challenge. Seeing the BRI through the lens of geopolitical competition invites real dangers. To assume that the BRI is primarily a competitor to the US-led order, and that the two can only exist in a win-lose relationship, is to invite conflict and become a self-fulfilling prophecy.

---

[7] Kent E. Calder, *Supercontinent: The Logic of Eurasian Integration* (Stanford: Stanford University Press, 2019).

[8] Calder, *Supercontinent*, p. 7.

Hasty Peace, Nasty Greed: Analyzing the Defects of the 1951 Treaty of San Francisco in Comparison with the 1919 Treaty of Versailles

Kim Sung Won

Abstract This article critically examines the 1951 Treaty of San Francisco by comparing it to the 1919 Treaty of Versailles, aiming to highlight the evolution and shortcomings of postwar peace treaties. The 1919 Treaty of Versailles marked a transformative point in international law by explicitly assigning war guilt and imposing punitive measures on Germany. In contrast, the 1951 Treaty of San Francisco adopted a more traditional and conciliatory approach, notably omitting explicit accountability for Japan's wartime actions. A central argument of the article is that the lack of detailed provisions regarding territorial settlements and reparations in the 1951 Treaty of San Francisco has contributed to ongoing disputes in East Asia, such as the Dokdo/Takeshima conflict. Utilizing the Third World Approaches to International Law (TWAIL) framework, the article asserts that the 1951 Treaty of San Francisco reinforced colonial and hegemonic power structures, prioritizing the interests of major powers over those of victimized and weaker nations. The article further demonstrates that Cold War dynamics and US strategic interests heavily influenced the formation of the 1951 Treaty of San Francisco, resulting in insufficient justice for Asian countries affected by Japanese aggression. The analysis underscores the need for a critical, interdisciplinary reassessment of the legacy of the 1951 Treaty of San Francisco and its broader implications for international law and regional stability.

Keywords Colonial legacy · Dokdo · East Asia · International law · San Francisco Treaty · TWAIL · Versailles Treaty

---

K. Sung Won (✉)
Law, School of Law at Hanyang University, Seoul, The Republic of Korea
e-mail: eastphalia@hanyang.ac.kr

Y.-H. Kim et al. (eds.), *Beyond the San Francisco System*,
https://doi.org/10.1007/978-981-95-3328-2_6

1 Introduction

International law has been instrumental in upholding peace and security within the global community. The challenging dynamics of international power politics often lead to inevitable conflicts over national interests among states, which historically have precipitated the onset of wars. Human history is replete with significant wars that have reshaped the international order. The genesis of warfare can be traced back to ancient times, predating the formal establishment of state systems. Typically, following a war, peace treaties are negotiated and signed by the involved parties or states to establish a framework for future relations and to prevent further conflicts. In this regard, it is reasonable to assert that human history and peace treaties represent two sides of the same coin.

Traditionally, peace treaties have encompassed reflections on past conflicts and aspirations for future peace. Notably, these treaties often exhibited a spirit of magnanimity toward the nations responsible for initiating wars. Such generosity was largely driven by the overarching objective of these treaties: the prevention of future conflicts. However, the nature of these agreements underwent a significant transformation with the 1919 Treaty of Versailles, which marked a stark departure from previous conventions in the aftermath of World War I.

The 1919 Treaty of Versailles embodied a stringent international stance toward Germany, attributing to it the responsibility for the war, partitioning its territories, and instituting penalties for war crimes. In contrast, the 1951 Treaty of San Francisco did not continue these revolutionary trends. Instead, it resembled earlier peace treaties, predating the 1919 Treaty of Versailles. Given that the 1951 Treaty of San Francisco is often cited as a root cause of ongoing territorial disputes in East Asia, a critical analysis contrasting it with the 1919 Treaty of Versailles is warranted.

This paper delves into the apparent regression encapsulated by the 1951 Treaty of San Francisco. The initial section scrutinizes the role and implications of peace treaties within international law. Subsequently, it analyzes the core components of the 1919 Treaty of Versailles and highlights how it diverged from classical peace treaties. The comparison reveals the problematic aspects of the 1951 Treaty of San Francisco. This paper also examines the lasting impact of the 1951 Treaty of San Francisco on the Dok-Do dispute, highlighting the necessity for a critical reevaluation of its legacy. Finally, the paper explores the issues inherent in the 1951 Treaty of San Francisco through the lens of the Third World Approaches to International Law (TWAIL).

2 Implications of the Peace Treaties in International Law

2.1 Peace Treaties and the International System

Peace treaties play a pivotal role in the evolution of international law. Concluded to terminate hostilities and establish frameworks for future peace, these treaties precipitate significant shifts in the geopolitical landscape both before and after a conflict. The resulting transformations in the international system serve as crucial benchmarks for periodizing studies in international law and international relations. For instance, the Peace of Westphalia, which marked the conclusion of the Thirty Years' War, was instrumental in fostering the state-centric international system.[1]

Similarly, the Congress of Vienna and the subsequent Concert of Europe, organized post-Napoleonic wars, were vital in maintaining the balance of power in Europe.[2] These events underscore how major peace treaties profoundly influence the structure of international society. Without the Peace of Westphalia, the state-centric system might not have emerged. Likewise, the expansion of what was once termed the "Public Law of Europe"—and later international law—could not have occurred without the colonial and imperial undertones of the Concert of Europe.

The function of peace treaties in restoring peace and security, which are often ravaged by war, can be seen as a general formula. The consistent nature of peace treaties throughout history extends beyond mere structural similarities; they address a broad spectrum of issues ranging from political and territorial disputes to economic, financial, and legal questions. Common elements of peace treaties include preambles; peace and friendship clauses; operational provisions for conflict resolution; clauses addressing the financial, economic, and juridical repercussions of war; amnesty provisions and the repatriation of prisoners; guarantee clauses; and mechanisms to ensure treaty implementation.[3]

---

[1] For a brief introduction to the Westphalian Peace, see, A. Nussbaum, *A Concise History of the Law of Nations*, rev. ed. (The Macmillan Company, 1961), pp. 115–117.

[2] T. Fitschen, "Vienna Congress (1815)", in R. Wolfrum (ed.), *The Max Planck Encyclopedia of Public International Law, Vol. X* (Oxford Univ. Press, 2012), pp. 678–683.

[3] C. Bell, *On the Law of Peace: Peace Agreements and the Lex Pacificatoria* (Oxford Univ. Press, 2007), p. 77.

2.2 *The Peace Treaties in Historical Context*

2.2.1 Pre-classical Period

Bell identifies the Treaty of Kadesh between the Hittite and Egyptian empires as a prototypical form of peace treaties in the pre-classical period.[4] The treaty is notable for its contemporary relevance, featuring a detailed preamble that establishes fraternal bonds and reaffirms previous commitments. It stipulates non-aggression, mutual defense against third-party attacks, the return of refugees, and the extradition of criminals to their home states for trial. Notably, the agreed borders were documented separately in another papyrus.[5]

Bederman highlights the existence of certain "norms" across treaties that ensured certainty and security in expectations related to war and peace: (1) the conduct of embassies, immunities granted to envoys, and protections for foreigners; (2) the sanctity of treaties and alliances; and (3) the regulations governing the declaration of war and limits on wartime actions.[6] In the context of early Roman Empire peace treaties, Baldus observes practices that included agreements on peace settlements, non-use of force, future friendships, and collateral agreements addressing territorial or security issues, such as hostage-taking and reparations.[7] This suggests a substantial consistency in the content of peace treaties.

There is significant continuity between peace treaties in antiquity and those of the early Middle Ages. From the early Middle Ages through the sixteenth century, peace treaties typically involved declarations by the parties and were solidified through mutual oaths. Future-oriented clauses aimed to prevent war and stabilize peace, often stipulating non-harm agreements between the parties and their allies, enforceable through reprisals. Regarding past conflicts, these treaties commonly addressed amnesties, restitution, and the removal of wartime restrictions on trade, restoration of privileges, and sometimes the return of prisoners of war.[8]

Lesaffer points to the 1540s as a pivotal period marking a crisis in the European international legal order, reflected in and driven by shifts in peace treaty practices. This era saw the breakdown of the feudal order and the rise of sovereign statehood, culminating in the norms that paved the way for the Peace of Westphalia.[9]

---

[4] *Id*, pp. 80–81.

[5] *Id.*, p. 81.

[6] D. Bederman, *International Law in Antiquity* (Cambridge Univ. Press, 2001), p. 22.

[7] C. Baldus, "Vestigia Pacis. The Roman Peace Treaty: Structure or Event?", in R. Lesaffer (ed.), *Peace Treaties and International Law in European History: From the Late Middle Ages to World War One* (Cambridge Univ. Press, 2004), pp. 114–115.

[8] K.-H. Ziegler, "The Influence of Medieval Roman Law on Peace Treaties", in Lesaffer, *supra* note 7, pp. 148–150.

[9] R. Lesaffer, "Peace Treaties from Lodi to Westphalia", in Lesaffer, *supra* note 7, p. 43.

2.2.2 Classical Period and Interwar Years

The classical period of international law is recognized as a critical phase during which the contemporary international legal system began to take clear shape. The Peace of Westphalia, concluded among Catholic and Protestant states and entities in Europe, is often heralded for establishing the foundational elements of today's international legal framework, notably the concept of a plurality of independent states under no superior authority.[10]

Prior to Westphalia, co-ratification was a significant feature of peace treaties, serving as an essential element for their effectiveness.[11] Throughout the classical period, peace treaties bolstered the narrative of sovereignty that Westphalia epitomized. However, the treaty-making practices of this era also reveal the complexities in the evolution of international law as a system among states. Notably, Indigenous groups were recognized as entities with treaty-making capacity until the turn of the nineteenth century and World War I. For instance, from 1778 to 1868, the United States ratified 367 treaties with Indigenous nations.[12]

The transition from viewing Indigenous peoples as "states" capable of treaty-making to domestic groups without such capacities marked a significant shift. This transition not only solidified the European model of statehood in international relations but also relegated State-Indigenous conflicts to domestic jurisdictions, thereby encapsulating them within the exclusive sovereignty of the state.

The modern period of international law was significantly shaped by the Peace Treaties of Paris.[13] These treaties introduced groundbreaking concepts, including political responsibility for initiating war and punitive measures for transgressions.[14] Furthermore, the Paris Peace Treaties catalyzed the formation of the League of Nations, challenging the efficacy of the traditional balance of power in maintaining global peace and security.

The interwar period witnessed innovative legal arrangements addressing the rights of minority groups and disputed border areas, facilitated by the League of Nations mandate system and the evolving discourse on self-determination. The regime established by the Paris Treaties included specific provisions for minority rights, addressing the challenges of nationalist divisions within the context of new international governance.[15]

---

[10] A. Cassese, *International Law*, second ed., (Oxford Univ. Press, 2005), pp. 22–25.

[11] Lesaffer, *supra* note 9, pp. 19–21.

[12] F. Prucha, *American Indian Treaties: The History of a Political Anomaly* (Univ. of California Press, 1994), p. 1.

[13] C. Tomuschat, "The 1871 Peace Treaty between France and Germany and the 1919 Peace Treaty of Versailles", in Lesaffer, *supra* note 7, p. 384.

[14] See, M. Schmoeckel, "Consent and Caution: Lassa Oppenheim and his reaction to World War I", in Lesaffer, *supra* note 7, pp. 270–274.

[15] See, S. Chesterman, *You, The People: The United Nations, Transitional Administration, and State-Building* (Oxford Univ. Press, 2004), pp. 13–25.

The interwar developments highlight the intricate links between the resolution of interstate and intrastate conflicts, illustrating how peace treaties and international administrative practices have historically shaped both international and domestic legal orders. This period exemplifies the challenges of addressing international conflicts without definitive decisions regarding national identity, foreshadowing contemporary debates on the relationship between international institutions and national sovereignty.[16]

3 The 1919 Treaty of Versailles as a Peace Treaty

3.1 A Historical Background

By April 1918, it became evident to German representatives that the Empire was facing an inevitable military defeat. In late September, Germany's political and military leaders resolved to approach President Woodrow Wilson to firstly request an armistice and secondly to negotiate peace. This outreach was grounded in Wilson's Fourteen Points. From October 29 to November 4, 1918, an inter-allied conference was held in Paris to discuss the terms of an armistice and a subsequent peace settlement. During this conference, Britain and France advocated for stringent conditions designed to dismantle Germany's remaining military capabilities. The conference's outcomes were relayed to the German delegation through a communication known as the Lansing Note, signed by the US Secretary of State on November 5, 1918. This document formed the basis of the armistice agreement, which was officially signed on November 11, 1918.[17]

Following the armistice, the Allied Powers deliberated on how to structure the final peace settlement. Driven by French proposals and after some debate over the venue, the United States, Great Britain, and France agreed to convene a peace conference in Paris. This conference formally commenced on January 18, 1919, and concluded its proceedings on August 10, 1920.[18]

The peace treaty was signed in the Hall of Mirrors at the Palace of Versailles on June 28, 1919. Prior to this, on June 22, 1919, the German National Assembly had voted to approve the treaty, with 237 votes in favor and 138 against. The 1919 Treaty of Versailles was signed by the United States, the British Empire, France, Italy, Japan, and other Allied and Associated Powers, with Germany on the opposing side. Notably, China was listed as a signatory but abstained from signing due to a dispute over the territorial provisions concerning Shantung and Kiaochow, where the Supreme Council favored Japanese interests.[19]

---

[16] Bell, *supra* note 3, p. 93.

[17] F. Schorkopf, "Versailles Peace Treaty (1919)", in Wolfrum, *supra* note 2, p. 658.

[18] *Id.*

[19] *Id.*, p. 659.

3.2 Content of the Provisions of the 1919 Treaty of Versailles

3.2.1 German Boundaries and Overseas Territories

The 1919 Treaty of Versailles notably lacked traditional peace provisions that typically reassured future peaceful relations beyond the mere absence of war.[20] Parts II to IV of the 1919 Treaty of Versailles addressed territorial alterations and their political repercussions. The borders of Germany were significantly redrawn, affecting Belgium, Luxembourg, France, Switzerland, Austria, Czechoslovakia, Poland, and Denmark.[21] The 1919 Treaty of Versailles imposed various political obligations on Germany, including the establishment of demilitarized zones, adherence to treaties between third parties, the organization of plebiscites, and the protection of minorities.[22]

Alsace and Lorraine, territories ceded to Germany in the 1871 peace treaty, were returned to French sovereignty. Demilitarized zones were set up along the left bank of the Rhine and 50 kilometers inwards from its right bank. France was granted exclusive rights to exploit coal mines in the Saar basin, while governance of the Saar was relinquished to the League of Nations for a 15-year period ending with a referendum to determine its future. Germany was also compelled to acknowledge the inalienable independence of Austria, contingent upon the consent of the Council of the League of Nations.[23] Additionally, Poland was granted access to the Baltic Sea through the cession of West Prussia and Pomerania, and the city of Danzig, along with its surrounding territory, was designated as a free city under the protection of the League of Nations.[24]

Part IV of the 1919 Treaty of Versailles detailed the surrender of Germany's overseas territories and rights established through international agreements. Germany renounced all claims to its colonies and treaty-based rights in several countries including Bulgaria, China, Egypt, Liberia, Morocco, Siam, the province of Shantung, and Turkey.[25]

3.2.2 Military and Penalties Provisions

Part V of the 1919 Treaty of Versailles mandated extensive disarmament measures.[26] The size of the German military was restricted to 100,000 army soldiers and 15,000 naval personnel, with prohibitions on military or naval air forces, tanks, and

---

[20] *Id.*, p. 660. See, *Treaty of Peace with Germany (Treaty of Versailles)*, Preamble.

[21] *Treaty of Versailles,* Part II, Arts. 27–30.

[22] *Id.*, Part III, Arts. 31–117.

[23] *Id*, Art. 80.

[24] *Id.*, Art. 100.

[25] *Id.*, Arts. 118–158.

[26] *Id.*, Part V, Arts. 159–213.

submarines. Detailed regulations and limitations were also set on armament, ammunition, and warship possession. Germany was further required to abolish compulsory military service in favor of voluntary enlistment, with these disarmament measures subject to supervision by an inter-allied commission.

The 1919 Treaty of Versailles also included penalty provisions.[27] Specifically, Article 227 mandates the extradition of the German Emperor Wilhelm II and others accused of violating the laws and customs of war. It also proposed the creation of a special tribunal to prosecute the former German head of state for supreme offenses against international morality and the sanctity of treaties.[28]

3.2.3 Reparations and Guarantees Provisions

The extradition provisions in the 1919 Treaty of Versailles marked a shift toward more punitive measures within the treaty's structure,[29] particularly highlighted in Part VIII of the 1919 Treaty of Versailles.[30] This part opened with the war guilt clause, which attributed sole responsibility for the war and its atrocities to Germany.[31] This clause not only imposed moral and financial blame but also laid the groundwork for subsequent reparations and legal actions against Germany.

To ensure the execution of the treaty provisions, the Allied and Associated Powers maintained the right to occupy German territories west of the Rhine, including four strategic Rhine bridgeheads: Koblenz, Cologne, Kehl, and Mainz.[32] This military occupation was set for a period of 15 years, with provisions for staged withdrawals after five and ten years, contingent upon Germany's compliance with the treaty conditions. This approach underscores the Allied commitment to securing long-term peace and adherence to the treaty, reflecting a blend of enforcement and conditional reconciliation strategies.

---

[27] *Id.*, Part VII, Arts. 227–230.

[28] Art. 227: The Allied and Associated Powers publicly arraign William II of Hohenzollern, formerly German Emperor, for a supreme offence against international morality and the sanctity of treaties.

In its decision the tribunal will be guided by the highest motives of international policy, with a view to vindicating the solemn obligations of international undertakings and the validity of international morality. It will be its duty to fix the punishment which it considers should be imposed.

[29] *Treaty of Versailles*, *supra* note 20, Arts. 227–230.

[30] *Id.*, Arts. 231–247.

[31] Art. 231: The Allied and Associated Governments affirms and Germany accepts the responsibility of Germany and her allies for causing all the loss and damage to which the Allied and Associated Governments and their nationals have been subjected as a consequence of the war imposed upon them the aggression of Germany and her allies.

[32] *Treaty of Versailles*, *supra* note 20, Part XIV, Arts. 428–433.

3.3 Implications for Peace Treaties in International Law

The 1919 Treaty of Versailles represented a groundbreaking shift in the traditional framework of peace treaties at the time of its adoption. While it incorporated standard elements such as territorial and financial compensation, which are customary in peace agreements, the Treaty also introduced significant modifications and novel provisions.

Unlike traditional peace treaties, which delineated a clear demarcation between a state of war and a future of amicable relations, the 1919 Treaty of Versailles departed from this concept. The "war guilt" clause specifically extended Germany's political, economic, and financial responsibilities indefinitely into the future, effectively maintaining Germany in a state of punitive subjugation.[33] Thus, the Treaty did not establish a baseline for a new, cooperative relationship between the former adversaries as might have been expected.

Additionally, the penalty provisions that called for the extradition of individuals accused of war crimes were seen, particularly by Germany, as unexpected and legal innovations. These provisions were not perceived as measures to address the moral implications of wartime actions but rather as mechanisms to further humiliate the German populace.[34]

Furthermore, the 1919 Treaty of Versailles was instrumental in introducing the principles of self-determination and minority protection into international law, albeit the relevant clauses fell short of fulfilling the expectations set by President Wilson's Fourteen Points. The Treaty also played a crucial role in the establishment of the League of Nations, which embodied the concept of a collective security system designed to maintain peace among nations.

In this vein, the Treaty deserves recognition for its contribution to the creation of the Permanent Court of International Justice. Article 14 of the 1919 Treaty of Versailles tasked the Council of the League of Nations with the responsibility of formulating plans for the establishment of a global court, marking a significant advancement in the institutional framework of international law.[35]

---

[33] Schorkopf, *supra* note 17, p. 663.

[34] *Id.*

[35] *Treaty of Versailles*, *supra* note 20, Art. 14: The Council shall formulate and submit to the Members of the League for adoption plans for the establishment of a Permanent Court of International Justice. The Court shall be competent to hear and determine any dispute of an international character which the parties thereto submit to it. The Court may also give an advisory opinion upon any dispute or question referred to it by the Council or by the Assembly.

4 The Legacy of the 1951 Treaty of San Francisco Judged from the 1919 Treaty of Versailles

4.1 Looking Forward, Moving Backward

While the effectiveness of the 1919 Treaty of Versailles in maintaining international peace and security remains a subject of intense debate, its attempt to enforce international justice by introducing political responsibility for the war through punitive measures is undeniable. The Treaty's novelty lies primarily in its explicit punitive approach toward Germany. It included detailed provisions for the delimitation of Germany's territory and the redistribution of its colonies, which, despite substantial criticism, clearly reflected the international community's intent to penalize Germany as the aggressor. In doing so, the Treaty diverged from traditional peace treaty elements that typically emphasized reconciliation and a forward-looking stance.

This deviation raises the question of whether the 1951 Treaty of San Francisco, also known as the Treaty of Peace with Japan, mirrors the revolutionary nature of the 1919 Treaty of Versailles. Investigating whether the 1951 Treaty of San Francisco incorporates similar revolutionary characteristics is crucial, particularly in the context of the Dok-Do dispute, which is often cited as a direct consequence of this treaty. This inquiry examines whether the 1951 Treaty of San Francisco includes detailed provisions for the redistribution of Japanese territories or assigns responsibility to Japan for its wartime actions, similar to those found in the 1919 Treaty of Versailles.

The 1919 Treaty of Versailles, for example, includes intricate details on the redistribution of German territories[36] and the specific delineation of borders, such as those concerning the Saar basin.[37] In contrast, the 1951 Treaty of San Francisco contains only a simplistic provision regarding the territories Japan was required to return to the affected states.[38] This lack of detailed territorial provisions has been identified as a primary factor contributing to ongoing territorial disputes in East

[36] See, *Treaty of Versailles, supra* note 20, Part II. Boundaries of Germany.

[37] *Id.*, Part III. Section IV.

[38] *The 1951 Treaty of San Francisco*, Chap. II. Territory

Art. 2

(a) Japan, recognizing the independence of Korea, renounces all right, title and claims to Korea, including the islands of Quelpart, Port Hamilton and Dagelet.

(b) Japan renounces all rights, title and claim to Formosa and the Pescadores.

(c) Japan renounces all right, title and claim to the Kurile Islands, and to that portion of Sakhalin and the islands adjacent to it over which Japan acquired sovereignty as a consequence of the Treaty of Portsmouth of September 5, 1950.

(d) Japan renounces all right, title and claim in connection with the League of Nations Mandate System, and accepts the action of the United Nations Security Council of April 2, 1947, extending the trusteeship system to the Pacific Islands formerly under mandate to Japan.

(e) Japan renounces all claim to any right or title to or interest in connection with any part of the Antarctic area, whether deriving from the activities of Japanese nationals or otherwise.

(f) Japan renounces all right, title and claim to the Spartly Islands and to the Paracel Islands.

Asia. Kang's analysis of the 1947 Treaty of Peace with Italy further supports the argument that the simplistic territorial clauses in the 1951 Treaty of San Francisco have significantly undermined the relationship between Japan and its former victims in Asia.[39]

Counterarguments suggest that the simplicity of the territorial provisions in the 1951 Treaty of San Francisco may be justified due to the different political and geographical contexts compared to Europe in 1919, which dealt extensively with central Europe and involved numerous neighboring states. Hence, a more detailed approach to territorial changes, like those seen in the 1919 Treaty of Versailles, might have been deemed unnecessary for Japan. However, despite recognizing these differences, it is difficult to ignore that the 1951 Treaty of San Francisco does not follow the precedential path set by the 1919 Treaty of Versailles in terms of detailed territorial reallocation and addressing war responsibilities.

4.2 The Unwillingness to Make Punishment of Japan as the War-Causing State

The 1919 Treaty of Versailles is distinguished from previous peace treaties primarily by its inclusion of the so-called "war guilt" provisions, which represent a departure from traditional treaty terms that typically seek to reconcile past grievances and look forward to a cooperative future. It is in this context that the 1919 Treaty of Versailles holds historical significance, reflecting the international community's unequivocal stance toward wartime accountability and the shaping of international law's approach to war responsibility in the early twentieth century.

This raises the question: does the 1951 Treaty of San Francisco echo the values of the 1919 Treaty of Versailles? Preliminary analyses suggest a negative response, especially concerning the assignment of war guilt. A thorough review of the negotiation history and political atmosphere surrounding the 1951 Treaty of San Francisco is essential for a comprehensive understanding, but initial indications suggest that the 1951 Treaty of San Francisco does not reflect the innovative characteristics of the 1919 Treaty of Versailles concerning accountability for war crimes.

Article 231 of the 1919 Treaty of Versailles explicitly assigned responsibility to Germany and its allies for all losses and damages incurred by the Allied governments and their nationals due to the war. In contrast, Article 14(a) of the 1951 Treaty of San Francisco acknowledges Japan's responsibility for war damages but notes Japan's insufficient resources to fully compensate for these damages while maintaining a viable economy. This article lacks a direct counterpart to Article 231,

[39] P. K. Kang, "A Comparative Study on the Provisions on Territories in the Peace Treaty with Italy in 1947 and the Peace Treaty with Japan in 1951", 63 *Korean Journal of International Law* 217 (2018), pp. 223–224. See also, K. Hara, *Cold War Frontiers in the Asia-Pacific* (Routledge, 2007), p. 7.

notably omitting any formal acknowledgment of Japanese responsibility for initiating the conflict.

The absence of explicit war guilt provisions in the 1951 Treaty of San Francisco may reflect strategic considerations during the Cold War, emphasizing the geopolitical importance of Japan in East Asia over the pursuit of historical accountability.[40] This oversight is arguably a root cause of ongoing territorial disputes in the region, as the treaty fails to address Japanese war responsibilities comprehensively and lacks detailed provisions on territorial restitution.[41]

The interval of three decades between the two treaties does provide some context for the differences in their content and objectives. While the 1919 Treaty of Versailles aimed to prevent future German aggression through punitive measures, its perceived failure may have influenced a more restrained approach in the 1951 Treaty of San Francisco, potentially to avoid the punitive excesses seen in 1919. However, considering the analysis by Kang on the 1947 Treaty of Peace with Italy, this argument of a simplistic approach based on previous failures does not hold strong.[42]

Further, Park's critique suggests that if the parties involved had been European rather than Asian, the 1951 Treaty of San Francisco might have contained more detailed provisions, similar to those of the 1919 Treaty of Versailles.[43] This perspective suggests a Eurocentric bias in treaty negotiations, which may have undervalued the significance of Japan's actions in East Asia. Moreover, unlike the 1919 Treaty of Versailles, which included provisions for the extradition of war criminals such as Wilhelm II, the 1951 Treaty of San Francisco lacks such measures, indicating a potentially lesser commitment to international justice and the establishment of a peaceful regime in East Asia. Instead, the treaty seems to have been hastily concluded primarily to re-establish Japan as a bulwark against the spread of communism, often at the expense of the interests of the victimized states.

4.3 A Critical Analysis of the 1951 Treaty of San Francisco from a TWAIL Perspective

When peace treaties reflect the colonial core of domination, subjugation, oppression, and obedience, these elements become the primary targets of critique by TWAIL. As a methodology of international law, TWAIL generally focuses on the colonial and imperialist origins and influences of international law. Regarding the theoretical origins of TWAIL, Mutua points to decolonization movements,

---

[40] H. N. Kim, "The U.S. and the Territorial Dispute on Dokdo/Takeshima between Japan and Korea, 1945–1954", 13 *International Journal of Korean Studies* 97 (2009), pp. 106–112.

[41] K. Hara, "50 Years from San Francisco: Re-Examining the Peace Treaty and Japan's Territorial Problems", 74 *Pacific Affairs* 361 (2001), pp. 368–375.

[42] See, Kang, *supra* note 39.

[43] The opinion of B. K. Park expressed in the third Seminar of the International Law and History (2018. 10. 19)

including the 1955 Bandung Conference, as foundational.[44] Gathii, on the other hand, traces the origins to a 1996 meeting of Harvard Law School graduate students discussing the accessibility of international law for Third World countries. He explains that the term TWAIL was coined by the participants of this meeting.[45] As a method of international legal studies, TWAIL criticizes the Western-centric bias in international law and aims to establish fair international legal norms. TWAIL argues that this inherent bias deliberately marginalizes the interests of Third World countries and peoples.[46]

From the perspective of TWAIL, a critical issue is how victorious nations seek to derive benefits through the oppression, domination, and exploitation of the defeated nations, and how these strategies of the victors are incorporated into peace treaties that shape the post-war international order. In essence, if the content of a peace treaty maintains and strengthens a dominator-dominated structure, no matter how ideally it prescribes conditions for peace and reconciliation, it remains an unjust international norm that perpetuates and intensifies hegemony and colonialism.

The conciliatory stance toward Japan stipulated in the 1951 Treaty of San Francisco can be traced back to Japan's recognition as a major nation, or so-called civilized nation, since World War I. However, considering the severe reparations imposed on Germany and Italy by the 1919 Treaty of Versailles and the 1947 Treaty of Peace with Italy, one could argue that the status of being a "civilized nation" did not significantly influence the specific contents of peace treaties. Yet, this raises a further issue: why Japan received exceptional treatment and what were the underlying reasons for this.

In the geopolitical context, it is possible that Western powers considered Asia less strategically important than Europe. However, the drafting process of the 1951 Treaty of San Francisco reflects the Cold War context, showing the significance of maintaining American hegemony in East Asia. Nonetheless, Dulles led the treaty's emphasis on reconciliation rather than punishment, resulting in the insufficient materialization of the rights and interests of the actual victim nations of Japan's wartime aggressions.

From the perspective of TWAIL, the 1951 Treaty of San Francisco can be seen as a peace treaty that inadequately considered the interests and rights of Third World nations and peoples, favoring those of the First World. TWAIL's critical stance can aid in addressing issues, particularly territorial disputes such as the Dokdo issue, which mainstream international law theories like legal positivism fail to resolve.

---

[44] M. Mutua, "What is TWAIL?" 94 *Proceedings of the American Society of International Law Annual Meeting* (2000), p. 31.

[45] J. Gathii, "TWAIL: A Brief History of Its Origins, Its Decentralized Network, and a Tentative Bibliography," 3 *Trade Law and Development* (2011), p. 28. For a detailed explanation of the latest trends in TWAIL discussions, see, J. Gathii, "Promise of International Law: A Third World View (Including A TWAIL Bibliography 1996–2019 as an Appendix," 114 *Proceedings of the American Society of International Law* (2020), pp. 165–187.

[46] D. Fidler, "Revolt Against or From Within the West? TWAIL, the Developing World, and the Future Direction of International Law," 2 *Chinese Journal of International Law* (2003), p. 31.

The legal positivist approach to the treaty focuses primarily on interpretation and typically neglects to consider the context and purposes behind its formation. This tendency, as Anthony Anghie points out, stems from the intrinsic connection between legal positivism's interpretative targets in international law and colonialism and imperialism.[47] In this context, TWAIL offers an alternative starting point for analyzing the 1951 Treaty of San Francisco.

Applying TWAIL to critically review the 1951 Treaty of San Francisco presents numerous challenges, which are not easily overcome. A fundamental issue within the TWAIL framework is its inception as a critique of Western-centric international legal methods, specifically legal positivism. A prerequisite for applying a critical perspective is the existence of a target for critique, meaning that a structure of binary opposition must be established and how such a structure is accepted becomes crucial.

Criticism from the TWAIL perspective of the 1951 Treaty of San Francisco has been somewhat accepted academically, and it is undeniable that this approach can offer new perspectives on complex issues triggered by the treaty, such as the territorial disputes over Dokdo. However, when disputes regarding the interpretation and application of the treaty are formalized and judicial resolution is sought, the extent to which TWAIL's critical view can be accepted remains questionable.

Utilizing TWAIL for developing new arguments requires a so-called framing of the issue, which has both strengths and weaknesses. TWAIL employs insights from adjacent disciplines such as history, political science, sociology, philosophy, and anthropology to critique the positivist approach in international law. Critiques of the 1951 Treaty of San Francisco's colonialist and imperialist legacies have primarily been attempted through historical studies focusing on the archival materials. In international law, issues discussed during the drafting process of the treaty, especially the negotiations between the United States and Japan regarding Japanese territories, are highlighted. Undoubtedly, examining the drafting history of the 1951 Treaty of San Francisco is valuable. However, this approach is fundamentally historical and may be seen as merely a historical approach to international law.

In this context, the utility of a historical approach to international law with respect to the 1919 Treaty of Versailles lies in understanding how this treaty differed from traditional peace treaties and why these differences arose. Studies of the 1951 Treaty of San Francisco's drafting history often employ a chronological structure, highlighting points raised or omitted at certain times. This approach reveals that US interests in East Asia played a significant role in shaping the treaty's lenient terms toward Japan, often at the expense of the interests and understanding of nations and peoples victimized by Japanese wartime aggression.

However, critics argue that despite these historical facts, the historical and legal aspects of the 1951 Treaty of San Francisco are distinct issues and should not be integrated into a singular approach. While purposive and intentional interpretations

---

[47] See, A. Anghie, *Imperialism, Sovereignty and the Making of International Law* (Cambridge Univ. Press, 2005).

beyond literal textual analysis are possible, such methods only substantiate claims that the treaty predominantly reflects the interests of Western nations, particularly the United States, without necessarily justifying claims of the treaty's illegality.

Thus, TWAIL's critique of the 1951 Treaty of San Francisco faces significant initial challenges. Consequently, a broader framing is required to ensure that issues associated with the treaty are not diminished to mere matters of treaty interpretation. This necessitates emphasizing the need for an interdisciplinary approach to address the legacies of colonialism while framing the 1951 Treaty of San Francisco itself as problematic. This strategy aims to challenge and potentially reframe the discourse around the treaty within the broader context of international law.

While the interdisciplinary approach inherent in TWAIL's framing can be beneficial, it also risks handling international law issues outside of the legal framework itself. Indeed, TWAIL has strengths in criticizing problems induced by legal positivism, but it struggles to offer viable solutions to these issues. The historical failures of TWAIL in areas such as the New International Economic Order, maritime law, development, and international investment cannot be overlooked.

The difficulty in proposing effective solutions within TWAIL arises from the structure of international law itself. If international law perpetuates and strengthens colonial tendencies, then TWAIL can critique this structure but realistically cannot propose effective solutions. Therefore, the only solution may be to dismantle the existing structure of international law and create a new one. However, such a grand strategy is not achievable in the short term, and it remains unclear what stance the primary actors in international law, the nation-states, will take on this strategy.

Recently, there have been legal approaches emphasizing anti-colonialism, as seen in the Dutch colonial reparations ruling for Indonesia and the CARICOM rulings related to anti-colonialism. These represent significant steps in the legal assessment of the legacies of colonialism under an anti-colonial framework. However, the Dutch case primarily addressed reparations for inhumane acts committed during colonial rule rather than a legal assessment of colonialism itself, highlighting the limitations of current approaches in truly addressing the roots and broad implications of colonial legacies within international law.

Certainly, the 2002 UN General Assembly's adoption of the Durban Declaration expressed concerns about racial discrimination, xenophobia, and intolerance, emphasizing the legacies of slavery and colonialism, with ongoing discussions highlighted in UNGA Resolution A/74/321, "Elimination of racism, racial discrimination, xenophobia and related intolerance: comprehensive implementation of and follow-up to the Durban Declaration and Programme of Action," dated 21 August 2019. This development is highly commendable in terms of an anti-colonial approach to international law.[48] However, the focus of such legal resolutions on reparations through human rights law,[49] coupled with the ongoing strong political

[48] UNGA, Res A/74/321, Elimination of racism, racial discrimination, xenophobia and related intolerance: comprehensive implementation of and follow-up to the Durban Declaration and Programme of Action, 21 August 2019.

[49] *Id.*, paras. 26–35.

and legal resistance to reparations,[50] indicates that forming an international legal structure advocating anti-colonialism remains a challenging issue.

From a TWAIL perspective, the critical review of the 1951 Treaty of San Francisco must start with an acknowledgment of TWAIL's intrinsic limitations. While TWAIL's strategy of highlighting the colonial legacies in the 1951 Treaty of San Francisco is of great utility, any subsequent legal approaches must involve careful modifications of TWAIL's claims. Determining the extent of these modifications, which must align somewhat with existing international law discourse and mechanisms based on legal positivism, presents a significant challenge. Such modifications risk diluting TWAIL's original character.

Ultimately, if the international community embraces the international legal structure proposed by TWAIL, the critical assertions regarding the 1951 Treaty of San Francisco from a TWAIL perspective are likely to gain support. This shift in perception of the international law structure could reveal that the 1951 Treaty of San Francisco is not merely a peace agreement for East Asia but a principal perpetuator of colonial legacies threatening peace in the region well into the twenty-first century.

5 Conclusion

An unresolved past constrains the present and impacts the future. As a foundational norm of international society, international law reflects changes within this community, and these changes in international law typically maintain a static nature until a significant event alters the structure of international society. In this context, peace treaties play a crucial role in the evolutionary development of international law because they address events that have shattered the existing international structure and provide blueprints for the newly forming structure of international society.

Looking back at the history of international society, efforts have been made toward establishing a safer and more peaceful international community. In this regard, the 1919 Treaty of Versailles represented a clear departure from traditional peace treaties, reflecting the international community's decisive will to prevent further devastation from war. Although it focused on post-war reparations, the so-called "war guilt clause" of the 1919 Treaty of Versailles, which held nations accountable for causing the war, has significant implications for the development of international law from the perspective of peace treaties.

While the political implications that the 1919 Treaty of Versailles may have indirectly triggered World War II cannot be ignored, the value of the Treaty as a peace treaty remains undeniable, given its intent to hold nations accountable for war. Although complex political contexts influenced its formulation, the absence of such a resolute will in the 1951 Treaty of San Francisco is a significant and regrettable departure in the structural nature of peace treaties and international law.

[50] *Id.*, paras. 45–54.

Indeed, the discontinuity of the 1919 Treaty of Versailles was politically contextualized, and the argument that this discontinuity was abandoned by the nations that led the war reparations clauses could also be used to undermine the value of the treaty. Furthermore, it could be strongly argued that the 1951 Treaty of San Francisco represented the best possible outcome given the political dynamics of the time. However, accepting such arguments might lead to a lack of direction in the development of international law. If international law is understood to be influenced by the geopolitical dynamics of the time, this poses a significant challenge to the very raison d'être of international law.

Unfortunately, the 1951 Treaty of San Francisco has become a historical cause of disputes in East Asia, including the Dokdo/Takeshima issue. From a TWAIL perspective, the treaty can be perceived as a peace agreement where the interests and rights of weaker nations were deliberately sacrificed for the restructuring of an international order dominated by the great powers. TWAIL's approach, which adopts a historical and critical stance on the international legal issues faced, identifies the treaty's nature as one where the rights of the actual victim nations, considered weaker, were overlooked by powerful countries. This perspective provides an alternative view that transcends the limitations of analyzing individual clauses of the treaty based on legal positivism.

While TWAIL may not offer the best solution to the problems addressed by the 1951 Treaty of San Francisco, and applying TWAIL to the treaty involves complex and challenging issues, the necessity for a critical review of the treaty from a TWAIL perspective remains. This is essential not only for reflecting on the past that continues to affect the present and will impact the future, but also for ensuring that international law evolves in a way that genuinely reflects the principles of justice and equity.

The omission of the "war guilt clause" from the 1951 Treaty of San Francisco, and why John Foster Dulles abandoned the stance he had advocated during the 1919 Treaty of Versailles, raises essential questions. Furthermore, the extent to which the Cold War dynamics decisively influenced the 1951 Treaty of San Francisco underscores the need for a more detailed study. However, as long as the character of the 1951 Treaty of San Francisco is perceived as a product of "Hasty Peace and Nasty Greed," it will remain under the scrutiny of TWAIL. The 1951 Treaty of San Francisco continually prompts questions about international law's capacity to address the issues it raises. It is time to respond to these questions, and in doing so, a comparative analysis of the 1919 Treaty of Versailles and the 1951 Treaty of San Francisco, combined with the TWAIL approach, could be instrumental in finding satisfactory answers.

The absence of a "war guilt clause" in the 1951 Treaty of San Francisco reflects a significant shift in international relations and legal priorities post-World War II, particularly under the influence of Cold War politics. Unlike after World War I, where the victorious allies sought to penalize Germany, the approach in the 1951 Treaty of San Francisco aimed more at integrating Japan into a new international order as a strategic ally against the spread of communism. This strategic shift was largely driven by the United States, with Dulles playing a pivotal role, prioritizing geopolitical stability and the containment of Soviet influence over punitive measures.

Understanding these dynamics through the lens of TWAIL could offer deeper insights into how power dynamics, rather than principles of justice and accountability, often dictate the content and direction of peace treaties. TWAIL's critical perspective highlights how such treaties can fail to address the interests and rights of weaker nations, perpetuating inequalities and injustices in international relations. This approach not only challenges the conventional narratives surrounding these treaties but also pushes for a reevaluation of how international law can better serve the global community's broader interests, rather than merely reflecting the will of the dominant powers.

Japanese Historical Position and the San Francisco System

The Political Situation Surrounding the "Trans-war Phenomenon" in Postwar Japan and the San Francisco Peace Treaty

Tae-Jin Yi

Abstract The article analyzes the political transformation of Japan from the Meiji era through the postwar period, focusing on the enduring influence of emperor-centered nationalism and its impact on Japan's democratization after World War II. It traces how the imperial system shaped prewar fascism and continued to affect postwar politics, particularly during the Allied occupation and the drafting of the new constitution. The study highlights the limited nature of Japan's acceptance of war responsibility in the San Francisco Peace Treaty, noting that reparations and accountability were largely restricted to Allied Powers, with little acknowledgment of Asian victims. The treaty, negotiated under Prime Minister Yoshida Shigeru, prioritized economic recovery and security cooperation with the United States, leading to the establishment of American military bases and the U.S.–Japan Security Pact. The article critiques the persistence of imperialist and conservative attitudes among Japanese leaders, which complicated reconciliation with neighboring Asian countries. It also discusses the internal and external debates over the treaty, the challenges of true democratization, and the legacy of unresolved historical issues in East Asia. Ultimately, the article argues that the San Francisco system institutionalized a new Pacific order centered on U.S. strategic interests, leaving many wartime legacies unaddressed.

Keywords Allied Powers · Cold War · Democracy · Emperor · Japan · Liberal Party · Peace Treaty · San Francisco · SCAP · Yoshida

T.-J. Yi (✉)
Department of History, Seoul National University, Seoul, Korea (Republic of)
e-mail: tjyi@snu.ac.kr

Y.-H. Kim et al. (eds.), *Beyond the San Francisco System*,
https://doi.org/10.1007/978-981-95-3328-2_7

1 Preface

At the 2019 Seoul Conference, I presented my research on the obstruction of South Korean representatives from attending the September 1951 San Francisco Peace Treaty with Japan. While it was generally believed to be the will of the U.S. government, an analysis of the "Dulles Document" revealed that it was the United Kingdom. Dulles was sent to the Far East by President Truman as an advisor to the U.S. Secretary of State and met with officials from South Korea and Japan. Dulles took it for granted from the outset that the Korean representative would attend the conference. Dulles even made such a statement five times on formal occasions. Per contra the U.K. government opposed this from the beginning considering the relationship with the People's Republic of China.

The U.K., having expended much of its power in World War II, sought to leverage the economic networks established in Southeast Asia and China during its colonial era to restore its postwar economic strength. From the adoption of the "Atlantic Charter" in 1941, Prime Minister Churchill clashed with President Franklin Roosevelt's desire to eliminate all colonies in the postwar period. In talks with Dulles, the U.K. officials were firm on the opinion that it was beneficial for the Allies to maintain some ties with Communist China as a means of checking Soviet strength within the communist camp.

Dulles asserted that South Korea's position on the front lines in the Korean War against communism alone justified its inclusion in the peace treaty conference. However, this situation changed in the lead-up to the July 1951 armistice talks. Starting from May, Dulles began to align with the views of the U.K., possibly due to the perceived urgency of reaching an amicable conclusion, particularly with Communist China becoming a party to the armistice talks as a combatant nation. After meeting with his U.K. counterpart, Dulles traveled to Japan, where Japanese Prime Minister Shigeru Yoshida strongly opposed South Korea's participation to the San Francisco Peace Treaty Conference. Yoshida argued that Japan's postwar economic recovery would be impossible if the issue of reparations to Koreans in Japan became a reality. Since then, Dulles remained silent on South Korea's participation.

While examining such landscapes of international relations, I recognized the need to examine Japan's internal affairs. I could not overlook the influence of the imperial consciousness of the emperor system ingrained in prewar Japanese bureaucrats on key figures at the Supreme Command of the Allied Powers (SCAP) in Tokyo, as revealed in Prime Minister Shigeru's remarks to Secretary of State Dulles, and the possible extended influence it may have had on the U.S. government in Washington. This awareness of the issue stemmed from my last six-year research on the development of "Tōyoshi (東洋史)" or "Oriental History" and "Tohōgaku(東方學)" or "Eastern Studies" in the Japanese Empire, projects I initiated in 2016.[1]

[1] I examined the formative process of the emperor-system fascism in the Meiji era in *The Development of "Oriental History" in the Japanese Empire and the Emperor-System Fascism* 『

Recently, I was introduced to Harvard professor Andrew Gordon's concept of the "interwar phenomenon," and it provided me with the confidence to write this article.[2]

2 The Political Landscapes of Prewar Imperial Japan and the Emperor-System Fascism

2.1 Establishment of the Emperor-Centered Nationalism During the Meiji Era (1868–1912)

The arrival of Perry's fleet in 1853 divided Japanese national opinion into proponents of the Tokugawa shogunate and advocates of restoring imperial rule. The supporters of restoration were primarily from the western domains that had lost to the eastern army under Tokugawa Ieyasu at the Battle of Sekigahara in 1600, focusing on Chōshū, Satsuma, and Tosa. In December 1867, they justified the overthrow of the Tokugawa shogunate through the "Great Proclamation of the Restoration of the Imperial Rule." The Boshin War, which began in January 1868, resulted in the defeat of the shogunate-supporting forces, paving the way for the Meiji era of monarchy. People from Chōshū, and Satsma became the core of the new government, and socially, the Westernization movement rapidly gained momentum.

Meanwhile, samurais from various regions who had supported the Tokugawa shogunate and lost the "Boshin War" came together in the 1870s to form the "Free Civil Right Movement," advocating for the establishment of a national assembly. Tosha moved to this movement since the Meiji govenment was siezed by the Chosu and Satsuma. In 1881, after defeating the British-style cabinet system proposed by Saga-ken councilor Ōkuma Shigenobu, a House of Councilors member, Itō Hirobumi was tasked by the emperor to establish the national constitution and traveled to Europe to gather data. During this period, he persuaded the emperor to commit to realizing the Free Civil Right Movement's demand for a national assembly within 10 years. This led to the establishment of the Liberal Party (1881), the Constitutional Progressive Party (1882), the Constitutional Enactment Party (1882), and so on. In 1885, Itō Hirobumi introduced a cabinet system and became the first prime minister. In 1889, he accomplished the long-standing task of enacting the "Constitution of the Empire of Japan." The Constitution aimed to establish a strong

일본제국의 '동양사' 개발과 천황제 파시즘』 (Social Criticism Academy, 2022), published as part of the collaborative research for the publication of the eight-volume *General Critique of Japanese Colonial History*; in Vol. 8 *Foreign Invasions and the Transformation of Eastern Classic Studies in the Japanese Empire*, 『일본제국의 대외침략과 동방학 변천』 (as above). I strongly felt the limitations of Taishō democracy and the government-patronized imperial historical science amid the development of imperial-metropolis fascism in the Shōwa era. I examined the lack of process of overcoming such criticism in the post-war period.

[2]Andrew Gordon, *History of Modern Japan: From the Tokugawa Era to 2001* on p. 636. A Modern History of Japan: From Tokugawa Times to the Present, Oxford University Press, 2002.

emperor-system state, with all power deriving from the emperor. It also declared that State Shinto, emphasizing the sanctity of a line of emperors unbroken for ages eternal, is not a religion, allowing it to reign supreme over all religions. The following year, the "the Imperial Edict on Education" was promulgated as the foundation for the education of subjects to perpetuate emperor-centered nationalism.

In 1890, the National Assembly was established as promised. However, the National Assembly was not a branch of the separation of the three powers but was convened by the emperor, the source of all power. In practice, its sole function was to annually review the government budget. Socially, it perpetuated the class system of *kazoku*, *shizoku*, and commoners, restricting the right to vote and be elected to the hereditary class. In the cabinet system, the prime minister was appointed by a small group of *genro* from Chōshū and Satsuma, who nominated candidates for the emperor's consideration. While political parties elected representatives, they operated outside the cabinet system. Although the Imperial Constitution had no provision for political parties, Chap. "A Case for the Modifiability of the San Francisco Peace Treaty: Examining the Varying Positions of the United States and Britain Over South Korean Participation", which specified the roles of "Minister of State and Privy Counselor," stipulates that the Minister of State is to assist the emperor (Article 55), and the Privy Counselor is to deliberate on state affairs following consultations with the emperor under the "Privy Counselor Control." As per these provisions, it became customary for the emperor to appoint a prime minister based on the recommendation of the Privy Counselor.

Under the guidance of Itō Hirobumi, emperor-centered nationalism aimed to exert dominance over neighboring countries. The Chōshū faction, led by Itō Hirobumi and Yamagata Aritomo, mainly comprised individuals from the Shoka Village School in Hagi, the center of Chōshū Domain. The teacher, Yoshida Shōin (1830–1859), a military scholar, was executed at 30 for advocating the overthrow of the Tokugawa shogunate. His disciples, who dominated the Meiji government's bureaucracy and military (land forces) from around 1890, established Shōin Shrine next to Shōka Village School. They published his writings and utilized the "Shōin spirit" as a guiding principle for the education of subjects.

In his 1854 book, *A Record of Imprisonment*, Yoshida Shōin outlined Japan's future as follows: to avoid becoming a colony of the Western powers, Japan should quickly learn their technological civilization and occupy the surrounding countries before them. He proposed a plan of action that called for the occupying and developing Hokkaido, annexation of the Ryukyu, followed by the occupation of Taiwan, Chosŏn, Manchuria, Mongolia, and China. The ultimate goal was to multiply Japan's power, extending influence to the Pacific Ocean and reaching as far as Australia and California. Surprisingly, Shōin's concept of "occupying neighboring countries" in *A Record of Imprisonment* was systematically implemented in this order by his disciples and followers.

The execution of the "occupying neighboring countries" required a military build-up. Yamagata Aritomo, a prominent military authority, successfully established a national army system and a division system capable of overseas deployment. This approach differed from the defensive national defense system of the late Tokugawa shogunate, which, under the guidance of French advisors, established Jintai or the defense bases in coastal areas. The Tokugawa shogunate, aspiring to be a maritime trading nation, had adopted a defensive national system.

The 1894 Sino-Japanese War marked a significant advancement in Japan's policy of "occupying neighboring countries" aimed at the continent. Despite Japan's victory in the war, U.S. intervention and the "Triple Intervention" prevented the Japanese empire from achieving its goals. Japan touted the war as one in which the "civilization" of the Japanese empire would rescue Chosŏn from the influence of the "barbaric" Qing dynasty. The empire planned to use the war to turn Chosŏn into a protectorate. However, Chosŏn's monarch, Gojong, resisted Japanese military pressure, and the Chosŏn legation in the United States requested intervention from President Cleveland based on the Treaty of Amity and Commerce between the United States and Korea in 1882. President Cleveland issued a warning to Itō Hirobumi's cabinet, creating a barrier that the Itō cabinet failed to overcome. Russia, France, and Germany compelled Japan to abandon the Liaodong Peninsula, acquired from the Qing empire as booty. At that time, Japan was bound by an "unequal treaty" with the Western powers, restricting its freedom to invade its neighbors' territories.

However, the Japanese empire persisted in its policy of "occupying neighboring countries." Over the following decade, Japan significantly increased its armaments and successfully shed the constraints of the "unequal treaties" in 1899. Through persuading President Theodore Roosevelt to align with them, Japan avoided repeating the mistakes made with President Cleveland. In the war with Russia that erupted in February 1904, Japan achieved its intended goals with the active cooperation of the U.S. president. This conflict resulted in the containment of Russian influence in the Far East and forced a "protectorate treaty" with wartime troops stationed in the Korean Empire or *Daehan Jeguk*. In June 1907, the Korean emperor dispatched three envoys to the International Peace Conference in Hague to inform the delegates of each country that he had never authorized a "protectorate treaty." However, they were unable to penetrate the diplomatic barriers erected by Japan.

The Korean emperor supported the Korean Independent Army (*Taehanŭigun*), which had gained ground in the Russian Maritime Province. The emperor observed that An Jung-geun, the leader of the commando unit formed by the army, shot Itō Hirobumi, the chairman of the Privy Counselor, to death at the Harbin railroad station. This incident lent credence to the "Korean annexation theory," which the Imperial Japanese military advocated in contrast to Itō Hirobumi's protectorate policy. In March 1910, following the conclusion of the trial of the commandos, Terauchi Masatake was appointed as the third resident general of Korea in May. In August of the same year, he forcibly "annexed" Korea to the Japanese Empire.

2.2 The Limits of "Democracy" and "International Cooperative Diplomacy" in the Taishō Era (1912–1926)

From the inception of the cabinet system in 1885 until Emperor Taishō's ascension to the throne in July 1912, the cabinet changed 15 times. Chōshū's cabinets totaled 8 (4 in Itō Hirobumi's cabinet and 2 each in Yamagata Aritomo's and Katsura Tarō's cabinets), while Satsuma's cabinets totaled 4 (2 each in Kuroda Kiyotaka's and

Matsukata Masayoshi's cabinets). The remaining one was Ōkuma Shigenobu's cabinet (June 30–November 8, 1898), representing the Saga clan. This period illustrates that the 44-year Meiji era was dominated by the two domain cliques of Chōshū and Satsuma. Notably, Ōkuma Shigenobu's cabinet is the only one labeled a "party cabinet." He referred to it as the "Constitutional Party Cabinet," aligning with the Constitutional Party he founded in September 1898. This did not necessarily imply that he assumed the role of prime minister as the leader of the parliamentary majority. As a non-mainstream figure, it was a means of expressing his critical awareness of the domain clique forces. To address this challenge, Itō Hirobumi, the founder of the Imperial Constitution, organized the Association of Friends of Constitutional Government in 1900 and formed the fourth cabinet the following year in 1901, leading to the "Association of Friends Cabinet." The emperor continued to appoint the candidate recommended by the Privy Counselor elders after discussion as the prime minister. The Meiji era cabinet was often characterized as a "beyond-party principle" because of its intended distance from political parties.[3] This situation persisted during the "Taishō Democracy Era."

After the death of Itō Hirobumi, the chairman of the Privy Counselor, on October 26, 1909, factions opposed to the Association of Friends of Constitutional Government, which he had organized, came together to establish the "Constitutional Nationalist Party" on March 14, 1910. This party emerged in response to the Association of Friends of Constitutional Government's perceived compromise with the domain clique forces. On December 21, 1912, Katsura's third cabinet was inaugurated as the first cabinet of the Taishō Era. At the suggestion of Yamagata Aritomo, Katsura's third cabinet aimed to increase the military expansion budget in preparation for the future "preemption" of Manchuria, Mongolia, and China. This move prompted the Constitutional Protection Movement, advocating for the overthrow of the clans, with leadership from Ozaki Yukio (1858–1954) of the Association of Friends of Constitutional Government and Inukai Tsuyoshi (1855–1932) of the Constitutionalist Nationalist Party.

Despite being a member of the Association of Friends of Constitutional Government, Ozaki was a liberal-leaning politician who championed party-centered politics. He and Inukai shared common ground at newspapers and magazines offices, as well as in political parties, developing a mutual determination to overcome domain clique politics. In particular, Ozaki aligned with Ōkuma Shigenobu's British-style cabinet system. He devoted his entire life to the constitutional movement, earning the titles of the "God of Constitutional Government" and the "Father of Parliamentary Politics." Inukai, as described subsequently, was sacrificed in the May 15, 1932 incident during his tenure as the cabinet's prime minister. The Constitution of the Empire of Japan does not contain any provision specifying a cabinet system of party politics. This absence might explain the challenges faced by the Constitutional Protection Movement.

[3] Yamada Eiko 山田央子, 1999, 『History of the Political Party During Meiji Period (明治政黨史)』, 創文社, pp. 194 ~ 195 [History of the Ming Dynasty Party].

In April 1914, Ōkuma Shigenobu's second cabinet was formed, representing an achievement of the "Constitutional Protection Movement." However, with the outbreak of World War in June of the same year, the movement's momentum inevitably subsided. The war presented an opportunity to expand the policy of "preempting neighboring countries," which had emerged a decade after the victory in the Russo-Japanese War. Chōshū elder Yamagata Aritomo capitalized on the wartime situation to recommend Chosŏn Governor Terauchi Masatake to the emperor, leading to the formation of Terauchi's cabinet in October 1916. Terauchi was a junior under Yamagata Aritomo in the Chōshū domain clique. The momentum of the Constitutional Protection Movement was unable to suppress the rising tide of emperor-system nationalism amidst World War I. However, the resources of the Privy Counselor elders, by this time, had dwindled considerably. As a result, Terauchi's cabinet was characterized as a "beyond-party principle," avoiding the pressure of the Constitutional Protection Movement.

In September 1918, Prime Minister Terauchi resigned due to rice riots, and Hara Takashi (1856–1921), a native of Morioka Domain in the Tōhoku region, was appointed as his successor. Hara Takashi was the first prime minister to be selected by political parties in the House of Representatives rather than by the Privy Counselor and presented to the emperor for appointment. By 1918, only three elders of the Privy Counselor remained: 80-year-old Yamagata Aritomo (died February 1922), 66-year-old Terauchi Masatake (died November 1919), and Saionji Kinmochi (1849–1940). Saionji came from an official family of Tokugawa shogunate and rarely showed factional colors. The weakening of the Privy Counselor allowed the Constitutional Protection Movement to realize its dream of party politics. Hara Takashi's political career was shaped through the Association of Friends of Constitutional Government. However, he was hailed as a "commoner chancellor" when he became prime minister, refusing to accept the service of attendance for his title of nobility from the imperial aristocracy kazoku. He was historically significant as the first party-nominated prime minister. He was attacked and killed at Tokyo Station by a young station attendant on November 4, 1921. This incident was linked to a complaint about the differential treatment the Empire of Japan received at the Washington Disarmament Conference. Hara Takashi stood for Taishō democracy, essentially demonstrating both the possibilities and limitations of liberal democracy.

In 1920, the League of Nations, proposed by U.S. President Woodrow Wilson, was established. The Empire of Japan became one of the four permanent members, elevating its international profile. However, the internal administration did not easily recover from the shock of Prime Minister Hara Takashi's assassination. Takahashi Korekiyo's cabinet (November 1921–June 1922) was formed from the Association of Friends of Constitutional Government. Subsequent cabinets, including those of Kato Tomosaburo (June 1922–August 1923), Yamamoto Gonnohyoe (September 1923–January 1924), and Kiyoura Keigo (January 1924–June 1924), were all labeled as "non-party cabinet." Under Kiyoura's cabinet, the Second Constitutional Protection Movement unfolded. Criticizing previous cabinets as privileged and unconstitutional cabinets, the three factions of the Constitutional Protection

Movement (Constitutional Association, Association of Friends of Constitutional Government, and Innovation Party) formed the Second Constitutional Advocacy Association. In the May 1924 general election, the Constitutional Advocacy Association secured a landslide victory, capturing 61% of the House of Representatives. Katō Takaaki's cabinet (June 1924–January 1926) was launched in June, marking the establishment of a true "party cabinet." However, the "regular constitutional way" came to an end on May 15, 1932, when naval officers murdered Inukai Kiyoshi, the prime minister of the cabinet, in the May 15th Incident. This incident marked the conclusion of an eight-year period since the establishment of a political party cabinet.

After the establishment of the League of Nations, Kato Takaaki's cabinet pursued "international cooperative diplomacy" in line with its status as a permanent member. Shidehara Kijuro was appointed foreign minister and promoted "the international cooperative diplomacy," including a policy of non-interference in the internal affairs of China, cooperation with the U.K. and the United States, and the restoration of diplomatic relations with the Soviet Union. He served as acting foreign minister on four occasions, including Wakatsuki Reijiro's first cabinet (January 1926–April 1927) and second cabinet (April–December 1931), as well as Hamaguchi Osachi's cabinet (July 1929–April 1931). His cooperative diplomacy earned him the nickname of "Shidehara Diplomacy." This diplomacy of international cooperation shared a similar fate to the end of the party cabinet.

2.3 "Imperial Way" Fascism in the Prewar Shōwa Era (1926–1945)

In December 1926, Emperor Shōwa was enthroned. The Meiji and Taishō emperors rarely revealed themselves to the public. This was the result of displaying the emperor's dignity. Emperor Meiji was even nicknamed the "Silent Emperor." By contrast, Emperor Shōwa often appeared before cheering crowds on a white horse in the plaza in front of the *Goko*, the imperial residence. There were numerous local patrols. Emperor Shōwa traveled to Europe in 1921 as a crown prince at the age of 20 (before he was crowned). The trip, which was associated with the Japanese empire becoming a permanent member of the League of Nations, received a great welcome from the royal families and governments of Europe. On his return, the crown prince stood before a crowd and waved, greatly impressed by the sight of the kings of European kingdoms standing on the second-floor verandas of buildings and waving to the citizens crowded in the square.[4] This unprecedented practice set the stage for the "direct politics" of the emperor after his ascension to the throne, paving the way for "Imperial Way"(皇道) fascism.

[4] Tae-Jin Yi, Volume 8, pp. 298–303.

Immediately after Emperor Shōwa's ascension, the government maintained a form of party politics. The first acting prime minister nominated was Tanaka Giichi (1864–1929), the first prime minister to be a reserve army captain from Chōshū Domain since Terauchi Masatake in the Taishō Era. His nomination as the cabinet prime minister was in the capacity of party leader. His cabinet, which lasted 805 days from April 1927 to July 1929, marked a return to domain-centered politics from party politics. Prime Minister Tanaka did not appoint a foreign minister but served the post himself. This was the end of "Shidehara Diplomacy." Subsequently, in Hamaguchi's cabinet and Wakatsuki's second cabinet, Shidehara was reinstated, but that was short-lived. Following the Manchurian Incident in September 1931, the Japanese empire distanced itself from the League of Nations, initiating the process of secession.

In April 1930, Prime Minister Hamaguchi Osachi (July 1929–April 1931) was seriously wounded in a right-wing sniper attack at Tokyo Station and died the following year. The prime minister was seen as a violator, undermining the emperor's supreme command. This act was considered radical partisan political misconduct. Wakatsuki Reiji's second cabinet followed, but the Kwantung Army's presence in Manchuria, regardless of the wishes of the central government at home, led to the Manchurian Incident. In December 1931, Inukai Tsuyoshi, president of the Association of Friends of Constitutional Government, became prime minister and formed a cabinet. Inukai was the spearhead of the Constitutional Protection Movement in the early 1910s. In the initial days of the new cabinet, in February 1932, the Blood Brotherhood's assassination of business leaders led to the declaration of Manchukuo under the leadership of the Manchukuo Kwantung Army. The central government had largely lost control of the military. In May of the same year, a group of young naval officers broke into the prime minister's residence and killed him (May 15th Incident).

In May 1932, Saito Makoto, a former naval captain, became prime minister and formed a new cabinet. Since then, the cabinet changed five times until Konoe Fumimaro's first cabinet launched in June 1937. All five cabinets were labeled "grand coalition cabinets" instead of being identified by the prime minister's party of origin. This marked the complete end of Taishō Democracy. It became common for an army or navy captain to be nominated prime minister. Konoe Fumimaro, a civilian nominated as prime minister, was an anomaly in this trend (June 1937–January 1939). He was a high-ranking *kazoku* and a vanguard of imperial metropolis that prioritized warring families as much as the military. His father, Konoe Atsumaro, was a leading proponent of Asiacentrism, envisioning an Asia dominated by the Japanese emperor.[5]

---

[5] Konoe Fumimaro was the 30th head of the Konoe family of the Five Regent Houses (Go-sekke: Fujiwara's main lineage and includes Konoe, Takatsukasa, Kujo, Ichijo, and Nijo) and the 12th oldest son of the crown prince of Emperor Koyozei (reigned: 1571–1617). Fumimaro became the heir to the family dukedom, a member of the noble council, and president of the Touadoubunka. He was a member of the study group in the House of Aristocrats and formed the Hwayokai, a social

Konoe Fumimaro actively implemented Emperor Shōwa's policy of foreign expansion. In his first cabinet, he led the "Great Unity Cabinet," which led to the opening of the Sino-Japanese War in July, the promulgation of the "National Mobilization Law" in April of the following year, and the announcement of the "Statement of Construction of a New Order in East Asia" in November. This envisaged an East Asian world order dominated by the Japanese emperor. In July 1940, he was again named prime minister and formed Konoe's second cabinet (July 1940–July 1941). In accordance with Emperor Shōwa's wishes, he issued a decree dissolving all political parties and formed the Imperial Rule Assistance Association as a national organization. In November of the same year, under the Imperial Rule Assistance Association, the Industrial Patriotic Council of Great Japan was formed, and all labor unions were disbanded. In March 1941, primary school was renamed "national school," and the "Maintenance of the Public Order Act" was revised in March.

During his second cabinet, Konoe Hiromaru pushed troops through the Northern French Indochinese Islands and formed a "triple alliance" with Germany and Italy. The re-entry of troops into French Indochina with the launch of the third cabinet in July 1941 marked the actual beginning of the Pacific War. Emperor Shōwa took on the appearance of a commander-in-chief of a war effort, issuing "imperial instructions" to specific fleet commanders. After all political parties were dissolved, instead of a prime minister who led the Imperial Rule Assistance Association, a national mobilization organization of all subjects, he served as the hand and feet of Emperor Shōwa's direct politics.

In October 1941, following Konoe's third cabinet, the cabinet of Army Chief Tojo Hideki (September 1941–July 1944) was launched. With the front expanding in all directions, the emperor needed an active-duty captain. Tojo Hideki, as prime minister, followed Emperor Shōwa's lead and made an amphibious raid in Peninsular Malaysia in December, followed shortly thereafter by an attack on Pearl Harbor in the U.S. state of Hawaii, launching the "Greater East Asia War" or Pacific War in earnest. On December 16, 1938, Konoe's first cabinet renamed the cabinet to *Kōain* (East Asia Development Board), as the Sino-Japanese War broke out, and worked to control the administration of the occupied territories. In November 1941, Tojo Hideki's cabinet changed the name of the *Kōain* to *Daitōashō* (Ministry of Greater East Asia) due to the expansion of the front, and he himself served as foreign minister, internal affairs minister, land minister, culture minister, etc. The cabinet's operating system was adapted for wartime, and the Pacific War began.

In 1853, Yoshida Shōin, a samurai of the Chōshū domain, wrote in *A Record of Imprisonment* that for the Japan Archipelagic State to avoid becoming a colony of the great powers of Europe and America, it must learn the advanced technological civilization of the West as early as possible and take over its peripheral countries before the great powers. They were to take Taiwan, Chosŏn, Manchuria, Mongolia,

---

and bargaining group, and served as vice chairman and chairman of the House of Aristocrats before becoming prime minister. He was a key player in the imperialist, or "imperial way" system.

and China, then head out to the Pacific Ocean to California, the rich land of the United States, and then on to Australia, which the British held only one-tenth of. Sixty-eight biographical books about the policy's founder, Yoshida Shōin, were published in the 77 years before the end of the war in August 1945. Of the 68 books, 57 were published in the Shōwa 20-year period, at a rate of 2.9 books per year. During the Pacific War period of 1941–1943, there were 9 to 10 books per year. Yoshida Shōin became the subject of urging soldiers to fight vigorously. One of the most popular of these books featured the following battle song. [Tae-Jin Yi, 2022, Volume 1, pp.317–318]:

Renounce individualism, disregard ego.
Our bodies are not our own; they belong to the emperor and our country.
Move with all your might, as far as your strength will take you.
This is the life of Shōinism and the path of the Japanese subjects.
If you don't embrace this principle, this spirit of being pro-Japanese while doing best in your job,
then the practice of Shinto will be incomplete.
Embrace Shōinism. And witness the revival of the original Japanese spirit.
-*Everydaylife of the Shōinism* (The Headquarters of the Shōinism Dissemination, 1942)-

3 The "Trans-war Phenomenon" in Postwar Japan

3.1 "End of War Protocol" Without Mentioning "Unconditional Surrender"

There are many existing studies on postwar Japanese democracy or a "peace system." Many scholars, including John Dower and Wada Haruki, discussed the problems of postwar Japan. I would like to conclude by surveying the historical trajectory of Japan from the Meiji period to the Shōwa period, during which the emperor-centered nationalism caused unprecedented wars in world history. My focus is on Japan's task of realizing liberal democracy that was thrown from the outside after the defeat and its political identity as a nation in the signing of the San Francisco Treaty, which marks the beginning of a "peace system". Let us begin with what Emperor Shōwa, who is said to be the reality of the Japanese Empire, looked like in the history of defeat.

In November 1943, the three leaders, Franklin Roosevelt, Winston Churchill, and Chiang Kai-shek, met in Cairo and decided to fight until Japan surrendered unconditionally. A year and a half later, in February 1945, when the three leaders met in Yalta to discuss the handling of the war with Germany, they pledged to cede the Japanese-held South Sakhalin and Chishima (Kuril Islands) to the Soviet Union. In July of the same year, the leaders of these countries met again in Potsdam. On July 26, Soviet General Secretary Stalin, British Prime Minister Clement Attlee, and U.S. President Harry S. Truman issued the Potsdam Declaration in the name of the United States, the U.K., and China, with the consent of China's Chiang Kai-shek. It recommended the unconditional surrender of Japan's armed forces and the postwar handling policy of Japan. The Soviet Union became a signatory to this declaration with the proclamation of war against Japan.[6]

The situation of the Pacific War turned on April 1, 1945, when U.S. forces landed on Okinawa, significantly narrowing the front lines. However, the island was not completely captured until June 23. In the mainland of the Japanese Empire, the theory of desperate resistance emerged, and the construction of a tunnel in the mountains of Nagano as a resistance headquarters began. The U.S. government, fearing the loss of both sides due to a protracted war on the Japanese mainland, proceeded to drop the atomic bombs on Hiroshima on August 6 and Nagasaki on August 9. Emperor Shōwa, who had been commanding the front hitherto, recorded an "End of War Declaration" on August 14 and broadcast it the next day. Commonly known as the "Jewel Voice Broadcast," it was named the "Protocol of the End of the Great East Asian War" (hereafter, the "End of War Protocol").

Emperor Shōwa's "End of War Protocol" reads, "I have directed the Imperial Government to notify of its acceptance of the joint declaration made by the four nations of the United States, Great Britain, China, and the Soviet Union. To promote the well-being of the subjects of the empire and to share in the enjoyment of the common good of all the people is an example set by our imperial ancestors, and I have not held back from it. In fact, the reason for the early declaration of war against the United States and Great Britain was based on imperial pride and a desire for stability in the East, and it was not my intention to reject the sovereignty of other countries and invade their territories." The sentences consistently avoid taking responsibility for the war.

Even for the reason of declaring the end of war, he stated, "The enemy has repeatedly killed innocent people by using new and cruel bombs, the effects of which are truly incalculable, and if we continue to engage, it will lead not only to the destruction of our people but also to the destruction of human civilization. In this case, what can I do to preserve the hundreds of millions of young people and apologize to the spirits of our imperial ancestors? It is for this reason that I have pushed the Imperial Government to respond to the Joint Declaration." He unilaterally attributed the reason for ending the war to the dropping of the atomic bombs by the United States.

As it has already been pointed out, the phrase "unconditional surrender" does not appear in Emperor Shōwa's "End of War Protocol." If it was to be looked for notwithstanding, "unconditional surrender" was indirectly indicated by the Emperor's instructions to comply with the "joint declaration" of the Potsdam Conference. The Potsdam Declaration stipulated in Article 13 the "unconditional surrender of the armed forces of Japan" and directed that it be accepted. Even so, the "End of War Protocol" is a serious distortion of the history of war accountability. For example, these were problematic expressions that the Japanese Emperor's decades-long

[6]The Potsdam Declaration stipulated (1) the elimination of militarists (Article 6), (2) the occupation of Japan by the Allies (Article 7), (3) the territory of Japan limited to Honshu, Hokkaido, Kyushu, and Shikoku (Article 8), and (4) the unconditional surrender of Japan's armed forces (Article 13).

aggression to build the (Great) East Asia was "to share in the enjoyment of the common good of all people" and "it was not my intention to reject the sovereignty of other countries and invade their territories." Isn't this a deception that should be condemned in the name of humanity?

What was the situation when the Emperor's "End of the War Protocol" was delivered to the people of the Empire? The issue of the Asahi Shimbun on August 15, 1945, carried the following subheadings under the large headline "The Great Announcement of the End of the War Spreads Through the World": "The Emperor's Great Decision on the Havoc of the New Bomb," "The Empire Accepts the Declaration of the Four Powers," and "Fear Brings Peace for a Long Life." It also included a photo of the subjects kneeling on the street to listen to the "Jewel Voice Broadcast." What is important is the comment, "There was neither a mentioning of the 'end of the war' nor 'defeat.'" Rather than a reference to an error or a puzzlement in the "End of War Protocol," it could have been read as a statement that the Emperor had not surrendered. The "trans-war phenomenon" in postwar Japan is a testament to this.

3.2 *Passivity of the "Emperor's Humanity Declaration"*

On January 1, 1946, the "Emperor's Humanity Declaration" was issued at the request of the General Headquarters (GHQ) of the Allied Powers. Even if Emperor Shōwa rode by on foot, rather than on a white horse, in front of the crowd with this declaration, it would not change the perception that the emperor was the ruler of the country. The Japanese people's worship of emperors, instilled in them by the "Imperial Constitution" of 1889 and the "Education Code" of 1890, was not something that could be changed overnight.

In accepting the Potsdam Declaration, the Japanese government demanded "national polity protection" or the condition that no changes be made to the constitutional status of the Emperor. This consciousness did not easily disappear in the postwar political reorganization either, and the "abolition of the emperor system" was eventually accomplished passively by the Allies. "Strengthening the revival of democratic tendencies" and "establishing respect for fundamental human rights" (Clause 10 above) and "establishing responsible governments with peaceful tendencies" (Clause 12) were defined in the Potsdam Declaration. In the realization of these points, the Japanese government remained passive until the end.

In accordance with the "Declaration of End of War," the surrender document was signed on September 2 of the same year aboard the U.S. battleship Missouri in Tokyo Bay by Imperial Japanese Foreign Minister Mamoru Shigemitsu and Chief of Staff Yoshijirō Umezu. Shigemitsu, the foreign minister, signed the document "by and in the name of His Imperial Majesty the Emperor and the Government of Japan," and Umezu, the chief of staff, signed it "by and in the name of the Imperial General Headquarters of Japan." The document reads, "Declaring the unconditional surrender of all the armed forces of the Japanese Empire and the allies of all the armed forces under the control of the Japanese Empire." It was signed by Douglas MacArthur, the Supreme Commander of the Allied Forces, and nine other representatives of each country to signify their acceptance. However, in Article 1, the document states that "All commanders of the Japanese armed forces, regardless of where they are currently stationed or where they are located, unconditionally surrender to the Allies and to military organizations cooperating with the Allies." Technically, this was an "unconditional surrender" of the Japanese military organization and cannot be seen as a surrender of the Japanese Empire. Article 4 reads, "The authority of the Cabinet of Japan and of the Japanese Emperor to govern the country shall be subject to the control and limitation of the Supreme Commander for the Allied Powers (SCAP) only as may be deemed suitable for the purpose of carrying into effect this treaty of surrender." Amid the taboo on the sanctity of the emperor, the question was whether the content of the future "Constitution of the Japanese Nation" could be prepared with the voluntary will to realize liberal democracy to some extent.

In the case of Germany, there was Konrad Adenauer, the former mayor of Köln, who opposed Nazism from 1933. He was imprisoned under the Nazi regime and only released in 1944, where he was a leading figure in the creation of the Christian Democratic Union and became the first chancellor of the postwar Federal Republic of Germany, a key figure in the construction of a liberal Germany. The only history of liberalism advocated in postwar Japan is the Constitution Protection Movement of the 1910s and 1920s. However, Tsuyoshi Inukai and Yukio Ozaki, who led this history, did not exist in the postwar period. Inukai was murdered by militaristic young officers on May 15, 1932, while serving as prime minister, and Ozaki was 87 years old at the time of defeat in 1945. Ozaki was elected to the House of Representatives as many as 25 times between 1889 and 1952 and held the honorary position for 63 years. In his old age, he was losing followers under the shackles of being a "god of constitutional government." In the absence of an impetus to abolish the emperor system that had regulated the entire political structure, as in postwar Japan, the Emperor's "Humanity Declaration" could never mean the true realization of liberal democracy. Article 1 of the Constitution of Japan, which was promulgated in November 1946 after the Emperor's "Humanity Declaration," stipulates, "The Emperor shall be the symbol of the State and of the unity of the People, deriving his position from the will of the people with whom resides sovereign power." It indicates that the Emperor remains the subject of sovereignty even in postwar Japan.

As a historian of a neighboring country, it is both strange and surprising to look at the list of Japanese cabinets or prime ministers and see that the sequence of cabinets that began in December 1885 (Meiji 18) remained unchanged after the war. Naruhiko Higashikuni, who was sworn in on August 17 in the aftermath of the "End of War Protocol," is listed as the 30th prime minister and the 43rd head of cabinet. It followed the 29th cabinet of Kantarō Suzuki, who had replaced the 29th prime minister just before the war. The "Shōwa era" was also continued to be used, increasing the number of years each year. Wasn't it the reality of postwar Japan, where even if the emperor system may have been removed outwardly, the worship of the emperor was still deeply embedded in their consciousness?

3.3 Establishment of the Supreme Command of the Allied Powers (SCAP) and the "Constitution of Japan"

The Allies, led by the United States, managed Japan for 6 years and 6 months, from August 14, 1945, to April 27, 1952. The Allied governing structure was organized so that the Far Eastern Commission (FEC) set basic policy, and under it was the U.S. government, which established the SCAP and its GHQ for command leadership. The FEC was headquartered in Washington, D.C., chaired by the United States and comprised 11 war-participating countries. In accordance with the basic policy set by the FEC, the U.S. government established the SCAP and GHQ in Tokyo to direct or recommend FEC policy to the Japanese government and to implement various measures against the Japanese people after the war. The four nations at the center of the Alliance—the United States, the U.K., China, and the Soviet Union—separately formed the Allied Council for Japan as an advisory body to the SCAP and GHQ, headquartered in Tokyo. The U.S. chaired this council as well. It was a postwar Japanese administration centered on the United States.

What was the state of internal affairs management on the Japanese side before and after the defeat? From the Pacific War to defeat, there were three successive cabinets: the 40th Prime Minister Hideki Tojo's cabinet (October 18, 1941, to July 22, 1944; 1009 days), the 41st Prime Minister Kuniaki Koiso's cabinet (July 22, 1944, to April 7, 1945; 260 days), and the 42nd Prime Minister Kantarō Suzuki's cabinet (April 7, 1945, to August 17, 1945; 133 days). Every prime minister has been an army or navy captain. With Emperor Shōwa's "Jewel Voice" Broadcast on August 15, 1945, the cabinet of Imperial Prime Minister Kantarō Suzuki concluded. It was on August 17 that the emperor named his successor, Naruhiko Higashikuni, an imperial family member with the status of an army commander, as prime minister. There was a two-day gap in the nomination of Japan's next prime minister.

On August 30, Supreme Commander MacArthur arrived in Tokyo. He entered through the Atsugi Naval Air Station. It was 13 days after the inauguration of the Naruhiko Higashikuni cabinet. The signing of the "Surrender Document" took place aboard the battleship Missouri in Tokyo Bay on September 2. On the same day, MacArthur, the U.S. Army Pacific Supreme Command, was sworn in as the SCAP and given full authority to administer the occupation under the Potsdam Declaration. This was followed by the establishment of the SCAP's GHQ in Tokyo on October 2. Within the GHQ was the Civil Affairs Bureau, which led Japan's democratization efforts. On October 4, the Higashikuni cabinet resigned after less than 2 months in office, citing the so-called "Order on Liberty" (English version) from GHQ as a major milestone, and on October 9, Kijūrō Shidehara was appointed as the 44th prime minister and formed the 31st cabinet.

The newly appointed Kijūrō Shidehara was a foreign minister who had practiced "international cooperation diplomacy" in the first decade of the Shōwa Era. Considering the plethora of diplomatic matters coming down from the GHQ in the immediate aftermath of the defeat, he was the best person for the job. The Shidehara cabinet lasted only 226 days, from its inauguration on October 24 when the United

Nations was established, to the start of the International Military Tribunal for the Far East on May 3 of the following year. The enactment of the "Constitution of the Japan" was the crowning achievement of the cabinet, and the general election under the new constitution resulted in the resignation of the Shidehara cabinet and the formation of the first Shigeru Yoshida cabinet.

On the evening of October 9, when the Shidehara cabinet was sworn in, Supreme Commander MacArthur met with Fumimaro Konoe, a minister without a portfolio in the former Higashikuni cabinet, to explain the need for constitutional revision. Konoe was a powerful politician of the high-ranking noble or *kazoku* who had served as prime minister thrice before the end of the war, and in the Higashikuni cabinet, he held the position of the Lord Keeper of the Privy Seal for the imperial office. Supreme Commander MacArthur first approached him because the most important issue in the constitutional revision was how to deal with Article 1, Section 1 of the Imperial Constitution, which stated that "The Empire of Japan shall be ruled by the Emperor for ever and ever." In other words, the measure was conscious of the importance of imperial approval. In response, Konoe, along with former Kyoto Imperial University professor Sōichi Sasaki,[7] launched an investigation into the constitutional amendment on the issue of government-patronizing. However, their work came out in two pieces: "Outline of Possible Results of the Examination on the Revision of the Imperial Constitution" on November 22, under the name of Fumimaro Konoe, and "Necessity of Revising the Imperial Constitution (Sasaki Constitution Draft)" on November 24. Two of the proposals had undergone the Emperor's reply process, but neither was acceptable to the GHQ. Sasaki, a constitutionalist, was known as a follower of Taishō Democracy's "constitutionalism," but he did not touch Articles 1–4 of the Imperial Constitution on the Emperor. Konoe's proposal was a revision within the framework of the constitution of the Meiji Empire. The 100-article amendment focused on the right to life, the establishment of a constitutional court, and local governance.

Meanwhile, 2 days later, on October 11, MacArthur met with Kijūrō Shidehara, the new Prime Minister of Japan, and mentioned the "liberalization of the constitution." On October 13, the Cabinet formally launched a constitutional research study as a government, in opposition to the Konoe and Sasaki's research projects on constitutional revision. On October 26, the Committee to Investigate Constitutional Issues (also known as the Matsumoto Committee) was organized with Secretary of State Jōji Matsumoto[8] as its head. On February 8, 1946, the Shidehara Cabinet

[7] Graduated from the Law School of Kyoto Imperial University in 1903; assistant professor at the university in 1906 and professor in 1913; conducted administrative law lectures; in charge of constitutional law since 1927; served as dean of the Law School twice since 1921. With a constitutional theory that combined strict literary interpretation with constitutionalism, he served as the theoretical leader of the Taishō Democracy alongside Minobe of the Tokyo Imperial University and established the Kyoto school in constitutional study. Resigned in 1933 in protest of the Takigawa Incident, an incident of suppression of thought. He worked to advocate for university autonomy, including serving as the center of a protest movement by the Law School faculty.

[8] After graduating from the Law School of Tokyo Imperial University, he became a counselor at the Ministry of Agriculture and Commerce, then returned to the university in 1903 as an assistant

submitted the "Matsumoto Proposal" prepared by this committee to the GHQ. However, this proposal also recognized the emperor's right to rule, so the GHQ rejected it. Instead, the GHQ drafted a "GHQ Constitution Draft" and presented it to the Shidehara cabinet on February 13. Based on this draft, the Shidehara cabinet prepared a "Constitutional Amendment Bill" and presented it following approval from Supreme Commander MacArthur. The fact that multiple proposals to amend the Meiji Empire Constitution were rejected by the GHQ means that the abolition of the emperor system was not possible within the Japanese political system itself.

3.4 *The Light and Shade of the Liberal Democratic Party, the First Postwar Conservative Party*

On April 10, 1946, the 22nd general election to the House of Representatives was held under the "New Election Act." Since the defeat, the election marked the first establishment of a new government through the parliamentary system. Party politics, which had disappeared after Taishō Democracy waned in the early 1930s, returned, with the head of the ruling party becoming the prime minister. It was also the first time women's suffrage was allowed, making it the first universal election with both men and women as voters. The Japan Cooperative Party (Dec. 1945, Party leader: Takeo Miki), Japan Progressive Party (formerly Democratic Justice Party, Nov. 1945, Machida Chūji), Liberal Party of Japan (Nov. 1945, Ichirō Hatoyama, Shigeru Yoshida), Japan Socialist Party (formerly Proletarian Party, Nov. 1945, Tetsu Katayama), and four other parties participated in the general election, and the Liberal Party became the majority party. However, the subsequent parties repeatedly reorganized themselves because there was no majority party.

Prime Minister Kijūrō Shidehara, who oversaw the general election, joined the Japan Progressive Party seemingly trying to keep the cabinet together. In response, all other political parties rebelled, initiating a movement to unseat the cabinet, and there was so much opposition within the cabinet as well that the entirety of the Shidehara Cabinet resigned on May 22, 1946. Thus, Ichirō Hatoyama, the leader of the majority Liberal Party (1845–48), prepared to form a new cabinet, but GHQ ordered him to be "purged from public office" for being a "militarist who

---

professor. He studied abroad in Europe from 1906–1909 and returned to Japan in 1910 and became a professor at Tokyo Imperial University. He also became a director of the Manchurian Railway Company in 1919, became its vice president, and in 1923, became the Minister of the Legal Affairs Bureau in the second Yamamoto cabinet. He was elected to the House of Peers by the Emperor in January 1924 and appointed as a member to the Imperial Academy. He served as president of Kansai University until 1928; a minister of commerce and trade in the Saitō cabinet in 1934; and drafted the constitution in 1945 in the Shidehara cabinet as minister of state. He was expelled from public office in 1946 for holding the office for inspecting Mantetsu (South Manchuria Railway).

collaborated with the rise of the military" with the cabinet organization ahead.[9] Shigeru Yoshida, the second in seniority within the Liberal Democratic Party (1948–50), became prime minister, and the First Yoshida Cabinet was sworn in on May 22, 1946. Yoshida was a foreign minister in the previous Shidehara Cabinet who had formed the Liberal Party of Japan with Hatoyama in preparation for the general election.

The First Shigeru Yoshida Cabinet existed for 368 days until May 22, 1947, and proceeded to revise the "Constitution of the Empire of Japan." In October 1946, the House of Representatives agreed to a House of Peers amendment to the Constitutional Amendment Bill, and the "Constitution of Japan" was established. Thus, "the Empire of Japan" eventually became "Japan." The House of Peers is disbanded at the end of this mission and replaced by the House of Councilors. The First Yoshida Cabinet, which began with a new constitution under GHQ's guidance, was not in the right position to end the imperial era on its own. Yoshida was, as stated by himself, a man imbued with an emperor-first mentality. And no politician or bureaucrat at the time was immune to the emperor system or militarism, as when Ichirō Hatoyama, the first president of the Liberal Party, was suddenly "expelled from office." In 1941, more than 380 politicians, who had become members of the Imperial Rule Assistance Association by the Third Fumimaro Konoe Cabinet, were targeted for the "purge from public office."

Ichirō Hatoyama (1883–1959) graduated from the Law School of Tokyo Imperial University in 1907 and entered politics in 1915, when he was elected to the House of Representatives after being recognized officially by the Association of Friends of Constitutional Government. His entry into politics during the Taisho Democracy was not without liberal orientation. However, in 1927, he served as cabinet secretary in the Tanaka Giichi Cabinet, who was far from the Democracy trend. Meanwhile, in 1931, he was appointed as the minister of culture and education when Tsuyoshi Inukai, who was at the center of the Constitution Protection Movement, formed a cabinet. After the Inukai Cabinet fell apart in the wake of the May 15 Incident and the end of the Taishō Democracy, he again became the minister of culture and education in the Saitō Makoto Cabinet, which was launched in 1932. Rather than leading the Constitution Protection Movement like Inukai, he played to the political status quo.

In 1939, Hatoyama belonged to the orthodox faction when the Association of Friends split in response to the rise of the military power in politics. In July 1940, the Second Fumimaro Konoe Cabinet was launched, dissolving all political parties

---

[9] In the later years of the Second Wakatsuki Cabinet (Apr.–Dec. 1931), Teijirō Yamamoto, Kaku Mori, and others, along with army chiefs such as Tetsuzan Nagata, Hitoshi Imamura, and Hideki Tojo, discussed overthrowing the cabinet, an extremely problematic behavior for parliamentarians. The proposal was reportedly rejected by the army as well. (Kiyotada Tsutsui,《昭和前期の政黨政治》, 2012, Chikuma Shinsyo 237). Other reasons cited for the expulsion included the statement that Adolf Hitler's administrative policies in Nazi Germany were successful when Wakatsuki was president of the Association of Friends prewar and criticizing the U.S. military's atomic bombing after the war.

in the name of national unity and forming a single party called the Imperial Rule Assistance Association. On April 30, 1942, in the 21st general election of the House of Representatives, the "Assistance Political System Council" was formed and nominated 466 candidates (same number as the quota), and 381 were elected, representing 81.8% of all seats. At this time, Hatoyama was not nominated by the council, so he ran as an "unnominated" candidate and won. However, the "unnominated" never meant being opposed to the totalitarianism of the Assistance Council. He was close to Fumimaro Konoe, who was named prime minister thrice in 1937, 1940, and 1941. He was never a champion of liberal democracy.

In October 1941 the army chief Hideki Tojo, representing the armed forces, was nominated as the prime minister. A three-time cabinet member, Konoe's family was one of the five regent houses that had been able to ascend to the highest levels of government, including regent, chief advisor, and grand minister of state, since the Kamakura Era[10] and was at the top of the *Kazoku* clan during the Meiji Era. His father, Atsumaro Konoe, was a leading advocate of Asianism. The gathering of bureaucrats like Hatoyama around Konoe was motivated by dissatisfaction with the fact that the cabinet had been handed over to the military power, not by any sense of criticism of the emperor system's fascistization. If it is true that Hatoyama was guilty of "the problem of interference with the prerogative of supreme command" (May 7, 1946), in which he proposed to overthrow the civilian cabinet to the military power before the war, as GHQ pointed out, it would surely be an unacceptable duplicity for a politician.

Hideki Tojo, who became the prime minister as an active-duty army captain, was the executor of the expanding front of the "Great East Asian War" spearheaded by Emperor Showa. In 1943, Hatoyama could no longer stay in politics, criticized the Tojo Cabinet, and retreated to the villa of a businessman (石橋正二郎) in the resort town Kawaizawa (耕井澤). If GHQ's earlier assumption on his proposal to the military power to form the cabinet is true, this escape was a bit of a cop-out. On August 15, 1945, Hatoyama broke down in tears as he listened to the "Jewel Voice Broadcast" at the villa and said, "The days of the military are over. This is our time" (*Autobiography*), and he left the cabin at dawn the next day and headed for Tokyo.

In October 1945, Ichirō Hatoyama formed the Liberal Party of Japan with his comrades Ichirō Kōno and Hitoshi Ashida, both from the orthodox faction of the former Association of Friends of Constitutional Government, and Bukichi Miki of the former Constitutional Democratic Justice Party. The tendencies of "comrades" Hatoyama met at his return to Tokyo did not differ too much from his.

Ichirō Kōno (1898–1965) entered politics in 1931 as secretary to the Minister of Agriculture and Forestry in the Inukai Cabinet and ran for and won the 18th House of Representatives general election the following year. After being elected, he joined the Association of Friends of Constitutional Government and got to know Hatoyama. Like Hatoyama, he was also elected as an "unnominated" in the 1942 Imperial Rule

[10]Yi, Tae-Jin, *Foreign Invasions and the Transformation of Eastern Classic Studies in the Japanese Empire*, Academy of Social Criticism, 2022. P. 155. The five regent houses (go-sekke) are Konoe, Takatsukasa, Gujo, Ichijo, and Nijo.

Assistance Association member election. Hitoshi Ashida (1887–1959) was a former diplomat who entered politics and served as a conduit to the Ministry of Foreign Affairs by joining the Association of Friends of Constitutional Government. Although he served as a "liberal" in the parliament during the rise of militarism, like Hatoyama, he showed no signs of a fighter. Liberal politicians of this era were liberals in the limited sense of opposing military rule, not in the sense of fundamental opposition to the emperor system.

Bukichi Miki (1884–1956) of the Constitutional Democratic Justice Party was Hatoyama's sworn friend and is credited the most with preventing the rise of the Japan Socialist Party in 1955, leading to a coalition of Liberal and Democratic parties. In June 1922, he entered politics when he was elected to the Tokyo Metropolitan Assembly, where he campaigned to clean up the municipal administration of the city. During this time, Hatoyama was on the opposite side of the political spectrum when it came to confronting the Association of Friends of Constitutional Government over the cleanup movement. After winning the election to the House of Representatives in 1924, Bukichi Miki was elected secretary-general of the Constituent Assembly at the age of 39. Spearheading the Constituent Assembly, he led the party to become the primary opposition in the year's general election in May. In June, the three factions of the constitution protection were formed (the Constituent Assembly, Association of Friends, and Innovation Club) and the First Takaaki Katō Cabinet was inaugurated. Miki left politics in 1928 after being involved in the "Suspicion around the Keisei Electric Railway" and became president of the Hoji Shimbun in 1939 after completing his sentence. In 1942, he ran as an "unnominated" candidate in the Imperial Rule Assistance Association election and won, returning to politics; the "unnomination" in the Imperial Rule Assistance Association election is a common element of Hatoyama Ichiro's "comrades" after the defeat in the war.

The Liberal Party of Japan, centered around Hatoyama, was the first postwar conservative party to emerge from the ranks of conservative politicians or businessmen. The party claimed to overthrow militarism, establish a democratically accountable political system, rebuild a free economy, ensure freedom of thought and scholarship, and promote culture as its platform, with the code of implementing the Potsdam Declaration, eradicating militaristic elements, and promoting free economic activity. It is clear that the Liberal Party is a party that is seeking a liberal democratic path in postwar Japan. However, as we have seen, in postwar Japan, conservative politicians advocating liberalism were limited in their ability to overturn the constitution of the emperor system on their own. True liberals would have stood up to the Taishō Democracy trend when it was being overthrown by young officers of the imperial metropolis school. Liberalism was not tolerated by the holders of the imperial absolutism spirit thought as it was too seen as a conduit for socialist ideas. They did not challenge this line of thinking. When the Third Konoe Cabinet dissolved all political parties in favor of the Emperor's totalitarian system and held the Imperial Rule Assistance as a collective association of subjects to select members of parliament, they could not deny this system and participated as the "unnominated." Were they afraid of having it pointed out to them that they were not the Emperor's subjects?

Hatoyama's discourse was published in the September 15, 1945 edition of the Asahi Shimbun. It stated that dropping the atomic bomb was a war crime in violation of international law. In all likelihood, this was in response to the Emperor's reference to the U.S. military's atomic bomb as "the enemy's new and cruel bombs" in the "End of War Protocol." The GHQ ordered Asahi Shimbun to suspend publication for 48 hours and blocked the way with a "public office purge decree" when Hatoyama won the first cabinet organization as the president of the ruling party in the general election the following year. (May 7, 1946) Hatoyama then named Shigeru Yoshida as his successor, and the First Yoshida Cabinet was formed on May 22.

This disruptive situation in the run-up to the inauguration of the first cabinet under the New Constitution was due to the limitations of human resources in the postwar political situation. The postwar political situation began in 1941 with the dissolution of the Imperial Rule Assistance Association, which was created as a mega-state organization after dissolving all political parties. More than 400 Assistance Association candidates were nominated to the people, and 381 were elected, making the Assistance Association mainstream. However, these nominees became prime targets for postwar "purges from public service." Thus, the "unnominated" became central figures in the resurgence party. It was similar to starting over from scratch with only a partial cut of the prewar base. In this regard, calling this the "trans-war phenomenon" is not incorrect.

4 The Yoshida Cabinet and the San Francisco Peace Treaty

4.1 Shigeru Yoshida's Emperor-Centrism

From the inauguration of the First Yoshida Cabinet under the New Constitution in May 1946 until the San Francisco Peace Treaty in September 1951, the cabinet changed five times: from Tetsu Katayama of the Japan Socialist Party from May 1947 and Hitoshi Ashida Cabinet (1887–1959) of the Democratic Party from March 1948 to the Second Yoshida Cabinet from October 1948, etc. The postwar cabinets changed parties composing the cabinet after their inauguration. The First Yoshida Cabinet switched from the Liberal Party to a coalition with the Progressive Party, the Katayama Cabinet switched from the Socialist Party to a Coalition of Social, Democratic, and National Cooperative Parties, and the Ashida Cabinet switched from the Democratic Party to a coalition of Democratic, Social, and National Cooperative Parties. The Second Yoshida Cabinet even changed its name from the Progressive Party to the Democratic Liberal Party.

The Socialist Party of Prime Minister Tetsu Katayama (1887–1978) was the first progressive party. The following Liberal Party of Japan under Prime Minister

Ashida was a conservative party formed in 1947 around the Japan Progressive Party. The two cabinets were short-lived, lasting only 292 days and 220 days, respectively, for a total of 2 years and 5 months. The Democratic Liberal Party of the Second Yoshida Cabinet was a coalition of the Comrade Club, the Democratic Club, and the opposition Liberal Party of Japan, made up of former Democratic Party members who opposed and broke away from the 1948 coalition government of the Japan Socialist Party. The San Francisco Peace Treaty was all done in the Second and Third Yoshida Cabinets. Yoshida was a mainstay of postwar Japanese politics, serving as prime minister for a whopping 6 years (2415 days) on three separate occasions. It was Yoshida who created the San Francisco system. The frequent changes in the parties that make up the cabinet indicate how weak the foundations of party politics were in the postwar period. The fact that Yoshida formed the cabinet as prime minister on three separate occasions suggests that postwar Japanese politics had virtually one orientation. Then, who was Shigeru Yoshida as an individual?

Shigeru Yoshida (1878–1967) was a diplomat-turned-politician. He was a big name politician who served as the Minister of Agriculture one time, the Minister of Foreign Affairs five times, and the Prime Minister of the cabinet five times. He also served as Minister of the First and Second Restoration Ministries, which reorganized the Army and Navy after the war. He was also a member of the House of Representatives (seventh term) and a member of the House of Peers, which qualifies him as a parliamentary politician.

He was born in 1878 in Kochi Prefecture, the fifth son of Tsuna Takeuchi. His father, Takeuchi, spent a long time in prison for participating in anti-government conspiracies as a revenge for the death of Daisuke Itagaki, a leading liberal civil rights activist of the time. His son, Shigeru Yoshida, became his adopted son in 1881 after being assisted by his father's close friend, Yoshida Kenzo, who was a wealthy merchant. Yoshida dropped out of Keio Gijuku and entered Gakushuin in 1897, graduating 4 years later. Gakushuin was the educational institution for children of the *Kazoku* clan, and at this time, it established a "university department" to train diplomats, and Yoshida enrolled in this department to pursue his dream of becoming a diplomat. In 1904, the department was abolished, so he transferred to Law School at Tokyo Imperial University without examination. Upon graduation in 1906, he passed the consular examination and entered the Ministry of Foreign Affairs. The fact that Yoshida began his higher education at Gakushuin likely played a role in making him an absolute believer in the emperor system.

In 1918, he served as consul in Jinan, Shantung Province, and attended the Paris Peace Conference in 1919 as a member of the delegation. His father-in-law, Nobuaki Makino, was named ambassador plenipotentiary and became a member of the delegation. Yoshida spent most of his 20 years in the Foreign Ministry in China, rather than being posted to Europe or the United States, as many diplomats of the time would have liked. Yoshida's views on imperial Japan's expansion into China, especially in Manchuria, were stronger than those of the military.

Yoshida's insistence on entering Manchuria was so extreme that he was restrained by Prime Minister Giichi Tanaka and the army in late 1927. He supported the so-called "Manchuria–Mongolia separatism" in solidarity with another hardliner, Gaku

Mori.[11] In the Tanaka Cabinet in 1928, Mori was named the vice-minister of foreign and political affairs and Yoshida the vice-minister of foreign affairs, respectively. To stop Kijūrō Shidehara's "international cooperative diplomacy" in line with the Taishō Democracy trend, Tanaka appointed himself foreign minister as well and appointed Mori and Yoshida as vice-ministers. It was the reactivation of Yoshida Shoin's "pre-emption of neighboring countries" policy, which had been dormant since the Russo-Japanese War, creating an outlet for the military's hardline approach to Manchuria–Mongolia and the Far North, including the Kwantung Army.

In the 1930s, Yoshida moved his workplace to Europe. He became ambassador to Italy in 1931 and to the U.K. in 1936. Diplomatically, he appeared to be a "pro--U.K.-U.S." faction that valued its relationship with the U.K. and the United States. He was close friends with Fumimaro Konoe, who formed the cabinet as prime minister on three occasions in 1937, 1940, and 1941. In the formation of the Kōki Hirota Cabinet in March 1936, he was slated to be the foreign minister and cabinet secretary as Konoe's "messenger," but he failed to join the cabinet due to opposition from the army, including Hisaichi Terauchi.[12] His confrontation with the military made him the center of attention at GHQ after the war.

In the run-up to the start of the Pacific War, he met frequently with U.S. Ambassador Joseph C. Grew and Foreign Minister Shigenori Tōgō in an unsuccessful attempt to prevent the outbreak of war. After the war, he served as a liaison for anti-war groups such as his father-in-law Nobuaki Makino and former Prime Minister Konoe and engaged in peacemaking. He saw the Japanese defeat at the Battle of Midway as an opportunity for peace negotiations and traveled with Konoe to Switzerland, home of the League of Nations, to try to spark peace talks. However, the U.S. military's advance was so rapid that they gave up. In 1945, as Japan's defeat loomed large, he and Shunkichi Ueda, Konoe's henchman, were working on the "Konoe's address to the throne" to review end-of-war measures when they were arrested and detained by the military police. The imprisonment also became a postwar badge of honor for "opposition to the military," a crucial factor in GHQ's credibility. However, when politicians rallied around Konoe after the military took power, it was only to oppose the military's rise to power and expansion, not for liberal democracy. There was no difference in consciousness between the two in the construction of the emperor-dominated "Tōyo (East)" and "East Asia (Tōa)." It was the same conflict composition that Itō Hirobumi's protectorate policy as to sieze the sovereignty of the Korean Empire before and after the Russo-Japanese War was faced with the immediate annexation policy by army force.

After the end of the war, when Emperor Shōwa tried to abdicate to take responsibility for the war, it was reportedly Yoshida who stopped him. When Emperor Shōwa tried to apologize to the people, Yoshida actively discouraged him. Yoshida

---

[11] The argument for independence of Manchuria and Mongolia from the Republic of China was to facilitate Japanese expansion or subordination to Japan. This is similar to the arguments made during the Qing-Japanese War to separate Korea from the Qing Empire's influential sphere and use Korea as a bridgehead for Japan's expansion into the continent.

[12] The son of Terauchi Masadake, the first governor general of Chosen Korea and the 18th prime minister.

seemed to think that if the emperor abdicated or atoned, Japan would fall apart. When Emperor Akihito was crowned in November 1952, the prime minister, Yoshida, reportedly referred to himself as "Vassal Shigeru." He was so obsessed with the sanctity of the imperial family that even the media at the time criticized it as an "anachronism."

In 1882 (Meiji 15), Kogakan was founded by Prince Kuni Asahiko, a master of religious rites for the Ise Shrine. It was established for the purpose of training teachers for the priesthood or Shinto. It was when Itō Hirobumi was working on the Imperial Constitution and national Shinto. After being a government vocational school in 1903, Kogakan became a government university under the Ministry of Education in 1940, growing into a major institution in the promotion of national Shinto. Thus, after the defeat, it was closed by edict in March 1946. Then, in September 1951, the Kogakan University Revival Movement took place in the festive atmosphere of the signing of the San Francisco Peace Treaty and the inauguration of Japan as a "truly independent nation." In the same year, a foundation called The Isuzukai (五十鈴會) was founded, and the following year, the "Shrine Imperial Academy Revival School-Supporting Association" was formed. It opened in September 1955 as Shrine Imperial Academy and was renamed Imperial Academy University in 1962. Shigeru Yoshida, a three-time prime minister, was inaugurated as the university's first president.

The San Francisco Peace Treaty was an international event in which the postwar "nation of Japan" erased its image as a defeated nation. The fact that Yoshida, who had served as prime minister and ambassador plenipotentiary at the event, was appointed as the first president of the Imperial Academy University, which was revived in the wake of the peace treaty, symbolizes his staunch devotion to the emperor system.

4.2 The Cabinet's Focus on Economic Issues in Negotiating the Peace Treaty

In April 1947, at the end of the First Yoshida Cabinet, the 23rd general election was held. The new constitution (Article 67, paragraph 1) made a member of the National Diet a requirement for the prime minister, and Yoshida ran for office in Kochi Prefecture, his biological father's hometown. He was elected, but the ruling Liberal Party of Japan lost its place as the dominant party to the Japan Socialist Party. Socialist Party leader Suehiro Nishio[13] was thrilled by the unexpected victory but felt the party was unprepared to take charge of the government. Hence, Nishio

[13] Suehiro Nishio (1891–1981) was elected as "unnominated" in the 1942 Imperial Rule Assistance Association election. He distanced himself from the Assistance Political Society and secretly joined the movement to overthrow the Tojo Cabinet. This career history kept him from the "purge from public office" after the war. In November 1945, he formed the Japan Socialist Party and distinguished himself as a right-wing socialist.

attempted to form a cabinet with a non-socialist prime minister and its majority of members from the Socialist Party. Specifically, he wanted Yoshida to continue as prime minister instead of the Liberal Party's current prime minister. However, Yoshida detested the pro-communist leftists within the Socialist Party and demanded that party leader Nishio exclude the left. When this proposal was not accepted, the First Yoshida Cabinet resigned on May 24.

The House of Representatives, which was formed by the 23rd general election, did not have an absolute majority party and thus held a nomination election for the head of a cabinet. The election was won by Tetsu Katayama, a former secretary-general of the Japan Socialist Party. On May 24, the Katayama Cabinet was sworn in as the first Socialist Party Cabinet in Japanese history. As mentioned earlier, the Katayama Cabinet was dismissed only after 292 days, and the cabinet of Hitoshi Ashida of the Democratic Party was sworn in on March 10, 1948. The Democratic Party's political base was also highly unstable. After the end of the war in 1945, a group of relatively progressive figures came together to form the Liberal Party of Japan, but with many of its cadres bound by the "purge from public service," the Liberal Party formed the Democratic Party in 1947 in alliance with factions within the Liberal Party that were unhappy with its president, Yoshida, and Ashida became the president. However, the Ashida Cabinet also dissolved the following year on October 15, 1948, after mere 220 days.

The Second Yoshida Cabinet, formed on October 15, 1948, was also formed amid a new reorganization of political parties and factions. The Ashida Cabinet fell apart due to a corruption scandal. In the meantime, former prime ministers Kijūrō Shidehara and Kakuei Tanaka, who were members of this party, and the "Democratic Club" merged with the Liberal Party to form the Democratic Liberal Party, with Yoshida as its president. In October 1948, Yoshida formed his second cabinet, but early the following year, a motion of no-confidence in the cabinet submitted by the Socialist Party and other opposition parties was passed, forcing Yoshida to dissolve the House of Representatives.

In the 24th House of Representatives general election held on January 23, 1949, Yoshida's Democratic Liberal Party won by a mile and formed a new third cabinet. The Third Yoshida Cabinet, which lasted from February 16, 1949, to October 30, 1952, had such an unstable party base that it had to undergo three "cabinet reshuffles" during its existence. Although the postwar political situation was largely a one-man show for Shigeru Yoshida's Cabinet, the three "reshuffled cabinets" in the third cabinet indicate that there was a great deal of political unrest. The large number of politicians tied to GHQ's "purge from public office" list was also a major cause.

The postwar Japanese political landscape, centered on Yoshida, was soon dominated by conservative politics, and its conservatism was not a conscious departure from the emperor system nationalism and thus far from the liberal democratic politics sought by the Allies. The San Francisco Peace Treaty with Japan of September 1951 was signed amid the Japanese regime's unwillingness to abandon its imperialist emperor-first mentality. It is an irony of the times that the U.S. government, a symbol of liberal democracy, would allow an emperor system devotee like Yoshida to negotiate a peace treaty with Japan that would define the course of postwar East Asia.

The San Francisco Peace Treaty was almost entirely driven by the U.S. government. Yoshida Shigeru, the prime minister, did not have much more to ask for politically, having succeeded in relegating the issue of abolishing the emperor system to a "humanity declaration" by the emperor. It was foolish to provoke GHQ and the U.S. government with unreasonable demands. In reality, it was a wise posture to seek cooperation for the Japanese economy, which was suffering from severe inflation. Prime Minister Yoshida was optimistic for Ikeda Hayato, the minister of treasury.

The Japanese plenipotentiary delegation that traveled to the San Francisco Peace Treaty site in September 1951 was composed of Shigeru Yoshida, chief plenipotentiary; Hayato Ikeda, minister of treasury; Gizō Tomabechi, supreme chairman of the National Democratic Party; Nirō Hoshijima of the Liberal Party; and Muneyoshi Tokugawa, president of the "Green Breeze Society." The prime minister and the minister of treasury represented the government, whereas the other three represented the House of Representatives and the House of Councilors. Tomabechi and Hoshijima represented the opposition and ruling parties in the House of Representatives, while Tokugawa, the chairman of the "Green Breeze Society," represented the House of Councilors.[14] One representative from opposition and ruling parties on each side of the House of Councilors and the House of Representatives traveled to San Francisco, along with other two, the prime minister and minister of treasury of the cabinet. The fact that the prime minister participated with assistance from the minister of treasury rather than the foreign minister indicates the importance of economic issues to the Japanese government.

Hayato Ikeda (1899–1965) was a longtime bureaucrat who entered politics after the war and served as the right-hand man of Shigeru Yoshida, involved in the foreign, security, and economic policies of the Yoshida Cabinet. Along with Eisaku Satō (1901–1975), he was a leading figure in the "Yoshida School." Yoshida was a master of diplomacy because he was committed to building trust with Supreme Commander MacArthur, but he needed a trustworthy expert on whom he could rely regarding finance and economics. Yoshida asked Seijirō Miyajima (1879–1963), an accomplished businessman, to become the new minister of treasury in his cabinet, but he declined and recommended Hayato Ikeda instead. The banking and finance sector was also experiencing a shortage of talent, with many people targeted for the purge from public office. Ikeda was a graduate of Kyoto Imperial University and was the first person to join the cabinet from Kyoto Imperial University before, during and after the war.

Ikeda graduated from Law School of Kyoto Imperial University's in 1924, and after passing the Higher Civil Service Examination, he entered the Ministry of Treasury. He was outside the mainstream as the core of graduates of the ministry

[14] When the first House of Councilors convened on May 20, 1949, a group of members of the House of Councilors formed the "Green Breeze Society (緑風会)" to symbolize the start of the new National Assembly.

was from Tokyo Imperial University. However, he soon left the ministry due to an incurable disease but was miraculously cured in 1934 and returned to the ministry after working in a general company. During the 1941 expansion, he worked on military financing as head of the State Taxation Bureau, where he successfully introduced an advertising tax to pay for temporary military expenses. After the war, he worked in postwar compensation, dealing with many munition companies and civilians. In September 1945, he briefed GHQ on Japan's tax system, which led him to begin working on postwar tax reform with GHQ. He excelled in the field of finance, including tax reform, due to his excellent memorization of numerals, and was selected as a minister of treasury in the Third Yoshida Cabinet. Ikeda was entrusted with the economy by Yoshida in the form of a plenipotentiary delegation and remained in office even through three "cabinet reshuffles," serving as minister of trade and industry (the Third Yoshida Cabinet) and minister of the economic council board (the Fourth Yoshida Cabinet).

In February 1949, Joseph Morrell Dodge, a special envoy of U.S. President Truman, came to Japan. He successfully addressed the problem of inflation in the German economy under Allied occupation. He then traveled to Japan at the behest of the Truman administration to learn about the country's economic problems. He often met with Ikeda, the minister of treasury, to discuss and recommend the implementation of the "Dodge Line." Ikeda originally planned to establish an active fiscal policy to revitalize the economy through tax cuts and public investment. However, Dodge and GHQ called for an ultra-balanced fiscal policy according to the "Dodge Line." As a result of the demand, a strict tight-money policy was implemented, and from April to June 1949, the Japanese economy plunged into a severe financial crisis. In 1950, as people of all classes faced increasing pressure to make ends meet, there were increasing calls for a relaxation of the "Dodge Line." Prime Minister Yoshida, concerned that negative public opinion was escalating, sent Ikeda to the United States to explore the intention of Dodge. By the way, Ikeda was being assigned more tasks.

Dodge and William Frederic Marquat, GHQ's Director of Economic and Scientific Affairs, had worked with Ikeda over the years and had seen his competence and had invited him to participate in intensified negotiations with the United States. On April 25, 1951, Ikeda traveled to the United States as Prime Minister Yoshida's special envoy, accompanied by Jirō Shirasu, Minister of Trade and Industry (now the Ministry of Economy, Trade and Industry), and Kiichi Miyazawa, Secretary of the Ministry of Treasury. It was his first trip to the United States as a postwar Japanese cabinet minister. On May 3, he visited the State Department to request a relaxation of the "Dodge Line" and verbally conveyed Prime Minister Yoshida's message: the Japanese government hopes for early strengthening, and if the U.S. military presence in Japan is necessary to ensure the safety of Japan and the Asian region after strengthening, the Japanese government is willing to sign a treaty to that end. The U.S. government responded with an offer of independence for Japan and a request for full cooperation in the Korean War. In effect, it was the moment when the framework for the San Francisco Peace Treaty was being formulated.

The "San Francisco Peace Treaty with Japan" of September 8, 1951, pursued the simultaneous realization of three complex tasks: to recognize Japan as an independent nation on the losing side of the Pacific War, to revive its economy to reduce the economic burden on the United States in East Asia, and to ensure that Japan would serve as an anti-communist bulwark in the impending war against communism through the signing of the U.S.–Japan Security Treaty. The proactivity of the Japanese government in this process was a welcome change for the U.S. administration at the time. The U.S. government was happy enough to forget the complete liquidation of colonialism as a historical task when they demanded Japan's "unconditional surrender."

On August 14, 1941, U.S. President Franklin Roosevelt, upon entering World War II, demanded that the U.K.'s Prime Minister Churchill agree to an "Anti-Colonialism" pledge that there should be no colonies on earth after the war was over. Roosevelt's beliefs were reaffirmed at the Cairo Conference and then developed into a proposal to create the United Nations. Upon his death in February 1945, the Truman administration was faced with the simultaneous challenge of Anti-Communism as postwar international relations quickly developed into the Cold War. Although the terms of the San Francisco Peace Treaty were to adequately coordinate two tasks, "Anti-Colonialism" was nearly forgotten. If this conclusion was the result of a deliberate inducement by the leading members of the Japanese government, imbued with the imperialist consciousness of the emperor system, then the Peace Treaty should be reconsidered for the sake of the honor of the U.S.

5 Closing: Japanese Bureaucrats' "Absurd Remarks" After the San Francisco Peace Treaty

So far, we have covered how the Japanese Empire, after the Meiji Restoration in 1868, established the construction of a new "East Asia" ruled by the Emperor of Japan as a national goal, using Yoshida Shōin's "idea of preempting neighboring countries" as the basis for the establishment of the emperor-centered nationalist system. Further, we have looked at how this goal was realized through the major and minor wars, and the details of the disappearance of the Taishō Democracy as an aspiration of the domestic liberal civil rights movement by the uprising of the idea of Yoshida's preemption in the early Shōwa period, and the remnants of imperial absolutism in the postwar Japanese political scenario after the final defeat of the Greater East Asia War, which was the culmination of the implementation of Yoshida's preemption of peripheral countries policy. The postwar Japanese political landscape revealed surprisingly strong remnants of fascism lingering from the prewar emperor system that ran counter to the liberal democratization envisioned by GHQ. Considering these limitations, it is highly doubtful that the San Francisco Peace Treaty of September 1951 could have functioned as a milestone in the realization of a postwar peace regime in East Asia.

President Franklin Roosevelt's "anti-colonialism" was the primary rationale for the United States' entry into World War II. The Pacific War, provoked by the Japanese Empire, made this cause and task solid. In its postwar dealings, the U.S. government saw itself as having a *zeitgeist* mission to prioritize the colonial problems created by fascism under the Japanese emperor system above all else. Only the realization of the policy of liquidating the various damages suffered by the countries colonized by the Japanese Empire could justify the first atomic bombing in human history.

However, the U.S. government and GHQ's lack of understanding of the emperor system defer the realization of this task, and the rush to establish a system to counter it in the face of the emerging Cold War resulted in the loss of the timely imperative task of the Pacific War. Clearing up the colonial liability issue was an essential part of the postwar transformation of Japan into a full-fledged liberal democracy. It was the emperor system's nationalist mentality that served as a pillar of the Japanese Empire's colonization of its neighbors. The first priority was the eradication of the aggressionist idea of the grace and glory of being ruled by the only imperial family "unbroken for ages eternal" in human history. After experiencing defeat, Emperor Shōwa even went so far as to consider abdication as a necessary next step. Nevertheless, the GHQ and the U.S. government were satisfied with the Emperor's "Humanity Declaration," allowing an emperor-worshiping consciousness to survive in postwar Japan. Allowing the man most responsible for maintaining and defending the emperor-system consciousness to become acting prime minister three times was the performance of GHQ's anti-colonial work. It is surely an incorrect answer that the credit goes to Shigeru Yoshida, who helped create the framework for the San Francisco Peace Conference in September 1951 and attended it himself as the head of Japan's plenipotentiary delegation, signing a peace treaty that focused on reviving the Japanese economy and securing a U.S.–Japan security system.

The sense of urgency resulting from the expansion of communist power in East Asia since late 1948 was undeniable. Even so, it was no excuse for adopting a historical "wrong answer." President Franklin Roosevelt highlighted the aim of anticolonialism in the Atlantic Charter and proposed the creation of the United Nations (UN) with the goal of realizing it. After his death, the UN's headquarters was established in New York. Ending colonialism and countering the Cold War were goals that had to be realized together—one could not be a substitute for the other. The absence of a political leader like Konrad Adenauer of Germany, who had fought Nazi fascism, in postwar Japan was also a factor for the United States' wrong call in the San Francisco system.

Even so, the U.S. government and GHQ should have immediately recognized these limitations of postwar Japan and taken steps to address them. In other words, the San Francisco system is rightfully criticized as a "wrong answer" that resulted from a lack of understanding of the reality of the Japanese Empire's fascism under the emperor system. Even if the policy of using Japan as an anti-communist bulwark was acceptable in the face of the reality of a communist invasion, it was an irreparable mistake on the part of the Truman administration to lose sight of another historical task. The so-called rants of Japanese politicians, which was a secondary act of aggression against Korea after the San Francisco Peace Treaty was finalized as a system, prove that it was a mistake.

After the San Francisco Peace Conference in September 1951, the U.S. government urged Korea and Japan to normalize diplomatic relations. Thus, on October 20, 1951, representatives of the two countries met in Tokyo for preliminary talks, and on February 15, 1952, the first round of (full-dress) talks began. The talks were held seven times over a 14-year period, but after a series of stalemates and ruptures, they finally ended in June 1965 with the signing of the Treaty on Basic Relations between the Republic of Korea and Japan. The repeated ruptures were all due to rants by Japanese representatives. Their remarks, premised on the legitimacy of annexing Korea, reveal Japanese politicians' mind in the postwar scenario and call into question the basic conditions of the San Francisco Peace Treaty. The "Record of Historical Remarks by the Japanese Government and Politicians, etc.," dated November 15, 1995, released by the Ministry of Foreign Affairs of the Republic of Korea, lists a total of 26 cases. Of these, we present only a few examples from the signing of the San Francisco Peace Treaty in September 1951 to the conclusion of the Korea–Japan talks in June 1965 to conclude this article.

In September 1951, with the first preliminary Korea–Japan talks ahead, Prime Minister Shigeru Yoshida addressed the Japanese Diet and said, "The most important issue in these talks is not to grant Japanese citizenship to Koreans in Japan, and the purpose of the talks is to prevent Japan from having immigrant ethnic minorities as worms in its stomach." This is a severely racist statement. In the third Korea–Japan talks on October 15, 1953, Kan'ichirō Kubota, the Japanese representative said, "The Cairo Declaration, which referred to the enslavement of the Korean people, was an expression of the Allies' wartime hysteria. Japan's 36 years of rule was a favor to the Koreans, and if Japan had not gone to Korea, the Chinese Communists or the Soviet Union would have gone in."

The Japanese side rejected Korea's demand for a retraction and an apology, and the two countries did not hold talks for four-and-a-half years thereafter. On July 28, 1958, Banboku Ōno, vice president of the Liberal Democratic Party, said, "Ultimately, Japanese diplomacy should focus on close cooperation with the United States, and in order to do this, Korea and Taiwan should be in close relations, and if possible, a United States of Japan should be formed with Korea and Taiwan." These words reflect an imperialist consciousness that sought to recreate the glory of imperial Japan. On July 21, 1961, Masuo Araki, Japan's Minister of Education, said, "Japanese people should take pride in the fact that they were fortunate not to be born as Africans or Koreans," revealing a deep-seated racist consciousness. The UN Commission on Human Rights should take action against such remarks. On October 5, 1962, Hayato Ikeda, Japan's Prime Minister, who had prioritized solving Japan's economic problems in the drafting of the San Francisco Treaty, had said, "Following the example of Itō Hirobumi, Japan should dig into Korea," indicating his intention to re-colonize Korea.

On January 7, 1965, Shinichi Takasuki, the head of the Korea–Japan talks, made a series of statements at a press conference that will make one's ears perk up, as follows: "Japan dominated Korea, but it was for the good of Korea"; "Japan's efforts were thwarted by the war, but it would have been nice to have had Korea for another 20 years or so”; and “The ‘change of name’ alone was a measure taken to assimilate Koreans and treat them like Japanese, and it cannot be said that it was a bad thing.” These comments made one wonder whether the era of the Japanese Empire persisted in 1965. On February 15, 1965, at a meeting of the House of Representatives of the Japanese Diet, a member of the Socialist Party exposed Foreign Minister Etsusaburo Shiina’s remarks in his new book *Assimilation and Politics* that “if the management of Taiwan, the annexation of Korea, and the dream of cooperation and peace among the five tribes in Manchuria are called Japanese imperialism, it is glorious imperialism.” Even other members of the same House of Representatives could not tolerate the colonialist postwar Japanese politics represented in such consciousness; this was the face of Japan in the San Francisco System.

References

Dulles, F. R., & Ridinger, G. E. (1955). The anti-colonial policies of Franklin D. Roosevelt. *Political Science Quarterly, 70*(1), 1–18. Oxford University Press.

Gunther, J. (1950). *Roosevelt in retrospect: A profile in history*. Harper & Brothers.

Hudson, M. O. (1922). *The United States and the new international court. World Peace Foundation Pamphlets Vol. I*. (2017 reprint, Facsimile Publisher, India).

Hudson, M. O. (1924). *American cooperation with the League of Nations. World Peace Foundation Pamphlets Vol. VII No.1*. (2017 reprint, Facsimile Publisher, India).

Hudson, M. O. (1925a). Amendment of the covenant of the League of Nations. *Harvard Law Review, 38*, 903.

Hudson, M. O. (1925b). The prospect for international law in the twentieth century. *Cornell Law Quarterly, 10*(4), 419.

Hudson, M. O. (1925c, April 25). Contemporary development of law. Address before the second conference of teachers of international law, Washington, DC.

Hudson, M. O. (1934). The post war development of international law and some contributions by The United States of America. International Conciliation, No. 301.

Hudson, M. O. (1935). *By Pacific means*. Yale University Press.

Link, A. S. (1974). *Wilson the diplomatist: A look at his major foreign policies*. New Viewpoints.

Messer, R. L. (1982). *The end of an alliance: James F. Byrnes, Roosevelt, Truman, and the origins of the Cold War*. University of North Carolina Press.

Poetker, J. S. (1969). *The fourteen points*. Charles E. Merril Publishing Co.

Stead, W. T. (1900). *Mr. Carnegie’s conundrum £40,000,000, what shall I do with it?* Review of Reviews Office.

シーボルト, W. J. (1965). 日本占領の外交回想 (野末賢三 譯). 朝日新聞社.

ジョン·ダウ. (1991). 吉田茂とその時代 (上)(下) (大窪愿二 譯). 中公文庫.

야마무로 신이치. (2009). 키메라, 만주국의 초상 (윤대석 역). 소명출판.

이태진. (2022a). 일본제국의 ‘동양사’ 개발과 천황제 파시즘. 사회평론아카데미.

이태진. (2022b). 일본제국의 대외침략과 동방학 변천. 사회평론아카데미.

三浦陽一. (1996). 吉田茂 サフラシスコ講和 (上· 下). 大月書店.

中山隆志. (2000). 關東軍. 講談社選書メチエ 180.

井上直樹. (2013). 帝國日本と<滿鮮史>: 大陸政策と朝鮮· 滿洲認識. 塙書房.

伊藤之雄. (2009). 山縣有朋: 愚直な權力者の生涯. 文春新書 684, 文藝春秋.

伊藤隆, & 季武嘉也 (編). (2005/2007). 近現代日本人物史料情報辭典. 吉川弘文館.

保阪正康. (2005). 昭和天皇. 中央公論新社.

千葉功. (2012). 桂太郎. 中公新書 2162, 中央公論社.
原田史. (2000). 大正天皇. 朝日新書 663.
原田史. (2015). 「昭和天皇實録」を讀む. 岩波新書 1561.
原田史, 吉田裕. (2005). 岩波 天皇·皇室辭典. 岩波書店.
古川隆久. (2011). 昭和天皇: 「理性の君主」の孤獨. 中公新書 2105.
吉川元. (2015). 國際平和とは何か: 人間の安全を脅かす平和秩序の逆說. 中公叢書.
吉田裕. (1995). 日本人の戰爭觀: 戰後史なかの變容. 岩波書店.
吉野誠. (2002). 明治維新と征韓論ー吉田松陰から西鄉隆盛へ-. 明石書店.
和田春樹. (2009). 日露戰爭: 起源と開戰 (上・ 下). 岩波書店.
和田春樹. (2015). 「平和国家」の誕生: 戦後日本の原点と変容. 岩波書店.
和田春樹 外. (2010). 日露戰爭と韓國併合; *19*世紀末-*1900*年代. 岩波講座・ 東アジア近現代通史 第2巻, 岩波書店.
坂本一登. (1991). 伊藤博文と明治國家形成: 「宮中」の制度化と立憲制の導入. 吉川弘文館.
堀内哲 (編・ 著). (2009). 天皇條項の削除を!. 有限會社JCA出版.
大江志乃夫. (1985). 日本の參謀本部. 中公新書 765, 中央公論社.
安丸良夫. (2001). 近代天皇像の形成. 岩波モダンクラシックス, 岩波書店.
安濃豊. (2017). 大東亞戰爭の開戰目的は植民地解放だった: 帝國政府の聲明發掘. 展轉社.
安田浩, & 趙景達 (編). (2005). 戰爭の時代と社會: 日露戰爭と現代. 靑木書店.
小林英夫. (1996). 滿鐵, 「知の集團」の誕生と死. 吉川弘文館.
山室信一. (2001). 思想課題としてのアジア: 基軸·連鎖·投企. 岩波書店.
岸本美緒 (編). (2006). 「帝國」日本の學知 第3巻 「東洋學の磁場」. 岩波書店.
川田稔. (2003). 原敬と山縣有朋. 中公新書 1445, 中央公論社.
平山龍水. (2002). 東アジア冷戰の起源: 朝鮮半島分斷の構圖. 株式會社 信山社.
後藤春美. (2016). 國際主義との格闘: 日本 國際聯盟 イキリス帝國. 中公叢書.
德川義寬. (1997). 侍従長の遺言: 昭和天皇との*50*年. 朝日新聞社.
戶部良一. (2010). 外務省革新派: 世界秩序の幻影. 中公新書 2059.
李鍾元. (1996). 東アジア冷戰と韓米日關係. 東京大學出版會.
松野賴三. (1985). 保守本流の思想と行動. 朝日新聞社.
林久治郎. (1978). 滿洲事變と奉天總領事: 林久治郎遺稿. 原書房.
海軍機關學校. (1942). 詔勅集.
渡辺昭夫, & 宮里政玄 (編). (1986). サフランシスコ講和. 東京大學出版會.
渡辺昭夫, & 宮里政玄 (編). (2010). 近代日本なかの「韓國併合」. 東京堂出版.
白鳥庫吉. (2004). 國史: 昭和天皇の歷史教科書 (出雲井品 譯). 講談社.
福永文夫. (2014). 日本占領史. 中公新書 2296, 中央公論社.
秦郁彦 (編). (1991). 日本陸海軍總合事典 *1868–2000*. 東京大學出版會.
秦郁彦 (編). (2001). 日本官僚制總合事典 *1868–2000*. 東京大學出版會.
窪寺紘一. (2009). 東洋學事始: 那珂通世とその時代. 平凡社.
立野信之. (1963). 昭和軍閥 勃興篇. 講談社.
笠原十九司. (2017). 日中戰爭全史 (上・ 下). 高文研.
笠原英彦. (2006). 明治天皇:苦惱する「理想的君主」. 中公新書 1849.
笹川紀勝, 金勝一, & 內藤光博 (編). (2010). 日本の植民地支配の實態過去の淸算-東アジアの平和と共生に向けて. ICU21世紀COEシリズ 第8巻, 風行社.
篠原初枝. (2010). 國際聯盟. 中公新書 2055, 中央公論社.
米原謙. (2003). 德富蘇峰. 中公新書 1711, 中央公論社.
關榮次. (2003). 日英同盟; 日本外交の榮光と凋落. 學研.
韓桂玉. (1996). 「征韓論」の系譜: 日本と朝鮮半島の*100*年. 三一書房.

A Study on Modern Japanese Colonialism and Ryukyu Restoration

Xu Yong

Abstract The external expansion of Modern Japan began with the annexation of the Ryukyu Kingdom and culminated in the formation of the colonial empire of "Greater East Asia Co-Prosperity Sphere". After Japan's defeat and surrender, due to complicated international factors, Ryukyu hasn't been unable to achieve national autonomy like Korea and other colonies, and remained under "dual colonial rule" of the Japanese county government and U.S. military occupation. The Ryukyu people's aspiration and endeavors for national restoration have persisted for a century and a half. The international community should adhere to international principles including the Cairo Declaration, draw on the experience and lessons from handling other Japanese colonies, respect the Ryukyu people's right to self-determination, and come up with a real solution to the international issue of the sovereignty of Ryukyu.

Keywords China-Japan relations · Japan · Ryukyu · Colonialism · National liberation

The annihilation of the Ryukyus in 1879 marks the starting point for Japan's external expansion and colonial rule in modern times. The Ryukyu people's ideas and actions for national restoration also began there, which received long-lasting and close attention from the international community. Around World War II, Japan's colonization of the Ryukyu islands was discussed at the Cairo Conference, followed by the occupation of the U.S. military and international arrangements such as the trusteeship coming out of the San Francisco Peace Conference, but the issue remains unsolved. Today, the Ryukyu islands are divided, with about 1/3 of its area, including Amami Oshima in the north, incorporated into the jurisdiction of Kagoshima Prefecture of southern Kyushu, Japan, and the remaining 2/3, about 2600 km^2

X. Yong (✉)
Department of History, Peking University, Beijing, People's Republic of China
e-mail: xuyong@pku.edu.cn

Y.-H. Kim et al. (eds.), *Beyond the San Francisco System*,
https://doi.org/10.1007/978-981-95-3328-2_8

including Okinawa's Main Island and the central & southern islands, forming the Okinawa Prefecture, Japan, which is now in a state of "dual colony".[1]

Broadly seen, among all the national liberation movements against colonialism in the Asia-Pacific region, only a handful such as the Korean National Independence Movement in East Asia and the Indian Nonviolent Resistance Movement in South Asia have delivered national independence and nation-building after World War II. Although the Ryukyu people have not achieved their goal of "saving the country" and "rejuvenation", they have not stopped their efforts. In the twenty-first century, they put forward new political appeals such as "Ryukyu independence", "renegotiation of sovereignty", and "self-determination".[2] The Ryukyu people's desire for national restoration and their endeavors matter to the survival of a thousand-year-old nation and is a major political event in the Asia-Pacific region. They're not, as the usual critics put it, the "independence theory of izakaya (Japanese bistro)".[3] The Ryukyu issue has been international in nature since the start, and is also one of the topics discussed in the joint historical study between China and Japan in the twenty-first century. The international community should learn from the basic principles of dealing with Japanese colonies since the end of World War II, as well as the experience and lessons of dealing with the Ryukyu issue and re-explore the solution to issues such as its sovereignty.

"The colonial rule that Ryukyus suffered lasted for more than 140 years, the longest in the world."[4] There is quite a lot of literature related to the Ryukyus in China and abroad. This article explores modern Japanese colonialism and the Ryukyu restoration based on the academic achievements and historical documents published around the twenty-first century. Criticism and suggestions are welcome.

---

[1] Regarding the Ryukyuans as a "nation", and the concepts of "colony" and "military colony" that describe the social attributes of Okinawa since modern times, can be traced back to the discussions of pre-war Ryukyu scholar Iha Fuyu and other Japanese civil rights thinkers; for the terms and descriptions commonly used after the war, one can refer to the works of scholars such as Namihira Tsuneo (波平恒男), Matayoshi Seikiyo (又吉盛清), Shiitada Atsushi (後田多敦), Matsushima Yasukatsu (松島泰勝), and Arakaki Takeshi (新垣毅) cited in this article, as well as media such as "Ryukyu Shimpo"(琉球新报) and "Okinawa Times"(沖縄タイムス).

[2] There are many political concepts and related studies about the Ryukyu people's struggle for "independence," "self-reliance", "autonomy", "sovereign self-determination", and "right to self-determination" after the war. For reference, see the 琉球新報社、新垣毅『沖縄の自己決定権』(高文研出版、2015 年), 松島泰勝『帝国の島———琉球·尖閣に対する植民地主義と闘う』(明石書店、2020 年), 後田多敦『琉球救国運動———抗日の思想と行動』(出版舎Mugen、2010 年), 波平恒男『近代東アジア史のなかの琉球併合』(岩波書店、2015 年), 新城俊昭『琉球·沖縄史』(株式会社東洋企画、2018 年), and又吉盛清『大日本帝国植民地下の琉 球沖縄と台湾』(株式会社同時代社、2018 年), etc. Apart from these, there are plenty of radical works supporting Ryukyu independence.

[3] This theory was proposed by scholars such as Shinzaki Shigeharu (新崎盛暉)、and Ukari Hizen (屋嘉比收), with the aim of criticizing the "independence theory" discussed in small bars. See 松島泰勝『琉球独立への道———植民地主義に抗う琉球ナショナリズム』、法律文化社、2013 年p. 6 and p. 211.

[4] 松島泰勝『帝国の島———琉球·尖閣に対する植民地主義と闘う』 p. 296.

1 The Demise of the Ryukyu Kingdom and the Formation of Modern Japanese Colonialism

The Ryukyu islands, where the ancient Ryukyu Kingdom is located, sit at the farthest east of Asia and in the western Pacific Ocean, stretching thousands of kilometers from north to south. The origin of the residents on the islands has not yet been determined, but many ancient human fossils have been discovered there, for example many complete fossils of the Minatogawa people have been discovered on the main island of Okinawa, estimated to have existed over 22,000 years ago, earlier than the Hamakita people in mainland Japan (about 14,000 years ago).[5] The Ryukyu Islands' geographical location, local products, and other natural conditions "not only provided a place and stage for the formation of culture and history" for human activities on the islands, "but also set the basic conditions for their culture and historical existence",[6] creating the unique ancient Ryukyu civilization.

With ancient villages and scattered cities, the ancient Ryukyu people were unified by the Shang Dynasty around the fifteenth century, hence began the history of the Ryukyu people "having a country of their own". The fifteenth and sixteenth centuries after the unification were a golden period of the Ryukyu Kingdom's internal development and external exchanges. According to Takara Kurayoshi (高良倉吉), neither the conferment of status by the Chinese emperor nor the power manipulation of the Japanese government were able to change the characteristics of the Ryukyu Kingdom as an independent country. The King of Ryukyu after unification "maintained his existence as the only master who reigned over the 'Ryukyu Era', that is, the Ryukyu Kingdom was a purely independent country that supported this 'master' as the apex, which was established in the ancient Ryukyu era".[7]

The Ryukyu people's national awareness and their political & cultural expressions can be seen from the "Bridge to All Nations Bell" cast by the Shang Dynasty in 1458, on which was the following Chinese inscription: "The Ryukyu Kingdom is a famous place in the South China Sea. Its beauty tops that of Three Kingdoms of Korea. It is like a Penglai Island sitting between Ming China and Japan. The passing ships and vessels serve like a bridge to all nations, bringing in exotic treasures from ten directions."[8] This inscription has been widely quoted and was also written on the folding screen in the Okinawa Prefectural Government Office. "Wan Guo Jin Liang (万国津梁) (meaning 'the bridge to all nations')" has become a term used by the residents of the Ryukyu Islands to identify themselves and represent the existence of Ryukyu history and culture.

Entering the seventeenth century, the "Satsuma Invasion" took place in 1609 initiated by Shimazu Iehisa (島津家久), the lord of Satsuma clan. The Ryukyu King

[5] 新城俊昭『琉球·沖縄史』pp. 8–9.

[6] 高良倉吉『琉球王国史の課題』、ひるぎ社、1989 年 p. 10.

[7] 高良倉吉「古琉球への誘い」、琉球新報社編『新琉球史』(古琉球編)、琉球新報社、1991年 p. 22.

[8] 新城俊昭『琉球·沖縄史』 p. 68.

was captured, and minister Zheng Tong (鄭迵) and others who refused to surrender were killed. In the following 200 years, the Ryukyu Kingdom was subject to Satsuma's constant economic plundering and political manipulation. Some Japanese scholars based their proposition that Ryukyu "belonged" to Japan on Satsuma's invasion and control. However, illegal and violent invasion should not become the basis for sovereignty, and the Ryukyu people actually retained their independent status as a country relative to "Yamato (Japan)". In the eighteenth century, the works of Japanese military scientist Hayashi Shihei (林子平) such as *Kaikoku Heidan* and *Sangoku Tsuran Zusetsu* described Korea, Ryukyu, and Ezochi (now Hokkaido) as "Japan's three neighboring countries." In the mid-nineteenth century, the Ryukyu Kingdom successively concluded international treaties with the U.S., France, and the Netherlands, which speaks to the international community's recognition of the political sovereignty of the Ryukyu Kingdom.[9]

In the late nineteenth century, Japan fundamentally changed the historical trajectory of Ryukyu. As a fellow island country in the Asia-Pacific region, Japan also suffered oppression from European and American colonial forces in the nineteenth century. After that, it experienced the restoration of the monarchy around 1868 and the Meiji Restoration, rebuilt the national regime, gradually established a militarist system, formulated a foreign expansion policy of "establishing national prestige over all directions", and embarked on a path of invading neighboring countries in East Asia together with Western powers.[10]

The Meiji regime quickly went to war when it was still young, and its first step was to set foot on the island nation of Ryukyu. A weak country without any armed force, Ryukyu fell victim to the Japanese military and police almost without any fighting, which was the beginning of the tragedy of the Ryukyu nation. Japan occupied Ryukyu by force in 1872 and changed Ryukyu to Okinawa Prefecture in 1879. As a late-comer colonial power, Japan's plundering and oppression of Ryukyu was far more heinous than that of those old-fashioned powers. In order to strictly control the Ryukyu colony and the thought of Ryukyu people, Japan jailed Sho Tai (尚泰), King of Ryukyu, in Tokyo, took away all the documents such as the original copies of foreign related treaties and census register from the King's residence, and then quickly published a large number of historical books based on Japan's official history "Imperial Chronicles",[11] in order to advertise the legitimacy of its colonial rule. Such publications include Otsuki Fumihiko's (大槻文彦) *Ryukyu Shinshi* (1873), Kobayashi Kyoukei's (小林居敬) *Ryukyu Hanshi* (1874), Ijichi Sadaka's (伊地知貞馨) *"Okinawa Shi"* (1877), Matsuda Michiyuki's (松田道之) "*Ryukyu Shobun*" (three volumes, 1879), etc. These publications vigorously promote the idea that the Ryukyus are part of the Japanese people, deny the national identity of the Ryukyuans,

[9] 琉球新報社、新垣毅『沖縄の自己決定権』,高文研出版2015,pp. 20–21.

[10] 徐勇《两战间的日本法西斯主义及其对外扩张理论》,《抗日战争研究》, No. 3, 2002; 《近代日本的军政关系研究》,《国际政治研究》, No. 1, 2015.

[11] "Imperial Chronicles" refer to official Japanese histories such as "Kojiki"(古事紀) and "Nihonshoki"(日本書記).

and claim that the history of Ryukyu is an integral part of Japanese history, and that Ryukyu history is to Japanese history what local history is to national history. Their purpose is to serve the policy of assimilating Ryukyu people into Japanese and annihilating the Ryukyu as a country.

Facing the invasion of Japan, the Ryukyu Kingdom, which was characterized by gentle and non-military culture, embarked on the journey of national salvation without military forces. The most intense resistance was around 1879. The Ryukyu government petitioned the Japanese government to preserve the old system, and meanwhile it asked for assistance from the Chinese, British, and American governments. In 1878, Mao Fenglai (毛凤来) and Ma Jiancai (马兼才), among the members of the Council of Three (Sanshikan) of Ryukyu submitted a petition to the embassies of various countries in Tokyo, stating "The Ryukyu Kingdom has been paying tribute to China since the 5th year of Hongwu in the Ming Dynasty. In the 2nd year of Yongle, our former King Wu Ning was canonized as the King of Zhongshan. Since then, Ryukyu has been listed as an outlaying vassal (of China). It adopts the Chinese era name, lunar calendar and characters, only autonomous with respect to its domestic policies… It has remained a vassal of China for more than 500 years." It stated that "although our country is small, it is a country of our own" and called on various countries to mediate, "Now things have come to a critical juncture, and we can only rely on the great powers to persuade Japan to keep the Ryukyu Kingdom the way it is. The people of the country would be most grateful to you. In addition to preparing separate petitions to the imperial envoy of the Great Qing Dynasty and the minister plenipotentiary of the Great France, we hereby submit our petitions and ask for your kind permission to implement them."[12]

Ryukyu also sent other envoys to the Qing government to ask for help. In 1879, Xiang Dehong (向德宏), a purple-turban official of Ryukyu sent a petition to Li Hongzhang (李鸿章), stating "I don't want to be Japanese live or dead".[13] Later, Xiang Dehong died in China. Lin Shigong (林世功), another envoy, sacrificed his life in Beijing on October 20, 1880 trying to his country, and left a poem before his martyrdom: "I'd rather give up my life for the survival of the country, and my parents I trust to my brothers." Lin Shigong "died at 40 years old. The Qing government mourned his ambition and gave 200 taels of silver to pay for his coffin. Lin was buried at Zhangjiawan in the evening of October 22, 1880".[14] Lin Shigong died in protest of Japan, which wakened his compatriots. Lin, along with Chen Tianhua (陈天华), a Chinese who jumped into the sea to protest against Japan in 1905, and An Jung-geun (安重根), a Korean hero who in 1909 assassinated Ito Hirobumi (伊藤博文), the first Japanese Resident General in Korea, are all typical heroes who resisted Japanese colonialism in East Asia.

---

[12] 西里喜行 編『琉球救国請願書集成』、東京法政大学沖縄文化研究所, 1992, pp. 39–40. The original text is in Chinese, with punctuation by the author. The phrase "2nd year of Yongle"(永乐二年) in the text may not be precise, but was quoted as it is in the book.

[13] 西里喜行編『琉球救国請願書集成』 p. 44.

[14]「沖縄歴史物語」、『伊波普猷全集』第2 巻、平凡社1974, pp. 441–442.

The Qing government had many discussions on the Ryukyu issue. Although it didn't send troops directly, it always agreed with Lin Shigong's proposal of "sustaining the country and supported the negotiations with Japan regarding "keeping everything in the Ryukyu Kingdom as it was" and "saving Ryukyu".[15] The "Ryukyu Restoration Movement"[16] and "Ryukyu National Salvation Movement"[17] launched by the Ryukyu gentry class came to fail after years of persistence. The Ryukyu royal family kept on resisting and did not sign any treaty with Japan regarding national sovereignty. But despite efforts of multiple parties, Ryukyu ultimately failed in front of Japanese military force. "The result of the Japanese government's 'conquest' was the elimination of the Ryukyu Kingdom and establishment of the colonial government of Okinawa Prefecture".[18] The Ryukyu Kingdom, which was originally "an independent country", became the first colony under Japan's foreign expansion.

The expansionist policy of annexing the Ryukyu Islands gathered strong support from militarists and populists within Japan, but were also vocally opposed by civil-right supporters and democratic-minded thinkers. Among them, the most influential and representative one was socialist Kawakami Hajime (河上肇). In 1911, Kawakami visited the Ryukyu Islands to give a speech, where he emphasized that the Ryukyu people had the right to confront imperialist Japan, which got him a shower of criticism from local pro-Japanese newspapers and driven away.[19] Kawakami's thoughts of opposing the invasion of Japan and colonization of Ryukyu produced a far-reaching influence, and contributed to the awakening of Iha Fuyu (伊波普猶), a native Ryukyu scholar who originally advocated the "Nichiryu Dosoron (The Japan-Ryukyu Common Ancestor Theory)". Ueki Edamori (植木枝盛), a contemporary thinker, believed that "sovereign equality (equalism) should be promoted among all Asian countries; militarism should be eliminated; and 'liberalism' should be implemented", and put forward the "Concept of Ryukyu Independence". Yanagita Kunio (柳田国男) described the situation in Ryukyu as "hell", "destruction and "starvation". Hirotsu Kazuo (広津和郎) pointed out that countries around the world paid attention to the tragic sufferings in colonies such as Korea, but no one knows the sufferings of the Ryukyu people.[20]

The above-mentioned opposition to the annexation of Ryukyu was at a disadvantage and failed to counter the expansionist ideological trend in Japan at the time. And the democrats were internally divided into two factions—one supporting the annexation of Ryukyu and the other opposing it. Furthermore, there were radical arguments attacking the Ryukyu people as "Ryukyu slaves", the Ryukyu King as a

[15] 戴东阳《甲中事变前后黎庶昌的琉球策略》,《历史研究》, No. 2, 2007.

[16] 赤嶺守「琉球復旧運動の一考察」、地方史研究協議会『琉球·沖縄———その歴史と日本史像』、雄山閣出版1987; 比屋根照夫『自由民権思想と沖縄』、研文出版1982.

[17] 後田多敦『琉球救国運動———抗日の思想と行動』.

[18] 松島泰勝『帝国の島———琉球·尖閣に対する植民地主義と闘う』p. 15.

[19] 松島泰勝『琉球独立への道———植民地主義に抗う琉球ナショナリズム』p. 8.

[20] 比屋根照夫『自由民権思想と沖縄』pp. 234, 34, 244–245.

"tribal chief", and demanding sending a punitive expedition against it.[21] This means the colonialist annexation of Ryukyu, both in concept and in action, garnered support from various political forces domestically, enjoying the advantage of cooperation between the ruling and opposition parties.

During the process of the annihilation of Ryukyu Kingdom, although there were national heroes like Lin Shigong who fought to the death for the country, and the support from external forces such as Japanese democratic anti-war peace activists and the Qing government of China, Ryukyu's own limitations, such as poor geographical conditions and small population, led to its failure in directly preventing Japan from establishing its colonial rule there. Afterwards, the Ryukyu nation's resistance movement entered a more difficult colonial period.

Japan's annexation of Ryukyu directly affected its subsequent national policy decisions and development direction. In 1887, Nakae Chomin (中江兆民), a philosopher, published *Three Drunkards on Government*, which was quite influential and had many versions of Chinese translation. The book describes the national policy debates between three characters. The first is "Mr. Hero", who advocates full military mobilization, foreign conquests and the seizure of neighboring territories; the second is "Mr. Gentleman", who advocates learning from the West and implementing full democracy and demilitarization; the third is "Mr. Nanhai", who advocates focusing on commercial trade with proper armament. Japanese researchers believe that the proposition of "Mr. Nanhai" was "most popular with the Japanese people in the 20th year of the Meiji era".[22] However, the development trajectory of Japan's domestic and foreign policies shows that since the annexation of Ryukyu, Japan has been rushing down the path of war. With "Mr. Hero" having the upper hand and completely suppressing "Mr. Nankai" and "Mr. Gentleman", his hegemonic policy of constantly invading the territories of neighboring countries and plundering the wealth of them accelerated the formation of Japan's state colonialism.

The dispute over peace and war on the Ryukyu issue kept bubbling up in Japanese politics in the following decades, and the anti-war democrats were often defeated. This was especially true during the Japanese invasion of China in the 1930s and 1940s, which sparked a nationwide war frenzy.

Japan's occupation of Ryukyu was the starting point of its modern colonialism, rather than the endpoint. While still in the process of annexing Ryukyu, Japan was promoting a more radical expansion theory, coveting a wider territory. For example, the *Ryukyu Shinshi* published in 1873 "cited ten pieces of evidence to argue" that not only Ryukyu, but also the major area of East Asia should belong to the Imperial State of Japan: "Alas! Today, with the prosperity of the Enlightenment, from the Thousand Islands of Karafuto to the Okinawa Islands, thousands of miles from north to south, the Imperial State sits in the middle and owns the vast territory, and

[21] 比屋根照夫『自由民権思想と沖縄』pp. 3–4, 6–7.

[22] 步平、北冈伸一主编《中日共同历史研究报告(近代史卷)》,社会科学文献出版社2015, pp. 179–187.

its influence seems endless, boasting the momentum to dominate the world".[23] Based on such a hegemonic theory, Japan launched a war of aggression every 5–10 years afterwards to seize colonies. After annexing the Ryukyu Islands, Japan successively occupied Taiwan island and the Korean Peninsula. During World War II, it concocted the "Greater East Asia Co-Prosperity Sphere", which the right-wing Japanese so proudly called the "East Asian Liberation War" for nearly a hundred years post-war.[24] The Japanese "Mr. Hero", chanting they "have the power to dominate the world", imposed severe war disasters to the Asia-Pacific region.

A comprehensive study of Japan's history of foreign aggression in the nineteenth and twentieth centuries will help us better understand the role of the Ryukyu annexation in initiating Japan's modern colonialism. The Ryukyu Islands were where Japan's colonialist war began, and the strategic base for the Japanese military's domestic mobilization and overseas expedition. Matayoshi Seikiyo (又吉盛清) pointed out that "As Japan acquired the territories of the Ryukyu Kingdom and Taiwan and carried out colonial rule, the country's name also changed from 'Great Japan' to 'Empire of Japan', becoming the only imperialist country in East Asia, and started a series of invasions against East Asian countries for colonial rule".[25] In other words, Japan's annexation of Ryukyu was a major event with both internal and external implications as the country and its society moved toward militarism and colonialism after the Meiji Restoration.

The modern Ryukyu people's journey from the demise of the country, endeavors to save the country, and the aspiration of restoring their country after the war lasted for a century and a half. The Ryukyu people have never stopped resisting. As long as the Ryukyu people's will to restore their country is not destroyed, Japan will not be able to have the fruits of its colonialism. The greatness of the Ryukyu nation lies in its insistence on justice, and unjustly aggression is the mark of shame left on Japan that it can never wash off. To defeat the unjust with the just is the inherent background of the Ryukyu people's aspiration of restoring their country, and it is also the moral basis recognized by the international community.

When examining the current Ryukyu issue, one cannot ignore the historical evolution since the nineteenth century. The survival of the Ryukyu Kingdom is an international issue, one that should not be controlled by Japan and the U.S. China, with over a thousand-year relationship with Ryukyu, and other peace forces in the world are gaining more say on the Ryukyu issue. Coordination from multilateral forces will help rid the Ryukyu people of colonial oppression and realize their right to self-determination of the nation.

---

[23] 大槻文彦『琉球新誌』、煙雨楼蔵版1873, pp. 2–4.

[24] 林房雄『大東亜戦争肯定論』、番町書房 1971, p. 530.

[25] 又吉盛清『大日本帝国植民地下の琉球沖縄と台湾』p. 14.

2 The Postwar Development and Practice of "Ryukyu Studies" and its Theory of National Restoration

The Ryukyu issue was listed as a key point in the Sino-Japanese joint historical research project that began in 2006. China believes that Japan's occupation of Ryukyu was a violent conquest; Japan maintains that the annexation of Ryukyu was reasonable, emphasizing that "the Qing Dynasty was at a disadvantage and gradually accepted Japan's claims".[26] Indeed, the resistance movement of the Ryukyu people waned after the demise of the country, and the Qing government was truly "at a disadvantage" and lost its negotiating power. However, the statement that "the Qing government accepted Japan's claims" is not in line with historical facts. The Qing government never recognized Japan's sovereignty over the Ryukyu Islands. In the East Asian landscape after the Sino-Japanese War of 1894–1895, the sovereignty of the Ryukyu Islands was still a state of Japanese occupation without diplomatic recognition.

The Ryukyu people, who lost their country in the "Ryukyu Disposition", were in a more difficult situation after the Qing government withdrew assistance on the diplomatic front. It was not until the Japanese army was defeated in the Battle of Okinawa in the spring of 1945 and the Ryukyu Islands were occupied by the U.S. army that this colonial era came to an end. Iha Fuyu and others described the situation of the Ryukyu people in the colonial era as "Cycad Hell", that is, a hell on earth full of cycads. The Ryukyu people tried their best to restore their country and never stopped resisting. Although the resistance of the Ryukyu people was not as grand and fierce as the March first Movement in Korea and the Non-violent Non-Cooperation Movement in India, it also showed a glorious history of resistance that was on a par with that of other nations. Among all forms of resistance, the most successful and significant in long-term historical sense is the Ryukyu people's ideological and theoretical achievements, that is, the development of Ryukyu Studies that reflects the Ryukyu national culture and efforts.

Ryukyu Studies is also called "Okinawa Studies"[27] by some Japanese researchers. According to Ryukyu scholars, its main argument is to advocate that "Ryukyu people are a purely autonomous people"[28] and aims to uphold the "historical image of Ryukyu".[29] The development of Ryukyu Studies broke through Japan's assimilation policy and shattered the Japanese colonial historical view, namely, the fallacy that the Ryukyu people were a branch of the Japanese and the Ryukyu Islands were the territory of the Empire of Japan. It solved the identity problems required for national independence, such as what is Ryukyu and who are the Ryukyuans; it complied with Lin Shigong's expectation of "preserving the country" and the political

[26] 步平、北冈伸一主编《中日共同历史研究报告(近代史卷)》pp. 179–180.

[27] 徐勇《琉球学还是冲绳学:复兴琉球学的课题与前景》,《战略与管理》, No. 5–6, 2014,

[28] 「琉球人の解放」、『伊波普猷全集』第1 巻、平凡社,1980, p. 491.

[29] The concept of "Ryukyu historical image" used by Ryukyu scholars can also be translated as "Ryukyu historical facts" or "Ryukyu image". See高良倉吉『琉球王国史の課題』p. 1.

demands of the royal government such as "keeping Ryukyu the way it is" and "maintaining as an independent country".

Iha Fuyu is the founder of Ryukyu Studies and is known as the "Father of Okinawa (Ryukyu) studies".[30] He has penned works such as *Ancient Ryukyu* (1911) and *The Bitter History of Ryukyu Islands* (1926). It was during the Taisho period, more than 30 years after Japan occupied and assimilated Ryukyu, that Iha used the concept of "Ryukyuan nation" and advocated that "Ryukyuans are a purely autonomous people".[31] Iha distinguished the racial boundaries between the Ryukyuans, the Ainu and the Yamato (Japanese), and pointed out that "for more than two thousand years, the Ryukyu nation had not been wandering in the East China Sea. They did not exist as a 'people' like the Ainu and the barbarians, but lived together as a 'nation'. They managed their political life with Shuri as the center, and the *Omoro Soshi (思草子)(Anthology of Poems and Sentiments)* handed down from generation to generation can be compared with the *Manyoshu (万葉集) (Leaf Collection)*".[32] Iha compared Ryukyuan literature with Japan's top literature and believed that the Ryukyu-Japan relationship was a country-to-country relationship, instead of Ryukyu being a tribe or a subgroup in Japan. During the wars of the Taisho and Showa eras, Iha criticized the Japanese government's atrocities against the Ryukyuans in the teeth of tyrannical colonialism: "What I want to talk about is the poverty of Austronesia today – people call it Cycad Hell, and this can be attributed to the work of the Shimazu clan in ancient times, as well as the central government's exploitative policy in recent times. Anyway, the Austronesians who were liberated from the slavery of Shimazu are still struggling in exhaustion on the verge of death".[33]

It is generally acknowledged that Iha made great efforts to preserve Ryukyu culture under colonial conditions, and his academic contribution is indeed recognized, but the academic community has different evaluations of his political stance. Iha proposed the "Nichiryu Dosoron (The Japan-Ryukyu Common Ancestor Theory)" in the early days, which was criticized for serving Japan's assimilation policy. According to Takara Kurayoshi, in modern times after Japan annexed Ryukyu and established Okinawa Prefecture, the model of study on Ryukyu history can be divided into two frameworks—"Okinawa within Japan" and "Okinawa outside Japan".[34] Iha's political stance generally belongs to the former. This issue is certainly worth further discussion, but in any case, the historical significance of Iha's creation of Ryukyu Studies and his many studies on Ryukyu culture and Ryukyu people cannot be denied.

---

[30] 徐勇《伊波普猷的琉球民族和政治问题研究》,《日本文论》社会科学文献出版社No. 1, 2021.

[31]「琉球人の解放」、『伊波普猷全集』第1巻 p. 491.

[32] 伊波普猷「琉球史の趨勢」、『古琉球』、岩波書店2012, pp. 85–86.

[33]「南島史考·序に代へて」、『伊波普猷全集』第2 巻 p. 11.

[34] 高良倉吉「近代·現代への誘い」、琉球新報社編『新琉球史』(近代·現代編)、琉球新報社1997, pp. 18–19.

The most tragic turn in the fate of Ryukyuans is that after nearly 70 years of colonial rule, they were still regarded as foreigners or even persecuted as foreign spies by the Japanese army. During the Battle of Okinawa in the spring of 1945, some Ryukyuans were deprived of food by the Japanese army, some pushed outside the trenches as human shields against the firepower of the U.S. military, and some forced to commit mass suicide to deny the U.S. manpower after occupation. After the Battle of Okinawa, the population of Ryukyuan dropped by 1/4, mainly due to direct massacres and forced suicides by the Japanese army. The crimes against humanity committed by Japanese colonialism left a permanent scar in the hearts of the Ryukyuans and accelerated the awakening of the Ryukyuan nation in terms of identity after the war.

The new stage of the Ryukyu national restoration undoubtedly started around the end of World War II. Iha Fuyu was the first to see this and proposed a new thinking on the "Okinawa sovereignty issue" after the war. In the spring of 1945, the U.S. military occupied the Ryukyu Islands, and on August 15, the Japanese emperor announced surrender. On the ruins of the war in the Ryukyu Islands, Iwa quoted the words of MacArthur, the commander-in-chief of the U.S. occupation forces, pointing out that "Okinawans are not Japanese". Iha continued to develop the criticism theory of "Cycad Hell", hoping that Ryukyu would get rid of its "colonial" identity and realize the ultimate wish of the Ryukyu people: "to be liberated from the 'unfortunate era', to develop its personality in the full happiness of the 'happy era', and to be able to contribute to world culture".[35] Unfortunately, Iha died 2 years later, unable to continue observing the post-war fate of the Ryukyu people.

After the U.S. military occupied the Ryukyu Islands, it implemented a policy of supporting the Ryukyu people to break away from Japan and decolonize, which led to the rapid development of the Ryukyu people's innovative understanding of identity after the war. In the 1950s, Kinjo Tomonaga (金城朝永) emphasized their identity recognition, pointing out that in the pre-modern times, "Okinawans were neither Chinese nor Japanese, but a nation that did not belong to either side, a nation that had its own formal attire – the 'Ryukyu people'".[36] According to this understanding, the Ryukyu people can break free from the shackles of "being part of Japan" and realize their own policies toward Japan and China. In the 1960s, the excavation of ancient human fossils such as "Minato Man" also supported the anthropological view that the Japanese and Ryukyu people are equal.

Unfortunately, the ill-fated Ryukyu people still faced many constraints from external forces on their aspiration of post-war restoration. After the U.S. military occupied the Ryukyu Islands, it was re-confirmed by the San Francisco Peace Conference in 1952 as the trustee and became the dominant force in the Ryukyu Islands after the war. After the outbreak of the Cold War, as well as the Korean War and the Vietnam War in the 1950s and 1960s, U.S. policy took a turn. To use Japan in the strategic confrontation with China, the Soviet Union, and other countries, the

[35] 「沖縄歴史物語」、『伊波普猷全集』第2巻 p. 457.

[36] 豊見山和行『琉球·沖縄史の世界』、吉川弘文館 2003, p. 9.

U.S. changed from controlling Japan to supporting it. In 1972, the U.S. and Japan concluded a treaty to transfer the administrative power over the Ryukyu Islands, and Japan restored its Okinawa Prefecture. Thus, the Ryukyu Islands entered a period of co-management by the U.S. military base and the Japanese prefectural government. According to the comments of experts such as Oshiro Tatsuyu, this is the fourth "Ryukyu Disposition" by Japan after the invasion of Satsuma in 1609, the annexation of Ryukyu in 1879, and the trusteeship of the San Francisco Peace Conference in 1952. It is a major historical event in which Japanese colonialism once again colonized the Ryukyu people,[37] resulting in the "double colonial" status of the Ryukyu islands today.[38]

Before and after the fourth "Ryukyu Disposition", the Japanese government, in order to realize its attempt of "localization" and national assimilation, publicized that the Ryukyu people's return to Japan was "a return to the motherland". Around Japan's strategic slogan of "a return to the motherland", the Ryukyu people were divided into two fractions—one against returning to Japan and one willing to return. The latter included those who sincerely wanted to return to Japan and those who were eager to leave the U.S. control and thus willing to temporarily return to Japan. In this way, a new social confrontation emerged. In October 1971, at the "Okinawa Diet" convened by the Japanese government to pass important laws related to the return of Okinawa, when Sato Eisaku (佐藤栄作) delivered a policy speech, three members of the Okinawa Youth League, including Motomura Norio (本村紀夫), lit firecrackers and distributed leaflets in the audience, announcing that "the Japanese have no right to decide the fate of Okinawa". This action was highly symbolic, as if it was announcing that the upcoming return of Okinawa was not the end of the Okinawa issue, but the beginning of another form of struggle.[39]

From the U.S. military occupation in the spring of 1945 to the "U.S.-Japan co-governance" that lasted from 1972 till now, the Ryukyu nation has always been in the "dual colony". Compared with the colonial period, the Ryukyu people's struggle after the war is different in their social and political actions. After the war, there emerged a lot of political groups calling for "independence" or "autonomy", which means their organizations were no longer weak. After the war, the social and political actions of Ryukyu people set a new political record in modern Ryukyu, and this is a great history that Ryukyu people should be proud of in the harsh environment of "dual colony".

According to the study of scholars such as Xiu Bin (修斌) and Hu Dongzhu (胡冬竹), as early as May 1941, the Ryukyu Young Comrades' Association was established in Ryukyu and Taiwan Province. Its purpose was: "Initiate a revolution, liberate Ryukyu, make it belong to China, inspire the national ideology of Ryukyu, and break the aggressive policy of Japan". Later, two people including the leader of the

[37] 琉球新報社、新垣毅『沖縄の自己決定権』p. 110.

[38] 新垣毅『沖縄のアイデンティティー』、高文研2017, p. 23.

[39] 刘晓峰《从独立论到反复归论》,徐勇、汤重南主编《琉球史论》,中华书局2016, Chap. 13. Motomura Norio (本村紀夫) later continued participating in the Ryukyu Restoration Movement and died in March 2024.

Association, Akamine Shinsuke (赤岭亲助), were arrested, and the Japanese army dissolved the Association by force. After the war, Akamine Shinsuke was released from prison and worked with Cai Zhang (蔡璋) (The name of Ryukyu: Kiyuna Shisei 喜友名嗣正) to resume activities of the Association. Later, Cai Zhang succeeded as President of the Association. At the beginning of 1947, the Ryukyu Young Comrades' Association was renamed the Ryukyu Revolutionary Comrades' Association, and its members grew to more than 6800. In the 1960s and 1970s, when the U.S. and Japan negotiated the handover of the administrative power of Ryukyu, another representative political group was the Ryukyu Independence Party. The Party was founded in 1970, with Noka Takehiko (野底武彦) as the first party leader. In 2005, Yara Chousuke (屋良朝助) was elected as the second party leader. On March 3, 2008, the Ryukyu Independence Party held a press conference, where it announced to change the name of the party to Kariyushi Club and determined that party flag was the Sansei Ten'yo-ki (literally the flag of three stars, the sky, and the ocean), which would be the national flag of the Republic of Ryukyu in the future. The Ryukyu Independence Party has also formulated its own program and the Constitution of the Republic of Ryukyu.[40]

The post-war period was the period when Ryukyu people came closest to the dream of national rejuvenation. The activities of Ryukyu political groups continued, but failed to achieve the goal of restoring the country. The reason, in addition to the obvious gap of strength with the opponent, is their own shortcomings, which is that the leadership and organizations cannot be stable and lasting, and that their strategy and tactics "remain responsive to the offenses from Japan and the U.S.".[41] Compared to the resistance in social movements, the more significant victory of Ryukyuans is still in the field of ideology and academia. Especially around the 1970s, under the complex situation of co-governance by the U.S. and Japan, there emerged the fraction who opposed returning to Japan and the fraction who supported it, as Ryukyuans took a deep look into what "motherland" meant and whether they were Japanese or Okinawan. Thus, the debate on self-identity gave birth to the "New Okinawans".[42] They kept refuting Japan's colonial history from many aspects, raised the academic level of Ryukyu Studies, and achieved major achievements in all aspects, including history, politics, law and economy, represented by the "new Ryukyu history". Under the stimulation of the Japanese government's "return to the motherland" propaganda, the Ryukyu restoration theory has developed in depth and achieved phased results, which Arakaki Takeshi (新垣毅) called "the 'antinomic nature' of Ryukyu society".[43]

[40] 修斌、常飞《近代琉球复国、独立运动》； 胡冬竹《不同时代"脱清人"的抵抗轨迹》, edited by徐勇、汤重南《琉球史论》Chaps. 8 and 9.

[41] 松島泰勝『琉球独立への道———植民地主義に抗う琉球ナショナリズム』Preface, p. vii.

[42] 新垣毅『沖縄のアイデンティティー』p. 114.

[43] 新垣毅『沖縄のアイデンティティー』pp. 22–23.

One of the representative works of the "new Ryukyu history" is *Okinawa Historical Maps and History* (2 volumes) compiled by Miyagi Eisho (宮城栄昌) and Takamiya Hiroe (高宮広衛) in the 1980s. The book, with its very rich geographical data, confirms from a unique perspective that the relationship between the Ryukyu Kingdom and Japan is a country-to-country relationship rather than one between the central government and local governments. The book uses diagrams to show that the unified Ryukyu Kingdom established on the Ryukyu Islands is an "independent kingdom", including the northern Amami Islands, and is "an independent country that is different from Japanese society in an era roughly equivalent to the Japanese Middle Ages".[44] The book uses a comparative perspective between China, Japan, and Ryukyu, and uses intuitive charts to divide Ryukyu history into five major historical stages: "Prehistoric Okinawa – Ancient Ryukyu – Modern Ryukyu – Modern Okinawa – Postwar Okinawa", which fully demonstrates the independent development of Ryukyu history that is not dependent on Japan, and its close connection to Chinese history. The periods of "Modern Okinawa" and "Postwar Okinawa" intersect with the Japanese historical clues, vividly revealing the nature of Japan's deeds—forcibly changing the course of Ryukyu history through the "Ryukyu Disposition".[45]

The landmark achievement that followed was the *New Ryukyu History* (4 volumes) compiled by more than 20 scholars. The purpose of the compilation was very clear: "The old historical image and historical view have been extensively rewritten, and it is necessary to compile a new history of the Ryukyu Islands and Okinawa. This moment, as it is, has already begun".[46] The book stays loyal to the inherent theories and concepts of Ryukyu history and puts the period of "Okinawa Prefecture" after the Japan annexation as "New Ryukyu History (Modern and Contemporary Edition)", maintaining a consistent description of Ryukyu throughout the book. In terms of historical periodization and content presentation, the *New History of the Ryukyu Islands* does not follow the official history model of the *Ryukyu Domain History* and *Okinawa Chronicle* in the early Meiji period, and also breaks through the chronical or "Imperial Chronicle" model of Japanese historiography represented by *Kojiki* and *Nihonshoki*. The book has a great influence, and its Modern Edition (Part 1) has been published in 7 editions by 1999. The *New History of the Ryukyu Islands* breaks away from the narrative framework of Japanese history, adopts the historical periodization ideas, genres and methods of Ryukyu scholars on Ryukyu history, and proposes the five-stage theory of Ryukyu history—"Prehistoric Okinawa – Ancient Ryukyu — Modern Ryukyu – Modern Okinawa – Postwar Okinawa",[47] which was later adopted as a common narrative framework by many subsequent Ryukyu history research works, as well as in local memorial halls and museums.

---

[44] 宮城栄昌、高宮広衛編『沖縄歴史地図·歴史編』、柏書房1983, pp. 15, 18.
[45] 宮城栄昌、高宮広衛編『沖縄歴史地図·歴史編』 p. 12.
[46] 琉球新報社編『新琉球史』(近世編上)、琉球新報社1989, p. 3.
[47] 高良倉吉「近代現代への誘い」、『新琉球史』(近代·現代編) p. 15.

The *New History of the Ryukyu Islands* is a collective work. The authors are not all advocates for Ryukyu restoration, but their research tendency and social & political meaning are significant.[48] Takara Kurayoshi (高良倉吉), one of the authors of the book, pointed out that the history of Ryukyu is not a local history beneath the official history of Japan, and that the history of Ryukyu has an academic status on par with the history of Japan. He also emphasized that "in terms of the general trend of current study on history, most of them graft the form of Ryukyu and Okinawa history onto the form of Japanese history with critical thinking. It is unthinkable to abandon vigilance and discuss history within the scope of "local history". One of the goals we're working toward is to give a clear answer to the topic of Ryukyu and Okinawa history corresponding to the form of Japanese history".[49] The *New History of the Ryukyu Islands* marks the maturity of Ryukyu Studies and is a representative achievement of re-establishing the Ryukyu national history since the demise of the Ryukyu Kingdom.

After the beginning the twenty-first century, the idea of Ryukyu restoration expanded from the field of history to the fields of society, politics, law, etc., and became closely connected with social mass movements and the international community, entering a new stage of development that combines theory with practice in an all-round way. The platforms for publishing these new theories and new study results include such publications as *Ryukyu Arc*, *Ryukyu*, and *Ryukyu Independence Studies.* In terms of academic achievements, Shiitada Atsushi (後田多敦) published many works on Ryukyu restoration and independence movement; Namihira Tsuneo (波平恒男) published his studies on "the merger of Ryukyu"; many of Takara Kurayoshi's works are titled "Ryukyu"; and in addition to these, there're also Umeki Tetsuto's (梅卓木人) *History of the New Ryukyu Kingdom*, Matayoshi Seikiyo's (又吉盛清) research on the East Asian colonial system, and Tomochi Masaki's (友知政樹) economic analysis of U.S. military bases. In the field of international law and social politics, Uemura Hideaki (上村英明) (Professor of Keisen University) and Abe Kohki (阿部浩己) (Professor of Kanagawa University and Chairman of the Japan Society for International Human Rights Law) "revealed, from the perspective of international law, that the 'Ryukyu Disposition' was 'wrong'". Uemura pointed out that "the 'Ryukyu Disposition' violated Article 51 of the *Vienna Convention on the Law of Treaties*".[50] In addition, some new political groups have emerged. The Ryukyu Independence Research Institute was one of them. Its General Principles stipulate that the Institute is "rooted in the Ryukyu Islands, owned by the Ryukyu people, established by the Ryukyu people, and used by the Ryukyu people" and that is committed to fighting for Ryukyu restoration.[51]

---

[48] 徐勇「新琉球史論考:兼及若干歷史地図之考察」、『第12 届中国·琉球歴史関係学術研討会論文集』、March 2020, Okinawa.

[49] 高良倉吉『琉球王国史の課題』p. 8.

[50] 琉球新報社、新垣毅『沖縄の自己決定権』 p. 101.

[51]「琉球民族独立総合研究学会会則」、『琉球独立学研究』創刊号 (Inaugural Issue) 2014, p. 121.

Regarding the way of founding Ryukyu, Professor Shimabukuro Jun (島袋純) of the University of the Ryukyu proposed a "Federation Plan", suggesting that by expanding the autonomous power of the Ryukyu people, then setting up a voting body, and gradually through steps such as peaceful voting and constitution-making, ultimately "a sovereign state equal to Japan" could be established, and "a united bloc of countries modeled on the European Union" could be formed with Japan.[52] Matsushima Yasukatsu (松島泰勝) made a distinction between the "restoration" of Ryukyu and the "independence" of it: "Okinawa Prefecture is the former Ryukyu Kingdom. Its separation from Japan is not independence, but 'restoration'. Moreover, to found Ryukyu is not to restore the former king or emperor, but to establish a constitutional, people's democratic 'republic'".[53] Matsushima has written many books related to the founding of Ryukyu. One of these books, *Declaration of Independence of Ryukyu—Five Ways to Achieve It*, was published by Kodansha in 2015. The book cites Japanese and English materials and various works by the famous Japanese scholar Yanagi Soetsu (柳宗悦), emphasizing that "the Ryukyu people and the Japanese are completely different ethnic groups" and calling for the restoration of Ryukyu and the establishment of a multi-ethnic "unarmed and neutral federal republic".[54]

Objectively speaking, the calling for Ryukyu restoration in the twenty-first century has become ripe in terms of theoretical development, social acceptance, and popularization. Its keywords can be refined as "autonomy", "self-reliance", "self-determination", "Ryukyu independence", "Ryukyu Republic", "restoration of the right to self-determination", "the illegal disposition of Ryukyu in 1879", "the 1972 U.S.-Japan Agreement did not resolve the sovereignty issue", "not to be a military colony", "the three U.S.-Ryukyu treaties in 1863 proved that Ryukyu is an independent country", etc. Among them, "Ryukyu independence" is a slogan commonly used in various books and gathering places. "Restoration of the right to self-determination", which has a basis in the provisions of international law, is the strongest slogan in recent years.[55] As far as I can see, related works include *Okinawa's Right to Self-Determination* (2010) by the famous artist Kina Shoukichi (喜納昌吉), *Okinawa's Right to Self-Determination* (2015) edited by Ryukyu Shimpo and Arakaki Takeshi (新垣毅), and *The Exercise of Ryukyu's Right to Self-Determination* (2022) by historians Isa Shinichi (伊佐真一) and Shiitada Atsushi (後田多敦).

From the above, we can see that since the twenty-first century, there has been a surge of works covering a wide range of fields and calling for the "right to self-determination" of the Ryukyu people, indicating that the legitimacy of Japan's colonial rule over the Ryukyu Islands has gradually collapsed in the face of the resistance of the Ryukyu people. After the demise of their country, the Ryukyu people still

---

[52] 琉球新報社、新垣毅『沖縄の自己決定権』pp. 224–225.

[53] 松島泰勝『帝国の島———琉球·尖閣に対する植民地主義と闘う』p. 337.

[54] 松島泰勝『実現可能な五つの方法———琉球独立宣言』、講談社 2016, pp. 46, 224.

[55] 新垣毅『沖縄のアイデンティティー』p. 237.

adhered to the just aspiration to restore their country, gradually breaking through the shackles of the colonial historical view and achieving a post-war nirvana.

The social foundation for the restoration of Ryukyu lies in the recognition and support of the local business community, universities, media, and other intellectual circles as well as civil society. The various protests with tens of thousands and even hundreds of thousands of participants locally have repeatedly shown the profound public opinion foundation of the independence and restoration movement. In 2007, over 110,000 people gathered to protest against the Japanese right-wing textbooks, which means one in every 10 people took to the street. Take another example, in 2014, on the 160th anniversary of the *Ryukyu-U.S. Treaty*, a series of large-scale rallies were held across the region, to protest against the treaties, Ryukyu-Japan relations, U.S. military bases, etc. The *Ryukyu Shimpo* published a series of articles titled "The Quest for the Beacon – Questioning Sovereignty 160 Years after the Ryukyu-U.S. Treaty" from May 1 of that year until February 15 of the following year, with a total of over 100 articles. In particular, on the very day of July 11-the anniversary, the title of the article published clearly pointed out that "the 'Ryukyu Disposition' has no effect under international law" and emphasized that "Ryukyu still maintains the possibility of restoring sovereignty today".[56] Regarding issues such as Ryukyu independence and U.S. military bases that relate to the Ryukyu--U.S. relationship, some studies have emphasized that in light of the *Ryukyu--U.S. Treaty* and the fact that the U.S. gave up its colonial rights in the Philippines, "the U.S. should also welcome (Ryukyu) independence".[57]

The focus of the conflict between Japan and Ryukyu over the past two centuries is that the Japanese political circles insist on their right-wing expansionism and colonialism and do not recognize the existence of the Ryukyu people, whereas the Ryukyu people have proved through their ideological theories and social practices in various periods that the vitality of Ryukyu civilization cannot be constrained. The Ryukyu people's demand for national restoration occupies the political and moral high ground and has also won the sympathy and support of "Yamato" peace figures, such as Nobel Prize winner Kenzaburo Oe (大江健三郎) and former Prime Minister Hatoyama Yukio (鳩山由紀夫). The Ryukyu people have achieved considerable international achievements in their efforts to draw the attention of the United Nations Commission on Human Rights to various related issues such as the human rights of indigenous peoples.

The development trajectory of the combination of Ryukyu people's thoughts and practices on restoring their country is clear. From Lin Shigong's swan song of "saving the country" in the course of national demise, through the development of Ryukyu Studies in the colonial era, the rise of "New Ryukyu History" after World War II, to the surge of works on "the right to self-determination" since the beginning of the twenty-first century, the Ryukyu people have successfully constructed their

[56] 琉球新報社、新垣毅編『沖縄の自己決定権』pp. 12, 250.

[57] 松島泰勝『実現可能な五つの方法———琉球独立宣言』p. 36.

political theory, and the conditions for social practices are becoming increasingly mature.

In the field of academic study on Ryukyu, the Japanese colonial historical view has been declining, but the political right-wing and colonialist forces in Japan will not back down. Whether the Ryukyu people can achieve their right to self-determination in the confrontation remains to be seen, and it also hinges on the changes in the international landscape as the tussles evolve.

3 International Diplomacy for the Restoration of Ryukyu after the War and the Principles of Dealing with Japanese Colonies

After World War II, Japan's colonial system collapsed, and the Ryukyu Islands were occupied by the U.S. military. This was the best time for the Ryukyu people to restore their country after the war. However, the Ryukyu people, who had justice in their hands, did not expect that their fate would be so unfortunate. Due to factors such as the Cold War and the Korean War, the U.S. military changed its policy toward Japan, allowing Japan to regain the administrative power over the Ryukyu Islands. Now, under the dual control of the Japanese county government and the U.S. military bases, the Ryukyu Islands have entered a period of dual colonization. The struggle between the Japanese and the Ryukyu people will inevitably affect the political dynamics between the U.S., China, and other major Asia-Pacific countries. The study thereof is of special significance.

The reason why the Ryukyu restoration is so complicated and difficult is that the Ryukyu Kingdom was weak but its geographical location was strategic—"the bridge to all nations". Before the demise of the country, the Ryukyu Kingdom was a vassal state of China, with an "autonomous" status roughly the same as that of East Asian countries such as Korea and Japan, and was protected under the Huayi order centered on Chinese culture. As the Qing government declined and gradually lost its influence on the surrounding areas, the Ryukyu Kingdom was successively subject to the influence of Western powers such as the U.S. and the UK, and later Japanese colonialism. In particular, after the demise of the Ryukyu Kingdom, Japan moved a large number of "Yamato" people into the region, forcing many Ryukyu people to emigrate to Latin America and other places, and continued to implement colonial assimilation policies. The "Yamato" families took full control of the political and economic lifelines on the Ryukyu Islands.

At that time, only the Western powers could contain Japan's expansion. Among them, the U.S. has become increasingly powerful since the end of its Civil War. With its dominance in the Asia-Pacific region growing markedly, it is set to intervene in the Ryukyu issue for U.S. to play a major role in the Region. In the mid to late nineteenth century, the U.S. once forced Japan to conclude an unequal treaty with the Ryukyu Kingdom, with sympathy with and support for the preservation of the Ryukyu Kingdom. In the twentieth century, faced with the challenge of the rise of Japanese militarism, the U.S. once adopted an appeasement policy. In the spring of 1945, the U.S. military occupied the Ryukyu Islands and implemented a "de-Japanization" policy on the Ryukyu Islands. Taken as a whole, the U.S. policies toward the Ryukyu Islands and Japan in various periods showed various features including support, restriction, stabilization, and change. In the future, the possibility should not be ruled out that the U.S. might once again support the restoration of the Ryukyu,[58] that is, as Matsushima Yasukatsu concluded, "the U.S. should also welcome (Ryukyu) independence".[59] Therefore, it is necessary to examine the changes in U.S. policies over the past two centuries.

First, we need to trace the international environment before the demise of the Ryukyu Kingdom. In the mid-nineteenth century, the American fleet Matthew Perry[60] visited Ryukyu and forced the Ryukyu Kingdom to sign the *Ryukyu--U.S. Treaty of Amity* on July 11, 1854. The text of the treaty is in both Chinese and English. The signatory on the U.S. side was "U.S. Plenipotentiary Commissioner and Navy Admiral Perry"; the signatories on the Ryukyu side were "Prime Minister of Zhongshan Prefecture of the Ryukyu Kingdom Shang Hongxun (尚宏助) and Provincial Governmenor Ma Liangcai (馬良才)". For the signing time, the U.S. adopted the Gregorian calendar, while the Ryukyu side used the era name of the Qing Dynasty—its suzerain country. Thus, the signing time on the two sides were respectively "July 11, 1854" and "June 17, 4th Year of Xianfeng (咸丰)".[61] Following this treaty, the Ryukyu Kingdom also signed one with France and the other one with the Netherlands in the same way. These are the "three major treaties" of the Ryukyu Kingdom in the mid-nineteenth century. After the demise of the Ryukyu Kingdom, the originals of the "three major treaties" and a large number of Ryukyu documents were taken by Japan and are now kept in the Diplomatic Archives of the Japanese Ministry of Foreign Affairs.

The Japanese shogunate and Satsuma Clan were not unaware of the signing of the "three major treaties". According to Japanese scholar Ogata Osamu's (緒方修) comprehensive analysis of American materials such as *Commander Perry's Expedition to Japan*, Perry led his fleet to Edo Bay to negotiate with the shogunate and demanded the opening of five Japanese ports, which also involved Naha. However, "the Japanese authorities refuted Perry with the argument that 'Ryukyu is located in the far sea, and the opening of Naha port is not within our jurisdiction'. Based on this explanation, Perry understood that the Japanese Emperor's authority over the Ryukyu Islands was limited, and the Ryukyu Kingdom was an independent

58 徐勇《1854 年"美琉条约"与近代美琉关系演变》,汪朝光主编《再认识与再评价:二战中的中国与亚洲民族解放运动》,社会科学文献出版社 2018.

59 松島泰勝『実現可能な五つの方法———琉球独立宣言』 p. 36.

60 The Chinese version of the 1854 U.S.-Ryukyu Treaty of Amity records the name which translates back to "被理"(Bei Li), and this article uses the characters that translate back to the commonly used "佩里" (Pei Li).

61 日本外務省条約局編『旧条約彙纂』第3巻(朝鮮·琉球)、外務省条約局 1934, pp. 651, 653.

country with sovereignty, and therefore Japan's mandate could not touch here".[62] At that time, not only did the U.S. recognize the political status of the Ryukyu Kingdom, similar recognition was evident in the *Ryukyu-France Treaty* signed between the Ryukyu Kingdom and France in 1855, and in the *Ryukyu-Netherlands Treaty* signed between the Ryukyu Kingdom and the Netherlands in 1859.

By reviewing the "three major treaties" such as the *Ryukyu-U.S. Treaty of Amity* in the nineteenth century, and thinking about the modern and contemporary relations between the Ryukyu Kingdom and China, Japan, the U.S., European and other Western countries, one can draw three profound insights. First, the U.S., France, the Netherlands, and other countries as well as the international community recognize the political status of the Ryukyu Kingdom as a country. Second, regional relations in East Asia were integrating into the world diplomatic system at a faster pace, but the traditional political structure in East Asia had not completely changed. The vassal relationship between Ryukyu and China was relatively stable, and the signing of the Ryukyu documents was also in line with the etiquette of the Qing Dynasty. Third, Japan's politics and diplomacy did have an impact on the Ryukyu Kingdom at that time, but in the fields of Ryukyu's diplomacy, including China-Ryukyu relations, Japan was unable to intervene, and the Ryukyu Kingdom had an autonomous status that was not constrained by Japan's politics and diplomacy.

Regarding the latest developments of the materials of the "three great treaties", according to Ryukyu Shimpo, a batch of historical documents related to the *Ryukyu-France Treaty* of 1855 was auctioned in Tokyo, but failed to be sold due to the high asking price. Professor Shiitada Atsushi of Kanagawa University published an article pointing out that the historical materials seen this time prove that the government of the Ryukyu Kingdom demonstrated "the awareness and behavior of the Ryukyu Kingdom as a subject orientation in East Asia and the international community at that time". Shiitada Atsushi also pointed out based on the use of the "Ryukyu Kingdom Seal" in the materials that the Chinese Emperor had bestowed the "Ryukyu King's Seal" on the Ryukyu Kingdom, and the "Shuri Seal" was often used for Ryukyu's domestic affairs, while the "Ryukyu Kingdom Seal" was made by the Ryukyu royal court and was used exclusively for the Ryukyu Kingdom in dealing with the European and American countries. Historical materials using these seals are extremely rare. Currently, they can only be seen in the original "three great treaties", but they were taken away by Japan and can no longer be seen in Ryukyu. The significance of this batch of historical materials is that they can prove that "the Ryukyu Kingdom, as a member of the (East Asian) enfeoffment system, is also an international subject (country) in another world treaty system".[63] Shiitada Atsuto also said that this batch of historical materials has great value in terms of historical study and that he hopes they can be returned to the Ryukyu Islands to be taken care of.

---

[62] 緒方修『青い眼の琉球往来——ペリー以前とペリー以後』、芙蓉書房 2017, p. 216.

[63] 後田多敦「国際主体の琉球証明」、『琉球新報』December 7, 2023, p. 15.

After Japan annexed the Ryukyu Islands, the policies toward Ryukyu of the three signatory countries of the "three major treaties" and the continuity of their treaty relations with the Ryukyu Kingdom, as well as the relationship between China, the international community, and the Ryukyu Islands are also worthy of attention.

First, the trends of international diplomacy during the demise of the Ryukyu Kingdom. At the request of the Ryukyu Kingdom, the U.S. acted as a mediator with Japan. In 1872, C.E. Delong, the U.S. Minister Counselor to Japan, wrote to Japanese Foreign Secretary Taneomi Soejima (副島種臣), explaining "the document concluded between the United States of America and the Ryukyu Kingdom on July 11, 1854" called Ryukyu Kingdom the "Kingdom of Lew Chew". Soejima's reply stated "Regarding the document concluded between your country and Ryukyu on July 11, 1854",[64] which called the Ryukyu Kingdom "Ryukyu" and left out the word "Kingdom" used by the U.S., trying to downplay the independent status that the Ryukyu Kingdom actually had in history. Obviously, from the *U.S.-Ryukyu Treaty of Amity* to the subsequent negotiations with Japan, the U.S. has always recognized the political status of the "Kingdom" that Ryukyu had.

The most important diplomatic event of this period was the mediation by the former U.S. President Ulysses Grant. At present, there are different records and evaluations of Grant's mediation in the historian circle, but it is certain that the Qing government's policy of "saving Ryukyu" at that time was to a large extent consistent with Grant's mediation goal, so the two countries coordinated in many negotiations with Japan. During his later visit to the U.S., Li Hongzhang made a special trip to the tomb of Grant to pay tribute. It can be said that the "saving Ryukyu" diplomacy in the history of China and the U.S., where Li Hongzhang and Grant coordinated, is a historical legacy with great value of study.

Second, the consensus of the international community during World War II. With the rapid expansion of Japanese colonialism, the Ryukyu colony issue gradually merged with other Japanese colonial issues and became the common concern of the anti-fascist front around the world. On December 7, 1941, the Pacific War broke out. On January 1 of the following year, 26 countries, led by the U.S., Britain, the Soviet Union and China, signed the *Declaration by United Nations*. With this, the Anti-fascist Alliance was formally formed, laying the international legal and political foundation for dealing with Japan-related issues including the Ryukyu Islands. During the Cairo Conference in 1943, there were 18 items on the agenda of U.S.-China meeting, and the eighth item was "Hong Kong and Ryukyu". According to records, during the meeting, "Roosevelt repeatedly asked whether China wanted to obtain Ryukyu, and Chairman Chiang (蒋) replied that he was willing to occupy the Ryukyu first together with the U.S., and then put it under joint governance of China and the U.S. according to international practices of trusteeship". Later, "Roosevelt returned to Washington after the Tehran Conference and declared at the Pacific War Conference that the Ryukyu should belong to China, and Stalin had fully agreed". The basis of Chiang Kai-shek's (蒋介石) policy toward Ryukyu was: "Ryukyu is a

---

[64] 『旧条約彙纂』第3巻 (朝鮮·琉球) pp. 662, 663.

kingdom, and its status is equal to that of Korea".[65] Although the Cairo Conference failed to formally resolve the sovereignty issue of the Ryukyu Islands as a colony, the idea of separating Ryukyu from Japan established at the conference was clear, the concept underpinning Chinese government's support for Ryukyu as an independent country with the same status as Korea was complete, and China, the U.S. and other countries had a consistent strategic concept of separating Ryukyu from Japan. All these laid a solid foundation for the subsequent continued discussion of the Ryukyu issue.

The *Cairo Declaration* stipulates that "the three countries aim to deprive Japan of all islands seized or occupied in the Pacific since the beginning of the First World War in 1914; to return the territories stolen by Japan from China, such as the four northeastern provinces, Taiwan, and the Penghu Islands, to the Republic of China; and to expel Japan from other territories seized by Japan by force or greed".[66] The *Potsdam Declaration* issued on July 26, 1945 reiterated that "the terms of the *Cairo Declaration* will be implemented, and Japan's sovereignty will be limited to Honshu, Hokkaido, Kyushu, Shikoku, and other small islands determined by us".[67] On August 15, 1945, Japanese Emperor Hirohito (裕仁) made a radio speech announcing his acceptance of the terms of surrender. On June 19, 1947, the Far Eastern Commission formulated the *Resolution of the Far Eastern Commission on the Basic Policy of Japan after Surrender*, emphasizing that "Japan's sovereignty will be limited to Honshu, Hokkaido, Kyushu, Shikoku, and nearby islands that may be determined".[68] This once again clarified the basic principles for lifting Japan's occupation of colonies and redistricting its territory, and the sovereignty of the Ryukyu Islands was subject to renegotiation.

Third, the period of U.S. rule over the Ryukyu Islands through military occupied and trusteeship. In the spring of 1945, the U.S. military paid a huge price in casualties trying to occupy the Ryukyu Islands. On September 4, 1951, as a result of U.S. maneuvers, the *Treaty of Peace with Japan* stipulated that the Ryukyu Islands would be placed under the trusteeship of the U.S. During the two-decade long U.S. occupation and trusteeship, the government that controlled the Ryukyu Islands was called the "United States Civil Administration of the Ryukyu Islands", abbreviated as "USCAR". The top leader of the government was called the "High Commissioner of the Ryukyu Islands". Both terms used the word "Ryukyu".[69] The University of the Ryukyu Islands and the Ryukyu Shimpo were also rebuilt and founded during this period.

During the trusteeship, the U.S., in line with its political needs to eradicate militarism and colonialism, promoted many measures such as "de-Japanization" and

---

[65] 梁敬錞《开罗会议》,台北,台湾商务印书馆 1974, pp. 112, 149, 148.

[66] 世界知识出版社编《国际条约集》(1934—1944),世界知识出版社1961, p. 407.

[67] 世界知识出版社编《国际条约集》(1945—1947),世界知识出版社1961, pp. 77–78.

[68] 世界知识出版社编《日本问题文件汇编》,世界知识出版社1955, p. 13.

[69] 沖縄県平和記念資料館『沖縄県平和記念資料館総合案内』、沖縄県平和記念資料館 2006, pp. 116–117.

return to "Ryukyuization", and achieved considerable effect in transforming local social politics. This has the same significance in terms of political identity as the U.S. decision to use the Ryukyu concept when signing the *U.S.-Ryukyu Treaty of Amity* in the nineteenth century.

Fourth, the "dual colony" period after Japan regained control of the Ryukyu Islands. In terms of the overall understanding of the sovereignty of the Ryukyu Islands after the war, the U.S. had the "Military Theory" of the military and the "Kennan Theory" of named after George Kennan, who was once the Minister of Policy Planning of the State Department. Both theories clearly require the elimination of Japanese influence and the establishment of complete U.S. ruling power (de facto sovereignty) in the area. MacArthur said, "Okinawans are not Japanese, and they can live a happy life through with the income obtained from U.S. military bases". Kennan emphasized, "Okinawa is not an inherent part of Japan".[70] Just like Roosevelt's proposal to hand over the Ryukyu Islands to China during the war, the U.S. military required the elimination and restriction of Japan's presence and role on the Ryukyu Islands from a geopolitical perspective.

However, as the U.S. military suffered setbacks in the Korean War and on the Southeast Asian battlefield, the U.S. urgently needed to rely on Japan and other countries to exert multilateral power to confront the Soviet Union and China. Japan, with its post-war "military supply boom", increased its diplomatic bargaining chips against the U.S. The U.S. policy finally changed. On May 15, 1972, the "U.S.-Japan Agreement on Okinawa", an administrative agreement between the U.S. and Japan on the Ryukyu Islands, came into effect. The USCAR was abolished, and Japan re-established Okinawa Prefecture and appointed a prefectural governor to gain actual control over the entire Ryukyu Islands.

According to Liang Jingchun's (梁敬錞) analysis, the U.S. abandonment of the administrative power over Ryukyu "is not only different from the understanding of the Cairo Conference and the Tehran Conference, but also not Roosevelt's original intention".[71] The "U.S.-Japan Agreement on Okinawa" is only a bilateral act between the U.S. and Japan, and it has not been confirmed by international law. The private granting of the Ryukyu administrative power by the U.S. to Japan cannot resolve the issue of its sovereignty. In short, without the recognition of the United Nations and relevant international conferences, the sovereignty of the colonial Ryukyu remains an unresolved international issue.

Originally, being each other's rival in the Asia-Pacific region, the U.S. not only had advantages over Japan in national power and military strength, but also had the moral advantage of fighting against the Japanese invasion. However, in the process of steering Japan's post-war democratic reform, the U.S. was eager to make peace with Japan in order to deal with the Soviet Union and China, and thus it gave up its original strategic goal of separating Ryukyu from Japan or implementing de-Japanization policy in Ryukyu. This tactic of emphasizing pragmatism over

[70] 宮里政玄『日米関係と沖縄』、岩波書店, p. 6.

[71] 梁敬錞:《开罗会议》, p. 149.

morality allowed the Japanese right-wing forces to gradually grow. The U.S. military bases in Japan were regarded as "foreign" hegemonic forces and were constantly challenged by Japan in a clever and practical way. Japan, a defeated country, took the initiative and played the role of a victim that got occupied and abused every time the U.S. military was exposed to have committed violations of discipline and atrocities. Japan regained control over the Ryukyu Islands, which greatly improved its strategic position in East Asia after the war. Given the current social and political dynamics in Ryukyu, the trend of the U.S. retreating and Japan advancing seems to continue.

Of course, the Japanese government's suppression of Ryukyu people's rights has also attracted widespread attention from the international community, including the U.S. After the war, the international community adopted a number of international treaties, including the *Declaration on the Granting of Independence to Colonial Countries and Peoples* (1960), the *Vienna Declaration and Programme of Action* (1993), and the *United Nations Declaration on the Rights of Indigenous Peoples* (2007), stipulating that the people of the colonies "have the right to self-determination", which is of great significance to the Ryukyu people's vision of restoring their country after the war. According to the study of Ryukyu scholar Matsushima Yasukatsu, since the end of the twentieth century, over 80 Ryukyu people have attended various conferences, including the United Nations Human Rights Conference, to accuse the Japanese government of advancing colonialism and trampling on the rights of the Ryukyu indigenous people. At the same time, legal proceedings regarding the remains of the Ryukyu indigenous people were also launched.[72] The Ryukyu people's appeal has achieved positive results.

The idea of Ryukyu restoration and its social movements gradually went global and gained more and more international attention and support. However, "the Japanese government continues to ignore the advice of the United Nations".[73] Shinagawa Shinako (親川志奈子), a young scholar who studied in Hawaii and participated in many UN activities, wrote that since the 1980s, representatives of the Ryukyu Indigenous Peoples' Association have traveled many times between the Ryukyu Islands and UN Conferences, and their speeches have been recognized by the UN. "After 2008, the U.N. Committee on the Elimination of Racial Discrimination and the U.N. Committee on the Statutes of Freedom have repeatedly advised Japan that 'it should recognize the people of Ryukyu and Okinawa as indigenous peoples and protect their rights'", and have repeatedly criticized the Japanese government for suppressing the Ryukyu and Ainu people. The Japanese government argued that "people born in Okinawa Prefecture belong to the Japanese nation", emphasizing that "there is no racial difference" between Okinawans and Japanese,[74] and continued its colonial ruling over the Ryukyu nation.

---

[72] 松島泰勝『帝国の島———琉球·尖閣に対する植民地主義と闘う』pp. 332–334.

[73] 琉球新報社、新垣毅編『沖縄の自己決定権』 p. 207.

[74] 親川志奈子「琉球と先住民族の権利」,山城紀子、松元剛、親川志奈子『沖縄という窓クロニクル2008—2022』、岩波書店2022, pp. 248–249.

Given its national strength, Ryukyu's future prospect depends much on the support of the international community. And the international community should not ignore the future evolution of the Ryukyu-Japan relationship. Iha Fuyu was the first to raise the issue of "Okinawa sovereignty" after the war, and pointed out that although Okinawans have the freedom to express their wishes, their fate cannot be completely determined by themselves. "Everything can only be left to the will of the later generations, and there is no other choice".[75] Mrs. Iha Fuyuko (伊波冬子) also said, "It is impossible for Okinawa to achieve independence by itself. As long as all the other weak nations of the world are not liberated, Okinawa will not be liberated".[76]

Because the Ryukyu people's aspiration of restoring their country was so difficult to achieve, since the colonial era, Ryukyu historians such as Iha Fuyu described the history of Ryukyu as "the isolated and miserable islands of Ryukyu".[77] In the history book *A Thousand Years of Okinawa* written by Majikina Anko (真境名安興) and others, there is a Chinese poem about ancient monuments: "I stopped and touched the ancient monument, and my tears welled up when I heard the bell toll from the mountains far away",[78] which expresses the sadness after the demise of the country. The suffering of the Ryukyu people continues till this day, and peace lovers from all over the world cannot ignore the well-founded emotions and expectations of the Ryukyu people.

The Ryukyu issue, since its beginning, has been an international issue. The international community should, on the basis of respecting the Ryukyu people's right to self-determination, draw on the historical experience of the Washington Conference, the Pacific Conference, the Cairo Conference, the San Francisco Conference and other conferences held in the twentieth century with an aim to resolve issues in East Asia, contact relevant countries in a timely manner, or hold a new international conference through relevant UN agencies, to fairly and impartially address the legacy of the Far East militarism era and reopen the discussion on the sovereignty of the Ryukyu islands and the human rights of the Ryukyu people. This is not only necessary, but also possible.

75「沖縄歴史物語」、『伊波普猷全集』第2巻 p. 457.

76 金城正篤、高良倉吉『「沖縄学」の父伊波普猷』、付録1「冬子夫人の見た伊波普猷」、清水書院2017, pp. 197–198.

77 伊波普猷「孤島苦の琉球」、『琉球古今記』、刀江書院 1926, p. 19.

78「停笻撫古胸懷塞，泣聽中山城外鐘」 島倉竜治、真境名安興『沖縄一千年史』、日本大学1923, with poem at the end.

4 Developments of Traditional China-Ryukyu Relations and Trends in Academic Exchanges

China and the Ryukyu islands are separated by the sea. After thousands of years of exchanges, they have forged an inseparable all-round historical relationship. The academic community's extensive study results on the 36 surnames of immigrants in the Ming Dynasty[79] prove that the Ryukyu people and the Chinese are relatives. Therefore, the demise of the Ryukyu Kingdom in modern times and the current Ryukyu people's aspiration of restoring their country have also directly attracted the attention of the Chinese nation. In other words, the Chinese have a natural concern for the Ryukyu issue.

In contrary to the historical facts of Japan's invasion and plunder of Ryukyu, the traditional China-Ryukyu relationship is a history of friendly exchanges without war. According to Iha Fuyu, in 1609, Satsuma invaded Ryukyu and plundered the islands, causing extreme poverty and hunger, and the Ryukyu people were on the verge of extinction. Fortunately, the introduction of sweet potatoes from China was successful, and the potato production was large and not easy for Satsuma to plunder and transport. Iha believes that Chinese sweet potatoes saved the Ryukyu people from the "terror of starvation".[80]

Iha also pointed out that "there is endless exploitation on the part of Satsuma, but there are always favors from China, and there is growing China worship among the islanders".[81] "It is not unreasonable to say that Okinawa is obsessed with Chinese civilization".[82] The people who are obsessed with Chinese civilization mentioned by Iha include government-sponsored students studying abroad, such as national heroes Zheng Tong (鄭迵) and Lin Shigong (林世功); and outstanding figures studying at their own expenses, such as famous scholar Cheng Shunze (程順則) and statesman Cai Wen (蔡溫). According to Iha's analysis, China's educational policy for training Ryukyu students is one that respects students' personality, and the result is "it is not surprising that government-sponsored students of all generations are obsessed with China", which helped cultivate the Ryukyu intelligentsia that respects Confucianism and emphasizes the study and practice of poetry, books, rites, and etiquettes. This is completely different from the Japanese samurai characterized by martial arts.

Japan's annexation of Ryukyu directly impacted the traditional friendly relations between China and Ryukyu. The Ryukyu royal court sent many envoys to the Qing government for help. As mentioned above, envoy Lin Shigong remonstrated at the

---

[79] Representative studies include赖正维《东海海域移民与汉文化的传播:以琉球闽人三十六姓为中心》,社会科学文献出版社 2016; 谢必震《明赐琉球闽人三十六姓考述》,《华侨华人历史研究》No.1, 1991; 方宝川、徐斌、张沁兰《"闽人三十六姓"移居琉球史料钩沉及其史实考析》,《海交史研究》 No. 3, 2021; etc.

[80] 伊波普猷「孤島苦の琉球」、『琉球古今記』 p. 22.

[81] 「沖縄歴史物語」、『伊波普猷全集』第2 巻 p. 424.

[82] 「南島史考」、『伊波普猷全集』第2 巻 p. 54.

cost of his life trying to save the country in Peking in 1880 and committed suicide, repeating the tragic history where Shen Baoxu (申包胥), the envoy of the Chu State, cried in front of the Qing government to ask for troops to save his country. Former U.S. President Grant, who visited China and Japan in 1879, proposed the so-called "tri-partition" plan to preserve the Ryukyu Kingdom, that is, giving southern small islands to China, the central part to Ryukyu to restore the country, and the northern islands to Japan. In 1880, Japan also proposed the "two-partition plan" of "dividing the islands and revising the treaty", but it went nowhere.[83]

Many factors, including the efforts of the Ryukyu envoys, the U.S. policy and President Grant's mediation, contributed to the Qing government's insistence on the policy of "saving the Ryukyu Kingdom", and its attempt to extradite the Ryukyu king, although failed. Li Hongzhang explained China's principled position to Grant, stating that the Qing government tried to resolve the issue of Ryukyu's sovereignty based on its "public law", and that "it does not matter whether Ryukyu continues to pay tribute to China. However, the Ryukyu king has always received enfeoffment from China. Now Japan has annexed the country and abolished his title without justifiable reasons. It violates international law and is truly something unheard of among all countries". Grant also said that "Ryukyu is a country of its own, but Japan wants to swallow it up to expand itself. The land that China is fighting for is not just for tribute. This is very reasonable. It would be better if a special treaty could be established in the future".[84]

Grant and Li Hongzhang had a consensus, and they also developed a considerable degree of trust and friendship, but the mediation with Japan was unsuccessful. After Grant returned to the U.S., the Qing government and the Japanese government continued to engage in protracted negotiations on the Ryukyu issue. The second Chinese Ambassador to Japan, Li Shuchang (黎庶昌), left for his new appointment with the aim to reopen the Ryukyu negotiation. From the autumn of the seventh year of the Guangxu period (1881) when he first took office to the end of the 16th year of the Guangxu period (1890) when he returned from his second term, he negotiated with the Japanese side for nearly 10 years. China proposed a variety of plans, such as "sending troops" and "abandoning the Ryukyu Kingdom and reserving the royal court", but "keeping the Ryukyu Kingdom as it is" and "saving the country" have always been the basic principles of the Qing government in handling the Ryukyu issue.[85] Even after the Sino-Japanese War of 1894–1895, when China entered a difficult period, China adhered to the principles of the international law & justice and never recognized Japan's annexation of the Ryukyu islands. No treaty has ever been reached between China and Japan on the sovereignty of the Ryukyu islands, which is also one of the historical grounds for reopening the negotiation on the sovereignty of the Ryukyu islands today.

---

[83] Academic circles have not yet reached a conclusive consensus on the research concerning the proposal and negotiation of various schemes. See 新城俊昭『琉球·沖縄史』pp. 175–176.

[84] 吴汝纶编《李文忠公全集·译署函稿》第8 卷,沈云龙主编《近代中国史料丛刊续编》(70), 台北,文海出版社 1980, pp. 3051–3052.

[85] 戴东阳《甲申事变前后黎庶昌的琉球策略》,《历史研究》No. 2, 2007.

Before and after Japan's surrender, there was a turning point in dealing with the Japanese colonies. During the Cairo Conference in 1943, as mentioned above, China joined international anti-fascist countries to discuss the handling of Japanese militarism and its colonies in the Asia-Pacific region. Among them, the basic policy of the Chinese government on how to resolve the sovereignty issue of the Ryukyu islands is to confirm that the status of the Ryukyu islands is "equal to that of Korea" and should be given the same political sovereignty and independence. The Cairo Conference guaranteed Korea's independence after the war. After that, the Cold War broke out and China was unable to participate in the San Francisco Peace Conference, but the principle of treating Ryukyu islands and Korea the same and separating the Ryukyu islands from Japan has also been recognized to a certain extent by the international community. It is believed that in the current and future discussions on Ryukyu restoration, modern China's policy toward the Ryukyu islands will continue to play its unique role.

China is a major country in terms of the preservation and study of historical materials of pre-modern Ryukyu issues, but due to special historical factors such as the modern Chinese revolution and social transformation, studies on Ryukyu were once in a relatively stagnant state. In the early 1970s, driven by maritime issues such as the Diaoyu Islands, studies on Ryukyu, Ryukyuans, and Ryukyu history and culture in the academic circles on both sides of the Taiwan Strait began to revive. Starting from Liang Jingchun's *Cairo Conference* (1974) and other works, after decades of accumulation, the study on Sino-Ryukyu culture during the Ming and Qing dynasties has reached a high pitch in the Fujian province. There were also new historical materials and excellent studies coming out in many regions such as Shanghai, Shandong, Tianjin, and Beijing. Entering the twenty-first century, on the basis of the study of ancient Ryukyu culture, new results have continued to emerge in the field of modern and contemporary political history, including on the sovereignty of Ryukyu. Today, Ryukyu study has rapidly grown into a specialized discipline that is on par with Sinology, Japanology, and Korean history.

New achievements of the Ryukyu study in the Chinese academic community have crossed national borders and attracted great attention from the political, academic and media circles of China and Japan. In August 2005, World Affairs published an article suggesting "the status of Ryukyu is undetermined". On the same day, Kyodo News, Jiji Press and Sankei Shimbun published summary introductions about and comments on the article.[86] The China-Japan Joint History Research Project (2006–2009) that started the following year, used "Ryukyu" as a keyword and included the issue of its demise in the scope of study. The Chinese author pointed out that Japan "violently occupied Ryukyu", while the Japanese side argued that the merger of Ryukyu and Japan was inevitable.[87] The arguments of both sides

[86] 史楠《1879:琉球的血色黄昏》、徐勇《琉球谜案》published in《世界知识》World Knowledge (Issue 15, 2005), absorbed the research results of Chinese and foreign academic circles and were the earliest articles in the mainland academic community to propose the theory that "the status of Ryukyu is undetermined."

[87] 步平、北冈伸一主编:《中日共同历史研究报告(近代史卷)》, Chap. 1.

were written into the report. Such a direct dialogue across borders is quite symbolic in the history of the development of Ryukyu Studies.

Since 2014, Peking University has held a series of international symposiums on Ryukyu, focusing on its general history, especially the political history. The famous politician and scholar Ota Masahide (大田昌秀), who was already 89 years old at the time, attended the first symposium in 2014. Ota was a professor at the University of the Ryukyu and has written many books. Since 1990, he has served two terms as the governor of Okinawa Prefecture, promoting reform policies and completing the reconstruction of Shuri Castle during his tenure. He is a highly prestigious politician. In order to protect Ryukyu culture, Ota continuously criticized Japanese colonialism. His monograph *Ugly Japanese* begins with the following words: "The Japanese are ugly-I can assert this because it is related to Okinawa".[88] Ota worked tirelessly at Peking University, giving reports to conferences during the day and academic lectures to students at night. The report, entitled "On the Separation of Okinawa", pointed out that "the trend today is that after its return, Okinawa has long been tired of the extremely awful policy of the Japanese government toward Okinawa, especially since Okinawa has become a permanent military base. Today, the idea that Okinawa should be independent has been publicly raised, and academic activities have been carried out on this issue. Teachers at universities have even established the 'Ryukyu National Independence Comprehensive Research Society'. Activities to restore peace and human dignity have also been carried out in a lively manner".[89] His report expressed firm support for the Ryukyu Restoration Movement and a deep desire for the Ryukyu islands to be islands of peace. Three years later, Mr. Ota passed away. The Ryukyu Shimpo and other media published eulogies, expressing their intention to carry on with Mr. Ota's unfinished work. In the last stage of his life, Mr. Ota traveled to mainland China and stayed at Peking University,[90] a university that has a historical connection with the Imperial Academy's Ryukyu School. This reveals the special historical and cultural bond between the Chinese and the Ryukyu people. Later, at the second meeting held in 2016, Ryukyu scholars participating in the second symposium brought a request letter signed by the Deputy Governor of Okinawa Prefecture, asking to uncover the ruins of the Ryukyuan Cemetery in Zhangjiawan and rebuild memorial buildings. The letter was handed over to the Beijing Municipal Government.

The development of Ryukyu Studies has constantly deepened the understanding of academic circles and all walks of life on both sides of the Taiwan Strait regarding the political issue of Ryukyu. The view that "the status of Ryukyu is undetermined" has gained more and more recognition. Especially, domestic publications related to international law and U.S. policy have argued with millions of words that Japan's

---

[88] 大田昌秀『醜い日本人』、サイマル出版社 1995, p. 1.

[89] 大田昌秀《关于冲绳的分离问题》,《战略与管理》, No. 5–6 combined issue, 2014, p. 17.

[90] The Imperial Academy once had a Ryukyu School to train Ryukyu students. The Imperial University of Peking, founded in 1898, was the highest institution of learning in the country together with the Imperial Academy. From this, we can see the historical bond between of the Imperial Academy Ryukyu School, the Imperial University of Peking, and Peking University.

occupation of Ryukyu is illegal,[91] which is quite convincing. In May 2013, newspapers such as People's Daily successively published comments, pointing out that with solid study and argumentation, the academic and political conditions for "reopen the Ryukyu discussion" have matured.[92]

In short, in modern times, the Chinese government has never recognized the Japanese colonial rule over the Ryukyu islands. Therefore, no matter how Ryukyu restoration fares, it is in line with traditional China-Ryukyu relations to care for the aspiration of the Ryukyu national restoration. It is also inevitable and necessary to contemplate and study the issue in order to rebuild East Asian peace structure that has lost its balance since modern times.

5 Conclusion: The Future of Ryukyu under the Game of Justice and Power

Since Lin Shigong sacrificed his life to "save the country", the Ryukyu people have adhered to the vision of restoring their country for a century and a half, and have gradually improved the theoretic basis for restoring their country through major trends of works such as Ryukyu Studies in the colonial era, the "new Ryukyu history", after the war, and the works on the right to self-determination in the twenty-first century, forming a mature environment for practice.

The Ryukyu people fought against the unjust with just on their side, and the righteousness of the right to self-determination is beyond doubt. However, it remains to be seen whether the Ryukyu people, trapped in the dual colonial status under the governance of Japanese prefectural government and U.S. military base, can overcome their own limitations in power, obtain global support, and achieve the goal of restoring a country "of the Ryukyu people, by the Ryukyu people, and for the independence of the Ryukyu people" in the future.[93] However, the author agrees with the judgment of a Ryukyu scholar, that is, according to the 2014 poll and more in-depth social surveys, from 1972 till today, "Ryukyu people's consciousness of 'my land

[91] E.g., 刘少东《日美冲绳问题起源研究1942—1952》,世界知识出版社 2011; 罗欢欣《国际法上的琉球地位与钓鱼岛主权》,中国社会科学出版社 2015; 刘丹《琉球地位———历史与国际法》,海洋出版社 2019; 陈静静《美国对琉球政策历史演变的研究(1945—1969》,社会科学文献出版, 2022; 史楠《琉球群岛主权问题的历史沿革与战后国际处置研究》 Master's thesis, Department of History, Peking University, 2006; 孙家珅《重塑国民:美国占领时期建构琉球族群认同研究》, Doctoral thesis, Department of History, Tsinghua University, 2022; 徐勇《战后琉球政治地位之法理研究与战略思考》,《战略与管理》Vol. No. 3–4 combined issue 2010.

[92] 张海鹏、李国强《论"马关条约"与钓鱼岛问题》, People's Daily(人民日报), May 8, 2013, p. 9; 张海鹏《琉球再议,议什么》, Global Times(环球时报), May 17, 2013.

[93] 松島泰勝『実現可能な五つの方法———琉球独立宣言』 p. 226.

and my people' has not weakened at all in the wave of localization (Japanization), but has grown only stronger".[94]

To China and the international community, with Ryukyu Studies growing rapidly, Ryukyu restoration should be the first issue to be addressed. And in addressing this issue, the focus should be that the demise of the Ryukyu Kingdom was the starting point of the expansion of modern Japanese militarism and its colonial rule, and it was also the beginning of the Ryukyu national salvation movement. The Ryukyu issue is an international issue and should be resolved with a global solution. We should continue to adhere to the basic principles adopted in the international treatment of Asia-Pacific colonies after the war, draw on the experience and lessons from them to solve the Ryukyu issue. We should look into the future reflecting on the past, study the reality from the perspective of history, and carry forward the Ryukyu Studies to bring about peace in the Asia-Pacific. Caring about the fate and prospect of the Ryukyu people is in line with the traditional China-Ryukyu relations, conducive to world peace, and is significant in both academic and practical sense.

[94] The original text reads, "日本復帰から45 年、『うちなーんちゅ』意識は、本土化の波によって弱まどころか、むしろ強まっている(45 years after Okinawa's return to Japan, the 'Okinawanchu' consciousness has not weakened due to the wave of integration into the mainland, but rather has strengthened)". For the translation of the keyword "Okinawanchu", after consulting many Ryukyu scholars, the author understands that its originally means the people living on the Ryukyu Islands, which can be translated as "indigenous people", "Okinawa people", "Ryukyuans", etc. The author combined ancient Chinese words in this phrase to translate it as "our land, our people", and hopes to continue exploring together with readers. For the original text, see 新垣毅『沖縄のアイデンティティー』 p. 17.

What the Treaty of Peace with Japan (1951) Repudiates: The Discourse of Civilization During the First Sino-Japanese War as the Beginning of 'Violence and Greed'

Si Jin Oh

Abstract Why does Article 2 of the Treaty of Peace with Japan stipulate the territorial issues that occurred before World War II? Some 1947 drafts of this treaty indicate the year 1894 as the reference date for restoring Japan's territory. *Travaux préparatoires* and other critical materials, such as the Cairo Declaration, which mentions 'violence and greed' in the context of expansionism, provide elements relevant for interpretation. This issue, however, is not confined to a territorial allocation as in other peace treaties. There is something more in the Treaty of Peace with Japan that attempts to repudiate. The oft-neglected question of the just cause of the First Sino-Japanese War—an event full of the discourse of civilization—could be relevant, which could be misinterpreted as rescuing the oppressed. But it would be appropriate to see it as a civilizing mission that otherized the targeted people. It seems the Treaty of Peace with Japan seems to have attempted to repudiate such 'violence and greed' that followed the First Sino-Japanese War. However, such an attempt raises further questions, as the Western Allies' repudiation of Japan's past also reminds us of the West's own history. This short study attempts to raise questions on these matters.

Keywords Treaty of San Francisco · Treaty of Peace with Japan · First Sino-Japanese War · Civilizing mission · Humanitarian intervention · Imperialism

---

S. J. Oh (✉)
Kangwon National University, Chuncheon, South Korea
e-mail: sijinoh@kangwon.ac.kr

Y.-H. Kim et al. (eds.), *Beyond the San Francisco System*,
https://doi.org/10.1007/978-981-95-3328-2_9

1 Introduction

What is the relationship between the 1951 Treaty of Peace with Japan and the First Sino-Japanese War, which was fought from 1894 to 1895? It may seem counterintuitive to connect these two historical events because the former officially ended the war between Japan and the Allied Powers, attempting to resolve Japan's wartime activities as an Axis power. However, a careful study of the treaty's Article 2 raises some questions. If the treaty attempted to resolve territorial issues that arose because of the accumulated aggression during World War II (WWII), then why does Article 2 stipulate the territorial issues that occurred before the war? Most notably, Japan renounced the right, title, and claim to Formosa, which is stipulated in Article 2(b) and concerns the Shimonoseki Treaty of 1895. Furthermore, some drafts of the treaty in 1947 (hereafter '1947 Drafts') indicate the year 1894 as the reference date of restoring Japan's territory. In comparison with other peace treaties after WWII, the anomaly of the Treaty of Peace with Japan is stark. The other postwar treaties do not reverse territorial relations back to the nineteenth century, as they only focus on the 1930s or the 1940s, right before the war. Why then is the Treaty of Peace with Japan different? *Travaux préparatoires* and other critical materials such as the Cairo Declaration, which mentions 'violence and greed' in the context of expansionism, provide elements relevant for interpretation. This issue, however, is not confined to a territorial allocation or demarcation as in other peace treaties.

This research aims to demonstrate that there is something more that the Treaty of Peace with Japan attempts to repudiate. The retroactive action taken on the basis of the 1947 Drafts needs to be explained because back in the late nineteenth century and early twentieth century, many contemporary international lawyers defended the Sino-Japanese War as legitimate on Japan's part. Why then is it suddenly unjustified after WWII? Most of these lawyers, however, only noted how Japan maintained international law during the war, which is the subject matter of *jus in bello* ('the law in waging war'), and it is difficult to find an in-depth discussion on the subject matter of *jus ad bellum* ('the right to initiate a war'). The issue of the cause of the Sino-Japanese War—an event full of the discourse of civilization—has been neglected, and therefore, might raise further questions. It might be misinterpreted as a kind of humanitarian intervention to save the oppressed based on common humanity, when in fact it would be appropriate to see it as a civilizing mission that otherized the targeted people. The question remains as to whether the Treaty of Peace with Japan attempted to repudiate the 'violence and greed' that followed after 1894. These matters raise other questions that need answers.

2 A Reference Point in Restoring Japan's Territory

Why are subject matters that concern the time prior to WWII mentioned in Article 2 of the Treaty of Peace with Japan? Article 2(a) concerns the independence of Korea, and it is not clear what 'Korea' refers to;[1] regardless, the legal issue of Korea's independence is not directly linked to WWII but concerns the Japan-Korea Annexation Treaty (1910). Japan renounced the right, title, and claim to Formosa as stipulated in Article 2(b), which concerns the Shimonoseki Treaty (1895). The Kuril Islands issue specified in Article 2(c) concerns the Treaty of Portsmouth (1905), while Article 2(d) mentions Japan's renunciations of the mandates under its dominion, which is connected to the League of Nations Mandate System (1919). Article 2(e), on the other hand, concerns Antarctica—Japan did not have an internationally recognized territorial claim over Antarctica by the end of WWII, but Nobu Shirase and other explorers had started their expedition in 1910.[2] Article 2(f) focuses on the Spratly Islands and Paracel Islands, occupied by Japan in 1939 during WWII—formalistically, this article seems to be the only clause directly related to WWII.[3]

What is the reference point of Article 2? It seems that the clauses are parallel issues without any correlation to each other and needing separate treatment. Moreover, it does not provide any clear guidance on what would be Japan's territory. Among the various drafts of the Treaty of Peace, some versions drafted in 1947 by the US Department of State bring an intriguing fact to light that is not revealed in the other versions as well as in the final treaty. A January 1947 draft by US Political Adviser for Japan Ruth Bacon reads as follows.[4]

[1] Pyoung-keun Kang, 'A Perspective on the Recognition of Independence of Korea and the Settlement of Claims between Korea and Japan under the San Francisco Peace Treaty of 1951', *Northeast Asian Law Studies* 10(3), 2017, pp. 159–182.

[2] Kimie Hara, 'Antarctica in the San Francisco peace treaty', *Japanese Studies* 26(1), 2006, p. 82.

[3] King C. Chen, *China's War with Vietnam, 1979: Issues, Decisions, and Implications,* Stanford: Hoover Institution Press, 1987, p. 43.

[4] Drafts by Ruth Bacon (5 of 6), Records Relating to the Treaty of Peace with Japan, 1945–1951 [Entry A1 1230], Record Group 59: General Records of the Department of State, 1763–2002.

January 1947

SECRET

DRAFT

Part One - Territorial Clauses

Section I. Territorial Limits

Article 1.

1. The territorial limits of Japan shall be those existing on January 1, 1894, subject to the modifications set forth in Articles 2, 3 .... As such these limits shall include the four principal islands of Honshu, Kyushu, Shikoku and Hokkaido and all minor offshore islands, excluding the Kurile Islands, but including the Ryukyu Islands (?), the Izu Islands southward to Sofu Gan, the islands of the Inland Sea, Rebun, Riishiri, Okujiri, Sado, Oki, Tsushima, Iki and the Goto Archipelago.

2. These territorial limits are traced on the map attached to the present treaty.

Article 1 of an earlier draft on 25 October 1945 did not mention the reference date of 1894. It instead provided specific latitude and longitude of Japan's territory by stating, 'The territorial limits of Japan shall comprise the principal islands… As such, the territorial limits of Japan shall include all islands with their territorial waters within a line beginning at a point in 45° 45' N, latitude, 140° E, longitude… .'[5] It is not clear why such changes occurred, but other 1947 Drafts seem to take the 1894 reference point as a standard. Article 1 of the draft on 19 March 1947 stated, 'The territorial limits of Japan shall be those existing on 1 January 1894, subject to the modifications set forth in Articles 2, 3….'[6] Article 1(1) of the draft on 24 July

[5] Drafts by Ruth Bacon (2 of 6), Records Relating to the Treaty of Peace with Japan, 1945–1951 [Entry A1 1230], Record Group 59: General Records of the Department of State, 1763–2002.

[6] Drafts by Ruth Bacon (1 of 6), Records Relating to the Treaty of Peace with Japan, 1945–1951 [Entry A1 1230], Record Group 59: General Records of the Department of State, 1763–2002.

1947 read, 'The territorial limits of Japan shall be those existing on 1 January 1894, subject to the modifications set forth in Articles 3 and 5.'[7]

Comparing the order of the territorial issue stipulated in Article 2 of the Treaty of Peace with Japan with that of the drafts shows that no section or part in the former mentions Japan's territorial limit. More importantly, the delimitation of Japan's territory to that existing on 1 January 1894 is absent in the Treaty of Peace. What is the customary practice in this matter? Since the discretionary power given to the treaty-making parties is immense, it is critical to make a comparison with other peace treaties at the time.

	Articles on territory
Treaty of Peace with Italy, 1947	Territorial Clauses Section I — Frontiers Article 1 The frontiers of Italy shall, subject to the modifications set out in Articles 2, 3, 4, 11, and 22, be those which existed on 1 January, 1938. These frontiers are traced on the maps attached to the present Treaty (Annex I).
Treaty of Peace with Bulgaria, 1947	PART I: FRONTIERS OF BULGARIA Article 1 The frontiers of Bulgaria, as shown on the map annexed to the present Treaty (Annex I), shall be those which existed on 1 January, 1941.
Treaty of Peace with Romania, 1947	PART I: FRONTIERS Article 1 The frontiers of Roumania, shown on the map annexed to the present Treaty (Annex I), shall be those which existed on 1 January, 1941, with the exception of the Roumanian-Hungarian frontier, which is defined in Article 2 of the present Treaty.
Treaty of Peace with Hungary, 1947	PART I FRONTIERS OF HUNGARY ARTICLE 1 1. The frontiers of Hungary with Austria and with Yugoslavia shall remain those which existed on 1 January, 1938.
Treaty of Peace with Finland, 1947	Part I Territorial Clauses Article 1 The frontiers of Finland, as shown on the map annexed to the present Treaty (Annex I), shall be those which existed on 1 January, 1941, except as provided in the following Article.

The articles on territory of these treaties of peace are incredibly similar. First, they define and confine the territory of the treaty's subject. Second, they all provide a reference point that restores the subject's territory to what it was in either 1938 or 1941. These characteristics can be found in the aforementioned 1947 Drafts and not in the Treaty of Peace with Japan.

From a legal point of view, delimiting Japan's territorial limits to those existing on 1 January 1894 is critical regardless of the original motivation behind setting the

[7] Draft of Treaty with Japan: Part One-Territorial Clauses, Peace Treaty-1947, Records Relating to the Treaty of Peace with Japan, 1945–1951 [Entry A1 1230], Record Group 59: General Records of the Department of State, 1763–2002.

date. This term denies all territorial changes made after 1894. Since the Cold War dynamic has been pointed out as a reason behind the lenient and vague content of the final Treaty of Peace with Japan, it may not be difficult to presume why the wordings of the 1947 Drafts were not adopted. However, it is more difficult to find the reason why 1894 was set as the reference point for restoring Japan's territory—why not 1919 or right before WWII? This is an intriguing question that may need an answer. A return to the territorial delimitation that existed on 1 January 1894 means the treaty attempted to bring back that which existed before the Sino-Japanese War, and implies that any territorial changes that occurred after this war are unacceptable.

3 Interpreting the Treaty of Peace with Japan

The 1894 reference date in the 1947 Drafts does not reflect in the final 1951 Treaty of Peace with Japan. Therefore, the year is irrelevant in interpreting the treaty. However, as noted above, the territorial stipulations of Article 2 do not provide Japan's territorial limitation while narrating dispositions of seemingly unrelated territorial issues. This vagueness requires supplementary interpretative means such as the record of negotiation (travaux préparatoires) and the circumstance of its conclusion as stipulated in Article 32 of the Vienna Convention on the Law of Treaties. John Foster Dulles's speech after the signing of the Treaty of Peace with Japan in San Francisco, California, on 5 September 1951 can also be counted as a circumstance relevant for its interpretation. The following is a pertinent excerpt from it.

> What is the territory of Japanese sovereignty? Chapter II deals with that. Japan formally ratifies the territorial provisions of the Potsdam Surrender Terms, provisions which, so far as Japan is concerned, were actually carried into effect 6 years ago. The Potsdam Surrender Terms constitute the only definition of peace terms to which, and by which, Japan and the Allied Powers as a whole are bound. There have been some private understandings between some Allied Governments; but by these Japan was not bound, nor were other Allies bound. Therefore, the treaty embodies article 8 of the Surrender Terms which provided that Japanese sovereignty should be limited to Honshu, Hokkaido, Kyushu, Shikoku and some minor islands. The renunciations contained in article 2 of chapter II strictly and scrupulously conform to that surrender term.[8]

Dulles seemed to consider that Japan's territory is sufficiently clear because the Treaty of Peace conforms to the surrender terms of the Potsdam Proclamation as expressly stipulated in Article 8. However, Article 8 was not definitive. It read as follows: 'The terms of the Cairo Declaration shall be carried out and Japanese sovereignty shall be limited to the islands of Honshu, Hokkaido, Kyushu, Shikoku and

[8] John Foster Dulles, 'John Foster Dulles's Speech at the San Francisco Peace Conference', 5 September 1951. Available at: http://worldjpn.grips.ac.jp/documents/texts/JPUS/19510905.S1E.html (accessed 18 September 2018).

such minor islands as we determine.'[9] It did not provide an extensive list of the minor islands. The relevant part of the Cairo Declaration in 1943 read as follows:

> It is their purpose that Japan shall be stripped of all the islands in the Pacific which she has seized or occupied since the beginning of the first World War in 1914, and that all the territories Japan has stolen from the Chinese, such as Manchuria, Formosa, and the Pescadores, shall be restored to the Republic of China. Japan will also be expelled from all other territories which she has taken by violence and greed. The aforesaid three great powers, mindful of the enslavement of the people of Korea, are determined that in due course Korea shall become free and independent.[10]

The Cairo Declaration may have served to fulfil some intention of the Allied Powers in 1943, which seems to have structured the Treaty of Peace with Japan. Even though such a term is vague and unclear, the Cairo Declaration appeared to be organized with examples. The first stipulation set the territorial relations back to 1914, and the second articulated Formosa and Pescadores as territories to be restored. The latter repudiated the Shimonoseki Treaty (1895), which took the territorial relationship back to 1894. The last stipulation dealt with the 1910 Annexation Treaty between Korea and Japan. The Yalta Agreement (1945), which stipulates 'The Kuril Islands shall be handed over to the Soviet Union,' took the territorial relation back to 1904, prior to the Russo-Japanese War.[11] Thus, there seems to be a similarity that can be compared.

Timeline	Cairo Declaration and the Yalta Agreement	Article 2 of the 1951 Treaty of Peace with Japan
The Sino-Japanese War (1894–1895)	…all the territories Japan has stolen from the Chinese, such as Manchuria, Formosa, and the Pescadores, shall be restored to the Republic of China (The Cairo Declaration)	(b) Japan renounces all right, title and claim to Formosa and the Pescadores.
The Russo-Japanese War (1904–1905)	2. The former rights of Russia violated by the treacherous attack of Japan in 1904 shall be restored, viz.: (a) the southern part of Sakhalin as well as all the islands adjacent to it shall be returned to the Soviet Union. 3. The Kuril Islands shall be handed over to the Soviet Union. (Yalta Agreement)	(c) Japan renounces all right, title and claim to the Kurile Islands, and to that portion of Sakhalin and the islands adjacent to it over which Japan acquired sovereignty as a consequence of the Treaty of Portsmouth of 5 September, 1905.

[9] Potsdam Proclamation, Proclamation Defining Terms for Japanese Surrender Issued, at Potsdam, July 26, 1945. Available at: https://www.ndl.go.jp/constitution/e/etc/c06.html (accessed 18 September 2018).

[10] Cairo Declaration, from the Conferences at Cairo and Tehran, 1943. Available at: http://digital.library.wisc.edu/1711.dl/FRUS.FRUS1943CairoTehran (accessed 18 September 2018).

[11] Crimea (Yalta) Conference, 1945: Entry of Soviet Union into War Against Japan, Agreement signed at Yalta February 11, 1945.

Timeline	Cairo Declaration and the Yalta Agreement	Article 2 of the 1951 Treaty of Peace with Japan
The Annexation of Korea (1910)	The aforesaid three great powers, mindful of the enslavement of the people of Korea, are determined that in due course Korea shall become free and independent. (The Cairo Declaration)	(a) Japan recognizing the independence of Korea, renounces all right, title and claim to Korea, including the islands of Quelpart, Port Hamilton and Dagelet.
The League of Nations Mandate System	Japan shall be stripped of all the islands in the Pacific which she has seized or occupied since the beginning of the first World War in 1914 (The Cairo Declaration)	(d) Japan renounces all right, title and claim in connection with the League of Nations Mandate System.
Other	Japan will also be expelled from all other territories which she has taken by violence and greed. (The Cairo Declaration)	(e) Japan renounces all claim to any right or title to or interest in connection with any part of the Antarctic area, whether deriving from the activities of Japanese nationals or otherwise. (f) Japan renounces all right, title and claim to the Spratly Islands and to the Paracel Islands.

The wording of Article 1 of the January 1947 Draft is almost identical to Article 8 of the Potsdam Proclamation. The latter has two parts—the first states the Cairo Declaration, and the second gives the names of the four prominent islands without mentioning the minor islands. If the first part of the Potsdam Proclamation is substituted with the first part of Article 1(1) of the 1947 Draft, the rest seems significantly similar. In other words, what the Cairo Declaration meant could be the first part of Article 1(1) of the 1947 Draft: 'The territorial limits of Japan shall be those existing on 1 January 1894.' In this regard, the stipulation in the Cairo Declaration, 'Japan will also be expelled from all other territories which she has taken by violence and greed' could have meant, until 1947, as reversing all territorial relations back to 1 January 1894. The wording of the two texts leads us to perceive the similarity, and makes us speculate a connection.

Objective	Potsdam Proclamation	The January 1947 Draft	The Basic Post-Surrender Policy for Japan
Sovereignty and territorial limitation of Japan	8. The terms of the Cairo Declaration shall be carried out and Japanese sovereignty shall be limited to the islands of Honshu, Hokkaido, Kyushu, Shikoku and such minor islands as we determine.	The territorial limits of Japan shall be those existing on 1 January, 1894, subject to the modifications set forth in Articles 2, 3 … As such these limits shall include the four principal islands of Honshu, Kyushu, Shikoku and Hokkaido and all minor offshore islands …	Japan's sovereignty will be limited to the islands of Honshu, Hokkaido, Kyushu, Shikoku and such minor outlying islands as may be determined.

The communique signed at the Moscow Meeting of Council of Foreign Ministers, 1945 agreed to establish the Far Eastern Commission to 'formulate the policies, principles, and standards in conformity with which the fulfilment by Japan of its obligations under the Terms of Surrender may be accomplished.'[12] On 19 June 1947, the Far Eastern Commission unanimously approved the Basic Post-Surrender Policy for Japan (hereafter 'the Basic Policy') 'with the object of fulfilling the intention of the Potsdam declaration….'[13] As noted, the draft prepared on 24 July 1947—drafted after the Basic Policy was designed—mentioned the same territorial limitation of Japan as that existing on 1 January 1894. This again implies that the intention of the Potsdam Proclamation in conjunction with the Cairo Declaration was to restore Japan's territory to what it was on 1 January 1894.

Indeed, the date 1894 was not included in the final wording of the Treaty of Peace with Japan. However, as noted, Dulles's speech after the signing of the treaty clearly emphasized the 'Potsdam Surrender Terms' as the binding peace terms in the context of Japan's territory. Therefore, considering the Potsdam Proclamation, which refers to the Cairo Declaration, it could be interpreted that the setting point of reference for the Treaty of Peace with Japan is implied as 1 January 1894. However, there is one unresolved legal issue. The 1947 Drafts take 1894 as the reference, and this could be modified only when it was explicitly indicated in the following Articles. This approach puts all other undiscussed territorial issues in the year 1894. However, this aspect is not clear in the wording of the Treaty of Peace. Therefore, one may need to argue that the territory in question was taken by violence and greed, as stipulated in the Cairo Declaration, to claim that year 1894 as the reference point applies to the case. The burden of proof is on those who argue for it.

4 Civilization and Its Difficulty in the Cause of the Sino-Japanese War

Regardless of the political motivation behind the scenes, there are legal consequences in setting the date back to 1894 because back in the late nineteenth century and early twentieth century, and many international lawyers recognized the Sino-Japanese War as legitimate on Japan's part.[14] The 1947 Drafts have a different view of such legitimacy. Therefore, an explanation of why it is suddenly unjustified after WWII is crucial. From the perspective of law, there is one question that has not been sufficiently discussed during and after the Sino-Japanese War. Previous studies narrate the historical background of the Convention of Tientsin (1885) that was

[12] Moscow Meeting of Council of Foreign Ministers, 1945, Communique and report signed at Moscow December 27, 1945. Available at: https://avalon.law.yale.edu/20th_century/decade19.asp (accessed: 25 February 2020).

[13] Anthony Best (ed.), *British Documents on Foreign Affairs—reports and Papers from the Foreign Office Confidential Print*, Vol. 3 Japan and China, January 1947–December 1947, University Publications of America, 2001, pp. 101–102.

[14] E.g., T. E. Holland, 'International Law in the War between Japan and China', *The American Lawyer* 3, 1895; John Westlake, 'Introduction', in Sakuye Takahashi, *Cases on International Law during Chino-Japanese War*, Cambridge: Cambridge University Press, 1899.

concluded between China and Japan in relation to the Min regime of Korea, seeking China's intervention in the Peasant Uprising.[15] However, they do not clearly discuss the issue of the cause of the Sino-Japanese War, which should be justified in terms of law rather than explaining why it occurred in terms of fact.

Unlike what many jurists assumed until recently, war could not be initiated indiscriminately in the late nineteenth century. This is often quoted as the indiscriminate thesis. The demise of the just war theory in terms of natural law and the rise of legal positivism confuses us in that the just cause element of *jus ad bellum* was anachronistic and irrelevant in the nineteenth century. However, such a position taken by four radical positivists—Oppenheim, Westlake, Lawrence, and Anzilotti—was not accepted by the majority until the end of WWI.[16] The end of the just war era does not mean the end of international law related to initiating wars. Ethical rules were already customarily accepted, and mainstream legal positivists recycled and reflected these into the right of self-preservation that was part of the fundamental rights of sovereign states.[17] In short, arbitrary aggression was not permitted, and a justified reason to violate other nations' sovereignty was necessary.[18]

Therefore, Japan had to formulate a reason that justified its war with China. If Japan cared to meet the standard of *jus in bello,* which circulated among the members of the family of nations, it is reasonable to speculate that it must also have been keen on the standard of *jus ad bellum.* The question then is: What kind of justification had Japan invoked? The formal declaration of war on 1 August 1894 could be relevant for the initial legal analysis, and there are critical points that cannot be neglected. First of all, Japan declared war on China—and not Korea—to defend the independence of Korea. Japan purported that it could send its military into Korea based on the previous treaty concluded with China for 'freedom from the calamity of perpetual disturbance,' as China circumvented Korea's reform and reeled in its position in the family of nations that was obtained 'through Japanese efforts.'[19] This portrays Korea as the victim that Japan is attempting to civilize and save from the perpetrator China. China, on the other hand, promptly declared that Korea has been

[15] Jae-gon Cho, 'The Connection of the Sino-Japanese War and the Peasant War of 1894', *Korea Journal* 34(4), 1994, pp. 45–58.

[16] Randall Lesaffer, 'Aggression before Versailles', *The European Journal of International Law* 29(3), 2018, pp. 790–791.

[17] Ibid.

[18] Nonetheless, the scope and notion of the use of force is not as clear as war and these two should be differentiated. (Sung-won Kim, "A Review on the Threat of Force in International Law", *Dong-A Law Review* 59, 2013, pp. 361–386.)

[19] Declaration of War against Qing Dynasty (1894) 清国ニ対スル宣戦ノ詔勅 < 原文>, 清国ニ対スル宣戦ノ詔勅日 (清戦争開戦の詔勅 明治27年8月1日), Navigator of the Historical term. Available at: http://teikoku-denmo.jp/history/kaisetsu/other/nisshin-kaisen-shousho.html (accessed 14 June 2020). Original Text: '帝国ハ是ニ於テ朝鮮ニ勧ムルニ其ノ秕政ヲ釐革シ内ハ治安ノ基ヲ堅クシ外ハ独立国ノ権義ヲ全クセムコトヲ以テシタルニ朝鮮ハ既ニ之ヲ肯諾シタルモ清国ハ終始陰ニ居テ百方其ノ目的ヲ妨碍シ剰へ辞ヲ左右ニ托シ時機ヲ緩ニシ以テ其ノ水陸ノ兵備ヲ整へ一旦成ルヲ告クルヤ直ニ其ノ力ヲ以テ其ノ欲望ヲ達セムトシ更ニ大兵ヲ韓土ニ派シ我艦ヲ韓海ニ要撃シ殆ト亡状ヲ極メタリ'

its tributary, and China is sending in troops following Korea's repeated requests to repress the recent peasant insurrection (of May), which it later changed to halt Japan's bullying attempt to change Korea's system of government.[20]

On 29 July 1894, just a couple of days before the day of the declaration of war, Fukuzawa Yukichi contributed his view to a newspaper that this war was a battle between the one who attempts to progress toward civilization and the one who will thwart the progress.[21] Uchimura Kanzo even argued that the war was a just war because it was justified not only in legal terms but also on an ethical level as it was a war of civilization.[22] Such is the well-known rhetorical frame of the Sino-Japanese War. *Harper's Weekly* on 11 August 1894[23] and *New York Times* on 28 July 1894[24] supported the argument of civilization versus barbarism in the war between Japan and China. At the heart of this war was the discourse on barbaric China violating the sovereignty and independence of vulnerable Korea, which then led Japan's intervention in the name of civilization to save Korea.

However, it should be noted that the scope of legal war confines the engagement between sovereign states belonging to the family of nations. If the war is between uncivilized nations or between civilized and uncivilized nations, the rules of international law do not apply in a strict sense because it is not exactly a war between sovereign nations defined by international law. Henry Wheaton explicitly noted that there is no universal international law, and that international law only applies to the members of the family of nations.[25] In 1844, Wilhelm Heffter noted, 'The European law of nations is, according to its historical roots, binding essentially only upon the Christian States... However, in relation to non-Christian States, it finds only a partially, carefully measured application according to the expected reciprocity....'[26] The British military manual of 1907 stated:

> The rules of International Law apply only to warfare between civilized nations, where both parties understand them and are prepared to carry them out. They do not apply in wars with uncivilized States and tribes, where their place is taken by the discretion of the commander and such rules of justice and humanity as recommended themselves in the particular circumstances of the case.[27]

---

[20] Franz Schurmann and Orville Schell, *Imperial China—China Reading 1,* London: Penguin Books, 1967, pp. 240–242.

[21] Kato Yoko, *Modern Japan's War Logic: Seinan Theory to the Pacific War,* Young-Jun Park, (trans.), Taehaksa, 2003, p. 111.

[22] Eung-soo Jeong, 'Uchimura Ganzo's Change of the Perspective of War', *Journal of Japanese Culture,* 15, 2002, pp. 20–31.

[23] 'The Chino-Japanese War in Korea', *Harper's Weekly*, August 11, 1894, p. 141.

[24] *New York Times*, July 28, 1894, p. 4.

[25] Henry Wheaton, *Elements of International Law*, James Brown Scott (ed.), The Classics of International Law, Washington: Carnegie Endowment for International Peace, 1866, p. 15.

[26] Indirectly cited from Wilhelm G. Grewe, *The Epochs of International Law*, Michael Byers (trans.), New York: Walter de Gruyter, 2000, p. 464.

[27] War Office, *Manual of Military Law,* London: H.M. Stationary Office, 1907, p. 456.

Elbridge Colby reiterated the same idea in 1927 in the *American Journal of International Law*.[28] In other words, warfare with uncivilized nations was not a proper war; rather, it was often called 'small wars.'

In this regard, Japan did not need to rigorously adhere to the rules of international law with the highest standard, as in the case of European nations facing so-called uncivilized nations in the nineteenth century. Notably, China was technically not a member of the family of nations, and Japan, too, had not been accepted as a full member by the international community when the Sino-Japanese War was initiated. Even though he defended that Japan meticulously abided by the laws of war, T. E. Holland noted, 'Antecedently to the war, therefore, we should have said that Japan was admitted on probation, while China was only a candidate for admission, to the "family of nations"'.[29]

Therefore, technically, it was not necessary for the two nations to comply with international law during their conflict. Presuming that Japan was a member of the family of nations, it was not obligated to abide by the rules of international law in a war with an uncivilized nation. Nevertheless, upholding these rules, including the law of war, is evidence that the state is indeed part of the family of civilized nations.[30] This is one of the reasons why Japan attempted to portray the Sino-Japanese War as Takahashi did, within the frame of civilized Japanese keeping to the rules of warfare with respect to international law against barbaric Chinese.[31]

5 Civilizational Discourse as in the Case of Humanitarian Intervention or Civilizing Mission?

There is a case that the cause of war could be justified even between civilized and uncivilized nations. That is, the civilized nations could initiate war or intervene with force in the name of civilization to fight against barbarism to save innocent people and guarantee independence. This consideration is relevant because Japan's rhetoric at the outbreak of the war seems to have been framed as something that reminds us of humanitarian intervention.[32]

[28] Elbridge Colby, 'How to Fight Savage Tribes', *The American Journal of International Law* 21(2), 1927, p. 279.

[29] T. E. Holland, 'International Law in the War between Japan and China', *The American Lawyer* 3, 1895, p. 387.

[30] Gerrit W. Gong, *The Standard of "Civilization" in International Society*, Oxford: Oxford University Press, 1984, pp. 15ff.

[31] Sakuye Takahashi, *Cases on International Law during Chino-Japanese War*, Cambridge: Cambridge University Press, 1899.

[32] Multiple publicists endorsed the legality of humanitarian intervention with diverging takes—Bluntschli, Mimiami, and Fiore took it as a legal right; Heffter endorsed it in civil war caused by oppression; Calvo took the stance that it is justified to cease 'crimes of a government against its subjects' (Samuel Herrick, 'Interference by one nation in the internal affairs of another nation on

The humanitarian intervention cases of the nineteenth century were closely related to the idea of Western powers rescuing Christian victims from merciless barbaric rulers.[33] In the case of the Greek War of Independence from 1821 to 1830, the Ottoman Empire was labelled as the uncivilized and despotic oppressor hindering the independence of the Greek nations.[34] In 1826, Tsar Nicholas I appealed for joint intervention; on 20 October 1827, the joint naval forces of Britain, France, and Russia wiped out the entire Ottoman fleet in the Battle of Navarino.[35] In the Civil War in Syria from 1860 to 1861, the Maronites initiated an uprising in May of 1860 that was retaliated against by the Druze, resulting in the killing of more than 15,000 Christians.[36] Later, France, Great Britain, Austria, Prussia, and Russia intervened, and this case was recognized as the singular incident of genuine humanitarian intervention in the nineteenth century by Ian Brownlie.[37] Atrocities were committed against Bulgarians during the April Uprising from 1876 to 1878—this was a Bulgarian revolt against the Ottoman Empire, which was then followed by a series of uprisings against the Empire in Bosnia-Herzegovina in 1875. In response, the Sublime Porte sent *bashi-bazouks* (irregular troops) to suppress the rebels, and subsequently, about 12,000 to 20,000 Bulgarians were massacred.[38] This case has often been mentioned as another representation of a nineteenth-century humanitarian intervention.

---

the ground of humanity', *The Brief* VI(3), 1906, p. 196.); Woolsey stated that there are only two instances that justify interference: self-preservation and the crime of a government against its subjects (Theodore D. Woolsey, *Introduction to the Study of International Law, designed as an aid in teaching, and in historical studies,* New York: Charles Scribner, 124 Grand Street, 1864, p. 57.); Halleck, Lawrence, Hall, and Oppenheim, on the other hand, were not fully convinced that humanitarian intervention is part of the international legal system. Halleck cited Phillimore: 'As an accessory to others, this [humanitarian ground] may be defensible, but it can scarcely be admitted into the code of international law...' (Henry Wager Halleck, *International Law,* San Francisco: H. H. Bancroft & Company, 1861, p. 340.) Citing Historicus, Lawrence perceived that intervention on the ground of humanity is 'a high act of policy above and beyond the domain of law' (T. J. Lawrence, *Principles of International Law,* 4th ed., Boston: D. C. Heath & Co., Publishers, 1910, pp. 128–129). Hall seemed to have argued that intervention on the ground of humanity is brought about by sentiment, to the exclusion of law. Oppenheim doubted the existence of the rule of humanitarian intervention even though public opinion and the attitude of the Great Powers approved it (Lasa Oppenheim, *International Law: A Treatise,* Vol. I, 2nd ed., New York: Longmans, Green and Co., 1912, pp. 194–195).

[33] Ibrahim Seaga Shaw, 'Historical Frames and the Politics of Humanitarian Intervention: from Ethiopia, Somalia to Rwanda', *Globalization, Societies and Education* 5(3), 2007, p. 354.

[34] Gary J. Bass, *Freedom's Battle: The Origins of Humanitarian Intervention,* New York: Vintage Books, 2008, p. 92.

[35] Alexis Heraclides, 'Humanitarian Intervention in the 19th Century: The Heyday of a Controversial Concept', *Global Society* 26(2), 2012, p. 222.

[36] Ibid., p. 223.

[37] Ian Brownlie, *International Law and the Use of Force by States,* Oxford: Oxford University Press, 1963, p. 340.

[38] Heraclides, 'Humanitarian Intervention in the 19th Century', p. 225.

In the nineteenth-century cases, the barbarism of the perpetrators is accentuated in a certain way that makes it justifiable to violate the sovereignty of the Turkish nation—that is, a perceived uncivilized nature is given as the justification for violating the state sovereignty of the targeted nation. As noted by Heraclides, the sovereignty of the uncivilized nations was 'delegitimated' and, accordingly, 'the infringements of non-intervention... were more acceptable if "civilized" states intervened in "non-civilized" countries.'[39] Lorimer, a social Darwinist international lawyer of the nineteenth century, even argued that a civilized nation has an obligation as well as right to interfere in the domestic matters of an uncivilized one for the latter's benefit.[40]

However, humanitarian intervention against barbarism to defend civilization cannot stand in the case of the Sino-Japanese War. What then was the manifested just cause here? The nineteenth-century publicists rarely discuss the just cause of humanitarian intervention in detail, but most point to the extreme humanitarian situations. In referring to the Greek independence case, Wheaton outlined that 'the general interests of humanity' are violated by 'the excesses of a barbarous and despotic government.'[41] Humanitarian intervention either frames the oppressor government as massacring its people or the people under its control. Yet, an extreme humanitarian situation such as unilateral massacring of civilians did not occur in the case of Korea. Moreover, Korea was not exactly under China's control. The Joseon Dynasty has often been depicted as China's vassal that caused the conflict between China and Japan, and led to the war. Imperial Japan even contended that Japan liberated Korea from Chinese oppression and made it a sovereign nation after the war. This premise is not based on the historical facts at the time. The Chinese policy of a tributary relationship with Korea respected Korea's autonomous status in both internal and foreign affairs.[42] The Governor of Hong Kong, Sir John Bowring, reported the following to the British government in 1854:

> There is a nominal dependence upon China, very similar to that recognized by Siam and Cochin China. Tribute is regularly sent. Acts of submission are from time to time recorded: but the Chinese Government exercise[s] no real authority, and seems never to interfere with the jurisdiction of Corean functionaries. The authority of the King is absolute.[43]

[39] Alexis Heraclides, 'Humanitarian Intervention in International Law 1830–1939. The Debate', *Journal of the History of International Law* 16, 2014, pp. 29–30.

[40] James Lorimer, *The Institutes of the Law of Nations,* Clark, New Jersey: The Lawbook Exchange, Ltd., 2005 (original 1883), p. 228.

[41] Henry Wheaton, *Elements of International Law,* Philadelphia: Carey, Lea & Blanchard, 1836, p. 91.

[42] Byong-gi Song, *A Study of Modern History of Korea and China Relations,* Seoul: Dankook Univ. Pub., 1985, p. 19.

[43] John Bowring, 'Bowring to FO, No. 122, August 25, 1854', in *Modern Korean Diplomatic Documents*, Vol. 5: Treaty of friendship and Commerce Between Great Britain and Corea, eds. Modern Korean Diplomatic Documents Compilation Committee, Seoul: Northeast Asian History Foundation, 2013, pp. 820–821.

Notably, certain images of Korea, such as the Hermit Kingdom, had been suggested and promoted by external entities, which caused further misunderstandings.[44]

However, the actual substance of historical independence may not have been an interest. What may be critical is their affinity to the European civilization. The Greeks depicted themselves as direct descendants of the ancient classical civilization that was the foundation of the European civilization.[45] In the case of the Syrian Massacres, the French had claimed the Maronite Christians as their protectees. During the Crusade of Saint Louis (1147–1149), the Maronite Christians were given the title of 'French-men' in return for service to France.[46] During the Bulgarian Atrocities, on the side of Russia, pan-Slavism of the Slavophiles played an important role.[47] The belief in the kinship between the Russians and Bulgarians seemed to have played a role in triggering the intervention.

What happens when the otherized victims of oppression are considered inferior and barbaric rather than beings sharing homogeneity as in the above three cases? A civilizing mission sometimes involved propaganda of liberating the oppressed inferior people from the barbaric despots. Despotism here meant 'a regime hindering progress, and therefore, civilization.' In the three cases noted above, despotism was connected to Ottoman barbarism and Islamic belief against Christian progress.[48] However, when the victims were not Christians, the liberation did not imply independence for their progress. There seems to be a correlation as the civilizing mission of the nineteenth-century French colonial policy was also based on values that promoted liberation from tyranny, slavery, and feudalism.[49] The republican ideology developed during the 1789 French revolution galvanized the French to colonize West African regions from 1895 to 1914, justifying it as liberation from oppression 'that they believed to exist.'[50] The non-Westerners comprised the others who were in need of enlightenment of Western democracy and freedom.[51] The British Empire's justification in colonizing India was also presented as humanitarianism to liberate the oppressed people of India from the 'Oriental Despotism' of the Mughals.[52]

---

[44] Yi Tae-Jin, 'Was Korea Really a "Hermit Nation"', *Korea Journal* 38(4), 1998, pp. 5–35.

[45] Davide Rodogno, *Against Massacre: Humanitarian Interventions in the Ottoman Empire, 1815–1914,* Princeton University Press, 2012, p. 75.

[46] Ibid., p. 93.

[47] Bass, *Freedom's Battle*, p. 244.

[48] Rodogno, *Against Massacre*, pp. 38–39.

[49] Lisa Moses Leff, 'Jews, Liberals and the Civilizing Mission in Nineteenth-Century France', *Historical Reflections / Réflexions Historiques* 32(1), 2006, p. 105.

[50] Alice L. Conklin, 'Colonialism and Human Rights, A Contradiction in Terms? The Case of France and West Africa, 1895–1914' 103(2), 1998, p. 420.

[51] Ibid., p. 422.

[52] Michael Mann, '"Torchbearers Upon the Path of Progress": Britain's Ideology of a "Moral and Material Progress" in India', in Harald Fischer-Tiné and Michael Mann (eds.), *Colonialism as Civilizing Mission: Cultural Ideology in British India,* London: Wimbledon Pub. Company, 2004, p. 5.

Before the 'Great Rebellion' of 1857–1859, the British colonial rule's legitimacy was questioned, but when a rebellion in India occurred, the British Empire, particularly the East India Company, depicted and labelled the Mughals as oppressive despots. Consequently, the non-Christian victims of the oppression were an object of the civilizing mission.

Such a civilizing mission was not exactly a cause for war between sovereign nations—instead, it was a cause for intervention, which often led to colonization. Arguably, therefore, Japan also went to war with the aim of colonization rather than seeing it as a war between sovereigns. *New York Herald,* on 11 October 1894, noted that Japan should be allowed to carry out a 'civilizing mission' in Korea.[53] It seems Japan otherized the Koreans while claiming it is intervening for their liberation from the despotism of China. This idea of a civilizing mission—which was a stepping stone to the Japan-Korea Annexation Treaty of 1910 and to the absorption of Manchuria—prevailed until the end of WWII.[54] In 1907, Seiji Hishida, a long-serving Japanese government official, claimed that Formosa is the first Japanese colony.[55] In 1924, Ralston Hayden briefly noted in *Foreign Affairs* that Formosa is the first large colony of Japan acquired in 1895, as if Japan is now a colonial power equal to the Western empires.[56] The Sino-Japanese War may not be the first case of Japan's expansion, but it must have been a watershed that the post-WWII Allies may have attempted to repudiate as the initiation of 'violence and greed' that lasted until the end of WWII.

6 Conclusion

What does the Treaty of Peace with Japan attempt to repudiate? There is a reason why its Article 2 stipulates territorial issues that occurred before WWII. Like other peace treaties at the time, the 1947 Drafts reveal the date the treaty's authors attempted to return to—1 January 1894, which was before the Sino-Japanese War. This rewind causes a legal issue because the international lawyers of the nineteenth and early twentieth centuries emphasized how Japan fought the war in accordance with international law, while China did not. However, *jus in bello* and *jus ad bellum* should be distinguished.

This research delved into the question of *jus ad bellum,* especially the cause of war, which has not been discussed sufficiently in previous studies. The cause of war on Japan's part was based on civilization against barbarism. However, such a

[53] *New York Herald,* October 11, 1894, p. 8.

[54] S. C. M. Paine, *The Sino-Japanese War of 1894–1895: Perceptions, Power, and Primacy,* Cambridge University Press, 2003, p. 325.

[55] Seiji Hishida, 'Formosa: Japan's First Colony', *Political Science Quarterly* 22(2), 1907, pp. 267–281.

[56] Ralston Hayden, 'Japan's New Policy in Korea and Formosa', *Foreign Affairs* 2(3), 1924, pp. 474–487.

formulation was counterintuitive because such a war, which required two or more members of the family of nations, was not exactly defined under international law. Accordingly, a sovereign nation was not obliged to abide by the rules of international law in a war with uncivilized nations.

The rhetoric used reminds us of the previous humanitarian intervention cases, as the frame of civilization versus barbarism was indeed established on military intervention for saving the victims from despotic suzerains. Nonetheless, such an action cannot be justified in this case as there was no actual humanitarian crisis, and the independence of Korea was customarily guaranteed. However, the implied question was the victims' status. Previous intervention cases identified the victims with homogeneous religious or ethnic affinity with the intervener, but when the victims were deemed inferior and not sharing racial or civilizational identity, as in the case of India and other civilizing mission cases, their liberation from the oppression was mere rhetoric, articulated to justify colonialism. The 'violence and greed' seems to refer to this colonial expansion of Japan—the date 1 January 1894 proposed in the 1947 Drafts seems to repudiate this colonialism.

The implication of this attempt, however, is more complex, and questions remain, because Japan, which had historically shared the East Asian civilization with Korean and China, could also be imitating the Western colonial powers otherizing the targeted people as inferior, not sharing the same humanity. Consequently, it obtained 'the ultimate status symbol' of the colonial empire when the Shimonoseki Treaty of 1895 was concluded[57] and it was finally treated as an equal worthy of 'membership in the family of civilized nations.'[58] In this regard, the Western Allies are trapped in an unfavourable situation by repudiating Japan's colonial past, in which the West is also culpable on the other side of the world. Perhaps unintended, but the repudiation consequentially implies disapproval of what the West has done. Or is it another level of discrimination against the non-whites? With the outbreak of the Russo-Japanese War (1904–1905), Western attitude toward Japan seems to have changed to Yellow Peril, a colour-metaphor toward East Asian people against the civilized Western world.[59] The first *War Plan Orange* for the US Navy to blockade the Japanese Archipelago was designed in 1906, which evolved later and prevailed until the end of WWII.[60] Ironically, when Pearl Harbor—the territory the United States annexed in 1898 by getting the Hawaiian ruler to abdicate—was attacked in 1941, the race war between the United States and Japan began. The Western Allies stressed the subhuman, inhuman, or barbaric nature of the Japanese enemy sufficiently, saying

---

[57] Mark R. Peattie, 'Introduction', in Ramon H. Myers and Mark R. Peattie (eds), *The Japanese Colonial Empire, 1895–1945,* New Jersey: Princeton University Press, 1984, p. 10.

[58] Kentaro Kaneko, 'The Yellow Peril Is the Golden Opportunity for Japan', *The North American Review* 179(576), 1904, p. 642.

[59] Ibid., pp. 642–643.

[60] Fumio Takahashi, 'The First War Plan Orange and the First Imperial Japanese Defense Policy: An Interpretation from the Geopolitical Strategic Perspective', *National Institute for Defense Studies(NIDS) Security Reports* (5), 2004, pp. 69–70.

it deserved to be exterminated.[61] While berating Nazi's racism and purporting democratic ideals on the other side of the globe, the Western Allies denied the equality of the human race in Japan's case. Thus, in finding justice, the Western Allies may also need to repudiate their history.

Acknowledgement This research was developed by revising the paper presented at the conference "*Beyond the San Francisco System—the 4th International Conference in Seoul*" held in Seoul on November 8, 2019.

[61] John W. Dower, *War Without Mercy: Race & Power in the Pacific War,* New York: Pantheon Books, 1986, pp. 10–12.

Japanese Second World War Memory and the San Francisco Peace Treaty

Chan Yang

Abstract Article 11 of the San Francisco Peace Treaty specifies: 'Japan accepts the judgments of the International Military Tribunal for the Far East and of other Allied War Crimes Courts both within and outside Japan'. The Japanese government signed the San Francisco Peace Treaty, and from its enactment in 1952, Japanese citizens were expected to remember the Second World War in accordance with the verdicts of the postwar tribunals. However, based on the nature of 'collective memory' and the empirical findings of this paper, neither the San Francisco Peace Treaty nor the Japanese government could alter the evolution of Japanese war memory or resolve its issues (e.g., victim mentality, amnesia, and the beautifying of war). These issues have developed through the interplay among Japanese individuals, non-official agents, the Japanese government, and the international community over an extended evolutionary period since the wartime.

Keywords Amnesia · Atomic bombing · Collective memory · Comfort women · Education · Hiroshima · Nationalism · Nanjing Massacre · San Francisco Peace Treaty · Victim mentality

Three types of literature address the topic of post-war Japanese World War Two memory. Firstly, the impact of the war and the Japanese response to their war history have been central themes in much historical writing on post-war Japan. This emphasis stems from the continuity between post-war and wartime Japan and the profound significance of the war itself; it was not only Japan's longest and most devastating conflict but also its first failed war since the Meiji Restoration.[1] Some

[1] E.g. Nakamura Masanori, *Sengoshi* [Postwar history] (Tokyo: Iwanami shoten, 2005) 中村政則, 戦後史 (岩波書店 2005). John W. Dower, *Embracing Defeat: Japan in the Aftermath of World War II* (London: Penguin, 2000).

C. Yang (✉)
Department of History, Shanghai Jiao Tong University, Shanghai, People's Republic of China
e-mail: yang.chan@sjtu.edu.cn

Y.-H. Kim et al. (eds.), *Beyond the San Francisco System*,
https://doi.org/10.1007/978-981-95-3328-2_10

scholars even suggest that by the mid-1990s, two unresolved questions—how to become a normal nation and how to confront the wartime past—still hindered Japan's transition to a post-war era.[2] Secondly, considerable research directly addresses the themes of 'war responsibility' or 'war memory', focusing exclusively on how the Japanese remembered the war at specific moments or throughout the period from 1945 to the present day.[3] These discussions are not always centered on the state.[4] Thirdly, understanding how the Japanese remembered the war can also be gleaned literature dealing with the evolutional history of specific controversies related to the war, such as education about the war in Japanese schools and debates about the Nanjing Massacre and Comfort Women Issue, or the remembrance of individual wartime events, such as the atomic bombings of Hiroshima and Nagasaki.[5]

---

[2] P. J. Bailey, *Postwar Japan: 1945 to the present* (Oxford: Blackwell, 1996). The time scale of the 'postwar era' is difficult to define. In terms of the historiography of postwar Japanese history, as early as the 1970s, when Japan was considered to have completed the process of reintegrating into the international community, publications addressing so-called postwar Japanese history began to emerge, see, M. Kosaka, *A history of postwar Japan* (Tokyo: Kodansha International, 1972). Works of postwar Japanese history boomed again in 1990s after Showa emperor died and the 1955 system collapsed', see, A. Gordon, *Postwar Japan as History* (Berkeley: University of California Press, 1993); M. Hane, *Eastern phoenix: Japan since 1945* (Oxford: Westview Press, 1996). After new millennium, there has been little comprehensive work on the topic, still, we can see works, like D. McCargo, *Contemporary Japan* (Basingstoke: Palgrave Macmillan, 2004).

[3] See, Sekizawa Mayumi (ed.), *Sensou kiokuron - boukyaku, henyou shoshite keishou* [War memory: forget, change and inherit] (Kyoto: Shouwadou, 2010) 関沢まゆみ,戦争記憶論—忘却、変容そして継承 (昭和堂,2010). Many works compare Japanese war remembrance with German's and America's, e.g. S. Conrad, 'Entangled Memories: Versions of the Past in Germany and Japan, 1945–2001', *Journal of Contemporary History,* 38 (2003), 85–99. However, there are only a few works, which compare China and Japan. For instance, Kushner's work did compare the war memory in China and Japan, nonetheless, since 1990, see, B. Kushner, 'Nationality and Nostalgia: The manipulation of memory in Japan, Taiwan and China since 1990', *The International History Review*, XXIX (2007): 709–944.

[4] For instance, Fujiwara discussed the evolution of the Japanese war remembrance through the themes such as the postwar Japanese anti-war pacifism and postwar Japanese democracy, which was mostly from the perspective of intellectuals and grassroots, Fujiwara Kiichi, *Sensou wo kiokusuru: Hiroshima, Horokosuto to genzai* [Remember the war, Hiroshima, Holocaust and the present] (Tokyo: Koudansha gendai shinsho, 2001) 藤原帰一, 戦争を記憶する 広島・ホロコーストと現在 (講談社現代新書,2001). Kosuge discussed how the World War Two legacies were dealt with through the discussion of the Japanese reconciliation with its former enemies (mainly the UK and China), mainly from the perspectives of individuals and unofficial organizations, or some periphery state organs (e.g. legations). Kosuge and Ishida also discussed the Japanese progressive intellectuals' changing perceptions towards the issue of 'war responsibility'. Nobuko Kosuge, *Sengo wakai* (Tokyo: Chuukou shinsho, 2005) 小菅信子,戦後和解 (中公新書, 2005). Ishida Takeshi, *Kioku to boukyakuno seijikaku - douka seisaku, sensou sekinin, shuugoteki kioku* [Politics of remembering and forgetting - assimilation policy, war responsibility and collective memory] (Tokyo: Akashi shoten, 2000) 石田雄, 記憶と忘却の政治学 - 同化政策・ 戦争責任・集合的記憶 (明石書店, 2000).

[5] See, P. Cave, 'Japanese Colonialism and the Asia-Pacific War in Japan's History Textbooks: Changing representations and their causes', *Modern Asian Studies* 47 (2013), 542–580. Kasahara Tokushi, *Nankin jiken ronsoushi* [History of Nanjing incident debate] (Tokyo: Heibonsha, 2007) 笠原十九司, 南京事件論争史 (平凡社, 2007).

Drawing from this extensive literature, several distinctive phases in the evolutionary history of Japanese war memory can be identified. Moreover, the contributions of all actors—be they state, ordinary people, social groups, or outside powers—to shaping the evolutional process of Japanese war memory, as well as the difference between national and local war memory, can be discerned as well. Similar to the present day, Japanese war remembrance over the past seven decades has been highly contested, and the problematic aspects of this war remembrance—such as the victim mentality, amnesia, and the beautifying of war—have also emerged during this period.

There was an opportunity for the 'contest nature' and problems of Japanese war memory to be addressed in the 1950s. The San Francisco Peace Treaty's article 11 specifies:

> Japan accepts the judgments of the International Military Tribunal for the Far East and of other Allied War Crimes Courts both within and outside Japan, and will carry out the sentences imposed thereby upon Japanese nationals imprisoned in Japan. The power to grant clemency, to reduce sentences and to parole with respect to such prisoners may not be exercised except on the decision of the Government or Governments which imposed the sentence in each instance, and on recommendation of Japan. In the case of persons sentenced by the International Military Tribunal for the Far East, such power may not be exercised except on the decision of a majority of the Governments represented on the Tribunal, and on the recommendation of Japan.

The Japanese government signed the San Francisco Peace Treaty, and from the time it took effect in 1952 on, Japanese citizens were expected to remember the Second World War according to the verdicts of the postwar tribunals. Why, then, did Japan fail to do so? Or, to phrase it differently, why has Japanese WWII memory remained contested and problematic, even though the Japanese government had already accepted a single version of war memory, which denounced imperial Japan as an undisputed 'victimizer' and was approved by Japan's wartime opponents? To answer this question, we must delve into the evolutionary history of Japanese War memory and the 'contest nature' of Japanese war memory in detail.

The core tenet of Japanese Second World War memory revolves around the concept of 'collective memory', defined as the shared recollection of a group of people, often passed down through generations and transcending individual memories.[6] European scholars played a pivotal role in advancing this concept and its association with war-related narratives. A significant insight gleaned from writings on European Second World War memory is the 'evolutionary nature' of war memory. These writings highlight how the current version of European war memory has evolved through changes during the early post-war period, the Cold War era, and the period after 1989. More precisely, in the immediate aftermath of the devastating war, most European nations employed various strategies to evade confronting the darker aspects of their Second World War past. With the onset of the Cold War, the memory of the Second World War became fragmented and distorted along the lines of communism, anti-communism, and antifascism. However, since the end of the Cold

[6] Whitehead, Anne, *Memory* (London: Routledge, 2009).

War, there has been a thawing process in the remembrance of the war in both Western and Eastern Europe.[7] Similarly, Japanese Second World War memory has traversed various distinct phases.

During wartime Japan, the general populace remained unaware of the numerous atrocities committed by its military. This lack of awareness stemmed not only from state censorship but also from the nation's collective reluctance to confront these realities, fostered by ultra-nationalist indoctrination and propaganda efforts by Japanese authorities.[8]

Following the war's conclusion on August 15th, there emerged a brief period during which many Japanese citizens began to introspect on their wartime actions and engage in discussions regarding war accountability in a diverse and progressive manner.[9] This shift can largely be attributed to the reforms implemented by the General Headquarters (GHQ), the US-led occupation authority in Japan. These reforms allowed for greater freedom of expression, enabling Japanese citizens to openly criticize aspects deemed detrimental, including the military, Shintoism, and ultra-nationalist education.[10] Additionally, the International Military Tribunal for the Far East (IMTFE) conducted by the GHQ revealed numerous wartime atrocities perpetrated by the Japanese military, including the infamous Nanjing Massacre. This revelation sparked widespread shock and prompted discussions, even leading to the incorporation of such events into school curricula.[11]

However, despite these efforts, scholars like Dower argue that the GHQ's decision of not prosecuting Emperor Hirohito and using a few military leaders to 'clean up' the crimes committed by the Japanese nation 'reinforced a strong popular inclination to ignore what the men of Yamato had done to others in their frantic quest for empire and security'.[12] Therefore, the emergency of a prevalent victim mentality in Japanese war memory should also be attributed to the GHQ. Shin also highlighted the United States' role in shaping the problematic Japanese war remembrance. This influence was evident through various channels, including the International Military Tribunal for the Far East (IMTFE), the San Francisco Peace Treaty, which exempted

---

[7] Lebow, 'The Memory of Politics' and T.C. Wolfe, 'Past as Present, Myth, or History? Discourses of Time and the Great Fatherland War' in Lebow and Kansteiner (ed.) *The Politics of Memory in Postwar Europe*, 249–283; Müller, *Memory and Power*; N. Bannister, *The Secret Holocaust Diaries: The Untold Story of Nonna Bannister* (Carol Stream: Tyndale House Publishers, 2010). D. Cesarani, 'Lacking in Convictions: British War Crimes Policy and National Memory of the Second World War' in Evans and Lunn (ed.), *War and Memory in the Twentieth Century*, 27–42.

[8] Yoshida Takashi, *The Making of the 'Rape of Nanking': History and Memory in Japan, China and the United States* (Oxford: Oxford University Press, 2006).

[9] Ishida, *Kioku to boukyaku.*

[10] E.g. details about these reforms, see: Hana, Eastern phoenix, p.13. Nevertheless, the freedom granted by the occupation authority came with great censorship, for example, discussion of wartime atrocities committed by the US force was forbidden in Yoshida, *the Making of the 'Rape of Nanking'*.

[11] Yoshida, *the Making of the "Rape of Nanking"*.

[12] Dower, *Embracing defeat*, p.27.

Japan from paying reparations for its wartime actions, and American crimes such as air raids and the use of atomic bombs.[13]

However, some scholars argue that the victim mentality among the Japanese was not solely imposed by the GHQ but rather emerged as a natural response among the Japanese people. Seraphim posited that the roots of this mentality were deeply embedded in a three-fold trauma: the hardships of war, the subsequent defeat, and the loss of sovereignty under foreign occupation. According to this perspective, these experiences primed the Japanese psyche for a sense of victimhood even before any official endorsement of such a mindset. Similarly, Gluck suggested that while the IMTFE may have presented elements of a victim narrative to Japan, it was not forcibly imposed. Instead, the Japanese populace willingly embraced it as it aligned with the nation's desire to disassociate from its wartime past.[14]

Following 1947, a noticeable shift occurred in the occupation authority's reformative agenda as the specter of the Cold War loomed. This shift ushered conservatives, who advocated for a war narrative steeped in national pride, back into power.[15] Furthermore, motivated by pragmatic considerations, the GHQ began to conceal certain Japanese wartime atrocities, such as the Japanese Biological Warfare program. Several scholars have discovered evidence suggesting that the United States had a covert agreement with Ishii Shiro, granting members of his Unit 731 immunity from being tried in the IMTFE and other war tribunals in exchange for their experimental data. Additionally, on 26 January 1948, a mysterious poison murder incident occurred at the Imperial Bank (*teigin jiken*帝銀事件). Evidence strongly indicates that this incident was related to former members of Unit 731. However, it is widely believed that both the US and Japanese governments obstructed the investigation of the incident due to their reluctance to publicize the activities of Unit 731.[16]

In April 1952, Japan regained its independence as the foreign occupation came to an end. The newly empowered conservative government sought to dismantle several early democratic reforms initiated by the GHQ. During this second 'reverse course' of the GHQ's democratic reforms, the conservative government earnestly

---

[13] G. W. Shin, 'Historical Disputes and Reconciliation in Northeast Asia: The US Role', *Pacific Affairs,* 83 (2010), 663–673.

[14] F. Seraphim, *War memory and social politics in Japan, 1945–2005* (Cambridge: Mass; London, Harvard University Press, 2006); C. Gluck, 'The Past in the Present' in Gordon, Andrew (ed), *Postwar Japan as History* (Berkeley: University of California Press, 1993).

[15] B. Cumings, 'Japan's Position in the World System' in Gordon, Andrew (ed), *Postwar Japan as History* (Berkeley: University of California Press, 1993), 34–64.

[16] Harris, Sheldon, *Japanese biological warfare experiments and other atrocities in Manchuria, 1932–1945, and the subsequent United States cover-up: a preliminary assessment* (Dordrecht: Kluwer Academic Publishers, 1991). Tsuneishi, Keiichi, 'Unit 731 and the Japanese Imperial Army's Biological Warfare Program'. <http://www.japanfocus.org/-Tsuneishi-Keiichi/2194>, date unknown, date accessed, 16 Mar 2014. H. Gold, *Japan's wartime human experimentation program: unit 731testimony* (North Clarendon: Tuttle Publishing, 1996); Tsuneishi Keiichi, 'Nanasanichi butai no bourei - teigenjiken zaidokuku' [Departed soul of Unit 731 - re-read the Imperial Bank Incident], *Gendai shisou*, 33 (2005), 154–160 常石敬一, 七三一部隊の亡霊 - 帝銀事件再読, 現代思想, 33 (2005), 154–160.

embarked on its policy of nurturing Japanese patriotism. Education became a prime target, culminating in an October 1956 decree from the Ministry of Education aimed at censoring leftist textbooks. Consequently, references to Japanese military atrocities, including the Nanjing Massacre, dwindled in school materials. Simultaneously, the government began utilizing war commemoration events, such as the 全国战没者追悼式 (from 1963), to foster a shared national narrative centered around the Second World War. Amidst these developments, the victim mentality gained further traction, particularly after Hiroshima and Nagasaki entered the national consciousness, symbolizing Japan's collective suffering following the 1954 Lucky Dragon Incident.[17]

Notwithstanding the conservative state's dominance in shaping war remembrance, Ishita contended that the latter half of the 1950s marked a transformative period for intellectuals grappling with wartime legacies. He proposed that this era witnessed a departure from the narratives promoted by the GHQ and the IMTFE, with intellectuals striving to engage with the war on their own terms. During this time, a spectrum of progressive perspectives on the war emerged among these intellectuals, exemplified by figures like Takeuchi Yoshimi 竹内好, who underscored Japan's responsibilities toward East Asian nations.

In 1960, Japan experienced widespread and disruptive demonstrations opposing the extension of the Japan-US Security Treaty.[18] Following this crisis, Prime Minister Ikeda shifted his focus away from the constitutional revision and rearmament pursued by his predecessors, opting instead for a strategy centered on economic expansion. During this phase, the government's priorities were largely oriented toward material development, resulting in a relatively diminished role in shaping Japan's collective memory of the Second World War. However, despite the government's emphasis on economic growth, certain revisionist intellectuals, including Hayashi Fusao 林房雄, sought to inflame nationalist sentiments among the Japanese populace by championing the perceived righteousness of the 'Great East Asian War'.[19]

Moreover, the economic prosperity achieved during the so-called Japanese postwar miracle period, largely facilitated by the Liberal Democratic Party (LDP), brought a sense of stability to Japan and shifted public focus away from political activism toward economic pursuits. There were still a few issues that prompted Japanese people to recall the war, such as environmental pollution. The rationale

---

[17] In 1955 an article The problem of Deplorable Textbooks accused the textbooks used then were leftist biased deplorable 'red textbooks', see, Yoshida, *the Making of the 'Rape of Nanking'*; Ishida, *Kioku to boukyaku*.

[18] Hane, *Eastern Phoenix*.

[19] Zhang, Shaozhe, Kang, Xianshu and Huang, Xiaochun, 'Chuugoku' [China], in Tetsu Nakamura (ed.), *Higashi Ajia no rekishi kyoukasyou wa dou kakareteiruka* [How the history textbooks have been written in East Asia] (Tokyo: Nihon hyouronsya, 2004) 張紹哲,康賢淑,黄孝春, 中国, 中村哲, 東アジアの歴史教科書はどう書かれているか (日本評論社, 2004), p.5–6; Hayashi's representative work, see, 'Daitoua sensou kouteiron' [Argument of affirming Great East Asian War 大東亜戦争肯定論], which was published serially in *Chuuo kouron* 中央公論 between 1963 and 1965. This work argues the war was not an invasion war, but a war for liberating Asia.

behind the rapid economic growth was developmentalism (*hattenshugi*発展主義), which was rooted in the same ideology that underpinned Japan's invasions in the 1930s. It argued that invading other East Asian countries was a necessary choice for Japan. Criticism of the rapid economic growth policies indirectly led people to question the righteousness of the 'necessity of invasion'.[20] However, public opinion, which used to sympathize with the progressives and their war views, gradually disappeared due to the rapid economic growth in the 1960s.

In the 1970s, Japan's economic achievements instilled a sense of national security among its people, prompting a more open examination of their wartime past. Several significant events further encouraged this re-evaluation, including the Vietnam War, the return of Okinawa, diplomatic normalization with China, and the Emperor's visits to England in 1971 and the United States in 1975.[21] On the other hand, however, the dominance of the Liberal Democratic Party (LDP) faced severe challenges during this period. The economic miracle was shaken by the Nixon Shock in 1971, when President Richard Nixon ended the Bretton Woods system, forcing the Japanese yen to appreciate. This led to an immediate change in the exchange rate from 360 yen per dollar to 308 yen per dollar. Additionally, the oil crisis in the 1970s further exacerbated the situation, coinciding with the exposure of scandals involving LDP politicians, such as the Lockheed Scandal in 1976.[22] Despite these setbacks, the LDP managed to recover from the leadership crisis in the early 1980s and reaffirmed its commitment to nationalism and constitutional revision, echoing the priorities of its predecessors before 1960. Consequently, the LDP reinstated patriotic education, with the history of the Second World War as a significant component, as a means to address various domestic and international challenges.[23]

The 1982 Textbook Incident occurred against this backdrop. It was the first large-scale diplomatic conflict between Japan and its wartime opponents, especially China and other East Asian countries, over World War Two history. Relevant scholars, mainly political scientists, consider it a watershed moment in terms of the nature and scale of WWII history-related problems. Before 1982, they did not regard the wartime history issue as prominently as it is now. Since then, it's evident that war history-related problems have become a significant and persistent element in Japan's foreign relations. Taking Sino-Japanese relations as an example, contemporary assessments suggest they encompass various levels: military, diplomatic/political, economic, and individual perspectives. However, amidst these dimensions, the issue of wartime history looms large, exerting significant influence and, in turn, being influenced by them.[24]

---

[20] Ishida, *Kioku to boukyaku*.

[21] Ishida, *Kioku to boukyaku*.

[22] R. Vietor, 'Japan: Deficits, Demography, and Deflation', *Harvard Business School Case*, 2005.

[23] *Hane, Eastern Phoenix*; K. Ide, 'The Debate on Patriotic Education in Post-World War II Japan', *Educational Philosophy and Theory*, 41 (2009), 441–452;

[24] E. Chanlett-Avery and D. K. Nanto, 'The Rise of China and Its Effect on Taiwan, Japan, and South Korea: U.S. Policy Choices', *CRS Report for Congress*, 2006. Iriye similarly suggests that

Following the 1982 Textbook Incident, international scrutiny significantly shifted the atmosphere in Japan in terms of the discussion of the war. Faced with foreign criticism and government concessions, problems surrounding Japan's wartime memory, such as victimization narratives and nationalist sentiments, were further inflamed.[25] Concurrently, conservative politicians in Japan also escalated efforts to promote patriotic education programs.

The impact of patriotic campaigns conducted by the Japanese government since the end of the 1970s, particularly following the 1982 Textbook Incident, on exacerbating the problems surrounding Japanese Second World War memory has been widely discussed.

For instance, He suggests that in Japan, through the patriotic campaigns, the conservative government managed to propagated 'self-glorifying' and 'self-whitewashing' myths in order to 'shake off the war stigma' and justify its more assertive foreign policies, like Nakasone Yasuhiro's *sengo seiji no soukessan* (settle all accounts on post-war political issues 戦後政治の総計算) movement. According to He, although 'often distorting historical facts', myths present 'a picture of the shared past that can evoke the deepest emotional resonance from the populace' and tend to 'lead different countries to interpret the same historical events with great discrepancy'; furthermore, elites use and make myths to 'justify national security policy or address domestic political concerns.' Once such myths are promoted by elites with short-term aims and accepted by the people, they become difficult to eliminate.[26]

Nevertheless, recent studies have raised doubts about the effectiveness of the Japanese government's sponsored patriotic campaigns since the late 1970s.[27] Scholars like Ide and Tanaka suggested that the patriotism campaign launched by the LDP, particularly patriotic education in school, faced fierce opposition within Japanese society. Additionally, some scholars, who initially proposed a correlation between the state-sponsored patriotic campaigns and Japan's problematic war memory, now indicate that the officially sponsored patriotic campaign failed to

there are security ties, economic ties, and cultural ties in the Sino-Japanese relationship, see, Iriye, Akira, 'Sino-Japan relations 1945–1990', *The China Quarterly*, 124 (1990), 624–638.

Caroline, Rose, *Interpreting history in Sino-Japanese relations: a case study in political decision-making* (London: Routledge,1998). Yang, Daqing, 'The Challenges of the Nanjng Massacre: Reflections on Historical Inquiry', in Fogel (ed.), *The Nanking Massacre in History,* 133–181.

[25] Nakamura, *Sengoshi.*

[26] He, Yinan, 'Remembering and Forgetting the War: Elite Mythmaking, Mass Reaction, and Sino-Japanese Relations, 1950–2006', *History & Memory*, 19 (2007), 43–74, p.45; He, Yinan, *The Search for Reconciliation: Sino-Japanese and German-Polish Relations since World War II* (Cambridge: Cambridge University Press, 2009), p.206.

[27] Ide, 'The Debate on Patriotic Education'; H. Tanaka, 'Kyouiku houki kaisei nimiru "aikokushin kyouiku"' [Review 'patriotic education'from the perspective of changing education law], *Ryuukyuu daigaku kyouiku gakubu kiyou*, 76 (2010), 67–76 田中洋, 教育法規改正にみる「愛国心教育」,琉球大学教育学部紀要, 76 (2010), 67–76; Chan and Bridge, 'China, Japan, and the Clash of nationalisms'.

cultivate patriotism or nationalism among the Japanese. Instead, it fostered cynicism or indifference toward Japan's wartime past among the populace.[28]

Contestation is a manifest aspect of the current Japanese Second World War memory. Unlike Germany, where a dominant theme of overcoming the past exists, or China, where themes of resistance, hatred, and condemnation toward Japan's wartime actions prevail, Japan lacks a unified narrative of war remembrance. The next section will delve into this contested nature in greater detail.

It's often held that Europeans have dealt with the memory of Second World War better than their East Asian counterparts. However, there are still various problems in European memory of the war, such as the neo-Nazism and the Eastern European countries' mentality of double victimization of Nazism and Stalinism. Writings on European Second World War memory often attribute responsibility for the creation of these problems not only to several high-ranking state leaders but to all individuals across various societal strata who embrace this problematic remembrance. Similar multi-players dynamics in shaping Second World War memory and its associated problems also exist in Japan.

In his empirical research within Japan, Seaton identifies five primary groups and their versions of war remembrance: progressives, progressive-leaning group, 'don't knows and don't cares' group, conservatives and nationalists/revisionists.[29] The problematic aspects of nationalists' war remembrance (beautify the 'Great East Asia War') and the revisionists' war remembrance (deny the atrocities) are easily seen by the outsiders as the dominant theme of Japanese war remembrance. The problem of the 'don't know and don't care' group—amnesia—is often criticized as well. However, the real worrying problem of Japanese war remembrance is the victim mentality, which is held by most Japanese people. Shimazu implies that by placing the burden of war responsibility on the shoulders of the military and others, the Japanese can be anointed forever as victims of the war; moreover, the intensely myopic victim mentality came at the cost of ignoring the real victims of Japanese aggression, especially in Asia.

The contested nature of Japanese Second World War memory was also fostered by the social-historical context of Japan. Various fundamentally different perspectives regarding the Second World War have coexisted within the country since wartime. Some assert the war's necessity for Japan's survival, while others justify it as a means to expel white imperialists from Asia and establish a Great East Asian Co-Prosperity Sphere. Conversely, there are those who vehemently oppose the war, citing its devastating toll in terms of lives lost, both Japanese and from other nations. Consequently, Japanese remembrance of the war remains highly contentious. Furthermore, a myriad of distinct wartime and post-war experiences among Japanese

[28] See, C. Rose, 'Patriotism is not taboo: nationalism in China and Japan and implications for Sino-Japanese relations', *Japan Forum,* 12 (2001),169–181.

[29] P.A. Seaton, *Japan's contested war memories: the 'memory rifts' in historical consciousness of World War II* (London: Routledge, 2007). Based on various quantitative data he collected in Japan, Seaton illustrates the contested Japanese war memory in ideology, popular stories, families, regional context, newspapers, museums and so forth.

people have only served to heighten this contested nature. Among these experiences, those of civilians and combatants stand out as the two primary categories, each with its own subdivisions.

Most Japanese civilians remained on the home front, where their experiences of the war primarily involved suffering from air raids and the devastation caused by atomic bombs, leading to extremely difficult lives during and immediately after the conflict. Additionally, there were Japanese subjects living in the empire's colonies, and their war experiences varied depending on their locations. For example, Japanese settlers in Manchuria (known as *manshuu kaitaku imin* 満州開拓移民) enjoyed comfortable and peaceful lives until the Soviet Union entered Manchuria on August 8, 1945, plunging them into hellish circumstances.

As for the combatants, while some primarily participated in the war as victimizers, the roles of others were much more complex, such as young students coerced into becoming *kamikaze* suicide attackers. The experiences of combatants after Japan's surrender also differed. Prisoners of war brought to Siberia by Soviet soldiers tended to view themselves as victims of the war. Conversely, some who were re-educated and repatriated to Japan by the CCP regime (e.g., members of *chuukiren* 中帰連) not only harbored sincere guilt but also became staunch exposers of the crimes committed by Imperial Japan in China.[30]

Moreover, the state and unofficial agents were often in contest with each other. Drawing from her discussion on Ienaga Saburo's three lawsuits against the Japanese textbook screening system and the domestic struggles over school history education and war memory, Nozaki suggested that Ienaga and his supporters represented the individual Japanese people who challenged the official line of war memory in the battle of school textbooks. She also argued that although Ienaga did not win all of the lawsuits or all of the points he disputed after several decades of struggle, he did succeed outside the courtroom and made a difference to Japanese war memory.[31] Furthermore, several scholars argued that apart from progressives, nationalists, and revisionists also defended their versions of war memory against the conservative LDP government, which was subject to external pressures. For instance, following the 1982 Textbook Incident, the Japanese government publicly promised to correct improper descriptions in the textbooks. Disturbed by the changes in the textbooks, several army veterans, including the famous revisionist Tanaka Masaaki, filed a lawsuit against the Ministry of Education (MOE) for allowing the textbooks to include 'misrepresentations' of the 'Nanking Incident' on March 13, 1984. During

[30] See relevant articles included in Naka Hisao, *Sengo Nihonno nakano 'sensou'* ['War' within postwar Japan] (Kyoto: Seikai shisousha, 2004) 中久郎, 戦後日本のなかの「戦争」(世界思想社, 2004). Testimonies about different wartime experience in different locations are collected in the NHK's War Testimony Archives, available online, see: <http://www.nhk.or.jp/shogenarchives/kioku/>, date accessed, 10 Mar 2014.

[31] Y. Nozaki, *War Memory, Nationalism and Education in Postwar Japan, 1945–2007: the Japanese history textbook controversy and Ienaga Saburo's court challenges* (London: Routledge, 2008).

the same period, the progressive textbook writer Ienaga Saburo filed a second lawsuit against the MOE for its censorship via its textbook screening system.[32]

The unofficial agents were also contested among themselves. Gluck identified four custodians of the past: progressive intellectuals, conservative intellectuals, purveyors of the popular past, and individuals with personal memories of the past. Among these custodians, the progressive and conservative intellectuals were often in contest with each other. Even within the purveyors of the popular past, different kinds of memories were presented to Japanese audiences.[33] Several military songs (*gunka* 軍歌) popular during the Second World War continued to be prevalent in post-war Japan. These military songs often reflected a specific events or aspects of the war and could evoke strong emotions in listeners. *Douki no Sakura* (Cherry Blossom in the Same Year 同期の櫻), for example, was always associated with *kamikaze* members. Artists who popularized these songs through albums, films, and other mediums injected nostalgia into Japanese remembrance of the war. Additionally, there were purveyors who beautified the war in their works, such as the nationalistic Second World War-themed films, such as Turbulent Showa History (*gekidou no shouwashi: gunbatsu*激動の昭和史:軍閥). However, numerous purveyors vehemently criticized the invasion war launched by Imperial Japan, shedding light not only on the suffering of Japanese people but also on that of people in other Asian countries. For instance, the film series *Ningen no Jouken* (the Human Condition 人間の条件) depicted the cruel treatment of local Chinese in Manchuria through the eyes of the main character, Kaji.

Moreover, individuals with personal memories of the past were often in contest with each other, especially when they emerged as social agents of Second World War remembrance. This contest was well illustrated by Seraphim, who traced the history of five social groups advocating different versions of the war memory and researched how social politics affected war memory in Japan. Among the five groups examined by Seraphim, the Japan Teachers' Union and the Japan-China Friendship Association were traditionally considered custodians of the progressive memory of the war. The Japan Memorial Society for the Students Killed in the War (*wadatsumi nokai わだつみの会*) was a famous custodian of the memory of young elite students who died in the war, serving as a backbone for the anti-war movement in post-war Japan. The remaining two groups, the Association of Shinto Shrines and the Japan Association of War-Bereaved Families (*izokukai* 遺族会), were traditionally seen as custodians of the nationalist memory of the war, due to their involvement in glorifying the military personnel sacrificed in the war (*eilei* 英霊). The latter group actively pushed the Japanese government to nationalize the Yasukuni Shrine (which failed in 1974) and requested that the Japanese Prime Minister make 'official' visits to the shrine. However, there were still disputes within the group. Sensing the danger of the nationalist stance reflected by the promotion of this kind of war memory and the actions carried out by the Izokukai, Christian bereaved

[32]Yoshida, *The Making of the 'Rape of Nanking.'* Ide, *'The Debate on Patriotic Education'*.

[33]Gluck, 'The Past in the Present'.

families established their own association in 1969 and initiated campaigns to withdraw their family members from being worshipped in the Yasukuni Shrine. Seraphim highly valued the practices of these unofficial social agents, who communicated their interpretations of war and post-war to their constituents, to the state, and to the larger public, making and negotiating war memory. She further pointed out that different individuals and groups used war memory, which has been deeply embedded in the post-war political structure, as a tool for advancing their particular interests in a changing context. These 'interests' could be practical, such as economic compensation, and spiritual, such as glorification of loved ones who died in the war.[34]

Moreover, because wartime experiences varied from place to place in Japan, the prevailing remembrance in each location was also distinctive. For example, the Battle of Okinawa resulted in the highest number of casualties in the Pacific Theatre and was regarded as the only battle in Japan's own land (although this popular perception was inaccurate). Furthermore, the battle led to various tragedies such as large-scale mass suicides and the US Occupation until 1972. Naturally, the memory of the Second World War for the people of Okinawa should have been dramatically different from those in other parts of Japan. Similarly, cities like Kyoto and Nara were spared from Allied air bombings due to their historical heritage. Therefore, the war memory of people from Kyoto and Nara could not be the same as those from places that suffered heavily from air raids, such as Tokyo, where around 100,000 people died on March 10, 1945 alone.[35]

The difference between Japanese national and local war remembrance could be observed. For example, Hiroshima's suffering from the Atomic Bombing has been used by all Japanese as a symbol of Japanese victimhood during the Second World War. Nevertheless, Hiroshima's local memory and Japanese national memory were not always in harmony.[36] Although there were various provocative responses to this

---

[34] Seraphim, *War memory and social politics*, p.5, and p.8. Aoki Yasue 青木康栄, 'Shizumerarenai sensouno kioku' [War memory that cannot be relieved 鎮められない戦争の記憶] in Naka Hisao, *Sengo Nihonno nakano 'sensou'* ['War' within postwar Japan] (Kyoto: Seikai shisousha, 2004) 中久郎, 戦後日本のなかの「戦争」(世界思想社, 2004).

[35] See, relevant testimonies in the NHK War Testimonies Archives, such as Watanabe 渡邉幸二's 'My postwar 私の戦後' which is about the author's memory about the Battle of Okinawa as a soldier; Oda 小田昌衛's 'My Tokyo Air Raid 私の"東京大空襲"', and Kobayashi 小林道夫's 'Toyama Air Raid 富山空襲'.

[36] Pre-6 August war memory in Hiroshima, such as the fanatic atmosphere in Hiroshima, the prevailing hatred towards the Americans, everyday life of ordinary residences, and the colonial subjects' lives: see, J. Hersey, *Hiroshima* (London: Penguin Books, 1985); K. Selden and M. Selden, *The atomic bomb: voices from Hiroshima and Nagasaki* (The East Gate Book,1989); K. Bird and L. Lifschultz, *Hiroshima's shadow* (Stony Creek: Pamphleteer's Press, 1993).

There were a large number of pre-1982 literature deal with the remembrance of August 6. The Hiroshima City Library and the Hiroshima Peace Research Institute are great places for this kind of sources. E.g. L. Yoneyama, *Hiroshima traces: time, space, and the dialectics of memory* (Berkeley; London, University of California Press, 1999). Okuda Hiroko, *Genbaku no kioku* [Memory of atomic bombing] (Keio gijyuku daigaku chuppankai, 2010) 奥田博子, 原爆の記憶 (慶応義塾大学出版会, 2010). Encyclopedia-type-of-books published by Hiroshima local apparatus, see: Hiroshima ken, *Genbaku sanjyunen* [Atomic bombing thirty years] (Hiroshima ken, 1981)

shocking weapon among Japanese people immediately after the disaster, discussions about the Atomic Bombs were generally censored after the press code was announced by the occupation authority in mid-September 1945. Furthermore, 'American isolation of the *hibakusha* (victims of the A-bomb 被爆者) was compounded by ostracism within Japanese society itself' at the time. Japanese people did not fully comprehend the human consequences of the Atomic Bomb until 1949 when the door to publish the accounts by the *hibakusha* was opened by the publication of *Nagasaki no kane* (the Bells of Nagasaki 長崎の鐘) that year. The Japanese government also did not provide special assistance to the *hibakusha* even after the ending of the occupation in 1952.[37] In this situation, the treatment of the *hibakusha* and the task of rebuilding the city largely relied on Hiroshima's local sources. Moreover, despite being neglected by other Japanese, remembrance activities were organized locally. For instance, in 1946, a mourning ceremony for people in academic or artistic careers who died as a result of the Atomic Bomb was held on February 10; a special volume about the Atomic Bomb was published by *Chuugoku Bunka* 中国文化 on 10 March; and a large-scale anniversary mourning ceremony was held on August 6. On August 6, 1947, the first Hiroshima Peace Memorial Ceremony (which is still held annually) was organized. Additionally, a mass grave on Ninoshima island (*Ninoshima sennintsuka* 似島千人塚) was built and an unveiling ceremony was held on November 13, 1947. The ceremony was banned by the occupation authority in 1950, following the outbreak of the Korean War. This sparked protests from the *hibakusha*, such as the *hibakushia* poet, Touge sankichi 峠三吉.[38]

広島県,原爆三十年 (広島県, 1981)；Chuugoku shinbunsha, *Hiroshima no kiroku* [Hiroshima's record] (Hiroshima: Chuugoku shinbunsha, 1986) 中国新聞社, ヒロシマの記録 (中国新聞社,1986). Similar to Nanjing, the Atomic Bombing was almost in every local realms of war memory. On local medias, see: Chugoku Shinbusha, NHK, *NHK to Chuugoku shinbun no genbaku houdou* [NHK and Chuugoku news's reports about atomic bombing] (NHK, 2003) 中国新聞社, NHK, NHKと中国新聞の原爆報道 (NHK, 2003). On commemorative ceremonies, like the Hiroshima Heiwasai (Hiroshima Peace Memorial Ceremony 広島平和祭), and other commemorative facilities throughout the city and centered around the Peace Park, see: Kosakai Yoshiteru, *Hiroshima tokuhon* [Hiroshima textbook] (Hiroshima heiwa bunka sentai, 1995) 小堺吉光, ヒロシマ読本 (広島平和文化センター, 1995). On literature, songs, films and victims' testimonies, see: Kuwajiro Mizuta, *Genbaku wo yomu* [Read atomic bombing] (Tokyo: Koudansha,1982) 水田九八二郎, 原爆を読む (講談社, 1982); J. W. Treat, *Writing ground zero: Japanese literature and the atomic bomb* (Chicago: University of Chicago Press, 1995). Hiroshima toongaku iinkai, *Hiroshima to Ongaku* [Hiroshima and music] (Tokyo: Choubunsha, 2006)「ヒロシマと音楽」委員会, ヒロシマと音楽 (汐文社,2006).

Also, there are many ready-made archives about the Hiroshima citizens' war remembrance activities, which were preserved in its municipal and prefectural archives, such as Imabori Seiji Archives.

[37] J. W. Dower, 'The Bombed: Hiroshimas and Nagasakis in Japanese Memory', in Michael J. Hogan (ed.), *Hiroshima in History and Memory* (Cambridge: Cambridge University Press, 1996), p.127.

[38] Chuugoku shinbunsha, *Hiroshima no kiroku.*

The turning point in incorporating Hiroshima's suffering from the Atomic Bomb into Japanese national memory was the Lucky Dragon Incident on March 1, 1954. This incident, where a Japanese fishing boat was contaminated by nuclear fallout from an American hydrogen bomb test at Bikini Atoll, was considered the genesis of the Japanese anti-nuclear movement.[39] However, despite being hailed as the center of the anti-nuclear movement by their compatriots, people in Hiroshima were not entirely enthusiastic about the ritualization and politicization of their experience.[40] The contrast between the Japanese activists, who flocked to Hiroshima and vociferously quarreled over political disputes in August, and the Hiroshima *hibakusha,* who bravely faced the difficulties caused by the Atomic Bombs and quietly lived their lives, was depicted by Oe Kenzaburo in his book 'Hiroshima Note'.[41]

Furthermore, the war remembrance culture promoted in Hiroshima differed from that promoted by the Japanese government and most other places in Japan. The central Japanese government maintained a generally conservative stance from 1945 to the early 1990s, with only a few exceptions. Several keywords abstracted from various accounts can summarize the conservative central regime's official line on how to remember the war: 'amnesia,' 'right-wing,' 'nationalist,' and 'denial.' Meanwhile, all six Hiroshima mayors during this period devoted themselves to building Hiroshima as the center of the Japanese post-war pacific movement and as an international city of peace, including Hamai Shinzo and Araki Takeshi, both of whom were *hibakusha.* Thus, people in Hiroshima not only considered the city's experience as a national suffering of Japan but also as a tragedy of the human race.

Consequently, while most Japanese were still focused on their own wartime sufferings during the 1960s and 1970s, Hiroshima had already begun paying great attention to the foreign victims of the A-bomb and of the Japanese military.[42] This was largely because, in publicizing the Hiroshima experience around the world, the social agents of the experience encountered criticisms and differences in war remembrance from other countries earlier than other Japanese, who were mostly inward-looking regarding war remembrance at the time. For instance, the painter Maruki was questioned by an American at an exhibition of his paintings about the Atomic Bomb in Los Angeles in 1970: 'if a Chinese artist painted the brutal massacre of Chinese in Nanking by the Japanese Occupation Army, and brought that painting to Japan, what would you do?' After this encounter, Maruki started seriously reflecting on Japan's role as a victimizer during the war and created several

---

[39] Mindy Haverson, 'Memory and Memorial: How the Hiroshima Bombing and its Korean Victims have Shaped and Challenged Postwar Japanese Identity', *Stanford Journal of East Asian Affairs*, 102 (2011), 69–80.

[40] Dower, 'The Bombed'.

[41] Dajiang Jiansanlang and Weng Jiahui (translator), *Guandao Zhaji* [Hiroshima Note] (Beijing: Zhongguo guangbo chubanshe, 2009) 大江健三郎,翁家惠译，广岛札记（中国广播出版社，2009) This book was originally published in Japanese in 1965.

[42] More information about the struggle of the Hiroshima municipal government, see, S. Tachibana, 'The Quest for a Peace Culture: the A-bomb Survivors' Long Struggle and the New Movement for Redressing Foreign Victims of Japan's war', *Diplomatic History,* 19 (1995), 329–346.

paintings to reflect this aspect, such as the Nanjing Massacre's Panel 南京大虐殺の図.[43]

Still, it has been reiterated by Japanese as well as foreign scholars that there was one thing shared by almost all groups in post-war Japanese society: the victim mentality. Even progressives who constantly reflected on war responsibilities exhibited signs of this victim mentality. For example, Ienaga Saburo believed that Imperial Japan was responsible for damaging people's freedom and rights and for causing a large number of deaths among Japanese people as a result of war, while also acknowledging the sufferings imposed on Japan by the Allied side, especially the United States and the USSR.[44]

In conclusion, the remembrance of the Second World War has been an integral part of Japanese domestic society. Furthermore, this remembrance extended into Japan's diplomatic arena. For instance, through the processes of reconciliation and negotiation for war repatriation, Japan sought to improve relationships with its former enemies.[45] The pacifism movement, stemming from the memory of victimhood during the war, was also occasionally used to criticize American policies.[46] The Japanese state and various agents of war memory with differing views toward the Second World War, as well as wartime/post-war experiences, often *competed* with each other in shaping the Japanese remembrance of the War. Additionally, remembrance of the war varied from place to place. As a result, Japanese remembrance of the war was contested and multi-layered, yet unified under the victimhood narrative of the war. This feature directly contributes to the problematic Japanese war remembrance of the Second World War nowadays.

Returning to the overarching research question of this paper: Why has Japanese WWII memory remained contested and problematic even though the Japanese government had already accepted article 11 of the San Francisco Peace Treaty? According to the nature of 'collective memory' and the empirical study on the evolution of Japanese WWII memory and its contested nature, neither the San Francisco Peace Treaty nor the Japanese government could alter the course of the evolution of Japanese war memory and eliminate its problems. These problems were shaped through interactions among normal Japanese people, Japanese non-official agents, Japanese government, and international community during the wartime, the past seven decades of postwar, and the present day.

---

[43] p.103 in Maruki Shun and Maruki Iri, '*Genbaku no zu*' [Atomic bombing's panel] (Tokyo: Komine shoten, 2000) 丸木位里,丸木俊, 原爆の図 普及版完本 (小峰書店, 2000).

[44] Fujiwara argued, the experience as victims have tied Japanese together and make talking the war as an Japanese experience possible, Fujiwara,*Senso wo kioku*; Ienaga Saburo, *Senso sekinin* [War responsibility] (Tokyo: Iwanami shoten, 2005) 家永三郎, 戦争責任 (岩波書店, 2005), this book was firstly published in 1985, the author drew a wider range of first and secondary sources which were mainly from the pre-1980s period.

[45] Barak Kushner, 'The Dissolution of the Japanese Empire and the Struggle for Legitimacy in Postwar East Asia, 1945–1965', which is a research project founded by the ERC.

[46] Fujiwara, *Senso o kioku*, p.131.

Unsolved Problems in the San Francisco System

Beyond the San Francisco System: An Inspiration from Canada

Kimie Hara

Abstract After World War II, the San Francisco System established in East Asia and the Pacific assured the dominant US influence and military presence. At the same time, it left a lasting legacy of conflicts and divisions between peoples and nations that continue to affect the region today. To break the cycle of recurring conflicts and escalating tensions and to promote peace and stability, it is crucial to understand the historical context and sincerely address and resolve the underlying issues. In recent years, Canada has made significant progress in its efforts toward historical reconciliation with Indigenous peoples and decolonization. This shift was also reflected in the resolution of its territorial dispute with Denmark in 2022. These efforts offer valuable insights for considering conflict resolution and reconciliation in East Asia.

Keywords San Francisco Peace Treaty · Cold War · East Asia · Territorial disputes · United States · Japan · Reconciliation · International law · Colonial legacy · Indigenous rights

---

This paper builds on the author's earlier work and contains overlapping content, particularly from the following publications: Kimie Hara (ed.), *The San Francisco System and Its Legacies: Continuation, Transformation, and Historical Reconciliation in the Asia-Pacific* (London: Routledge, 2015); *Reconciliation and Symbiosis in East Asia from Comparative Perspectives* (Kitchener, Pandora Press, 2025); Kimie Hara, *Cold War Frontiers in the Asia-Pacific: Divided Territories in the San Francisco System* (London: Routledge, 2007); "The San Francisco Peace Treaty and Frontier Problems in the Regional Order in East Asia: A Sixty-Year Perspective," *The Asia-Pacific Journal* 10, no. 17, issue 1 (2012).

K. Hara (✉)
Keiko and Charles Belair Centre for East Asian Studies, Renison University College, University of Waterloo, Waterloo, ON, Canada
e-mail: khara@uwaterloo.ca

Y.-H. Kim et al. (eds.), *Beyond the San Francisco System*,
https://doi.org/10.1007/978-981-95-3328-2_11

1 The San Francisco System: The Post–World War II Order and Regional Conflicts in East Asia

The Cold War structure that emerged in the post–World War II era is often attributed to the Yalta System, which resulted from agreements between the United States, the UK, and the USSR on the construction of the postwar international order at the Yalta Conference in February 1945. However, with regard to the regional international order in East Asia and the Pacific, the Yalta blueprint gave way to the San Francisco System. Following a series of East–West tensions, notably those centered on the communization of Eastern Europe, the Yalta System was consolidated in Europe. The status quo received international recognition in the 1975 Helsinki Accords. By the early 1990s, however, the Yalta System had collapsed, accompanied by significant changes such as the democratization of Eastern Europe, the independence of the Baltic states, the reunification of Germany, and the demise of the Soviet Union. Since then, many have viewed the collapse of the Yalta System as synonymous with the end of the Cold War.

The Yalta System, however, was never established as an international order in East Asia. The post-war international order was discussed and some secret agreements affecting Japan were concluded at Yalta. The terms "Yalta System" and "East Asian Yalta System" are sometimes used to refer to a regional post-war order based on those agreements.[1] But it was a blueprint that would have taken effect only if such agreements had been faithfully implemented. By 1951, when the peace treaty with Japan was signed in San Francisco, the Yalta agreements had been in part distorted or made equivocal. Under the new circumstances of escalating East–West confrontation that had begun in Europe, post-war Asia took a profoundly different path from that originally planned.

The San Francisco Peace Treaty was an international agreement that in significant ways shaped the post–World War II order in the region. With its associated security arrangements, it laid the foundation for the regional structure of Cold War confrontation: the San Francisco System fully reflected the strategic interests and the policy priorities of the peace conference's host nation, the United States. The System assured the dominant influence and lasting presence of the United States, or "Pax Americana", and brought Japan democracy and economic prosperity, but at the expense of lasting divisions among peoples and countries in East Asia.

The Cold War developed differently between the Atlantic and Pacific sides of the Eurasian continent. While falling short of "hot" war, it was "Cold War" in Europe and the US-USSR context. By contrast, in Asia it was "hot" in places, and more complex. After the Japanese withdrawal, the postwar liberation and independence movements in some parts of the region turned to civil war over the governing principles for the new states, where competition over spheres of influence between the superpowers supervened. Instead of a direct clash between the United States and the USSR, Asian

[1] Akira Iriye, *The Cold War in Asia: A Historical Introduction* (Englewood Cliffs, NJ: Prentice Hall, 1974), 93–97; Yoshihide Soeya, *Nihon gaiko to chugoku 1945–1972* [Japanese Diplomacy and China 1945–1972] (Tokyo: Keiko Gijuku Daigaku Shuppan-kai, 1995), 33–38.

lands became surrogate battlefields between Capitalism and Socialism. In 1951, while failing to form a multilateral regional alliance like NATO, the United States signed a mutual defense treaty with the Philippines on August 30, a tripartite security treaty with Australia and New Zealand (ANZUS) on September 1, and a security treaty with Japan on September 8 on the same day as the peace treaty. The "San Francisco Alliance System" of US hub-and-spoke military alliances came into being then.[2]

Along with political and military conflicts, significant elements within the Cold War structure in East Asia are the regional conflicts among its major players. Confrontation over national boundaries and territorial sovereignty emerged from the disposition of the defeated Axis countries. Whereas Germany was the only divided nation in Europe, several Cold War frontiers emerged to divide nations and peoples in East Asia. The San Francisco Peace Treaty played a critical role in creating or mounting many of these frontier problems. Vast territories that Japan once ruled or advanced into, extending from the Kurile Islands to Antarctica, and from Micronesia to the Spratlys, were disposed of in the treaty. The treaty, however, specified neither their final disposition nor their precise geographical limits, thereby sowing the seeds of multiple "unresolved problems" throughout the region.

The regional conflicts derived from the post-war territorial disposition of the former Japanese empire may be classified into three kinds: (1) insular territorial disputes such as those pertaining to the Northern Territories/Southern Kuriles, Dokdo/Takeshima, Senkaku/Diaoyu, Spratly/Nansha and Paracel/Xisha Islands; (2) divided nations as seen in the Korean Peninsula and cross–Taiwan Strait problem;[3] and (3) status of the territories concerning Okinawa and Taiwan.[4] These problems did not necessarily originate solely in the San Francisco Peace Treaty. For example, a secret agreement to transfer the Kuriles and Southern Sakhalin from Japan to the USSR was reached at the Yalta Conference in February 1945. However, the problem emerged at San Francisco, since the peace treaty specified neither final disposition

[2]The United States made similar arrangements with South Korea in 1953, Taiwan in 1954, and Thailand in 1961. For a detailed analysis of the San Francisco Alliance System, see William T. Tow, Russell B. Trood, and Toshiya Hosono, eds., *Bilateralism in a Multilateral Era: The Future of the San Francisco Alliance System in the Asia-Pacific* (Tokyo: Japan Institute of International Affairs, 1997).

[3]The peace treaty alone did not divide China and Taiwan (Formosa). However, by leaving the status of the island undecided, it left various options open for its future, including possession by the People's Republic of China (PRC) or the Republic of China (ROC), or even its independence. The peace treaty also left the final designation of "Korea" unclear. Although Japan renounced "Korea" and recognized its independence in the treaty, no reference was made to the two governments established in the divided peninsula, then at war with each other. There was then, and still is, no state or country called "Korea," but two states, the Republic of Korea (ROK) in the south and the Democratic People's Republic of Korea (DPRK) in the north.

[4]Okinawa (the Ryukyus), together with other Japanese islands in the Pacific, was addressed in the treaty's Article 3. This article neither confirmed nor denied Japanese sovereignty, but guaranteed sole US control—until such time that the United States would propose and affirm a UN trusteeship arrangement over these islands. "Administrative rights," if not full sovereignty, of all the territories specified in this article were returned to Japan by the early 1970s, without having been placed under UN trusteeship. However, long after the "return," the majority of US forces and military bases in Japan remain concentrated in Okinawa.

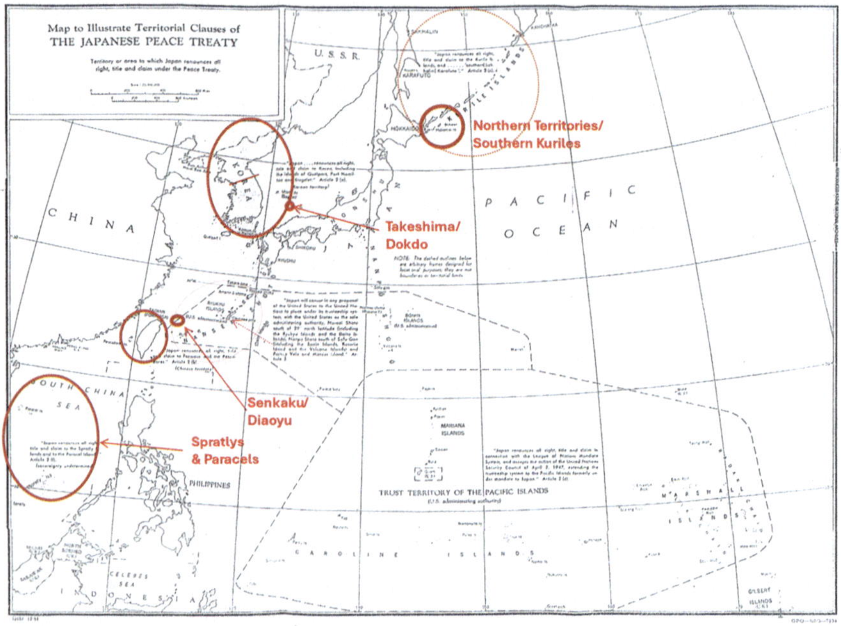

Fig. 1 The San Francisco Peace Treaty and the regional conflicts. Source: United States, 82nd session, SENATE, *Executive Report No.2, Japanese Peace Treaty and Other Treaties relating to Security in the Pacific/Report of the Committee on Foreign Relations on Executives, A, B, C and D*. Washington: United States Government Printing Office, 1952), with related regional conflicts in East Asia marked in red by the author

nor precise boundaries of these territories that Japan renounced.[5] There is neither a post-WW II peace treaty nor a resolution to the territorial or border problem between Japan and Russia/USSR (Fig. 1).

2 "Unresolved Problems" in the San Francisco System

The ambiguity of the Japanese peace settlement, particularly the equivocal wording of its territorial clauses, was closely tied to the developments of the Cold War in the region. Prior to the final draft of the San Francisco Peace Treaty, signed in 1951—six years after the Japanese surrender—multiple treaty drafts were prepared by the US State Department, the primary drafter. Early versions were largely shaped by US wartime studies and aligned with the Yalta spirit of inter-Allied cooperation.[6] These

[5] Hara, "The San Francisco Peace Treaty and Frontier Problems in the Regional Order in East Asia: A Sixty Year Perspective."

[6] Hara, "The San Francisco Peace Treaty and Frontier Problems."

drafts reflected the Allies' "punitive" and "rigid" policy toward Japan, treating it as a defeated enemy to be stripped of its conquered territories and weakened both militarily and economically. As for territorial dispositions, those early drafts were lengthy and detailed, providing clear border demarcations and specifying the names of small islands near Japan's post-war borders, such as Takeshima, Habomai, and Shikotan, specifically to avoid future territorial conflicts.

However, against the background of the intensifying Cold War, which became "hot" in East Asia with the outbreak of the Korean War in June 1950, the peace terms with Japan changed in sync with the new strategic interests of the United States. Specifically, Japan and the Philippines, soon to be the most important US allies in East Asia, were to be secured for the non-communist West with pro-US governments, whereas the communist states were to be contained.

In this context, drafts of the Japanese peace treaty underwent numerous revisions, eventually becoming more simplified. The names of the countries, namely China and de south union, intended to receive territories such as Formosa (Taiwan), the Kuriles, and other islands were removed from the text. This simplification lest behind various "unresolved problems" between regional neighbors. The ambiguous wording of the treaty was not the result of oversight or error, but rather a product of extensive deliberations and revisions.[7] It is no coincidence that the territorial disputes derived from the San Francisco Peace Treaty—the Northern Territories/Southern Kuriles, Takeshima/Dokdo, Senkaku/Diaoyu (Okinawa),[8] Spratly/Nansha, and Paracel/Xisha problems—all line up along the "Acheson Line," the United States' Cold War defense perimeter of the western Pacific, announced in January 1950. With the outbreak of the Korean War, the United States altered its policy toward Korea and China, which it had once written off as "lost," and intervened in both nations' civil wars. However, in order to avoid further escalation of these regional conflicts, which could possibly lead to a nuclear war or the next total war, the "containment line" came to be fixed at the Military Demarcation Line and Taiwan Strait, respectively.

As for the Spratlys and Paracels, disposed of in Article 2(f) of the peace treaty and located in the South China Sea at the southwest end of the Acheson Line, to varying degrees, Chinese ownership was considered for these territories in US wartime preparations for a post-war settlement. Their final designation was not specified in the San Francisco Treaty, not simply because it was unclear, but, more importantly, to prevent them from falling into the hands of China. Disputes over the sovereignty of these islands in the South China Sea existed before the war. However, the pre- and post-war disputes differ in terms of the countries involved and the

[7] Hara, *Cold War Frontiers in the Asia-Pacific*.

[8] The territorial problem between Japan and China originally centered on the Ryukyu Islands (Okinawa), as part of which the Sankakus were placed under US control. Chiang Kai-shek's Republic of China (ROC), representing "China" at the UN, was actively demanding the "recovery" of the Ryukyus up to the early post-war years. With the reversion of administrative rights to Japan in 1972, however, the focus of the dispute shifted to the Senkakus. (Hara, *Cold War Frontiers in the Asia-Pacific*, 161).

nature of the disputes—that is, pre-war colonial frontiers were reborn as Cold War frontiers in Southeast Asia.[9]

Meanwhile, the United States tactically negotiated the terms of UN trusteeship for its advantage and secured exclusive control of its occupied islands, making the Pacific north of the Equator "an American Lake."[10] Among those islands, Micronesia, disposed of in the peace treaty's Article 2(d), was used for US nuclear testing, whereas Okinawa became one of the most important US military bases in the region.[11]

Besides the handling of territories, the US Cold War strategy was also reflected in other aspects of the peace settlement with Japan. For instance, the peace treaty specified Japan's acceptance of the judgments of the International Military Tribunal for the Far East, the so-called Tokyo Tribunal (1946–1948). However, the tribunal overlooked the responsibility of the Japanese government for the torture and abuse of Chinese and Koreans, in such matters as the Nanjing massacre, the use of Korean and Chinese forced labor in Japanese mines and factories, and the forced prostitution of Korean, Chinese, and other nations' "comfort women" by the Japanese military.[12]

To transform Japan as a pro-US nation, the peace terms to be presented by the United States had to be more attractive to Japan than those by the communist nations, which would attempt to estrange Japan from the United States. Consequently, the peace terms with Japan became "generous" rather than punitive, with the focus placed on economic recovery of post-war Japan. This "reverse course" led to the eventual return of conservative politicians, who were purged or prosecuted as war criminals during the occupations period.

Neither of the governments of China (PRC or ROC) nor Korea (ROK or DPRK) was invited to the peace conference. The Soviet Union participated in the peace conference but did not sign the treaty. The Japanese peace treaty was prepared and signed multilaterally, making the forty-nine signatories the "concerned states." Except for Japan, however, none of the countries directly concerned with territorial settlements were participants in the treaty. The result was to bequeath multiple unresolved conflicts to the countries directly concerned and to the region.[13]

The peace treaty with Japan was meant to end World War II and usher in a "post-war" era in the Asia-Pacific. Instead, it became a by-product of the Cold War,

---

[9] Before World War II, the countries primarily involved in disputes in the South China Sea were China and two colonial powers, Japan and France. After the war, Japan and France withdrew; the islands came to be disputed by the two Chinas (PRC and ROC) and the newly independent neighboring Southeast Asian countries. Chapter 6 in Hara, *Cold War Frontiers in the Asia-Pacific*.

[10] John W. Dower, "Occupied Japan and the American Lake" in America's Asia, edited by Edward Friedman and Mark Selden (New York: Vintage, 1971), 146–197. For Western imperial powers' control of the world's oceans, see Peter Nolan, "Imperial Archipelago," *New Left Review* 80 (March–April 2013).

[11] Chapters 4 and 7 in Hara, *Cold War Frontiers in the Asia-Pacific*.

[12] Gi-Wook Shin, "Historical Disputes and Reconciliation in Northeast Asia: The RUS Role," *Pacific Affairs* 83, no. 4 (December 2010), 664.

[13] Hara, "The San Francisco Peace Treaty and Frontier Problems."

entangling Japan and the region in its dynamics. Unresolved issues rooted in this context have continued to divide East Asia, effectively perpetuating a new form of "divide and rule" under the San Francisco System.

3 Transformation and Contemporary Legacy of the San Francisco System

More than 70 years since the San Francisco agreement, the world has undergone profound transformations. Following periods of East–West tensions and subsequent relaxation, including the Cold War thaw of the 1950s and the détente of the 1970s, the Cold War was widely perceived to have ended by the early 1990s.

In the Asia-Pacific, however, the Cold War unfolded differently from the bipolar structure in the Euro-Atlantic region. A tri-polar structure emerged with the US–China–USSR dynamic, particularly after the Sino–Soviet split in the early 1960s. China had been a target of the US containment strategy since its intervention in the Korean War. With its nuclear development in 1964 and participation in the Indochina Wars, China assumed a larger role in the Asian Cold War. Similar to how the emergence of nuclear weapons fundamentally altered the character of post–World War II international relations and played a major role in shaping the US–Soviet Cold War, the US–China confrontation evolved into a true "Cold War" without direct military conflict. Instead, surrogate wars were fought on China's periphery. Despite a series of Sino–US rapprochements and the normalization of relations in the 1970s, the United States maintained its security commitment to Taiwan through the introduction of the Taiwan Relations Act, even after severing official diplomatic relations.

From the late 1980s to the early 1990s, the "end of the Cold War" brought significant political de-escalation and reconciliation to the region. Sino–Soviet/Russian border negotiations began in the late 1980s and were finalized through mutual concessions in the 2000s. Despite the Soviet Union's collapse, however, the Cold War structure in the region endures. Along the Military Demarcation Line of the Korean Peninsula, the Taiwan Strait, and the disputed territories along the Acheson Line, conflicts continue to divide nations in the region. In China, the communist regime survived despite adopting capitalist reforms and a market economy. Surpassing Japan to become the world's second-largest economy in the twenty-first century, China has embraced a modern version of "rich nation, strong military" (富国強兵), reminiscent of pre-World War II Japan, but on a far larger scale. This transformation is viewed by the United States and its allies as an increasing security threat.

The relaxation of tensions during the Cold War thaw in the 1950s and détente in the 1970s both ultimately led to a subsequent deterioration of East–West relations. Similar patterns have emerged in East Asia, such as the US–China conflicts following the 1989 Tiananmen incident and, more recently, in response to China's economic and military rise. Other examples include military tensions across the Taiwan Strait and Korean Peninsula, stalled negotiations between Japan and North Korea to normalize relations, and territorial and historical disputes involving Japan, China, and their neighbors. While the 1975 Helsinki Accords recognized the political status quo and borders in Europe, East Asia remains fragmented by ongoing territorial and historical conflicts, preventing it from achieving the level of détente seen in 1970s Europe.

Despite political divisions, historical conflicts, and unresolved borders, East Asia has grown increasingly interconnected through economic, cultural, and other relations. China's economic reforms in the late 1970s marked the beginning of a partial dissolution of regional Cold War confrontations. Over the past seven decades, East Asia has undergone remarkable economic recovery and transformation, transitioning from the devastation of war. Starting with Japan in the 1950s, followed by the newly industrializing economies (NIEs) in the 1970s and 1980s, and culminating in China's rise in the twenty-first century, the region has become one of the world's most dynamic economic centers.

Multilateral economic cooperation and institution-building in East Asia have also advanced, especially since the 1990s. Inspired by the end of the Cold War and European regional integration, regionalism gained momentum, leading to the emergence of the broader "Asia-Pacific" concept. This was built on foundations like the Pacific Economic Cooperation Council (PECC), Asia-Pacific Economic Cooperation (APEC), and the ASEAN Regional Forum (ARF). Following the global economic crises of 1997 and 2008, new forums involving China (PRC), Japan, and South Korea (ROK), such as ASEAN+3 and the PRC–Japan–ROK Trilateral Summit, emerged. Economic relations have become the key factor binding the region, contributing to what Stein Tønnesson calls "East Asia's Developmental Peace."[14]

In the twenty-first century, particularly since the 2010s, a broader regional concept known as the "Indo-Pacific" has emerged. Unlike "Asia-Pacific," however, this term is used in the context of a shift from easing tensions to a new cycle of deteriorating relations, often framed as the "US-China New Cold War." A key difference from the past is the rise of China on the global stage and North Korea's acquisition of nuclear weapons. In response, the United States has sought to curb Beijing's influence and maintain its own regional dominance by forming new partnerships, such as AUKUS, QUAD, and Five Eyes, under its "Indo-Pacific" strategy. This strategy involves collaboration with friendly nations and Western allies across the broader region, reinforcing its post–World War II regional alliances, notably the San Francisco Alliance System. Meanwhile, since the outbreak of the war in Ukraine in February 2022, Russia has intensified its confrontation with the West, strengthening its ties with China and North Korea. These developments have contributed to growing uncertainties in East Asia, leaving the region in a more precarious position than during the Cold War era of the twentieth century – a tendency accentuated with the return of the US Trump administration in 2025.

---

[14] Stein Tønnesson, "Explaining East Asia's Developmental Peace: The Dividends of Economic Growth," *Global Asia* 10, no. 4 (Winter 2015): 10–15.

4 Beyond the San Francisco System: An Inspiration from Canada

Interpretations of the "Cold War" and the "end of the Cold War" vary, as do those of the San Francisco System.[15] Regardless of these differing perspectives, tensions stemming from these conflicts have periodically intensified and are likely to continue as long as they remain unresolved. To break this vicious cycle, prevent these negative legacies from passing further onto future generations, and secure peace and stability in the region, the principal sources of conflict must be addressed and resolved.

The United States wields significant influence on the resolution of regional conflicts, just as it played a key role in their origins. However, resolving these conflicts could alter the regional security balance and potentially lead to a US withdrawal or reduced influence in the region. This may not always align with US strategic interests. Given that these conflicts help justify US presence and sustain its influence in the region, it may be more strategically advantageous for the United States to manage and maintain tensions between regional states, while avoiding direct conflict between great powers.

The structural binding force of the San Francisco System remains strong and deeply entrenched. However, as seen with past developments in the "Thaw," "Détente," and the "End of the Cold War," changes in domestic conditions, shifts in international political dynamics, and the reevaluation of existing policies could lead to future changes. Meanwhile, both governmental and non-governmental actors seeking to resolve, rather than merely managing, these conflicts can engage in cross-border dialogue and cooperation at various levels to explore and prepare mutually acceptable solutions.

There are many historical precedents around the world that can serve as valuable references. Notable examples include the Åland Islands Arbitration (1921), the first conflict resolution by the League of Nations, and the Helsinki Accords (1975), the Final Act of the first Conference on Security and Cooperation in Europe (CSCE) during the East-West détente period.[16] These examples continue to provide important insights and lessons when considering potential solutions to regional conflicts in East Asia.

---

[15] For relevant discussions, see "Introduction: Rethinking the 'Cold War' in the Asia-Pacific" in Hara, *Cold War Frontiers in the Asia-Pacific*, 2–13. The term "San Francisco System" is used in different ways. Some define it as Japan's position in the post-war world, based on the San Francisco Peace Treaty and the US-Japan bilateral security alliance, while others see it in a broader context of the US-led post–war regional and Cold War order in the Asia-Pacific, as also seen in this paper. The term has also, though to a lesser degree, been used to refer to the US security alliance system in the region, the "San Francisco Alliance System" mentioned earlier.

[16] "Envisioning Åland-Inspired Solutions for the Northern Territories Problem," in Hara and Jukes, eds., *Northern Territories, Asia-Pacific Regional Conflicts and the Åland Experience: Untying the Kurillian Knot* (London: Routledge, 2009), 113–124; Hara, "Preparing Ideas for Future: Envisioning a Multilateral Settlement," in Hara, ed., *San Francisco System and Its Legacies: Continuation, Transformation, and Historical Reconciliation in the Asia-Pacific* (London: Routledge, 2015), 264–271.

In addition to Europe, Canada offers another important case. Canada's engagement with these conflicts is not without precedent. Canada bears historical responsibility, as it proposed that the post-war Japanese peace treaty not specify final designation of the territories in the treaty drafting process, thus contributing to sow the seeds of various disputes.[17] Canada is both a Pacific and Atlantic nation, and a member of the Organization for Security and Cooperation in Europe (OSCE), formerly CSCE that participated in the Helsinki Accords. While always mindful of its relationship with its neighboring superpower, the United States, Canada has historically pursued a path of internationalism and multilateralism, building a reputation as a peace-builder on the global stage.

Despite its relatively positive international standing, Canada has a long history of colonial and settler colonial practices. Its relationships with Indigenous peoples have been forged through treaties as well as trade and military alliances. Over time, however, these relationships were undermined by colonial and imperial paternalistic policies enshrined in law. Indigenous peoples were deprived of their land, language, and culture, and their children were taken from their families and placed in so-called Residential Schools, where they were forcibly assimilated by white settlers. This systemic abuse continued for many years, even after World War II.

In the 1990s, the Royal Commission on Aboriginal Peoples issued recommendations for dispute resolution, but these efforts fell short of meeting the expectations of Indigenous peoples. In 2007, the Indian Residential Schools Settlement Agreement, the largest class-action settlement in Canadian history, was implemented. One key aspect of the agreement was the establishment of the Truth and Reconciliation Commission (TRC), which, in 2015, released its final report after conducting inquiries across Canada. The report included 94 "Calls to Action" to further reconciliation between Canadians and Indigenous peoples in a wide range of areas. The then Prime Minister Justin Trudeau accepted the report on behalf of Canada, and since then, there has been a renewed focus on rectifying past injustices and achieving historical reconciliation. Notably, the "Territorial Acknowledgment" or "Land Acknowledgment" has become a common practice across Canada.[18] There have also been significant developments at various levels of Canadian society, including federal, provincial, territorial, municipal governments, and in the private sector.

Some may argue that these issues are now domestic matters within Canada and are irrelevant to international reconciliation and dispute resolution. However, historical agreements and treaties between the Canadian government and Indigenous peoples (First Nations, Métis, and Inuit), which respect their sovereignty, are central

---

[17] Hara, *Cold War Frontiers in the Asia-Pacific*, 94; Hara, *San Francisco System and Its Legacies: Continuation, Transformation, and Historical Reconciliation in the Asia-Pacific*, 12.

[18] This practice involves recognizing and paying respect to the ancestral lands of specific indigenous groups or nations where actions occur. It is commonly observed during various events, meetings, and in public documents as a gesture of acknowledgment and honor. Similar practices have been observed in other settler colonial countries, such as New Zealand, Australia, and Perhaps, lesser degree at present (2025), the United States.

to the relationship. Today, these agreements are recognized as part of "nation-to-nation relations."

The groundwork for the United Nations Declaration on the Rights of Indigenous Peoples (UNDRIP)—a key element of the TRC's "Calls to Action"—can be traced back over a century, to 1923, with the efforts of Haudenosaunee (commonly known as the Iroquois or Six Nations) Chief Deskaheh. He sought to draw international attention to Canada's failure to uphold treaties at the League of Nations, the predecessor of the United Nations. Deskaheh traveled to Europe carrying a passport issued by the Six Nations, not Canada. This contrasts with East Asia at a time when both Korea and Taiwan were under Japanese colonial rule and regarded as Japans "domestic affairs" – and provides valuable insights into the intertwined dynamics of imperialism and decolonization.

In 2007, when UNDRIP was adopted by a vast majority of 144 in favor (with 4 against and 11 abstaining), Canada opposed the declaration. However, in 2016, a year after the Canadian government accepted the TRC report and its 94 Calls to Action, Canada officially withdrew its objection to UNDRIP.[19] In 2021, the UNDRIP Act (Bill C-15) became law in Canada. This marked a significant shift in Canada's approach to Indigenous rights, reflecting the government's commitment to upholding the rights of Indigenous peoples and advancing reconciliation.

Furthermore, in June 2022, Canada peacefully resolved a territorial dispute with Denmark over Tartupaluk/Hans Island, a small uninhabited island in the Arctic, in a manner that reflects the spirit of the UNDRIP Act. The agreement on the island's sovereignty followed consultations with the Indigenous Inuit peoples from both Nunavut and Greenland. They will retain hunting rights and freedom of movement on the island, which has been part of their hunting grounds for centuries. This resolution ensures the protection of Indigenous rights, allowing them to maintain their traditional way of life.[20] This conflict resolution is particularly noteworthy because it acknowledges and reflects the interests and voices of the Indigenous Inuit peoples—who have historically inhabited the area—not merely a bilateral agreement between the central governments in Ottawa and Copenhagen.

Despite facing strong resistance and challenges from time to time, reconciliation efforts in Canada continue. This ongoing journey may offer valuable insights and serve as an inspiration for considering dispute resolution and reconciliation in East Asia, where territorial issues are deeply intertwined with historical conflicts.

---

[19] Australia, New Zealand, and the United States, which had opposed the declaration in 2007, reversed their positions and expressed support between 2009 and 2010. However, all three countries have recognized UNDRIP as a non-binding international standard rather than fully aligning it with their domestic laws.

[20] "'Whiskey war' with Denmark over tiny Arctic island ends peacefully with deal ", CTV News, June 14, 2022. Apostolos Tsiouvalas and Endalew Lijalem Enyew, "The Legal Implications of the 2022 Canada-Denmark/Greenland Agreement on Hans Island (Tartupaluk) for the Inuit Peoples of Greenland and Nunavut," *The Arctic Institute, Center for Circumpolar Security Studies*, January 24, 2023, https://www-thearcticinstitute-org.translate.goog/legal-implications-2022-canada-denmark-greenland-agreement-hans-island-tartupaluk-inuit-peoples-greenland-nunavut/?_x_tr_sl=auto&_x_tr_tl=ja&_x_tr_hl=ja&_x_tr_pto=wapp. Accessed November 21, 2024.

The political and security environment in contemporary East Asia has been profoundly shaped by its historical evolution, which dates back to the pre-World War II period, when the region became integrated into the Western-led world order, largely defined by imperialism and colonialism. In this context, Japan, uniquely among Asian nations, expanded its territorial domains and joined the ranks of Western imperialist powers. However, as a consequence of the Asia-Pacific War (World War II), Japan lost much of the territories it had acquired or advanced into, as stipulated in the San Francisco Peace Treaty. The Cold War further shaped the region's political and security landscape, leaving a lasting legacy of conflicts and divisions between peoples and nations. Throughout these processes, the roles and impacts of the West, particularly the United States, were significant, though they are often overlooked.

While Asia is distinct in many ways, the experiences, wisdom, and lessons drawn from efforts to address and overcome historical challenges and negative legacies can hold relevance beyond regional boundaries. Just as the order and concepts of modern international relations spread from the West to the rest of the world, so too may the solutions and strategies for overcoming historical conflicts find resonance across different regions.

References

Dower, J. W. (1971). Occupied Japan and the American lake. In E. Friedman & M. Selden (Eds.), *America's Asia* (pp. 146–197). Vintage.

Hara, K. (2007). *Cold war frontiers in the Asia-Pacific: Divided territories in the San Francisco system*. Routledge.

Hara, K. (2012). The San Francisco Peace Treaty and frontier problems in the regional order in East Asia: A sixty year perspective. *The Asia-Pacific Journal, 10*(17), e1.

Hara, K. (2015). *The San Francisco system and its legacies: Continuation, transformation, and historical reconciliation in the Asia-Pacific*. Routledge.

Iriye, A. (1974). *The Cold War in Asia: A historical introduction*. Prentice Hall.

Nolan, P. (2013). Imperial archipelago. *New Left Review, 80*, March–April.

Soeya, Y. (1995). *Nihon gaiko to chugoku 1945–1972 [Japanese diplomacy and China 1945–1972]*. Keiko Gijuku Daigaku Shuppan-kai.

Tow, W. T., Trood, R. B., & Hosono, T. (Eds.). (1997). *Bilateralism in a multilateral era: The future of the San Francisco alliance system in the Asia-Pacific*. Japan Institute of International Affairs.

Tsiouvalas, A., & Enyew, E. L. (2023, January 24). The legal implications of the 2022 Canada-Denmark/Greenland agreement on Hans Island (Tartupaluk) for the Inuit peoples of Greenland and Nunavut. The Arctic Institute, Center for Circumpolar Security Studies. https://www-thearcticinstitute-org.translate.goog/legal-implications-2022-canada-denmark-greenland-agreement-hans-island-tartupaluk-inuit-peoples-greenland-nunavut/

US State Department (1943). *Foreign Relations of the States (FRUS) Diplomatic Papers, the Conference at Cairo and Tehran*. Washington, DC: Government Printing Office.

Transcending the San Francisco System Requires the Elimination of Colonial Remnants: With a Focus on Post-war Territorial Disputes in Northeast Asia

Dekun Hu

Abstract This article analyzes how the post-war San Francisco System, established by the United States through the 1951 peace treaty, fundamentally altered Allied agreements on the disposition of Japanese territory and entrenched sources of ongoing territorial disputes in Northeast Asia. It details how wartime declarations such as the Cairo and Potsdam agreements set clear principles for returning territories seized by Japan, but the San Francisco Treaty replaced these with ambiguous provisions, often favoring U.S. strategic interests and Japan's claims. The exclusion of China and the Soviet Union from the treaty process, and the shift from "return" to "renounce" regarding territories, led to unresolved disputes over areas such as the Diaoyu/Senkaku Islands, Dokdo/Takeshima, and the Kuril Islands. The article argues that these changes institutionalized colonial remnants and Cold War divisions, impeding regional cooperation and reconciliation. It further contends that Japan's incomplete reckoning with its colonial past and the U.S. pursuit of hegemony have perpetuated instability. The study calls for Northeast Asia to abandon Cold War thinking, eliminate colonial legacies, and pursue a community of shared destiny. Ultimately, it suggests that only through regional cooperation and historical justice can the obstacles created by the San Francisco System be overcome.

Keywords Allied Powers · Cairo Declaration · Cold War · Colonial legacy · Dokdo · Northeast Asia · Potsdam Proclamation · San Francisco System · Territorial disputes · United States

The territory issue was an important aspect of establishing the post-war international order by the anti-fascist alliance. It involved liberating territories occupied by fascist forces, reclaiming lands seized by fascist nations through colonial expansion and external aggression, and delineating the territorial boundaries of fascist states.

D. Hu (✉)
Institute of Boundary and Ocean Studies, Wuhan University, Wuhan, China
e-mail: dkhu@whu.edu.cn

Y.-H. Kim et al. (eds.), *Beyond the San Francisco System*,
https://doi.org/10.1007/978-981-95-3328-2_12

These actions were crucial components of constructing the post-war international order by the Allies. Therefore, as early as wartime, the Allies deliberated on measures to address territorial changes resulting from fascist aggression in a series of important meetings; and the Cairo Declaration and the Potsdam Proclamation established the basic principles and guidelines for post-war disposition of Japanese territory. However, after World War II, the United States, in pursuit of hegemony in East Asia under the pretext of the Cold War, intentionally sought to alter the common provisions of the Allies regarding the disposition of Japanese territory. On September 8, 1951, the United States led the unilateral signing of the San Francisco Peace Treaty, establishing the San Francisco system dominated by the United States and centered around the U.S.-Japan alliance. This action left serious consequences, becoming the source of territorial disputes between Japan and China, South Korea, Russia, and between China and her neighboring countries in the South China Sea, and a major obstacle to cooperation and development in Northeast Asia.

1 Punishing the Aggressor Country: Provisions of the United States, the United Kingdom, the Soviet Union, and China Regarding the Disposition of Japanese Territories During the War

For the needs of the anti-fascist war, on January 1, 1942, 26 anti-fascist countries led by China, the United States, the United Kingdom, and the Soviet Union signed the United Nations Declaration in Washington, which stipulated, "Each Government pledges itself to cooperate with the Governments signatory hereto and not to make a separate armistice or peace with the enemies."[1] In October 1943, the four countries of China, the United States, the United Kingdom, and the Soviet Union issued the Declaration of the Four Nations on General Security, announcing that the unanimous determination of the four major countries is to "take joint action" in defeating the enemy and handling surrender matters of the enemy.[2] Therefore, the principle of unanimity among the major powers of the Allies and the principle of not "negotiating peace without consulting one's allies" became the common agreement of the four major anti-fascist countries.

The Cairo Conference was a product of the development of the World Anti-Fascist War into the stage of strategic counterattack. From the second half of 1942 to the first half of 1943, the anti-fascist allied forces achieved strategic turning points respectively on the Eastern Front, the North African-Mediterranean Theater,

[1] *Guojifa Tiaoyueji (1934–1944)* (Beijing: Shijie Zhishi Chubanshe, 1961), p.343 [《国际条约集》(1934–1944)，北京:世界知识出版社，1961年，第343页].

[2] Faxue jiaocai bianjibu (ed.), *Guoji Guanxi Ziliao Xuanbian* (Shangce, Dierfence) (Wuhan: Wuhan Daxue Chubanshe, 1983), p.175. [法学教材编辑部审定:《国际关系资料选编》(上册，第二分册)，武汉:武汉大学出版社，1983年，第175页].

and the Pacific Theater. On the Eastern Front, from July 1942 to February 1943, a series of major battles such as the Battle of Stalingrad took place, and the Soviet army achieved a decisive victory, not only leading to a strategic turnaround from strategic stalemate to strategic counterattack on the Eastern Front but also marking a strategic turning point in the entire anti-fascist war. In the North African-Mediterranean Theater, from October 1942 to May 1943, the British army carried out the Battle of El Alamein in Egypt, defeating the German-Italian "Afrika Korps", and subsequently the Anglo-American Allied forces annihilated the remnants of the German-Italian "Afrika Korps" in Tunisia, opening the gateway to the Mediterranean. In the Pacific Theater, in June 1942, the U.S. military achieved a complete victory in the Battle of Midway, gaining control of the Pacific. In February 1943, the U.S. military captured the strategic position of Guadalcanal Island in the Solomon Islands, opening the passage for a comprehensive counterattack in the Pacific Theater. In short, by the middle of 1943, the situation was developing in favor of the anti-fascist allied forces, and the task facing the Allies was to coordinate their strategies, launch a comprehensive strategic counterattack, defeat fascism as soon as possible to achieve victory in the war, and begin planning for the post-war disposition of fascist countries. The Cairo Conference was convened against this backdrop.

From November 22 to 26, 1943, the leaders of China, the United States, and the United Kingdom, Chiang Kai-shek, Roosevelt, and Churchill, held a summit in Cairo, the Egyptian capital. The conference produced the Cairo Declaration, which was formally issued on December 1 in the name of China, the United States, and the United Kingdom after obtaining the agreement of Soviet leader Stalin. In reality, it was a joint declaration of the four major anti-fascist powers, the contents of which were:

> The several military missions have agreed upon future military operations against Japan. The Three Great Allies expressed their resolve to bring unrelenting pressure against their brutal enemies by sea, land, and air. This pressure is already rising.
>
> The Three Great Allies are fighting this war to restrain and punish the aggression of Japan. They covet no gain for themselves and have no thought of territorial expansion. It is their purpose that Japan shall be stripped of all the islands in the Pacific which she has seized or occupied since the beginning of the first World War in 1914, and that all the territories Japan has stolen from the Chinese, such as Manchuria, Formosa, and The Pescadores, shall be restored to the Republic of China. Japan will also be expelled from all other territories which she has taken by violence and greed. The aforesaid three great powers, mindful of the enslavement of the people of Korea, are determined that in due course Korea shall become free and independent.
>
> With these objects in view the three Allies, in harmony with those of the United Nations at war with Japan, will continue to persevere in the serious and prolonged operations necessary to procure the unconditional surrender of Japan.[3]

The core content of the Cairo Declaration is, "The three great powers are fighting this war to stop and punish Japan's aggression". The main content of stopping and punishing Japanese aggression includes: firstly, the coordination of allied forces in

[3] *Guojifa Tiaoyueji,* p.407 [《国际条约集》(1934–1944)，北京:世界知识出版社，1961年，第407页].

planning operations against Japan, cooperating with each other until Japan surrenders unconditionally. Secondly, the deprivation of territories acquired through Japanese colonial aggression and expansion since modern times, which is a prerequisite for the reconstruction of a new order in East Asia after the war. The Cairo Declaration states, "It is their purpose that Japan shall be stripped of all the islands in the Pacific which she has seized or occupied since the beginning of the first World War in 1914, and that all the territories Japan has stolen from the Chinese, such as Manchuria, Formosa, and The Pescadores, shall be restored to the Republic of China. Japan will also be expelled from all other territories which she has taken by violence and greed". The phrase "all other territories which she has taken by violence and greed" refers to the territories of China, Korea, and other Asian countries, including the Ryukyu Islands, seized by Japan through "violence or greed" since the Meiji Restoration, all of which fall within the scope designated for deprivation by the Allies. Regarding the territories occupied by Japan in China, the Cairo Declaration points out, "It is their purpose… that all the territories Japan has stolen from the Chinese, such as Manchuria, Formosa, and The Pescadores, shall be restored to the Republic of China". This passage means that Manchuria, Taiwan, and the Pescadores Islands seized by Japan, including all territories illegally occupied by Japan such as the Diaoyu Islands seized in 1894 and the South China Sea Islands seized in 1939, must be returned to China. The Cairo Declaration also stipulates "The aforesaid three great powers, mindful of the enslavement of the people of Korea, are determined that in due course Korea shall become free and independent". This means overthrowing Japanese colonial rule and granting independence to Korea, so Japan must return all occupied Korean territories.

On July 26, 1945, China, the United States, and the United Kingdom, in the Proclamation Defining Terms for Japanese Surrender (the Potsdam Declaration), urged Japan to surrender unconditionally, reaffirming that "Japanese sovereignty shall be limited to the islands of Honshu, Hokkaido, Kyushu, Shikoku, and such minor islands as we determine, as had been announced in the Cairo Declaration in 1943".[4] The Potsdam Declaration confirmed that the Cairo Declaration was a document that the Allies must implement, while also delineating the territory of Japan. Like the Cairo Declaration, the Potsdam Declaration also received the agreement of the Soviet Union, indicating it was a joint decision of the four powers: China, the United States, the United Kingdom, and the Soviet Union.

During the initial phase of the United States' occupation of Japan, the handling of the Japanese territorial issue was largely in accordance with the provisions of the Cairo Declaration and the Potsdam Declaration. On January 29, 1946, Directive No. 667 issued by the Supreme Commander for the Allied Powers (SCAP) indicated that, after Japan's defeat and withdrawal from the territories it had occupied in China and other countries, the scope of Japan's territory, as stipulated by the Allies, was defined as, "the four main islands of Japan and about 1000 smaller adjacent

[4] *Guojifa Tiaoyueji,* p.78 [《国际条约集》(1934–1944)，北京:世界知识出版社，1961年，第78页].

islands, the Tsushima Islands, and the Ryukyu (Nansei) Islands north of the 30th parallel north (excluding Kuchinoshima Island)".[5] On the same day, the SCAP issued the Memorandum on the Separation between Japan and the Governments and Administrations of Certain Outlying Areas (referred to as the Memorandum), which specifically defined Japan's territorial scope: "Japan is limited to the four main islands of Japan (Hokkaido, Honshu, Kyushu, and Shikoku) and approximately 1000 smaller adjacent islands, including the Tsushima Islands, the Ryukyu Islands north of the 30th parallel North (excluding Kuchinoshima Island); it does not include: (a) Ulleungdo Island, Takeshima Island (Dokdo Island), and Jeju Island; (b) the Ryukyu Islands south of the 30th Parallel north, Ogasawara Island, and the Bonin Islands… (c) the Kuril Islands…"[6] According to the specific provisions of the Memorandum, the Chinese delegation in Japan drew up a map of Japanese territory, depicting the territorial scope defined by the SCAP as "the four main islands of Japan (Hokkaido, Honshu, Kyushu, and Shikoku) and about 1000 smaller adjacent islands", while the Ryukyu Islands, Ogasawara, Bonin Islands, etc., did not belong to Japan, and the Kuril Islands (referred to as the "four Northern islands" by Japan) belonged to the Soviet Union, and Takeshima (referred to as Dokdo by Korea) belonged to Korea. The Chinese delegation in Japan also noted "This map is based on Memorandum No. 667 issued by the Deputy Director of the Deputy Office of the Allied Headquarters on January 29, 1946, to the Japanese government".[7]The SCAP's definition of Japan's territory was communicated to all Allied countries, and no objections were raised by the Allies, indicating that at this time the United States' delineation of Japan's territorial scope followed the provisions of the Cairo Declaration and the Potsdam Declaration and reflected the consensus of the Allies. It should also be noted that the Chinese delegation in Japan also drew a map of the Ryukyu Islands, which clearly indicated that China's Diaoyu Islands (referred to as the "Senkaku Islands" by Japan) did not belong to the Ryukyu Islands.[8]

[5]Taiwan "Zhongyang yanjiuyuan jindaishisuo danganguan", Waijiaobu danan, ref.419/0004 [台湾"中央研究院近代史所档案馆"，《外交部档案》，档案号:419/0004].

[6]Taiwan "Zhongyang yanjiuyuan jindaishisuo danganguan", Waijiaobu danan, ref. 012.6/0138 [台湾"中央研究院近代史所档案馆"，《外交部档案》，档案号:012.6/0138].

[7]Taiwan "Zhongyang yanjiuyuan jindaishisuo danganguan", Waijiaobu danan, ref. 012.6/0138 [台湾"中央研究院近代史所档案馆"，《外交部档案》，档案号:012.6/0138].

[8]Taiwan "Zhongyang yanjiuyuan jindaishisuo danganguan", Waijiaobu danan, ref. 012.6/0138 [台湾"中央研究院近代史所档案馆"，《外交部档案》，档案号:012.6/0138].

2 Serving Colonial Aggression: The San Francisco Peace Treaty Changed the Provisions of the Allied Powers Regarding the Disposition of Japanese Territory

After the war, Japan was occupied solely by the United States, so the United States led the policy of occupation and the signing of peace treaties with Japan, as well as the disposition of Japanese territory. In the early post-war period, the United States largely followed the basic principles of the Allied Powers regarding the handling of Japanese territorial issues. However, after the Cold War began, there was a significant change in U.S. policy toward Japan: from punishing the aggressor nation Japan to bolstering it as a fortress in the Asian Cold War. U.S. policy toward Japanese territory also changed accordingly: from depriving Japan of "all other territories which she has taken by violence and greed" to accommodating Japan's demands for territories that had already been deprived by the Allies.

Firstly, it changed the principle of major powers'unanimity in negotiating with Japan. In October 1943, Declaration of the Four Nations on General Security, issued by China, the United States, the United Kingdom, and the Soviet Union, declared that the joint determination of the Four Powers was to "take joint action" in defeating the enemy and handling surrender matters.[9] This was the principle of "major power unanimity" in not negotiating peace individually with the fascist Axis powers or signing peace treaties individually with the defeated countries, and it was a solemn agreement among the four major anti-fascist countries. On December 26, 1945, at the Moscow Conference, the foreign ministers of the Soviet Union, the United States, and the United Kingdom decided to establish the Far Eastern Commission and the Allied Control Council, stipulating that the Supreme Commander of the Allied Powers should be responsible for implementing the directives of the Far Eastern Commission; all orders of the SCAP must be submitted to the Far Eastern Commission. The decisions of the Far Eastern Commission must be approved by a majority of all representatives, and among the approving representatives, there must be representatives of the Big Four: the United States, the United Kingdom, the Soviet Union, and China.[10] The conference reaffirmed the principle of "major power unanimity". However, the United States, which dominated the San Francisco Peace Treaty conference, bypassed the Far Eastern Commission, refused to invite the Chinese government, disregarded the objections and abstentions of countries like the Soviet Union, and forcibly pushed through the San Francisco Peace. These actions violated the principle of "major power unanimity" Treaty, and exacerbated the division and confrontation among the Allies.

---

[9] Faxue jiaocai bianjibu (ed.), *Guoji Guanxi Ziliao Xuanbian* (Shangce, Dierfence) (Wuhan: Wuhan Daxue Chubanshe, 1983), p.751. [法学教材编辑部审定:《国际关系资料选编》(上册，第二分册)，武汉:武汉大学出版社，1983年，第751页].

[10] He Chunchao et al. (ed.), Guojiguanxishi ziliao xuanbian (1945–1980) (Beijing: Falv chubanshe, 1988), p.15–17 [何春超等主编:《国际关系史资料选编(1945–1980)》，北京:法律出版社1988年版，第15–17页].

Secondly, it changed the provision of the Cairo Declaration regarding the return of territories occupied by Japan to China. At the Cairo Conference, Chinese Nationalist Government Chairman Chiang Kai-shek and U.S. President Franklin Roosevelt clearly stated during their discussions that "the land Japan has acquired from China should be returned to China". Later, this was agreed upon by British Prime Minister Winston Churchill. Therefore, the Cairo Declaration solemnly announced, "that all the territories Japan has stolen from the Chinese, such as Manchuria, Formosa, and The Pescadores, shall be restored to the Republic of China". This means that the declaration stipulated that Japan must return all territories it had occupied in China since modern times, including the Diaoyu Islands and the South China Sea Islands, to China. The Potsdam Declaration reiterated that the conditions set forth in the Cairo Declaration must be implemented. After the war, the Chinese government, based on the Cairo Declaration and the Potsdam Declaration, had already recovered Taiwan, the Pescadores Islands, and the South China Sea Islands. However, the San Francisco Peace Treaty stipulated: "Japan renounces all right, title and claim to Formosa and the Pescadores" and "Japan renounces all right, title and claim to the Spratly Islands and to the Paracel Islands".[11] This change from "returning" to "renouncing" altered the provisions of the Cairo Declaration. The Cairo Declaration was a joint agreement of the four major Allied Powers: China, the United States, the United Kingdom, and the Soviet Union, and had the force of international law. However, the San Francisco Peace Treaty was forcibly passed without the participation of China and with the Soviet Union's refusal to vote, which was obviously illegal. The consequences of this change were the current territorial dispute between Japan and China over the Diaoyu Islands, as well as the illegal occupation of the South China Sea islands and reefs by countries like the Philippines and Vietnam, resulting in territorial disputes in the South China Sea. Therefore, before the San Francisco conference was held, on August 15, 1951, Chinese Foreign Minister Zhou Enlai solemnly pointed out: the peace treaty draft "deliberately stipulated that Japan renounces all right to the Nanwei Island and the Xisha Islands without mentioning the issue of returning sovereignty. In fact, the Xisha Islands and Nanwei Island are, like the entire Nansha Islands, Zhongsha Islands, and Dongsha Islands, part of Chinese territory. Although they fell under Japanese imperialism during the aggression war, they were all received by the Chinese government after Japan surrendered. The Central People's Government of the People's Republic of China hereby declares: The inviolable sovereignty of the People's Republic of China over the Nanwei Island and Xisha Islands is not affected by whether or not and how the peace treaty draft of the United States and Britain stipulates".[12] After the signing of the peace treaty, on September 18, the Chinese

[11] Tian Huan(ed.), Zhanhou Zhong Ri guanxi wenxianji (1945–1970) (Beijing: Zhongguo shehuikexue chubanshe, 1996), p.105 [田桓主编:《战后中日关系文献集(1945–1970)》，北京:中国社会科学出版社，1996年，第105页].

[12] Tian Huan(ed.), Zhanhou Zhong Ri guanxi wenxianji (1945–1970) (Beijing: Zhongguo shehuikexue chubanshe, 1996), p.99 [田桓主编:《战后中日关系文献集(1945–1970)》，北京:中国社会科学出版社，1996年，第99页].

government issued a statement stating that the peace treaty with Japan "is illegal, invalid, and therefore absolutely unacceptable".[13] On July 16, Taiwan authorities leader Chiang Kai-shek angrily pointed out in a speech, "There is a commitment to "no separate peace" among the Allied countries", the treaty "though signed, is hypocritical and untrue", and "there are no such hypocritical, illegal, and immoral precedents in history, ancient and modern, at home and abroad".[14] It can be seen that the views of Chinese people on the San Francisco Peace Treaty across the Taiwan strait are consistent.

Thirdly, it changed the provisions of the Yalta Agreement regarding the division of Soviet and Japanese territories. On February 11, 1945, the Soviet Union, the United States, and the United Kingdom signed the Agreement on Japan (Yalta Agreement), which stipulated regarding the Soviet-Japanese territorial issue: "The southern part of Sakhalin and all the islands adjacent to it must be returned to the Soviet Union", and "the Kuril Islands must be transferred to the Soviet Union".[15] However, the San Francisco Peace Treaty stipulated, "Japan renounces all right, title and claim to the Kurile Islands, and to that portion of Sakhalin and the islands adjacent to it over which Japan acquired sovereignty as a consequence of the Treaty of Portsmouth of September 5, 1905".[16] The consequence of changing "returning" to "renouncing" is one of the root causes of the current territorial disputes between Japan and Russia.

Fourthly, the San Francisco Peace Treaty changed the provisions of the Cairo Declaration regarding the territory of Korea. The Cairo Declaration stipulated, "Japan will also be expelled from all other territories which she has taken by violence and greed. The aforesaid three great powers, mindful of the enslavement of the people of Korea, are determined that in due course Korea shall become free and independent".[17] The declaration is very clear that Japan must return all territories it has occupied in Korea to make Korea free and independent. The Memorandum of SCAP No. 667 clearly stipulates that "Japan is limited to the four main islands of Japan (Hokkaido, Honshu, Kyushu, and Shikoku) and approximately 1000 smaller adjacent islands" and it does not include "Ulleungdo Island, Takeshima Island

[13] Tian Huan(ed.), Zhanhou Zhong Ri guanxi wenxianji (1945–1970) (Beijing: Zhongguo shehuikexue chubanshe, 1996), p.104 [田桓主编:《战后中日关系文献集(1945–1970)》，北京:中国社会科学出版社，1996年，第104页].。

[14] Taiwan "Guoshiguan": Geminwenxian – dui Ri heyi (2), ref. 002000000458A [台湾"国史馆": 革命文献—对日和议(二)，档案号: 002000000458A].

[15] Tian Huan(ed.), Zhanhou Zhong Ri guanxi wenxianji (1945–1970) (Beijing: Zhongguo shehuikexue chubanshe, 1996), p.3 [田桓主编:《战后中日关系文献集(1945–1970)》，北京:中国社会科学出版社，1996年，第3页].

[16] Tian Huan(ed.), Zhanhou Zhong Ri guanxi wenxianji (1945–1970) (Beijing: Zhongguo shehuikexue chubanshe, 1996), p.105 [田桓主编:《战后中日关系文献集(1945–1970)》，北京:中国社会科学出版社，1996年，第105页].

[17] Tian Huan(ed.), Zhanhou Zhong Ri guanxi wenxianji (1945–1970) (Beijing: Zhongguo shehuikexue chubanshe, 1996), p.3 [田桓主编:《战后中日关系文献集(1945–1970)》，北京:中国社会科学出版社，1996年，第3页].

(Dokdo Island), and Jeju Island".[18] However, the Peace Treaty stipulated that "Japan, recognizing the independence of Korea, renounces all right, title and claim to Korea, including the islands of Quelpart, Port Hamilton and Dagelet". The usage of "renounce" instead of "return" became the cause of the territorial dispute between Japan and South Korea. More importantly, the SCAP Directive No. 667 stipulates that Takeshima (Dokdo) is excluded from Japan's territorial jurisdiction and belongs to South Korea rather than Japan. However, the treaty deliberately avoids mentioning Japan's return of Dokdo, which is another cause of the territorial dispute between Japan and South Korea.

It should also be noted that after the war, in dealing with the division of Korean and Japanese territories among the Allied Powers, the proposal of the Chinese government explicitly stated that Dokdo belongs to South Korea. However, China was blocked from the San Francisco conference, unable to fight for the complete return of Chinese territory at the conference, nor could it support Korea's territorial integrity.[19]

Fifthly, it changed the provisions regarding islands such as the Ryukyu Islands. The Kingdom of Ryukyu was an independent country that existed for hundreds of years on the Ryukyu Islands, and since the Ming Dynasty, its kings had been appointed by the Chinese emperor. After the Meiji Restoration, Japan started external colonial expansion and forcibly annexed the Kingdom of Ryukyu in 1879, incorporating the Ryukyu Islands into the territory of Japan and establishing Okinawa Prefecture. At the Cairo Conference, U.S. President Roosevelt had asked Chiang Kai-shek about the ownership of the Ryukyu Islands, and Chiang Kai-shek replied that the Ryukyu Islands had once had the Kingdom of Ryukyu and were a vassal state of China, so they should be granted independence after the war, similar to what was given to Korea.[20] Although the Cairo Declaration did not write the Ryukyu Islands into it, the Ryukyu Islands were certainly included in the Cairo Declaration's provision that "Japan will also be expelled from all other territories which she has taken by violence and greed", and should be deprived. The Memorandum of SCAP No. 667 clearly stipulates that Japan's territory does not include the Ryukyu Islands south of the 30th parallel North, the Ogasawara Islands, and the Sulphur Islands, etc.[21] Regarding this, the San Francisco Peace Treaty made two changes: one was to change the Ryukyu Islands south of the 30th parallel North to South of the 29th parallel North, expanding Japan's territory to the area north of the 29th parallel North; the other was that although the treaty stipulated that the United States would administer the Ryukyu Islands south of the 29th parallel North,

[18] Taiwan "Zhongyang yanjiuyuan jindaishisuo danganguan", Waijiaobu danan, ref. 012.6/0138 [台湾"中央研究院近代史所档案馆"，《外交部档案》，档案号:012.6/0138].

[19] Taiwan "Zhongyang yanjiuyuan jindaishisuo danganguan", Waijiaobu danan, ref. 072.4/0001 [台湾"中央研究院近代史所档案馆"，《外交部档案》，档案号:072.4/0001].

[20] Taiwan "Guoshiguan": Kailuo huiyi (2), Ref. 档案号: 002000001245A [台湾"国史馆": 开罗会议(二)，档案号: 002000001245A].

[21] Taiwan "Zhongyang yanjiuyuan jindaishisuo danganguan", Waijiaobu danan, ref. 012.6/0138 [台湾"中央研究院近代史所档案馆"，《外交部档案》，档案号:012.6/0138].

the Ogasawara Islands, and the Sulphur Islands, U.S. representative Dulles announced at the San Francisco conference, "The best solution for the United States is for the United States to administer these islands and exercise administrative rights over them, while allowing Japan to retain residual sovereignty."[22] The U.S. announcement that Japan has "residual sovereignty"over the Ryukyu Islands, Ogasawara Islands, and Sulphur Islands changed the provision of the Potsdam Declaration regarding Japan's territorial scope, which "shall be limited to the islands of Honshu, Hokkaido, Kyushu, Shikoku, and such minor islands as we determine", laying the groundwork for the United States to privately hand over these islands to Japan in the future.

Sixthly, the United States refused to return the Diaoyu Islands to China. As mentioned earlier, the Cairo Declaration's provision on the disposition of Japanese territory is to deprive Japan of "all other territories which she has taken by violence and greed" since the Meiji Restoration. The Diaoyu Islands were secretly incorporated into Japanese territory during the Sino-Japanese War in 1895, so they clearly belong to the lands "taken by violence and greed" since the Meiji Restoration and should be returned to China. In the early post-war period, China requested that the Diaoyu Islands be returned to China from the Allied Powers. There are two maps drawn by the Chinese delegation in Japan in 1947. The first map discusses the formation of the territorial boundaries of the Kingdom of Ryukyu, without the Diaoyu Islands; the second map is the original territorial boundaries of Ryukyu, without the Diaoyu Islands. However, for political reasons, the United States included the Diaoyu Islands under the jurisdiction of the Ryukyu region, and then, despite opposition from both sides of the Taiwan Strait, unilaterally handed over the administration of the Diaoyu Islands to Japan during the transfer of Okinawa to Japan, seriously infringing on China's territorial sovereignty and maritime rights and interests, causing the current dispute between China and Japan over the Diaoyu Islands and affecting the development of China-Japan friendship.

The six changes made by the San Francisco Peace Treaty to the Allied Powers'provisions on territorial matters have directly led to territorial disputes between Japan and China, Korea, and Russia, as well as between China and countries around the South China Sea. "When the snipe and the clam fight, it is the fisherman who benefits", and this is what the United States hopes for.

[22] (Ri) Waiwusheng, *Riben waijiao wenshu: jiujinshan heyue – qianzi yu shengxiao*, 2009, p.69 [(日)外务省:《日本外交文书:旧金山和约—签字与生效》，2009年版，第69页].

3 Source of Northeast Asian Territorial Disputes: The San Francisco System with the Core of the U.S.-Japan Alliance

In the period following the end of World War II, the United States was still able to handle the disposition of Japanese territory in accordance with the provisions of the Allied Powers, as evidenced by documents such as the SCAP Directive No. 667 and its Memorandum issued on January 29, 1946. However, with the onset of the Cold War, the United States, seeking to establish an East Asian order under its leadership, and Japan, seeking to avoid punishment from the Allied Powers, began to mutually utilize each other, drawing closer from former enemies to allies, and thus utilizing the San Francisco Peace Treaty to change the Allied Powers'provisions regarding the disposition of Japanese territory.

Under the sole occupation of Japan by the United States after the war, Japan's break with fascism was incomplete, leading to Japan's bargaining with the Allied Powers over territorial issues. In his memoirs, Prime Minister Yoshida Shigeru, who served twice as Japanese Prime Minister after the war, wrote that to address the Allied Powers' disposition of Japanese territory, Japan expended great effort in compiling English-language materials, "elaborating on the inseparable relationship between islands such as Okinawa, Ogasawara, Sakhalin, the Kuril Islands, Shikotan, and Etorofu and Japan, from historical, geographical, ethnic, economic, and all other possible perspectives",[23] with the purpose of reclaiming these lands that had been stripped away by the Allied Powers. On January 26, 1946, the Japanese Foreign Ministry drafted a Comparative Study of the Allied Peace Treaty Plan and Our Desired Plan, in an attempt to reject returning the Kuril Islands and Southern Sakhalin to the Soviet Union on the grounds of denying acquisition by "violence or greed", and to oppose "unconditionally recognizing China's sovereignty over Ryukyu" through methods such as local voting. On February 1 of the same year, the Japanese Foreign Ministry's Treaty Bureau drafted a Principled Study of the Content of the Peace Treaty and a Comparison of the UN Plan with Our Desired Plan. It decided to make a fuss over "such minor islands as we determine" as stipulated in the Potsdam Declaration, hoping to ensure that "the small islands related to Japan in geographical, historical, ethnic, and economic aspects" would be assigned to Japan. In May 1946, the Japanese Peace Treaty Research Committee submitted the First Research Report on the Japanese Peace Treaty Issue, outlining Japan's countermeasures: regarding the nearby small islands of Japan, "efforts should be made to allow our country to expand its scope"; regarding the Ryukyu Islands, they should be placed under joint trusteeship by the Allied Powers or solely by the United States, opposing their belonging to China; regarding Southern Sakhalin and the Kuril Islands, as the Yalta Agreement was a secret pact, Japan was not obligated to abide by it and should discuss additional conditions such as determining ownership

---

[23] (Ri) Jitian Mao, Shinian huiyi Disanjuan (Beijing: Shijiezhishi chubanshe, 1965) p.6–7 [(日)吉田茂:《十年回忆》第三卷，北京:世界知识出版社，1965年，第6–7页]。

through local resident voting.[24] On July 24, 1947, the Japanese Foreign Ministry formulated Japanese Desired Plan for the meeting with Acheson, the Political advisor of the U.S. State Department to SCAP, which comprehensively outlined the Japanese demands for peace making. Regarding territorial issues, it requested that when the Allied Powers decided on the small islands around Japan, they could "fully consider the historical, racial, economic, and cultural ties between these islands and Japan."[25] This document was submitted to Acheson and Whitney, the Director of Civil Affairs of SCAP, but was rejected by both of them. On July 28, Acheson explicitly stated: I don't want Japan to start discussing conditions with the Allied Powers before Japan knows the latter's conditions. On the same day, Whitney also replied, "I have submitted this document to General MacArthur. In the view of the general, Japan's attempt is to impose its own views on the peace treaty during peace conference… It is likely to provoke other countries, especially those opposing Japan, and may be detrimental to Japan". Whitney also reminded Japan, "For present-day Japan, the wisest course of action is to remain silent until the peace conference begins."[26] At this time, the United States believed that Japan was completely disregarding the attitudes of other countries and only sought to impose its views through American-led peace talk, therefore could not approve its requests.

The People's Republic of China was established in October 1949, and with the outbreak of the Korean War in June 1950, the Cold War escalated into a hot war. The dramatic changes in the Asian situation led to a major shift in U.S. policy toward Japan: from punishing the aggressor nation Japan to bolstering it as a fortress in the Asian Cold War. This accelerated the pace of the United States bolstering Japan to contain China and the Soviet Union, providing an opportunity for Japan to seek territory.

After the outbreak of the Korean War, Japan believed that the division among the Allied Powers had become inevitable and thus decided on a policy of relying on the United States for separate peace talk. On December 3, 1949, the Japanese Foreign Ministry stated in the Basic Policy for Security Guarantees under Reconciliation with the Majority of Countries that the possibility of Soviet Union and China's participation in the peace talk had completely disappeared, and in order to ensure its own security, Japan could use the following condition to exchange agreements with countries like the United States: Japan could allow contracting parties to station troops and establish military bases on islands outside Japan's mainland, but the main body of foreign troops was the U.S. military.[27] On October 4, 1950, the Japanese Foreign Ministry drafted a Countermeasure Policy on the US Concept of

---

[24] (Ri) Waiwusheng, *Riben waijiao wenshu: jiujinshan heyue – duice zhunbei*, 2006, p.95–96 [(日)]外务省:《日本外交文书:旧金山和约—签字与生效》，2006年版，第95–96页].

[25] (Ri) Waiwusheng, *Riben waijiao wenshu: jiujinshan heyue – duice zhunbei*, 2006, p.245–247 [(日)]外务省:《日本外交文书:旧金山和约—签字与生效》，2006年版，第245–247页].

[26] (Ri) Waiwusheng, *Riben waijiao wenshu: jiujinshan heyue – duice zhunbei*, 2006, p.262–264 [(日)]外务省:《日本外交文书:旧金山和约—对策准备》，2006年版，第262–264页].

[27] (Ri) Waiwusheng, *Riben waijiao wenshu: jiujinshan heyue – duice zhunbei*, 2006, p.441–442 [(日)]外务省:《日本外交文书:旧金山和约—对策准备》，2006年版，第441–442页].

the Peace Treaty with Japan. Regarding territorial issues, Japan stated that it had no objection to relinquishing rights related to the independence of Korea, Taiwan, the Pescadores, the Kwantung Leased Territory, the Mandated Territories in the South Seas, and the Southern Sakhalin Island. However, it made the following demands: first, the Kuril Islands could not be handed over to the Soviet Union. Although there was already a secret agreement at Yalta to return the Kuril Islands to the Soviet Union, this contradicted the "principle of not expanding territory" in the Atlantic Charter. At the same time, the Habomai Islands and Shikotan are part of Hokkaido and do not belong to the Kuril Islands, so they cannot be subject to territorial disposition. Second, Japan hoped that Ryukyu, the Ogasawara Islands, and the Sulphur Islands would not be separated from Japan's territory, as this was a matter of national sentiment. The document also noted in the comments that although Japan agreed to have some areas administered by the United States, it must be limited to the smallest possible range. Furthermore, it stipulated that "Japan and the United States act as co-administrators of the trusteeship", "after the trusteeship ends, the nationality of the territory will be determined by a vote of the Japanese people", and "after the trusteeship ends, the United States will transfer the administrative authority of the trusteeship to Japan".[28]On the same day, the Japanese Foreign Ministry formulated a Statement to the United States, disagreeing with the return of the Kuril Islands to the Soviet Union, and also disagreeing with the separation of the Southwest Islands (including Okinawa), the Ogasawara Islands and the Sulphur Islands from Japan's mainland after being placed under U.S. trusteeship, because these islands were not "taken by violence and greed" by Japan.[29]

On October 14, U.S. Secretary of State Dulles confirmed during a meeting with reporters that the U.S. State Department had proposed seven principles for the peace treaty with Japan, with the third clause regarding the principle of territorial disposition in Japan: "Japan recognizes the independence of Korea; agrees to the United States as the administering authority for the United Nations to trust the Ryukyu Islands and the Ogasawara Islands; commits to accept the decision on the status of Taiwan, the Pescadores, the Southern Sakhalin Island and the Kuril Islands, by the United Kingdom, the Soviet Union, China, and the United States, and if there is no decision within 1 year after the treaty comes into effect, the United Nations General Assembly will make the decision; Japan renounces its privileges and interests in China."[30] Japan strongly objected to the lack of clear statement from the United States regarding the sovereignty of its trusteeship areas. On October 25, the Japanese Foreign Ministry wrote in a document titled Regarding the Seven Principles of the U.S. for Reconciliation with Japan, "Regarding Korea, Taiwan, and the Pescadores, it is necessary to give up all rights; separating the Ogasawara and Ryukyu Islands

[28](Ri) Waiwusheng, *Riben waijiao wenshu: jiujinshan heyue – duimei jiaoshe*, 2007, p.18–20 [(日)]外务省:《日本外交文书:旧金山和约—对美交涉》，2007年版，第18–20页].

[29](Ri) Waiwusheng, *Riben waijiao wenshu: jiujinshan heyue – duimei jiaoshe*, 2007, p.18–20 [(日)]外务省:《日本外交文书:旧金山和约—对美交涉》，2007年版，第18–20页].

[30](Ri) Waiwusheng, *Riben waijiao wenshu: jiujinshan heyue – duimei jiaoshe*, 2007, p.97[(日)]外务省:《日本外交文书:旧金山和约—对美交涉》，2007年版，第97页].

from Japan is difficult for the Japanese people to accept emotionally; efforts should be made to minimize the area under trusteeship; separating the Kuril Islands, which are part of Japan's territory, is difficult for the national sentiment to accept".[31]On January 19, 1951, the Japanese Foreign Ministry stated in a revised version of the aforementioned document (i.e., the D task revised edition) that it was willing to "first conclude a peace treaty with the United States alone."[32] "Under the situation where Okinawa and the Ogasawara Islands must be placed under trusteeship, … Japan wants to become a co-administrator and then have these islands return to Japan when the trusteeship is lifted."[33] "Japan has equal status with the United States in terms of the ownership of the islands, their administration, and the rule over the islanders."[34]Japan requested to jointly administer the Ryukyu Islands and other areas with the United States and requested that they be transferred to Japan after the trusteeship ends, essentially turning Japan into a "victorious country", which grossly violated the provisions of the Allied Powers.

Even the United States found Japan's demands excessive. On January 31, 1951, during the second meeting between U.S. Secretary of State Dulles and Japanese Prime Minister Yoshida, Dulles stated, "I understand the feelings of the Japanese people very well, but this is already clearly stipulated in the surrender terms, and I hope Japan will consider it as something that has been decided."[35] Japan's demands were flatly rejected. However, at this point, the United States had decided to turn Japan into its ally in the Far East Cold War. Although it did not agree with Japan's excessive demands, it still tried to consider Japanese requests as much as possible. As Dulles said, "This time we are not formulating the treaty as winners and losers, but as friends of Japan considering the entire treaty."[36]The United States gave Japan two major gifts in the treaty: one was to change the southern boundary of Japan from the 30th parallel North to the 29th parallel North, extending Japan's southern boundary southward by 1 degree; the other was to leave "room for maneuver" in the U.S.-administered Ryukyu Islands and other areas, namely the "residual sovereignty" promised by Dulles to Japan.[37]The so-called "residual sovereignty" was actually a product of political deals between Japan and the United States. The

[31] (Ri) Waiwusheng, *Riben waijiao wenshu: jiujinshan heyue – duimei jiaoshe*, 2007, p.75 [(日)]外务省:《日本外交文书:旧金山和约—对美交涉》, 2007年版，第75页].

[32] (Ri) Waiwusheng, *Riben waijiao wenshu: jiujinshan heyue – duimei jiaoshe*, 2007, p.137 [(日)]外务省:《日本外交文书:旧金山和约—对美交涉》, 2007年版，第137页].

[33] (Ri) Waiwusheng, *Riben waijiao wenshu: jiujinshan heyue – duimei jiaoshe*, 2007, p.140 [(日)]外务省:《日本外交文书:旧金山和约—对美交涉》, 2007年版，第140页].

[34] (Ri) Waiwusheng, *Riben waijiao wenshu: jiujinshan heyue – duimei jiaoshe*, 2007, p.162–163 [(日)]外务省:《日本外交文书:旧金山和约—对美交涉》, 2007年版，第162–163页].

[35] (Ri) Waiwusheng, *Riben waijiao wenshu: jiujinshan heyue – duimei jiaoshe*, 2007, p.189 [(日)]外务省:《日本外交文书:旧金山和约—对美交涉》, 2007年版，第189页]

[36] (Ri) Waiwusheng, *Riben waijiao wenshu: jiujinshan heyue – duimei jiaoshe*, 2007, p.175 [(日)]外务省:《日本外交文书:旧金山和约—对美交涉》, 2007年版，第175页].

[37] (Ri) Waiwusheng, *Riben waijiao wenshu: jiujinshan heyue – duimei jiaoshe*, 2007, p.611 [(日)]外务省:《日本外交文书:旧金山和约—对美交涉》, 2007年版，第611页].

United States was unwilling to express Japan's sovereignty over the U.S.-administered areas in public terms, fearing difficulty in justifying it to the international community. Therefore, through the interpretation of ambiguous terms, the United States acknowledged Japan's "residual sovereignty" over the administered areas, laying the groundwork for future clandestine transfers of the Ryukyu Islands and other areas between the United States and Japan. Japan was overjoyed. On September 7, Japanese Prime Minister Yoshida Shigeru delivered the Speech on the Acceptance of the Japanese Peace Treaty at the San Francisco Conference, saying uncontrollably, "This is not a treaty of revenge, but a document of 'reconciliation and trust'", "In the name of the Japanese people, and with extreme joy, I accept it".[38]

From this, it can be observed that after the war, the United States, out of the need to contain China and the Soviet Union during the Cold War, reciprocally utilized Japan, changed the common provisions of the Allied Powers regarding territorial issues, caused a series of territorial disputes in East Asia. This became the root cause of the instability in the international order in East Asia and its repercussions persist to this day. If present-day Japan is truly sincere about resolving its territorial disputes with China, Korea, and Russia, it should return to the original provisions agreed upon by the Allied Powers.

4 Beyond the San Francisco System: Abandoning Cold War Thinking and Clearing the Residuals of Colonialism

The above demonstrates two major shortcomings of the San Francisco System:

Firstly, the remnants of colonialism. As mentioned earlier, post-war Japan was solely occupied by the United States, thus violating the principle of unity among the major Allied Powers. In illegally excluding China from the conference and with the Soviet Union refusing to sign the treaty, the United States dominated the policies of occupation and the signing of treaties with Japan, as well as the disposition of Japanese territory, and established the San Francisco System. It has been 73 years since the end of World War II, and the vast majority of former colonial and semi-colonial countries in Northeast Asia have gained national independence. However, Japan, the former colonial power, has not undergone thorough reflection, nor has it completely abandoned colonial thinking. It still regards former colonial and semi-colonial countries with a colonial mindset and perspective. For example, Japan's territorial disputes with China and South Korea over the Diaoyu Islands and Dokdo, respectively, as well as Japan's illegal occupation of the Ryukyu Islands with the support of the United States, are all manifestations of Japan's strong desire to maintain the territories it acquired through colonial expansion. Furthermore, Japan's reflection on its aggressive war is severely insufficient, and it refuses to offer war

---

[38] (Ri) Waiwusheng, *Riben waijiao wenshu: jiujinshan heyue – qianzi yu shengxiao*, 2009, p.136 [(日)]外务省:《日本外交文书:旧金山和约—对美交涉》，2009年版，第136页].

apologies and compensation to countries like China that suffered its aggression, which also reflects the influence of colonial thinking. Therefore, we should continue to adhere to the basic principles of the Cairo Declaration and the Potsdam Proclamation, and continue to eliminate colonial thinking, which is a common task for all countries in Northeast Asia.

Secondly, abandoning Cold War thinking. World War II was a joint victory for the anti-fascist allies. In human history, never before has a war, like the World Anti-Fascist War, mobilized such extensive and thorough efforts from countries and peoples worldwide, connecting them so closely and firmly. The common mission enabled humanity to overcome the obstacles between the two opposing social systems of socialism and capitalism, break down the barriers between the metropolis and the colony, and overcome the differences between different religions and beliefs. Under the banner of the anti-fascist united front, seeking common ground while reserving differences and uniting in battle, countries around the world achieved an unprecedented level of depth and breadth in political, economic, military, diplomatic, and technological exchanges. Humanity's interdependence, interconnection, interaction, and mutual support entered a new era. After the war, countries should have united and cooperated to heal the wounds of war. However, led by the United States, the Western camp launched the Cold War for its own selfish interests, becoming the root cause of global unrest and severely hampering the development of countries, especially developing countries, for half a century. Although the Cold War has ended, the Cold War thinking still persists. Therefore, only by thoroughly abandoning the Cold War thinking can Northeast Asia move toward cooperation and development.

Therefore, Northeast Asia must thoroughly eliminate the remnants of colonial thinking and decisively abandon the Cold War thinking in order to transcend the San Francisco System and move toward cooperative and win-win development. Of course, the complete eradication of the remnants of colonial thinking and the decisive abandonment of Cold War thinking will not be achieved overnight; it will be a lengthy process. Therefore, in order to transcend the San Francisco System, Northeast Asia must unify three aspects of cognition. Under this premise, effective measures should be taken to promote the transition from the San Francisco System to cooperative and win-win development.

Firstly, we must establish the concept of a Northeast Asian community of shared destiny. The world is vast enough to accommodate the common development of all countries. Northeast Asia, too, is vast enough to accommodate the common development of all Northeast Asian countries. Western Europe was once the main battlefield of two world wars, and historically, nations there fought each other for centuries. After the war, on the basis of reconciliation between Germany and France, Western Europe promoted unity and established the European Community, thus facilitating the development of Europe. Southeast Asia was also once the focus of the Cold War, but since the establishment of the Association of Southeast Asian Nations (ASEAN) in 2002, the region has developed rapidly and has successfully replaced the United States as China's largest trading partner. Since Western Europe and ASEAN have been able to establish communities, why can't Northeast Asia? It should be said that the success of China, Japan, and South Korea is an opportunity for each other. We should add more to the construction of the community of shared destiny, rather than subtract from it, and jointly promote it rather than regress.

Secondly, we must adopt an overall perspective and strive to resolve or set aside disputes to create a favorable atmosphere for cooperation in Northeast Asia. Northeast Asian countries are not numerous, but they are full of Cold War confrontations, territorial disputes, and historical differences. The outbreak of any conflict is sufficient to affect the overall situation in Northeast Asia. Therefore, countries in Northeast Asia should adopt an overall perspective, strive to resolve disputes rather than exacerbate conflicts, and both sides of the dispute should downplay or set aside the dispute, keeping it within the scope that does not affect cooperation between countries. If a dispute cannot be resolved in the short term, decisive measures should be taken to set it aside, in order to create a favorable atmosphere for cooperation in Northeast Asia.

Thirdly, Northeast Asia has a good foundation for cooperation. In September 1972, China and Japan signed the Treaty of Peace and Friendship between China and Japan, normalizing diplomatic relations between the two countries. In August 1978, the two countries concluded the "China-Japan Peace and Friendship Treaty", opening a new chapter in China-Japan cooperation. In 1992, China and South Korea established diplomatic relations, and economic exchanges between the two countries developed rapidly. Since then, the connections between China, Japan, and South Korea have become increasingly close. In 2002, the leaders of China, Japan, and South Korea proposed the idea of establishing a China-Japan-South Korea free trade area. In May 2012, China, Japan, and South Korea signed the Agreement on the Promotion, Facilitation, and Protection of Investment in Beijing. In November of the same year, the three countries officially launched negotiations for the China-Japan-South Korea Free Trade Agreement (FTA). However, due to the implementation of the Asia-Pacific Rebalance Strategy by the United States, aimed at containing China, Japan was incited to provoke the Diaoyu Islands dispute and Sino-Japanese relations quickly deteriorated, leading to the suspension of negotiations for the China-Japan-South Korea FTA. In June 2015, China and South Korea officially signed the China-South Korea Free Trade Agreement and formally launched it on December 20th of the same year. On May 9, 2018, the seventh China-Japan-South Korea leaders' meeting was held in Tokyo, and it was unanimously agreed to promote economic and trade cooperation among the three countries, promote the construction of the East Asian Economic Community and regional integration process, and achieve sustained and stable economic growth in the region. However, since then, due to the "decoupling" and other sanction policies adopted by the United States toward China, which directly affected Japan and South Korea's policies toward China, economic and trade cooperation between China, Japan, and South Korea has stalled. If external factors are excluded, China, Japan, and South Korea can achieve trilateral economic and trade cooperation, which will greatly promote Northeast Asia's transition to cooperative and win-win development and the construction of a community of shared destiny for humanity.

In summary, Northeast Asia must thoroughly eliminate the remnants of colonial thinking and decisively abandon the Cold War thinking in order to transcend the San Francisco System. We must establish the concept of a Northeast Asian community of shared destiny, adopt an overall perspective, and strive to resolve or set aside disputes to create a favorable atmosphere for cooperation. Northeast Asia has a good foundation for cooperation, and if China, Japan, and South Korea can lead the way in achieving trilateral economic and trade cooperation, it will greatly promote the process of Northeast Asia's transition to cooperative and win-win development, and the process of building a community of shared destiny for humanity, and each country can also realize its respective dream in the process of building a community of shared destiny in Northeast Asia.

It should be noted that my ideas are just academic discussions and theoretical propositions, and the path for Northeast Asia to move toward cooperation and development depends on the joint efforts of governments and civil society in each country.

The San Francisco Peace Treaty and Territorial Issues: *Information Pamphlets on Territorial Issues From the Japanese Ministry of Foreign Affairs and Their Impact*

Byung Joon Jung

Abstract This paper deals with the preparation and documentation activities of the Japanese Ministry of Foreign Affairs (JMOFA) for the San Francisco Peace Treaty of 1951. Between 1946 and 1949, JMOFA produced seven volumes of pamphlets on territorial issues in the preparation process leading up to the peace treaty. Among them, a series of four pamphlets under the title of Minor Islands Adjacent to Japan Proper was published. These pamphlets were distributed to the Allied Powers to good effect. Focus was placed on the Southern Kuriles, Ryukyus, and Liancourt Rocks (Dokdo), which Japan felt should be recognized as Japanese territory by the Allies. After the San Francisco Peace Treaty, Japan restored peaceful relations with the United States and its major allies, but hostile relations between Japan and its neighbors in East Asia persisted. It was natural that the Soviet Union (Russia), China, and Korea, excluded from the Peace Treaty, later came to engage in territorial disputes with Japan.

Keywords San Francisco Peace Treaty · Japanese Ministry of Foreign Affairs · *Minor Islands Adjacent to Japan Proper* · Southern Kuriles · Ryukyus · Senkaku (Diaoyu) · Dokdo (Liancourt Rocks)

1 Introduction

Since the San Francisco Peace Treaty of 1951, Northeast Asia has had several island disputes: the Kuril Islands or Northern Territories dispute between Russia and Japan, the Dokdo or Takeshima (Liancourt Rocks) dispute between Korea and Japan, and the Senkaku or Diaoyu Islands dispute between China and Japan.

B. J. Jung (✉)
Department of History, Ewha Womans University, Seoul, South Korea
e-mail: bjjung@ewha.ac.kr

Y.-H. Kim et al. (eds.), *Beyond the San Francisco System*,
https://doi.org/10.1007/978-981-95-3328-2_13

Neither China nor Korea was invited to the San Francisco peace negotiations. The USSR was invited and did participate but did not sign the resulting peace treaty. China at the time was divided into the People's Republic of China and the Republic of China (Taiwan) as a result of its civil war, while Korea was divided into South and North Korea and descended into war in the course of the treaty talks. The absence of these three nations manifests the reality that the peace talks were not aimed at the restoration of peace for the people of Northeast Asia.

After the settlement of the San Francisco Peace Treaty in 1951, many questions and issues emerged regarding territories in Northeast Asia, and more than a few suspicions and conspiracy theories have been raised as a result. One of these theories in Korea asserts that the Dokdo issue came to the surface when the island group was marked as Japanese territory in the 1949 peace treaty draft by the US Department of State and that there may have been some Japanese lobbying at work behind the scenes. At the center of these maneuvers was William J. Sebald, who served as political adviser (POLAD) to the Supreme Commander for the Allied Powers (SCAP), Chief of the Diplomatic Section of SCAP Headquarters, and US representative to the Allied Council for Japan (Lee, 2001; Yoshida, 1958, 25–26, 60–70).

One study has argued that the cause of post-war territorial issues in Northeast Asia lies with the United States' tactical handling of the territorial disposition of Japan in the San Francisco Peace Treaty, a result in turn of the American Cold War strategic objective of preventing the communization of the Korean Peninsula and expanding American influence over Japan (Hara, 2005, 29–71).

From 1946, the Japanese Ministry of Foreign Affairs (JMOFA)[1] began to produce materials on territorial issues based on Japan's selective strategic priorities and provided these to the US Department of State through the SCAP Diplomatic Section. Through everyday contact, Japan turned the United States into its advocate and, further, into a practical channel for promoting Japan's interests. The officials of the SCAP Diplomatic Section, including its chief, Sebald, and the officials of the POLAD-Japan office, were sympathetic to Japan's concerns and demands and made active efforts to accommodate its interests. The opinions of the Japanese government were deemed reasonable, there was a stable channel to deliver them to the Department of State, and American diplomats and officials who relayed them were friendly toward Japan. This is the truth about the diplomatic and lobbying efforts by JMOFA between 1947 and 1951 regarding territorial issues (Jung, 2010, 322–331). This paper looks into the effects and significance of the territory reports produced by JMOFA from 1946 to 1949 (Cheong, 1991; Hara, 1998; Lee, 1998; Hara, 2005; Jung, 2010; Wada, 2013).

[1] During the years of 1946–1947, the government department called the Gaimushō in Japanese had the English title of Foreign Office. The English name was later changed to the Ministry of Foreign Affairs. To avoid confusion, except when citing actual works, I use the term Ministry of Foreign Affairs (JMOFA) regardless of year.

2 Measures by Japan's Ministry of Foreign Affairs on Territorial Issues and the Production of Information Pamphlets

2.1 Measures on Territorial Issues

After the end of the Pacific War, regarding the peace settlement, the JMOFA undertook research into the three areas—general, political, and economic clauses—with the focus of political clauses being territorial issues. Japan accepted there was nothing it could do about the terms of the Cairo Declaration (December 1943), Potsdam Declaration (July 1945), and General of the Army Douglas MacArthur's Instruction to his Commands Concerning the Basic Purpose of the Allied Occupation of Japan and the Manners in which They are Carried Out by the Allied Forces (December 19, 1945), namely, to "limit Japanese territory to the islands of Honshu, Hokkaido, Kyushu, Shikoku, and minor islands";[2] strip Japan of all its former islands in the Pacific; and oblige Japan to return Manchuria, Formosa, and the Pescadores to China, withdraw from all occupied territories, and free Korea.[3] What mattered regarding postwar territorial issues was how to secure some one thousand minor islands in the vicinity of Japan, whose fate the Allies would determine.

The basic stance of the JMOFA was that Japan was responsible for the Pacific War, but not for what had happened prior to that conflict (Jo, 2008, 46). Its stance on territorial issues was that it was even willing in principle to surrender territories acquired in ways that had been recognized as conventional under international law and practices at the time of their acquisition and which had long been regarded as Japanese territory by the international community. But it would not accept the international community's judgment that Japan's retention of these was criminal and that they must be separated from Japan as a punitive measure (Takasaki, 1998, 7–8).

According to the guidelines and principles on territorial issues completed by the JMOFA in May 1946, we know that the territories that interested Japan the most were Amami Oshima, Izu Oshima, the Ryukyu Islands (Okinawa), Southern Sakhalin, the Kurils, and Iwo Jima. Its goal was to have these islands acknowledged by the Allies as "minor islands adjacent to Japan proper."[4]

The final position of the Japanese government on territorial issues is suggested in the "Statement to the US (draft)" it wrote in October 1950: it first declares that Japan conformed to the principles of the Atlantic Charter and was thereby fully willing to surrender its title to Formosa and the Pescadores, free Korea, and give up its

[2] "Territorial Clauses" (領土條項), January 31, 1946 (JMOFA, 2006, 46–47).

[3] "Comparison and Analysis of the Allied Powers' Presumable Proposals and Japan's Own Desired Outcomes" (想定される聯合國側平和條約案と我か方希望との比較檢討), January 26, 1946 (JMOFA, 2006, 19).

[4] "Expected Political Clauses in a Peace Treaty and Countermeasures for Possible Discrepancies (draft)" (對日平和條約に於ける政治條項の想定及對處方案), May 1946 (JMOFA, 2006, 95–96).

mandatory rule over the Micronesian islands in the Pacific (Nanyo). However, it contended that it should be allowed to retain islands that had always been historically and ethnically Japanese territory because they were not seized through war by Japan but had been part of Japanese territory continuously and for a long time. The islands listed by the JMOFA were the Kuril Islands, Habomai Islands and Shikot*an, the Nansei Islands, the Ogasawara Islands, and Iwo Jima.[5]

2.2 Information Pamphlets on Territorial Issues: Minor Islands Adjacent to Japan Proper Series

During its preparations for the peace talks from 1946 to 1949, the JMOFA produced information pamphlets on the islands it wished to have acknowledged as Japanese territory and distributed them to SCAP Headquarters and the Allied Powers. According to Yoshida Shigeru and Nishimura Kumao, director of the Ministry's Treaties Bureau, the JMOFA produced a total of seven volumes on territorial issues (Yoshida, 1958, 25–26, 60–70; Nishimura, 1971, 45–47).

From its first publication on territorial issues, *The Kurile Islands, the Habomais, and Shikotan* (November 1946), to *Japanese Economy in Asia* (December 1950), the JMOFA forwarded 36 volumes to the Department of State (Nishimura, 1971, 45). Rather than books, these were more like pamphlets of dozens of pages (Table 1).

There were in all seven volumes on territorial issues, with four of them published as a series under the English title, *Minor Islands Adjacent to Japan Proper* (日本の附屬小島) (Jung, 2010, 331–342). Their availability to the public is as follows (Table 2):

The four volumes (Parts I–IV) of the *Minor Islands Adjacent to Japan Proper* series are in the collection of the US National Archives and Records Administration (NARA).[6] The Diplomatic Archives of the Ministry of Foreign Affairs of Japan recently made public only Part II (Wada, 2013, 232), and it is known that Australia has Part I in its possession (Hara, 1998; Wada, 2013, 100, 232).

The other three volumes are as follows: V. *Sakhalin*, VI. *South Kuriles, Habomai Islands, Shikotan Island,* and VII. *Tsushima*, the last of which was made public in the United States and Japan.[7] Volumes V and VI have not yet been actually seen. The Japanese titles of the *Nihon no fuzoku kojima* 日本の附屬小島 (Minor Islands Adjacent to Japan Proper) series appear in JMOFA documents.[8]

[5] "Statement to the US (draft)" (對米陳述書[案]), October 4, 1950 (JMOFA, 2007, 25–26)

[6] NARA, RG 84, Foreign Service Posts of the Department of State, Office of the US Political Adviser for Japan-Tokyo, Classified General Correspondence, 1945–1949, Box 22; RG 59, Decimal File, 894.014/7–1447, 894.014/9–2347.

[7] NARA, RG 59, Decimal File, 794.022/1–2450; Wada (2013, 237–238).

[8] "Statement to the US (draft)" (對米陳述書[案]), October 4, 1950 (JMOFA, 2007, 24–30).

Table 1 List of 36 reference works in English forwarded to the US Department of State by the Japanese Ministry of Foreign Affairs

Classification		Item	Publication date
1. General issues		1. Japan's status quo (politics)	Feb. 1950
		2. Japan's status quo (economy)	Dec. 1949
2. Territorial issues		1. The Kurile Islands, the Habomais, and Shikotan	Nov. 1946
		2. South Kuriles, Habomai Islands, Shikotan Island	Apr. 1949
		3. Sakhalin	Jan. 1949
		4. Ryukyu and other Nansei Islands	Mar. 1947
		5. The Bonin Island group, the Volcano Island group	June 1947
		6. Minor Islands in the Pacific and in the Japan Sea	June 1947
		7. Tsushima	June 1949
3. Political issues		1. Jurisdiction of the international court of justice	Feb. 1948
		2. Japanese nationals in the territories to be separated from Japan and foreigners who originated from those territories and reside in Japan	Feb. 1948
		3. Japan's police system	June 1948
		4. Status of foreigners in Japan	June 1950
		5. Japan and international treaties	Mar. 1949
		6. Treatment of Japanese nationals overseas	Oct. 1949
4. Economic issues	A. Related to the future	1. Minimum quality of life that should be allowed for Japan	Aug. 1948
		2. Actual quality of life in Japan	Dec. 1947
		3. Attachment to the above no. 2	Dec. 1947
		4. Fisheries	Jan. 1948
		5. Japan's shipping industry	Mar. 1948
		6. Problems with Japan's civil aviation	Jan. 1948
		7. Japan's population problems	June 1948
		8. Japan's whale hunting	Jan. 1949
		9. Damage/losses Japan suffered in the Pacific war (attachment: Damage/losses by the atomic bombs)	Apr. 1949
	B. Related to existing claims	1. Japan's overseas debts and Japan's claims and obligations in the territories to be separated from Japan	June 1948
		2. Status of rooted property	Sept. 1948
		3. Occupation costs	July 1948
		4. Industrial property rights	Oct. 1948
		5. Foreigners' copyright issues	Apr. 1948
		6. Capture and inspection	Feb. 1949
		7. Allied property in Japan	Sept. 1950
		8. Reparations	May 1950

(continued)

Table 1 (continued)

Classification		Item	Publication date
5. Special issues		1. Submarine cables	May 1948
		2. Weather and oceanographic observation in Japan	May 1948
		3. Narcotics	Feb. 1950

Source: Nishimura (1971, 45–47)

3 Impact of the *Minor Islands Adjacent to Japan Proper* Series, the Japanese Ministry of Foreign Affairs' Information Pamphlets on Territorial Issues

Part I of the series was published and distributed in November 1946, Parts II and III in March 1947, and Part IV in June 1947. The series title was the same throughout, with the names of the islands given as subtitles for each respective pamphlet. This order of publication may indicate the degree of importance and priority given to the islands by Japan.

The islands discussed in these first volumes in the series are: (1) the Kuril Islands, the Habomai Islands, and Shikotan; (2) the Ryukyu and other Nansei Islands; (3) the Ogasawara Islands and the Iwo Islands (the Bonin Islands and the Volcano Islands); and (4) minor islands in the Pacific (the Daito Islands, Marcus Island [Minami-Tori-shima], and Parece Vela [Okinotorishima]) and Minor Islands in the Japan Sea. This order reflected the degree of importance set by the JMOFA (Jung, 2010, 331–365).

According to POLAD-Japan, 20 copies of these pamphlets were sent to the US Department of State via POLAD-Japan on three occasions (February, July, and September 1947),[9] and different sections of SCAP Headquarters also received them. These reference materials had already been delivered to the Bureau of Far Eastern Affairs' Working Group on Japan Treaty and geographers from early 1947, when the Department of State began composing drafts for the peace treaty with Japan.

The JMOFA is also believed to have sent these pamphlets to other nations besides the United States, including Australia, the United Kingdom, and other Allies belonging to the Far Eastern Commission.

[9] United States Political Adviser for Japan, Despatch no.1296, Subject: Minor Islands Adjacent to Japan (Sept. 23, 1947) (NARA, RG 84, Office of the US Political Adviser for Japan-Tokyo, Classified General Correspondence, 1945–1949, Box 22).

Table 2 List of seven reference works in English on territorial issues forwarded to the Department of State by the Japanese Ministry of Foreign Affairs

	Japanese title	English title	Publication date	Language available	Countries where public access is allowed
①	日本の附屬小島I,千島齒舞及び色丹島	Minor Islands Adjacent to Japan Proper, Part I: The Kurile Islands, the Habomais, and Shikotan	Nov. 1946	English	United States, Australia
②	日本の附屬小島II, 琉球及び他の南西諸島	Minor Islands Adjacent to Japan Proper, Part II: Ryukyu and Other Nansei Islands	Mar. 1947	English	United States, Japan
③	日本の附屬小島III, 小笠原及び火山列島	Minor Islands Adjacent to Japan Proper, Part III: The Bonin Island Group, the Volcano Island Group	Mar. 1947	English	United States
④	日本の附屬小島IV, 太平洋及び日本海小諸島	Minor Islands Adjacent to Japan Proper, Part IV: Minor Islands in the Pacific, Minor Islands in the Japan Sea	June 1947	English	United States
⑤	樺太	(Unknown)	Jan. 1949		
⑥	南千島, 齒舞, 色丹島	South Kuriles, Habomai Islands, Shikotan Island	Apr. 1949		
⑦	對馬	Tsushima	July 1949	English	United States, Japan

Source: Compiled by author based on Nishimura (1971, 45–47); "Statement to the US (draft)" (對米陳述書[案]), October 4, 1950 (JMOFA, 2007, 24–30); NARA, RG 84, Foreign Service Posts of the Department of State, Office of the US Political Adviser for Japan-Tokyo, Classified General Correspondence, 1945–1949, Box 22; NARA, RG 59, Decimal File, 894.014/7–1447, 894.014/9–2347

3.1 Minor Islands Adjacent to Japan Proper, Part I: The Kurile Islands, the Habomais, and Shikotan (November 1946)

Minor Islands Adjacent to Japan Proper, Part I treats the Kurils (Kuriles), Shikotan, and the Habomais north of Hokkaido. As is widely known, the Yalta Accord (February 1945) stipulated that Southern Sakhalin be returned and the Kurils handed over to the Soviet Union. The problem was the scope of the Kurils.

This pamphlet, published in November 1946, divided the Kuril Islands into the northern and southern Kurils, and argued the southern Kurils (Etorofu-to and Shikotan) had been Japanese territory "since early days," while the Habomai Islands and Shikotan were not part of the Kurils, but of Hokkaido (Jung, 2010, 340).

JMOFA explained the Kuril Islands as a combination of the northern Kurils north of Uruppu (Urup) and the southern Kurils, which consisted of Yetorofu (Etorofu) and Kunashiri. It argued that the northern Kurils were peacefully acquired through the 1875 Treaty of Saint Petersburg, and the southern Kurils had always been Japanese territory, with Japan's sovereignty over them confirmed in the 1854 Treaty of Commerce and Navigation between Japan and Russia (Treaty of Shimoda) (FO, Japanese Government, 1946, 2–7). It claimed that if the intent of the Yalta Conference was to restore Japan's territorial borders as they were just prior to the Russo-Japanese War (1904–1905),[10] the return of Southern Sakhalin would suffice, but the return of the entire Kurils, including the southern Kurils, could not be accepted (Jung, 2010, 340).

Regarding Shikotan and the Habomai Islands, JMOFA contended that these islands were not part of the Kurils but extensions of Hokkaido's Nemuro Peninsula, which the Soviets occupied after the war (FO, Japanese Government, 1946, 9–10; Jung, 2010, 340). In other words, JMOFA argued that the Kuril Islands, to be handed over to the Soviet Union under the Yalta Conference, did not include Etorofu and the Kunashiri Islands, which belonged to the southern Kurils, and Shikotan and the Habomai Islands, extensions of the Nemuro Peninsula, were illegally occupied by the Soviets only after the end of hostilities.[11]

Nevertheless, this pamphlet differs from the official view held by the Japanese government since 1956 in a few ways:

First, though JMOFA distinguished between the northern and southern Kurils and claimed Japan's sovereignty over the southern Kurils, it admitted to Etorofu-to and Kunashiri being part of the southern Kurils, thereby falling under the overall scope of the Kurils to be handed over to the Soviet Union. They marked the northern and southern Kurils with different patterns (▩and ▩) in the attached map (Fig. 1) but made it clear that the southern Kurils were still part of the Kuril Islands.

Second, the JMOFA colored all of Shikotan and the Habomai Islands black to mark them as extensions of Hokkaido. But here, it is unclear whether Shikotan is an extension of Hokkaido or the Kurils. Even materials referred to by the JMOFA described Shikotan and the Habomai Islands as belonging to the Kurils.

The *Russian Encyclopedia* (I. E. Andreevsky, ed., 1890) described the Habomai Islands and Shikotan as part of the Kurils, while the *Grand Russian Encyclopedia* (P. N. Milyukov, ed., 1904) excluded about half of the Habomai Islands from the Kurils (FO, Japanese Government, 1946, 7n1). The *American Sailing Directory* (1930) separated the Habomai Islands and Shikotan from the Kurils and featured them under the heading of Hokkaido, while the *British Sailing Directory* (1940), after describing the Kuril Islands, gave a separate paragraph to the Habomais and Shikotan. The longitudinal and latitudinal scope of the Kurils as defined by the *Encyclopedia Britannica* (1911) excluded the Habomai Islands and Shikotan, but

[10] "Statement to the US (draft)" (對米陳述書[案]), October 4, 1950 (JMOFA, 2007, 26).

[11] "The General Order No. 1 issued on September 2, 1945 by the Supreme Commander for the Allied Powers did not specify to whom the Japanese forces in the Habomais and Shikotan should surrender. However, the fourth Brigade stationed in these islands, being under the command of the 89th Division in Kunashiri Island, surrendered to the Soviet Commander-in-Chief. The Habomais and Shikotan have since been under Soviet occupation as well as the Kurile islands" (FO, Japanese Government, 1946, 9n5).

still in the main text, Kunashiri and Shikotan were referred to as being among the principal islands of the Kurils (FO, Japanese Government, 1946, 8n3).

Third, though *Minor Islands Adjacent to Japan Proper, Part I* cited Shikotan together with the Habomai Islands, even Japan itself recognized Shikotan as belonging not to Nemuro province, an extension of Hokkaido, but to Chishima, namely, the Kurils. When the Development Commission was established in Hokkaido in 1869 and 11 provinces were founded, Shikotan became part of Nemuro province but was incorporated into Chishima province of Nemuro prefecture in 1885. Shikotan's relations with Kunashiri and Etorofu subsequently deepened, with the trio often called the "three minami Chishima Islands" (Park, 2014, 154–155). To increase the odds of Shikotan remaining in Japanese possession, the JMOFA identified Shikotan, which belonged to the southern Kurils in actuality, as part of Nemuro province and described it as part of Hokkaido.

After the publication of Part I of the series on the Kuril Islands, Habomai Islands, and Shikotan in November 1946, the POLAD-Japan office and the Department of State held different discussions on how to handle the southern Kurils, Shikotan, and the Habomais (Wada, 2013, 89–105). Treaty drafts written by the Bureau of Far Eastern Affairs from 1947 and those by the British Foreign and Commonwealth Office in 1951 all disputed the scope of the Kuril Islands: they generally agreed that Etorofu-to and Kunashiri belonged to the Kurils but disagreed on whether Shikotan and the Habomai Islands did as well (Wada, 2013, 96–97).[12]

In 1949, POLAD-Japan, led by Sebald, strove to accommodate the view of the JMOFA on the Kuril Islands. Sebald forwarded two reports to the Department of State, "Economic Importance to Japan of Etorofu, Kunashiri, Habomai, and Shikotan Islands" (December 12, 1949)[13] and "Japanese Petition for Return of Southern Kuril Islands" (December 31, 1949),[14] arguing that historic grounds for these four islands being part of the Kurils were weak, and thereby, they should not be incorporated by the Soviet Union.

Having received Sebald's reviews of the drafts, the Bureau of Far Eastern Affairs requested the Office of the Legal Adviser for a legal review of the southern Kurils. This was because the draft treaty dated October 13, 1949, treated these islands as Japanese territory, and the draft treaty dated November 2, 1949, had them as Soviet territory, while a telegram dated November 14, 1949, from Sebald argued that they

[12] Working Group on Japan Treaty, Notes of Meeting on Friday, August 1, 1947 (NARA, RG 59, Office of Northeast Asia Affairs, Records Relating to the Treaty of Peace with Japan—Subject File, 1945–1951, Lot 56D527, Box 5); "Treaty of Peace with Japan" November 2, 1949 (NARA, RG 59, 740.0011PW(Peace)/11–1449); FO 371/92535, FJ 1022/171, "Japanese Peace Treaty: Second revised draft of the Japanese Peace Treaty," March 1951; FO 371/92538, FJ 1022/222, "Provisional Draft of Japanese Peace Treaty (United Kingdom)," April 7, 1951, The National Archives (TNA), United Kingdom.

[13] Despatch by Sebald to the Secretary of State, Subject: Economic Importance to Japan of Etorofu, Kunashiri, Habomai, and Shikotan Islands. (Dec. 12, 1949), no.866 (NARA, RG 59, Decimal File, 740.0011PW(Peace)/12–1249).

[14] Despatch by Sebald to the Secretary of State, Subject: Japanese Petition for Return of Southern Kuril Islands (Dec. 31, 1949) (NARA, RG 59, Decimal File, 740.0011PW(Peace)/12–3149).

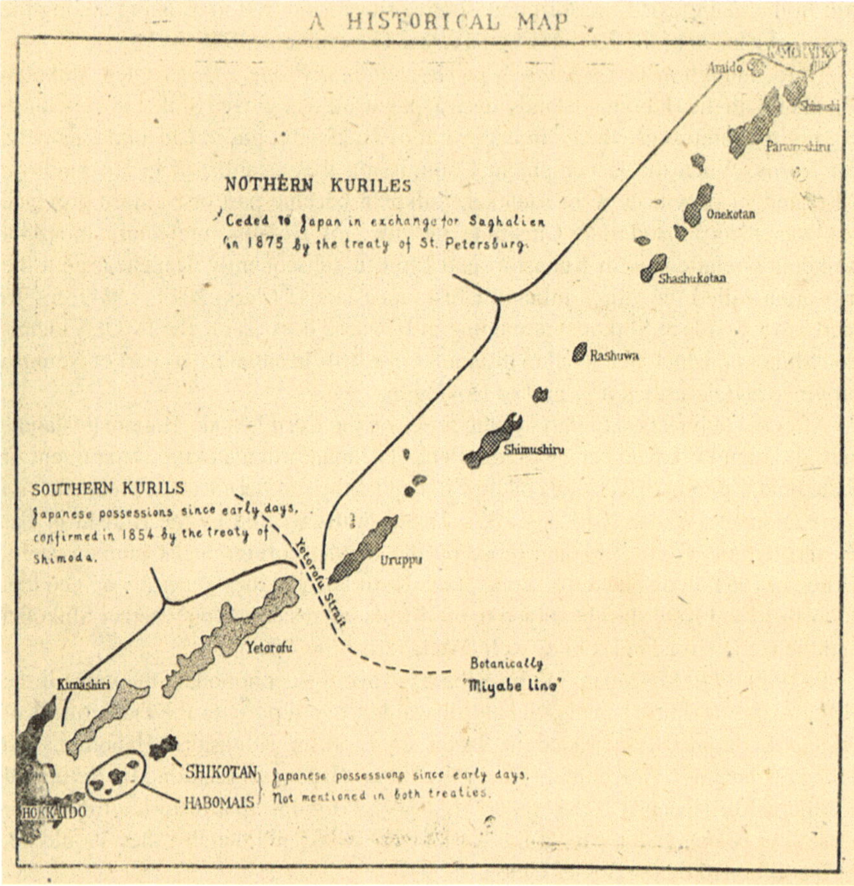

Fig. 1 Map attached to *Minor Islands Adjacent to Japan Proper, Part I* (Nov. 1946) (distinguishing between the southern Kurils and northern Kurils, Shikotan, and the Habomais). *Source*: FO, Japanese Government (1946)

belonged to Japan.[15] The Bureau provided nine documents as references, which included two important ones written by the JMOFA.[16] Neither documents nor other information produced by the USSR were available to the Department of State. Such materials often defined the Habomai Islands and Shikotan as constituents of the Kurils, along with the islands of Etorofu and Kunashiri.

The Office of the Legal Adviser determined that the Habomai Islands and Shikotan were not part of the Kurils to be handed over to the Soviet Union, but

[15] Memorandum by Hamilton (FE) to Fisher (L), Subject: Southern Kurile Islands (Nov. 22, 1949) (NARA, RG 59, Decimal File 740.0011PW(Peace)/11–2249.

[16] Japanese Government, "South Kuriles; Habomai Islands; Shikotan Island" (Apr. 1949); *Minor Islands Adjacent to Japan* (1947).

Kunashiri and Etorofu-to were. Namely, it ruled that the former two islands were Japanese territory while the latter two were Soviet territory.[17] As a result, the Department of State decided that the Habomai Islands and Shikotan were to be Japanese territory and Kunashiri and Etorofu Soviet territory.

In the process leading up to the conclusion of the San Francisco Peace Treaty in 1951, the Japanese government accepted that the Kurils to be handed over to the Soviet Union included Kunashiri and Etorofu, or the southern Kurils. Nevertheless, backed by the United States, it contended that the Soviets were wrongfully occupying the Habomai Islands and Shikotan.

In 1956, the Soviet Union and Japan signed the Soviet-Japanese Joint Declaration and agreed to the return of Shikotan and the Habomai Islands after the conclusion of a peace treaty. Shikotan and the Habomai Islands are relatively small in size and adjacent to Japanese Hokkaido, but Etorofu and Kunashiri are large and more grounds existed to contest ownership. Later, faced with severe criticism by domestic political circles for having surrendered Kunashiri and Etorofu, the Japanese government came, by 1961, to claim that they were not part of the Kurils (Wada, 2013, 109–118, 145–178). These territorial issues remain unresolved to this day.

3.2 Minor Islands Adjacent to Japan Proper, Part II: Ryukyu and Other Nansei Islands (March 1947)

Minor Islands Adjacent to Japan Proper, Part II, deals with the Ryukyu Islands, which are known as Nansei Shoto or Ryukyu Retto in Japanese, and came under potential US trusteeship after the San Francisco Peace Treaty. This pamphlet divided Nansei Shoto into Kagoshima prefecture (Satsunan Islands) and Okinawa prefecture (Ryukyu Islands): the former included the Osumi Islands and Amami Oshima, and the latter included Okinawa and the Sakishima Islands.

Japan expected it could not refuse the placement of the Ryukyu Islands under the trusteeship of the United States or another Allied power, should that be decided upon.[18] Instead, Japan emphasized its sovereignty over Amami Oshima, an important, densely populated island south of the 30th north latitude. Amami Oshima-related petitions accounted for the largest share of the petitions that inundated the office of American special envoy John Foster Dulles, the Department of State, and SCAP Headquarters during the peace treaty process. Amami Oshima was excluded from Japanese administration by the San Francisco Peace Treaty but returned to Japan in December 1953 (Yoshida, 1958, 66–67). In *Minor Islands Adjacent to*

---

[17] Memorandum by Conrad E. Snow (L/P) to Hamilton (FE), Subject: Southern Kurile Islands and the Shikotan Archipelago (Nov. 25, 1949) (NARA, RG 59, Decimal File, 740.0011PW(Peace)/11–2549).

[18] "Expected Political Clauses in a Peace Treaty and Countermeasures for Possible Discrepancies (draft)" (對日平和條約に於ける政治條項の想定及對處方針[案]), May 1946 (JMOFA, 2006, 95–96).

Japan Proper, Part II, JMOFA, on alert for any sign of transfer of the Ryukyus to China, provided historical evidence of Japanese sovereignty over the islands. But JMOFA also commented on the Diaoyu Islands (Senkaku Islands), whose ownership is currently being disputed with China. This group is called the Senkaku Shoto (Senkaku Islands) in Japanese, the Diaoyu Islands in Chinese, the Diaoyutai Islands in Taiwanese, and the Pinnacle Islands in English. This English name, Pinnacle Islands, written in Chinese characters, became Sento 尖頭 or Senkaku 尖閣. This pamphlet described the islands as follows:

> …the Sento Islands (total area 2 sq. m.) lying north of Sakishima sub-group are uninhabited and of little importance. (FO, Japanese Government, 1947a, 2)

The JMOFA recorded the Senkaku Islands as the "Sento Islands" and ascribed to these uninhabited islands "little importance," which is very unusual considering the current dispute over them (Fig. 2). This reveals what Japan really thought of them at that time.

As noted, the name Sento Shoto, or Sento Islands, is a translation of the English name Pinnacle Islets. This first appeared in 1908 in Japanese naval records, which recorded them as 6 *li* (24 km) east of Gyocho Jima (Hoa pin su in English, Diaoyu Yu in Chinese). (Unryu, 2000, 91).

Then, what impact did Part II of the series, created by the JMOFA, have on the US Department of State? First of all, the Japanese name, Nansei Shoto, was officially used in the San Francisco Treaty. The official draft treaty, dated March 1951, mentioned the "Ryukyu Islands south of 29th north latitude," which the Japanese government requested be replaced with the "Nansei Islands south of 29th north latitude." As far as rationale, it explained, "The Amami Islands, which do not belong to the Ryukyu Islands, but to the Satsunan Islands, lie south of 29th north latitude, while the Nansei Islands include both the Satsunan and Ryukyu Islands, that is, all the islands between Kyushu and Formosa (Taiwan)."[19]

Sebald forwarded this request to the Department of State by telegram the same day he received it, together with his report that the Japanese government's suggestion for Nansei "…appears historically correct according (to) Jap[anese] usage. 'Ryukyu Islands' not coextensive with 'Nansei Islands,' former term applying only to those islands formerly included within Okinawa prefecture (Okinawa and Sankishima sub-groups, including Daito and Sento Islands)."[20]

This opinion of Sebald's is very noteworthy because he firstly considered Nansei as an accurate name and secondly explained that the Ryukyu Islands included the Sento Islands. His opinion, a representation of Japan's position, can be regarded as a US record that backed up Sento/Senkaku as Japanese territory. Still, he quoted incorrect information that Sento belonged to "Sankishima" (i.e., Sakishima).

---

[19] "Observations on the Provisional Draft of a Japanese Peace Treaty" (平和條約草案に對するわが方意見), April 4, 1951 (JMOFA, 2006, 351–352).

[20] Telegram by Sebald to the Secretary of State, no. 1750 (April 4, 1951) (NARA, RG 59, Decimal File, 694.001/4–451).

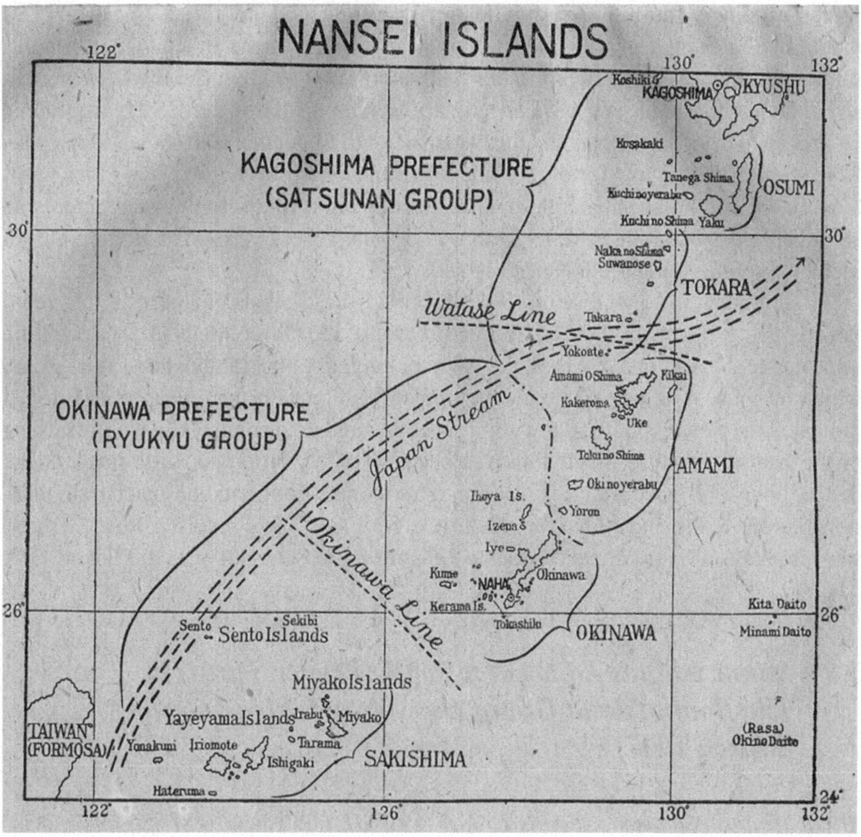

Fig. 2 Nansei Islands map attached to *Minor Islands Adjacent to Japan, Part II* (March 1947). *Source*: FO, Japanese Government (1947a)

Upon receipt of Sebald's telegram, Robert A. Fearey, a working-level official at the Department of State, consulted with Samuel W. Boggs, a Department of State geography specialist, on the question. From his study of the *US Hydrographic Report,* Boggs found that "the Nansei Islands extend in an arc form off the north-eastern coast of Taiwan to the southern end of Kyushu. This chain of islands is divided into five groups called, from south to north, Sakishima Gunto, Okinawa Gunto, Amami Gunto, Tokara Gunto, and Sumi Gunto." As such, he responded that "Nansei was technically more accurate" and should be used.[21]

Fearey accurately pointed out that "Ryukyu" was a much more familiar name and that it was likely that the Japanese government had suggested "Nansei," because it was a Japanese name ("Ryukyu" derives from the Chinese "Loochoo") and they

[21] Memorandum by Fearey to Allison, Subject: Nansei Shoto (April 5, 1951) (NARA, RG 59, Decimal File, 694.001/4–551.

wanted to hint at future ownership. Fearey marked six island groups, including five mentioned by Boggs and the Daito Group next to them, on the attached map. On this same map, Fearey wrote Sento under Sekibisho (赤尾嶼), but Sekibisho was actually a different island. What was used here was a portion of the US Hydrographic Office (HO) Chart 1500, used by the Department of State, that also showed Japanese, Korean, and Taiwan territories, but not such small places as Sento. This was a problem related not only to the large scale of the map but also due to the weak interest in "uninhabited islands of little importance." In any case, Fearey and Boggs did not include Sento as part of the Nansei Islands.[22]

In summary, the JMOFA in 1947 described the Senkaku Islands as the Sento Islands lying north of the Sakishima subgroup and as uninhabited and of little importance. Sebald in 1951 thought Sento belonged to the "Sankishima" subgroup, which he viewed as part of Okinawa prefecture. For their part, Fearey and Boggs indicated the Sento Islands at the wrong location and determined they did not belong to the Nansei Islands. All of this was because they were given little importance: hence the use of inaccurate names (Sento and Sankishima) and an inaccurate location (below Sekibisho). Of course, Article 3 of the San Francisco Peace Treaty, wherein Nansei Shoto appears, does not mention the Senkaku or Sento Islands.

3.3 Minor Islands Adjacent to Japan Proper, Part III: The Bonin Island Group, the Volcano Island Group (March 1947)

Minor Islands Adjacent to Japan Proper, Part III, published in March 1947, deals with the Bonin Islands, or Ogasawara Islands, and the Volcano Islands (Kazan Retto or Iwo Islands in Japanese). Japan argued that the former were incorporated into Japanese territory in 1875 and the latter in 1891.

This pamphlet was mainly meant to explain when Japan found these islands and how it came to take possession of them after disputes with European states and the United States (FO, Japanese Government, 1947b, 1–8) (Fig. 3).

The Battle for Iwo Jima was a major battle of the Pacific War, after which the Iwo Islands were occupied by the US Navy. The United States considered both the Bonin and Iwo Islands as strategic locations and planned to place them under its trusteeship.

The Soviet Union opposed the US trusteeship of the Ryukyu, Bonin, and other islands. The United States forwarded the official treaty draft to the Soviet Union in March 1951, to which the latter sent back its comments on May 7. When seen only from a logical perspective, ironically, the Soviet suggestion was the most reasonable and advantageous to Japan. It suggested that (1) a meeting of the Council of Foreign

[22] Telegram by Sebald to the Secretary of State, no. 1750 (April 4, 1951) (NARA, RG 59, Decimal File, 694.001/4–451).

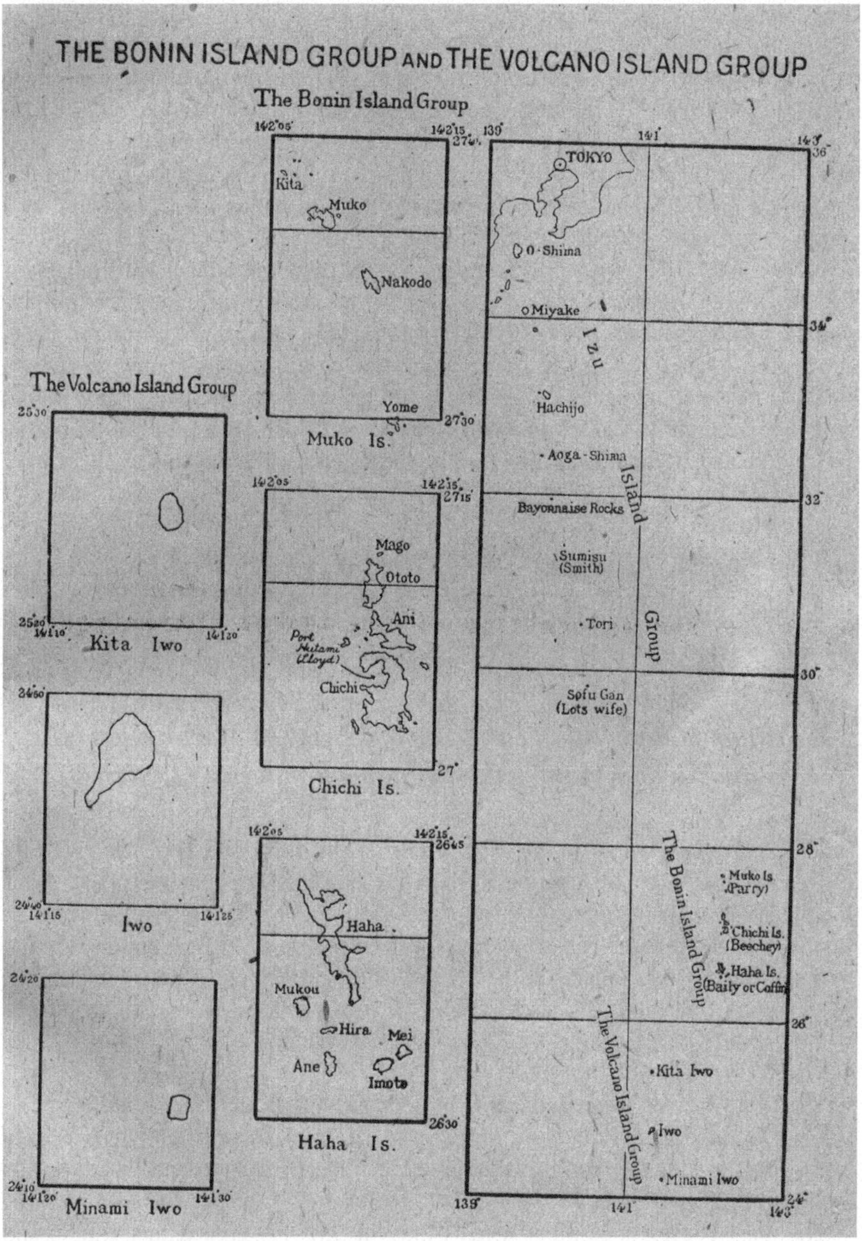

Fig. 3 Map attached to *Minor Islands Adjacent to Japan, Part III* (March 1947). *Source*: FO, Japanese Government (1947b)

Ministers, composed of representatives of the United States, United Kingdom, USSR, and the People's Republic of China, be convened in June or July 1951, to begin preparation of the peace treaty with Japan; (2) Formosa and the Pescadores be returned to "China"; (3) there was no legal justification that could be adduced for removing the Ryukyu and Bonin Islands from Japanese control; (4) the treaty contain guarantees against the restoration of Japanese militarism, including limitations on the size of the Japanese armed forces; (5) the occupation forces be withdrawn within a year of the formal conclusion of peace; (6) there be no limitations on the development of Japan's peaceful economy; (7) the treaty prohibit Japan from entering into any coalition directed against any of the states which fought with their armed forces against Japan; and (8) the signatories to a treaty agree to support Japan joining the United Nations.[23] These suggestions were meant mainly to have a Japanese peace settlement examined at a foreign minister conference that would include representatives of the People's Republic of China, and to object to turning the Ryukyu and Bonin Islands into military bases under US trusteeship. In its reply (May 19, 1951), the US side rejected the proposal for a meeting of the Council of Foreign Ministers.

In the end, the two islands were placed under potential US trusteeship under Article 3 of the San Francisco Peace Treaty, but eventually, trusteeship was not accomplished. These islands were returned to Japan in 1968.

3.4 Minor Islands Adjacent to Japan, Part IV: Minor Islands in the Pacific, Minor Islands in the Japan Sea (June 1947)

Minor Islands Adjacent to Japan Proper, Part IV, the last of the series, begins with a cover and one-page map, continues with a one-page table of contents and 12 pages of text, and ends with another one-page map. It discusses, (1) the Daito Islands, (2) Marcus Island (Minami-Tori-shima), and (3) Parece Vela Island (Okinotorishima) in the portion "Minor Islands in the Pacific" and (1) Liancourt Rocks (Takeshima, Dokdo) and (2) Utsuryo (Dagelet Island, Ulleungdo) in the portion "Minor Islands in the Japan Sea (East Sea)" (FO, Japanese Government, 1947c; Jung, 2010, 342–365) (Fig. 4).

The Daito Islands, Marcus Island, and Parece Vela Island were not covered in *Minor Islands Adjacent to Japan Proper, Part III*, and *Minor Islands Adjacent to Japan Proper, Part IV,* was also the first to include Ulleungdo and Dokdo in the East Sea.

The most conspicuous point here is that the JMOFA argued that Dokdo and Ulleungdo fell under the scope of islands adjacent to Japan in this pamphlet

[23] "Summary of Negotiations Leading Up to the Conclusion of the Treaty of Peace with Japan," by Robert A. Fearey (Sept. 18, 1951), 9 (NARA, RG 59, Records Relating to the Treaty of Peace with Japan, Subject File, 1945–1951, Lot 56D527, Box 1).

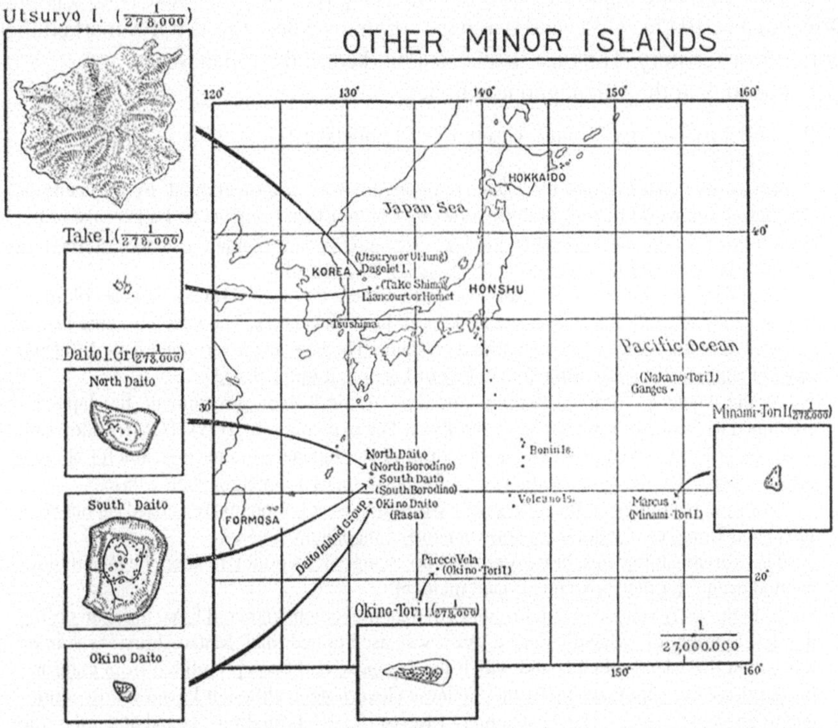

Fig. 4 Map attached to *Minor Islands Adjacent to Japan, Part IV* (June 1947). *Source*: FO, Japanese Government (1947c)

officially published for the Allies in June 1947. As other pamphlets in the series did, this one consistently talked about islands over which Japan deemed sovereign ownership to be contested and which it wanted to be recognized as its adjacent islands. The JMOFA did not feature any of the islands that were clearly Japanese territory in this series, such as Tsushima Island, Iki Island, and the Oki Islands, but only those contested islands where the JMOFA saw a chance of claiming them as Japanese territory. While *Minor Islands Adjacent to Japan Proper, Part III,* talked about the Ryukyus, it makes no mention of Taiwan because, of course, it was not Japanese territory. On the other hand, Ulleungdo and Dokdo were included among Japan's adjacent islands together with the numerous islands along its east coast (Jung, 2010, 342–350).

It is surprising to find Dokdo, and even Ulleungdo, among the islands over which Japan claimed sovereignty. This is probably the reason Part IV has not been made public in Japan. Despite its complete lack of claim over Ulleungdo, Japan still included it because it had clear intentions for the island. That is, by denying or damaging Korea's unquestionable sovereign ownership of Ulleungdo, it intended to deny Korea's ownership of Dokdo, islets adjacent to Ulleungdo. While attacking Ulleungdo, Japan's true target was Dokdo.

Dokdo and Ulleungdo are covered in five pages of body text (FO, Japanese Government, 1947c, 8–12) and two pages of maps where the JMOFA marked them as Japanese territory. The East Sea is also marked as the Japan Sea.

Let us look at the Ulleungdo text first:

> II. Dagelet Island (Matsu-shima, Utsuryo, or Ul-lung Island).
>
> 2. History
>
> It was only in 1787 that the island [Ulleungdo] was first mentioned, by the name of Dagelet, in the world history of discoveries by Captain Jean François de La Pérouse of the French navy. In Japanese documents, however, reference was made as early as 1004 to Uruma Island, an old Japanese equivalent for Ul-lung Island.
>
> The Island was known to Koreans also from ancient times. Several attempts at colonization were made by Koreans after the middle of the 13th century. The island became later a convenient hiding-place by criminals and brigands. The Korean Government from 1400 and onward adhered for a long time to a policy of keeping it uninhabited.
>
> As the island was thus virtually abandoned by the Korean government, the Japanese continued to frequent it in increasing numbers. The expedition of TOYOTOMI, Hideyoshi, to Korea in 1592 served to accelerate activities of the Japanese in this area, and for about a century thereafter, the island remained in all appearances a Japanese fishing base.
>
> From the beginning of the 17th century repeated negotiations were carried on between Japan and Korea on the question of ownership of the island. …
>
> The Korean authorities, however, made no change in its policy to keep the island uninhabited even after the above mentioned incident. …
>
> … in the early years of Meiji (around 1868), a movement gathered force in Japan urging the development of "Matsu-shima"…As it was ascertained that "Matsu-shima" was none other than the island which…and which the Japanese had been prohibited from entering, the petitions were not taken up by the Japanese Government, although Japanese still continued to go to the island…The Annexation of Korea in 1910 brought the island under the rule of the Government-General of Chosen (Korea). (FO, Japanese Government, 1947c, 10–12; underline added)

As seen in the underlined parts above, the JMOFA demonstrated its intent to clearly describe Ulleungdo as Japanese territory or under Japanese rule. According to the pamphlet, Japan first recognized Ulleungdo in the eleventh century, and Korea attempted to colonize it only after the middle of the twelfth century and adhered to a policy of keeping it uninhabited from the fifteenth century onward. For a century after the Japanese invasion of Korea in 1592, the Japanese ruled the island. At the end of the seventeenth century, Korea's ownership of Ulleungdo was recognized after a long dispute, but the Korean authorities continued to keep the island uninhabited, while the Japanese never stopped fishing near the island. Also, in the latter part of the nineteenth century, there was a movement and petitions urging the development of Ulleungdo, and despite the government's disapproval, the Japanese still continued to go to the island. That is to say, the pamphlet claims that Japan first recognized Ulleungdo and had it under its rule for a century, there had been disputes over sovereignty, and while Korea practically left it unattended, Japan developed the island (FO, Japanese Government, 1947c, 9–10).

This tone completely disregarded the historical records regarding Ulleungdo, widely known in Korea, which begin with its conquest and incorporation by Korea's ancient Silla kingdom in 512 (Ulleungdo was then the autonomous nation of

Usan-guk), but instead posits the eleventh-century Japanese record as the oldest. This hints at why Japan added Ulleungdo to its list of adjacent islands.

As these pamphlets were designed to assert Japan's ownership of certain islands, Ulleungdo, which was undoubtedly Korean territory then as it is now, should not have been featured. Most of the islands included in the pamphlets were those the Allies excluded from Japanese administration or over which sovereignty was disputed. As the Japanese title of the series, "Japan's Adjacent Islands," implied, it is beyond question that Japan viewed Ulleungdo as one such island.

It was impossible, then as now, to have Ulleungdo recognized as Japanese territory in consideration of both historical facts and common sense. Then, why was it included among Japan's adjacent islands in the JMOFA's official territory references for the Allies? Two reasons can be thought of in this regard.

First, from the latter half of the nineteenth century, Japan exhibited ambitions of ownership over Ulleungdo, not Dokdo. But they had to turn their attention to Dokdo, Ulleungdo's adjacent island, because history undoubtedly established Ulleungdo as Korean territory. In premodern Japanese materials, where Dokdo is mentioned, it appeared together with Ulleungdo as its annexed island. It never appears alone and was deemed to function only through its affiliation with Ulleungdo. The actual reason the Korean Empire declared Ulleungdo a county in 1900 was to make clear its ownership of the island in response to Japan's growing encroachment (Song, 1999, 93–132). The first book Japan published after the declaration of its illegal incorporation of Dokdo in 1905 was *Takeshima oyobi Utsuyōtō* (Dokdo and Ulleungdo) (Okuhara, 1907). This recognition of Ulleungdo and Dokdo as one entity naturally continued up to 1947.

Second, the JMOFA attacked Korea's lax policy toward the inhabited Ulleungdo despite Korea's clear ownership of it and thereby intended to reveal that Korea did not even have a policy on the uninhabited Dokdo. This was a calculated move to take Dokdo by ostensibly attacking Ulleungdo.

The pamphlet's description of Dokdo is false and fraudulent. Let us look at a portion of it:

> I. Liancourt Rocks (Take-shima)
>
> 2. History
>
> … the Japanese knew the existence of the Liancourt Rocks from the ancient times …..
>
> As for European acquaintance with the Rocks, it was in 1849 that the *Liancourt*, a French whaling ship, first sighted them and gave them their present name…..It should be noted that while there is a Korean name for Dagelet, none exists for the Liancourt Rocks and they are not shown in the maps made in Korea.
>
> On February 22, 1905, the Governor of Shimane prefecture, by a prefectural proclamation, placed the Liancourts under the jurisdiction of the Oki Islands Branch Office of the Shimane prefectural government. (Note 3: *The United States Hydrographical Survey* at present deals with Liancourt Rocks under the head of Oki group of islands.)
>
> 3. Industry
>
> In 1904, however, the inhabitants of Oki Islands began to hunt sea-lions on these islets and thereafter each summer the [Oki] islanders, using Dagelet as their base, went regularly tso the Rocks and built sheds as temporary quarters for the season. (FO, Japanese Government, 1947c, 9–10; underline added)

According to the JMOFA, the Japanese had known of the existence of Dokdo from ancient times, naming it Matsu-shima in 1667, and the Europeans named it Liancourt Rocks only in 1849. Unlike with Ulleungdo, the pamphlet claims there was traditionally no Korean name for the Liancourt Rocks, and they were not shown on Korean-made maps. If Japan alone had had historical and geographical evidence on the islets and if they had been undoubtedly Japanese territory, as they claimed, there would be no reason to bring up Korea in the text. By referring to Korea here, Japan essentially admitted that there was indeed material evidence that Dokdo was Korean territory, and it had concerns in this regard. This also explains why Ulleungdo was featured in the pamphlet. Without explaining the situation surrounding Ulleungdo, they could not explain Dokdo.

The account that there was no Korean name for Dokdo and that these rocks were not shown on Korean-made maps is an entirely fraudulent claim. Dokdo (Usan-do) has appeared in countless Korean maps and geography books since at least the seventeenth century. The name Dokdo is often found even in Japanese materials. Another name, Seokdo, can be seen in Imperial Decree No. 41 of 1900.

The assertion that the Japanese began fishing from the Liancourt Rocks in 1904 and Shimane prefecture incorporated them on February 22, 1905, was meant to justify the Japanese invasion. The fact that Oki islanders had to use Ulleungdo as their base to fish at Dokdo over a long period only proved that Dokdo was already considered as affiliated with Ulleungdo, so that they had to start from there. As this was a time when Imperial Japan was encroaching on Korea, the Oki islanders were able to use Ulleungdo for their fishing operations at Dokdo.

As is well known, in September 1904, Nakai Yozaburo 中井養三郎, a fisherman from Shimane prefecture, requested that the Japanese government incorporate Dokdo as Japanese territory and lease it to him. On January 28, 1905, the Japanese government did so by naming Dokdo Takeshima and promulgated this through a Shimane prefecture public notice. Nakai and the Japanese government were aware that Dokdo was Korean territory. The Korean Empire was belatedly informed of the situation through a report by the magistrate of Ulleungdo, Sim Heung-taek, in 1906. However, the royal palace had been invaded by Japanese troops in the turbulence of the Russo-Japanese War, and Korea's sovereign diplomatic rights had been lost. The outcry raised by the Korean press regarding what was happening to Dokdo is well known. Dokdo was seized by violence and greed during the first phase of Japan's invasion of Korea.

Some 40 years later, while the two halves of Korea were still occupied by American and Soviet troops and under their respective military administrations, Japan published this pamphlet claiming Dokdo and Ulleungdo to be its adjacent islands. At that time, Korea was standing at a crossroads between national division and unification. Koreans had yet to have their own government. The two powers on the Korean Peninsula decided to establish provisional governments and trusteeship rule through the US-Soviet Joint Commission as a way to establish peace on the peninsula, but this was when Korean hopes for unification and true independence were dashed with the full-blown emergence of the global Cold War. Without Koreans knowing or having their own government to represent them, their territorial sovereignty was being threatened by none other than Japan, the country from which Korea had just been liberated.

Further, Japan lied without compunction to advance its territorial interests. The lie that "while there is a Korean name for Dagelet, none exists for the Liancourt Rocks and they are not shown in the maps made in Korea" vividly demonstrates Japan's stance on Korea, its just-liberated colony.

This Japanese stance had an impact on SCAP Headquarters and the Department of State from 1947, and this pamphlet, Part IV, was used as rational evidence for rejecting Korea's claims on several occasions during the peace treaty process. SCAP Headquarters used this pamphlet to reject Korean claims and interests on largely two occasions. In August 1948, the Patriotic Old Men's Association of Korea (Uguk noinhoe) appealed to General MacArthur regarding Korea's sovereign ownership of Dokdo and Ulleungdo.[24] Richard Finn of the POLAD-Japan office reviewed the petition but rejected the Korean claim, citing the information in the Japanese pamphlet. The POLAD-Japan office was already well-informed of the pamphlets and deemed them credible.[25]

In his review of a draft treaty sent by telegram to the Department of State in November 1949, Sebald suggested that Dokdo (Liancourt Rocks, Takeshima) be specified part of Japanese territory and that security considerations be made as the installation of weather and radar stations on them.[26] Though he did not mention it, there is no doubt that Sebald had consulted *Minor Islands Adjacent to Japan Proper, Part IV.*

As a result, the US draft treaties produced between 1949 and 1950 recorded that (1) Takeshima had been formally claimed by Japan in 1905, apparently without protest by Korea, and placed under the jurisdiction of the Oki Islands Branch Office of Shimane prefecture, and (2) unlike Dagelet Island, Takeshima had no Korean name and did not appear ever to have been claimed by Korea.[27] These views mirrored the claims of the pamphlet. Sebald's argument, made in November 1949, had a decisive influence on the Department of State's decision regarding sovereign ownership of Dokdo at that time.

The Department of State had organized the Working Group on Japan Treaty and had been preparing for a peace treaty since August 1946, beginning to compose drafts on territory clauses in early 1947. As evidenced by Department of State

[24] US Political Adviser for Japan no. 612 (Sept. 16, 1948). Subject: Korean Petition Concerning Sovereignty of "Docksum," Ullungo Do, Tsushima, and "Parang" Islands (NARA, RG 84, Entry 2828, Japan: Office of US Political Adviser for Japan [Tokyo], Classified General Correspondence [1945–1949, 1950-], Box 34).

[25] GHQ, FEC, Check Sheet, G-2 to Diplomatic Section, Subject: Petition of Patriotic Old Men's Association of Seoul, Korea. Sept. 27, 1948.

[26] William J. Sebald, POLAD-Japan to W. Walton Butterworth, Nov. 14, 1949 (NARA, RG 59, Decimal File, 740.0011PW(Peace)/11–1449); Sebald to the Secretary of State, Subject: Comment on Draft Treaty of Peace with Japan, Nov. 19, 1949 (NARA, RG 59, Decimal File, 740.0011PW(Peace)/11–1949).

[27] "Draft Treaty of Peace with Japan," Dec. 29, 1949 (NARA, RG 59, Lot 56D527, Box 6); "Commentary on Draft Treaty of Peace with Japan" (RG 59, Decimal File, 694.001/7–1850).

geographer Boggs, who used the Part I pamphlet as a major reference in July 1947,[28] these pamphlets prepared by the JMOFA became official references for the Working Group. As of July 1947, they accepted Japan's claims by including the Ryukyus as Japanese territory and adjudging that Kunashiri and Etorofu-to, "which ethnically, economically, and historically have been part of Japan," did not fall under the scope of the Kurils defined under the Yalta Conference.[29] In just 7 months since the JMOFA produced these pamphlets, specialists and policymakers at the Department of State were using them as "objective and rational references" (Jung, 2010, 362–365). Prime Minister Yoshida recalled how the JMOFA sent Japanese information booklets to Washington from 1948 by courtesy of the Diplomatic Section, SCAP, but in a strictly unofficial mode. These booklets and their contents were appraised as "very good reference data" by Washington. "By the time the US government started writing draft peace treaties the same year [1950], Japanese-prepared documents had already been delivered to them in sufficient quantity" (Yoshida, 1958, 25–26).

When Korea and the United States were discussing a peace treaty with Japan in July and August 1951, this Part IV pamphlet was used as an "objective" reference. Boggs wrote reports about the Liancourt Rocks (Dokdo) on three occasions and had to rely on the JMOFA's pamphlet, the only available literature in English on the subject.[30]

Consequently, Assistant Secretary of State Dean Rusk wrote in a memorandum on August 10, 1951, that "this normally uninhabited rock formation was according to our information never treated as part of Korea and, since about 1905, has been under the jurisdiction of the Oki Islands Branch Office of Shimane prefecture of Japan. The island does not appear ever before to have been claimed by Korea."[31] The JMOFA's 1947 pamphlet was used as the most important basis for the Department of State's conclusion.

[28] "Draft of Treaty with Japan," Jul. 24, 1947, by Samuel W. Boggs (SA-E/GE) (NARA, RG 59, Records of the Office of Northeast Asian Affairs Relating to the Treaty of Peace with Japan, Lot 56D527, Box 5); Memorandum by Boggs (SA-E/GE) to Fearey (FE) Jul. 24, 1947 (NARA, RG 59, Decimal File, 740.0011PW(Peace)/7–2447).

[29] Working Group on Japan Treaty, Notes of Meeting on Friday, Aug. 1, 1947 (NARA, RG 59, Lot 56D527, Box 5).

[30] Memorandum by Boggs, OIR/GE to Fearey, NA, Subject: Spratly Island and the Paracels, in Draft Japanese Peace Treaty, Jul. 13, 1951 (NARA, RG 59, Decimal File, 694.001/7–1351); Memorandum by Fearey to Allison, Subject: Proposed Changes for August 13 Draft, Jul. 30, 1951. p. 3 (NARA, RG 59, State Department, Records Relating to the Japanese Peace and Security Treaties, 1946–1952, Lot 78D173, Box 2).

[31] Letter by Dean Acheson to You Chan Yang, Ambassador of Korea, Aug. 10, 1951 (NARA, RG 59, Japanese Peace Treaty Files of John Foster Dulles, 1946–1952, Lot 54D423, Box 7; RG 59, Decimal File, 694.001/8–1051).

3.5 *Tsushima (July 1949)*

Of the pamphlets on territorial issues produced by the JMOFA between 1946 and 1949, the circumstances around the writing of *Tsushima* are clearer. It was written in response to ownership claims over Tsushima and demands for its return raised in Korea before and after the establishment of the ROK government in 1948. ROK President Rhee Syngman's demand for the return of Tsushima in August 1948 generated great press, which covered reactions and rebuttals in Japan.[32] The Chinese media of Taipei issued reports that, as the Ryukyus and Tsushima, which had been Chinese and Korean territory, respectively, three hundred years ago, were taken by Japan, they should be returned to their respective owners (*Dong-A Ilbo*, August 19, 1948). As such, some Chinese media associated the return of the Ryukyus to China with that of Tsushima to Korea. The demand for the return of Tsushima by President Rhee and other Korean government officials continued until early 1949, and Japan saw a need to respond. In the end, the JMOFA took up the job in mid-1949 and completed *Tsushima* in July 1949, which was forwarded to the Department of State in late December 1949.[33]

This pamphlet consists of a cover, a one-page table of contents, and 33 pages of text. Its highlight was exchanges between Korea and Japan (JMOFA, 1949b, 6–16). By virtue of its geographic location, Tsushima had played an important role in Korean-Japanese communication since ancient times. The island's *wako* ("Japanese raiders") had an impact on Korean-Japanese relations. It also served as a relay base for Korean diplomatic missions after the Japanese invasions of Korea from 1592 to 1598.

Overall, *Tsushima* did not deal with the grounds Korea provided for its claim but instead placed emphasis on illegal activities by Korean residents on Tsushima. This was probably because Tsushima was clearly Japanese territory in terms of both history and international law. Its supplement provided statistics on Korean residents, illegal Korean entrants, and other types of Korean criminals. Its claims included that Koreans accounted for 3 percent (or 2140 people) of the Tsushima population and were involved with the heavily leftist Korean Residents' League (Jaeil joseonin yeonmaeng) there and that the biggest problem the island faced was illegal Korean entrants and arrestees, with 60 percent of illegal entrants detained in Nagasaki prefecture being Korean nationals arrested on Tsushima.

The *Tsushima* pamphlet was submitted to the Department of State in late December 1949, and Sebald, the political adviser for Japan, forwarded it to the

[32] "Tsushima henkan wa gensoku ni kaesu" (Return of Tsushima Goes against Principle), *Asahi shimbun*, August 2, 1948; "Tsushima no henkan, Rhee daitōryō yōkyū" (President Rhee Demands Return of Tsushima), *Asahi shimbun*, August 19, 1948. For more information on Tsushima, see Jung (2012).

[33] Japanese Ministry of Foreign Affairs, "Assignment of Work on a Peace Treaty" (平和條約問題作業分擔), November 12, 1949 (JMOFA, 2006, 453–454).

Department of State on January 24, 1950.[34] But, in reality, Japan was not really concerned about its ownership of the island because this had already been confirmed in General of the Army Douglas MacArthur's Instruction to his Commands Concerning the Basic Purpose of the Allied Occupation of Japan and the Manners in which They Are Carried Out by the Allied Forces (December 19, 1945). This pamphlet was produced and distributed to refute the Korean government's claim and was also propagandistic in nature. The ownership over the island itself was never seriously disputed.

4 Conclusion

Thus far, this paper has examined how the JMOFA came up with pamphlets on territorial issues as part of the preparation process leading up to the peace treaty talks between 1946 and 1949, as well as examined the contents and characteristics of these pamphlets, which were distributed to the Allied Powers.

In 1946, the JMOFA launched full-scale preparations on territorial issues that would be reflected in the eventual peace treaty and, as part of these endeavors, produced a total of seven volumes of reference material on major territorial issues alone for distribution to the United States and other Allies. The focus of these publications was on "minor islands" that the Allies would allow Japan to retain. Between November 1946 and June 1947, the JMOFA published a series of four pamphlets under the series title, *Minor Islands Adjacent to Japan Proper*. The wording of the series title, "Minor Islands Adjacent to Japan," clearly reflected the Potsdam Declaration's article: "Japanese sovereignty shall be limited to the islands of Honshu, Hokkaido, Kyushu, Shikoku, and such minor islands as we determine." The order in which the contents were published reflects the degree of importance of the islands as determined by the JMOFA: the Kuril Islands, the Ryukyu Islands (Okinawa), the Bonin Islands, and finally Dokdo and Ulleungdo. Additional references on territorial issues also appeared, which included *Sakhalin* (January 1949), *South Kuriles, Habomai Islands, Shikotan Island* (April 1949), and *Tsushima* (July 1949).

The JMOFA went ahead and produced sufficient references on territorial issues that were regarded as proper by the Allies. This production of references was possible thanks to a vast collection of backup data in existence, securing grounds for ownership in terms of both history and international law, the development of plausible arguments, and the availability of human resources dedicated to territorial issues. Not only that, the Japanese government managed to get these references into the hands of those who were handling Japanese territorial issues in the US government and the governments of other Allied Powers. Thereupon, Japan was able to

[34] Subject: Proposed Development of Iki and Tsushima Islands, Jan. 24, 1950 (NARA, RG 59, Decimal File, 794.022/1–2450).

express its concerns on territorial issues during the process of preparing a peace treaty, as well as after that treaty was concluded.

Though having been defeated in the war, Japan was still in possession of diplomatic experience, relevant systems, and well-trained personnel and was able to predict possible approaches on Japanese territorial issues by such powers as the United States, Great Britain, and the Soviet Union. The JMOFA understood the importance of territorial issues, collected and analyzed relevant data, identified historical and legal grounds for its claims, and developed logic to finally produce and deliver references to those in charge of territorial issues on the Allied side. The Japanese even managed to persuade the Allied policymakers of the justification of their references and arguments. The production and distribution of reference materials on territorial issues was at the core of the JMOFA's campaign to induce a favorable outcome from the Allies regarding its territories. Between 1946 and 1947, it successfully produced and distributed English references on major territorial issues, thereby overwhelming other interested countries, which were not making any such preparations, let alone putting their thoughts into writing.

With the United States reversing its policy toward Japan in 1948 and with the outbreak of the Korean War in 1950, concluding a peace treaty with Japan and the rearmament of Japan became inevitable. With the appointment of John Foster Dulles as a special envoy to the peace treaty talks with Japan in 1950, the movement for an early peace without the consent of Soviets, such as an announcement of Dulles' "Seven Principles," gained full momentum.

While Japan was officially and formally ending hostile relations with the victorious countries of World War II and restoring peace, the situation was different for its two neighbors, Korea and China. Despite being one of the victors, China was mired in its own civil war, which became serious in Manchuria in 1946, leading by 1949 to the Chinese Communist Party gaining control of almost the entire mainland with the Kuomintang withdrawing to Taiwan. The political and military standoff on the two sides of the Taiwan Strait did not allow China to properly respond to the San Francisco Peace Treaty.

Korea was divided, with two separate governments established in 1948 in the southern and northern halves of the peninsula. When the Korean War broke out in 1950, the United States/United Nations, the Soviet Union, and China entered the conflict, turning it into the largest international war in East Asia since the end of World War II. When Dulles made his second official visit to Tokyo in February 1951, Seoul had been recaptured by enemy forces, this time the Chinese. The Korean government was in crisis, as it faced possible evacuation to Jejudo or Okinawa. The overwhelming goal of Korea's diplomats was simple survival. That is, while Japan was regaining peace, Korea and China, previously colonized and occupied by Japan, were mired in civil war. Ironically, the communization of China and the Korean War prompted the conclusion of the peace treaty with Japan. Another irony is that Japan's peace came because of wars in the two nations it had previously invaded.

In the end, the desires of the Japanese government were to some extent reflected in the San Francisco Peace Treaty. Its stance on the southern Kurils gained the approval of POLAD-Japan and the Department of State, but the treaty, in which the Soviet Union did not participate, left the relevant clause vague. Japan's suggestion for the Ryukyus—the use of such names as Nansei Shoto and Nanpo Shoto—was accommodated in the treaty text. The Senkaku or Diaoyu Islands, which JMOFA spelled "Sento" Islands in the pamphlet, were not mentioned in the treaty, and neither was Dokdo, which Japan supposedly laid claim to.

Since his appearance at the negotiating table in 1950, Dulles pursued a simpler treaty document, and this was achieved. Different interests and conflicts among the various nations were not resolved but simply patched up, with territorial clauses greatly simplified. The United States introduced the handling of the ex-mandatory territories in the South Pacific and Okinawa (the Ryukyus) that concerned its own interests and let the other territorial clauses remain vague.

With the conclusion of the San Francisco Peace Treaty, peace was formally restored between Japan and the United States and its major allies, but hostile relations persisted between Japan and its neighbors in East Asia. It was only natural that Russia, China, and Korea, excluded from the San Francisco Peace Treaty, later came to engage in territorial disputes with Japan. On the surface, these seem to be conflicts with Japan only, but in truth, the United States, which attempted to use Cold War logic to deal with the outcomes of World War II, was a hidden cause.

References

Primary Sources

FO=Foreign Office (Gaimushō), Japanese Government. (1946). *Minor Islands Adjacent to Japan Proper, Part I. The Kurile Islands, The Habomais, and Shikotan.* In NARA, RG 84, Foreign Service Posts of the Department of State, Office of the US Political Advisor for Japan, Tokyo, Classified General Correspondence, 1945–1949, box 22.

FO=Foreign Office (Gaimushō), Japanese Government. (1947a). *Minor Islands Adjacent to Japan Proper, Part II. Ryukyu and Other Nansei Islands.*) In NARA, RG 84, Foreign Service Posts of the Department of State, Office of the US Political Advisor for Japan, Tokyo, Classified General Correspondence, 1945–1949, box 22.

FO=Foreign Office (Gaimushō), Japanese Government. (1947b). *Minor Islands Adjacent to Japan Proper, Part III. The Bonin Island Group, the Volcano Island Group.* In NARA, RG 84, Foreign Service Posts of the Department of State, Office of the US Political Advisor for Japan, Tokyo, Classified General Correspondence, 1945–1949, box 22.

FO=Foreign Office (Gaimushō), Japanese Government. (1947c). *Minor Islands Adjacent to Japan Proper, Part IV. Minor Islands in the Pacific, Minor Islands in the Japan Sea.* In NARARG 84, Foreign Service Posts of the Department of State, Office of the US Political Advisor for Japan, Tokyo, Classified General Correspondence, 1945–1949, box 22.

JMOFA=Ministry of Foreign Affairs (Gaimushō), Japanese Government. (1949a). *South Kuriles, Habomai Islands, Shikotan Island.* Ministry of Foreign Affairs.

JMOFA=Ministry of Foreign Affairs (Gaimushō), Japanese Government. (1949b). *Tsushima.* Ministry of Foreign Affairs.

JMOFA=Ministry of Foreign Affairs (Gaimushō), Japanese Government. (2006). *Nihon gaikō bunsho: Sanfuranshisuko heiwa jō yaku junbi taisaku (Japanese diplomatic documents:*

Preparations for the San Francisco Peace Treaty). Japanese Ministry of Foreign Affairs. https://www.mofa.go.jp/mofaj/ms/da/page25_001056.html

JMOFA=Ministry of Foreign Affairs (Gaimushō), Japanese Government. (2007). *Nihon gaikō bunsho: Sanfuranshisuko heiwa jōyaku taibei kōshō (Japanese diplomatic documents: Negotiations with the US for the San Francisco Peace Treaty)*. Japanese Ministry of Foreign Affairs. Available online https://www.mofa.go.jp/mofaj/ms/da/page25_001057.html

National Archives and Records Administration, United States (NARA). RG 84, Foreign Service Posts of the Department of State, Office of the US Political Advisor for Japan, Tokyo, Classified General Correspondence, 1945–1949, Box 22.

National Archives and Records Administration, United States (NARA). RG 59, Records Relating to the Treaty of Peace with Japan, Subject File, 1945–1951, Lot 56D527, Box 1.

National Archives and Records Administration, United States (NARA). RG 59, Records Relating to the Japanese Peace and Security Treaties, 1946–1952, Lot 78D173, Box 2.

National Archives and Records Administration, United States (NARA). RG 59, State Department, Decimal File, 694.001 series, 794.022 series, 740.0011PW(Peace) series, and 894.014 series.

The National Archives, United Kingdom (TNA). (1951). FO 371/92535, FJ 1022/171, "Japanese Peace Treaty: Second revised draft of the Japanese Peace Treaty," March 1951; FO 371/92538, FJ 1022/222, "Provisional Draft of Japanese Peace Treaty (United Kingdom)," April 7.

Secondary Sources

Cheong, S.-H. (1991). *The politics of anti-Japanese sentiment in Korea: Japanese-South Korean relations under American occupation, 1945–1952*. Greenwood Press.

Hara, K. (1998). *Japanese-soviet Russian relations since 1945: A difficult peace*. Routledge.

Hara, K. (2005). *Sanfuranshisuko heiwa jōyaku no mōten: Ajia Taiheiyō chiiki no reisen to "sengo mikaiketsu no shomondai" (Cold War Frontiers in the Asia-Pacific: The troubling legacy of the San Francisco Treaty)*. Keisuisha.

Jo, S.-H. (2008). Je 2 cha segye daejeon hu miguk-ui daeil jeollyak-gwa dokdo gwisong munje (US strategy toward Japan after the Second World War and the Dokdo issue). *Gukje jiyeok yeongu (Review of International and Area Studies), 17*(2), 41–80.

Jung, B.-J. (2010). *Dokdo 1947 (Dokdo 1947)*. Dolbegae.

Jung, B.-J. (2012). 1953–1954 nyeon dokdo-eseo-ui han-il chungdol-gwa hanguk-ui dokdo suho jeongchaek (Korea-Japan confrontation over Dokdo from 1953 to 1954 and Korea's policy to guard Dokdo). *Hanguk dongnip undongsa yeongu (Research on the History of the Korean Independence Movement), 41*, 389–450.

Lee, S.-U. (1998). *Ilbon-ui yeongto bunjaeng-gwa saenpueuransisueuko pyeonghwa joya (Japan's territorial disputes and the San Francisco Peace Treaty)*. Inha University Press.

Lee, J.-H. (2001). Dok-do gatgetda ilbon paejeon dwi daemi robi (The defeated Japan lobbied the US for ownership of Dokdo), *Joongang Ilbo*, December 23.

Nishimura, K. (1971). *Nihon gaikō-shi 27: Sanfuranshisuko heiwa jō yaku (Japan's diplomatic history 27: The San Francisco Peace Treaty)*. Kajima Research Institute Press.

Okuhara, H. (1907). *Takeshima oyobi Utsuyōtō (Takeshima and Utsuryoto)*. Hokosha.

Park, B.-S. (2014). Daeil ganghwa joyakwa Dok-do Jeju-do Kuril Ryukyuje-do, (San Francisco Peace Treaty and Dokdo, Jejudo, the Kuril Islands, and the Ryukyu Islands). *Dokdo yeongu (A Study of Dokdo), 16*, 154–155.

Sebald, W. J., & Brines, R. (1965). *With MacArthur in Japan: A personal history of the occupation*. W. W. Norton & Company.

Sin, B.-R. (2001). *Hanguk bundansa yeongu, 1943–1953 (A study of Korea's history of division, 1943–1953)*. Hanul Academy.

Song, B.-G. (1999). *Ulleungdo-wa Dokdo (Ulleungdo and Dokdo)*. Dankook University Press.

Takasaki, S. (1998). *Geomjeung han-il hoedam (Verification: Japan-Korean Talks)* (K. Yeong-jin, Trans.). Cheongsu seowon. Originally published as *Kenshō nikkan kaidan* (Iwanami shoten, 1996).

Takeso, S. (1984). *Sengo nihon gaikō no shōgen: nihon wa kōshite saisei shita 1 (Testimony to Japan's postwar diplomacy: How Japan revived 1).* (N. Nagan, Ed.). Research Institute for Public Administration.

Unryu, S. (2000). *Sovereign rights and territorial space in Sino-Japanese relations: Irredentism and the Diaoyu/Senkaku Islands.* Association for Asian Studies and University of Hawai'i Press.

Wada, H. (1990). *Hoppō ryōdo mondai o kangaeru (Thoughts on the northern territories dispute).* Iwanami shoten.

Wada, H. (2013). *Dongbuk asia yeongto munje, eotteoke haegyeolhal geosinga (How to resolve Northeast Asian territorial issues)* (I. Gyeong-taek, Trans.). Sakyejul. Originally published as *Ryōdo mondai o dō kaiketsu suruka: tairitsu kara taiwa e* (Heibonsha, 2012).

Yoshida, S. (1958). *Kaisō jūnen (Reminiscence of ten years)* (Vol. 3). Shinchosha.

The San Francisco System and The Human Right

Unlawfulness of Japan's Colonization of Korean Peninsula: Korea's Declaration of January 21, 1904, and Japan's Violation of International Law

Etsuro Totsuka

Abstract This article examines the illegality of Japan's colonization of the Korean Peninsula, focusing on the period from the 1904 declaration of neutrality by the Korean Empire through the 1910 annexation. It argues that Japan's military invasion and occupation of Korea constituted a serious violation of customary wartime international law, particularly the law of neutrality, as Korea's neutrality was internationally recognized but disregarded by Japan. The paper analyzes the An Chunggun case, highlighting how Japanese courts ignored wartime international law and instead applied domestic criminal law, undermining Korea's sovereignty. The study demonstrates that key treaties, such as the 1904 Protocol and the 1905 Protectorate Treaty (Eulsa Treaty), were invalid due to coercion, lack of ratification, and procedural defects. It further contends that the 1910 Annexation Treaty was also null and void, as it was based on these illegitimate agreements and lacked proper authorization. The article draws on historical and legal sources to show that Japan's occupation was unlawful under both contemporary and modern international law. This conclusion aligns with the 2018 ruling of the Republic of Korea's Supreme Court. The paper underscores the importance of recognizing these violations for historical justice and future reconciliation in East Asia.

Keywords An Chunggun · Annexation · Coercion · Eulsa Treaty · International law · Japan · Korea · Neutrality · Protectorate Treaty · Sovereignty

The Judgment of the Republic of Korea's Supreme Court of October 30, 2018, ruled that Japan's military occupation of the Korean Peninsula was illegal and that the

---

E. Totsuka (✉)
International Human rights Law, Ryukoku University Law School, Kyoto, Japan
e-mail: etsuro@jcom.zaq.ne.jp

Y.-H. Kim et al. (eds.), *Beyond the San Francisco System*,
https://doi.org/10.1007/978-981-95-3328-2_14

colonization of Korea was unlawful.[1] This ruling was based on the Constitution of the ROK. One may ask, then, what about under international law? Was Japan's occupation of the Korean Peninsula illegal under international law?

The large troops of the Japanese Empire landed at Incheon, which was the territory of the Korean Empire, on February 8, 1904, and continued their military occupation of the Korean Peninsula till August 15, 1945. It took place, however, before wars were generally banned by the Kellogg-Briand Pact of 1928.[2] Even so, was this military invasion by Japan against Korea illegal under any international law?

"Yes, it was," thinks this speaker.

He considers that it was a serious violation of then customary wartime international law of neutrality,[3] which guaranteed inviolability of the territory of a neutral country. One must not forget that the Korean Empire made the declaration of neutrality on January 21, 1904, which the Japanese Empire completely ignored.

It is essential to understand this Japan's military invasion against Korea was "WAR" under wartime international law. This speaker presented the following views in Daegu lately at AAS-Asia Conference.[4]

1 The Judgment of An Chunggun Case

The Judgment (February 14, 1910) by the Regional Court of the Kwantung of the Empire of Japan (Lushun) was published in the Diplomatic Bulletin by MOFA of Japan.[5]

The main text said, "Defendant An Chunggun shall be executed." Lieutenant General An Chunggun of the Korean Voluntary Corps did not appeal the ruling. He

[1] 金昌禄『韓国大法院強制動員判決、核心は「不法強占」である』参照。著者が2022年8月に韓国の知識産業社を通じて出版した「大法院の強制動員判決、核心は『不法強占』である」を日本語に翻訳し、「法律事務所の資料棚アーカイブ」に掲載したものである。 http://justice.skr.jp/documents/nocciolo.pdf 2023年5月14日閲覧。

[2] The Kellogg-Briand Pact was an agreement to outlaw war signed on August 27, 1928.

[3] Convention (V) respecting the Rights and Duties of Neutral Powers and Persons in Case of War on Land. The Hague, 18 October 1907. Article 1. The territory of neutral Powers is inviolable. This principle had already existed as customary international law, which was confirmed by the 1907 Hague Peace Conference. It was known before 1904 by the Japanese scholars, who published academic works. See: 戸塚悦朗「韓半島植民地支配の不法性(その4——1904年1月21日大韓帝国中立宣言と「不法強占」」龍谷法学56巻4号2024 (in print)。

[4] Etsuro Totsuka, "Violence and Anti-Violence in Early Twentieth-Century China, Japan, and Korea, On the Judgment of the Trial of Lieutenant General An Chunggun of the Voluntary Corp." The 8th AAS-in-Asia Conference, 2023 AAS-in-Asia, June 24–27, 2–23, Daegu, Korea, Session Id: 3344, Session Title: Violence and Anti-Violence in Early Twentieth-Century China, Japan, and Korea, Date: Sunday, June 25, 2023, Time: 2:00 PM – 3:50 PM.

[5] 関東都督府地方法院判官真鍋十蔵「安重根外三名に対する判決」明治43年2月14日、外交要報第12号明治43年3月31日外務大臣官房、101–113頁。 https://www.jacar.archives.go.jp/aj/meta/listPhoto?LANG=default&BID=F2013090216110010414&ID=M2013090216110110424&REFCODE=B13080611200 2022年12月5日閲覧。

was executed by hanging in Lushun Prison on March 26, 1910, 5 months after the date of the shooting death of Duke Hirobumi Ito in Haolbin (October 26, 1909).

What were the findings? The part of the judgment in the reasons for the judgment related to the act of Lieutenant General An Chunggun of the Voluntary Corps is as follows.

> On October 26, 1909, shortly after 9:00 AM at the Haolbin Station of the Dongshing Railway in Russia, the defendant, An Chunggun, aimed at the Chairperson of the Privy Council, Duke Hirobumi Ito, and his entourage with the intention of killing them, and fired a series of pistols that belonged to him, three of which fell on the Duke and killed him.

Although An Chunggun asserted that the court should apply wartime international law, as he was fighting to defend his own country as a member of the Korean Voluntary Corps against war waged by Japan, the court completely ignored his arguments; instead, the judge wrongly applied the Japanese domestic criminal code (Art. 199) instead of wartime international law.

We need to give a thorough thought to the hidden reason why the court avoided to applying wartime international law. This speaker speculates that Japan might have thought that it was vital to let peoples of the world give no attention to wartime international law, which could reveal the real nature of Japan's illegal invasion against Korea under wartime international law.

Recently, President Park Geun Hye of the ROK welcomed the decision of China to erect a monument of An in Haolbin. Then, the Japanese government protested, and the government of Japan labeled An Chunggun as a "criminal" and "terrorist".[6] Is this legally right?

There were only very few research on the legal aspects of the An Chunggun vs. Ito Hirobumi case in Japan or elsewhere.[7] The speaker will explore the reasons why An Chunggun shot Ito and the legal nature of the An Chunggun trial by Japan, as an example of an antiviolence case made by the people defending his own country from unlawful, huge systematic military violence, namely, war.

2 Why Did An Chunggun Shoot Ito?

Having been arrested shortly after he shot Hirobumi Ito on October 26, 1909, An was interrogated by prosecutor Mizobuchi, who was a Japanese, about the reason why he shot Ito. In response, he wrote 15 articles about Hirobumi Ito's guilt in Chinese at Lushun Prison. It contained a brief description of important events of violence that symbolized the extremely violent process of Japanese colonization of

---

[6] Japan protest over Korean assassin Ahn Jung-geun, 20 January 2014 BBC https://www.bbc.com/news/world-asia-25808437 visited on 4 June 2023.

[7] TOTSUKA, Etsuro, The An Chunggun Trial and Peace in the East, in Yi Tae-Jin et al. (ed.) Peace in the East: An Chunggun's Vision for Asia in the Age of Japanese Imperialism, Lexington Books, 2017, pp. 85–109.

Korea. Taken together, this clearly showed that Ito's idea of peace in the East was based on constant and systematic military violence against An's country, the Korean Empire.

Was such military violence, as accused by An Chunggun, lawful under wartime international law?

3 Unlawfulness of Japan's Occupation of Korea: "Korean War" (1904–1945)

This speaker wishes to focus on the historical fact that the invasion and occupation by the military forces of Imperial Japan against Korea constituted of serious violation of international law of neutrality.

Professor Emeritus Wada Haruki, in his article "The Russo-Japanese War and the Annexation of Korea: Thinking from the Russia Factor," states that the Chosun War existed alongside the Russo-Japanese War.[8]

Russia did not think of occupying Korea and supported the Korean Empire's policy of neutrality. If a neutral Korean Empire had been realized, it would have provided a buffer zone and greatly reduced Russia's threat to Japan. It was a rational foreign policy, considering Switzerland's permanent neutrality policy in Europe and later Sweden's.

Philosophers had already unveiled their vision for peace, and it was a major international challenge whether the international community of the twentieth century could achieve world peace by curbing imperialist wars that had taken territorial competition for granted. This issue was discussed at the first international conference in the Hague held in 1899, which was followed by the Second in 1907. The first Hague Peace Conference, held immediately after Gojong declared the establishment of the Korean Empire, failed to decide on a general ban on war. However, the first conference succeeded in adopting important treaties that codified the laws of war and institutionalized the rules for the peaceful settlement of international disputes, and the second conference in 1907 made many treaties, including one for the law of neutrality. The conferences basically confirmed and codified preexisting customary wartime international law.

According to Article 1 of the Hague Convention (V) respecting the Rights and Duties of Neutral Powers and Persons in Case of War on Land, the Hague, October 18, 1907, signed at the Second Hague Peace Conference, "The territory of neutral Powers is inviolable."[9]

---

[8] 和田春樹「日露戦争と韓国併合——ロシアという要因から考える」笹川紀勝監修=邊英浩・都時煥編著『国際共同研究韓国強制併合一〇〇年: 歴史と課題』明石書店2013年、81–101頁。

[9] Convention (V) respecting the Rights and Duties of Neutral Powers and Persons in Case of War on Land. The Hague, 18 October 1907. https://ihl-databases.icrc.org/en/ihl-treaties/hague-conv-v-1907 visited on June 4, 2023.

Therefore, it was not unreasonable for Gojong, who became the Emperor of the Korean Empire, and the people of Korea to hope that in the twentieth century, international law might guarantee world peace and to survive peacefully by adopting a policy of neutrality. It is necessary to recall that it was such a new era.

According to Wada's essay, "At this time, the Korean Emperor, Gojong, was the first to formally lay out the line that Korea could be seen as a neutral country and asked the Japanese government for its approval. In August of nineteen hundred, Cho Byung-shik was sent to Japan as Minister. In response, the Russian Minister to Japan, Isvolsky, strongly supported the idea, and he persuaded both the Russian foreign minister, Lamsdorff, and the Emperor to support it. ・・・ When Isvolsky formally made a proposal to the Japanese government in January 1901, Kato firmly rejected the proposal, also after hearing the opinion of Komura, the Japanese Minister to Qing. ・・・ It can be seen that the confrontation between Japan and Russia became decisive from this moment."

The world powers supported the Korean Empire's policy of neutrality. "On January 21, (1904) external neutrality was actually declared. ・・・・ The United Kingdom and Germany sent their acceptance responses to the declaration on January 22, France on the 25th, and Italy on the 29th," said Professor Emeritus Yi Tae-jin.[10]

Had they succeeded in such a shift at this time in the early twentieth century, there was a good chance that Japan could have avoided becoming engulfed in a violent and disastrous foreign policy that would then lead to the Manchurian Incident, the Sino-Japanese War, and the Asia-Pacific War.

Japanese leaders, however, adhered to the teachings of Shoin Yoshida and never abandoned their aggressive policy of attempting to rule the Korean Empire by force. Hirobumi Ito was one of its key leaders. Wada's essay describes the situation just before the outbreak of the Russo-Japanese War as follows: "This is where the negotiations between Japan and Russia begin. The basic point of conflict in these negotiations is that Japan sought recognition for having 'superior interests' in Korea and recognition for making Korea a protectorate, while Russia refused to recognize Japan's unrestricted control over Korea. This was expressed in the Russian provision that 'no part of Korean territory is used for strategic purposes.' The Japanese finally did not accept the clause, and the Russians did not lower it. Russia did not claim sovereignty over Korea itself."

The Russo-Japanese War was preceded by the start of the Korean War, an invasion by the Empire of Japan against the Korean Empire, which had declared itself war-time neutrality, and the subsequent military action by the Empire of Japan against Korea in violation of international law, thus illegal 'forced occupation' continued until August 15, 1945.

"On February 6, 1904, Japan notified the Russian government of the end of negotiations, the severance of diplomatic relations and declared that it reserved the right to act independently."

---

[10] 李泰鎮「一九〇四 ~ 一九一〇年、韓国国権侵奪条約の手続き上の不法性」笹川紀勝=李泰鎮 (共編著)『国際共同研究・韓国併合と現代——歴史と国際法からの再検討 』明石書店、2008年、122頁。

Wada's essay continues.

"The war known as the Russo-Japanese War began with the Japanese Navy's occupation of Chinhae Bay and the Masan City Telegraph Office on February 6, 1904. The Japanese landed at Incheon in the evening of February 8 and advanced to Seoul the next morning. The above can be seen as an act of open aggression against the Korean Empire, which declared its wartime neutrality, and the start of the Korean War. … The Japanese occupation extended to Pyongyang, and in March, the occupation forces were given the name resident army in Korea. The size was two divisions."

4 The Protocol of February 23, 1904, was *null and void* ab initio

The policy of neutrality, as the major foreign policy established by Emperor Gojong, has been given some attention in research on Korean modern history.[11] In Japan, the neutrality of Korea was also researched by Japanese historians.[12] However, more rigorous works are welcome, as it has decisive legal importance when we scrutinize the unlawfulness of Japan's colonization of the Korean Peninsula.

The Korean Empire made the declaration of neutrality on January 21, 1904. Although the territory of the neutral independent state, namely, the Korean Empire, was inviolable under the customary wartime international law, having ignored the rule of international law, the large troops of the Japanese Empire invaded at Incheon on February 8, 1904, and they soon occupied the whole Korean Peninsula.

On February 22, 1904, Russia severely accused of this illegal aggression by Japan.[13]

The Japanese Empire had to act quickly in addressing its violation of international law, and, on the next day, they demanded that the Foreign Minister of the Korean Empire sign the Protocol of February 23, 1904.[14] The Protocol included a provision that the Japanese military could use any Korean territory for strategic purposes. If this Protocol had been legally effective, the Korean Empire would have

---

[11] 엄찬호「高宗의對外政策研究」(A Study on the Foreign Policy of King Kojong) 한글로보기 http://www.riss.kr/link?id=T8052535. 韓国語の研究(英文サマリーあり) = 博士論文を参照 (URLは、http://www.riss.kr/search/detail/DetailView.do?p_mat_type=be54d9b8bc7cdb09&control_no=05a19e321d27fd24 2023年10月11日閲覧。

[12] 大澤博明「明治外交と朝鮮永世中立化構想の展開: 一八八二~八四年」熊本法学83巻 1995年、289–341頁。https://kumadai.repo.nii.ac.jp/records/26183 2023年10月9日閲覧。

[13] 和田春樹「日露戦争と韓国併合——ロシアという要因から考える」前掲笹川ほか『国際共同研究韓国強制併合一〇〇年』81–101頁。なお、この論文の基礎になる研究としては、和田春樹『日露戦争:起源と開戦(上)』岩波書店2009年12月及び同『日露戦争:起源と開戦(下)』岩波書店2010年2月がある。

[14] 総督府編纂『韓国条約彙纂』(明治四十一年十月、1908年)「日韓議定書(明治三十七年二月二十三日調印)」https://lab.ndl.go.jp/dl/book/798123?page=10 2023年10月14日閲覧。

been regarded as an allied state of Japan, and then Korea's neutrality would have ended on the day.[15] As a result, the question of whether this Protocol is legally effective or not has a significant impact on our research, whether Japan's occupation of the Korean Peninsula is illegal or not.

Besides serious defects in the process of treaty-making, such as bribery and violence,[16] it had similar problems to other old treaties between the Japanese Empire and the Korean Empire as follows. The full power of Emperor Gojong was not issued to the foreign minister, who signed the Protocol as the representative of the Korean Imperial Government, and the treaty was not ratified by Gojong, who had the authority to conclude the treaty. It must therefore be considered that the Protocol of February 23, 1904, did not enter into force and was not legally concluded.[17]

As a result, this Protocol, legally speaking, was ***null and void*** **ab initio**, and neutrality of the Korean Empire must have continued even after February 23, 1904.

Thus, the Korean War, by the Empire of Japan, continued even after that.

5 Illegality of the Nikkan-Kyoyaku of November 17, 1905

What took place in the midst of this war was the military occupation of the royal palace by Duke Hirobumi Ito in order to press for the compulsory conclusion of the Protectorate Treaty, dated November 17, 1905, referred to as the "Nikkan-Kyoyaku" (日韓協約) according to the Book of Treaties published by the Ministry of Foreign Affairs.

An Chunggun was one of the members of the Korean Voluntary Corps, who tried to defend their own country against such unlawful, huge, systematic military violence inflicted by Japan.

The speaker has been studying since 1992 the illegality of the Nikkan-Kyoyaku of November 17, 1905, and the illegality of the trial of An Chunggun.

The conclusions are summarized as follows.

1. Both the League of Nations study (the Harvard draft) and the 1963 report to the General Assembly of the United Nations International Law Commission (ILC) stated that the 1905 treaty (the so-called Protectorate Treaty) was absolutely ***null***

---

[15] 遠藤源六『日露戦役国際法論全』明治大学出版部, 明41年(1908年)7月、438頁は、「然ルニ二月二十三日ニ至リ日韓議定書成立シ韓國皇室ノ安寧又ハ領土ノ保全ニ危險アルトキハ我國カ臨機必要ナル措置ヲ取ルヘク韓國ハ我國ノ行動ヲ容易ナラシムル為メ十分便宜ヲ與フルコト竝此ノ目的ヲ達スル為メ軍略上必要ナル地點ヲ臨機収用スルノ權ヲ我國ニ與フルコトヲ約シタリ故ニ韓國の地位ハ該議定書ニ因リテ一變シ我攻守同盟國トナレリ・・・」としている。

[16] 李泰鎮「一九〇四 ~ 一九一〇年、韓国国権侵奪条約の手続き上の不法性」笹川紀勝=李泰鎮 (共編著)『国際共同研究· 韓国併合と現代——歴史と国際法からの再検討 』明石書店、2008年、113–124頁。

[17] 白忠鉉「日本の韓国併合に対する国際法的考察」前掲『国際共同研究· 韓国併合と現代』、389頁。

and void because of threats against individual representatives of the Korean Empire.

2. There exists no original copy of the "Nikkan-Kyoyaku" dated November 17, 1905. The existing document is only a draft treaty with a blank line instead of the title. Therefore, the existence of a treaty with this title cannot be proven.
3. The full power of Emperor Gojong was not issued to the foreign minister, Park Sai-jun, who signed the treaty as the representative of the Korean Imperial Government, and the treaty was not ratified by Emperor Gojong, who had the authority to conclude the treaty. It must therefore be considered that the treaty did not enter into force and was not legally concluded.

Therefore, we must conclude that the trial by the court, which found the jurisdiction to try a Korean subject, An Chunggun, citing the "Nikkan-Kyoyaku" (日韓協約)dated November 17, 1905, was unlawful, namely, ***null and void***, as the court had no legal basis for legitimate jurisdiction.

It was the same as a mock trial.

As a result, the execution of An Chunggun (March 26, 1910, at Lushun Prison) was due to the death sentence imposed by an unlawful trial that lacked a legitimate legal jurisdiction, and it was an unlawful killing of a person by the state.

On top of that, the Empire of Japan failed in legally making the Empire of Korea a protectorate state, and its independence was unchanged. Further, the Treaty of Annexation of the Korean Empire to the Japanese Empire of August 22, 1910, didn't take any effect, as it was made on the basis of the Nikkan-Kyoyaku of November 17, 1905, which doesn't exist.

For details, please refer to the literature in the list of articles this speaker made at the end of this paper.

6 Conclusion

These legal judgments make Japan's military occupation of the Korean Peninsula illegal, and the colonization of Korea was unlawful under international law. This conclusion supports the Judgment of the Republic of Korea's Supreme Court of October 30, 2018.

戸塚悦朗著文献リスト
1905年**11**月**17**日付日韓協約の不存在及び安重根義軍**参**謀中**将**裁判の不法性
2022年**11**月**17**日現在
(論文)

1. 「統監府設置100年と乙巳保護条約の不法性——1963年国連国際法委員会報告書をめぐってーー」『龍谷法学』39巻1号、2006年6月、15–42頁。

2. 「安重根裁判の不法性と東洋平和」龍谷法学42巻2号、2009年、1–27頁。 https://mylibrary.ryukoku.ac.jp/iwjs0005opc/TD00069008
3. 「最終講義に代えて—「韓国併合」100年の原点を振り返る-一1905年「韓国保護条約(?)」は捏造されたのか」龍谷法学42巻3号、2010年、311–336頁。(「韓国併合」100年市民ネットワーク編『今、「韓国併合」を問う ~ 強制と暴力· 植民地支配の原点 ~ 』アジェンダプロジェクト、2010年、45–65頁に、「1905年「韓国保護条約(?)」は捏造だったのか)として転載) https://mylibrary.ryukoku.ac.jp/iwjs0005opc/TD00070024
4. 「東アジアの平和と歴史認識—安重根東洋平和論宣揚の必要性をめぐって」龍谷法学、45巻3号、2012年12月、957–993頁。 https://mylibrary.ryukoku.ac.jp/iwjs0005opc/TD00373001
5. 「龍谷大学における安重根東洋平和論研究の歩み: 100年の眠りからさめた遺墨(上)」、龍谷大学社会科学研究所社会科学年報第44号、2014年5月、57–66頁。 https://mylibrary.ryukoku.ac.jp/iwjs0005opc/TD00493015
6. 「龍谷大学における安重根東洋平和論研究の歩み: 100年の眠りからさめた遺墨(下)」、龍谷大学社会科学研究所社会科学年報第44号、2014年5月、67–78頁。 https://mylibrary.ryukoku.ac.jp/iwjs0005opc/TD00493010

(著書)

7. 『「徴用工問題」とは何か?——韓国大法院判決が問うもの』明石書店、2019年10月、1–209頁。
8. 『歴史認識と日韓の「和解」への道——徴用工問題と韓国大法院判決を理解するために』日本評論社、2019年11月、1–248頁。
9. 『日韓関係の危機をどう乗り越えるか?—植民地支配責任のとりかた』アジェンダ· プロジェクト、2021年4月、1–69頁。

Remedies for the Victims of Crimes Against Humanity: The Case of Comfort Women and Forced Labor

Tae-Ung Baik

Abstract The United Nations Committee on Enforced Disappearances expressed its concern about the lack of statistical information on the number of so-called comfort women, who may have been subjected to enforced disappearance, and about the absence of investigations, prosecutions, and convictions of perpetrators in its Concluding Observations on December 8, 2018. However, Japan vigorously denied its responsibility. On October 30, 2018, the Supreme Court of the Republic of Korea issued a decision ordering a Japanese firm to pay approximately $88,000 in damages to each of the four forced labor victims of World War II. The Seoul Central District Court and the Civil Division 33 of the Seoul High Court, on January 8, 2021, and November 23, 2023, respectively, also concluded that the Japanese government should pay damages to the Korean women forced into sexual slavery for Japan's military. Japan again protested that these decisions are unacceptable under international law, arguing that the claims had already been "completely and finally" settled. This article discusses the rights of victims of crimes against humanity, namely comfort women and forced labor victims to demand truth, justice, reparation, and guarantees of non-recurrence and the obligations of Japan to provide effective remedies for the victims.

This article is a revised and edited version of the author's presentation given at the Beyond San Francisco Treaty System Conference held in Seoul on December 15, 2023. It is also based on the article written in Korean, *The Victims of Crimes Against Humanity and the 1965 Settlement Agreement Between Japan and the Republic of Korea (*Iljeha Banindobeomjoi Pihaejaua 1965 Han Il Chongugwon Hyupjeong), which was published as a book chapter in GOING BEYOND THE SAN FRANCISCO SYSTEM (San Francisco chejereul neomeoseo) (476-96 (Young-ho Kim ed., Medichi, 2022*)*. This work was in part supported by the Strategic Research Institute Program for Korean Studies of the Republic of Korea Ministry of Education and by the Korean Studies Promotion Service at the Academy of Korean Studies (AKS-2020-SRI-2200001).
Former-Chair Rapporteur of the UN Human Rights Council Working Group on Enforced or Involuntary Disappearances.

T.-U. Baik (✉)
William S. Richardson School of Law, University of Hawaii at Manoa, Honolulu, HI, USA
e-mail: tubaik@hawaii.edu

Y.-H. Kim et al. (eds.), *Beyond the San Francisco System*,
https://doi.org/10.1007/978-981-95-3328-2_15

Keywords Japan · Korea · South Korea · Supreme Court · Comfort women · Crimes against humanity · Forced labor · Reparations · Sovereign immunity · Victims

1 Introduction

On November 6, 2018, the United Nations Committee on Enforced Disappearances considered Japan's initial state-party report. The Committee, established under the International Convention for the Protection of All Persons from Enforced Disappearance (CED), reviews the implementation of the provisions of the Convention. In its Concluding Observation issued on December 8, 2018, the Committee expressed its concern about the lack of statistical information on the number of so-called comfort women, who may have been subjected to enforced disappearance, and about the absence of investigations, prosecutions, and convictions of perpetrators in these cases.[1]

However, the government of Japan responded with a complete denial. Japan asserted: "Although Japan had conducted full-scale fact-finding studies on the issue of comfort women [......], forceful taking away of comfort women by the military and Government authorities could not be confirmed in any of the documents in those studies."[2] While the Committee expressed concerns about the lack of adequate reparation for the victims, Japan's position was that the issue "was resolved finally and irreversibly."[3] The Committee expressed concern about the attitude, pointing out that it perpetuates impunity for perpetrators and denies victims their rights to truth, justice, reparations, and guarantees of non-repetition.[4] The Committee particularly highlighted (i) the lack of compensation for comfort women victims, (ii) the lack of efforts to uncover the truth about disappearances, (iii) the lack of statistics on potentially disappeared comfort women, and (iv) issues of forced abortions, emphasizing the need to enhance the protection of victims' human rights under international human rights law. Japan's vehement denial of the committee's judgments and evaluations led to friction with the UN treaty body. Japan's significant influence through financial contributions to the UN has sparked considerable controversy.

Regarding the lawsuits for compensation filed by victims of Japanese military sexual slavery (so-called comfort women) and forced labor during the Japanese occupation, more rulings in South Korean courts are awarding remedies to the

---

[1] Committee on Enforced Disappearances(UN), *Concluding Observations on the Report Submitted by Japan under article 29(1) of the Convention*(2018.11.12). CED/C/JPN/CO/1 Dec 5, 2018.

[2] Id.

[3] Id.

[4] Cho Ki-weon and Park Min-hee, *UN declares Japan's compensation to comfort women as inadequate,* Hankyoreh Daily Nov 21, 2018. http://english.hani.co.kr/arti/english_edition/e_international/871186.html (last visited 2/1/25).

victims. One of the most notable rulings was made on January 8, 2021, by the Civil Division 34 of the Seoul Central District Court (Presiding Judge Kim Jeong-gon) in a lawsuit filed by 12 victims of Japanese military sexual slavery, including the late Ms. Bae Chun-hee, against the Japanese government.[5] The court ruled that the issue of Japanese military sexual slavery was a premeditated, systematic, and widespread crime against humanity that violated international peremptory norms and that state immunity could not be applied even if it was a sovereign act of the state.[6] The court recognized the jurisdiction of the South Korean court over the defendant and ordered Japan to compensate each victim with 100 million won.[7] This rulings was a result of the long-standing efforts of the victims and civil society to realize human rights protection through the South Korean judiciary over the past decades.

On the other hand, on April 21, 2021, in a lawsuit filed by 20 victims of Japanese military sexual slavery, including Ms. Lee Yong-soo and the late Ms. Kwak Ye-nam, against the Japanese government, the Civil Division 15 of the Seoul Central District Court (Presiding Judge Min Seong-cheol) ruled that the South Korean court did not have jurisdiction over the case based on Japan's sovereign immunity. This ruling was overturned on November 23, 2023 by the Civil Division 33 of the Seoul High Court (Judges Goo Hoi-geun, Hwang Seong-mi, Heo Ik-su). The High Court rejected the District Dourt's ruling stating, "We cancel the first trial's decision and fully recognize the plaintiffs' claim amount." The court awarded victims and families of the Japanese military's comfort women compensation of 200 million won per person.[8]

Similarly, on June 7, 2021, in a compensation lawsuit filed by forced labor victims during the Japanese occupation against 16 Japanese companies, the Civil Division 34 of the Seoul Central District Court (Presiding Judge Kim Yang-ho) dismissed the case, stating that "the individual claims of South Korean citizens against Japan or Japanese nationals cannot be considered to have been extinguished or waived by the Claims Agreement," but that "their exercise through litigation is restricted."[9] The ruling highlighted the Court's conservative approach concerning state immunity even in the face of the worst crimes against humanity. It clearly demonstrated the limitations that the South Korean legal community must overcome. This case was again overturned, on February 1, 2024, in the appellate court proceeding, by the Civil Division 33 of the Seoul High Court (Judge Koo Hoe-geun, Hwang

---

[5] Seoul Central District Court, 34th Civil Division, 2016GaHap505092 (S. Kor.).

[6] Id.

[7] Id.

[8] *See Comfort women win appeal for damages against Japan..."Full amount claimed"* (Uianbu Pihaeja Ilbon Sangdae Sonhaebaesang Hangsosim Seungso… Cheonggu Geumaek Jeonbu Injeong), SBS News, Nov. 23, 2023 https://news.sbs.co.kr/news/endPage.do?news_id=N1007435489&plink=COPYPASTE&cooper=SBSNEWSEND (last visited 2/1/25).

[9] Seoul Central District Court, 2015 Ga-hap 13718, 2021. 6. 7. (S. Kor.).

Sung-mi, and Heo Ik-soo), which found the trial court's dismissal to be flawed and remanded the case to the Seoul Central District Court.[10]

Through these various rulings of South Korean courts, the judicial stance on the lawsuits for damages filed by victims of Japanese military sexual slavery and forced labor during the Japanese occupation appears to be moving toward awarding legal damages to the victims.

Nevertheless, the Yun Suk Yeol government tried to solve the problem of compensation through a third-party reimbursement plan regardless of the courts' decisions. In other words, the South Korean government was proposed to pay for the damages out of South Korean funds on behalf of Japan and Japanese corporations. Some victims have decided to accept the compensation from the South Korean government, while others are still seeking judicial remedies from Japan.[11]

The international political repercussions surrounding this issue have not yet been fully resolved, and the South Korea-Japan bilateral relationship is still somewhat entangled like a complex web. The logic of courts' rulings appears to reflect these complex internal and external circumstances. Hence, it is crucial to carefully examine the fundamental approaches of various courts in exploring the solutions to the serious human rights violations.

2 Court Rulings in South Korea

2.1 Japanese Military Comfort Women Victims

One of the major rulings related to the claims of Japanese military sexual slavery victims by the Constitutional Court of Korea was made on August 30, 2011. The Constitutional Court ruled that the Korean government's failure to make efforts to resolve the claims for damages by Japanese military comfort women victims through diplomatic channels under Article 3 of the "Agreement on the Settlement of Problems Concerning Property and Claims and Economic Cooperation between the Republic of Korea and Japan" (hereinafter referred to as the "Claims Agreement") was unconstitutional.[12] This ruling provided a significant turning point.

[10] Seoul High Court, 2012Na2031703, Feb.1.2024 (S. Kor.). *See also* Jaeho Lee, *The High Court Remands the District Curts Decision that Dismissed Forced Labor Victims Claims against the Supreme Court Decision* (Daebeop Panrye Ggaego Gangjedongwon Sonbaeso Gakhahaetdeon Pangyeol, 2simseo Pagi Hwansong) HANKYOEREH DAILEY Feb. 1.2024. https://www.hani.co.kr/arti/society/society_general/1126900.html (last visited 2/1/25) .

[11] *See* Hyeri Kim and Hyeri Lee, *'Third-party reimbursement'legal battle inevitable—Yoon's government ignores 'victims' rights'* (Je3ja byunje beopjeok datum bulgapi… Pihaeja kwonri oimyunhan Yun Suk Yeol jeongbu), Kyunghyangsinmun, Mar. 6, 2023, https://www.khan.co.kr/article/202303061749001 (last visited 2/1/25).

[12] *See* 2006 Hun-Ma 788, Aug. 30, 2011 (23-2(A) KCCR, 366) (S. Kor.).

Following this ruling by the Constitutional Court, the Korean government established the "Task Force on Measures for the Korea-Japan Claims Agreement" within the Ministry of Foreign Affairs and Trade in September 2011 and sent a verbal note requesting bilateral consultations on the issue of comfort women victims' claims, but Japan did not respond actively. During the Korea-United States-Japan summit on March 25, 2014, the two countries agreed to director-general-level consultations on the comfort women issue and held high-level confidential consultations. After the 8th high-level consultation meeting between Korea and Japan, which were conducted confidentially on December 28, 2015, Korean Foreign Minister Yun Byung-se and Japanese Foreign Minister Fumio Kishida announced at a joint press conference that the issue of apology and compensation for the comfort women had been resolved. The announcement, based on a closed-door agreement between the two foreign ministries, declared that the issue of Japanese military comfort women was "finally and irreversibly" resolved. The problem was that this agreement was made without comprehensive consultation with the victims and civil society, thus providing grounds for ongoing controversies.[13]

Despite the joint press conference of the Korean and Japanese governments, the comfort women victims and civil society did not agree to the resolution and continued to file lawsuits for damages through the Korean courts.

One of the key results of these judicial efforts was the ruling by the Seoul Central District Court's Civil Division 34 (Presiding Judge Kim Jeong-gon) on January 8, 2021, which is mentioned in the introduction to this article. The court ruled in the lawsuit that the acts of the Japanese military in the comfort women case constituted crimes against humanity that violated international peremptory norms and that state immunity could not be applied. The court also ruled that the Korean court had jurisdiction over the defendant exceptionally and ordered Japan to pay 100 million won per comfort woman victim.[14] This ruling of the Korean court, grounded in the constitution and legal order, comprehensively considered domestic law, international law, and the dynamic development of international customary law. The court confirmed that the damage to Japanese military comfort women was a specific example of the limitation of sovereign immunity under international customary law, making it as a significant achievement in human rights trials.

The ruling of the Seoul Central District Court on January 8, 2021, clearly explains the domestic and international legal grounds for Korea's claim of Japan's responsibility.[15] This ruling aligns with new human rights practices established in countries like Belgium, Spain, and Italy, which have actively responded to human rights violations, thereby reflecting the post-World War II trend of expanding human rights protection and remedies. This makes a significant milestone that demonstrates the

[13] Ever since this Agreement was reached, concerning the demands for apologies and compensation by the former Comfort Women victims, the Japan government has been arguing that the issues were "finally and irreversibly resolved" by the closed-door agreement with the Park Geun-hye government in 2015.

[14] Seoul Central District Court, 34th Civil Division, 2016GaHap505092 (S. Kor.).

[15] Seoul Central District Court, 34th Civil Division, 2016GaHap505092 (S. Kor.).

Korean judiciary's commitment to upholding human rights based on the principles of international human rights law. The international community has developed great human rights jurisprudence through the Nuremberg Trials, the Former-Yugoslavia Tribunal, Rwandan Tribunal, and other international courts around the world, along with the development of the International Criminal Court to respond to crimes against humanity and war crimes. This ruling can be characterized as a monumental human rights decision, grounded in the Korean constitution and its laws, concerning the internationally recognized violations committed against the comfort women.

To make matters more confusing, a completely opposite decision was made on April 21, 2021, shortly after the aforementioned ruling, by the Seoul Central District Court's Civil Division 15 (Presiding Judge Min Seong-cheol). The case was a lawsuit filed by 20 comfort women victims and their families, including Lee Yong-soo and the late Kwak Ye-nam, against the Japanese government. The Civil Division 15 decided that the Korean court did not have jurisdiction over this case.[16] This court ruled that, under the customary international law of state immunity and the legal precedents established by the Supreme Court, claiming damages against a foreign defendant for its sovereign acts is impermissible. Furthermore, the court held that such a result does not violate the Korean constitution, and that the resolution of the comfort women issue should be achieved through Korean government's efforts, including diplomatic negotiations with Japan. This ruling delivered a very narrow judgment based on international norms regarding state immunity and mechanically applied the concept of sovereign acts recognized by the Supreme Court's precedents, ultimately concluding that the Korean court lacked jurisdiction over the Japanese military comfort women case.

The court ruled that state immunity should be recognized if the act was a sovereign act, even if it was illegal within the territory of the forum state. This court does not recognize the evolution of the customary international law on state immunity. Consequently, it rendered the highly inappropriate judgment to uphold Japan's state immunity in the context of the Japanese military comfort women case. Based on this position, the jurisdiction of the Korean court to provide remedies for these unprecedented crimes against humanity was essentially negated.

However, this was not the final outcome. Following the victims' appeal, on November 23, 2023, the 33rd Civil Division of the Seoul High Court (Judges Koo Hoe-geun, Hwang Sung-mi, and Heo Ik-soo) issued a ruling that rejected Japan's state immunity and fully accepted the claims of the victims of Japanese military sexual slavery.[17] The ruling was finalized on January 23, 2021, as Japan did not appeal.

Regarding the Seoul Central District Court's ruling on January 8, 2021, which ordered Japan to pay 100 million won to each comfort woman victim, the Japanese government did not file an appeal either. However, the Japanese government took action to implement the court's decision. Consequently, the comfort women victims filed a request with the court seeking the disclosure of Japanese assets in Korea for

[16] *See* Seoul Central District Court 15th Civil Division, 2016GaHap580239 (S. Kor.).

[17] Seoul High Court, 2021NA2017165, 2023.11.23. (S. Kor.).

compulsory execution. On June 9, 2021, Judge Nam Seong-woo of the Seoul Central District Court's Civil Division 51 ordered, "The debtor shall submit a list of assets specifying the state of the assets at the asset specification date."[18] The court ruled that "if state immunity is invoked for serious human rights violations such as state-sponsored murder, rape, and torture, the common interests of the international community will be threatened" and that "it may rather result in harming friendly relations between countries."[19] The court also ruled that "if a state violates peremptory norms, it is appropriate to confiscate the privileges given to the state as it has crossed the boundaries set by the international community itself, and the debtor's actions fall under the exception to state immunity, so compulsory execution is lawful."[20] The court explicitly stated that the potential diplomatic ramification of relations with Japan or subsequent economic retaliation following the compulsory execution of a final judgment is a matter within the exclusive domain of the executive branch, which oversees diplomatic affairs, and thus excluded from consideration."[21]

2.2 *Forced Labor Victims During the Japanese Occupation*

Regarding the victims of forced labor, the Supreme Court of Korea ruled on May 24, 2012, that the individual claims of forced labor victims had not expired and that Japanese companies were liable for damages.[22] Following this ruling, continued efforts were made to secure reparations for the victims. These efforts culminated on October 30, 2018, when the Supreme Court of Korea delivered a final judgment, ordering Nippon Steel & Sumitomo Metal Corporation to compensate the four victims of forced labor with 100 million KRW (approximately $88,000) each.[23] Following this ruling, conflicts related to historical issues between Korea and Japan intensified.

On June 7, 2021, the Civil Division 34 of the Seoul Central District Court (Presiding Judge Kim Yang-ho) ruled in favor of Japan in a damage lawsuit filed by forced labor victims against 16 Japanese companies. The court stated:

> This ruling is based on the premise that the illegality of Japan's colonial rule is irrelevant to the interpretation of the Claims Agreement, and that the forced labor victims' claims for damages are included under the scope of the Claims Agreement...... The phrase "completely and finally resolved" in the Claims Agreement means not only that the contracting states waived diplomatic protection rights against each other, but also that the plaintiffs' right to pursue individual claims through lawsuits was restricted.

---

[18] Seoul Central District Law, 2021KaMyeong39, Decided June 9, 2021 (S. Kor.).

[19] Id.

[20] Id.

[21] Id.

[22] *See* Supreme Court of Korea, 2009 Da 68620, Decided on May 24, 2012 (S. Kor.).

[23] Supreme Court of Korea, 2013 Da 61381, Decided on Oct. 30, 2018 (S. Kor.).

The court's interpretation of the Claims Agreement reveals a flawed understanding of the legal principle about the relationship between domestic and international law. The ruling asserted, "when domestic courts handle international law, they must interpret and apply it as a legal system that governs the international community, which differs in nature from the domestic legal order." This ruling directly contradicted the Supreme Court's ruling on October 30, 2018, and caused significant controversy.

In the appellate court proceeding, the Civil Division 33 of the Seoul High Court (Judge Koo Hoe-geun, Hwang Sung-mi, and Heo Ik-soo) found the trial court's dismissal to be flawed and remanded the case to the Seoul Central District Court on February 1, 2024.[24]

2.3 *Japan's Position on Compensation Claims*

Regarding the issues raised by South Korean comfort women and forced labor victims, the Japanese government has consistently maintained that it does not recognize any legal responsibility. Former Japanese Prime Minister Shinzo Abe stated in 2018 that the South Korean Supreme Court's ruling, which required Japanese companies to compensate forced labor victims, was "unacceptable under the international law"[25] and argued that the 1965 Treaty on Basic Relations Between Japan and the Republic of Korea and the Claims Agreement[26] had "completely and finally resolved" the claims issue.[27] Denying the claims of the forced labor victims, which arise out of crimes against humanity and war crimes, Japan claims that the issue has already been resolved through the Claims Agreement. Japan argues that there is no responsibility for the actions of the Japanese military or companies and that the victims' rights have been extinguished, asserting that this is in accordance with international law.

Japan's response to its wartime atrocities, such as the comfort women issue and forced labor committed during the Japanese occupation, is highly reprehensible and

[24] Seoul High Court, 2012Na2031703, Feb.1.2024 Decision. *See also* Jaeho Lee, *The High Court Remands the District Curts Decision that Dismissed Forced Labor Victims Claims against the Supreme Court Decision,* Hankyoreh Dailey Feb. 1.2024. https://www.hani.co.kr/arti/society/society_general/1126900.html (last visited 2/1/25) .

[25] *See* Irak Choi, *Abe, Korean Supreme Court Decision, an Acceptable Judgement against the International Law,* (Abe, Han Deabeopwon Pangyeol, Gukjebeopsang Isseulsu Eobneun Pandan) Yonhap News (2018.10.30). https://www.yna.co.kr/view/AKR20181030136900073 (last visited 2/1/25) .

[26] Agreement on the Settlement of Problem concerning Property and Claims and the Economic Cooperation between Korea and Japan, 1965 Art. 2.

[27] Ever since this Agreement was reached, concerning the demands for apologies and compensation by the former Comfort Women victims, the Japan government has been arguing that the issues were "finally and irreversibly resolved" by the closed-door agreement with the Park Geun-hye government in 2015.

inconsistent with its current standing in the international community. Despite the undeniable reality of severe human rights violations perpetrated by Japan during the Pacific War, the Japanese government consistently ignores these violations and attempts to evade responsibility by invoking the outdated shield of sovereign immunity. This stance falls far short of modern international human rights standards. For such serious international human rights violations, the state should explicitly waive sovereign immunity and consent to lawsuits concerning illegal acts, rather than merely claiming immunity. Actively realizing transitional justice and opening the way for victims to seek legal remedies through litigation is the clear trend in contemporary international law and sovereign immunity jurispurdence. By continually relying on the outdated shield of sovereign immunity without offering reflection or apology for past actions, Japan demonstrates a shameful and shortsighted approach, especially when considering the possible proactive role it could otherwise play in East Asia.

The principle of sovereign immunity has developed under the principle of sovereign equality since the Treaty of Westphalia and has held the status of customary international law. However, the principle of sovereign immunity has gradually changed, being replaced by the new customary international law that recognizes exceptions to sovereign immunity for commercial activities and waivers. Official wartime acts directly performed by the government are generally covered by sovereign immunity. However, claims of sovereign immunity for international crimes, including war crimes or crimes against humanity, such as torture, rape, and acts of terrorism, systematically carried out by government agencies against civilians are losing ground.

The trial process becomes legally complex when a state commits illegal acts, such as crimes against humanity or war crimes, that do not constitute commercial activities and for which the state has not explicitly waived sovereign immunity. The assertion that international law unconditionally recognizes sovereign immunity for sovereign acts is inaccurate. Today, there is a growing number of cases in various international courts, including the International Criminal Court, where sovereign immunity is not mechanically recognized. Furthermore, the scope of interpreting exceptions to sovereign immunity has broadened with the prosecution and conviction of former and incumbent heads of state. The specific principles for applying exceptions to sovereign immunity are still evolving through judgments and practices in various international lawsuits and national courts. The individual's right to sue the state for its illegal acts is increasingly recognized compared to the past. Professor Erwin Chemerinsky of the University of Southern California even argues that the principle of sovereign immunity should no longer be recognized.[28] In this context, the rulings established by South Korean courts to protect human rights are significant milestones in this evolutionary process.

---

[28] Erwin Chemerinsky, *Against Sovereign Immunity*, STANFORD LAW REVIEW (vol.53) (2001.5).

3 Legal Issues for the Victims

3.1 1965 Claims Agreement Between Japan and Korea and Crimes Against Humanity

One of the most important principles of modern international law is that victims of serious human rights violations, such as crimes against humanity or war crimes, hold rights to demand truth, reparation, and guarantees of non-recurrence of the violations. The perpetrators of the violations owe international and domestic obligations to provide effective remedies to the victims for their sufferings. It contravenes international human rights standards to argue that the victims of the Japanese military's sexual slavery and forced labor cannot demand reparation by citing Japan's agreements with South Korean government.

On December 16, 2005, the UN General Assembly adopted the "Basic Principles and Guidelines on the Right to a Remedy and Reparation for Victims of Gross Violations of International Human Rights Law and Serious Violations of International Humanitarian Law."[29] This emphasizes that states must respect and implement international human rights and humanitarian law. Victims, whether individually or collectively, who have suffered physical, mental, economic harm, or serious violations of fundamental rights due to gross acts or omissions, are entitled to effective legal remedies, restitution, compensation, rehabilitation, satisfaction, and guarantees of non-repetition.

If the Claims Agreement fundamentally justifies content contrary to important international norms, the relevant provisions or the treaty itself must be reexamined for validity, as per the "Vienna Convention on the Law of Treaties." Article 53 of the Vienna Convention states that "a treaty is void if, at the time of its conclusion, it conflicts with a peremptory norm of general international law."[30] Therefore, treaties conflicting with norms such as the abolition of slavery, torture, war crimes, and crimes against humanity lose their validity.

In the Supreme Court ruling on October 30, 2018, regarding forced labor victims, the majority opinion held: "During the negotiation of the Claims Agreement, the Japanese government essentially denied legal compensation for forced labor damages without acknowledging the illegality of its colonial rule, and as a result, the governments of Japan and South Korea were unable to reach an agreement on the nature of Japan's rule over the Korean Peninsula, and it is difficult to believe that forced labor compensation claims were included in the scope of the Claims Agreement."[31] The minority opinion also interpreted that the Claims Agreement did

[29] Basic Principles and Guidelines on the Right to a Remedy and Reparation for Victims of Gross Violations of International Human Rights Law and Serious Violations of International Humanitarian Law, [UNGA, A/RES/60/147, 2006.]

[30] Vienna Convention on the Law of Treaties, 1155 U.N.T.S. 331, 8 I.L.M. 679, entered into force Jan. 27, 1980. Art 53.

[31] Supreme Court of Korea, 2013 Da 61381, Decided on Oct. 30, 2018 (S. Kor.).

not deny individual claims, even if it waived diplomatic protection rights.[32] Thus, the Korean Supreme Court's ruling that private companies must compensate forced labor victims is not a violation of international law.

Japan has not fulfilled its civil responsibilities, to say nothing of criminal punishment, for crimes such as the establishment of military comfort women or the human rights violations and unjust enrichment related to forced laborers. The Japanese government's claim that victims of international crimes cannot demand compensation from corporations is contrary to international law. If the Japanese government obstructs the provision of human rights remedies, it is committing a further human rights violation because victims maintain the fundamental right to demand justice and appropriate reparation.

3.2 Additional Human Rights Violations by Japan

Nippon Steel & Sumitomo Metal Corporation, a war criminal company, could potentially reach a settlement with the victims according to the Supreme Court ruling. However, the Japanese government's intervention to block this settlement is putting pressure on the victims. From the perspective of international human rights law, this is a typical act of human rights violation. When a state obstructs the perpetrator's obligation to provide remedies to the victims, it is not only perpetuating past wrongs but also committing new ones. This is an unacceptable as it runs counter to recent trends in international law and human rights law.

The Japanese government argues it has previously established a peace fund through private entities or issued formal apologies by government representatives. However, there were no genuine apologies to the actual victims. The victims argue that the crimes committed against 20 million neighboring citizens during the 35 years of colonial rule cannot be washed away without full acknowledgement of wrongdoing. A true apology involves revealing the truth about human rights violations, providing compensation and reparations, and taking substantial measures to prevent recurrence. Instead of focusing diplomatic efforts on removing the Comfort Women statues, Japan may choose to erect statues in the heart of Tokyo and establish museums to commemorate the tragic deaths, disappearances, and painful youth of comfort women and forced laborers under colonial rule. These actions would

[32] Justice Kim So-Young, Justice Lee Dong-Won, and Justice No Jung-Hee argue, "it cannot be assumed that individual right to claim of A etc. itself is discharged rightly by the establishment of Claims Agreement, and it is only the right to diplomatic protection of the Korean government about that right to claim that is discharged by the establishment of Claims Agreement." On the other hand, dissenting opinions by Justices Kwon Soon Il and Cho Jae Yeon argue, "although it is not valid to assume that the Korean people's individual right to claim against Japan or the Japanese people was nullified or relinquished by the Agreement, since exercising the right by litigation was restricted by the agreement, it is reasonable to deem that Party A and others' right to claim damages in Korea against New Nippon Steel Corporation, which is the Japanese people, for forced labor is restricted."

continuously educate the Japanese public and foster dialogue with the Korean people. When Japan takes the lead in guaranteeing human rights, it may also play a rightful role in improving human rights in other Asian countries. If a regional organization for Asia is formed in the future, where countries cooperate as a regional community, it should be based on the guarantee of human rights. When Japan sets an example in protecting human rights, it will be able to exercise a certain leadership as a proud and influential power in the region.

3.3 Unilateral Export Restrictions

Japan's decision to impose export restrictions, based on the assertion that rulings of South Korea's Constitutional Court and Supreme Court violated international law, was widely regarded as a direct affront to the international norms of free trade.[33] The abrupt and aggressive imposition of export restrictions, executed without sufficient prior consultation or adherence to established dispute resolution procedures with the counterpart was widely viewed as a shocking action. From an economic perspective, Japan's aggressive behavior raised concerns about the potential resurgence of militarism, reminiscent of past nightmares, especially when coupled with Japan's ongoing movement to revise its pacifist clause in the constitution. Although Japan maintains that the export restrictions were not directly connected to the South Korean Supreme Court's ruling on forced labor, these retaliatory measures were seen as a direct violation of the World Trade Organization (WTO) principle of free trade principles and are difficult to justify given their relance on the ambiguous rationale of South Korea's violation of interenational law.

The Japanese government has neither criminally prosecuted nor held any civil responsibility for the perpetrators' crimes such as the establishment of comfort women stations and the human rights abuses and unjust enrichment of forced laborers. They have denied any government responsibility and have not provided compensation or reparations. In fact, Japan's attempts to deny the wartime wrongdoing are found in multiple places.

As a response to the South Korean Supreme Court decision, Japan took drastic economic retaliation measures against South Korea, condemning the government's action concerning the forced labors case. There was no prior consultation.[34] Subsequent effort for diplomatic dialogue between the two governments did not work. South Korea eventually responded by taking similar economic restrictions.

[33] *"Japan uses trade restrictions as a weapon against South Korea"* Los Angeles Times, By Victoria Kim and Don Lee July 21, 2019. https://www.latimes.com/world-nation/story/2019-07-21/japan-trade-restrictions-hit-south-korea (last visited 2/1/25).

[34] Mina Polmann, *What's Driving Japan's Trade Restrictions on South Korea?* The Diplomat, July 29, 2019. https://thediplomat.com/2019/07/whats-driving-japans-trade-restrictions-on-south-korea/

The case was then referred to the WTO arbitration panel.[35] South Korea had also announced that it would suspend the extension of the GSOMIA(General Security of Military Information Agreement).[36] South Korea reverted its decision to terminate GSOMIA,[37] but dark shadows started to cover Seoul-Tokyo relations and are not completely cleared yet.

4 Changing Asia and Japan's Options

4.1 Japanese Militarism

Former Japanese Prime Minister Shinzo Abe, when he was first elected to the office in 2006, promoted the slogan of creating a "beautiful country." However, the policies he actually pursued were overtly militaristic. By making the issue of North Korea's abduction of Japanese citizens a central pillar of his administration and aligning with U.S. President George W. Bush's hardline stance on North Korea, he heightened military tensions across Asia. This ultimately led to a loss of public support, forcing him to step down in 2007 after just 1 year. When Abe returned to power in late 2012 through the House of Representatives election, his administration continued on the path of militarism until he handed over the baton to Yoshihide Suga.[38]

As China's influence in Asia rapidly grows, the United States hopes that Japan will exert some level of restraint and take on more military responsibilities. Leveraging this strategic situation, Japan aims to shed its past image as a war aggressor and become a key nation in Asia. As part of this effort, the Abe administration reinterpreted Article 9 of the Constitution, claiming that exercising collective self-defense outside Japanese territory was not unconstitutional, thereby seeking to expand the role of the self-defense forces. This militarization of Japan naturally raises tensions and concerns among various East Asian countries.

The growing far-right racism and disregard for human rights within Japan also cause serious concern. The so-called "Citizens' Group That Does Not Allow Special Privileges for Koreans in Japan" holds anti-Korean or hate-Korean rallies, inciting sentiments like "Children of spies, go back to the Korean Peninsula," thus revealing

---

[35] Yoon-seung Kang, *WTO to Discuss Opening Panel over Seoul-Tokyo Trade Row*, Yonhap News Agency, June 29, 2020 https://en.yna.co.kr/view/AEN20200629002300320 (last visited 2/1/25).

[36] Choe Sang-Hun, Motoko Rich and Edward Wong, *South Korea Says It Will End Intelligence-Sharing Deal With Japan, Adding to Tensions*, The New York Times, Section A, Page 9, Aug 22, 2019. https://www.nytimes.com/2019/08/22/world/asia/south-korea-japan-intelligence.html (last visited 2/1/25).

[37] Reiji Yoshida & Satoshi Sugiyama, *GSOMIA survives as South Korea reverses decision to exit intel pact with Japan*, The Japan Times Nov. 22, 2019.

[38] *Japan Announces a Military Shift to Thwart China,* The New York Times, Section A, Page 1, Jul 2, 2014. https://www.nytimes.com/2014/07/02/world/asia/japan-moves-to-permit-greater-use-of-its-military.html (visited 2/1/25).

extreme right-wing racism.[39] The ruling Liberal Democratic Party's 2012 constitutional amendment proposal seeks to entirely delete Article 97 of the current constitution, which enshrines human rights as the highest law, stating that they are the result of humanity's long struggle for freedom and are inviolable, permanent rights.[40] Additionally, by inserting expressions in Article 12 that freedom and rights come with responsibilities and duties, the proposal shows an intention to restrict civil liberties.[41] Consequently, the LDP's constitutional proposal has even been criticized as a Japanese version of the South Korean Yushin Constitution adopted in 1972 by the authoritarian Park Chung-hee regime.[42]

4.2 The Need for Cooperation Centered on Human Rights

Today, conflicts exist on multiple levels, in Europe, Asia, Africa, and other part of the world. Global conflicts have become more severe than ever. Despite the end of World War I, World War II, and the decades-long Cold War, the world continues to face challenges to peace. The wars in Iraq and the War on Terror, which intensified after the 9/11 attacks, have turned Afghanistan, Libya, and Syria into battlefields and heightened tensions with Iran and North Korea. The war between Russia and Ukrane is still continuing.

In the absence of a new alternative system after the Cold War, localized conflicts under the guise of the War on Terror or the prevention and control of weapons of mass destruction have created a new confrontation between China and Russia against the United States and its allies. The United States now views the strategic competition with China in Asia and threat from Russia in Europe as greater than those from Al-Qaeda or ISIS. As seen in Russia's growing interests in Asia and China's opposition to the deployment of THAAD and enhancing regional tensions, international conflicts centered on anti-terrorism have shifted to traditional conflicts among major powers, which could ignite a third world war if intensified.

With China's rapid growth in Asia as well as Russia's aggressive roles in Europe, including the ongoing Russia-Ukraine war, the United States has restructured its national security strategy focus from the war on terrorism to its traditional rivals,

---

[39] Ayako Hatano, *Can Strategic Human Rights Litigation Complement Social Movements? A Case Study of The Movement Against Racism and Hate Speech in Japan*, 14 U. Pa. Asian L. Rev., 228 (2019).

[40] Takao Suami, *Global Constitutionalism for East Asia: Its Potential to Promote Constitutional Principles* in Global Constitutionalism from European and East Asian Perspectives 562 (Takao Suami et al. eds., 2018).

[41] *See* Yun-Hyung Gil, *with a Provision on No Abuse of Freedom, Japan aims at Reinvigorating the Emperor and Defense Forces* ("Jayu Namyong Andoae" Johang Neoeuimyeo Cheonhwang Gundae Saligieh Onhim) Hankyoreh Dailey, Jan 16, 2014.

[42] The Yushin Constitution (유신헌법/維新憲法) was enforced during the dictatorship of President Park Chung-hee from December 27, 1972, to October 26, 1980.

China and Russia. This strategic position shift is found in the National Defense Authorization Act (NDAA), adopted by Congress.[43] For the first time, the 2019 NDAA defined China as the US "strategic competitors."[44] The US Congress believes that China's challenge to the US hegemony and its growing influence on foreign countries threatens the US national security and prosperity. The report also indicates that Russia wants to disable the North Atlantic Treaty Organization (NATO) trying to change the international order and global economic system of Europe and the Middle East in its favor.[45] The US Congress also believes that North Korea is a dangerous country with nuclear weapons, ballistic missiles, and other weapons of mass destruction, and that it is a significant security threat to the United States along with Iran.[46] Russia built a strong alliance with North Korea, and North Korean military is deployed to Ukraine.

In this way, the challenging situations for the countries in East Asia are far from simple. Facing the security challenges from China and Russia and North Korea's nuclear and missile development, the United States is strengthening its military alliances with Japan and Australia to pressure North Korea and China. The United States is also working with Vietnam, the Philippines, and Thailand to curb China's influence in the South China Sea. As a result, Asia is facing increased nationalism and military tensions, raising the possibility of localized conflicts.

The South China Sea disputes, along with China's nine-dash line, are ongoing in the Senkaku and Spratly Islands, and there is a possibility of similar territorial or maritime disputes arising in other parts of Asia, even in Yellow Sea with South Korea and in Northeast Asia. The United States has been responding to these tensions with strong actions, such as the construction of the Gangjeong Naval Base in Jeju, the relocation and reconstruction of the Okinawa base, and the deployment of THAAD in Seongju, South Korea. These may not be just diplomatic disputes, but they are reflecting ongoing changes in the military dynamics within the region, which will likely impact the fate of the Korean Peninsula for a considerable period.

North Korea, with its nuclear weapons and ICBMs, presents a challenge that provides space for the United States, China, Russia, and Japan to pursue their interests. South Korea is called upon to play a leading role in response to these changing circumstances. Beyond short-term measures, South Korea must pursue a new regional order through close cooperation with neighboring countries for the ultimate peace, which possibily aimed at re-unification of the Korean Peninsula. Without trust in humanity, common values in a society, and the fairness of state institutions, conflicts cannot be resolved.

[43] John S. McCain National Defense Authorization Act for Fiscal Year 2019, PUBLIC LAW 115–232—AUG. 13, 2018

[44] Id. Sec.1261 states, "Congress declares that long-term strategic competition with China is a principal priority for the United States that requires the integration of multiple elements of national power, including diplomatic, economic, intelligence, law enforcement, and military elements, to protect and strengthen national security."

[45] Id. Sec.1248

[46] Id. Sec.1265.

The new world order after the Cold War continues to evolve. In Southeast Asia, the Association of Southeast Asian Nations (ASEAN) is moving toward a political-security community, an economic community, and a sociocultural community encompassing the ASEAN region. The East Asia Summit (EAS), attended annually by leaders from major countries in Northeast Asia, South Asia, and the Pacific, including the 10 ASEAN countries, South Korea, China, Japan, Australia, New Zealand, India, the United States, and Russia, serves as a forum for discussing Asia's future. Regional cooperation and integration in Asia are expected to continue steadily. In this process, a regional human rights organization in Asia should be part of it. At this time, Asia is the only region without a regional human rights organization, but there is ample possibility that a new regional system may emerge in Asia.

Without proactive and constructive efforts to guarantee human rights, a system that ensures human rights cannot be established. Human rights, which emphasize the fundamental dignity and value of human beings, differ from the concept of security, which emphasizes personal safety. Beyond defensive measures, human rights involve sharing values and expanding true personal and social peace based on the common cause. The role of human rights is crucial in resolving conflicts. Efforts to address issues begin where problems exist, and the guarantee of human rights becomes possible within movements for such changes. Human rights aim to be a universally shared norm in human society. While human rights strive for universality, they must also encompass particularities. They are not fixed values but concepts in the process of change and development. To promote universal human rights norms and organizations to protect human are movements of incorporating others and building solidarity with them rather than excluding them.

5 Conclusion

While other continents have regional human rights courts, such as the European Court of Human Rights and the Inter-American Court of Human Rights, Asia still lacks a regional political organization and a regional human rights court. Asia needs a regional human rights court where individuals or NGOs can file lawsuits against states for human rights violations. When a human rights cooperation organization is properly established in Asia, the continent, which has existed only as the "other" to Europe, can actively contribute to the world with its own identity and significance.

At this time, Japan is not playing any important role in such activities . However, Japan may be able to take a more proactive role in promoting human rights cooperation in Asia if it properly deal with past historical issues. Japan can become a global leader not only in economics but also in values by healing the past human rights issues, reexamining the victims of the Pacific War, such as comfort women and forced laborers. It can also contribute to the creation of new human rights norms for the future. It may also help to restore the currently challenged Korea-Japan relationship. If Japan truly wants to play an important role in Asia, it should focus on building soft power rather than pursuing militarization. Japan cannot earn the respect of neighboring countries with an anachronistic historical perspective that denies the existence of comfort women, glorifies Class A war criminals as patriots, and condemns colonial independence fighters as criminals. If the Japanese government truly wants to create a beautiful country, it should heal the wounds of war crimes and human rights violations instead of strengthening militarism. For such a change, Korea and Japan should place human rights at the center of problem-solving and approach past issues in a new way.

The Continuity of Statehood and Peoplehood in Modern Korea: How the Republic of Korea Has Defined Its Citizenry

Chulwoo Lee

Abstract This article explores the legal and political foundations of the Republic of Korea's statehood and citizenship, illuminating the ROK's assertion of its identity and continuity with the pre-annexation Korean state. The ROK government has consistently asserted that Japan's annexation of Korea was null and void ab initio and that, therefore, Korean statehood persisted despite Japanese rule. The article shows to what extent this position has manifested itself in the Korean state's definition of the boundaries of its people. While the main purpose of the study is to examine the official discourses of the ROK government in explaining the continuity of the citizenry from the pre-annexation Empire of Korea to the post-1948 Republic of Korea, it also sheds light on how the Empire of Korea and the Provisional Government of the Republic of Korea addressed issues of membership. The article highlights the underlying conviction in the identity and continuity of statehood held by the framers of the 1948 Nationality Act and examines the position, within the ROK legal system, of the Temporary Provisions Concerning the Law of Nationality adopted under the US Army Military Government shortly before the establishment of the Government of the Republic of Korea, which was seemingly ignored by the framers. The study concludes that, while the interpretation and application of nationality rules have revealed certain gaps and inconsistencies, the ROK government and judiciary have maintained and developed a commitment to the identity and continuity of statehood between the Empire of Korea and the present Republic of Korea.

Keywords Citizenship · Nationality law · Statehood · Diaspora · Japanese rule · Republic of Korea · Empire of Korea

C. Lee (✉)
Yonsei University Law School, Seoul, South Korea
e-mail: chulwoo.lee@yonsei.ac.kr

Y.-H. Kim et al. (eds.), *Beyond the San Francisco System*,
https://doi.org/10.1007/978-981-95-3328-2_16

1 Introduction

Many political considerations drove the United States and its allies, the United Kingdom in particular, to preclude the Republic of Korea (hereinafter ROK) from the conference toward the San Francisco Peace Treaty of 1951. The geopolitical situation played a significant part—the division of Korea and the presence of two separate governments, the Korean War, and so forth. The complex political interest of the United Kingdom following its recognition of the communist government in China was behind its advice to the United States against inviting the ROK, moving the United States to withdraw its initially positive attitude to the ROK's participation. With all these political factors, the explanation why the ROK should be excluded was that Korea had been part of Japan (Yi Tae-Jin, 2022; Jung Byung-joon, 2020; Cheong, 1990). The denial of Korean statehood was set forth in Art. 2(a) of the San Francisco Treaty: "Japan, recognizing the independence of Korea, renounces all right, title and claim to Korea, including the islands of Quelpart, Port Hamilton and Dagelet." This was premised on the belief that Japan's annexation of Korea was valid. The position of the ROK has been against that presupposition. The ROK government advanced its position in negotiating for the 1965 Treaty on Basic Relations between Japan and the Republic of Korea. The ROK claimed that the treaties leading to the annexation were null and void ab initio. Japan opposed. The result was Article 2, which stipulated that "it is confirmed that all treaties or agreements concluded between the Empire of Japan and the Empire of Korea on or before August 22, 1910, are already null and void," which the ROK and Japan interpret in different ways (Yoo Euysang, 2022: 105–108).[1]

On a number of occasions, the ROK government put forward its position that the treaties leading to the annexation of 1910 were null and void ab initio and that there were identity and continuity between the current ROK and the pre-annexation Korean state. For instance, in 1986, the ROK government confirmed the validity of three multilateral treaties that the Empire of Korea (Daehanjeguk) had signed in 1903 and 1904 and communicated its confirmation to the Netherlands, the depository, and the Federal Republic of Germany, which made an enquiry.[2] In that context, the Ministry of Government Legislation made the following statement.

[1] United Nations Treaty Series, No. 8471, signed at Tokyo on 22 June 1965.

[2] The 1899 Convention (II) with Respect to the Laws and Customs of War on Land, to which Korea acceded in 1903, and the 1904 Convention for the Exemption of Hospital Ships in Time of War, from the Payment of All Dues and Taxes Imposed for the Benefit of the State, signed by Korea in 1904 and ratified in 1907, had continued to be valid, and the 1899 Convention (III) for the Adaptation to Maritime Warfare of the Principles of the Geneva Convention of August 22, 1864, to which Korea acceded in 1903, was replaced by a 1907 convention and later the 1948 Geneva Convention (Lee Soon-Chun, 2010: 237–239). In 1900, the Empire of Korea acceded to the Universal Postal Convention and the Universal Postal Union, and in 1949 the Union recognized the ROK's membership. The Empire of Korea also acceded to the First Geneva Convention of 1864, and Switzerland, the depository, recognized its effect on the ROK. The Second Geneva Convention of 1906 was signed and ratified by Japan on behalf of Korea (Lee Soon-Chun, 2010: 245–247).

> Japan's annexation of Korea was null and void and the Empire of Korea did not lose its statehood but retained its legal existence; it was only that its capacity to act (*Geschäftsfähigkeit*), in other words, the power to effectively govern its territory and people was unlawfully exercised by Japan acting as its proxy. The Empire of Korea's capacity of government was recovered by the establishment of the Government of the Republic of Korea on 15 August 1948, preceded by the US Army Military Government. It is an established principle in international law that the form of state, the form of government or the change of the name of the state in no way affect the identity and continuity of a state. The establishment of the Government of the Republic of Korea was not a change of statehood predicated on the extinction of the Empire of Korea, but a change in the form of state, the form of government, and the name of the state within the same subject in international law, and thus the identity of the state has continued. (Quoted in Lee Keun-Gwan, 2020: 169).[3]

There is quite a rich literature on the legality/illegality of Japan's seizure of Korea in light of international law and on Korean statehood in the first half of the twentieth century (Yi Tae-Jin and Sasagawa, 2009; Park Pae Keun, 2010; Lee Keun-Gwan, 2020; Kang Pyoung-keun, 2018; Na In-Gyun, 1999; Chon Jong-ik et al., 2016). This essay contributes to this discussion but with a particular focus. It examines how the above self-understanding of the Republic of Korea has manifested itself in the definition of its *Staatsvolk*, in other words, in explaining who are its citizens and what are the grounds for them being so. It brings to light some of the discursive practices of the ROK executive, legislature, and judiciary and examines how consistent the ROK's practice has been in insisting on its identity and continuity with the pre-annexation Korean state. This kind of *ex post facto* rationalization of state-peoplehood is an essential component of legal discourse denying the validity of annexation by a foreign power, as seen in the experiences of the Baltic states after achieving independence from the Soviet Union (Bauböck et al., 2009: Chaps. 1–3; Mälksoo 2022). The essay is more about the post-independence ROK's practices than about the legal status of pre-independence Koreans under either the Japanese imperial system or the law of any Korean political organization that Koreans might have regarded as authoritative during Japanese occupation, although the following section offers an outline of the pre-independence state of affairs.

2 The Status of Koreans During Japanese Occupation

In 2005, three legislative bills were introduced in the National Assembly. Two of the three purported to amend the Nationality Act, and the third one had the title Special Act on the Recovery of Nationality for Persons of Merit for Contribution to National

---

[3] This statement was based on "The Ascertainment of the Validity of Three Treaties Concluded by the Empire of Korea," Memorandum submitted by the Ministry of Foreign Affairs to the State Council, July 7, 1986, https://theme.archives.go.kr/viewer/common/archWebViewer.do?singleData=Y&archiveEventId=0028775688. For an account of the MOFA official who prepared the memorandum, see Lee Soon-Chun (2025).

Independence.[4] The three bills were tabled with the objective of granting ROK nationality to patriots who had fought for national independence and died in foreign countries or acquired foreign nationality before the establishment of the ROK Government in 1948 without having been entered on the family register.[5] The assumption behind the bills was that such people had died stateless or as foreign nationals without acquiring ROK nationality. The Review Reports of the three bills submitted to, and adopted by, the Legislation and Judiciary Committee (2005) rebutted that idea. The reports explained that such people were not stateless but possessed Korean nationality until they died. The ground was a law made at the turn of the century by the Empire of Korea, which disallowed expatriation. According to the reports, one could not lose nationality before December 20, 1948, the day when the Nationality Act of the ROK came into force.

The above mentioned law of the Empire of Korea was Rules on the Punishment of Persons Harming the Integrity of the State by Relying on a Foreign State, as amended in 1900, which contained a provision punishing under the Ming Code the act of having oneself registered as a national of a foreign state without obtaining permission from the government for deregistration (Chung In Seop, 2024: 276).[6] This rule was aimed at preventing Koreans from acquiring foreign nationality and acting as if they were outside of Korea's personal jurisdiction. The Legislation and Judiciary Committee reports cited the law as the best ground because there were few rules on nationality made and applied by the traditional Korean state. Historical documents of the Joseon dynasty show instances of naturalization to Korea, but no law was issued to define who the subjects of the kingdom were. It was no better under the Empire of Korea, which promulgated a nascent constitution—*Daehanguk gukje*—in 1899. This lack of a comprehensive set of rules on nationality is not surprising given that Japan enacted a nationality law in 1899 and Qing China did as late as in 1909 (Chung, 2024: 262; Dan, 2009).

The Review Reports reasoned that, because Japan's annexation of Korea was unlawful under international law and was declared null and void by the 1965 Basic Treaty, the Korean state had continued to exist and it was a new government, not a new state, that was established in 1948. . Hence, all Koreans who had been subjects of the Empire of Korea possessed ROK nationality.

---

[4] Bill No. 2430 (August 19, 2005); Bill No. 2467 (August 24, 2005); Bill No. 2527 (August 30, 2005).

[5] Although citizenship and nationality do not square with each other in some jurisdictions, the two terms are used interchangeably in this writing, as everyone who possesses the nationality of the Republic of Korea is recognized as a full citizen of the republic, except when alluding to the Japanese nationality of Koreans under the Japanese imperial legal system, which did not entail the full rights of citizens.

[6] The law was first issued in 1898, but the aforementioned provision was inserted by the second amendment in 1900. Although this law was replaced by Article 200 of *Hyeongbeop daejeon* (the Great Code of Penal Law) issued in 1905, the provision prohibiting expatriation was not included in that article. For the texts of laws of premodern Korea, see the Joseon law section in the Database of Korean History administered by the National History Compilation Committee, https://db.history.go.kr.

Then, how were the members of this population "grasped" by the Korean state before 1910 and during Japanese occupation? How were they treated by Japan and its governing authorities in Korea?

While the traditional Korean state lacked a law that defined who its subjects were, the households of the kingdom were to be registered for tax purposes, and surveys were to be conducted every three years. In the late stage of the Joseon dynasty, however, surveys were not regularly carried out. Whereas popular rhymes had it that Korea was a nation of 20 million people,[7] only five million subjects were identified when Japan took control of the government of Korea after the Treaty of 1905. The number increased to 13 million by 1910 as a result of new surveys conducted between 1905 and 1910 (Seo Ho-Chul, 2007). The population was recorded on a new Civil Registry (*minjeok*) introduced in 1909, which was carried over into the Korea Family Registry (*chōsen koseki*) in 1923.[8] Unlike the Joseon system that recorded only the situation at a particular temporal cross-section, the new system of registration reflected diachronic changes. The population was recorded to be 25 million at the end of Japanese rule (Park Keong-Suk, 2009: 37).

This system of registration, a product of Japanese rule, fairly accurately embraced the ethnonational Korean populace and was used later by the ROK as evidence of one's membership in the nation and state. In the meantime, Koreans in the anti-Japanese struggle took the composition of the Korean nation for granted without making rules and standards for determining who were Korean nationals. The Provisional Charter of the Republic of Korea, promulgated in April 1919 by the Provisional Government of the Republic of Korea in Shanghai, declared the establishment of a provisional government in the name of the "Korean nation (*daehan minjok*)" and made the "people (*inmin*) of the Republic of Korea (Daehanminguk)" subjects of constitutional rights. Article 5 of the Charter provided, "Those people of the Republic of Korea who have the quality of *gongmin* (citizens) have the right to elect and the right to be elected." Later that year, when three provisional governments in different places merged, a Provisional Constitution was proclaimed, with its first article declaring that the Republic of Korea was constituted by "the Korean people (*daehan inmin*)."[9] A government organization law enacted immediately after the establishment of the Provisional Government envisioned a "survey of nationality and population," but without practical power to govern the territory, it was impossible to subsume the populace under an institutionalized framework of nationality or citizenship.[10] The election of the Provisional Assembly was to be by direct

---

[7] "20 million people, a territory of 3000 *ri*, and a history of 4000 years" (Seo Ho-Chul, 2007: 119).

[8] *Hojeok* (*koseki* in Japanese) is best translated as the "household" register or registry, but *koseki* under Japanese rule is translated in this writing as the "family" register or registry, following the translation adopted by the US Army Military Government in its official documents.

[9] Full texts of the constitutions and official documents of the Provisional Government are available on the website of the National Legislation Information Center as well as the Database of Korean History. See https://www.law.go.kr/LSW/main.html.

[10] Special edition, the Official Gazette of the Provisional Government of the Republic of Korea (in Korean), November 5, 1919.

voting, but soon indirect voting or proxy voting became the practice (Lim Dong-hyun, 2018). In short, although popular sovereignty became the norm in 1919 and the Provisional Government was committed to representative democracy, it was practically impossible to make "we the people" in a substantive sense (Hahm & Kim, 2015). This impracticability may have discouraged the making of concrete rules for delimiting the boundary of the Korean citizenry. Furthermore, political conditions were unfavorable to such legislation: not only were there many political groups challenging the authority of the Provisional Government, but most anti-Japanese movements, including the nationalists, were tolerant of acquiring the nationalities of other countries, mainly China and Russia (later the Soviet Union).[11] An increasing number of Koreans in the Russian Far East acquired Russian nationality, and most of them acquired USSR citizenship as the Soviet Union unilaterally imposed its citizenship in 1924 and 1930 on persons who failed to assert and prove their foreign citizenship (Chung In Seop, 1998: 244–245; Ginsburgs, 1968: 13–14). A smaller percentage of Koreans in Manchuria acquired Chinese nationality, because until 1929 China's nationality law required the loss of the existing nationality of a person seeking naturalization (League of Nations, 1932: 57). Nevertheless, by the end of the Second World War, about 250,000–350,000 Koreans, that is, 15–25 percent of the Korean population in Manchuria, were presumed to have acquired Chinese nationality (Choi Kye-Soo, 2009: 468–480).

Japan, however, treated Koreans as Japanese subjects regardless of their naturalization to another country. It did so without applying its Nationality Law of 1899, unlike what it did in Taiwan. Instead, Japan explained that Koreans had become Japanese as a result of annexation and in accordance with custom and reason (Chen, 1984: 245–246). This was to block Koreans from escaping Japan's jurisdiction. Had Japan's Nationality Act been applied, one would have lost his/her nationality *ipso iure* if s/he acquired the nationality of another country (Chung, 2024: 278–279; Egawa et al., 1989: 191). Whereas the Empire of Korea's law against expatriation was not strictly put into practice from the outset and was not seriously considered by Koreans fighting against Japanese imperialism, Japan invoked that law and applied it against Koreans seeking expatriation. The Government-General of Korea recognized the validity of Korean laws at the time of annexation as having the same effect as decrees issued by the Governor-General unless those laws were replaced by new laws, and the law against expatriation was among those laws (Chung, 2024: 279; Mizuno 2000: 216–217).[12]

While Koreans were treated as Japanese nationals, they were separated from the Japanese and the other ethnonational groups in the empire. Japan discriminated between the people of *naichi* (inner land, Japan proper) and those of *gaichi* (outer

[11] As for the strategic approaches of Koreans in Manchuria and the Russian Far East toward naturalization to China or Russia (later the Soviet Union) in their anti-Japanese struggle, see Park Young-Suk (2010); Ban (1998).

[12] In 1908, the Empire of Korea notified foreign governments that it prohibited expatriation without permission (Chung, 2024: 277 note 48). By that time, Korea had been forced to sign the Treaty of 1905 to become Japan's protectorate.

land), and subjected the Japanese proper, Koreans, Taiwanese, and the people in Karafuto to separate family registries.[13] Former subjects of Joseon and the Empire of Korea were unable to move from *chōsen koseki* to another group's registry, *naichi koseki* in particular, except when the person became a member of a family belonging to that group, and vice versa.[14] One may find it ironic that this discriminatory system imposed by the authorities which the independent ROK did not recognize as lawful was used by the ROK in determining who its citizens were.

3 Institutionalizing "We the Citizens of Korea"

When the United States occupied the southern half of Korea and established a military government (United States Army Military Government, USAMGIK), it faced several tasks that required a definition of who Koreans were. Firstly, USAMGIK had to sort out Japanese residents in Korea. It imposed a travel ban on "all persons of Japanese nationality" and ordered them to register.[15] Facing Korean hostility toward these people, USAMGIK decided to repatriate all of them to Japan. It ordered all Japanese nationals other than those who had been brought under Japanese sovereignty by annexation in 1910 to be repatriated. Such people and native Koreans were distinguished by different family registries, and yet even the Japanese spouses of Korean men who had been entered on the Korean register were excluded from automatic entitlement to residence in Korea; they needed permission to stay (Chung In Seop, 1988: 664). As a result of this drastic measure, only 242 Japanese were reported to be remaining in Seoul shortly before the end of the US military government in 1948 (Kim Soo-ja, 2009: 118).

Another significant undertaking was to confiscate "enemy property." USAMGIK ordered that all property owned or controlled by Japanese nationals be vested in USAMGIK.[16] Those Japanese nationals were defined as persons who were "in possession of full civil and political rights" under the laws of Japan (Chung, 2024: 289).[17] In sorting out such persons, USAMGIK resorted to the family registry. Although this was congruent with the reality of membership in the prewar and wartime Japanese empire, USAMGIK faced many complaints, particularly from

---

[13] The Common Law (*Kyōtsuhō*), a Japanese statute enacted in 1923 to provide rules on the application of laws in different parts of the empire, included Karafuto in *naichi*. Karafuto ultimately became part of *naichi* in 1943 (Chen 1984: 265).

[14] A woman was transferred to her husband's family register upon the registration of marriage.

[15] USAMGIK Ordinance No. 10, Registration of Japanese Nationals. See Hanguk beopje yeonguhoe (1971) for all USAMGIK laws and ordinances cited in this chapter.

[16] USAMGIK Ordinance No. 33, Vesting Title to Japanese Property Within Korea.

[17] Charles Pergler, a legal consultant to USAMGIK, gave an opinion on the definition of "national of Japan" in Ordinance No. 33: "A formal definition of a 'national' of the 'Government of Japan' therefore would be, a person who, under the laws of Japan, was in possession of full civil and political rights." Opinion #67, United States Army Forces in Korea (1948: 14).

Koreans recorded on the Japanese register.[18] This prompted USAMGIK to request the Korean Interim Legislative Assembly to make a nationality law to be applied until a proper Korean legislature enacted one (Chung, 2024: 293–294).

The Korean Interim Legislative Assembly, the law-making body of the South Korean Interim Government under the control of USAMGIK, had been constituted through an election—an indirect election—despite the lack of a law that determined the boundary of the citizenry. The election rules had it that a member of the electorate should be a "Korean (*joseonin*)" residing south of the 38th parallel. No definition was given to who a Korean was. Somehow 45 delegates were elected, joined by another 45 appointed by USAMGIK (Seo Ho-Chul, 2017; Hahm & Kim, 2015: 254).

The biggest task of the Korean Interim Legislative Assembly was to make an election law for the forthcoming full legislature for Korea. That election law—the 1947 Law for the Election of Members of the Korean Interim Legislative Assembly—put "*gungmin*" meaning "citizen" in the place of "*joseonin*."[19] The law's implementing regulations defined the "citizen" as (1) any person who is registered in a Korean family register, (2) any person born of Korean parents, or (3) any person born of a Korean father and not possessing a foreign citizenship.[20] The law was, however, shelved for a number of reasons. A new election law was issued in the form of an USAMGIK ordinance.[21] It gave the right to vote to "any citizen twenty-one or more years of age" (Sect. 1), and its implementing regulations defined that person in the same way as the implementing regulations for the shelved law.[22] As to the meaning of "a person born of Korean parents" or "a Korean father," which the law did not define, the chairperson of the National Election Committee explained that it meant a person who could be deemed Korean by "common-sensical judgement in accord with sound national consciousness" (Chung, 2024: 292). This was perhaps the same attitude that was shared by the independence campaigners who regarded being Korean as natural and self-evident and thus made no deliberate efforts to define Korean nationality by way of a law.

The nationality law that the Interim Legislative Assembly enacted upon the request of USAMGIK was promulgated on May 11, 1948, a day after the first

---

[18] Although separate family registries institutionalized discrimination along ethnic lines, territorial distinction overlaid ethnic discrimination. While ethnic Japanese settlers enjoyed many privileges in *gaichi*, such as in schooling, local representation, and the application of laws, they were not politically represented at national level unless they went to *naichi* to vote. On the other hand, Koreans could exercise political rights if they resided in *naichi* (Oguma, 1998: 367–373). Nevertheless, given the lack of freedom of movement from *gaichi* to *naichi*, territorial discrimination did not much diverge from ethnic discrimination, and USAMGIK's recourse to the family registry to determine persons who enjoyed "full civil and political rights" was not a distortion of reality.

[19] USAMGIK Public Act No. 5.

[20] Section 2, Temporary Regulations for Implementing the Law for the Election of Members of the Legislative Assembly, January 5, 1948.

[21] USAMGIK Ordinance No. 175, Law for the Election of Representatives of the Korean People.

[22] Section 2, Regulations for Implementing the Law for the Election of Representatives of the Korean People, March 22, 1948.

National Assembly election. It was named the Temporary Provisions Concerning the Law of Nationality.[23] The purpose of the legislation was to "define those who are Korean nationals, in order to clarify legal relationships" (Sect. 1).[24] It provided for a "Korean (Joseon) nationality" and defined a person possessing Korean nationality at birth as a person i) whose father was Korean (*joseonin*), ii) whose mother was Korean and whose father was unknown or stateless, or iii) who was born in Korea and whose father and mother were unknown or stateless (Sect. 2). Again, the law did not define who were the Koreans (*joseonin*) whose descendants acquired Korean nationality *iure sanguinis*. Therefore, even if it had been effective since earlier, it would not have provided any standard on who a *joseonin* was in identifying the voters for the first National Assembly election.

The Temporary Provisions differed from the existing norm in that it recognized loss of nationality due to the acquisition of foreign nationality by naturalization (Sect. 4). Hence, Koreans who were naturalized in other countries were no longer Korean nationals, unlike under the rule against expatriation in pre-annexation Korea and the law under Japanese rule. Those who had lost Korean nationality could have their lost Korean nationality "restored" by "waiving" his/her foreign nationality.[25] The restoration of nationality retroactively took effect on August 9, 1945. That provision, Sect. 5, also provided for the restoration of Korean nationality by persons who had been entered on the Japanese family register; they could have their Korean nationality restored by cancelling their Japanese family registration.[26] This rule presupposed the validity of the family registration system under Japanese occupation. It recognized the effect of the Korean family registry as proof of one being Korean and distinguished between Koreans and Japanese by reference to their separate family registries. One of the strategic purposes of this provision that the drafters of the law had in mind was to reassign the property of Koreans who returned from the Japanese family register to the Korean register so that their property did not get vested in USAMGIK. The return to the Korean register would have been retroactively effective from August 9, 1945, a few months before USAMGIK began to confiscate enemy property. This embarrassed USAMGIK, which countered the attempt by

---

[23] USAMGIK Public Act No. 11. In my previous publications (Lee, 2010, 2012, 2015), I translated the title of this law as Provisional Rules on Nationality. It should be corrected to the title above, the official English title of the law adopted by USAMGIK.

[24] The wordings of the English version does not fully square with those of the Korean version. According to the Korean version, the law purported to "clarify legal relations by establishing a nationality for Koreans (*joseonin*) for the period up to the enactment of a nationality statute."

[25] "Waiver" in the official English text is understood as renunciation. But it did not mean a complete loss of the foreign nationality in question in pursuance of that country's law. Many Koreans who had acquired foreign nationality would not have been able to go through the relevant procedure for loss of nationality (Chung, 2024: 296; Kim Soo-ja 2009: 122–127).

[26] The official English text of the article: "Any person who obtained foreign nationality or was entered in a Japanese family register and has waived such nationality or cancelled such Japanese family registry on the effective date, or shall waive or cancelled hereafter, shall be deemed to be restored to Korean nationality as of, and prior to, 9 August 1945." USAMGIK Official Gazette, May 11, 1948.

issuing an ordinance (Ordinance No. 191) that disallowed reassignment of already vested property (Chung, 2024: 298).

USAMGIK came to an end 4 months later as the Government of the Republic of Korea was established. The Constitution of the Republic of Korea was promulgated on July 17, 1948. Its preamble proclaimed, "We, the citizens of Korea (*Daehan gungmin*), established the Republic of Korea (Daehanminguk) by the March First Movement in 1919." It enunciated popular sovereignty (Article 2) and stipulated that the conditions for becoming a citizen of the republic should be provided for by statute (Article 3). Pursuant to this provision, the National Assembly passed the Nationality Act in December 1948.

Under the Nationality Act of 1948, a person acquired the "nationality of the Republic of Korea" *iure sanguinis* provided that i) his or her father was a citizen (*gungmin*) of the ROK, ii) his father was a citizen of the ROK at the time of death if the father died before the birth of the person, iii) his or her mother was a citizen of the ROK if his or her father was unknown or stateless, or iii) he or she was born in the ROK if his or her father and mother was unknown or stateless (Article 2). Instead of a "Korean" (*joseonin*), the Nationality Act stipulated a "citizen of the Republic of Korea" as the reference person from whom nationality was to be transmitted.

When the draft of the Nationality Act was debated in the National Assembly, the phrase "citizen of the Republic of Korea" aroused controversy. Some representatives asked whether the ROK had existed before liberation. If "the Republic of Korea" were the country that was liberated from Japanese rule in 1945 or whose government was established in 1948, most people would be excluded from the citizenry because their fathers were born earlier. The Legislation and Judiciary Committee proposed that the "citizen of the Republic of Korea" be replaced by "*hanin* (Korean)" (Kim Soo-ja, 2009: 129–131; Chung, 2024: 271–272). To this challenge, justice minister Yi In responded by saying,

> We, according to the Preamble of the Constitution, carry on the spirit of the March First independence declaration and believe that we had a state before 15 August. There are cases where a state exists without a government… We have continued to exist both spiritually and legally. Although we did not state clearly, we made this statute because we have had nationality both spiritual and legal since a long time ago… We must say that the Republic of Korea have constantly been here in both spirit and law. The Republic of Korea had been here before 15 August… The Provisional Government in Shanghai became the Government of the Republic of Korea.[27]

In sum, the "Republic of Korea" in the Nationality Act simply means the Korean state past and present—the historic Korean state as well as the new republic born in 1948. The drafters deliberately omitted an extra provision that would define who the "initial citizens" were, because they believed that the Korean state had never ceased to exist despite Japanese occupation.[28]

---

[27] Minutes of the Constituent National Assembly, 1st Session, No. 118, December 1, 1948.

[28] This contrasts with many countries that achieved independence from colonial rule and were born as new states. For example, Article 5 of the 1950 Constitution of independent India defined who were the citizens of India at the time when the constitution came into force.

Out of 110 representatives, 64 supported the original phrasing; only ten voted in favor of "*hanin*" (Kim Soo-ja, 2009: 131). The *Staatsvolk* of the Republic of Korea was thus institutionalized. The initial citizens of the new republic were descendants of the members of the historic Korean polity, which was coextensive with the kingdom of Joseon (1392–1897), whose name changed to the Empire of Korea (Daehanjeguk, 1897–1910). The members of the "Korean nation" (*daehan minjok*) and "the people of Korea" (*daehan inmin*) whom the Provisional Government of the Republic of Korea claimed to represent were naturally carried over into the citizenry of the new Republic of Korea. The logic behind the Nationality Act manifests the most resolute assertion of continuity of Korean statehood and peoplehood.[29] How consistently has this position been followed by the government of the Republic of Korea?

4 Practices of the Government of the Republic of Korea

After Japan surrendered, the Supreme Commander for the Allied Powers (SCAP) faced the problem of treating Korean and Taiwanese people in Japan. In 1946, China's Kuomintang government issued a law to embrace the Taiwanese in Japan as Chinese nationals and communicated its position to SCAP. Korea lacked such a government and could not take any action on the matter. SCAP, whose main concern was internal security, took capricious approaches to Koreans, but on the whole, it treated Koreans as Japanese nationals, which was the Japanese government's position as well. In contradiction to this, however, Koreans were denied suffrage and were subjected to alien registration (Chung In Seop, 1996: 21–38).

Both SCAP and the Japanese government continued to regard Koreans as Japanese nationals even after USAMGIK developed a concept of Korean (Joseon) nationality and treated all persons entered on the Korean family register as Korean nationals pursuant to the Temporary Provisions Concerning the Law of Nationality. When the ROK Government was established and the ROK came to have a Nationality Act, SCAP took the stance that the nationality issue should be settled between Korea and Japan by a treaty (Chung, 1996: 24–27).

As the San Francisco Peace Treaty came close, Japan insisted that Koreans should be treated as aliens and, as the peace treaty came into force, the Japanese government definitely treated Koreans as aliens, invoking Article 2(a) of the treaty.

---

[29] Koreans in Manchuria, as foreigners vis-a-vis the Chinese, faced many disadvantages (see League of Nations 1932: Chap. 3). Voices emerged in favor of the application of Japan's Nationality Law, which would enable those Koreans to acquire Chinese nationality. In the early 1930s, Yi In also joined those voices (Chung In Seop 2024: 280–282). Apparently, this contradicts his later position as justice minister defending the original wordings of the Nationality Act. Yet his position as a lawyer advocating the interests of Koreans in Manchuria should be distinguished from his role as justice minister acting in official capacity.

Whether Article 2(a) could be a ground for denying Koreans' Japanese nationality have been subjects of controversy among advocates of *zainichi* rights (Onuma, 1986), but for the ROK, nationality was not an issue for contestation. The first draft Agreement on the Nationality and Treatment of Koreans in Japan (1952) provided, "The Republic of Korea confirms that Koreans in Japan are citizens of the Republic of Korea" (Chung, 1996: 41). Neither was the choice of nationality an option for the ROK. The ROK's concern was to press Japan to stabilize the residential status of Koreans in Japan. In negotiating with the Japanese government toward the normalization of relations, the ROK government claimed compensation for the forcible mobilization of labor, arguing that it was an unlawful conscription of nationals of a foreign country.[30] The nature of the state membership of Koreans under Japanese rule, another side of the same question whether the annexation was lawful and valid, has thus been at the heart of the ROK's and the victims' tort claims against Japan for labor mobilization, which the ROK Supreme Court and civil society advocates underlined as a governing element in disputes concerning that issue (Supreme Court 2018.10.30. 2013 Da61381; Kim Chang Rok, 2022).[31]

In contrast to this clear stance against Japan, there have been some confusing practices in domestic administration. Much confusion has derived from the place of the Temporary Provisions Concerning the Law of Nationality. The Temporary Provisions was one of the "existing laws" that retained effect in the new republic.[32] What was its relationship with the Nationality Act? What implications did it have in respect of the issue of Korean statehood before the establishment of the ROK Government in 1948?

By recognizing that pre-independence Koreans could lose nationality by acquiring foreign nationality, the Temporary Provisions disregarded, whether deliberately or unknowingly, the law of the pre-annexation Korean state. Yet it also departed from the law under Japanese rule. Literally, the Temporary Provisions has little to do with the question of legality or illegality of Japanese occupation. Yet it used the term "Joseon" in the stead of "the Republic of Korea." If this should not be taken as refusing to recognize a Korean statehood before the establishment of the ROK Government, neither can it be read as supporting the view that Korean statehood continued throughout Japanese occupation and USAMGIK administration. Indeed, USAMGIK was of the position that Korea was no more than "a state in the making."[33]

---

[30] The 13th conference of the General Compensation Committee, April 17, 1961 (Yoo Euysang 2019).

[31] Denial of the claim as in the dissenting opinion does not mean the recognition of Japanese rule as lawful and valid. The question is whether the agreement on the preclusion of claims is valid and a positive stance on this question does not conflict with the view that Japan's seizure of Korea was unlawful.

[32] "Existing laws and regulations shall be in effect to the extent that they do not conflict with this Constitution" (Article 100 of the Constitution of the Republic of Korea 1948).

[33] According to Charles Pergler, "Since Korea had been a part of the Japanese empire until the surrender of the Japanese and the latter's sovereignty over Korea had been terminated by the Potsdam Declaration of July 1945, in fact, Koreans ceased to be Japanese nationals. Korea being still a state in the making..." (Foreword to US Army Forces in Korea 1948). Ernst Fraenkel, another legal

Interestingly, the framers of the Nationality Act of 1948 disregarded the Temporary Provisions Concerning the Law of Nationality. Yi In never mentioned the Temporary Provisions in explaining the legislative intent, to assert the unbroken peoplehood of the ROK. No addendum was attached to the Nationality Act on the effect of the Temporary Provisions despite the fact that the Temporary Provisions professed to be provisional in anticipation of a nationality statute enacted by the forthcoming legislature of the new republic.[34]

A memorandum of the Ministry of Justice (MOJ) in 1954 made no reference to the Temporary Provisions in determining the nationality of a Korean who had acquired US citizenship during Japanese rule. The memorandum, which the MOJ issued as an advisory opinion for the Seoul High Court, followed the old rule against expatriation and regarded the person as a Korea-US dual national (Loh Yeong Don, 1996: 60). Had the Temporary Provisions been applied, he should have been treated as having lost his Korean nationality. This opinion was cited and followed in the aforementioned Legislation and Judiciary Committee's Review Reports on the laws for granting ROK nationality to patriots who had died in foreign countries without being entered on the family register (Legislation and Judiciary Committee, 2005).

Citing this memorandum among others, Loh Yeong Don devalues the Temporary Provisions as a source of binding rules on nationality issues prior to the Nationality Act of 1948. This position is part of his critique of the ROK's nationality law, in which he finds no definition of the initial citizens of the Republic of Korea (Loh, 1996). Loh's critique has been countered by Chung In Seop. Chung contends that the Temporary Provisions was the binding nationality law of Korea preceding the Nationality Act and has been respected by the ROK judiciary. Chung enumerates a number of court decisions of the 1960s and 1970s that applied the Temporary Provisions Concerning the Law of Nationality (Chung, 1998, 2024: 293–300). Four of those cases expressly applied the Temporary Provisions. Those cases involved persons whose family registration changed from Japanese to Korean or Korean to Japanese due to divorce from Japanese or Korean spouses respectively during the USAMGIK period (Supreme Court 1962.1.18. 4294HaengSang86; 1962.1.31. 4294MinSang651; 1976.4.23. 73Ma1051; Seoul High Court 1967.6.30. 67Na15). The key question related to the vesting of property, which depended on the nationality of the owner of the property, was conditioned by the restriction imposed by the

advisor to USAMGIK, even characterized Korea as a terra nullius (Lee Keun-Gwan, 2009: 151–152).

[34] If the ROK recognized the Temporary Provisions as a valid law, the Nationality Act would replace the Temporary Provisions even without an addendum to that effect, thanks to the principle that *lex posterior derogat legi priori*. Nevertheless, it is unnatural that the Nationality Act was completely silent on the Temporary Provisions, given that the restoration of nationality could be effected upon return from the Japanese family register to the Korean register, which was obviously a transitional arrangement. The Temporary Provisions, on the other hand, made it clear in its text that the law was transitional.

USAMGIK Ordinance 191.[35] In these cases, the Temporary Provisions was used for the narrow purpose of providing a ground for identifying Korean and Japanese by reference to the family registry. The remaining cases enumerated by Chung contained no reference to the Temporary Provisions, although the main question and reasoning were the same—discerning Korean and Japanese nationals on the basis of the family registry (Supreme Court 1963.11.21. 63Nu130; 1974.8.30. 74Do1668; 1976.4.23. 73Ma1051). Chung nevertheless categorized those cases as ones in which the Temporary Provisions was applied because it was the Temporary Provisions that officially recognized the validity of the family registry for distinguishing between Korean and Japanese nationals.

While the Temporary Provisions provided a binding guideline for the unmixing of the Korean and Japanese populations amid the disintegration of the Japanese empire and clarifiedy the boundaries of the Korean citizenry, the utility of the family registry was so obvious that it would have been used for differentiating Koreans and Japanese even if it had not been for the Temporary Provisions Concerning the Law of Nationality.[36] With Korea's independence, Koreans and Japanese needed to be differentiated and their human boundaries finalized anyway, and recourse to the family registry for that purpose was natural and inevitable. In other words, the Temporary Provisions need not be heralded as a big novelty for making the family registry the main device for separating Koreans from Japanese. It simply did a job that was necessary for a country that achieved independence, regardless of whether or not the foreign rule was legal and valid.

By contrast, the treatment of people who had acquired the nationalities of foreign countries other than Japan was where the Temporary Provisions differed from the pre-independence law, either the pre-annexation Korean or the Japanese imperial. The courts have made no decision expressly applying the Temporary Provisions in recognizing the loss of Korean nationality as a result of acquiring foreign (other than Japanese) nationality. But Chung In Seop cites a case to show that the Supreme Court recognized the Temporary Provisions as providing governing rules on that issue. The case, decided in 1981, concerned the nationality of a Korean who had acquired US citizenship in 1925. The Supreme Court ruled that the person was a foreigner because he had acquired US citizenship and should be treated as such in applying the Alien Land Act of 1961, which restricted the ownership of land by foreigners (Supreme Court 1981.2.10. 80Da2189). Although the decision made no mention of the Temporary Provisions, Chung interpreted it as applying the Temporary Provisions, because otherwise the person would not have been treated as having lost Korean nationality.

[35] In three of the four cases, return from the Japanese family register to the Korean register, and hence the change of nationality, was trumped by the application of Ordinance 191, which blocked the removal of property already vested. In the fourth case, a Japanese woman who divorced her Korean spouse was still treated as Korean because she was yet to be moved from the Korean family register to the Japanese register.

[36] The Korea Family Registration Ordinance, first issued in 1922, was recognized as a binding law under Article 100 of the 1948 Constitution.

This case should be analyzed in conjunction with a 1973 case in which the Supreme Court affirmed the ROK nationality of a Korean born in 1910 in the United States to permanent resident parents. The Supreme Court applied the Nationality Act retroactively to that person and held that he had acquired ROK nationality *iure sanguinis* according to Article 2 of the Act and remained an ROK-US dual national (Supreme Court 1973.10.31. 72Da2295).[37] The decision made no mention of the Temporary Provisions Concerning the Law of Nationality. Indeed, the court may have found no rule in the Temporary Provisions as well as any set of rules preceding the Temporary Provisions that would apply to a person who acquired foreign nationality by birth and had to rely on the Nationality Act to find a governing principle. Nevertheless, the retroactive application of the Nationality Act to an incident that had happened 48 years before its enactment sounds striking. One may conjecture that the Supreme Court did the same in its 1981 decision, since the decision squared with Article 12(iv) of the then Nationality Act while the court was silent on the source of the governing rule. Yet Chung In Seop has come up with a construction combining the 1973 and 1981 Supreme Court cases to explain the nationality status of Koreans prior to the Nationality Act of 1948. According to Chung, one should distinguish between Koreans who acquired foreign nationality by birth and those who voluntarily acquired foreign nationality; the former would retain their Korean nationality, but the latter would lose their Korean nationality upon the acquisition of foreign nationality (Chung, 2024: 299–300). In short, Chung has developed a construction congruent with the Nationality Act for clarifying the rules of the Temporary Provisions. In any case, however, the Supreme Court's position conflicted with the pre-independence rules as ascertained by MOJ.

Hence, until this point, the status of the Temporary Provisions was not fully settled as a source of rules on the nationality relations of Koreans before the enactment of the Nationality Act of 1948. In the meantime, the Cold War faded and reunion with coethnics in and from China and the Soviet Union posed a new challenge that begged the question of what the coethnics' nationality was. While the immigration authorities treated coethnics from China and the Soviet Union who entered the ROK through very limited routes as foreigners, the admission of "permanent returnees" from China and the Soviet Union in the late 1980s and early 1990s affirmed continuing nationality without the intervention of the Temporary Provisions. The "permanent return (*yeongju gwiguk*)" program for Koreans in the former communist countries was introduced to enable patriots distinguished for their service to national independence and their family members remaining in those countries to return and settle permanently in Korea. After the first case in 1989, MOJ drew up a Scheme on the Nationality of Coethnics Living in Communist Countries and devised a special procedure for nationality determination (*gukjeok panjeong*) outside of the Nationality Act, by which it ascertained the ROK nationality of permanent returnees. The permanent return procedure was streamlined by the Ministry of Foreign

[37] This case involved a conflict of laws question regarding the application of which country's law to a person who had gone missing during the Korean War.

Affairs' 1990 Guidelines on the Permanent Return of Persons Distinguished for Services to National Independence (Lee, 2012: 89–90).[38]

In 1995, the foreign ministry (MOFA) adopted Guidelines for the Permission of Permanent Return of Coethnics from China to expand the permanent return program to include coethnics from China in some circumstances other than patriotic backgrounds. Nevertheless, only a total of 355 persons had been recognized as permanent returnees by the end of 1996, along with about 200 Koreans from Sakhalin (Lee, 2012: 90, Jung and Yeom, 1999: 254). Since there were only a very few narrow routes for migration to Korea available to the Korean diaspora in China and the former Soviet Union, the permanent return program was under mounting pressure to broaden its gate and, in the end, proved to be unsustainable. In 1997, MOFA's 1995 Guidelines were replaced by MOJ's Guidelines on the Nationality Affairs of Coethnics from China. In the same year, the Nationality Act was amended, and the nationality determination procedure gained a statutory ground. Yet, its use was now limited to examining the nationality of returnees from Sakhalin and persons claiming to be North Korean.

The permanent return program up to 1997 was striking in that it not only treated Koreans under Japanese rule as having possessed Korean (or ROK) nationality but also implied that the members of the Korean diaspora in China and the former Soviet Union possessed ROK nationality regardless of their current citizenship of the country of residence. This was a logical outcome of recognizing permanent returnees as ROK nationals instead of granting them ROK nationality upon recovery of nationality or naturalization. Although it was never fully articulated, the permanent return program embodied the view that the Korean citizenry was coextensive with the historic Korean nation encompassing those who had migrated to China and Russia during or before Japanese occupation and their descendants.[39] In treating the members of this pre-independence diaspora, the ROK government affirmed the continuity of Korean nationality, and therefore Korean state-peoplehood, throughout Japanese rule.

Ironically, this seemingly inclusive approach was coupled with an exclusionary treatment of the members of the old diaspora. Only a tiny minority were given permanent returnee status, while the rest of the diaspora were denied any chance to have their ROK nationality recognized, nor were their applications for recovery of

[38] It required a potential returnee to obtain an opinion of recognition from the Ministry of Patriots and Veterans Affairs, which was taken into account when the Minister of Foreign Affairs decided whether to grant permanent returnee status. When one was granted that status, the MOJ ascertained the person's ROK nationality (C. Lee, 2012: 90).

[39] The motivation seems to have been more practical and technical than nationalistic. The Nationality Act at the time required one who acquired ROK nationality after birth to renounce his or her previous nationality within 6 months; otherwise, the person would lose his or her newly acquired ROK nationality. Before the 1998 amendment of the Enforcement Decree for the Nationality Act, there was no exception to this requirement. In the early 1990s, the renunciation of PRC nationality was almost impossible. Thus, if return migrants from China had been given the chance to acquire ROK nationality as foreigners, they would not have been able to keep their ROK nationality thus acquired because of the failure to renounce their PRC nationality.

nationality or naturalization accepted.[40] The ROK government was aware that it was unjustifiable to make nationality determination available only to a tiny minority and simultaneously found it impracticable to make it available to all. It also considered the risk of diplomatic friction with the People's Republic of China (PRC) because of its treatment of the Korean minority in China as part of the Korean *Staatsvolk* (Chulwoo Lee, 2010: 236, 2012: 90–91).

By adopting the Guidelines on the Nationality Affairs of Coethnics from China, the ROK government began to treat the members of the Korean minority in China as having lost their ROK nationality. When? The day when the People's Republic of China was proclaimed—October 1, 1949. MOJ created a fiction that the Koreans in China acquired PRC nationality and simultaneously lost their ROK nationality on that day. Hence, those born before October 1, 1949 should apply for recovery of nationality to regain their ROK nationality and those born on that day or after should go through the naturalization procedure to acquire ROK nationality.[41]

The Guidelines on the Nationality Affairs of Coethnics from China was challenged by way of a constitutional complaint, but the Constitutional Court dismissed the complaint on the grounds that intra-ministry guidelines were nonjusticiable and the contested guidelines had already been repealed (Constitutional Court 2006.03.30. 2003HeonMa806). Indeed, the Guidelines on the Nationality Affairs of Coethnics from China was repealed in 2005 and replaced by the Guidelines for the Administration of Recovery of Nationality by Coethnics of Foreign Nationality. The new guidelines retain the same provision on the date when Koreans in China lost their ROK nationality.[42] In comparison to Koreans in China, the administrative practice regarding the nationality of Koreans in the former Soviet Union, namely, Central Asia and Russia except Sakhalin, has been opaque, but few disputes have arisen because Koreans in those regions, who are many generations away from their emigrant ancestors, have less interest in claiming ROK nationality.[43]

---

[40] Only a very few narrow migration routes to Korea were available to the members of the Korean diaspora in China and the Soviet Union. At some point, those migrants were given visas, which suggests that they were regarded as foreigners, and were treated as illegal migrants if they overstayed their visas. For the changing procedures and treatments of immigration administration in the early stage of reunion with the old diaspora, see Chulwoo Lee (2012: 89–91).

[41] Article 3(2), Guidelines on the Nationality Affairs of Coethnics from China. Yet MOJ refused applications for naturalization or recovery of nationality by Koreans from China until 2001, and for some time after 2001 continued to subject them to stricter requirements than applicants from other countries (C. Lee, 2012: 91).

[42] Article 3, Guidelines for the Administration of Recovery of Nationality by Coethnics of Foreign Nationality.

[43] Interpretations vary as regards when Koreans in the former Soviet Union lost their Korean nationality. In some respects, the government gave an impression that it was treating them as having lost their Korean nationality when they acquired Russian nationality or USSR citizenship. Some scholars questioned this position (Loh, 1990; Chung, 1998: 244–245). Later, the HiKorea website stated as if the same criterion as Koreans in China applied to Koreans in the former Soviet Union (www.hikorea.go.kr/pt/index.html). It disappeared at some point. In response to my enquiry, an MOJ official in charge of nationality affairs opined that Koreans in the former Soviet Union

MOJ's new approach to the nationality of Koreans in China did not affect its position on the nationality of Koreans during Japanese rule. Those Koreans possessed ROK nationality, just like Koreans in the ROK, until almost a year after the enactment of the Nationality Act. Yet, shortly before MOJ adopted its new policy, a new legal construction emerged, which explained how Koreans in general had become ROK nationals. The watershed was a court dispute involving a woman from North Korea.

The plaintiff Yi Yeongsun was born in Korea during Japanese rule and lived in North Korea until moving to China in 1960. Yi entered South Korea in 1992 on a Chinese passport and visa with her husband, who was a Chinese citizen of Korean descent. The couple worked in restaurants and motels until a drunken man killed Yi's husband. Then, Yi decided to settle permanently in South Korea and reported to the police that she was North Korean. The police and immigration authorities, however, regarded her as Chinese, and the MOJ decided to deport her and detained her for deportation. Yi brought an action to have the orders declared null and void and, in the alternative, annulled because she was North Korean and, therefore, an ROK citizen. She submitted her North Korean citizen card and alien resident card issued by the Chinese government as proof. The Seoul High Court ruled that Yi was a ROK citizen and the deportation order and detention order should be annulled, although it refused to declare the orders null and void (1995.12.08. 94Gu16009). The Supreme Court affirmed the Seoul High Court decision (1996.11.12. 96Nu1221).

The crux of the decision was that Yi was North Korean and, therefore, an ROK citizen. In clarifying Yi's legal status, the Seoul High Court gave its interpretation of the legal grounds on which Koreans in general had become citizens of the Republic of Korea. In so ruling, the court recognized the Temporary Provisions Concerning the Law of Nationality as the source of governing rules prior to the Nationality Act of 1948. It explained that Koreans had possessed Joseon nationality pursuant to the Temporary Provisions and "acquired" the nationality of the Republic of Korea when its Constitution came into force on July 17, 1948. The Supreme Court accepted this construction.

Some commentators take issue with the use of the word "acquired" because it sounds like denying Korean statehood before July 17, 1948, and treating the ROK as a new state in international law (e.g., Kim Myung-Ki, 1997: 203–204). Yet, while the Yi Yeongsun decision has been cited in subsequent cases and various other official statements, the wording "acquired" has not been corrected or contested, even where the underlying premise is that Korean statehood did not cease during Japanese occupation. In other words, even in speech contexts where it is assumed or argued that Joseon nationals were merely carried over into the citizenry of the Republic of Korea and did not acquire ROK citizenship de novo, Koreans are described as having "acquired" ROK nationality.

---

retained their ROK nationality until the time when the republics of the Soviet Union became new states and one's citizenship of the new state in which the person resided was recognized.

The Yi Yeongsun holding became the standard legal explanation of how Koreans became ROK citizens, as it was cited in subsequent cases (e.g., Constitutional Court 2000.8.31. 97HeonGa12). Notwithstanding the problematic wording, the Yi Yeongsun case etched an image of the Temporary Provisions that is inclusive and protective. Its rationalization of the transition from Joseon nationality to ROK nationality has been invoked as a supporting ground for arguing the continuing possession of ROK nationality by the members of the Korean minority in China. A constitutional complaint against the Guidelines on the Nationality Affairs of Coethnics from China underlined the Temporary Provisions Concerning the Law of Nationality in claiming the continuing possession of ROK nationality by the claimants, who were undocumented Chinese migrants of Korean descent. The claimants argued that they were ROK-PRC dual nationals and that the ROK government had neglected its duty to make a law for them to choose their nationality or to make a treaty with China to resolve their nationality conflict. The Constitutional Court dismissed the complaint without a definite ruling on the claimants' alleged ROK nationality, but a dissenting justice partly embraced the claimants' logic.[44] According to the dissenting opinion, the contested Guidelines unconstitutionally treated as foreigners those who were recognized as having been "granted" Joseon nationality by the Temporary Provisions Concerning the Law of Nationality and "acquired" ROK nationality upon the 1948 Constitution coming into force. The dissenting justice further opined that "the initial citizens of the Republic of Korea" were the *joseonin* under the Temporary Provisions (Constitutional Court 2006.3.30. 2003HeonMa806).[45] It is problematic whether the dissenting opinion is congruent with the belief in the continuity of Korean state-peoplehood, because it uses the terms "granted" and "acquired" as if Koreans became Joseon nationals as well as ROK nationals de novo. Yet, it simultaneously cited the Provisional Constitution (1919) and the Provisional Constitutional Charter (1944) of the Provisional Government of the Republic of Korea, and thereby affirmed the continuity of "the people of the Republic of Korea."

The aforementioned 2005 Review Reports of the Legislation and Judiciary Committee of the National Assembly cited the Yi Yeongsun *ratio* in a positive way in affirming the ROK nationality of patriots who died abroad without being entered on the Korean family register (Legislation and Judiciary Committee, 2005). These reports adamantly deny that Koreans prior to the Nationality Act of 1948 could lose Korean nationality by acquiring foreign nationality; thus, while the Temporary Provisions was treated as a source of supporting grounds, its significant underlying proposition was forgotten or ignored.

---

[44] The opinion of the court offered its observation that Korean coethnics in China were "generally being deemed as foreigners possessing Chinese nationality," but it added that the claimants' complaint could not stand even if they had continued to hold ROK nationality because they had little choice but to acquire Chinese nationality.

[45] The Constitutional Court had already accepted the Yi Yeongsun *ratio* as the governing rule and hence the majority opinion in this case probably did not differ from the dissenting opinion as regards the status of the Temporary Provisions, although it did not mention that issue.

A stream of cases in the 2010s strengthened the status of the Temporary Provisions Concerning the Law of Nationality. The Seoul Administrative Court applied the Temporary Provisions in explaining the ROK nationality of a Korean in Japan who refused to register as a ROK national and stuck to "Joseon" in alien registration (2012.5.4. 2012GuHap3217).[46] The Seoul Administrative Court valorized the Temporary Provisions in rendering a declaratory judgment on the ROK nationality of a Korean in Sakhalin erstwhile treated as stateless by the Russian authorities (Seoul Administrative Court 2014.6.19. 2012GuHap26159). It was followed by a case that referred to the Temporary Provisions as rationalized by the Yi Yeongsun decision in recognizing the eligibility of a North Korean to compensation for forced labor mobilization during Japanese rule (Supreme Court 2016.1.28. 2011Du 24675).

The ROK's practices canvassed so far have exposed many gaps and discrepancies. How serious are those gaps and discrepancies? Has the ROK been inconsistent in asserting the continuity of its state-peoplehood?

5 Conclusion

Independence campaigns led by the Provisional Government of the Republic of Korea were predicated on the belief that the treaties that led to annexation were null and void, and therefore, Korea retained its legal statehood despite Japanese occupation. Rhee Syngman was perhaps the leader with the strongest commitment to that position. Political leaders who viewed the Provisional Government of the Republic of Korea as the greatest source of legitimacy expressed their commitment by using an era name based on the ROK's history from the establishment of the Provisional Government in 1919.[47] This attitude explains the ROK government's insistence on phrasing Article 2 of the 1965 ROK-Japan Treaty on Basic Relations in such a way as to make it clear that Japan's annexation of Korea was null and void ab initio. How consistently has the ROK put this position into action and discourse? Many arguments can be made with regard to various areas of state practice, but this chapter is concerned only with the ROK's definition and delimitation of its *Staatsvolk* and administration in respect of state membership.

While the Provisional Government of the Republic of Korea took it for granted that the population of the Joseon kingdom and the Empire of Korea became the citizenry of the Republic of Korea proclaimed in 1919, it did not go beyond declaring

[46] The decision was affirmed by the Seoul High Court (2012.5.4. 2012Nu15304) and the Supreme Court (2013.12.12. 2013Du7216). But the main issue in this case was whether the government's refusal to issue the plaintiff a special travel document for coethnics was lawful, and the courts ruled that it was lawful.

[47] Rhee Syngman, as Speaker of the first National Assembly inaugurated in 1948, put the date for his speech as May 31 in Republic Year 30.

that sovereignty lay with the Korean people; few efforts were made to provide detailed criteria for delimiting the boundaries of the citizenry. After Japan's surrender, practical needs arose for defining who Koreans were, and USAMGIK adopted somewhat differing criteria for different purposes, but in many cases, the family registration system implemented by the Japanese played a central part in differentiating Koreans and Japanese because that system had already institutionalized separation by putting the two groups in different registers. Although "Koreans" and "citizens" were defined for different purposes, including voter registration for the National Assembly election, no nationality law had been available until the Temporary Provisions Concerning the Law of Nationality came into force. The Temporary Provisions provided for a "Joseon" nationality. Whether this signifies a denial of Korea's continuing statehood is debatable, but it was at least not openly supportive of the status and official authority of the Provisional Government of the Republic of Korea; otherwise, there would have been no reason why the term "ROK nationality" should not be used. The Temporary Provisions also collided with the Empire of Korea's law that prohibited expatriation without permission, as it treated persons who had acquired foreign nationality as having lost Korean nationality.

The Nationality Act of 1948 was the clearest and strongest assertion of Korea's unbroken statehood. Its deliberate lack of definition of initial citizens is based on the premise that the Republic of Korea is a new name adopted in 1919 for the historic Korean state; therefore, "the citizen of the Republic of Korea" existed before 1948, and there was no need to define who a citizen was.

The framers of the Nationality Act disregarded the Temporary Provisions Concerning the Law of Nationality, and some subsequent governmental practices did so too. The Temporary Provisions was invoked in court decisions, but its use was limited to discerning Koreans and Japanese after Korea was liberated. Despite its provisions overriding the old rule against expatriation, the courts seldom applied the Temporary Provisions openly to cases involving the nationality of persons who acquired foreign nationality during Japanese rule. However, the Yi Yeongsun case, whose *ratio* the Seoul High Court developed and the Supreme Court affirmed, made the Temporary Provisions a stepping stone toward ROK nationality. Since then, the Temporary Provisions has been heralded as the first nationality law of Korea. Furthermore, it is now invoked in nationalistic statements that emphasize the continuing possession of ROK nationality by the members of the Korean diaspora.

Despite some gaps and discrepancies, the ROK has been quite adamant in asserting the continuity of state-peoplehood from the pre-annexation Korean state through Japanese rule and US military government to the current Republic of Korea. Although the Temporary Provisions Concerning the Law of Nationality contains nothing that supports the continuity of Korean statehood thesis, it is now positively referred to in nationalistic statements asserting continuity. Should the ROK be more consistent, the now routinely employed phrasing that Koreans "acquired" ROK nationality should be revised to signify that Joseon nationality, if that term should be used, was "converted" to ROK nationality.

References[48]

Ban, B. Y. (1998). *Seongjae Yi Donghwi ildaegi* [A biography of Seongjae Yi Donghwi]. Beomusa.

Bauböck, R., Perchinig, B., & Sievers, W. (Eds.) (2009). *Citizenship policies in the new Europe* (Expanded and updated ed.). Amsterdam University Press.

Cheong, S.-H. (1990). The issue of Korean participation in the San Francisco peace treaty in 1951. *Korea Journal, 30*(5), 16–26.

Chen, E. I.-t. (1984). The attempt to integrate the empire: Legal perspectives. In R. H. Myers & M. R. Peattie (Eds.), *The Japanese colonial empire, 1895–1945* (pp. 240–274). Princeton University Press.

Choi, K.-S. (2009). Migyihwan jaejung hanin eui gukjeok gwisok munje [The problems of the nationality status of unreturned Chinese Koreans]. *Hangukhak nonchong, 32*, 463–489.

Chon, J., et al. (2016). *Daehanjeguk eui jugwon mit yeongto seunggye e gwanhan beopjeok yeongu* [Legal studies in the sovereignty and territorial succession of the Empire of Korea]. Report submitted to the Ministry of Foreign Affairs, Republic of Korea.

Chung, I. S. (1988). Beopjeok gijun eseo bon hangugin eui beomwi [Legal boundaries of Koreans in light of legal criteria]. In *Sahoegwahak eui jemunje* [Problems in social sciences] (Festschrift for Professor Im Wontaek). Beommunsa.

Chung, I. S. (1996). *Jaeil gyopo eui beopjeok jiwi* [The legal status of Koreans in Japan]. Seoul National University Press.

Chung, I. S. (1998). Uri gukjeokbeopsang choecho gungmin hwakjeong gijun e gwanhan geomto [Inquiry into the criteria for finalizing the initial citizens under Korean nationality law]. *Gukjebeophakhoe nonchong, 43*(2), 235–248.

Chung, I. S. (2024). *Daehanminguk surip gwa gukjebeop* [The establishment of the Republic of Korea and international law]. Bagyeongsa.

Dan, S. (2009). Chinese by definition: Nationality law, jus sanguinis, and state succession, 1909–1980. *Twentieth Century China, 35*(1), 7–30.

Egawa, H., Yamada, R., & Hayada, Y. (1989). *Kokusekihō* [Nationality Law]. Yūbigaku.

Ginsburgs, G. (1968). *Soviet citizenship law*. A. W. Sijthoff.

Hahm, C., & Kim, S. H. (2015). *Making we the people: Democratic constitutional founding in postwar Japan and South Korea*. Cambridge University Press.

Hanguk Beopje Yeonguhoe. (1971). *Migunjeong beomnyeong chongnam* [Collected laws and regulations of the US military government] (English ed.).

Jung, K., & Yeom, M. (1999). Diaspora, gwihwan, chulhyeonjeok jeongcheseong: Sakhalin hanin eui yeonksajeok gyeongheom [Diaspora, return, emergent identity: The historical experiences of Sakhalin Koreans]. *Jaeoe hanin yeongu, 9*, 235–248.

Jung, B. (2020). Hanguk eui San Francisco Pyeonghwa hoedam chamga munje wa baeje gwajeong [The issue of Korea's participation in the San Francisco peace conference and the process of exclusion]. *Hanguk gwa gukje jeongchi, 36*(3), 1–42.

Kang, P. (2018). 19 segimal 20 segi jeonbangi 'Hanguk' eui gukgajeok jiwi e gwanhan gukjebeopjeok gochal [A perspective on the legal status of Korea in late 1890s and in the first half of the 20th century]. *Gukjebeop pyeongron, 49*, 1–33.

Kim, C. R. (2022). *Daebeobwon gangjedongwon pangyeol: Haeksimeun 'bulbeop gangjeom' ida* [The Supreme Court decision on forced labor mobilization: The crux of the question is "illegal occupation"]. Jisiksaneopsa.

Kim, M.-K. (1997). Bukhan jumin eul Daehanminguk gungmin euro bon daebeobwon pangyeol eui beobiron [The jurisprudence of the Supreme Court decision that regarded a North Korean as a citizen of the Republic of Korea]. *Justice, 30*(2), 186–205.

Kim, S.-J. (2009). Daehanminguk jeongbusurip jeonhu gukjeokbeop jejeong noneui gwajeong e natanan kungmin gyeonggye seoljeong [The delimitation of the boundaries of the 'citizenry'

[48] See notes for cited materials of which the author(s) cannot be specified.

in the discussion of nationality law enactment before and after the establishment of the government of the Republic of Korea]. *Hanguk geunhyeondaesa yeongu, 49*, 114–203.
League of Nations (1932). *Report of the Commission of Enquiry appointed by the Council of the League of Nations*, League of Nations Doc. C.663.M.320, Series of League of Nations Publication VII. Political, League of Nations.
Lee, C. (2010). South Korea: The transformation of citizenship and the state-nation nexus. *Journal of Contemporary Asia, 40*(2), 230–251.
Lee, C. (2012). How can you say you're Korean? Law, governmentality and national membership in South Korea. *Citizenship Studies, 16*(1), 85–102.
Lee, C. (2015). The law and politics of citizenship in divided Korea. *Yonsei Law Journal, 6*(1&2), 3–31.
Lee, K.-G. (2009). 1948 nyeon ihu nambukhan gukka seunggye eui beopjeok geomto [A legal examination of state succession by North and South Korea after 1948]. *Seoul gukjebeop yeongu, 16*(1), 143–166.
Lee, K.-G. (2020). Gukjebeopsang Hanguk eui dongilseong mit gyesokseong e daehan gochal [An inquiry into the identity and continuity of Korea under international law]. *Seouldaehakgyo beophak, 61*(2), 143–182.
Lee, S.-C. (2012). *Joyak eui gukga seunggye* [The state succession in treaties]. Yeollin chaekdeul.
Lee, S.-C. (2025). "Yeoksa wa gukjebeop eun mosun doeji ana: Daehanminguk gwa Daehanjeguk eun dongilhan gukkada [History and international law do not contradict each other: The Republic of Korea and the Empire of Korea are an identical state]." *Jugan Chosun*, 2837, 44–47.
Legislation and Judiciary Committee [Beopjesabeopwiwonhoe], National Assembly of the Republic of Korea. (2005). *Gukjeokbeop gaejeong beomnyuran geomto bogoseo* [Review reports on the Nationality Act amendment bills] (Bill Nos. 2430, 2467, and 2527).
Lim, D. (2018). Daehanminguk imsijeongbu eui 'daehaeng seongeo' yeongu [A study on the 'proxy election' of the Korean Provisional Government]. *Hanguk dongnipundongsa yeongu, 64*, 83–120.
Loh, Y. D. (1990). Jaeso hanin eui gukjeok e gwanhan yeongu [A study of the nationality of Koreans in the Soviet Union]. *Gukjebeophakhoe nonchong, 35*(1), 163–183.
Loh, Y. D. (1996). Urinara gukjeokbeop eui myeotgaji munje e gwanhan gochal [Inquiry into a few problems in Korean nationality law]. *Gukjebeophakhoe nonchong, 41*(2), 49–64.
Mälksoo, L. (2022). *Illegal Annexation and State Continuity: The Case of the Incorporation of the Baltic States by the USSR* (2nd revised ed.). Brill.
Mizuno, N. (2000). Kokuseki o meguru Toajia kankei [East Asian Relations Surrounding Nationality], In T. Huruya and S. Yamamuro (eds.), *Kindai Nihon ni okeru Toajia mondai* [East Asia Questions in Modern Japan] (pp. 211-237). Yoshikawa kobunkan.
Na, I.-G. (1999). Daehanminguk gwa Dehanjeguk eun beopjeok euro dongilhanga? [Are the Republic of Korea and the Empire of Korea legally identical]. *Gukjebeophakhoe nonchong, 44*(1), 127–140.
Oguma, E. (1998). *Nihonjin no kyōkai* [The boundaries of the Japanese]. Shiny sa.
Onuma, Y. (1986). Legal status of Korean residents in Japan: Past, present and future. *Seouldaehakgyo beophak, 27*(1), 8–29.
Park, K.-S. (2009). Singminji sigi (1910–1945) Joseon eui ingu dongtae wa gujo [The trends and structure of population in colonial Korea (1910–1945)]. *Hanguk inguhak, 32*(2), 29–58.
Park, P.-K. (2010). Discussions concerning the legality of the 1910 'annexation' of Korea by Japan. *Korea Journal, 50*(4), 13–41.
Park, Y.-S. (2010). *Manjujiyeok hanin sahoe wa hangil dongnip undong* [The Korean society in Manchuria and the anti-Japanese independence movement]. Gukhakjaryowon.
Seo, H.-C. (2007). 1890–1930 nyeondae jumin deungnok jedo wa guendaejeok tongshiseong eui hyeongseong [The resident registration system and the formation of modern governmentality 1890–1930] (Unpublished doctoral dissertation). Seoul National University.
Seo, H.-C. (2017). Nuga gungmin igo nuga yugwonja ga doeneunga? Namhan eui choecho chongseongeo wa jumin eui jagyeok, bunryu, deungnok [Who were the citizens and who should be

the electors? The first general election of South Korea and the registration and classification of residents]. *Sahoe wa yeoksa, 113*, 269–310.

United States Army Forces in Korea. (1948). *Selected legal opinions of the Department of Justice, United States Army Military Government in Korea.* Headquarters, United States Army Military Government in Korea.

Yi, T.-J. (2022). Hanguk chamga munje reul dulleossan Miguk gwa Yeongguk eui euigyeon chai: San Francisco pyeonghwa joyak eui gabyeonseong [The difference between the United Kingdom and the United States as regards the participation of Korea: The variability of the San Francisco Peace Treaty]. In Y. H. Kim et al. (Eds.), *San Francisco cheje reul neomeoseo: Dong Asia naengjeon gwa singminji · jeongjaeng beomjoe eui cheongsam* [Beyond the San Francisco system: The liquidation of the Cold War, colonialism and war crimes in East Asia] (pp. 181-204). Medici.

Yi, T.-J., & Sasagawa, N. (Eds.) (2009). *Hanguk byeonghap gwa hyeondae* [The annexation of Korea and modernity]. Taehaksa.

Yoo, E. (2019, September 19). Gangje dongwon daebeobwon pangyeol gwa cheonggugwon munje, geurigo bug-il sugyo eui gwaje [The Supreme Court decision on forced labor mobilization and the problem of tort claims, and the tasks of the normalization of diplomatic relations between North Korea and Japan]. Paper presented at a Gyeonggi Research Institute Conference.

Yoo, E. (2022). *Hanil gwageosa munje eui eoje wa oneul – singmin jibae wa jeonjaeng dong-won e daehan Ilbon eui chaegim* [The yesterday and today of the Korea-Japan history problems: Japan's responsibility for colonial rule and war mobilization]. Northeast Asian History Foundation.

Righting the Wrongs of the Past Between the Republic of Korea and Japan as a Retrial of the "San Francisco System"

Chang Rok Kim

Abstract The article examines the unresolved historical and legal conflicts between the Republic of Korea and Japan stemming from Japan's colonial rule over Korea from 1910 to 1945. It highlights how the 1951 San Francisco Treaty, while addressing war-related issues, neglected Japan's colonial responsibilities and excluded Korea from the peace settlement. The 1965 Korea-Japan Claims Agreement resolved financial and property matters but did not provide reparations for colonial injustices or acknowledge the illegality of Japanese rule. Korean victims of forced labor and "comfort women" have continued to seek justice through lawsuits, leading to landmark rulings by Korean courts that affirm Japan's occupation was illegitimate and that individual claims remain valid. These rulings have fueled diplomatic tensions, as Japan maintains that all claims were settled by the 1965 agreement. The article critiques the Cold War-era settlement, which prioritized geopolitical interests over historical justice, and discusses the ongoing "retrial" of the San Francisco System in Korean courts. It underscores the importance of legal activism and democratization in challenging established narratives. The study calls for a comprehensive reevaluation of the treaty system and recognition of colonial wrongs. Ultimately, it portrays the ongoing struggle for historical accountability and reconciliation between Korea and Japan.

Keywords 1965 Claims Agreement · Allied powers · Cold War · Colonial Rule · Japan · Korea · San Francisco Treaty · Supreme Court · Treaty interpretation · Victims

C. R. Kim (✉)
Kyungpook National University Law School, Daegu, South Korea

Y.-H. Kim et al. (eds.), *Beyond the San Francisco System*,
https://doi.org/10.1007/978-981-95-3328-2_17

1 Introduction

The 「Treaty of Peace with Japan」 (hereinafter 「San Francisco Treaty」), which was signed on September 8, 1951, and took effect on November 28 of the following year, created a new system (hereinafter "San Francisco System") that brought up many issues for which various critical reviews exist. The issues include the aggravation of the Cold War, vast deployment of the US Forces in Asia, Japan's separation from Asia, and territorial disputes in Asia (between Russia and Japan, China and Japan, China and Taiwan, and China and Southeast Asian countries, etc.).[1]

Here, the focus is on "historical conflicts," especially, the righting of the wrongs of the past between the Republic of Korea (hereinafter "Korea") and Japan. The issue of Japanese imperialism's invasion of the Korean Peninsula since the end of the nineteenth century, especially the issue of the responsibilities it should take for the colonization of the Korean Peninsula from 1910 to 1945, still remains unsolved even after 70 years since its ending. Even though the relationship between Korea and Japan was normalized in 1965, the issues of the past were not handled sufficiently and dealt with only vaguely. The issues have once again gained attention since the 1990s, when the Korean victims of colonization actively asked for their righting, becoming one of the main tasks for Korea-Japan relations by adding numerous issues to take a look at. Moreover, as the first historical step toward the establishment of a new peace order in Northeast Asia has been set with the 「Panmunjom Declaration」 on April 27, 2018, North Korea-Japan and even the Korean Peninsula-Japan relations are entering a new phase.

I believe that the righting of wrongs of the past between Korea and Japan, the two countries lying under the abovementioned situations, and the surrounding conflicts are not only closely related to the San Francisco System but also reveal the problems of the system. The purpose of this presentation is to review the issues while focusing on legal aspects.

2 San Francisco System, Neglecting the Responsibilities of Colonial Rule

The 「San Francisco Treaty」, as clearly mentioned in its preamble, has been signed to "settle questions still outstanding as a result of the existence of a state of war" between the Allied Powers and Japan. This shows that the purpose of the treaty is the post-war settlement of World War II.

As a result, in the 「San Francisco Treaty」, the Japanese imperialism's 35-year colonial rule over the Korean Peninsula from 1910 to 1945 has not been set as an

[1] John W. Dower, "The San Francisco System: Past, Present, Future in U.S.-Japan-China Relations," *The Asia-Pacific Journal*, Vol. 12, Issue 8, No. 2, February 24, 2014. (https://apjjf.org/2014/12/8/John-W-Dower/4079/article).

agenda to handle. The word "colony" never appears anywhere in the treaty. The two Koreas could not even participate as signatories of the treaty.

But, the「San Francisco Treaty」, even though the two Koreas were absent, regulated that "Korea [shall be entitled] to the benefits of Articles 2, 4, 9 and 12."

First, Article 2(a) provides that "Japan, recognizing the independence of Korea, renounces all right, title, and claim to Korea." This is in line with the「Cairo Declaration」of November 27, 1943, when the leaders of the United States, China, and the United Kingdom declared that "the aforesaid three great powers, mindful of the enslavement of the people of Korea, are determined that in due course Korea shall become free and independent."[2] However, the meaning of "independence" in Article 2(a) is unclear. Still, considering the purpose of the「San Francisco Treaty」, it is difficult to see that it includes asking Japan to take responsibility for its wrongdoings during colonization.

Second, in Article 4(b), it is regulated that "Japan recognizes the validity of dispositions of property of Japan and Japanese nationals made by or pursuant to directives of the United States Military Government in any of the areas referred to in Articles 2." The disposition of property regarding the Korean Peninsula includes Ordinance number 33, which was proclaimed by the Headquarters of United States Army Forces in Korea on 6 December 1945. Section 2 of the Ordinance provides that "property of Japan and Japanese nationals located within the jurisdiction of this Command on or since 9 August 1945 are vested in Military Government of Korea as of 25 September 1945, and all such property is owned by the Military Government of Korea." These Japanese public and private properties were transferred to the Korean Government under the Initial Financial and Property Settlement between the Government of the Republic of Korea and the Government of the United States of America, which was signed on September 11, 1948, and took effect on September 20 the same year.

Next, in Article 4(a) of the「San Francisco Treaty」, it is regulated that "the disposition of property of Japan and of its nationals in the areas referred to in Article 2, and their claims, including debts, against the authorities presently administering such areas and the residents (including juridical persons) thereof, and the disposition in Japan of property of such authorities and residents, and of claims, including debts, of such authorities and residents against Japan and its nationals, shall be the subject of special arrangements between Japan and such authorities." Here, the meaning of "property," "claims," and "special arrangement" are also unclear. However, just like Article 2(a), it is hard to understand that the terms include the purpose of asking Japan to take responsibility for its colonial rule.

In short, the purpose of the「San Francisco Treaty」was to ask Japan to take responsibility for the war it committed, not for its colonial rule over the Korean Peninsula. The issues of "property" and "claims" between Korea and Japan were forwarded to a "special arrangement," but it was set to be concluded under the US-led system based on the「San Francisco Treaty」.

---

[2]This declaration was reaffirmed by Article 8 (the terms of the Cairo Declaration shall be carried out) of the "Potsdam Declaration (Proclamation Defining Terms for Japanese Surrender)" of July 26, 1945.

3 1965 System as a Substructure of the San Francisco System

On October 21, 1951, a preliminary conference for the normalization of the relations between Korea and Japan began with the mediation of the foreign affairs director of the Allied Forces Supreme Commander William J. Sebald. The talk between Korea and Japan took place because the United States needed the normalization of the relations between the two countries located at the front line in Northeast Asia during the time of escalating Cold War. The fact that the talk began only a month after the signing of the「San Francisco Treaty」shows its correlation with the US-led San Francisco System.

Since then, as a result of seven talks during almost 14 years of repeated suspension and resume, several treaties, including the「Treaty on Basic Relations between Japan and the Republic of Korea」(hereinafter「Basic Treaty」) and the「Agreement on the Settlement of Problems Concerning Property and Claims and on Economic Cooperation」(hereinafter「Claims Agreement」), were signed on June 22, 1965. The agreements were ratified in December of the same year and took effect, and the diplomatic ties between Korea and Japan were normalized.

When taking a look at the treatises' relation with the「San Francisco Treaty」, the first one to focus on is the「Claims Agreement」. Article 1 of the「Claims Agreement」regulates that Japan provides "Japan's products and Japanese nationals' service" worth 300 million dollars for free and a loan of 200 million dollars with a long-term low interest rate, and Article 2 regulates as mentioned below.

> Art. 2, para. 1: "[The] problem concerning the property, rights and interests of the two Contracting Parties and their nationals (including juridical persons), and concerning claims between the Contracting Parties and their nationals, including those provided for in Article IV, paragraph (a) of the Treaty of Peace with Japan signed at the city of San Francisco on September 8, 1951, is settled completely and finally."

> Art. 2, para. 3: "[No] contention shall be made, with respect to the property, rights and interests of each Contracting Party and its nationals, to measures within the jurisdiction of the other Contracting Party as of the date of the signing of the present Agreement; or, with respect to the claims of each Contracting Party and its nationals against the other Contracting Party and its nationals, to claims arising from incidents which occurred on or before the said date."

As we can see that "Article 4, paragraph (a) of the Treaty of Peace with Japan" is mentioned in the above-cited Article 2, paragraph 1, the「Claims Agreement」is one of the "special arrangements" in Article 4(a) of the「San Francisco Treaty」. Of course, Korea is not obliged to the「San Francisco Treaty」since it is not one of the signatories. However, it is possible for Korea to exercise the right to be benefited mentioned in Article 4 of the「San Francisco Treaty」, and Korea did so with the signing of「Claims Agreement」.

If the「Claims Agreement」conforms to the "special arrangement" of Article 4(a) of the「San Francisco Treaty」, it is natural to interpret that issues regarding colonization are not included in problems solved with the Agreement. That is because, as explained above, the purpose of「San Francisco Treaty」was to deal with war-related issues, and the ones related to colonial rule were excluded.

However, unlike in the「San Francisco Treaty」, where the target range is clearly provided through the sentence, "[to] settle questions still outstanding as a result of the existence of a state of war," it is difficult to recognize the range in the「Claims Agreement」. Neither the preamble nor the text suggests the cause of the solved rights. This is clearly in contrast with the treaties Japan signed with other countries regarding "righting the wrongs of the past" after the Second World War, where the cause of the rights is clearly seen. For example, Article 6 of the Joint Declaration by the Union of Soviet Socialist Republics and Japan (19 October 1956) provides that "The USSR and Japan agree to renounce all claims by either State, its institutions or citizens, against the other State, its institutions or citizens, which have arisen <u>as a result of the war</u> since 9 August 1945," and Article 5 of the Joint Communique of the Government of Japan and the Government of the People's Republic of China (September 29, 1972) provides that "The Government of the People's Republic of China declares that in the interest of the friendship between the Chinese and the Japanese peoples, it renounces its <u>demand for war reparation</u> from Japan." However, in the「Claims Agreement, even though it provides that problems regarding rights be solved, it mentions nothing about the cause of the rights.

As the cause of handled rights is not provided, can we say that "all" rights are dealt with? Actually, given the legal common sense that all legal agreements should have a clear subject, it is difficult to draw such an interpretation. Moreover, there is a special reason why the「Claims Agreement」cannot be interpreted that way.

The reason can be seen from the Korean and Japanese governments' discrepancy in interpretation of Article 2 of the「Basic Treaty」. Article 2 of the「Basic Treaty」provides that "It is confirmed that all treaties or agreements concluded between the Empire of Japan and the Empire of Korea on or before August 22, 1910, are already null and void."[3] Regarding the Article, the Korean government interpreted that "all treaties or agreements concluded between the Empire of Japan and the Empire of Korea on or before August 22, 1910, are already null and void... Regarding the moment when they were nullified, without any additional explanation, the terms null and void mean all the treaties and agreements do not have any effect "from the beginning" in principle, and moreover, since it is emphasized with the term "already," it is retroactively Null and Void."[4] The basis of such interpretation is that

---

[3] The "Basic Treaty" was written in Korean, Japanese, and English, and the text itself states, "In case of any divergence of interpretation, the English text shall prevail." The Korean text's "already null and void" is written as "もはや無効" in Japanese. "もはや" in Japanese means "now" and in that sense, it can be seen as a term that places the time frame in the present rather than the past. As can be seen in the text below, such differences actually led to "differences in interpretation" between Korea and Japan. Therefore, the English text is significant in this regard, and "already" in English includes both "already" and "now." Therefore, even if the English text is followed, the difference in interpretation is not resolved.

[4] 대한민국정부, 『한일회담백서』, 1965, p. 19.

the treaties are "the products of Japanese imperialism's aggression."[5] On the contrary, the Japanese government interpreted that "'null and void' is just stating the objective fact that the treaties and agreements are null and void at this moment in the present... Regarding the moment when they were nullified, the treaties before annexation treaty took effect with their own achievement of conditions provided in them or with the coming into effect of the annexation treaty, and the annexation treaty lost effect on 15 August 1948, the day when Korea became independent."[6] The basis of Japanese Government's interpretation is that "the treaty was concluded under a legitimate procedure,"[7] that is, "the treaty was concluded by countries of equal position or under free will."[8] In short, according to the interpretation of the Korean government, the Japanese imperialism's 35 years of colonization of the Korean Peninsula was "illegitimate and forceful occupation," whereas according to that of the Japanese government, it was a "legitimate governing." Therefore, there is a difference in the range of rights to be dealt with for both sides. That is the reason why we cannot interpret that "all" rights have been solved by the 「Claims Agreement」.

Eventually, the rage of right handled by the 「Claims Agreement」 cannot be verified by reflecting the first standard of the General rule of interpretation of treaties, "the ordinary meaning to be given to the terms of the treaty in their context and in the light of its object and purpose," which is provided in Article 31 paragraph 1 of the 「Vienna Convention on the Law of Treaties」 (hereinafter "「Vienna Convention」").

On the contrary, it can be clearly identified under another standard stated in Article 31 paragraph 3(b) of the 「Vienna Convention」, which is the "subsequent practice in the application of the treaty which establishes the agreement of the parties regarding its interpretation." Right after the signing of the 「Claims Agreement」, regarding the range of right solved by the 「Claims Agreement」, the Korean government interpreted that "the cost of the 36-year colonial rule of the Japanese imperialism" was not the subject and only "financial and property settlement issues deriving

---

[5] Remarks by Minister of Foreign Affairs Lee Dong-won at the Special Committee for the Review of the Korea-Japan Treaty and Agreement and the Ratification Bill on August 8, 1965. 高麗大學校　亞細亞問題研究所　日本研究室編, 韓日關係資料集<第一輯>, 高麗大學校出版部, 1976, p. 252.

[6] 谷田正躬・辰巳信夫・武智敏夫編, 『日韓條約と國內法の解說』, 大藏省印刷局, 1966, p. 14. While this book states in its "Preface" that "all opinions in the commentary are the personal opinions of the author" (p. 5), considering the facts that the editors are the officers of the Ministry of Foreign Affairs, the Ministry of Justice and the Ministry of Agriculture and Forestry, and that those in such special positions "attempt to provide a comprehensive explanation to help achieve as accurate an understanding as possible" of the 1965 "Basic Treaty" and "Agreement" (p. 5), it can be said that it is without a doubt a reflection of the Japanese government's position at the time.

[7] Ibid, p. 14.

[8] Remarks made by Prime Minister Eisaku Sato at the Japan-Korea Special Committee of the House of Representatives on November 5, 1965. 『第50回 國會 衆議院 日本國と大韓民國との間の條約及び協定等に關する特別委員會議錄 第10號』, 1965.11.5, p. 2.

from the separation and partition of territory" have been dealt with,[9] and the Japanese government also interpreted that settlement issues on "Korea's secession" have been handled.[10] That is, both governments' interpretations reached an agreement that "settlement issues on territorial separation" have been solved. Moreover, both governments have made no modification to such an interpretation since then. Therefore, this constitutes the "subsequent practice in the application of the treaty which establishes the agreement of the parties regarding its interpretation."

In brief, considering the standards of international law on the interpretation of treaties, it is the "financial and property settlement issues deriving from the separation of territory," which have been dealt with by the 「Claims Agreement. Here, it is difficult to say that "separation of territory" implicates illegitimate forceful occupation of the territory before its separation. Eventually, just like in the case of the 「San Francisco Treaty」, the issues regarding the responsibilities that Japanese imperialism should take for the colonization of the Korean Peninsula have not been solved by the 「Claims Agreement」.

4 Retrial

4.1 Background

Under a new social environment formed from the late 1980s to early 1990s, the unsolved issue of righting the past wrongs between Korea and Japan arose once again. It was a result of the collapse of the Cold War system and its substructure, authoritarianism in Korea, which brought up the demands of the victims of colonization who have been oppressed under the logics of Cold War, saying "in times of war, one should not point a gun at the same side," and the logics of authoritarianism, saying "the benefits of the government outweighs the rights of individuals."

"Comfort women" victims and other Korean victims of colonization not only asked for help all around the world on the streets, during lectures, and in international organizations but also filed lawsuits in the courts of Japan, the United States, and Korea, asking the Japanese government and companies to take responsibility. These could be regarded as a retrial in the actual courts on the 「San Francisco Treaty」, which is similar to a sentencing asking for Japan to take responsibility for the wrongs it committed during the Second World War, and on the San Francisco System, the treaty's result.

[9] 대한민국정부, op cit, pp. 40–41.

[10] 谷田正躬・辰巳信夫・武智敏夫編, op cit, pp. 61–62.

4.2 Lawsuits in Japanese Courts

A total of a hundred lawsuits have been filed in Japanese courts asking Japan to take responsibility for its invasion and colonial rule. About 90 of them were processed or are being processed since the early 1990s, and about half of them were filed by Korean nationals.[11]

The biggest issues in the lawsuits in Japan vary, including the responsibilities for compensation of damages for violation of international law, responsibilities for compensation of damages for legislative omissions, extinction of rights based on extinctive prescription or exclusion period, exemption according to the legal principle of government irresponsibility, solution of right issues based on bilateral treaties, etc. During the past two decades, there were diverse rulings of Japanese courts, but still, the overall tendency was that core issues usually ended up being related to the handling of rights issues according to the bilateral treaties.

Eventually, on April 27, 2007, the Supreme Court of Japan came up with its final decision during the ruling on the case of Nishimatsu Construction Ltd.'s forced mobilization of the Chinese and on the case of rape of the Chinese.[12] Basically, the intent of both decisions is identical. Regarding the former case, the decision of the Supreme Court of Japan can be summarized as below.

According to the Supreme Court of Japan, 1) under the premise that all claims occurred during war, including that of individuals' be renounced, the「San Francisco Treaty」has set a post-war settlement outline for Japan which is to accept Japan's obligation of war reparation to the Allied Powers and leave the disposal of overseas asset in the jurisdictions of the Allied Powers to the Allied Powers and conclude concrete treaties individually with each Allied Powers on war reparation including service indemnity. 2) This outline should serve as an outline when Japan deals with post-war settlement issues, including by signing peace treaties with other countries or regions rather than the signatories of the「San Francisco Treaty」. 3) Such an outline was set since signing a peace treaty, if various wartime claims related issues are left to be handled through ex post individual exercise of right with civil trials, there might be confusion from the huge burden that has not been expected at the moment when the treaty was concluded and therefore stand in the way of achieving the goals of peace treaties. 4) Therefore, the "abandonment" of the right of claim does not mean an actual extinction of the right but a loss of the power to exercise a right through a trial. 5) However, the discretionary and voluntary action of the debtor is fine.

In short, the final stance of the Supreme Court of Japan is that "the claims right have not been eliminated substantially, but since the right to file a lawsuit has been

---

[11] For a summary of the trials, see「日本戦後補償裁判総覧」(http://justice.skr.jp/souran-jp-intro.html) written by attorney Yamamoto Seita. For a detailed analysis of lawsuits filed by Korean victims, see 김창록,「일본에서의 대일과거청산소송 -한국인들에 의한 소송을 중심으로 -」,『법사학연구』35, 2007.

[12] 最高裁二小法廷判決平成16年(受)第1658号; 最高裁一小法廷判決平成17年(受)第1735号.

eliminated, aid through court ruling cannot be provided. However, it is possible for the debtor to handle the issue voluntarily." By doing so, the Court withdrew itself from the issue, meanwhile passing the ball to the perpetrators, the Japanese government and companies, saying their voluntary action is fine, which is no different from the stance of the Japanese government, since victims could not receive any aid without the "voluntary action" of the debtor.

The final stance of the Supreme Court of Japan is as stated above, but the question is whether it can be applied to the 「Claims Agreement」 between Korea and Japan. The abovementioned decision is about "war reparation," but Japan does not recognize Korea as a member of the Allied Forces, and moreover, Korea is asking Japan to take responsibility for the damages it brought during colonization not during the Second World War. In the final ruling, the Supreme Court of Japan listed a number of treaties signed with countries or regions other than the signatories of the 「San Francisco Treaty」 that are applied with the same logic for their claims settlement, such as the 「Treaty of Peace between Japan and India」, but the 「Claims Agreement」 is not included in the list. Considering these, it is possible to interpret that the above-stated final decision is not applied to the 「Claims Agreement.

However, given that the final decision was made after the Supreme Court's complete review of the settlement of claims, which has repeatedly been the main issue during the hundred "ligations for war reparation," and the Court would not accept the claims based on illegitimate forceful occupation since it sees the Japanese imperialism's ruling of Korea as a legitimate one, it is possible to summarize that the Japanese Supreme Court's idea is that the so-called "outlines of the 「San Francisco Treaty" can be applied to the 「Claims Agreement」 as well. Then, it means that under the premise that the Japanese imperialism's ruling of Korea was legitimate, the Japanese Supreme Court sees the claims issue deriving from the separation of territory has been solved in the form of extinction of the right to bring action in a court.

4.3 *Lawsuits in Korean Courts and the Constitutional Court*

In Korea, regarding the righting of the past wrongs between the Korea and Japan, mainly the "comfort women" and forced mobilization victims filed lawsuits against the Constitutional Court and other courts from the late 1990s. Two of the most noticeable cases are the constitutional appeal filed by the comfort women victims against the Korean government in 2006 and the damage compensation suit by the forced mobilization victims against Mitsubishi Heavy Industries, Ltd. In 2000.

4.3.1 The Decision of the Constitutional Court in 2011

First, the former case has a close link with the decision made by the private and public joint committee,[13] formed to deal with the follow-up measures after the Korean government opened documents of the Korea-Japan talks from 1951 to 1965 to the public on 26 August 2005. In the decision, the Korean government made it clear that since "basically, the intention of the 「Claims Agreement」 between Korea and Japan was not to demand for reparation of colonial ruling, but to settle the financial and property claim and obligation issues based on Article 4 of the 「San Francisco Treaty」, it cannot be seen that the anti-humanitarian illegal activities, such as the comfort women issues, where Japanese authorities including its government and military engaged in, have been dealt with the 「Claims Agreement」, and the legal responsibilities of the Japanese government still remain." This is a reaffirmation of the government's stance in 1965, and even more, a declaration that legal responsibilities of the Japanese government still remain on the anti-humanitarian illegal activities, such as the comfort women issues, where the Japanese authorities were engaged in despite the 「Claims Agreement」.

However, despite the announcement of such a decision, the Korean government did not take active measures to ask the Japanese government about its legal responsibilities. Therefore, the "comfort women" victims filed a constitutional appeal against the government for its omission, and on August 30, 2011, the Constitutional Court ruled that the government's omission was against the Constitution. On the case, the Constitutional Court declared that "the Court affirm that the claimee's omission of not dealing with the conflict in interpretation between Korea and Japan about whether the right to demand compensation is eliminated by Article 2 paragraph 1 of the 「Claims Agreement」 according to the procedures provided by Article 3[14] of the same Agreement is against the constitution."[15]

Such a decision by the Constitutional Court, stating that "not dealing with the conflict according to the procedures by the agreement is against the constitution," just affirms that "not following the procedure is against the constitution." However, the decision was made under the premise that there is a conflict between Korea and Japan regarding the interpretation of the Claims Agreement, and therefore, it is actually an affirmation of the above-mentioned decision of the Korean government in 2005.

---

[13] 국무조정실, 「[보도자료] 한일회담 문서공개 후속대책 관련 민관공동위원회 개최」, 2005.8.26.

[14] It is stipulated that the issue will first be resolved through diplomatic channels, and if that is not possible, it will be resolved through arbitration procedures.

[15] 헌법재판소 2011.8.30 선고 2006헌마788 결정.

4.3.2 The Decision of the Supreme Court of Korea in 2012

The ruling by the Supreme Court of Korea[16] made on May 24, 2012, was quite epoch-making. Through the judgment of appellate court trial filed by the forced labor victims during the ruling of Japanese imperialism against Nippon Steel Corporation, the Court declared a quite epoch-making and historically noticeable "legal decision" regarding the overall righting of the past wrongs between Korea and Japan.

The first noticeable point of this Supreme Court ruling on the righting of the past wrongs between Korea and Japan is the part where it stated that "the overall responsibilities for colonial ruling" including the forced mobilization has not been solved despite the「Claims Agreement」. That is, the decision has declared that, first, "the「Claims Agreement」is not a negotiation to claim reparation for colonial ruling by Japan, but an agreement to deal with financial and property settlement between Korea and Japan according to political agreement based on Article 4 of the「San Francisco Treaty」," and "it is difficult to see that the right to demand compensation for anti-humanitarian or colonization-related illegal activities where the Japanese authorities were involved in can be applied with the「Claims Agreement」." This is beyond the level of the decision made in 2005 by the Korean government. In the 2005 decision, when the Korean government provided that "the responsibilities still remain for the Japanese government," it referred only to "the anti-humanitarian illegal activities, such as the comfort women issues, where Japanese authorities including its government and military were engaged in." Regarding this, the judgement of the Supreme Court affirmed that the claims right for neither "anti-humanitarian illegal activities where the Japanese authorities were engaged in" nor "colonization-related illegal activities" have been eliminated and, moreover, made it clear that "the diplomatic protection right of the Republic of Korea has not been abandoned." Such expansion of coverage has a significant meaning. That is because it means the "claims right on overall responsibilities for colonial ruling" has not been eliminated and its diplomatic protection right has not been eliminated, too.

What is more noticeable is that the ruling of the Supreme Court has affirmed the overall illegitimacy of the forceful occupation and the "colonial ruling responsibilities" of the Japanese imperialism. That is, by stating that "the First Constitution of Korea, providing in its preamble that 'We, the people of Korea, proud of a resplendent history and traditions dating from time immemorial, upholding the great spirit of independence by establishing the Republic of Korea with the March First Independence Movement of 1919 and reestablishing a democratic and independent nation,' and in its Article 100 that 'Acts, decrees, ordinances and treaties in force at the time this Constitution enters into force, shall remain valid unless they are contrary to this Constitution,'" and the current Constitution stating in its preamble that "the people of Korea, proud of a resplendent history and traditions dating from time immemorial, upholding the cause of the Provisional Republic of Korea Government

[16] 대법원 2012.5.24. 선고 2009다68620 판결.

born of the March First Independence Movement of 1919 and the democratic ideals of the April Nineteenth Uprising of 1960," the ruling has provided that "Japan's ruling over Korea during the time of Japanese imperialism's forceful occupation, is no other than an illegitimate forceful occupation, and the legal relations deriving from Japan's illegitimate occupation that are incompatible with the Constitutional spirit of Korea are excluded from their effect."

In brief, the ruling has legally affirmed that the Japanese imperialism's ruling over Korea was "illegitimate forceful occupation." Moreover, in that sense, the decision declared that "if legal relations deriving from illegitimate occupation are incompatible with the constitutional spirit of the Republic of Korea, their effects are excluded." That means all the laws created by the Japanese imperialism during the time of forced occupation and any legal relations based on them are null and void if they are "incompatible with the constitutional spirit of Korea." If so, all the Japanese imperialism's arrest, imprisonment, and punishment of the independence activists based on that law are null and void. Also, any activities that brought damage to Korean nationals, including the forced draft and conscription of Koreans, are illegal.

Likewise, the Supreme Court of Korea clearly stated that the Japanese imperialism's ruling of Korea was "illegitimate forceful occupation," and the claims right for "the illegal activities directly related to colonial ruling" has not been eliminated despite the「Claims Agreement」. This binds all the national organizations of Korea. However, it is needless to say that this idea is totally in contrast with the San Francisco System, the argument of the Japanese government, which relies on the "1965 System," the San Francisco System's substructure, and the judgement of the Japanese court, which accepted the stance of its government.[17]

5 Conclusion

The「San Francisco Treaty」was a sentencing of the international community in Japan. However, there, the responsibilities Japan should take for its colonial rule were missing. That was how the US-centered new system after the Second World War 'sealed" the issues of Japan's responsibilities for its colonial rule. That "seal" was in effect during the Cold War era.

However, with the collapse of the Cold War and its substructure, the authoritarian system in Asia, including Korea, and the "seal" could not be maintained. Korean victims of colonization stood forward to "unleash the seal," and they went through an extremely difficult time to achieve their goal while filing lawsuits in Japan, the United States, and Korea.

Japanese courts tried their best to keep the "seal" with a poor logic of "elimination of the right to file litigation." Although it is not mentioned here, the US courts

[17] For a more detailed analysis of the 2012 Supreme Court ruling, see 김창록, 「한일「청구권협정」에 의해 '해결'된 '권리' - 일제 '강제동원' 피해 관련 대법원 판결을 소재로」, 『법학논고』 49, 2015.

also joined to maintain the "seal" by setting aside their decision with "sovereign immunity" or "political issue" as their reasons.

That is why the decisions of the Constitutional Court and the Supreme Court of Korea especially gain attention. Their rulings meant opening the "seal" the「San Francisco Treaty」put in place 60 years ago. Such a change was possible, thanks to the intense judgment on numerous types of illegitimacy that appeared during the past authoritarian regimes in the process of democratization since the 1987 Democratization Movement. The "retrial" experience in the modern history of Korea led to the "retrial" of the San Francisco System.

The "retrial" is still ongoing. Also, as it has been the case until today, unless "justice" is served, "retrials" will continue endlessly. The history written by the Korean victims seeking the true righting of past wrongs and the people all over the world who heard their voice is telling us so.

(2018.10.27.)

[Postscript]

On October 30, 2018, 3 days after the above presentation was made, the Supreme Court of Korea delivered its final ruling[18] in favor of the plaintiffs in a lawsuit brought by Korean victims of forced labor against Nippon Steel Corporation. This ruling was the final decision on a reappeal by Nippon Steel Corporation, following the Seoul High Court's July 10, 2013, ruling,[19] which was in line with the 2012 Supreme Court decision. The 2018 Supreme Court ruling upheld the reasoning of the 2012 ruling.

However, on the day of the ruling, the Japanese government issued a statement by the Minister of Foreign Affairs,[20] claiming that the 2018 Supreme Court ruling "clearly violates Article II of the [Claims] Agreement." Despite this claim, the Japanese government provided no supporting arguments. The only "reference" attached to the statement was the text of the Claims Agreement, which the 2018 Supreme Court ruling had interpreted with sufficient and reasonable grounds under the Vienna Convention on the Law of Treaties.

While continuing these baseless accusations, the Japanese government also claimed that the "issue of workers from the Korean Peninsula" had been resolved by the Claims Agreement. However, the 2018 Supreme Court ruling was specifically about "forced mobilization," so raising the "issue of workers from the Korean Peninsula" was off target.

Despite the unjust nature of this backlash, the Japanese government demanded that "Korea take appropriate measures, including immediate actions to remedy such breach of international law." The only conceivable "measure" would be for the Korean government to invalidate the Supreme Court ruling, which would effectively

[18] 대법원 2018.10.30. 선고 2013다61381 전원합의체 판결.

[19] 서울고등법원 2013.7.10 선고 2012나44947 판결.

[20] "Regarding the Decision by the Supreme Court of the Republic of Korea, Confirming the Existing Judgments on the Japanese Company (Statement by Foreign Minister Taro Kono)," October 30, 2018.

amount to Japan's anachronistic demand that the Republic of Korea in the twenty-first century recognize extraterritoriality for Japanese companies.

Nonetheless, the Japanese government launched two trade attacks in July and August of 2019 in response to the 2018 Supreme Court ruling, prompting the Moon Jae-in administration to take countermeasures. As a result, Korea-Japan relations deteriorated to what was called "the worst state since the normalization of diplomatic relations."

After the Korean government changed from the Moon Jae-in administration to the Yoon Suk Yeol administration in 2022, the Yoon government announced on March 6, 2023, what it called a "solution to forced labor," under which the Foundation for Victims of Forced Mobilization under the Ministry of Interior and Safety would pay the damages owed by Japanese companies. This "solution" was the "appropriate measure" that the Japanese government had demanded.

Since the "solution" involved the executive branch overturning the judiciary's final rulings on specific disputes, it clearly violated the principle of separation of powers enshrined in the Constitution of the Republic of Korea. It also directly contravened the president's duty to "uphold the Constitution," rendering it unconstitutional.

Nevertheless, the Yoon Suk Yeol administration pushed the "solution" forward, but some of the forced labor victims who had won their cases rejected it. While the Yoon government attempted to force it through by depositing compensation into court, court officials refused to accept the application, and appeals against the refusal were all dismissed by the court. Furthermore, Japanese companies, following the Japanese government's position, did not donate to the foundation, and most Korean companies, except one, refrained from making donations to the controversial "solution," leading to its collapse due to a lack of funds.

Meanwhile, in lawsuits filed by Korean victims of the Japanese military "comfort women' system seeking damages from the Japanese government, the Seoul Central District Court ruled in favor of the plaintiffs on January 8, 2021, and the Seoul High Court similarly ruled in favor on November 23, 2023. Both rulings became final as the Japanese government did not appeal.

On the key issue of state immunity, the 2021 ruling[21] held that "when a state has inflicted severe harm on victims through inhumane acts that destroy the universal values of the international community," exceptions to state immunity should be recognized. The 2023 ruling[22] similarly denied Japan's claim of state immunity, stating that "in the case of illegal acts committed against nationals within the territory of the forum state, state immunity is not recognized, regardless of whether the act is considered sovereign."

These rulings reflect the evolution of state immunity, which began in the nineteenth century with the doctrine of absolute immunity for all state actions and shifted in the twentieth century to a restrictive immunity doctrine that excludes

[21] 서울중앙지방법원 2021.1.8. 선고 2016가합580239 판결.

[22] 서울고등법원 2923.11.23. 선고 2021나2017165 판결.

private law acts. The rulings are seen as actively participating in the evolving process of state immunity by incorporating human rights exceptions, reflecting the international community's shift from a state-centric worldview to a human rights-centered one. They also pioneer the future direction of state immunity by suggesting that immunity should be excluded for all unlawful acts of the state, drawing global attention.[23]

However, the Japanese government, which had not responded at all since the lawsuits were filed, continues to criticize these rulings, citing "the principle of state immunity under international law," and demands that the Korean government "take appropriate measures to correct the violation of international law." The Yoon Suk Yeol administration has not responded to the rulings, and the forced execution procedures by the victorious plaintiffs are ongoing.

Thus, the retrial of the San Francisco System through Korean courts continues as of 2024. The retrial proceeds step by step, overcoming persistent attempts to "seal" the issue.

[23] See, Kim Chang-Rok, "Korea's Court Denies Japan's State Immunity Again", *The Asia-Pacific Journal*, Vol. 22, Issue 1, No. 1, January 13, 2024.

Beyond the San Francisco System

Beyond the San Francisco System: A Japanese View

Wada Haruki

Abstract This article analyzes the origins, evolution, and consequences of the San Francisco System, the post-World War II order established by the 1951 San Francisco Peace Treaty, and the US-Japan Security Pact. It argues that the system did not achieve true peace in Northeast Asia but instead institutionalized a framework for ongoing conflict, especially on the Korean Peninsula. Excluding key regional actors such as China and the two Koreas, the treaty's partial nature left many disputes unresolved and enabled the United States to maintain a dominant security presence in Japan and Okinawa. The San Francisco System was further reinforced during the Vietnam War and only began to shift with the US-China rapprochement in the 1970s. Despite the end of the Cold War and US-Soviet reconciliation, North Korea remained isolated and developed nuclear weapons, escalating regional tensions. The article highlights how the Singapore Summit between the United States and North Korea in 2018 opened possibilities for dismantling the system and pursuing a new peace regime. Ultimately, the author envisions the replacement of the San Francisco System with a Northeast Asian community based on cooperation, denuclearization, and mutual security.

Keywords Cold War · Japan · Korean Peninsula · Northeast Asia · Peace Treaty · San Francisco System · Security · United States · Vietnam War · Washington

W. Haruki (✉)
Institute of Social Science, University of Tokyo, Tokyo, Japan
e-mail: fwjg0575@nifty.com

Y.-H. Kim et al. (eds.), *Beyond the San Francisco System*,
https://doi.org/10.1007/978-981-95-3328-2_18

1 The San Francisco System

The San Francisco Peace Treaty was concluded on September 8, 1951, by 49 countries, including Japan. The key signatories were six Western nations (the United States, the United Kingdom, Australia, New Zealand, the Netherlands, and France) and five Southeast Asian nations (Indonesia, the Philippines, South Vietnam, Cambodia, and Laos). The Soviet Union was present at the peace conference but refused to sign the treaty. Neither the "two Chinas"—the People's Republic of China (PRC) and the Republic of China (ROC)—nor the "two Koreas"—the Republic of Korea (ROK) and the Democratic People's Republic of Korea (DPRK)—were invited to attend. In the absence of these five countries, the treaty's implementation proved to be partial and imperfect, failing in its primary goal of assuring a lasting peace in Northeast Asia.

A few hours after initialing the San Francisco instrument, US treaty envoy John Foster Dulles and Prime Minister Yoshida Shigeru signed the Japan-US Security Treaty, allowing the United States to maintain its troops in Japan *indefinitely*. The San Francisco Peace Treaty and the bilateral security pact went into effect in April 1952 *as the US Occupation ended*, forming the core of the American bloc's postwar settlement with Japan. I call this peculiar power arrangement the San Francisco System (below, SFS). The SFS allowed the United States and its Free World allies to continue the war in Korea until an armistice was signed in 1953. The wartime consolidation of that system assigned Japan a central role in Washington's Far Eastern security strategy.

The SFS is an international state system. But not only did it fail to establish an effective peace, it set the stage for conditions that generated new armed conflicts involving the United States. Facing off against the US-dominated Western bloc was the so-called Communist bloc, consisting of the DPRK in North Korea, "Red China" on the Chinese mainland, and implicitly the USSR. The vanguard of the US military presence in Asia included American forces in the Republic of Korea and the ROK Army, as well as the Republic of China's Nationalist army in Taiwan. The US military command was headquartered in Japan and Okinawa, where the bulk of American troops and their logistical bases were deployed. Japan's nascent self-defense forces, *created in 1950 at the start of the Korean War*, were not counted in assessments of the US camp's war potential because the Japanese Constitution's Article 9 forbade the maintenance of a standing army. The SFS system encompassed the entire Japanese archipelago, including Okinawa, *which was under direct US military rule until 1972*, and secured the country's territorial integrity and security. Inside this system, Japan became the primary rear-area supply base for US forces in Asia.

It was the San Francisco System that permitted the United States, *aided by a token contingent of UN Forces*, to expand military operations against Chinese and North Korean armies in 1952 and 1953. After the armistice of July 27, 1953, the SFS was responsible for perpetuating a state of permanent hostilities along the Demilitarized Zone that divided South and North Korea at the 38th parallel.

2 Supplementary Efforts to Strengthen the San Francisco System

After the San Francisco peace conference, the Japan government, prodded by Washington, embarked on a series of difficult bilateral initiatives designed to shore up the SFS. I mention three in particular. First, on April 28, 1952, the day the SFS went into effect, Tokyo concluded the Sino-Japanese Peace Treaty (Treaty of Peace between Japan and the Republic of China) with the Chinese Nationalist regime in Taiwan, which had been excluded from the San Francisco conference. Dulles compelled Prime Minister Yoshida to negotiate this bilateral treaty with ROC President Chiang Kai-Shek.

The first official meeting was held in Taipei on February 20, 1952. During the talks, the Taiwan representative demanded that Japan recognize its obligation to pay reparations to the Republic of China and promised to waive the payment of all such benefits if a reparations clause were written into the Taipei treaty.[1] The Japanese representative, however, stubbornly refused to comply. Taking advantage of the ROC's ambiguous position in the San Francisco System, the Japanese side forced the Taiwan government to drop all reparations claims. Nevertheless, the 1952 Sino-Japanese Treaty greatly enhanced the international standing of ROC-Taiwan as the sole legal representative of China. Taipei was propped up by the United States and defended by the US-equipped ROC Army.

The second initiative was the interim Joint Declaration that Japan and the Soviet Union signed on October 19, 1956, ending hostilities and restoring diplomatic recognition as the prelude to an eventual peace settlement. Then-Prime Minister Hatoyama Ichirō had intended to sidestep the San Francisco System when he began normalization talks with Moscow in June 1955. The San Francisco Treaty obliged Japan to renounce its rights to the Kuril Islands and Sakhalin Island, which had been occupied by the Soviet Red Army in the closing days of World War II. The Hatoyama government instructed its plenipotentiary, Matsumoto Shun'ichi, to approach Moscow and propose the return of the Habomais and Shikotan, which were not included in the Kuril Islands. Prime Minister Yoshida had stated clearly during the San Francisco talks that those islands belonged to Hokkaido and could not to be included in the Kurils. *Having replaced Yoshida*, Hatoyama believed that renewing diplomatic relations with Moscow would counter Tokyo's subordination to the SFS.

When Soviet Premier Nikita Khrushchev hastily ordered his representative Yakov Malik to accept the Japanese request, however, Hatoyama's foreign minister, Shigemitsu Mamoru, and other leading officials of the Foreign Ministry's Yoshida faction moved to prevent the Japan-USSR rapprochement. They put together a more ambitious demand that Moscow was sure to reject: the return of all four islands in the southernmost Kurils (the so-called Northern Territories) or nothing: the Habomai

[1] Exceptions were such services of the Japanese people as salvaging and other work for the Allied Powers, as designated in the San Francisco Treaty's Article 14.

Group, Shikotan, Etorofu, and Kunashiri, all of which lay off the Hokkaido coast. Bilateral negotiations then underway in London broke down immediately.

Hatoyama engineered a compromise, and the two countries initialed the Joint Declaration in Moscow in October 1956, normalizing ties but without resolving the territorial issue, which was deferred until the conclusion of a final peace agreement. In the Joint Statement, Khrushchev, "desiring to meet the wishes of Japan and taking into consideration the interests of the Japanese State," promised to transfer the Habomais and Shikotan to Japan after the signing of a final peace settlement. The Japanese government, however, continued to insist on its demand for four islands further, contending that Etorofu and Kunashiri were not part of the Kurils. Tokyo's false arguments and unilateral claims have continued to block Japanese-Soviet reconciliation, exactly as the San Francisco System would have it.

A third initiative was the opening of preliminary talks between Japan and the Republic of Korea under American auspices on October 20, 1951. The ROK representative demanded an apology from for its colonial subjugation of Korea (1910–1945), but the Japanese government hewed adamantly to its official policy that colonial rule was justified under international law and that no contrition was required.

Fifteen years later, on June 22, 1965, after resigning itself to Tokyo's obstinacy, Seoul compromised and signed the Treaty on Basic Relations between Japan and the Republic of Korea. Article II of the treaty reads: "It is confirmed that all treaties or agreements concluded between the Empire of Japan and the Empire of Korea on or before August 22, 1910, are already null and void." South Korea and Japan each interpreted this article differently, however. Seoul's reading was that the 1910 annexation treaty was "null and void" from the outset, while Tokyo considered the text to mean that it was legally valid until the Republic of Korea came into existence in August 1948. Such radically differing interpretations of the 1965 bilateral treaty's most important stipulation should be deemed a fatal defect, and Article II should have been amended or expunged as soon as possible.

The Basic Relations Treaty also included the Agreement on the Settlement of Problems Concerning Property and Claims and on Economic Co-operation between Japan and the Republic of Korea. Under this accord, Japan pledged to give South Korea US$300 million unconditionally and lend it another $200 million at low interest. Article II of the agreement also confirmed that all issues arising from claims made by both sides had been "finally and completely resolved." At that moment, the Korean government decided to shelve the territorial question. As a result, the ROK's possession of Dokto (Takeshima in Japanese), an isolated island equidistant between Japan and South Korea, remains a source of bitter contention between the two countries. On the positive side, the Japan-ROK Basic Relations Treaty led to bilateral economic cooperation, inaugurating an era of rapid industrial growth in South Korea.

3 The Expansion of the San Francisco System

In late 1960, the main theater of hostilities between the US camp and the Communist camp shifted from the Korean peninsula to the Indochina peninsula. Opposing the United States was North Vietnam, which had declared Vietnam's independence from France in 1945, and liberation forces in South Vietnam, which had been separated from the North in 1954 by the Geneva Accords. In December 1960, the National Front for the Liberation of South Vietnam was formed to overthrow the US-backed Saigon regime, and armed resistance broke out against US forces who had replaced French colonial troops there. The year 1960 signaled the true onset of the Vietnam War, a conflict that can be viewed as an extension of the Korean War.

The San Francisco System became deeply involved in this new war. The 1965 Japan-ROK Treaty had paved the way for rapid economic growth in South Korea. Against this backdrop, Seoul dispatched ROK combat units to help American troops in Vietnam, and some 50,000 Korean soldiers were dispatched annually to the front lines in South Vietnam, totaling 300,000 soldiers in all.

Moscow and Beijing provided Hanoi with generous financial and military aid. North Korea also hoped to assist the Vietnamese by opening a second front in South Korea. From 1967, Pyongyang began building what I have called a "partisan state" (Korean, *yugyokdai gukka*),[2] and on January 21, 1968, an armed guerrilla unit was dispatched to infiltrate Seoul and attack the South Korean Presidential Palace there. The commandos were annihilated by ROK forces, however, and the scheme collapsed. Later, Pyongyang sent pilots to North Vietnam to assist in the air war over Vietnam. On the SFS side, Okinawa became one of the main staging areas for US long-range bombers and other military forces in the Indochina Theater, and Japan itself became a permanent logistics base and "rest and recreation" center for American soldiers in Asia. The war ended in defeat for the United States and its allies in 1975.

4 The 1972 Revision to the San Francisco System

Between 1971 and 1972, at the height of the Vietnam War, leaders of the PRC and the United States sat down to discuss their differences and reached a common understanding that the Korean War, in which both had participated on opposing sides, had ended in a draw. The joint Shanghai Communique signed by the People's Republic of China and the United States during President Richard Nixon's Beijing

[2]The post-independence model of North Korea as a partisan state is derived from the saga of Kim Il-sung's revolutionary partisan faction in Manchuria during the 1930s. See Wada Haruki, *Kita Chosen: Yugekitai kokka no genzai* (North Korea's Partisan State Today), (Tokyo: Iwanami Shoten, 1998).

visit on February 28, 1972, established bilateral ties, marking a decisive transformation of the fraught PRC-US relationship.

Caught by surprise, Tokyo rushed to match this gambit and, acting on its own, boldly signed a Joint Statement on September 29, 1972, that normalized relations with the PRC, expressed the desire for a peace treaty, and recognized the PRC as the "sole and lawful government" of China. The statement specified that "Japan feels deeply responsible for the enormous damage it has inflicted on the people of China through war in the past, and expresses its deep remorse." Finally, 27 years after the end of *World War II*, this single sentence was Japan's first formal apology to an Asian nation victimized by Imperial Japan during the war. The People's Republic of China apparently prevailed on Tokyo to formally acknowledge its war responsibility.

On the other hand, the PRC was obliged to waive all war reparation claims because of the 1952 Sino-Japan Peace Treaty that had deprived ROC-Taiwan of its war reparations rights. The earlier treaty should have been simply annulled. At the same time, Beijing decided to shelve its territorial dispute with Tokyo over ownership of the Diaoyu (Senkaku in Japanese) Islands, which were claimed by both countries. In 1978, Japan and the PRC signed the Treaty of Peace and Friendship, and Tokyo began to provide Beijing with economic aid. In 1979, Prime Minister Ōhira Masayoshi followed up by visiting China with the offer of a US$150 million loan.

In 1972, the United States returned administrative control over Okinawa to Japan, but the American bases increased. The enormous burden of supporting those enormous military facilities, which account for more than 70% of all US bases in Japan, continues to weigh heavily on the people of Okinawa. Thus, the SFS has undergone a subtle transformation, but to date, many of the changes have been superficial.

5 The End of the Cold War and the San Francisco System

In the late 1980s, a world-historical change took place as Moscow and Washington appeared to reconcile their differences following the end of the Cold War and the various revolutions that swept the Soviet Union and Eastern Europe. Committed to détente, the government of Mikhail Gorbachev sought to change radically not only the USSR's political system but its foreign policy, as well. To that end, he decided to begin by establishing truly peaceful relations with Washington. Moscow also hoped to establish diplomatic ties with Seoul.

It seemed that the Cold war would also end in Northeast Asia, but that was not to be. Hostilities between the DPRK and the San Francisco System, for instance, were not only intractable but intensified in the worst possible way.

In late 1991, Gorbachev was deposed, and the USSR was dissolved, becoming the Russian Federation. After losing its Soviet protector, the North Korean state faced severe economic dislocation. At this historical juncture, the Pyongyang leadership fell back on two emergency measures to stem the crisis. First, to compensate for the loss of the Soviet nuclear "umbrella," it decided to develop its own nuclear weapons program. Secondly, North Korea played a diplomatic card and attempted to normalize relations with its archenemy Japan. Washington tightened its grip on the SFS, vehemently denounced the first initiative, and labored mightily to stymie the second.

Japan attempted to negotiate with the DPRK between 1991 and 1992, but the first round of talks failed because of US interference, which succeeded in derailing the establishment of formal relations. In 2000, 8 years later, a second round of bilateral overtures took place, but these, too, were in vain. After a year of secret talks, however, Japanese Prime Minister Koizumi Jun'ichirō and DPRK Chairman Kim Jong Il arranged to meet in the North Korean capital on September 17, 2002, to sign the Pyongyang Declaration. The two finally agreed to create a framework for normalization. But this brief success could not parry the vehement opposition that erupted in Japanese political circles[3] and vigorous American obstructionism. The peace process was suspended once again.

North Korea's diplomatic option could not be achieved, so it doubled down on its first option and tested its first nuclear device in 2006, an event that sparked a harsh, volatile clash of key national interests. In 2016 and 2017, DPRK's new leader Kim Jong Un successfully pursued not only a nuclear weapons program but also a long-range ballistic missile project. The Pentagon and US intelligence community were highly alarmed, and Washington spared no effort to frustrate these endeavors.

The San Francisco System, which had undergone transformations, was now restructured to minimize those changes by Prime Minister Abe Shinzō and the new US President Donald Trump, who had taken office in January 2017. The two leaders made every effort to increase sanctions on North Korea and intimidate the Kim Jong Un government by deploying US military forces near Korean waters, especially after 2017. Preparing new security laws, Prime Minister Abe announced that he would support US saber-rattling against the North, including joint US-South Korean naval exercises. Japan seemed determined to upgrade its position in an overhauled San Francisco Treaty System.

6 Efforts to Avert the War Crisis of 2017

By 2017, the US-DPRK conflict had reached crisis proportions. North Korea moved full throttle ahead with its atomic weapons systems and ballistic missile technology. On March 6, Pyongyang test-launched four medium-range missiles, three of which landed 300 km off the northwest coast of Japan's Akita Prefecture, inside Japan's

[3] A contributing factor in this opposition was public shock at Kim Jong Un's unexpected recognition that in the 1970s and 1980s, special Korean commando units had arbitrarily entered Japan and abducted 13 Japanese citizens. Kim apologized candidly and noted that those responsible for the "appalling incident" had been duly punished, but the incident poisoned bilateral relations.

exclusive economic zone. On March 7 and 28, Pyongyang's Korean Central News Agency announced that these tests had been conducted by the Korea People's Army artillery detachment charged with attacking US military facilities in Japan in the event of a military contingency.

In his September 2017 address to the UN General Assembly and during his trip to East Asia in November, President Trump publicly warned Kim Jong Un that if he refused to comply with US demands for "complete, verifiable, irreversible denuclearization," our armed forces would have "no choice but to totally destroy North Korea." Prime Minister Abe always proclaimed himself in complete agreement with Trump on North Korea. During Trump's November visit to South Korea, he arranged for three US nuclear aircraft carriers to stage a drill in the Sea of Japan and flaunt their prowess.

On November 29, 2017, Pyongyang test-fired a new "Hwasong 15" ICBM with an estimated range of over 14,000 km—more than enough to reach North America. DPRK authorities lauded their "historical accomplishment of [achieving] state nuclear forces and [becoming] a strong rocket state." With these developments, the US-North Korea conflict entered a critical phase: the world now faced the prospect of a full-blown war between the two powers. In December, concerned people searched frantically for a way out of this imbroglio.

In mid-November, on the eve of the Pyeongchang Winter Olympics to be held in South Korea, the UN General Assembly had adopted an "Olympic Truce" resolution,[4] and this was now utilized by many parties to convince the North Korean government to participate in the event and dial down tensions. The resolution urged the world to remember that:

Pyeongchang 2018 marks the first of the three consecutive Olympic and Paralympic Games to be held in Asia, to be followed by Tokyo 2020 and Beijing 2022, offering possibilities of new partnership in sport and beyond for the Republic of Korea, Japan and China.

This message was conveyed by the South Korean government to the DPRK leader Kim Jong Un through various channels.

Kim Jong Un, who was staring into the maw of a nuclear abyss, was persuaded to return to the position taken by his father: nuclear diplomacy. We can recall here the memorable words of Kim Jong Il to Prime Minister Koizumi on the occasion of their second summit: "We came to have nuclear weapons for the sake of the right of existence. If our existence is secured, nuclear weapons will no longer be necessary." "We wish to sing a *duet* with the Americans through the Six-Party Talks.[5] We wish to sing songs with the Americans until our voices become hoarse."

Kim Jong Un made his new thinking public in his 2018 New Year's address, in which he signaled Pyongyang's willingness to join the Pyeongchang Winter

---

[4] UN Resolution 72/6: Building a peaceful and better world through sport and the Olympic ideal. November 13, 2017.

[5] The Six Party Talks were begun in 2003 to peacefully negotiate and resolve the issues surrounding North Korea's nuclear and missile programs: The participants are North and South Korea, China, the United States, Japan, and the Russian Federation.

Olympics. Later, he expressed the wish to hold a bilateral summit with President Trump. Trump, too, was facing the unthinkable. When South Korean President Moon Jae-In's special envoy conveyed this proposal to him on March 8, 2018, he jumped at the chance, accepting Kim's overture immediately.

On June 12, 2018, President Trump and Chairman Kim held their first summit in Singapore. They conducted a comprehensive and sincere exchange of opinions on the establishment of a new US-DPRK relationship and the construction of a lasting and robust peace regime on the Korean peninsula. President Trump committed to providing security guarantees to the DPRK, and Chairman Kim reaffirmed his unwavering determination to complete the denuclearization of the peninsula. Here, two tasks were laid on the table. The first was how to definitively end the Korean War by replacing the 1953 armistice with a constructive peace treaty, and the second was how to denuclearize. I took this turn of events to mean that the San Francisco System should be demolished. From another perspective, the Singapore Summit seems to have put an end to the war fears of the United States and the DPRK, opening a space for a fresh peace dialogue in Northeast Asia.

7 A Ray of Hope: The US-DPRK Peace Process

Finally, the time seems ripe to move beyond the San Francisco System. All the nations and peoples of Northeast Asia should now assume responsibility for bringing Washington-Pyongyang negotiations to a successful conclusion. Naturally, President Trump and Chairman Kim will bear the heaviest burden of accountability. They should formulate a program of peace and denuclearization and always strive to find areas of agreement, whatever the difficulties.

And yet nearly a year and a half has passed since Singapore. The two countries have not been able to concur about a mutually suitable modus vivendi. If they are to negotiate *effectively* and reach consensus on an equal footing, they must honor Clause 5 of the Joint Statement of the Fourth Round of the Six-Party Talks, Beijing (September 19, 2005), which commits the parties to coordinate efforts "to implement the [proposed] consensus in a phased manner in line with the principle of 'commitment for commitment, action for action'."

To me, it seems that this autumn (2019), the US and DPRK representatives have finally began to adhere to the Six Party Talks rule as they consider the fate of Pyongyang's Yongbyon nuclear facilities and the temporary lifting of a ban on North Korean coal and textile exports. Neither side has accepted the other's proposals in a balanced manner. A deeper reexamination of each other's position is in order if preparations for the next meeting are to proceed smoothly.

But these talks will be truly difficult. I think that North Korea will renounce nuclear weapons only if the United States completely removes its nuclear umbrella from South Korea and Japan. And while US troops in Japan and South Korea are not armed with strategic or tactical nukes per se, they remain under the aegis of the American nuclear arsenal, as are both Japan and South Korea. In other words, the complete denuclearization of the Korean peninsula depends as much on the permanent retraction of the US nuclear guarantee in South Korea and Japan as on North Korea's elimination of its atomic warheads and missiles. This observation inevitably raises the issue of *the role and status of* US military bases in both countries.

Stated differently, the task of completely ridding the Korean peninsula of the nuclear threat cannot be divorced from the task of denuclearizing the Japan Sea and the Japanese archipelago itself, including Okinawa. Now, we must focus urgently on the first task of the US-North Korea peace process: the final settlement of the Korean War through a just and viable peace accord. Barring this, people who have lived under the San Francisco System will not authorize the withdrawal of US forces from their country.

Seoul has taken great pains to promote reconciliation between the two Koreas. The two joint declarations adopted at the Panmunjom Truce Village in the DMZ and in Pyongyang over the past year were resounding successes. Today, however, the North is uneasy about the slow pace of change in South Korean policymaking toward the DPRK, and the once positive mood between the two sides has deteriorated. Today, no one in South Korea entertains the possibility of a new war on the peninsula, but neither does anyone feel a sense of genuine mutual trust. Koreans, South and North, do not share a common historical understanding of the Korean War. Without such consciousness, war memories will continue to haunt the two peoples.

The current situation is rather primitive. The South Korean government is unable to readjust its policy toward the Kaesong Industrial Zone's collaborative projects and the Mount Kumgang Tourist Region's joint venture because Washington will not go along with it. As for Japan, the policies of the Abe government pose a real obstacle to the Moon Jae In administration in the South.

Prime Minister Abe was stunned when President Trump abruptly accepted Kim Jong Un's summit proposal in March 2018. He immediately telephoned President Trump to explain that sanctions should not be relaxed until Pyongyang had totally abandoned its nuclear program and released a dozen Japanese that the North had criminally kidnapped, a preeminent national concern for Japan. Abe's policy toward the abductions, including *economic reprisals*, has long kept Japan from entering into formal relations with North Korea.

In 2006, when the first Abe Cabinet took office, the new premier proclaimed three principles for dealing with the abduction issue. The first is that the abduction problem is the single most important task facing Japan. The second principle is that without a resolution of the abduction question, there can be no normalization of Japan-DPRK relations. The third is that Japan presumes all abductees to be alive and insists stubbornly that all be returned.

In 2002, when Kim Jong Il informed Prime Minister Koizumi of the abductions and apologized, North Korean officials reported that a total of 13 Japanese had been seized, but that eight were dead and only five still living. Between 2002 and 2003, Pyongyang repatriated the five survivors and their families to Japan. The third principle, however, was tantamount to calling the North Koreans liars. That blunder, together with the imposition of sanctions, has made it impossible for talks to resume.

After the Singapore Summit, Abe said that he was willing to "break the shell of mutual distrust" and meet Chairman Kim face-to-face in order to resolve the abduction question, but he has never taken positive steps to further the US-DPRK peace process.

That is the real obstacle. Scrapping Abe's three principles would enable Tokyo to act quickly and open diplomatic relations with Pyongyang unconditionally. If embassies were set up in the two capitals, both countries could begin discussions on nuclear arms and ICBMs, the abduction quandary, sanctions, and economic cooperation, interacting calmly and without apprehensions. A prime example of such an effort is President Barack Obama's establishment of diplomatic ties with Cuba in 2014. The normalization of Japan-DPRK relations would produce irreversible security guarantees to North Korea and offer strong support for continuing US-DPRK and US-ROK negotiations.

Should Japan become such an ally, Seoul would be able to engage Pyongyang more actively and seek the common ground necessary to cultivate true mutual understanding. For that reason, the South Koreans, too, have a stake in winning the trust of the Japanese people.

8 The Common House of Northeast Asia

People have long pondered various concepts for building a regional community in Northeast Asia. In July 1990, I unveiled my idea for "A Common House where peoples of the world can live together" at a symposium of that name hosted by the Seoul daily *Dong-A Ilbo*. In February 2003, Roh Moo Hyun, the new South Korean president, announced his intention to construct a "Northeast Asian community" that would become a "community of peace and prosperity." Encouraged by President Roh's proposal, the same year, I went out on a limb and published a book called *The Common House of Northeast Asia: A Regionalist Manifesto.*[6] All of my proposals were the product of sheer imagination.

As a new era of history dawns, a positive vision of regional community is emerging. Since 1996, Professor Umebayashi Hiromichi has cherished the idea of a "Northeast Asian Nuclear Free Zone." According to him, Japan and South and North Korea could pledge to neither produce nor introduce nuclear weapons in their own countries, and the United States, Russia, and China could promise not to attack those countries with nuclear weapons. This, too, is a product of the imagination.

But the situation today leaves little room for optimism. North Korea openly expresses its commitment to full denuclearization and yet continues to upgrade its nuclear weapons capability. Japan and South Korea abide by the principle of non-possession of atomic armaments while depending on the protection of America's

---

[6] Wada Haruki, *Tōhoku Ajia kyōdō no ie*. Tōkyō: Heibonsha, 2003.

nuclear shield. The Russian Federation, the People's Republic of China, and the United States remain nuclear superpowers.

Should the US-North Korea peace process finally achieve its goal of nuclear disarmament in the Korean peninsula, the Japanese archipelago, and Okinawa, the two Koreas and Japan will be entirely free of atomic weapons, and their mutual enmity will be neutralized. Regardless of whether they maintain regular or minimal military forces, all should also have Article 9 outlawing war in their constitutions. These conditions point the way toward a union of peace-loving states.

The Koreas and Japan should also form a Northeast Asian security community with the three nuclear powers surrounding them. The nuclear states should be united by an oath of non-aggression and non-intervention toward the peninsula and the archipelago and bound by a no-war agreement with each other. This is the ultimate image of a real Northeast Asian Community—the future that beckons from beyond the moribund San Francisco System.

Beyond the San Francisco System, to Where? Contending Visions for the Region-Building in East Asia

Jong Won Lee

Abstract This article examines the evolution of East Asian regional order from the Cold War-era San Francisco System to present-day rival visions for regional integration. It argues that the San Francisco Peace Treaty institutionalized Cold War divisions and prioritized US strategic interests, enabling Japan's reintegration while neglecting historical reconciliation. The emergence of the ASEAN Plus Three framework and the East Asian Community vision in the 1990s reflected aspirations for greater regional autonomy and cooperation. However, US opposition and growing US–China rivalry have hindered the realization of a cohesive East Asian community. The study highlights the role of middle powers, like ASEAN and South Korea, in promoting inclusive regionalism while noting how mega-regional projects, such as China's Belt and Road Initiative and the US–Japan-led Indo-Pacific strategy, have complicated regional unity. The article traces the shift from Asia-Pacific to Indo-Pacific frameworks, emphasizing the impact of great power competition on regional diplomacy. It also explores the challenges and setbacks faced by trilateral and multilateral cooperation in Northeast Asia. Ultimately, the article contends that the region stands at a crossroads, with the risk of renewed division under a "San Francisco System 2.0" unless inclusive, community-based approaches prevail.

Keywords ASEAN Plus Three · Belt and road initiative · Cold War · East Asia · Indo-Pacific · Japan · Regionalism · San Francisco System · United States · US–China rivalry

J. W. Lee (✉)
Waseda University, Tokyo, Japan
e-mail: jwlee@waseda.jp

Y.-H. Kim et al. (eds.), *Beyond the San Francisco System*,
https://doi.org/10.1007/978-981-95-3328-2_19

1 Introduction

From the viewpoint of the regional order in East Asia, the San Francisco System is synonymous with the Cold War division. Concluded in September 1951, the San Francisco Peace Treaty was a direct product of the Korean War. To rebuild Japan as the regional bulwark against communism, the United States pushed forward the so-called "katamen kowa" (one-sided peace), over the objection of the Soviet Union and the People's Republic of China. As a result, it was a "lenient peace" for Japan, particularly in terms of addressing wartime atrocities and militarism. The Treaty provided a framework for Japan to be exempt from the burden of confronting and correcting historical injustices. In the 1965 ROK-Japan Normalization Treaty, the Cold War imperatives were given priority over historical issues, which became sources of continuing conflict between the two countries until today.

The region-building in East Asia is a way to overcome the Cold War division and to achieve regional reconciliation. In the early 1990s, moves toward regional cooperation became conspicuous, which culminated with the inauguration of the ASEAN Plus Three (ROK, China, and Japan) in 1997, and the proposal of the East Asian Community as its long-term goal. However, since after the early 2000s, the regionalist aspirations in East Asia have lost momentum, under the shadow of emerging conflicts between the United States and China.

Now East Asia is at a historical crossroads, caught between contending visions for regional frameworks. On the one hand, pan-Eurasian mega-regionalism seems to be gaining momentum under the influence of the overwhelming economic power of China. As a counter to this Chinese ambition, the United States and Japan promote the strategy of "Free and Open Indo-Pacific." Regional states in East Asia are pressed to choose sides in the intensifying "New Cold War."

This chapter examines how the vision of the East Asian Community emerged and progressed, focusing on the role of *middle powers*, such as the ASEAN countries and South Korea. It also attempts to analyze the impact of the global power struggles on the *region-building* in East Asia. The word of region-building is here used as an historical analogy with the nation-state building in the modern period.

2 The Rise of East Asia, Competing with the Asia-Pacific

In East Asia, the Cold War was essentially the confrontation between the United States and Communist China. In the Korean War, it was China and the United States that fought the war. The Soviet Union was, in fact, the main actor but remained behind the scenes. For the United States, Chinese influence on the regional states was a more direct and serious security threat.

In that sense, the US-China rapprochement with Nixon's historical visit to China in 1972 meant a virtual end of the Cold War in Asia. Japan hastily followed suit by normalizing relations with China in the same year. China established diplomatic relations with most of the regional states during the 1970s. Except in the Korean Peninsula, which failed to consummate the North-South dialogue, the Cold War confrontation in East Asia was put to a de facto end. In the late 1970s, US-China relations were deepened even in military affairs. In Africa, the former enemies behaved as if allies, fighting against pro-Soviet groups.

It was this changed situation that contributed to the "East Asian Miracle," as the title of the World Bank report in 1993. As the Cold War barriers were lowered, East Asia became the region of economic growth and prosperity. Successful entities such as South Korea, Taiwan, Singapore, and Hong Kong were touted as East Asian NIES (Newly Industrializing Economies).

Based upon such phenomenal economic performance, political moves toward regional institutionalization came to the fore. Malaysian Prime Minister Mahathir bin Mohamad proposed the East Asian Economic Group (EAEG) in 1990, which would be the first official suggestion of a regional framework in East Asia. EAEG was later renamed EAEC (East Asian Economic Caucus) to soften the image of an economic bloc. Stimulated by emerging regionalism in Europe and North America, Mahathir argued that economically vibrant East Asia needed its own regional grouping. The creation of the European Union (EU) and the signing of the North American Free Trade Agreement (NAFTA) in 1992 were important factors behind the Mahathir proposal. For Mahathir, the region of East Asia should be composed of the ASEAN countries and the three Northeast Asian nations, China, Japan, and South Korea. The implication was to exclude the United States and Australia. He wanted to establish a new regional organization that would replace the Asia-Pacific Economic Cooperation (APEC).

American reaction was swift and fierce. Washington would not allow the formation of an exclusive economic bloc in East Asia, with the United States being outside of it. The main targets of diplomatic pressure to crush the EAEG idea were South Korea and Japan. As economic powerhouses in the region, their participation was thought critical for the success of the Mahathir proposal. However, they were heavily dependent on the United States politically and militarily. In November 1991, the US Secretary of State James Baker travelled to East Asia to join the APEC meeting in Seoul. When he met Japanese Foreign Minister Watanabe Michio in Tokyo, he gave a strong warning not to join Mahathir's idea. His words were blunt: "EAEC is a plot to draw a line in the Pacific and split Japan from the United States. It is unacceptable" (*The Asahi Shimbun*, January 18, 1992).

His warning to Seoul was more straightforward. In his memoir, Baker boasted how he flexed diplomatic muscle to "kill" the East Asian plan:

In private, I did my best to kill it. Some East Asian APEC members were inclined to go along with it merely to placate the insistent Mahathir. At the APEC meeting in Seoul, Korean Foreign Minister Lee Sang Ok suggested this country might support Mahathir's proposal out of Asian solidarity. I reminded Lee that it was Americans, not Malaysians, who had shed their blood for Korea 40 years before. My message was simple: All countries are *not* equal. The South Koreans got it, and did not press for an EAEG.

Without strong Japanese backing, the EAEG represented less of a threat to our economic interests in East Asia (Baker & DeFrank, 1995: 610–611, emphasis in original).

This is how the first attempt to form an East Asian framework was frustrated. Concerned about the rise of independent regionalism in East Asia, the United States decided to reinforce APEC by enhancing it to the summit level. The Clinton administration held the first APEC Summit meeting in Seattle. Accordingly, the agenda was also expanded from economic to political and security issues. It was an attempt to pit *the Asia-Pacific* against the rising *East Asia* as the regional framework. In fact, the concepts such as the Asia-Pacific and the Pacific Basin were the ones coined by policymakers in Japan and Australia in the 1970s to emphasize the connection, strategic and economic over geographical, between the United States and East Asia (Dirlik, 1998: 7–9). Regarding the contending visions for region building in East Asia and the Asia-Pacific, the main difference is whether the United States is included or not. In other words, the issue is whether and how East Asia will construct an independent regional framework.

3 Vision for the East Asian Community

Even after the Mahathir proposal was aborted, ASEAN countries did not abandon the idea. It is worthwhile to note the critical role ASEAN, as a sort of collective middle power, played in the process of East Asian region-building. It is often said that regional integration is the product of a crisis. Wartime devastation and the threat from the Soviet Union urged the Western European countries to build the European Community. In the late 1990s, the same dynamics seemed to get in motion in East Asia.

In December 1997, ASEAN invited the three neighbors in Northeast Asia, the ROK, China, and Japan, to the ASEAN 30th Anniversary Commemorative Summit held in Kuala Lumpur, Malaysia. It was the first opportunity for the heads of state in the whole East Asia, comprising both Southeast and Northeast subregions, to gather together under one roof. It was supposed to be a ceremonial event. However, history often works in an unexpected way. Shortly before the Summit, the financial crisis began in Thailand in July 1997 and immediately spread to most of the region. South Korea was pushed to the brink of national bankruptcy, only to be saved by the IMF emergency bailout.

In the midst of a spreading crisis, the supposedly ceremonial summit turned out to be the highest-level meeting to discuss regional cooperation. As the crisis continued the next year, the leaders had to meet again in 1998. The meeting was institutionalized in 1999 as the ASEAN Plus Three (APT) Summit. Comprising the 10 ASEAN countries and three Northeast nations, South Korea, China, and Japan, the geographic scope is exactly the same as that of the Mahathir proposal. The APT still functions as the main framework for regional cooperation. According to its annual report, the APT has now 60 mechanisms from summit to ministerial and high-officials levels covering wide range of regional cooperative issues (ASEAN Secretariat, 2024).

Another middle power, South Korea, played a leading role in enhancing the APT cooperation into the vision of the East Asian Community. At the 2nd APT Summit in 1998, South Korean President Kim Dae Jung proposed establishing a committee to discuss the future visions for regional cooperation. Thus, in 1999, the East Asia Vision Group (EAVG) was created with the participation of representatives from the 13 countries. Former South Korean Foreign Minister Han Sung Joo was elected as chairperson. After 2 years of discussion, the EAVG published the final report titled "Towards an East Asian Community" in 2001 (Lee, 2019). It was the first official document which presented the vision for the East Asian Community as the ultimate goal to be achieved in the region.

4 From Peak to Decline: Rise and Fall of the East Asia Summit

One of the major recommendations by the EAVG for the vision of the East Asian Community was to evolve the annual APT Summit into the East Asian Summit (EAS). The EAS was expected to be a big step towards the goal of the East Asian Community. Ironically, the inauguration of the EAS resulted in the decline of community-building momentum in East Asia.

In the process leading to the EAS, dissension among the member states erupted. The main point of contention was the scope of the membership. Malaysia and China argued for the original 13 members, 10 ASEAN countries, and the three Northeast nations. They were called the "status quo school." As a counterargument, Japan, Singapore and others demanded an "expanded East Asia," including India, Australia, and New Zealand. The logic behind this "expansionist school" was the concern over the ever-increasing power of China. They thought that they needed to invite regional powers such as India and Australia as a counterbalance to China. Ultimately, the expansionist logic prevailed over the status quo argument. In 2005, the East Asia Summit was inaugurated with the membership of 16 countries (ASEAN+3 + 3). As a result of the geopolitical tug-of-war, the scope of East Asia was stretched beyond the usual geographical boundary to include part of South Asia and Oceania.

Yet even the inclusion of India and Australia was insufficient to balance the rapidly growing Chinese political and economic influence. At the initiative of Indonesia and Singapore, the United States and Russia were invited to become official members in 2011, when Bali hosted the 6th East Asia Summit. The Obama administration was more than willing to join the regional grouping, as it was reengaging in East Asia under the slogan of "Pivot to Asia." The East Asia Summit, along with the Trans-Pacific Partnership (TPP) Agreement, was posited as a main pillar of Obama's rebalance strategy. With the United States itself becoming a part of East Asia, *the*

Asia-Pacific was about to replace *East Asia.* And the function of the East Asia Summit began to alter.

Ironically, shortly after the inauguration of the Summit, the momentum for the vision of the East Asian Community began to wane. The annual Summit, which was expected to be a high-level forum for sharing views on regional community building, turned out to be an arena where big powers would clash over regional disputes. American and Japanese delegates, for instance, took a lead in criticizing Chinese behaviors in the South China Sea. Heads of state of regional countries gather together once a year at the Summit, which has historic significance in and of itself. However, lack of substance and progress, it is rarely covered in the regional media and languishes in low, if any, popular recognition.

Middle power diplomacy by ASEAN and South Korea, in particular, was the main driving force for regional community-building in East Asia (Lee, 2023). However, the process so far shows that there is a long way to realize the vision.

5 East Asia Torn Between Eurasia and the Indo-Pacific

As stated above, two visions of region-building were competing with each other in the earlier period: *East Asia* versus *the Asia-Pacific*. The main point of contention was how to deal with the rapid rise of China and subsequently whether the United States would be included. Regionalism in East Asia had to walk a fine line between the two powers. With the advent of the "New Cold War," now East Asia is being torn apart by the two newly emerging mega-regions: *Eurasia* versus *the Indo-Pacific*. For those in the region, the concept of East Asia has the connotation of overcoming old and new, historical and ideological divisions to build a peaceful community of nations. Yet, now East Asia is retrogressing to the battlefield of global power rivalries.

While the middle power diplomacy for East Asian regionalism waned, big powers began to impose their own regional ambitions, bringing cleavages into the region. In the early 2000s, China shed initial cautiousness and began to show active interest in the emerging regional diplomacy. In 2003, China took the initiative in launching the Six-Party Talks in Beijing to deal with the nuclear crisis in the Korean Peninsula. Along with Malaysia, China was one of the most earnest proponents of the early inauguration of the East Asia Summit in 2005.

However, recognizing that the Summit turned out to be a stage for China-bashing by the United States and Japan, Beijing rapidly lost interest in community-building in East Asia. Emboldened by the tremendous economic power at its disposal, China instead sought to build mega-regional frameworks beyond East Asia. The financial crisis caused by the collapse of Lehman Brothers in 2008 further convinced Beijing to envision an alternative global order to replace the old one governed by the West.

China worked closely with Russia to establish BRICS: a comprehensive cooperation among the five emerging powers, such as Brazil, Russia, India, China, and South Africa. The BRICs mechanism started as a foreign ministerial meeting in

2006, soon to be elevated to the summit level in 2009. When South Africa joined in 2011, the name changed from BRICs to BRICS. In 2015, the BRICS Development Bank (later renamed the New Development Bank) was established as a potential rival to the World Bank. BRICS is now emerging as a central rallying forum for the Global South. In 2024, Egypt, Ethiopia, Iran, and the United Arab Emirates joined the BRICS grouping, showing dramatically the decline of the US influence in the Middle East region.

President Xi Jinping, who became China's new leader in 2012, put forth ambitious visions under the slogan of One Belt One Road (later renamed Belt and Road Initiative, BRI) in 2014. Chinese regionalist design was no longer confined to East Asia. The focus was put on connecting China with not only countries in Asia but also those in the Eurasian continent and ultimately in Europe and beyond. Now the Belts and Roads are being extended to almost every corner of the globe. Putin's geostrategic vision of Eurasianism functions as an additional force to facilitate region-building on the Continent.

Based on deepening economic relations, regional security cooperation is also on the agenda. Upgrading of the Conference on Interaction and Confidence-Building Measures in Asia (CICA) proposed by Xi Jinping is one such effort in that direction. In 1992, at the initiative of Kazakhstani President Nazarbayev, CICA started as a regional security dialogue forum for countries in the Eurasian continent and remained minimal in scope. However, when China took over the chairmanship in 2014, President Xi proposed an ambitious plan to upgrade the forum to a solid regional security cooperation body modeled after the Organization for Security and Cooperation in Europe (OSCE). In his speech to the CICA Summit held in 2014 in Shanghai, Xi presented the "new Asian security concept" and argued for "Asian security by the Asians," implicitly criticizing the U.S. involvement in Asian affairs (Xi, 2014).

China also seems to be intent on reinforcing the Shanghai Cooperation Organization (SCO) as a more solid and comprehensive regional security framework on the Continent. It originally began as Shanghai Five, a cooperative mechanism among China, Russia, and three Central Asian nations (Kazakhstan, Kyrgyzstan, Tajikistan) in 1997, to deal with subregional security issues after the fall of the Soviet Union. In 2001, with the admission of Uzbekistan, it became institutionalized and renamed the SCO. In 2017, it expanded to eight states, including India and Pakistan. Iran and Belarus joined the group in 2023 and 2024, respectively. The SCO now covers vast areas of the Eurasian continent, even to the part of Eastern Europe. In addition to economic cooperation, the SCO states conduct joint military exercises regularly.

It was in this context that Japan and the United States put forward the Indo-Pacific as a new regional framework. They needed to realign regional countries to counterbalance increasing Chinese influence. In the process, Japan's initiative was outstanding. To a certain extent, we can say that Japan has been a major proponent of the New Cold War in East Asia, out of concern over power transition in the region, that is, rapidly rising China and retreating America.

When he was reelected as prime minister in late 2012, Abe Shinzo argued for close security cooperation among the United States, Japan, India, and Australia, calling it "Asia's democratic security diamond" to contain Chinese expansion (Abe, 2012). This proposal laid the foundation of the Quadrilateral Security Dialogue (QUAD), which was officialized in 2017. The first QUAD summit was held in 2021 and subsequently became institutionalized.

As a broader framework, the Free and Open Indo-Pacific (FOIP) concept was advocated by Japan and the United States. The slogan of the FOIP was first raised by Prime Minister Abe in 2016 in a speech made in Nairobi, Kenya. China was not mentioned directly in the speech; however, there was no doubt that Japan intended to compete with the Belt and Road Initiative in Africa. Soon, Japan succeeded in persuading the United States to accept the geopolitical plan. When President Trump visited Tokyo in 2017, Japan and the United States agreed to take the FOIP concept as the "US-Japan common strategy." In 2018, the United States changed the name of the Asia-Pacific Command based in Hawaii to the Indo-Pacific Command. Along with military reorganization, overall reconfiguration has been in progress in the regional strategies of Japan and the United States.

As big powers with different geopolitical visions compete among each other for influence, the region of East Asia is on the verge of being torn apart. Symbolically speaking, East Asia is, so to speak, caught between Eurasia and the Indo-Pacific: continental versus maritime nations.

6 Efforts to Maintain the Regional Unity

Faced with intensifying competition among big powers and widening cleavages in the region, middle powers such as ASEAN and South Korea strived to maintain regional unity and momentum toward community building. Focus was put on presenting alternative views on the emerging concept of the Indo-Pacific.

It was Indonesia that took leadership in rallying the ASEAN members for the united voice. When Trump and Abe declared the Free and Open Indo-Pacific initiative as the common strategy of the United States and Japan in 2017, ASEAN countries became increasingly concerned that the intensifying US-China rivalry could "jeopardize the long period of peace, stability and prosperity that the Asia-Pacific region has enjoyed." To preserve Southeast Asia's "regional autonomy," they preferred to "engage both the United States and China." Indonesia urged ASEAN to assume an active role in the discourse about this new Indo-Pacific strategic concept. For ASEAN, it was critical to retain its centrality in the evolving Indo-Pacific construct and architecture. After "18 months of intensive lobbying by Jakarta," ASEAN leaders finally adopted ASEAN Outlook on the Indo-Pacific (AOIP) in 2019, the draft of which was proposed by Indonesia (Anwar, 2020: 111–113). In the AOIP, the leaders declared that the Indo-Pacific should aim for a "region of dialogue and cooperation instead of rivalry," with such principles as ASEAN centrality, openness, inclusivity, equality, nonintervention, mutual respect, and so on. It also suggested that the existing regional mechanisms such as the East Asia Summit and ARF be used as platforms for dialogue and cooperation.

ASEAN countries did not remain only in words, with just issuing a declaration. They promoted the "mainstreaming" of the AOIP, which means the efforts to persuade the major regional powers to respect the principles of the AOIP. So far, ASEAN has issued joint declarations on the AOIP with the United States, China, South Korea, and Japan. As a result, the AOIP principles such as ASEAN centrality, inclusivity, and equalness are introduced into official documents of major powers, thus becoming a sort of norm in the discussion on the Indo-Pacific region. They are no doubt rhetorical. However, norm-building is an important aspect of the middle power diplomacy of ASEAN.

South Korea, another aspiring middle power in the region, also sought a balanced diplomacy amid the emerging "New Cold War" between the United States and China during the Moon Jae-in administration. For South Korea, the road to middle power diplomacy was far more rugged compared to that of ASEAN. Indonesia has a long history of independent diplomacy, as a leader in the nonaligned movement during the Cold War period. In contrast, South Korea was a product of the Cold War, born out of the division of the peninsula, and has been dependent on the United States for its security. For a long time, there was little room for autonomous diplomacy.

The dramatic end of the Cold War provided a historic chance for South Korea to broaden its diplomatic horizon. The Roh Tae Woo administration did not miss it by advocating and practicing *Nordpolitik*. It succeeded in normalizing relations with most of the former socialist bloc countries, including the Soviet Union and China, in a couple of years. President Kim Dae Jung's regionalist diplomacy in promoting the East Asian Community was in the same vein.

It would be worthwhile examining the efforts of the Moon Jae-in administration, which strived for balanced diplomacy in the face of the emerging New Cold War. Despite a close relationship with the United States, President Moon would not join directly the Free and Open Indo-Pacific initiative. He instead proposed the New Southern Policy along with the New Northern Policy. The latter was a direct descendant of *Nordpolitik*. The subregion of Northeast Asia was at the center of successive ROK administrations' diplomacy in the post-Cold War era. In contrast, Southeast Asia was given little attention, except for Kim Dae Jung's active engagement in the ASEAN+3 diplomacy. In fact, the Moon administration was the first in presenting regionalist strategy in a comprehensive and systematic way, connecting the two subregions of Northeast and Southeast Asia.

This came partly from the ambition of the Moon administration to play an active role in regional affairs as a rising middle power. More directly, it had to devise its own strategy vis-à-vis emerging Indo-Pacific policy discussions. Just like the ASEAN leaders, President Moon and his advisors were concerned about the rising tension among big powers, which would force the regional nations into binary choices between the United States and China. In a speech made in 2019, President Moon defined the role of South Korea as a "bridge nation that connects the continent and the ocean" (Moon, 2019).

The FOIP initiatives by Japan and the United States had a confrontational tone vis-à-vis China. For that reason, the Moon administration was cautious in adopting the concept. President Moon instead planned an independent strategy towards the region of Southeast Asia, which was becoming a battlefield in the emerging New Cold War. One of his presidential election campaign agendas was to "upgrade the relations with ASEAN and India to the same level with that of the four countries around the Korean Peninsula." The "four countries around the Korean Peninsula" was a term commonly used to denote China, Japan, Russia, and the United States and implied that said four countries held special significance for ROK diplomacy.

Shortly after he won the election in May 2017, Moon put the campaign pledge into practice and dispatched a special envoy to the Philippines, Vietnam, and Indonesia. Until then, it was a custom for the president-elect to send special emissaries only to the "four powers." It was the first time the ROK president-elect sent special envoys to Southeast Asian nations. Moon was serious in expressing his eagerness for strategic engagement in the ASEAN region. Within 2 years after the inauguration, he made official visits to all 10 ASEAN countries, nine of which were state visits.

It was at the state visit to Indonesia in November 2017 that President Moon unveiled his New Southern Policy (NSP). Indonesia was chosen for the nation's importance in the ROK's middle power diplomacy in the region. In the address made in Jakarta on November 10, 2017, Moon put forth the vision for a "3P community" between ASEAN and South Korea, which would be composed of three pillars: people community, peace community, and prosperity community. In addition to bilateral cooperation with Indonesia, he disclosed an ambitious plan for strategic engagement in the ASEAN region, ranging from political, security, and economic cooperation to sociocultural exchanges. For the details of his New Southern Policy, President Moon contributed an article titled "Toward a People-Centered ASEAN Community" to the online journal *Project Syndicate* on the same date as his speech (Moon, 2017). As stated above, Prime Minister Abe used the same journal to disclose his proposal for "Asia's democratic security diamond," which would later be realized as QUAD. Moon's choice of the journal was not accidental and clearly had the implication of presenting an alternative vision for the Indo-Pacific region.

Moon's strategy was to align closely with the ASEAN nations, particularly with Indonesia, to form a coalition of middle powers. In an internal report on the New Southern Policy made in December 2019, the Foreign Ministry defined the role of the ROK in the region as a "bridge nation" that would contribute to the "regional prosperity and peace" by "pursuing to cooperate with any regional vision … such as the Indo-Pacific strategy of the United States and the One Belt One Road Initiative by China" based upon the principle of "ASEAN centrality" (Lee, 2020: 74).

While searching for a balanced regional policy as a bridging middle power, the Moon administration strived to align its New Southern Policy with the FOIP strategy of the United States. President Trump made a state visit to South Korea on November 7, the day after he declared in Tokyo that the FOIP was the common strategy of the United States and Japan. Naturally, the FOIP became a major agenda of the Trump-Moon meeting. In the joint press release, Trump emphasized that "the US-ROK Alliance, built upon mutual trust and shared values of freedom, democracy, human rights, and rule of law, remains a lynchpin for security, stability, and prosperity in the Indo-Pacific." This was the first high-level US-ROK document in which the term Indo-Pacific was mentioned. However, the catchword of the Free and Open Indo-Pacific was carefully avoided and paraphrased indirectly.

After the summit, the two countries worked to find ways for functional collaboration between their respective strategies of FOIP and NSP. In the process, according to a ROK internal report, the "mutual complementarity" of the two strategies was emphasized (Lee, 2020:83). In the summit meeting in July 2019, Trump and Moon agreed to "deepen cooperation between the US Indo-Pacific Strategy and the ROK New Southern Policy," in areas such as "development assistance, energy and digital network security, maritime law enforcement capacity building, and natural disaster resiliency." They also agreed to support the centrality of ASEAN. Most of the areas for cooperation belonged to the socio-economic and nontraditional security agenda, which reflected ROK's cautious approach to the US-Japan FOIP initiative. Moon's New Southern Policy was an attempt to find a way to bridge the split between China's BRI and the United States' FOIP, aligning with other middle powers such as Indonesia.

However, Moon's New Southern Policy was under severe criticism from the conservatives both in and abroad. They denounced Moon's balanced diplomacy as tilting toward China, edging away from the United States. With the advent of the conservative Yoon Suk Yeol administration, South Korean regional diplomacy retrogressed instantly to the old-fashioned confrontational posture. From the year one of his presidency, Yoon and his advisors took the lead of "China exodus" chant, denouncing Moon's weak-kneed diplomacy toward China. In December 2022, the ROK government announced its own Indo-Pacific strategy, in the same vein with those of the United States and Japan. In practice, the Yoon administration pushed forward the reinforcement of security cooperation with the United States and Japan, thus actively committing to a formation of de facto regional alliance against China. To promote the security relations with Japan, President Yoon even made a controversial decision to virtually nullify the ROK Supreme Court decision on the case of the conscripted laborers during the colonial period, by making the ROK government to take over the compensation from the defendant Japanese companies. The ROK courts so far ruled that the subrogation was unlawful. The conservative administration, urged by the United States and Japan, again placed security imperatives of the New Cold War over historical justice.

7 The Community-Building Versus the New Cold War

At present, there are two triangles of nations, representing the contending dynamics in the region. One is the ROK-US-Japan relations, which are a pillar of the emerging New Cold War structure. The other is the ROK-China-Japan triangle born out of the process toward the East Asian Community. The former is on a vigorous wax, while the latter is at a standstill, if not on the wane, since the change of government in South Korea.

To consummate the trilateral relations among South Korea, the United States, and Japan into a comprehensive regional alliance was a long-cherished goal of the US strategy toward East Asia. In the early Cold War years, the United States hoped to create a collective alliance in Asia, after the model of NATO. However, the plan for an "Asian NATO" was aborted by objections from regional allies. It was not just because of Syngman Rhee's fierce anti-Japanese attitudes. Those countries invaded by Japan during the war, Australia and the Philippines in particular, were opposed to the idea of forming a collective security framework comprising Japan. As a result, the United States had to conclude a bundle of bilateral security pacts with respective allies: Japan, the Philippines, Australia, New Zealand in 1951, South Korea in 1953, and Taiwan in 1954. It came to be termed the hub-and-spoke alliance system (Cha, 2016).

The problem with this hub-and-spoke system was that the spokes were not linked with each other, incurring additional burden on the United States. That was why Washington took so great pains in pushing Seoul and Tokyo to normalize relations in 1965. Thereafter, America would not miss a chance to reinforce the trilateral security cooperation into a military alliance. When the nuclear crisis erupted in the Korean Peninsula in the 1990s, the Clinton administration created the Trilateral Coordination and Oversight Group (TCOG) to deal with the problem. This was the first formal security cooperation mechanism among the three nations, though confined to the North Korean nuclear issue. The Obama administration, having China as well as North Korea in mind, tried to expand the scope of the trilateral security cooperation to regional and global issues such as maritime security. Summit and foreign ministerial meetings were regularized, with the agreement to establish the trilateral secretariat in Washington, D.C. in 2011. However, all these efforts were neglected with the advent of the unilateralist Trump administration (Lee, 2018).

Returning to power, the Democratic Biden administration picked up where Obama left off. In August 2023, Biden invited ROK President Yoon and Japanese Prime Minister Kishida to Camp David for a summit. With Biden's call for a "new era of cooperation," the three leaders declared commitment to conduct annual joint military exercises, share intelligence, and hold the trilateral summit on an annual basis. The summit fell short of producing a three-way collective defense agreement but took a giant step toward it.

In summary, the Camp David agreements were 1) to expand the geographical scope of the trilateral cooperation beyond the Korean Peninsula to the Indo-Pacific, 2) to militarize the security cooperation to the level of alliance, and 3) to institutionalize the trilateral consultation mechanism. The US officials emphasized that the focus of the summit was to "lock-in" the trilateral cooperation, making the agreements irreversible. However, foreign policy orientation can shift with the change of government in a democracy. In South Korea, in particular, the majority are opposed to close military cooperation with Japan. A progressive government would try to take distance from it. The South Koreans, who have suffered for so long from living on the frontline of the Cold War, are not willing to be in the forefront again in the emerging New Cold War. Rather, they would strive to find a way to avert it, or to mitigate it at least.

Though weakened, the other triangle of the ROK-China-Japan is still expected to be a basis for maintaining the momentum for regional community-building. The trilateral cooperation mechanism was established in the process of the ASEAN+3 (APT). At the 2nd APT summit held in 1998, Japanese Prime Minister Obuchi Keizo suggested to having a meeting of the three Northeast Asian countries, Japan, South Korea, and China. President Kim Dae Jung agreed instantly, but the Chinese response then was reluctant. After a series of diplomatic endeavors by both Seoul and Tokyo, China finally agreed the next year. Thus, the first-ever trilateral summit-level meeting of South Korea, Japan, and China was held in 1999, at the margin of the APT summit. There, they agreed to meet on an annual basis.

Throughout the process, the collaboration of President Kim and Prime Minister Obuchi was conspicuous. They shared a vision for the regional community in East Asia. The two leaders are well-known for the Kim-Obuchi Joint Declaration in 1998, which is considered to have opened a new chapter for the Korea-Japan relations. The core spirit of the declaration was to "squarely face the past" and "build a future-oriented relationship." In this context, Prime Minister Obuchi voiced his "deep remorse and heartfelt apology" for Japan's "colonial rule" (Kim & Obuch, 1998). The declaration was the first written official apology made by the highest leader of the Japanese government. The regional community-building progressed hand in hand with historical reconciliation, which shows the way to go beyond the divisive San Francisco system.

Though launched as a historic step toward regional community in Northeast Asia, the ROK-China-Japan cooperation floundered from the outset. When the rightist Koizumi Junichiro became the Prime Minister and paid a visit to the Yasukuni Shrine, the trilateral summit was boycotted by South Korea and China in 2005 and 2006. When South Korea introduced the THAAD missile, China was opposed to holding the summit. In recent years, Japan rejected the meeting as a protest to the Moon administration's handling of the issue of the conscripted laborers. The process of trilateral cooperation has been swayed by conflicts over history, strategy, and emotion.

Despite continuing collision of interests, the three countries have promoted to institutionalize trilateral cooperation. Since 2008, the summit has been held as an independent meeting, separated from the APT. In 2011, the Trilateral Cooperation Secretariat was established in Seoul to promote comprehensive exchanges among the three countries.

After 5 years of suspension, the trilateral summit was held in Seoul in May 2024. It is significant that the leaders in the three countries shared the necessity to reinforce the trilateral cooperation in the face of the ever-intensifying New Cold War in the region. Though with different strategic perspectives, they have common interest in deepening economic interdependence and expanding social exchanges in the region. The power of functionalist cooperation is still effective in keeping the vision for the East Asian Community alive.

8 Conclusion: The Rise of the San Francisco System 2.0?

In 2015, Prime Minister Abe made a speech to the US Congress, set as a commemorative event of the 70th anniversary of the end of World War II. He began his address with an apology the Americans for starting the Pacific War. He concluded his speech by saying that "In the end, together with the US and other like-minded democracies, we won the Cold War." And he emphasized that the two countries, as the victors, shared responsibility to establish a new order "in the vast seas stretching from the Pacific to the Indian Oceans seas of peace and freedom" (Abe, 2015a). The implication is clear: Japan was a war criminal and defeated nation in terms of World War II, but a victor from the perspective of the Cold War, thus freed from the shackles of the past to assume the leadership in a new era.

This was the logic with which Abe put forth the slogan of the Free and Open Indo-Pacific. In the sense that the FOIP initiative is an attempt to introduce a new Cold War division into the region, we can call it the San Francisco System 2.0. The United States was the main architect of the San Francisco System 1.0, and Japan was a passive beneficiary. Now, Japan is a main proponent of the San Francisco System 2.0, actively inviting the New Cold War division into the region.

We should also pay attention to the close connection between the San Francisco System 2.0 and the rise of historical revisionism in Japan. Shortly after the address to the US Congress, Abe issued a statement for the occasion of the 70th anniversary of the end of World War II. In the statement, he carefully differentiated between apology for war and colonialism. Abe expressed "deepest remorse" and "sincere condolences" to Japan's wartime victims, while he justified its colonial rule as the same as that with other imperialist powers at the time. He apologized for the "aggression" against China, but not for the colonization of Korea. He moved on to assert that the future generations in Japan, "who have nothing to do with that war," should not be "predestined" to apologize themselves (Abe, 2015b). In short, he tried to put an end to the official apology by the Japanese government, suggesting his statement as the final one. It was an attempt to overwrite the Murayama statement in 1995, thus virtually replacing and erasing it from history. Abe's historical revisionism has a close relationship with Japan's ambition to play a central role in the emerging New Cold War. The emergence of the San Francisco System 2.0 poses a great challenge for the South Koreans to cope with.

References

Abe, S. (2012, December 27). Asia's democratic security diamond. Project Syndicate.

Abe, S. (2015a, April 29). Toward an alliance of hope: Address to a joint meeting of the U.S. Congress. Ministry of Foreign Affairs of Japan. https://www.mofa.go.jp/na/na1/us/page4e_000241.html. Accessed September 25, 2024.

Abe, S. (2015b, August 14). Statement by Prime Minister Shinzo Abe. Cabinet Secretariat, Government of Japan. https://japan.kantei.go.jp/97_abe/statement/201508/0814statement.html. Accessed September 26, 2024.

Anwar, D. F. (2020). Indonesia and the ASEAN outlook on the Indo-Pacific. *International Affairs, 96*(1), 111–129.

ASEAN Secretariat. (2024, June 12). Overview of ASEAN Plus Three cooperation. https://aseanplusthree.asean.org/wp-content/uploads/2024/06/APT-Overview-Paper-12-June-2024.pdf. Accessed September 20, 2024.

Cha, V. (2016). *Power play: The origins of the American alliance system in Asia.* Princeton University Press.

Baker, J. A., III, & DeFrank, T. M. (1995). *The politics of diplomacy: Revolution, war and peace, 1989–1992*. G. P. Putnam's Sons.

Dirlik, A. (Ed.). (1998). What is in a rim? Critical perspectives on the Pacific region idea. Rowman & Littlefield Publishers, Inc.

Kim, D. J., & Obuchi, K. (1998). Japan-Republic of Korea joint declaration: A new Japan-Republic of Korea partnership towards the twenty-first century. Ministry of Foreign Affairs of Japan. https://www.mofa.go.jp/region/asia-paci/korea/joint9810.html. Accessed September 20, 2024.

Lee, J. W. (2018). The origins of the US-Korea-Japan triangle: Intersection of diplomatic history and IR theories. *Ajiataiheiyo Tokyu, 33*, 19–41. In Japanese.

Lee, J. W. (2019). Kim Dae Jung's initiative for the East Asian community and Korea-Japan-China triangle. *Ajiataiheiyo Tokyu, 36*, 19–42. In Japanese.

Lee, J. W. (2020). Moon Jae-in's regionalist diplomacy and the new southern policy: An attempt for middle power diplomacy between FOIP and BRI. *Ajiataiheiyo Tokyu, 39*, 61–91. In Japanese.

Lee, J. W. (2023). A dolphin caught between whales? ROK's regionalist diplomacy as a middle power strategy. In Peking University-Waseda University Joint Research Initiative (Ed.), *Cooperation, competition, and integration in Asia-Pacific* (pp. 198–213). Waseda University Press.

Moon, J. (2017, November 10). Toward a people-centered ASEAN community. Project Syndicate.

Moon, J. (2019, August 15). Address by President Moon Jae-in on Korea's 74th liberation day. Ministry of Foreign Affairs of the Republic of Korea. https://overseas.mofa.go.kr/gr-ko/brd/m_6996/view.do?seq=1344766. Accessed September 20, 2024.

Xi, J. (2014, May 21). New Asian security concept for new progress in security cooperation: Remarks at the Fourth Summit of the Conference on Interaction and Confidence-building Measures in Asia. China.org.cn. http://www.china.org.cn/world/2014-05/28/content_32511846.htm. Accessed September 20, 2024.

Trouble Among East Asian Allies? America's Troubling Past

Alexis Dudden

Abstract This article explores the persistent tensions in Northeast Asia rooted in American foreign policy, particularly its influence on Japan–South Korea relations. It highlights how unresolved legacies of Japanese colonial rule and the division of Korea continue to shape diplomatic and social conflicts. The study examines the limitations of the 1965 Treaty on Basic Relations, which failed to address forced labor, comfort women, and broader historical injustices. It critiques the United States' tendency to prioritize strategic interests, often favoring Japan and sidelining Korean grievances. The article discusses how historical memory and nationalist sentiment fuel ongoing disputes, including territorial issues and public protests. It underscores the importance of confronting historical truths for reconciliation and regional stability. The analysis addresses Cold War dynamics that shaped treaty negotiations and left many issues unresolved. It calls for a reassessment of the San Francisco System and more inclusive recognition of history. The article concludes that unresolved historical issues remain central to contemporary security and diplomacy in Northeast Asia. Ultimately, it argues for a more honest and comprehensive engagement with the past to foster lasting peace.

Keywords 1965 Treaty · Allied occupation · Cold War · Diplomatic tensions · Historical memory · Japan · Korea · San Francisco Treaty · Treaty on Basic Relations · United States

Even before the horrible COVID-19 pandemic erupted in late 2019, it was tempting to blame everything wrong with American foreign policy on Donald Trump's presidency. However, the problem for Americans is that in some instances, the Trump administration has simply unveiled the crass and often racist practices that have long informed US government behavior. Put differently, Donald Trump and his supporters exacerbate bad situations, yet some of the situations were bad to begin with.

A. Dudden (✉)
Department of History, University of Connecticut, Mansfield, USA
e-mail: alexis.dudden@uconn.edu

Y.-H. Kim et al. (eds.), *Beyond the San Francisco System*,
https://doi.org/10.1007/978-981-95-3328-2_20

This is abundantly clear with regard to American policy toward mutual Northeast Asian allies, South Korea, and Japan.

Beginning in July 2019, a standoff between the governments in Seoul and Tokyo over trade restrictions and security arrangements spilled onto the streets in both countries, encouraging ongoing protests—South Koreans boycotted Japanese cars, beer, and tourism among other things while Japanese cancelled school trips abroad and Korean-related art installations at home—and prompting many to declare relations as the "worst ever" since Japan's occupation of Korea ended in 1945. Notwithstanding the lack of comparative consideration, even Donald Trump seemed surprised: "It's like a full-time job getting involved between Japan and South Korea… If they need me, I'm there." All the while, Washington pundits rolled out hackneyed mantras about the importance of "our allies working things out among themselves" as if rocky relations between these nations were a novel annoyance and as manageable as changing a playlist on an iPhone.

Absent in the preponderance of this recent discussion is awareness of the structural fractures undergirding Japan and South Korea's perennially precarious post-1945 relations. It is always important to bear in mind that until the very end of Japan's colonization of Korea (1910–1945), no Korean imagined that their country would be divided in half (no Japanese did either, and Americans were not even thinking about it). Yet, as is now well-known, late at night on August 10, 1945, two Americans working in Washington, Dean Rusk and Charles Bonesteel, looked at a map of Korea and drew a line through the 38th parallel, keeping Seoul under American control and offering anything north of the line to the Soviet Union (Moscow's leaders anticipated receiving the northern half of Japan as a war prize, having entered World War II against Japan not the nation's Korean colony). Several years later, with the Korean War ending in the July 1953 armistice, the line hardened into fact. Meanwhile, yet seemingly further and further out of reach, any post-1945 history of Korea does not erase the pre-1945 past, no matter how many expedient political efforts would seek to make it so. And this is where Washington's actions to this day have increasingly involved the United States in this process, regardless of ongoing efforts to imagine them away.

Lack of criticism from Seoul and Tokyo is not surprising since both South Korea and Japan rely on the United States as a security guarantor. Yet America's perennial and expedient favoritism of Japan over South Korea equally infuses the situation. In 1965, American diplomats worked behind the scenes to broker a "Treaty on Basic Relations" between Japan and South—known as the "Normalization Treaty"—that sought to address the colonial era's wrongs. From the start, however, this treaty was fatally flawed if only for the obvious historical impossibility of sidelining North Korea in a deal intended to solve this history, which the United States insisted. Put differently, there was no divided Korea under Japanese occupation, so any arrangement to address its substance—such as slave labor or the appropriation of property—would be moot from the start. Nonetheless, this is what Washington demanded in 1965, and this elision of Pyongyang's existence only assured that at some point history would bite back. This happened during the summer of 2019, making it imperative again to re-examine ways in which the United States fashioned the post-1945 geometry of Northeast Asia in its treaty arrangements for the region if any hope for a calm and progressive future is desired.

Importantly, neither economic nor security needs are driving the current moment: History is. Specifically, competing understandings of the history of forced and slave labor under Japan's colonial and wartime occupation of Korea propel today's iteration of the ongoing "history problems" as they are collectively known. The major touchstones primarily revolve around territorial disagreements and how best to compensate individuals who suffered under Japanese rule (in the current manifestation, the territorial component is in the background; in 2012, however, it was front and center, and at the time, pundits also declared relations as "at their worst ever"). Noticeably, American involvement in these core components has only exacerbated already contentious histories because of an ongoing determination to see history as background noise rather than elemental to the present. In this vein, American diplomatic efforts in the two main legal settlements concerning Japan's pre-1945 national past locate how the structural difficulties began. While Washington prefers to treat history as background music to the present, Seoul has now openly challenged this perennial policy myopia. The United States needs to grapple with the volatile histories at stake because Korean and Japanese public perceptions of shared pre-1945 histories have, in fact, become actionable security threats.

At first pass, the 2019 Japan-South Korea standoff began with Japan's early July 2019 imposition of economic restrictions on South Korea, claiming "national security reasons." Both governments fanned mutually constitutive and oppositional nationalist fires, while Washington made tepid interventions, enjoining the countries to work together. Ultimately, Seoul decided it was a no-win situation—if you cannot trust us, we cannot trust you—and ditched an American-structured military sharing pact with Tokyo. Defense analysts were flabbergasted, and South Koreans became more sharply divided over the course of their country given North Korea's pleasure at the news and its resumption of an "all missiles all the time" approach to global diplomacy.

In November 2018, a South Korean court ruled in favor of three 90-plus-year-old men seeking compensation from Japan's Mitsubishi Heavy Industries for their suffering over 75 years ago. Japanese historians estimate that roughly 800,000 Koreans were forcibly mobilized to labor in Japan between 1939 and 1945, and court cases, including this one, began as early as the 1970s within Japan to no avail. Finally, therefore, with the 2018 determination, a court made it possible for these plaintiffs' efforts to receive roughly US$80,000 by freezing assets of descendant corporations working in South Korea today (in related cases, some plaintiffs seek no money or one yen). The Japanese government balked at the ruling and, although South Koreans largely disagreed, maintained that the 1965 bilateral treaty had "entirely settled the past" and retaliated by delisting South Korea from a roster of preferred trading partners. The South Korean government followed suit and, together with the population at large, has brought to an effective halt all economic, diplomatic, and security relations between the two countries since. Japanese reports indicate that within three months, Korean tourism to Japan was down by nearly 50%, Nissan and

Honda, respectively, witnessed an over 80% drop in sales, and Japanese beer manufacturers saw a 97% decline in their products.

Many might raise eyebrows and wonder why any of these issues matter anymore. After all, American diplomats quickly point out: shouldn't North Korea's missiles be the focus? Even during the COVID-19 outbreaks, Pyongyang persists in launching missiles to appear relevant. In many ways, however, North Korea's unproductive and bellicose behavior only serves as Washington's perfect foil: each missile launch deflects attention away from how the United States failed those who suffered under Japanese rule by ignoring their demands for compensation from Japan following the surrender. Notably, in addition to Koreans, Chinese, and other Asians, this includes American POWs forced to labor at Japanese corporations — still without reparations or compensation. From various angles, therefore, it remains vital to the dignity of those who suffered under Japanese rule to make clear that the treaties intended to atone for their suffering were problematic from the start. This includes both the 1951 San Francisco Treaty ending the Allied occupation of Japan, as well as the bilateral 1965 agreement between Seoul and Tokyo.

Among other matters, in terms of the territorial component of the "history problems" between Japan and South Korea, decisions that American officials made during the United States occupation of Japan (1945–1952) remain central to the problems today. For example, the Allies—led by the United States under the direction of President Harry Truman's special representative John Foster Dulles—decided *not* to name sovereignty in the 1951 San Francisco Treaty over a small group of islands that both nations claim. This final determination not to name an owner—despite intense lobbying by both Korean and Japanese interests—went into effect in the form of a new map of Japan and its surrounding region in April 1952 (what the American government adheres to today).

The United States' decision not to make a decision at the time is not at all made clear now by Washington's repeated assertions that Japan and Korea should solve this problem for themselves. The current American position at once serves to define the United States as exceptional by removing it from its own history and also further entrenches already rigid positions in Japan and Korea to dig in their heels deeper, seemingly requiring the United States to ride in to the rescue.

The "San Francisco System," as it is known, rested on two developments: 1) the Allies' total destruction of the physical shape of what had been the Empire of Japan and 2) on the Japanese government's acceptance, while under US occupation, of the judgments of the Far Eastern Tribunals—including the guilty verdicts for 25 individuals charged as Class A war criminals. At the time, Japanese Prime Minister Yoshida Shigeru signed his name in agreement on behalf of Japan and the Japanese people while Emperor Hirohito was also satisfied with the outcome. A little-known April 26, 1952, telegram from General Matthew Ridgeway in Tokyo to John Foster Dulles (President Harry Truman's special representative in charge of the treaty process) reads as follows:

> His Majesty the Emperor of Japan, on his own initiative, graciously called upon me this morning and personally expressed his gratitude… (in) making it possible for Japan to regain her sovereignty next Monday.[1]

With this, the Empire of Japan's once massive reach that had spanned from North China to the South Pacific was reduced to what looks familiar today as the sea-horse shaped archipelago that the world knows as "Japan," floating in the North Pacific just to the east of the Asian mainland.

Significantly, the Korean War was being fought at the time, a war that caught most of the Americans involved in the occupation of Japan wholly by surprise when it broke out on June 25, 1950. This remains important to today's discussion of the island standoff if only because the bulk of the San Francisco Treaty's territorial determinations would set the stage for new geographical rifts throughout the areas of Japan's former empire, which, in American officials' thinking at the time, clearly included Korea.

Considering this moment solely through the official American diplomatic record at the time reveals that conversations and discussions among American occupation officials in Japan *prior* to the outbreak of the Korean War—chief among them General Douglas MacArthur—had gradually grown to favor Japanese recommendations concerning the islands, or they ignored the issue entirely. This is not surprising given that the Americans involved were living and working in occupied Tokyo and had become friendly with certain Japanese officials in the course of their duties.

Notwithstanding, important exceptions to Japan's territorial requests outside the four main islands of Honshu, Shikoku, Kyushu, and Hokkaido—territories that Japanese officials regularly described to the American occupation officials as "lost" or "stolen"—included first and foremost the southern Kuril Islands, which Tokyo continues to contest with Moscow today (known in Japan as the Northern Territories). In addition, the Americans would wholly ignore Japan's requests for the reversion of the Ryukyu islands at the time—known more commonly as Okinawa—which Japanese officials much more willingly sacrificed to the Americans than the southern Kurils anyway. Finally, no American discussion ever arose at the time—at least in the public record—in favor of Japan's regaining control over the Bonin Islands (known today as the Ogasawara and since America's 1968 reversion to Japan under Japanese sovereign control).

Many scholars and others have long pointed to Secretary of State Dean Acheson's famous so-called "perimeter speech" at the National Press Club in Washington, D.C., on January 12, 1950, as critical to setting the stage. It has long been argued that Acheson's omission of the Korean peninsula as a strategic necessity for the United States in his speech, suggesting to some that it lay outside the US defense perimeter, served as a green light for North Korea's invasion of South Korea several months later. Yet, the *lack* of mention by Acheson of the islands Koreans and Japanese contest today—let alone any of the other islands around Korea—is

---

[1] Ridgeway to Dulles, April 26, 1952; catalogued in the John Foster Dulles Papers, Seeley Mudd Manuscript Library, Princeton University.

revealing. When taken together, Acheson and MacArthur's general view of the region's territories—especially its islands—and their relationship to naming them at this specific historical moment is key to understanding why doing so was tabled at the Treaty of San Francisco's signing. The territories that General MacArthur emphasized in "Top Secret," "Secret," and "Confidential" diplomatic correspondence *before* the outbreak of the Korean War as "the Asiatic littorals" and "the Asiatic fringe"—his terms for the arc of islands running alongside continental Asia's coastline—make crystal clear what he viewed as critical to the defense of the west coast of the United States.[2] The territory that Japan continues to contest with Korea did not fit this category.

Key to today's controversies over historical perception, for American policy planners, MacArthur's hierarchy of certain territories would shape regional planning: no more, no less. For MacArthur, the Ryukyu Islands (Okinawa) were primary, followed by Taiwan. That said, because the islands contested by Korea and Japan today were absent to MacArthur's thinking, when mention of them arose in contemporaneous diplomatic correspondence among other American planners, it was noticeable because it was *not* in terms of MacArthur or Acheson's "line of defense." Rather, official mention of these particular islands at the time indicates that certain Americans saw them as a means of gaining political favor with Japanese politicians.

The American diplomatic record reveals intense Japanese lobbying for control over these islands—as the Koreans would, too, eventually—yet the difference between efforts in Seoul and Tokyo boiled down to the Americans in Tokyo simply echoing back to Washington, often verbatim and unsubstantiated, whatever their Japanese hosts asked them to. Thus, what creates tension today to a great degree rests on the 1951 Treaty of San Francisco's lacunae regarding what a number of Japanese officials presumed they were getting in the deal. Although quite a number of other islands are mentioned in the treaty, the ones disputed today were not because when the treaty went into effect, strategic thinking prevailed at the expense of Japanese lobbying. Therefore, what some Japanese disparage today as "Korean deceit" rests with determinations and omissions that Americans made.

A significant behind-the-scenes player was William J. Sebald, who held several important positions between 1946 and 1952, including as MacArthur's chief political adviser in Tokyo during the American occupation of Japan. In May 1965—on the eve of the controversial treaty's signing—Sebald published his memoirs, *With MacArthur in Japan: A Personal History of the Occupation*.[3] Sebald had cultivated personal relations with powerful Japanese political figures, and those ties appear to

[2] For example, see "Memorandum of Conversation, by the Chief of the Division of Northeast Asian Affairs (Max Bishop)," Washington, February 16, 1949 (Participants General of the Army Douglas MacArthur, William J. Sebald, Acting U.S. Political Adviser for Japan, Max W. Bishop, Chief, Division of Northeast Asian Affairs), in *Foreign Relations of the United States* (FRUS), 1949, Volume VII, p. 657.

[3] William Sebald, *With MacArthur in Japan: A Personal History of the Occupation* (New York: Knopf, 1965).

have led him to internalize their positions about "Korea"—the term he continued to use, even then, well after the Korean Peninsula had been divided. He reconciled them with his own understanding of America's interests, namely, "the clear United States objective of keeping Japan out of Communist orbit." Notably, his book bleeds unabashed contempt for Koreans as a people.

In simplest terms, what emerges in Sebald's memoirs in astonishingly clear ways is the disdain and occasional contempt with which he personally regarded Korea and Koreans. It is important to remember that Sebald's recollections were published in 1965, long after his personal withdrawal from Japan—a moment that shocked his hosts because he failed to say goodbye to friends and colleagues with whom he had worked and lived for decades. Moreover, Sebald's *With MacArthur in Japan* appeared during the moment of normalization of relations between Japan and South Korea, underscoring his personal aims to present Japan—and particularly Japan's post-1945 outlook—in the best possible light to his American readers (and particularly his former colleagues in Washington).

Unsurprisingly, no mention of territorial disputes or Korea's reparations claims appears in the book's 318 pages. In terms of the territorial component of today's "history problems," more than anything, this confirms that, regardless of the weight that the Japanese government gives today to several telegrams Sebald sent to Washington to promote Tokyo's position, Sebald himself did not regard the matter worth mentioning in his self-styled history. Instead, his contempt for Korea and Koreans is paramount. Sebald's Koreans—never Japanese—are inclined to violence but are also sweepingly "hapless" and "incapable." Sebald makes this nowhere clearer than in his description of the outbreak of the Korean War on what he called "the unhappy peninsula," which, rather unfortunately for him, was "one of his responsibilities."[4] With astonishing lack of self-awareness or self-reflection given how completely unprepared he and MacArthur and the entire American occupation staff in Japan appear to have been for North Korea's invasion of South Korea on June 25, 1950—again, noticeable because it fell under his area of responsibility to "know" such matters—Sebald goes on to describe how the war came to what he calls "a nation of sad people—oppressed, unhappy, poor, silent, and sullen."[5] Never once does he mention that the Japanese had "oppressed" the Koreans during the first half of the twentieth century—let alone that the internal divisions in Korean society were a lingering colonial legacy that powerfully shaped the "unhappy" terrain and ambiance he disdained.

Finally, having portrayed the Koreans as "fortunate" to have been taken over by the Japanese, Sebald arrives at the San Francisco Treaty moment. Replete with details of the inner workings of the Japan/China versus the Japan/Taiwan problems as well as the intricacies of dealing with Moscow, Sebald glides through the other "'peace' effort which caused many difficulties and some embarrassment:" the "Korean-Japanese conference to settle some of the outstanding difficulties between

---

[4] Sebald, p. 177.

[5] Sebald, p. 181.

those two nations…convened, with SCAP's approval, on October 20, 1951."[6] Sebald's downplaying of the Japan-Korea negotiations is a reminder that he failed to help Japan achieve its postwar ambitions. He failed not because of sympathy toward Korea's claims; rather, US Secretary of State John Foster Dulles, together with American military planners, decided that the United States should maintain legal maneuverability to hold onto this tiny piece of territory for strategic purposes—and, for all intents and purposes, the situation is the same today.

Japan's post-1945 relations with South Korea reveal that the government of Japan has long been preoccupied with preventing some of the nation's more troublesome histories from undermining the present or future. In other words, the "history problems" do not spring out of nowhere when particular standoffs arise. Chap. V, Article 14 of the San Francisco Treaty is clear:

It is recognized that Japan should pay reparations to the Allied Powers for the damage and suffering caused by it during the war. Nevertheless it is also recognized that the resources of Japan are not presently sufficient…

With this, the American architects of this treaty established the fractious pattern of Tokyo's establishment of bilateral relations not only with the former wartime allied power nations but also with countries formerly under its colonial control, beginning with Korea (by then the Republic of Korea and the Democratic Republic of Korea). As is now well known in large part to an effort by the South Korean government beginning in 2002 to declassify documents relating to the 1965 establishment of relations with Japan, Japanese officials refused to consider that any of the money Japan would transfer was legal compensation or reparations. As is equally and abundantly clear—and over the concerns of Japanese officials—Americans did not object when then South Korean President Park Chung-hee elected to use the funds (roughly US$800 million) that would be transferred from Japan as part of the deal solely to target certain industries and not for the range of Korean victims such as forced laborers and "comfort women" (military sex slaves) seeking individual compensation. At the same time, Japan takes any of the funds that were appropriated from forced laborers and makes them available to victims of its empire. Washington did not press these issues, leaving them to linger, and now we find ourselves again in the middle of a debate over how to remember the past—that is, a memory war, which is far more difficult to unravel than a debate over history.

In June 1965, after 13 years of protracted negotiations, Japanese and South Korean diplomats established relations that many describe as "normalizing" or as "coming to terms with the past." This moment thus officially began Japan's decolonization process with Korea. It is important to understand that the 1965 agreement inaugurated—not recommenced—South Korea and Japan's relations as independent states. Before Japan's 1910 colonization of Korea, Tokyo had relations with the entire peninsula, which it then usurped by annexing the country into the Japanese empire. In August 1945, the creation of American and Soviet occupation zones carved Korea in two, meaning that, in essence, there were no official relations

[6] Sebald, p. 287.

between occupied Japan and occupied South or North Korea, only relations between the various occupation authorities involved, and even those were quite confusing at best. In 1948, South and North Korea respectively came into existence, a condition made further real after the Korean War by the terms of the 1953 armistice between Pyongyang and Washington, which, as far as North Korea was concerned, gave it greater legitimacy than the South, which had to rely on the Americans' signature to end the fighting. Therefore, in 1965, South Korea's decision to begin relations with the country's former overlord without the North's participation generated additional tensions between Seoul and Pyongyang, not in the least because the UN-sanctioned 1965 Treaty on Basic Relations declared South Korea the sole legitimate government of the peninsula in terms of international conventions and protocols at the time. This, too, is out of step with today's inter-Korean peace initiatives, yet something which Washington appears also unprepared to confront.

Significantly, Washington was far from absent in the process at the time. As American interests in Vietnam grew in the early 1960s, Washington wanted to free up some of the funds it was spending on development and military aid in South Korea to use to defend its latest bulwark against communism, and it wanted to transfer some of the Korea burden to Tokyo. America's famous ambassador to Japan, Edwin O. Reischauer, had watched the years of failed negotiations between Japan and South Korea and strongly emphasized to Tokyo the need to formally address Korean resentment over colonization for progress to be made. Despite Tokyo's reluctance to get things going, Reischauer held firm to his position that Japan should make some sort of statement about the colonial era, and, in the months leading up to normalization, Japanese officials made statements revealing the critical role the United States played in the development of Japan's apology politics with South Korea.

Of subtle yet monumental importance, Reischauer, during this time, offered the phrase "unhappy history" to describe the recent past of Japanese-Korean relations. In pragmatic terms, it was pure genius to freeze the past into an indeterminate time period for which no one was to blame. This, however, is precisely what continues to anger those seeking recognition of specific histories, because, ever since then, Japanese and South Korean diplomats and politicians have repeatedly "regretfully" dissolved "the past" into equally vague phrases concerning the nations' future together. This vocabulary took root and emerged as the most powerful apologetic technique in play, and Japanese leaders finally solidified it in writing during the 1990s when similar terms flourished worldwide.

In September 1964, Reischauer wrote a memo to Secretary of State Dean Rusk acknowledging that a "clear Japanese apology for their colonial oppression of Korea in the past" was difficult, because "Japanese officials and public simply do not feel they owe any apology to Koreans." In November, he sent a telegram to Rusk to report on his breakfast meeting with Foreign Minister Shiina Etsusaburo during which he urged Japan to make "some sort of apology to Koreans for colonial past." When Shiina's secretary suggested that the foreign minister's upcoming visit to Korea would come "as close to expression of apology as was feasible," Reischauer urged that "some sort of forward-looking statement about turning backs on past unhappy history. .. might assuage Koreans' feelings without irritating Japanese public."

Early the following winter, in February 1965, Shiina visited Seoul for several days. Socialists in Japan protested the ruling party's decision to launch relations with Seoul at the expense of Pyongyang by organizing a no-confidence vote in the Diet, and students in both countries held demonstrations to protest North Korea's exclusion from the settlement. Japanese Prime Minister Sato Eisaku and South Korean President Park Chung-hee, however, were determined to make Shiina's visit a success at all costs. When Japan's foreign minister arrived at Seoul's Kimpo airport, he immediately declared Japan's "regret" for "the unfortunate period" the countries shared.

Shiina told waiting reporters, "I believe we should reflect deeply on the truly regrettable circumstances of the unfortunate period in the midst of our nations' long history.... It is in these hopes that we establish future-facing permanent and friendly relations on which we can build a new respectful and prosperous history." The countries had not yet established diplomatic relations, and this moment marked the first Japanese official public statement in Korea—South or North—about the colonial era. Asahi newspaper special correspondent, Imazu Hiroshi, noted Shiina's statement as highly significant, and he conveyed his own hopes for improvement. At the same time, James C. Thomson Jr., of Lyndon B. Johnson's National Security Council Staff, remarked that "Shiina came as close as a Japanese can to apologizing for Japan's sins, and everyone—including State—is thoroughly pleased."

The rigidity of such a formulation is clear, and until recently, victims were left with no option for protest other than running along a spinning wheel of the state's creation in courts that ultimately would remain indifferent to their claims. Thus, the October 2018 ruling in South Korea on behalf of several forced laborers could also extend beyond this particular effort to others, such as Chinese, North Koreans, or even Americans forced to labor for Japan's war effort. In this regard, Washington only continues to enable Japan's out of step behavior. What was legal in 1965—or rather, what Tokyo today contends "entirely settled the past"—is now no longer considered an international norm. Today, instead, forced labor is considered illegal from the start and impels state responsibility. On this note, then, the United States could do more to understand America's involvement in sustaining the deeply counter-productive standoffs over the "history problems" in Northeast Asia.

From the Joint Statement by Korean and Japanese Intellectuals to the End of the San Francisco System Evaluation Conferences: Toward a Durban Conference of East-Asian Intellectuals

Young-Ho Kim

Abstract This paper reflects on the evolution and significance of the San Francisco System through a series of international conferences held since 2016, involving Korean, Japanese, and global intellectuals. It traces the efforts to challenge the postwar order established by the 1965 Korea-Japan Basic Treaty and the San Francisco Treaty, highlighting the impact of joint statements and legal decisions declaring Japan's colonial rule over Korea as illegal. The paper draws parallels to the Durban Declaration, advocating for an East Asian movement against colonial legacies and for reparatory justice. It analyzes how the San Francisco System, originally intended as postwar atonement, shifted toward anti-communist alliances, exacerbating regional divisions and hindering East Asian community building. The study underscores the role of academic and legal activism in reshaping historical narratives and influencing diplomatic relations. It also examines the recent diplomatic tensions between Korea and Japan, particularly around compensation for forced labor, and critiques the Korean government's adoption of a third-party reimbursement model. The paper concludes by emphasizing the need for genuine reconciliation and historical atonement, drawing inspiration from global justice movements. Ultimately, it calls for a new East Asian "Durban Declaration" to overcome the limitations of the San Francisco System and foster lasting peace and justice in the region.

Keywords Colonial legacies · Civil society movements · East Asian reconciliation · Historical justice · Intellectual activism · International law · Korea-Japan relations · Postwar order · Reparatory justice · Durban Declaration · Japan-Korea intellectual joint statement

Y.-H. Kim (✉)
Department of Economics, Kyungpook National University,
Daegu, Korea (Republic of)

Y.-H. Kim et al. (eds.), *Beyond the San Francisco System*,
https://doi.org/10.1007/978-981-95-3328-2_21

1 Framing the Issue

Although my paper was written as a closing speech for the conference, it is being delivered now to serve as a potential reference for the general discussion. The panelists may also choose not to refer to our paper if they see fit.

When this conference was held for the first time at Columbia University in 2016, China proposed making it a continuing meeting instead of a one-off event. Many of the participants supported this idea, and the second meeting was subsequently held at UPenn, the third at Wuhan University in China, and the fourth at the Koreana Hotel in Seoul. The conference could not be held for the next three years due to COVID-19. This year's conference was originally scheduled to be held at the University of Waterloo in Canada, but Prof. Hara Kimie fell ill from excessive work while preparing for the event. Accordingly, the fifth and final meeting of this conference is being held here thanks to a hastily organized collaboration with the Korea University Asiatic Research Center.

Most of today's participants have attended at least two prior conferences, and I would like to extend my gratitude to Prof. Wada Haruki, Prof. Tae-Jin Yi, Prof. Alexis Dudden, and Prof. Xu Yong for being with us all the way since the beginning. I would also like to propose giving a big round of applause for the Northeast Asian History Foundation, which have generously provided us with financial support for all five conferences.

Although this conference began in 2016, there are efforts that predate its inception. Following on from the signing of the Joint Statement by Korean and Japanese Intellectuals in 2010, a series of five meetings was held between Seoul and Tokyo under the joint theme "The Promise of 2010 and Hope for 2015." These meetings sought to overturn the system established under the 1965 Treaty on Basic Relations Between Japan and the Republic of Korea (Basic Treaty). However, the rise of Prime Minister Abe Shinzo led to a resurgence of imperialism in Japan, and the dream embodied in the joint statement grew more distant.

With a view to tackling more fundamental issues, we chose "Beyond the San Francisco System" as the theme at that time. Accordingly, today we are holding the fifth and final conference. As the hosting group, the concept of an East Asian Durban Conference is a theme that runs through both of these issues. While the original African Durban World Conference was held in partnership with the UN and a number of national governments, we sought to hold an East Asian Durban Conference centered around ordinary citizens, and intellectuals in particular.

2 The Durban Conference and a Durban Conference for East Asian NGOs

From August to September 2001, the UN hosted a groundbreaking meeting in Durban, South Africa, called the World Conference Against Racism, Racial Discrimination, Xenophobia, and Related Intolerance. This meeting stipulated that slavery and the xenophobia of colonialism were "crimes against humanity "and that colonialism should be subject to censure and prevented from occurring again. The conference adopted the Durban Declaration and Program of Action that called for a historic end to colonialism. It is well known that the concept of a crime against humanity was born out of the process of overcoming the Nazi holocaust. This concept has now been expanded to include slavery and colonialism. The Durban Declaration is perhaps the most "UN-like" statement adopted since the inception of the United Nations. On the 20th anniversary of the declaration in 2021, the UN General Assembly adopted a statement that reaffirmed the original declaration. In 2014, the Caribbean Community (CARICOM) released the Ten Point Plan for Reparatory Justice based on the Durban Declaration, and 59 nations reaffirmed their support for the concept of reparatory justice at the third EU-CELAC Summit 2023. The Durban Declaration is alive and kicking and is actively spreading the concept of reparatory justice.

2.1 But What About East Asia?

The 2010 Joint Statement by Korean and Japanese Intellectuals was signed by 1139 scholars[1]and declared that the treaties leading up to the Japanese colonization of Korea were null and void. In particular, the fact that this statement was jointly signed by historians and filled the headlines in Korea for several days straight made it a monumental event that caused changes in the public perception of these issues. Even in China, up to 400 scholars of Korean and Japanese studies released a statement in support of the joint statement. The Prime Minister Kan-Naoto Statement was released directly after the joint statement. The Kan-Naoto Statement went further than the partnership between Korea and Japan proclaimed in the Murayama Statement of 1995, signed by Kim Dae-jung and Keizo Obuchi. This was followed by Constitutional Court of Korea rulings on wartime sex slavery (2011) and forced conscription (2012 and November 2018).

According to one study,[2] cases on sex slavery and forced conscription had followed the established rulings by the Supreme Court of Japan up until the release of the joint statement. Even directly prior to the statement's release in February and July of 2009, the Korean High Court followed the ruling set out in a 2007 case from the Supreme Court of Japan. However, in a 2011 case, the Constitutional Court of Korea held in a case on sex slavery that the state's nonfeasance was unconstitutional, and in 2012, the Supreme Court quashed and remanded a case on forced conscription after stipulating that colonial rule was illegal.

[1]Although more potential signatories to the statement continued to come forward, online signatures were closed at some point through consultation with Wada Haruki. If the statement had been left open, the number of signatures would have risen by several hundred.

[2]Do, S.-h. (2020, August). *The 2010 joint statement by Korean and Japanese intellectuals and the issue of historical justice*. Northeast Asian History Foundation.

A ruling on the illegality of Japan's colonial rule subsequently came out in 2018. The Supreme Court held that the Agreement Between Japan and the Republic of Korea Concerning the Settlement of Problems in Regard to Property and Claims and Economic Cooperation (Settlement Agreement) signed as part of the 1965 system was "not concluded for the purpose of seeking compensation over Japan's illegal colonial rule, but for resolving the issue of civil debt claims between Korea and Japan through political agreement based on Article 4 of the Treaty of San Francisco. The Treaty of San Francisco and the ensuing Basic Treaty and Settlement Agreement were agreements aimed at resolving financial and civil disputes stemming from the division of Korea's territory. The Supreme Court's decision affirmed the long-held Korean view that the issue of crimes committed during the colonial period still remained to be solved. The fact that groups of extreme right-wing Japanese protesters held frequent protests denouncing Wada Haruki, who had played a central role on the Japanese side in the signing of the joint statement, was a testament to the statement's destructive power.

According to my knowledge, 70 or so statements were released around this time. Several of these left a strong impression on us. There was the 2015 Joint Statement by Intellectuals of Korea, Japan, and the World that was facilitated by a group of the same name at a lecture on the tenth anniversary of Article 9 of the Japanese Constitution in September 2014. Later that year, Prof. Alexis Dudden led 187 world historians in releasing a joint statement. In 2018, 170 Japanese lawyers expressed support for this statement, including Prof. Totsuka Etsuro, who had been involved in the Supreme Court case on forced conscription. During the 100th anniversary of the March 1st Movement in 2019, Japan's largest NGO, the "Abolish War, Save Article 9 Action Coalition," released a statement in partnership with a collection of Korean civic groups, including the People's Solidarity for Participatory Democracy and YMCAs. Titled the "Korean and Japanese People's Joint Declaration of Peace," this statement expressed support for the 2010 Joint Statement by Korean and Japanese Intellectuals and was read aloud by Korean and Japanese representatives at a ceremony attended by 50,000 to commemorate the 100th anniversary of the March 1st Movement. A citizens' platform between the two countries was subsequently created in accordance with the statement and has been held every year since then in Seoul and Tokyo. That same year, a joint statement titled "Is Korea the Enemy?" was released by 78 Japanese civilian scholars, including Prof. Wada Haruki.

We dreamed of an East Asian Durban Declaration "rainbow" that would link all these pieces together, from the initial Joint Statement by Korean and Japanese Intellectuals to the Kan-Naoto Statement, the Supreme Court's decision on forced conscription, and the Korean and Japanese People's Joint Declaration of Peace. This was a rainbow that went beyond both the Basic Treaty (1965) system and the San Francisco System that served as its inspiration. To borrow a metaphor from poet Yi Yuk-sa, it was a "steel rainbow" in history.

3 The San Francisco System 2.0

The countercurrents of history were strong. At the second conference on "Beyond the San Francisco System," I compared the San Francisco Treaty with the Treaty of Versailles, noting that the sanctions imposed on Germany as the vanquished nation after World War I were so severe that they incited the backlash of Nazism. While national reflection on Nazism has led to atonement for the past in Germany, the treatment of war criminals in the Treaty of San Francisco was so lenient that it caused an almost complete revival of the prewar ruling class in Japan. I concluded that this had undermined historic atonement and caused East Asia to become entangled in the San Francisco System in an area not covered by the Durban Declaration.

Over the last five conferences, we shared the perception that the nature of the Treaty of San Francisco has changed from atonement for World War II to being more akin to an East Asian Anti-Communist war treaty. However, there was a lot of space that could not be explained purely through the establishment of a war against Communism, and it came out that alliances, corruption, conspiracy, and ignorance on the part of Japanese fascists and pro-Japan Americans were rampant in this space.

To paint a vivid picture of this, Prof. Jeong Byeong-jun played a video during the Columbia University conference that depicted those involved at the time holding a kimono party.[3] Professor Dudden called this the dirty secret of American diplomacy.[4] It has also been pointed out that this encouraged and even took advantage of Japan's "Datsu-A Ron" (Goodbye Asia) ethos of discrimination against Asia. A study by Prof. Hara Kimie found that this created points of conflict between Japan and the Soviet Union, Japan and China, and Japan and Korea, thereby "intentionally" hindering the formation of an East Asian community in the future.[5] The issue of land restitution, often mentioned as the unsolved problem of the Treaty of San Francisco, faced great criticism from the Chinese delegation, who claimed it was a violation of the Cairo Declaration and Potsdam Declaration.

In Korea, Prof. Tae-Jin Yi was at the center of accumulated research claiming that the treaties signed with Japan in the late Joseon period were invalid as they failed to satisfy the necessary conditions of a treaty.[6] Pioneers of international law with no relation to Korea, including French PhD Francis Ray and Manley Ottmer Hudson of Harvard, have stated that the Japan–Korea Protectorate Treaty of 1905 should be considered null and void under the pure logic of international law. It has

[3] Jung, B. J. (2025). The San Francisco Treaty and Territorial Issues: Information Pamphlets on Territorial Issues from the Japanese Ministry of Foreign Affairs and Their Impact. In *Beyond the San Francisco System*. Springer.

[4] Dudden, A. (2025). Trouble Among East Asian Allies? America's Troubling Past. In *Beyond the San Francisco System*. Springer.

[5] Hara, K. (2025). Beyond the San Francisco System: An Inspiration from Canada. In *Beyond the San Francisco System*. Springer.

[6] Yi, T.-J. (2025). The Political Situation Surrounding the "Trans-war Phenomenon" in Postwar Japan and the San Francisco Peace Treaty. In *Beyond the San Francisco System*. Springer.

been confirmed that this argument was acknowledged at a League of Nations General Assembly in 1935 and at UN General Assembly in 1963.

It was an unforgettable moment of excitement at the Wuhan Conference when Prof. Totsuka Etsuro reported that an actual copy of the 1905 treaty did not exist even in Japan, according to his research following on from the research of Prof. Tae-Jin Yi.[7] It was also noteworthy that on the issue of the Korean and Japanese government's differing interpretations of the word "already" in Article 2 of the Basic Treaty, Prof. Wada found in favor of the Korean government's view.

Rooted purely in academics and international law, the outcry from foreign scholars including Ray, Hudson, Wada, and Totsuka was like a sound of thunder that roared in the East Asian sky. This went beyond the realm of academic research and become a diplomatic incident. As one of the main premises of the Treaty of San Francisco collapsed, this lent weight to the Durban Declaration for East Asian intellectuals.

We believe the Korean Supreme Court decision in the forced conscription case represents the peak for an East Asian Durban Declaration that spans intellectuals and NGOs. At the fourth conference in 2019, Prof. Tae-Ung Baik spoke highly of the Supreme Court's decision to set a precedent of upholding human rights, noting that the ruling and similar precedents from district courts were similar in nature to human rights cases in Europe. On the other side, the Abe administration that grew unabated through the San Francisco System was one of the peaks for Japanese fascists. The "Abe regime" consisted of the 2015 Abe Statement released on the 70th anniversary of the end of World War II, as well as the "coup d'etat" of establishing the right of collective self-defense that neutralized Article 9 of Japan's peace constitution.[8] Japan's military power shifted from a defensive to an offensive system, and this was topped off through policies of faithful cooperation with America's strategy of confronting China. These two peaks clashed with one another, and the dramatic conflict between Korea and China reached a pinnacle during the COVID pandemic of the past few years. The San Francisco System 2.0 has been gradually extended through the Quad alliance between the United States, India, Australia, and Japan formed in the Asia Pacific region and the signing of the US-led Indo-Pacific Economic Framework for Prosperity (IPE) decoupling agreement with China.

However, there was one important caveat for the establishment of the San Francisco System 2.0. A dramatic diplomatic measure had to be implemented at the height of the diplomatic spat between Korea and Japan. Bilateral relations needed to become closer, which required a resolution to historical issues. To resolve such issues required either Japan to atone for the past in a manner akin to Germany, or Korea to set these historical issues aside.

---

[7] Totsuka, E. (2025). Unlawfulness of Japan's Colonization of Korean Peninsula—Korea' Declaration of January 21,1904 and Japan's Violation of International Law. In *Beyond the San Francisco System*. Springer.

[8] Uchida, M. (2022). The Armitage reports that encouraged Abe's constitutional reforms: The exercise of a right to collective self-defense alters Article 9 of the Constitution. In *Beyond the San Francisco System*. Medici Media.

Something very dramatic happened at this peak. The crux of the Supreme Court's decision revolved around the illegality of colonial rule. However, the newly elected Yoon Suk-yeol administration completely ignored the accumulated achievements of intellectuals through our version of the Durban Conference and chose to take issue only with the reimbursement model of direct compensation paid by Japanese companies. The government ultimately decided to adopt a system of third-party reimbursement. This was akin to a historical coup d'état. A clause in the Korean Civil Code stating that "debts may be repaid by a third party" was used to legally change the nature of a Supreme Court decision. The third-party reimbursement system is designed to include Japanese companies in the process, but the Japanese government has completely ignored the system, and the companies concerned have yet to pay a cent of compensation. The only company to have actually reimbursed victims through the system is the Korean firm POSCO.

This process has led to human rights violations on two fronts, with the Korean government ignoring the spirit of the Supreme Court's decision that colonial rule was illegal and victims must be compensated and the Japanese government continuing to ignore the right to individual claims that it previously acknowledged. As a result, although the ideals embodied in the Supreme Court's ruling on forced conscription opened a new horizon beyond the 1965 system and the San Francisco System, it has ended as nothing more than a summer night's dream. The 2015 Abe Statement represented a regression from the progress shown in Japan's stance through the 1995 Murayama Statement, the 1998 Japan–South Korea Joint Declaration between Kim Dae-jung and Keizo Obuchi, the 2002 Japan–North Korea Pyongyang Declaration, and the 2010 Kan-Naoto Statement, and it feels as if this momentum has been lost ever since.

The illegality of Japanese colonial rule, as recognized by the Supreme Court, has reverted to the stance that colonial rule was legal. The reparatory justice for victims of forced conscription and sex slavery has been relegated to the level of civil debt claims, and the victim-centered approach has regressed to a perpetrator-centered approach. In this sense, the 1965 system has almost been fully reinstated. Directly after the precedent set by the Supreme Court, the US State Department noted that the ruling went against international law. I believe this statement was made in reference to the Treaty of San Francisco. When linked with analysis by attorney Masatoshi Uchida, who has looked into the close relationship between developments in the US Armitage Reports and changes to Japan's military and security policy, it offers a glimpse into the dark side of the hawkish triangular alliance between the United States, Korea, and Japan.[9]

The Camp David US-Japan-Korea trilateral summit held in May this year led to what has been dubbed the Camp David Manifesto. During our fourth conference in Seoul, Prof. Lee Jong-won noted this was a sign of the San Francisco System 2.0.

[9] Uchida, M. (2022). Abe 'encouraged' the Armitage Report: The 'revision' of Article 9 of the Constitution to allow the exercise of the right of collective self-defence(아베 '개헌'을 '독려'한 아미티지 리포트: 집단적 자위권 행사 용인은 헌법 9조의 '개변'), In *Beyond the San Francisco System* (샌프란시스코 체제를 너머서) (Korean version). Medichi Media.

Three years later, this can be viewed as the birth of a system that runs completely counter to our East Asian Durban Declaration for NGOs.

Western Europe has served as a comparative model for dealing with history and atoning for the legacy of colonization. In partnership with the UN, Africa, and the South American empires are making every effort to implement reparatory justice for slavery and colonialism through the Durban Declaration. How can it be that postwar East Asia has been forced to endure the legacy of the San Francisco System, a system that wholeheartedly rejects the UN's values, and that this system is being perpetuated through the San Francisco System 2.0?

In an appellate decision on a case brought by victims of sex slavery against the Japanese government, Seoul High Court recently followed the customary international law of leading European nations in human rights. The court ruled that under the premise that Japanese colonial rule was illegal, the Japanese government cannot be exempt from liability and should provide reimbursement. This was a moving judgment that affirmed the human rights and right to life of women violated by the illegal war of aggression should be championed above state sovereignty.

Similar to the 2018 Supreme Court ruling on forced conscription, there is a high likelihood that this decision will ultimately become embroiled in diplomatic conflict, but we cannot expect to see any solution that is aligned with the Durban Declaration and moves beyond the San Francisco System.

4 Moving Toward 'Beyond'

"The path to paradise begins in hell."—John Wick: Chap. 3.

More rigorous research is needed into the relationship between East Asia's San Francisco System and economic development in the postwar period. What is clear is that a Japanese version of America's Marshall Plan was implemented under the San Francisco System at the time, and growth in the Japanese economy took off as a result of the benefits of special procurement from the Korean War. The East Asian empire formed from the areas surrounding the Japanese revival, and Japanese assets frozen within the empire combined with aid and loan grants from the US to lay a foundation for dependent rapid growth in East Asia. The unlimited supply of labor that enabled agricultural reforms in each country, the unlimited supply of US and Japanese capital and the unfettered opening of the American import market for industrial goods to prevent domestic inflation all came together to create an economic miracle in East Asia. Newly industrializing countries emerged during these two decades of rapid growth, and this period saw budding developed nations appear that were home to mature civic societies and flourishing democracy.

As a democracy matures, people become more sensitive to human rights issues, and human rights issues in the present tend to bring up related issues from the past. This is how the issues of sex slavery and forced conscription came to the fore in Korea, along with the problems of the 1965 system and the need to move past the San Francisco System. In addition, the level of regional trade coupling surpassed

50% and financial coupling became more advanced. We saw the launch of the Chiang Mai Initiative and the establishment of the ASEAN +3 community and the Trilateral Cooperation Secretariat, which paved the way for discussions on an East Asian community.

Things appeared to be progressing in accordance with Karl Deutch's theory that more frequent interpersonal and interstate relations between countries led to greater integration. The world talked about the East Asian era, and we dreamed of a Civil Asia. These trends were pushing us beyond the San Francisco System. "The path to paradise begins in hell" is a famous line in the film John Wick: Chap. 3. The path to moving beyond the San Francisco System began from within that very system. If the system had been fairer, the path would have opened up in a healthier way. We define the reactionaries who sought to conquer the postwar regime and revive the regime of the prewar ruling class that remained intact in Japan as making a 'leap backward' to the San Francisco System. If this is the case, the Civil Asia trends that sought to move beyond this system represent a "leap forward." In this contest, the United States ultimately chose to side with those who sought to leap backward. That is the identity of the San Francisco System 2.0—thwarting those who sought to move beyond the San Francisco System from within the system itself.

During the Columbia University conference, the Helsinki Process was considered as a means of moving beyond the San Francisco System. The Philadelphia Process, which refers to democratic reforms to the San Francisco System, was subsequently raised during the UPenn conference, and Prof. Wada Haruki stressed that the process of establishing diplomatic relations between Japan and North Korea could also offer a breakthrough. During the Seoul conference, Prof. Gavan McCormick and Prof. Wada Haruki pointed out that North Korea's denuclearization was intrinsically linked to the denuclearization process under the San Francisco System as a whole (including the Okinawa base).

The revitalization of the Trilateral Cooperation Secretariat in Seoul and the contentious issue of the trilateral summit meeting between Korea, China, and Japan could be part of a leap forward, and I believe the disarmament movement and antinuclear and peace movements in Northeast Asia could also be part of that process. To move beyond the San Francisco System, there are a surprisingly large number of forces under the system that must be brought into a coalition.

This leads to the so-called East Asian paradox that has put paid to any talk of an East Asian community. Japan was the first East Asian nation to achieve advanced industrialization, but Japan's civil society has matured at a slower pace, and democracy has become distorted. China has caught up to Japan in GNP while moving even further away from democracy. The level of trade and financial coupling in the region is on the rise, absolute mutual dependence is growing, and there is more exchange and cooperation than ever, but integration is becoming more distant. The US-China conflict, the demonization of neighboring countries, and the expansion of armaments are intensifying day by day, turning East Asia into the stage for an advanced weaponry contest and a region where it would not be surprising if war broke out at any moment. The path to paradise may begin in hell, but there are still forces remaining in hell that seek to demolish that path.

I once had the opportunity to speak alongside Prof. Kenzaburo Oe at a public rally of 50,000 people gathered to protect Article 9 of the Japanese constitution. I said that if the Japanese people succeeded in defending the peace constitution, it would be the first people's revolution to take place in Japan, and the success of the people's revolution in Japan would expedite the creation of a Civil Asia. I believe there is a path toward a forward leap beyond the San Francisco System by defending Japan's peace constitution.

The Korean government has distorted the Supreme Court's ruling into a system of third-party reimbursement, while the Japanese government is effectively ignoring the system altogether. Some Japanese citizens may have welcomed this as a victory for Japanese diplomacy, but how many more were concerned that the country had missed out on an opportunity to atone for the country's history of aggression and colonialism? I am curious how many were worried about the future of a country that embraces the past and allows the past to dominate the future.

Has the establishment of the San Francisco System 2.0 as a return to the 1965 system truly put an end to the situation? We believe the situation has not ended, but rather shifted from a diplomatic matter to a public issue regarding the history of civilization in East Asia. I frequently spoke at gatherings of Tokyo citizens seeking to uphold Article 9 of the constitution and was impressed by the level of civilizational capacity shown by the Japanese people. On one occasion, I exclaimed that Japan's movement to defend Article 9 should advance in partnership with the candlelight vigils taking place in Korea at the time. I noted that even if Japan claims to be a war victim due to the bombing of Hiroshima, there is no way this will be universally accepted, and I established the "Hapcheon process" based on Hapcheon, the county where the majority of innocent Korean victims of the bombing were from. However, this is evolving into a unified Hiroshima/Hapcheon process, thanks to a joint visit to Hiroshima Peace Park during the latest summit meeting between Korea and Japan.

Linking Hiroshima with Hapcheon would allow the movement to obtain greater legitimacy, and Hapcheon could gain strength from an alliance with Hiroshima. It is believed that the Hapcheon/Hiroshima process was activated to some degree during a forum on global nuclear victims in a recent Treaty on the Prohibition of Nuclear Weapons meeting held at UN Headquarters. I hope to see a "dove alliance" between those in Japan who seek to protect Article 9 of the constitution, Koreans who took part in the candlelight vigil protests, Hong Kong nationals from the yellow umbrella protests, and Chinese citizens from Tiananmen Square. This dove alliance could dream of a path toward the Durban system rather than the San Francisco System 2.0 perpetuated through the hawkish alliance between the United States, Japan, and Korea.

In a recent appellate case brought against the Japanese government by victims of sex slavery, the Seoul High Court followed the customary international law of leading European nations in human rights. The court held that, based on the premise that Japanese colonial rule was illegal, compensation had to be paid by the Japanese government, and any reimbursement from the Korean government could not be recognized. This was a thundering statement affirming that the human rights and right to life of women violated in Japan's illegal war of aggression should take precedent over state sovereignty.

In East Asia, the Japanese have already established grounds for individual claims in the process of seeking redress for the bombing of Nagasaki in lawsuits brought against the United States, and the Chinese established the same right in the trial process. For Koreans, the Japanese Ministry of Foreign Affairs has confirmed on multiple occasions that individual claims are still valid and separate from a nation's right to diplomatic protection. This is a fundamental verification of relative autonomy from the state for East Asian peoples, and I have always believed it speaks to the possibility of a Civil Asia. However, the individual rights of claim for Korean victims of sex slavery and forced conscription have been effectively ignored, and the San Francisco System 2.0 has come about as a result of this. This is a dramatic illustration of the difference in the level of human rights under the Durban system and the San Francisco System 2.0.

I once referred to Japan as a "whale inside a well" as opposed to a "frog inside a well," an expression for a person with a narrow view of the world. This refers to the fact that Japan is a whale-sized economic powerhouse yet remains confined to the narrowness of a well in terms of worldview. One of the frames Japan remains trapped in is the frame of historical perceptions. The whale needs to leave the well and find its way to the sea. In other words, atoning for the past is not simply an issue of the history of Japan's civilization, but a matter of economic growth. If we fail to connect the variety of possibilities that could overcome the San Francisco System, we will fail to get off the ground.

5 The UN and the San Francisco System

The Treaty of San Francisco consists of a full text, seven chapters, and 27 articles in total, with the signatures of the 48 nations invited to the meeting affixed at the end. As the greatest victims of Japan's policy of aggression, Korea and China were excluded from this process. Korea was not a signatory to the treaty yet remains confined within the system, while China refuses to acknowledge the treaty at all.

The main text of the treaty states, "In all circumstances to conform to the principles of the Charter of the United Nations and strive to realize the objectives of the Universal Declaration of Human Rights." The full text stipulates that the UN Charter and the objectives of the Universal Declaration of Human Rights must be respected, and that the subsequently established victim-centered approach should follow the same principles.

The UN gave rise to the idea of atoning for colonialism from the perspective of Lenin and Wilson's principle of national self-determination. In this respect, the Treaty of San Francisco is not only completely silent on the issue of colonial crimes, but the San Francisco System that effectively prohibits such crimes violates the treaty's own provision about conforming to UN principles as laid out in the full text.

Furthermore, the Settlement Agreement is limited to the issue of civil property claims stemming from the geographical division of Korean and Japanese territory as a result of World War II, which is diametrically opposed to the objectives of the Universal Declaration of Human Rights. This treaty failed to establish a historical or legal basis for human rights violations stemming from colonial crimes, including sex slavery and forced conscription. Accordingly, the Basic Treaty and Settlement Agreement that served as the basis for the 1965 system left the issue of colonial crimes to be resolved at a later date. From this perspective, the Treaty of San Francisco prevents further examination of colonial human rights violations and has effectively provided an international law basis for not recognizing individual rights of claim.

In this respect, the treaty blatantly violates the principle of conforming to the objectives of the Universal Declaration of Human Rights and runs counter to the Vienna Convention. The victim-centered approach is an important principle that was unanimously passed at a UN General Assembly in 2005 and is diametrically opposed to the Treaty of San Francisco. What should be done with a treaty that goes against the principles stated in its own full text? In the same way that the UN General Assembly decided in 1963 that international treaties which cannot be recognized as such were null and void, would it not be possible for us to bring the Treaty of San Francisco before the UN for censure and use statements signed by intellectuals around the world to call for an East Asian Durban system to replace the San Francisco one?

In this sense, although today marks the end of our time together, I hope this conference will continue in one form or another. (End).

Appendix: Treaty of San Francisco

the Allied Powers and Japan

Exported from Wikisource on September 12, 2025

No. 1832. TREATY[1] OF PEACE WITH JAPAN. SIGNED AT SAN FRANCISCO, ON 8 SEPTEMBER 1951

Whereas the Allied Powers and Japan are resolved that henceforth their relations shall be those of nations which, as sovereign equals, cooperate in friendly association to promote their common welfare and to maintain international peace and security, and are therefore desirous of concluding a Treaty of Peace which will settle questions still outstanding as a result of the existence of a state of war between them;

Whereas Japan for its part declares its intention to apply for membership in the United Nations and in all circumstances to conform to the principles of the Charter of the United Nations; to strive to realize the objectives of the Universal Declaration of Human Rights; to seek to create within Japan conditions of stability and well-being as defined in Articles 55 and 56 of the Charter of the United Nations and already initiated by post-surrender Japanese legislation; and in public and private trade and commerce to conform to internationally accepted fair practices;

Whereas the Allied Powers welcome the intentions of Japan set out in the foregoing paragraph;

The Allied Powers and Japan have therefore determined to conclude the present Treaty of Peace, and have accordingly appointed the undersigned Plenipotentiaries, who, after presentation of their full powers, found in good and due form, have agreed on the following provisions:

CHAPTER I

Peace

Article 1

(a) The state of war between Japan and each of the Allied Powers is terminated as from the date on which the present Treaty comes into force between Japan and the Allied Power concerned as provided for in Article 23.

Y.-H. Kim et al. (eds.), *Beyond the San Francisco System*,
https://doi.org/10.1007/978-981-95-3328-2

(b) The Allied Powers recognize the full sovereignty of the Japanese people over Japan and its territorial waters.

CHAPTER II

Territory

Article 2

(a) Japan, recognizing the independence of Korea, renounces all right, title, and claim to Korea, including the islands of Quelpart, Port Hamilton and Dagelet.

(b) Japan renounces all right, title, and claim to Formosa and the Pescadores.

(c) Japan renounces all right, title, and claim to the Kurile Islands, and to that portion of Sakhalin and the islands adjacent to it over which Japan acquired sovereignty as a consequence of the Treaty of Portsmouth of September 5, 1905.[2]

(d) Japan renounces all right, title, and claim in connection with the League of Nations Mandate System, and accepts the action of the United Nations Security Council of April 2, 1947, extending the trusteeship system to the Pacific Island formerly under mandate to Japan.[3]

(e) Japan renounces all claim to any right or title to or interest in connection with any part of the Antarctic area, whether deriving from the activities of Japanese nationals or otherwise.

(f) Japan renounces all right, title, and claim to the Spratly Islands and to the Paracel Islands.

Article 3

Japan will concur in any proposal of the United States to the United Nations to place under its trusteeship system, with the United States as the sole administering authority, Nansei Shoto south of 29° north latitude (including the Ryukyu Islands and the Daito Islands), Nanpo Shoto south of Sofu Gan (including the Bonin Islands, Rosario Island and the Volcano Islands) and Parece Vela and Marcus Island. Pending the making of such a proposal and affirmative action thereon, the United States will have the right to exercise all and any powers of administration, legislation and jurisdiction over the territory and inhabitants of these islands, including their territorial waters.

Article 4

(a) Subject to the provisions of paragraph (b) of this Article, the disposition of property of Japan and of its nationals in the areas referred to in Article 2, and their claims, including debts, against the authorities presently administering such areas and the residents (including juridical persons) thereof, and the disposition in Japan of property of such authorities and residents, and of claims, including debts, of such authorities and residents against Japan and its nationals, shall be the subject of special arrangements between Japan and such authorities. The property of any of the Allied Powers or its nationals in the areas referred to in Article 2 shall, in so far as this has not already been done, be returned by the administering authority in the condition in which it now exists. (The term nationals whenever used in the present Treaty includes juridical persons.)

(b) Japan recognizes the validity of dispositions of property of Japan and Japanese nationals made by or pursuant to directives of the United States Military Government in any of the areas referred to in Articles 2 and 3.

(c) Japanese-owned submarine cables connecting Japan with territory removed from Japanese control pursuant to the present Treaty shall be equally divided, Japan retaining the Japanese terminal and adjoining half of the cable, and the detached territory the remainder of the cable and connecting terminal facilities.

CHAPTER III

Security

Article 5

(a) Japan accepts the obligations set forth in Article 2 of the Charter of the United Nations, and in particular the obligations

(i) to settle its international disputes by peaceful means in such a manner that international peace and security, and justice, are not endangered;

(ii) to refrain in its international relations from the threat or use of force against the territorial integrity or political independence of any State or in any other manner inconsistent with the Purposes of the United Nations;

(iii) to give the United Nations every assistance in any action it takes in accordance with the Charter and to refrain from giving assistance to any State against which the United Nations may take preventive or enforcement action.

(b) The Allied Powers confirm that they will be guided by the principles of Article 2 of the Charter of the United Nations in their relations with Japan.

(c) The Allied Powers for their part recognize that Japan, as a sovereign nation, possesses the inherent right of individual or collective self-defense referred to in Article 51 of the Charter of the United Nations, and that Japan may voluntarily enter into collective security arrangements.

Article 6

(a) All occupation forces of the Allied Powers shall be withdrawn from Japan as soon as possible after the coming into force of the present Treaty, and in any case not later than 90 days thereafter. Nothing in this provision shall, however, prevent the stationing or retention of foreign armed forces in Japanese territory under or in consequence of any bilateral or multilateral agreements which have been or may be made between one or more of the Allied Powers, on the one hand, and Japan, on the other.

(b) The provisions of Article 9 of the Potsdam Proclamation of July 26, 1945, dealing with the return of Japanese military forces to their homes, to the extent not already completed, will be carried out.

(c) All Japanese property for which compensation has not already been paid, which was supplied for the use of the occupation forces and which remains in the possession of those forces at the time of the coming into force of the present Treaty, shall be returned to the Japanese Government within the same 90 days, unless other arrangements are made by mutual agreement.

CHAPTER IV

Political and economic clauses

Article 7

(a) Each of the Allied Powers, within one year after the present Treaty has come into force between it and Japan, will notify Japan which of its prewar bilateral treaties or conventions with Japan it wishes to continue in force or revive, and any treaties or conventions so notified shall continue in force or be revived, subject only to such amendments as may be necessary to ensure conformity with the present Treaty. The treaties and conventions so notified shall be considered as having been continued in force or revived three months after the date of notification and shall be registered with the Secretariat of the United Nations. All such treaties and conventions as to which Japan is not so notified shall be regarded as abrogated.

(b) Any notification made under paragraph (a) of this Article may except from the operation or revival of a treaty or convention any territory for the international relations of which the notifying Power is responsible, until three months after the date on which notice is given to Japan that such exception shall cease to apply.

Article 8

(a) Japan will recognize the full force of all treaties now or hereafter concluded by the Allied Powers for terminating the state of war initiated on September 1, 1939, as well as any other arrangements by the Allied Powers for or in connection with the restoration of peace. Japan also accepts the arrangements made for terminating the former League of Nations and Permanent Court of International Justice.

(b) Japan renounces all such rights and interests as it may derive from being a signatory power of the Conventions of St. Germain-en-Laye of September 10, 1919,[4] and the Straits Agreement of Montreux of July 20, 1936,[5] and from Article 16 of the Treaty of Peace with Turkey signed at Lausanne on July 24, 1923.[6]

(c) Japan renounces all rights, titles, and interests acquired under, and is discharged from all obligations resulting from, the Agreement between Germany and the Creditor Powers of January 20, 1930,[7] and its Annexes, including the Trust Agreement, dated May 17, 1930;[8] the Convention of January 20, 1930,[9] respecting the Bank for International Settlements; and the Statutes of the Bank for International Settlements. Japan will notify to the Ministry of Foreign Affairs in Paris within six months of the first coming into force of the present Treaty its renunciation of the rights, title, and interests referred to in this paragraph.

Article 9

Japan will enter promptly into negotiations with the Allied Powers so desiring for the conclusion of bilateral and multilateral agreements providing for the regulation or limitation of fishing and the conservation and development of fisheries on the high seas.

Article 10

Japan renounces all special rights and interests in China, including all benefits and privileges resulting from the provisions of the final Protocol signed at Peking on September 7, 1901,[10] and all annexes, notes, and documents supplementary thereto, and agrees to the abrogation with respect to Japan of the said protocol, annexes, notes, and documents,

Article 11

Japan accepts the judgments of the International Military Tribunal for the Far East and of other Allied War Crimes Courts both within and outside Japan, and will carry out the sentences imposed thereby upon Japanese nationals imprisoned in Japan. The power to grant clemency, to reduce sentences, and to parole with respect to such prisoners may not be exercised except on the decision of the Government or Governments which imposed the sentence in each instance and on the recommendation of Japan. In the case of persons sentenced by the International Military Tribunal for the Far East, such power may not be exercised except on the decision of a majority of the Governments represented on the Tribunal and on the recommendation of Japan.

Article 12

(a) Japan declares its readiness promptly to enter into negotiations for the conclusion with each of the Allied Powers of treaties or agreements to place their trading, maritime, and other commercial relations on a stable and friendly basis.

(b) Pending the conclusion of the relevant treaty or agreement, Japan will, during a period of four years from the first coming into force of the present Treaty

(1) accord to each of the Allied Powers, its nationals, products, and vessels

(i) most-favored-nation treatment with respect to customs duties, charges, restrictions, and other regulations on or in connection with the importation and exportation of goods;

(ii) national treatment with respect to shipping, navigation and imported goods, and with respect to natural and juridical persons and their interests—such treatment to include all matters pertaining to the levying and collection of taxes, access to the courts, the making and performance of contracts, rights to property (tangible and intangible), participation in juridical entities constituted under Japanese law, and generally the conduct of all kinds of business and professional activities;

(2) ensure that external purchases and sales of Japanese state trading enterprises shall be based solely on commercial considerations.

(c) With respect to any matter, however, Japan shall be obliged to accord to an Allied Power national treatment, or most-favored-nation treatment, only to the extent that the Allied Power concerned accords Japan national treatment or most-favored-nation treatment, as the case may be, in respect of the same matter. The reciprocity envisaged in the foregoing sentence shall be determined, in the case of products, vessels, and juridical entities of, and persons domiciled in, any non-metropolitan territory of an Allied Power, and in the case of juridical entities of, and persons domiciled in, any state or province of an Allied Power having a federal government, by reference to the treatment accorded to Japan in such territory, state, or province.

(d) In the application of this Article, a discriminatory measure shall not be considered to derogate from the grant of national or most-favored-nation treatment, as the case may be, if such measure is based on an exception customarily provided for in the commercial treaties of the party applying it, or on the need to safeguard that party's external financial position or balance of payments (except with respect to shipping and navigation), or on the need to maintain its essential security interests, and provided such measure is proportionate to the circumstances and not applied in an arbitrary or unreasonable manner.

(e) Japan's obligations under this Article shall not be affected by the exercise of any Allied rights under Article 14 of the present Treaty; nor shall the provisions of this Article be understood as limiting the undertakings assumed by Japan by virtue of Article 15 of the Treaty.

Article 13

(a) Japan will enter into negotiations with any of the Allied Powers, promptly upon the request of such Power or Powers, for the conclusion of bilateral or multilateral agreements relating to international civil air transport.

(b) Pending the conclusion of such agreement or agreements, Japan will, during a period of four years from the first coming into force of the present Treaty, extend to such Power treatment not less favorable with respect to air-traffic rights and privileges than those exercised by any such Powers at the date of such coming into force, and will accord complete equality of opportunity in respect of the operation and development of air services.

(c) Pending its becoming a party to the Convention on International Civil Aviation [11] in accordance with Article 93 thereof, Japan will give effect to the provisions of that Convention applicable to the international navigation of aircraft, and will give effect to the standards, practices, and procedures adopted as annexes to the Convention in accordance with the terms of the Convention.

CHAPTER V

Claims and property

Article 14

(a) It is recognized that Japan should pay reparations to the Allied Powers for the damage and suffering caused by it during the war. Nevertheless, it is also recognized that the resources of Japan are not presently sufficient, if it is to maintain a viable economy, to make complete reparation for all such damage and suffering and at the same time meet its other obligations.

Therefore,

1. Japan will promptly enter into negotiations with Allied Powers so desiring, whose present territories were occupied by Japanese forces and damaged by Japan, with a view to assisting to compensate those countries for the cost of repairing the damage done, by making available the services of the Japanese people in production, salvaging and other work for the Allied Powers in question. Such arrangements shall avoid the imposition of additional liabilities on other Allied Powers, and, where the manufacturing of raw materials is called for, they shall be supplied by the Allied Powers in question, so as not to throw any foreign exchange burden upon Japan.

2. (I) Subject to the provisions of sub-paragraph (II) below, each of the Allied Powers shall have the right to seize, retain, liquidate, or otherwise dispose of all property, rights, and interests of

(a) Japan and Japanese nationals,

(b) persons acting for or on behalf of Japan or Japanese nationals, and

(c) entities owned or controlled by Japan or Japanese nationals,

which on the first coming into force of the present Treaty were subject to its jurisdiction. The property, rights, and interests specified in this sub-paragraph shall include those now blocked, vested, or in the possession or under the control of enemy property authorities of Allied Powers, which belonged to, or were held or managed on behalf of, any of the persons or entities mentioned in (a), (b), or (c) above at the time such assets came under the controls of such authorities.

(II) The following shall be excepted from the right specified in sub-paragraph (I) above:

(i) property of Japanese natural persons who during the war resided with the permission of the Government concerned in the territory of one of the Allied Powers, other than territory occupied by Japan, except property subjected to restrictions during the war and not released from such restrictions as of the date of the first coming into force of the present Treaty;

(ii) all real property, furniture, and fixtures owned by the Government of Japan and used for diplomatic or consular purposes, and all persona furniture and furnishings and other private property not of an investment nature which was normally necessary for the carrying out of diplomatic and consular functions, owned by Japanese diplomatic and consular personnel;

(iii) property belonging to religious bodies or private charitable institution and used exclusively for religious or charitable purposes;

(iv) property, rights, and interests which have come within its jurisdiction in consequence of the resumption of trade and financial relations subsequent to September 2, 1945, between the country concerned and Japan, except such as have resulted from transactions contrary to the laws of the Allied Power concerned;

(v) obligations of Japan or Japanese nationals, any right, title, or interest in tangible property located in Japan, interests in enterprises organized under the laws of Japan, or any paper evidence thereof; provided that this exception shall only apply to obligations of Japan and its nationals expressed in Japanese currency.

(III) Property referred to in exceptions (i) through (v) above shall be returned subject to reasonable expenses for its preservation and administration. If any such property has been liquidated, the proceeds shall be returned instead.

(IV) The right to seize, retain, liquidate, or otherwise dispose of property as provided in sub-paragraph (I) above shall be exercised in accordance with the laws of the Allied Power concerned, and the owner shall have only such rights as may be given him by those laws.

(V) The Allied Powers agree to deal with Japanese trademarks and literary and artistic property rights on a basis as favorable to Japan as circumstances ruling in each country will permit.

(b) Except as otherwise provided in the present Treaty, the Allied Powers waive all reparations claims of the Allied Powers, other claims of the Allied Powers and their nationals arising out of any actions taken by Japan and its nationals in the course of the prosecution of the war, and claims of the Allied Powers for direct military costs of occupation.

Article 15

(a) Upon application made within nine months of the coming into force of the present Treaty between Japan and the Allied Power concerned, Japan will within six months of the date of such application, return the property, tangible and intangible, and all rights or interests of any kind in Japan of each Allied Power and its nationals which was within Japan at any time between December 7, 1941 and September 2,

1945, unless the owner has freely disposed thereof without duress or fraud. Such property shall be returned free of all encumbrances and charges to which it may have become subject because of the war, and without any charges for its return. Property whose return is not applied for by or on behalf of the owner or by his Government within the prescribed period may be disposed of by the Japanese Government as it may determine. In cases where such property was within Japan on December 7, 1941, and cannot be returned or has suffered injury or damage as a result of the war, compensation will be made on terms not less favorable than the terms provided in the draft Allied Powers Property Compensation Law approved by the Japanese Cabinet on July 13, 1951.

(b) With respect to industrial property rights impaired during the war, Japan will continue to accord to the Allied Powers and their nationals benefits no less than those heretofore accorded by Cabinet Orders No. 309 effective September 1, 1949, No. 12 effective January 28, 1950, and No. 9 effective February 1, 1950, all as now amended, provided such nationals have applied for such benefits within the time limits prescribed therein.

(c) (i) Japan acknowledges that the literary and artistic property rights which existed in Japan on December 6, 1941, in respect of the published and unpublished works of the Allied Powers and their nationals have continued in force since that date, and recognizes those rights which have arisen, or but for the war would have arisen, in Japan since that date, by the operation of any conventions and agreements to which Japan was a party on that date, irrespective of whether or not such conventions or agreements were abrogated or suspended upon or since the outbreak of war by the domestic law of Japan or of the Allied Power concerned.

(ii) Without the need for application by the proprietor of the right and without the payment of any fee or compliance with any other formality, the period from December 7, 1941, until the coming into force of the present Treaty between Japan and the Allied Power concerned shall be excluded from the running of the normal term of such rights; and such period, with an additional period of six months, shall be excluded from the time within which a literary work must be translated into Japanese in order to obtain translating rights in Japan.

Article 16

As an expression of its desire to indemnify those members of the armed forces of the Allied Powers who suffered undue hardships while prisoners of war of Japan, Japan will transfer its assets and those of its nationals in countries which were neutral during the war, or which were at war with any of the Allied Powers, or at its option, the equivalent of such assets, to the International Committee of the Red Cross which shall liquidate such assets and distribute the resultant funds to appropriate national agencies, for the benefit of former prisoners of war and their families on such basis as it may determine to be equitable. The categories of assets described in Article 14 (a) 2(II) (ii) through (v) of the present Treaty shall be excepted from transfer, as well as assets of Japanese natural persons not residents of Japan on the first coming into force of the Treaty. It is equally understood that the transfer provision of this Article has no application to the 19,770 shares in the Bank for International Settlements presently owned by Japanese financial institutions.

Article 17

(a) Upon the request of any of the Allied Powers, the Japanese Government shall review and revise in conformity with international law any decision or order of the Japanese Prize Courts in cases involving ownership rights of nationals of that Allied Power and shall supply copies of all documents comprising the records of these cases, including the decisions taken and orders issued. In any case in which such review or revision shows that restoration is due, the provisions of Article 15 shall apply to the property concerned.

(b) The Japanese Government shall take the necessary measures to enable nationals of any of the Allied Powers at any time within one year from the coming into force of the present Treaty between Japan and the Allied Power concerned to submit to the appropriate Japanese authorities for review any judgment given by a Japanese court between December 7, 1941, and such coming into force, in any proceedings in which any such national was unable to make adequate presentation of his case either as plaintiff or defendant. The Japanese Government shall provide that, where the national has suffered injury by reason of any such judgment, he shall be restored to the position in which he was before the judgment was given or shall be afforded such relief as may be just and equitable in the circumstances.

Article 18

(a) It is recognized that the intervention of the state of war has not affected the obligation to pay pecuniary debts arising out of obligations and contracts (including those in respect of bonds) which existed and rights which were acquired before the existence of a state of war, and which are due by the Government or nationals of Japan to the Government or nationals of one of the Allied Powers, or are due by the Government or nationals of one of the Allied Powers to the Government or nationals of Japan. The intervention of a state of war shall equally not be regarded as affecting the obligation to consider on their merits claims for loss or damage to property or for personal injury or death which arose before the existence of a state of war, and which may be presented or re-presented by the Government of one of the Allied Powers to the Government of Japan, or by the Government of Japan to any of the Governments of the Allied Powers. The provisions of this paragraph are without prejudice to the rights conferred by Article 14.

(b) Japan affirms its liability for the prewar external debt of the Japanese State and for debts of corporate bodies subsequently declared to be liabilities of the Japanese State, and expresses its intention to enter into negotiations at an early date with its creditors with respect to the resumption of payments on those debts; to encourage negotiations in respect of other prewar claims and obligations and to facilitate the transfer of sums accordingly.

Article 19

(a) Japan waives all claims of Japan and its nationals against the Allied Powers and their nationals arising out of the war or out of actions taken because of the existence of a state of war, and waives all claims arising from the presence operations or actions of forces or authorities of any of the Allied Powers in Japanese territory prior to the coming into force of the present Treaty.

(b) The foregoing waiver includes any claims arising out of actions taken by any of the Allied Powers with respect to Japanese ships between September 1, 1939, and the coming into force of the present Treaty, as well as any claims and debts arising with respect to Japanese prisoners of war and civilian internees in the hands of the Allied Powers, but does not include Japanese claims specifically recognized in the laws of any Allied Power enacted since September 2, 1945.

(c) Subject to reciprocal renunciation, the Japanese Government also renounces all claims (including debts) against Germany and German nationals on behalf of the Japanese Government and Japanese nationals, including intergovernmental claims and claims for loss or damage sustained during the war, but excepting (a) claims in respect of contracts entered into and rights acquired before September 1, 1939, and (b) claims arising out of trade and financial relations between Japan and Germany after September 2, 1945. Such renunciation shall not prejudice actions taken in accordance with Articles 16 and 20 of the present Treaty.

(d) Japan recognizes the validity of all acts and omissions done during the period of occupation under or in consequence of directives of the occupation authorities or authorized by Japanese law at that time, and will take no action subjecting Allied nationals to civil or criminal liability arising out of such acts or omissions.

Article 20

Japan will take all necessary measures to ensure such disposition of German assets in Japan as has been or may be determined by those powers entitled under the Protocol of the proceedings of the Berlin Conference of 1945 to dispose of those assets, and pending the final disposition of such assets will be responsible for the conservation and administration thereof.

Article 21

Notwithstanding the provisions of Article 25 of the present Treaty, China shall be entitled to the benefits of Articles 10 and 14(a)2; and Korea to the benefits of Articles 2, 4, 9, and 12 of the present Treaty.

CHAPTER VI

Settlement of disputes

Article 22

If in the opinion of any Party to the present Treaty there has arisen a dispute concerning the interpretation or execution of the Treaty, which is not settled by reference to a special claims tribunal or by other agreed means, the dispute shall at the request of any party thereto be referred for decision to the International Court of Justice. Japan and those Allied Powers which are not already parties to the Statute of the International Court of Justice[12] will deposit with the Registrar of the Court, at the time of their respective ratifications of the present Treaty, and in conformity with the resolution of the United Nations Security Council dated October 15, 1946,[13] a general declaration accepting the jurisdiction, without special agreement, of the Court generally in respect of all disputes of the character referred to in this Article.

CHAPTER VII

Final clauses

Article 23

(a) The present Treaty shall be ratified by the States which sign it, including Japan, and will come into force for all the States which have then ratified it, where instruments of ratification have been deposited by Japan and by a majority, including the United States of America as the principal occupying Power, of the following States, namely Australia, Canada, Ceylon, France, Indonesia, the Kingdom of the Netherlands, New Zealand, Pakistan, the Republic of the Philippines, the United Kingdom of Great Britain and Northern Ireland, and the United States of America. The present Treaty shall come into force for each State which subsequently ratifies it, on the date of the deposit of its instrument of ratification.

(b) If the Treaty has not come into force within nine months after the date of the deposit of Japan's ratification, any State which has ratified it may bring the Treaty into force between itself and Japan by a notification to that effect given to the Governments of Japan and the United States of America not later than three years after the date of deposit of Japan's ratification.

Article 24

All instruments of ratification shall be deposited with the Government of the United States of America which will notify all the signatory States of each such deposit, of the date of the coming into force of the Treaty under paragraph (a) of Article 23, and of any notifications made under paragraph (b) of Article 23.

Article 25

For the purposes of the present Treaty the Allied Powers shall be the States at war with Japan, or any State which previously formed a part of the territory of a State named in Article 23, provided that in each case the State concerned has signed and ratified the Treaty. Subject to the provisions of Article 21, the present Treaty shall not confer any rights, titles, or benefits on any State which is not an Allied Power as herein defined; nor shall any right, title, or interest of Japan be deemed to be diminished or prejudiced by any provision of the Treaty in favor of a State which is not an Allied Power as so defined.

Article 26

Japan will be prepared to conclude with any State which signed or adhered to the United Nations Declaration of January 1, 1942,[14] and which is at war with Japan, or with any State which previously formed a part of the territory of State named in Article 23, which is not a signatory of the present Treaty, a bilateral Treaty of Peace on the same or substantially the same terms as are provided for in the present Treaty, but this obligation on the part of Japan will expire three years after the first coming into force of the present Treaty. Should Japan make a peace settlement or war claims settlement with any State granting that State greater advantages than those provided by the present Treaty, those same advantages shall be extended to the parties to the present Treaty.

Article 27

The present Treaty shall be deposited in the archives of the Government of the United States of America which shall furnish each signatory State with a certified copy thereof.

↑ In accordance with article 23 (a) the Treaty came into force initially on 28 April 1952 with respect to the following States by virtue of the deposit by those States with the Government of the United States of America of their respective instruments of ratification on the dates indicated: {

↑ De Martens: Nouveau Recueil général de Traités, deuxième série, tome XXXIII, p. 3.

↑ United Nations, Treaty Series, Vol. 8, p. 189.

↑ League of Nations, Treaty Series, Vol. VII, p. 332.

↑ League of Nations, Treaty Series, Vol. CLXXIII, p. 213.

↑ League of Nations, Treaty Series, Vol. XXVIII, p. 11.

↑ League of Nations, Treaty Series, Vol. CIV, p. 243.

↑ League of Nations, Treaty Series, Vol. CIV, p. 328.

↑ League of Nations, Treaty Series, Vol. CIV, p. 441.

↑ De Martens: Nouveau Recueil général de Traités, deuxième série, tome XXXII, p. 94.

↑ United Nations, Treaty Series, Vol. 15, p. 295; Vol. 26, p. 420; Vol. 32, p. 402; Vol. 33, p. 352; Vol. 44, p. 346, and Vol. 51, p. 336. No. 1832

↑ League of Nations, Treaty Series, Vol. VI, p. 390.

↑ Official Records of the Security Council, first year, second series, No. 19, p. 467.

↑ League of Nations, Treaty Series, Vol. CCIV, p. 381.

The manufacturer's authorised representative in the EU is Springer Nature Customer Service Centre GmbH, Europaplatz 3, 69115 Heidelberg, Germany. If you have any concerns regarding our products, please contact ProductSafety@springernature.com

Printed and bound by CPI Group (UK) Ltd, Croydon, CR0 4YY
21/09/2026
02220010-0016